Inland Waterways
of
Great Britain

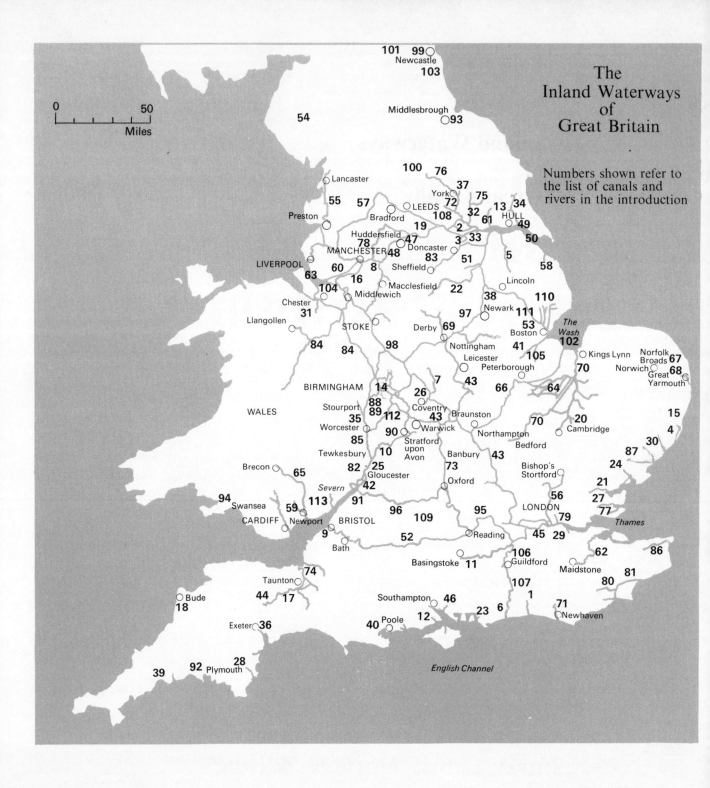

The
Inland Waterways
of
Great Britain

Numbers shown refer to
the list of canals and
rivers in the introduction

0   50
Miles

101   99
Newcastle
103

54

Middlesbrough
93

100   76
Lancaster
37
York 75
55   57   72   13   34
Preston   LEEDS   32   61   HULL
Bradford   108   2   49
19   33   50
Huddersfield   47   3
78   Doncaster
MANCHESTER 48   83   5
LIVERPOOL   8   Sheffield   51   58
63   60   Macclesfield   Lincoln
16   22   38   110
104   Middlewich   97   Newark 111
Chester   53
31   Derby   69   Boston
Llangollen   STOKE   41   102   The Wash
84   98   Nottingham   105
84   Leicester   70   Kings Lynn   Norfolk Broads 67
Peterborough   Norwich 68
BIRMINGHAM   14   7   43   66   64   Great Yarmouth
Stourport   26   15
35   88   Coventry   4
WALES   89 112   43   Braunston   20   30
Worcester   90   Warwick   70   Cambridge   87
85   Stratford   Northampton   24
upon   Bedford   21
Tewkesbury   10   Avon   Banbury   43   27
Brecon   82 25   73   Bishop's   77
65   Gloucester   Oxford   Stortford   56
94   42   95   LONDON 79
Swansea   59   113   91   96   109   45   29   62   86
CARDIFF   Newport   9   BRISTOL   52   Reading   106   Maidstone   81
Bath   Guildford   80
74   11   107   71
Taunton   Basingstoke   1   Newhaven
Bude   44   17   Southampton   46   23   6
18   Exeter   36   Poole   12
40
39   92   Plymouth
28

Severn
Thames
English Channel

Inland Waterways
of
Great Britain

England, Wales and Scotland

by

L.A.Edwards M.I.S.T.C.

Hon. Secretary of the Inland Waterways Association (1950-58)
and Hon. Consultant to the Inland Waterways Association (1958-)
and other bodies.

Imray Laurie Norie & Wilson

Published by
Imray, Laurie, Norie & Wilson Ltd
Wych House, St. Ives, Huntingdon, Cambridgeshire PE17 4BT, England

First edition	1939
Second edition	1947
Third revised and enlarged edition	1950
Fourth edition	1962
Fifth revised and reset edition	1972
Sixth revised and enlarged edition	1985
Reprinted	1988

© L. A. Edwards and Imray, Laurie, Norie & Wilson Ltd. 1985

Edwards, Lewis A.
  Inland waterways of Great Britain — 6th ed.
  1. Inland navigation — Great Britain
  2. Boats and boating — Great Britain
  3. Great Britain — Description and travel — 1971-
  I. Title
  386'.0941 HE663

  ISBN 0-85288-081-2

CAUTION

Printed at The Bath Press, Avon

Foreword

By the late Right Hon. Sir Geoffrey de Freitas, K.C.M.G.*
President of The Inland Waterways Association

This sixth edition of the standard work of reference to our waterway system comes at a critical time in our waterway development. The narrow canals, in particular, are carrying traffic in some cases greater then ever before, and the strain on tunnels, aqueducts and locks has led to an immense back log of maintenance problems. The Fraenkel Report issued in December 1975, which was commissioned by the Department of the Environment to study the operating and maintenance costs, gave a recommended programme, which from the year 1974 for a 15 year period totalled over £168,000,000 for operation and maintenance costs. Another survey is now planned and will soon be under way.

The canal network, still capable of expansion for commercial carrying, has become a major tourist asset and the Sheffield and South Yorkshire improvement scheme should really show that canal transport has still a major carrying function to relieve our sorely taxed road system. It is still rarely understood that a canal is a multi-functional unit with transport and recreation linked with other functions, such as fishing and, above all, drainage. The system has a valuable water supply function, and above all the network forms an essential component of the country's drainage system. The cost rendered to the community has never been calculated, and the Fraenkel Report made no attempt to assess the value to the country. It is clear that the cost is enormous and should be recognised by generous financial aid to the canal and river system.

A most valuable feature has now become an essential part of the waterway recovery system, that is of course, the great voluntary movement, the do-it-yourself canal navvy, co-ordinated by the Waterways Recovery Group, now part of the Inland Waterways Association. We have seen the River Avon re-opened through to Stratford; locks restored on the Montgomery; restoration of the Basingstoke Canal in sight with the help of the manpower creation schemes; the Buxworth Basin project; the Kennet and Avon Canal restoration is going well with the help of funds raised by local authorities and the local Trust. The Droitwich, Rochdale and other waterways are getting help from enthusiastic volunteers but they need more help as they perform a very useful function and youth requires something that gives scope for initiative and enterprise and is related to helping the environment.

A most welcome development is the interest shown by local authorities and the Manpower Services Commission. Work has been created for unemployed young people, some in areas of severe unemployment, and this has led to canal restoration going forward at a much greater pace.

Since the fifth edition we have lost the founder and vice-president of the Inland Waterways Association, Robert Aickman, and Tom Rolt, the I.W.A.'s first honorary secretary and author of *Narrow Boat,* the book which sparked off the canal revival. Their first meeting at Tardebigge aboard N.B. *Cressey* has been marked by a plinth with an engraved plaque recording that event in 1946.

The future holds a great challenge to us all and by a united effort we should see the canal system slowly restored and better than ever before. I warmly welcome Teddy Edwards' 6th edition, enlarged and more useful than ever to river and canal users.

---

*Shortly after writing this foreward, in 1982, Sir Geoffrey died. His loss to Conservation in general, and waterways in particular, is a very sad one indeed.

Preface

A complete change of attitude towards our inland waterways has come into being since my first edition of this book was published in 1950. Then we were just beginning to get used to the nationalised waterway organisation set up in 1948. There have been a number of upheavals, not all for the best, in the structure of the nationalised authority, but the happiest portent for the future was in 1963 when the waterways were under an organisation free from railway control. The Transport Act of 1968 brought further changes with a new concept of cruising waterways and, unsatisfactory though maintenance and financial matters were, the idea of a national waterways body seemed to meet with popular approval.

In the preparation of this volume I would like to thank officials of the British Waterways Board, and the many other navigation authority owners in this country for their help and co-operation. I am also indebted to the many waterway enthusiasts of The Inland Waterways Association Limited and other bodies, who it is impossible to thank individually. The Inland Waterways Association and its associates have been largely responsible for the public change of attitude to inland waterways.

The value of this work was greatly enhanced when in the 1950 edition I was able to incorporate the Distance Tables, suitably amended, and a Glossary of Canal Terms from Bradshaw's Canals and Navigable Rivers (1928 edition) compiled by the late Rodolph de Salis after a personal survey. I am very much indebted to Messrs. Henry Blacklock & Co. Ltd., Manchester and Major Count A. de Salis for their permission to reproduce these. These tables were further improved by four British Waterways Board officials who largely in their own time incorporated the locks in the tables, and I should like to again record appreciation to Messrs. Gater, Hendrick, Tasker and the late S. G. Craske. Alan Faulkner has kindly undertaken the Herculean task of revising the whole of the Grand Union Distance Tables and others.

The editor of *Waterways News* (British Waterways Board), Sheila Doeg has been most helpful and I must express appreciation at work done. The B.W.B. *Journal* is a most useful means of updating this work. The selection of photos for this book has been greatly helped by Vanessa Wiggins who has sorted some photos with care from the B.W.B. Library for this volume. Philip Daniell of B.W.B. has greatly improved the derelict waterways list.

The Birmingham Canal Navigations section has been greatly improved by reproduction of a section from the Cruising Guide to the B.C.N. written by K. D. Dunham and R. B. Mannion. This guide is invaluable to the Navigation of this unique area.

For details of the Scottish Waterways I am indebted to Mr Douglas G. Russell.

I should like to thank all the authorities for their permission freely given, to reproduce matter from their various publications, and in particular T. F. Christie at the Thames Water Authority, the Port of London Authority and the Manchester Ship Canal Company for the data which has greatly increased the value of this volume to the serious student.

In conclusion my thanks to Charles Collier, the late Chief Inspector, and Christopher Groves, also late Chief Inspector of the Yare, Bure and Waveney Commissioners, for rendering enormous help with the Broads section. Thanks also to John Gagg who has sent in frequent notes of his waterway cruises with data. John uses this book in connection with the I.W.A. *Silver Sword Scheme,* an award to encourage not only canal cruising but use of the little used waterways. This scheme is at present suspended.

Finally, may I thank my publishers for their help and forebearance at all stages of this work, and my wife, whose labours have made its production possible.

L. A. Edwards   *April 1985*
Ashtead

Contents

List of Canals and Rivers

SCOTLAND

INDEX
to
Nichols & Company's
SIX SHEET MAP
of the
INLAND NAVIGATION
and
Rail Roads
of
GREAT BRITAIN.

NOTE. The Roman Numerals in each Division refer to the corresponding Number in the Six Sheet Map; and the dotted Lines denote the Extent of each.
The Asterisks on the several Navigations and Railways shew the Points of Communication; and the Figures refer to the Index at the End of the Book.

Engraved on Steel by Frank & Johnson, Wakefield.

General
Historical Notes

The history of man's use of our rivers began with the stone net weight rings of prehistoric man and the hide-covered coracles of the Celt, examples of which, little changed through a millenium, still survive on the Severn, Teifi and Towy. But the first artificial cuts or canals were made by the Romans some of whose canal construction can be seen today running from Peterborough to the Trent; the first portion of this is called Caer-dyke (or Carr Dike) and sections of it can be seen near Bourne in Lincolnshire and elsewhere, the other part of this ancient route between Lincoln and the Trent is still in use being known as the Fossdyke Canal. This Roman waterway, although not used to a great extent now, has carried a great volume of traffic in the past, and as far back as 1121 records exist of King Henry 1 having improvements carried out on the canal.

No major canals for navigation were constructed until the middle of the 18th century, the beginning of the canal era, although great strides in inland waterway communication had been made on the continent. Improvements were made to rivers however, to facilitate navigation, long before the canal era and as early as 1065, Edward the Confessor made a decree regarding four rivers; he ordered that mills and fisheries should be destroyed on the Rivers Thames, Trent, Severn and Yorkshire Ouse and the rivers made navigable.

In these early days mention was made of the 'New River' at Winchester, Hampshire which was an artificial cut made to improve the navigability of the River Itchen. This ancient navigation is now derelict but Alresford Dam can still be inspected, it forms Alresford Pond and was used as a reservoir to provide a head of water to enable craft to navigate through flash locks to Alresford in Hampshire. This ancient specimen of civil engineering was constructed by Bishop Godfrey de Lucy (1189—1204). About the same time the care of the Thames was entrusted to the Corporation of the City of London by King Richard 1. Magna Carta referred to the crude weirs on the Thames and Medway and ordered their removal. Various acts were placed on the statute book after the signing of Magna Carta and at the end of the Middle Ages the following were some of the rivers which were in use for navigation over part of their courses: Ouse (Yorkshire), Tyne, Ure, Great Ouse, Itchen, Exe, Dart, Ouse (Sussex), Western Rother, Cuckmere, Witham, Stour (Suffolk), Thames, Lee, Humber, Avon (Somerset) and Stour (Kent). Our inland waterways, which were developed under the Tudors and Stuarts, made considerable progress as the early roads made transport by pack horse the only real alternative to transport by river. With the introduction of the lock to England some further progress was made, but the greatest progress came with the 'canal era'.

The inland water way system early in the nineteenth century Drawn by John Walker, land and mineral surveyor, for Joseph Priestley's book on railways and canals, 1831

Although John Trew had started construction of the Exeter Canal in 1563 and the Newry Canal and the Shannon Navigation in Ireland were constructed before the canal era, as were also pound locks on the Thames, British canal history virtually commenced with the opening of the Duke of Bridgewater's Canal from Worsley to Manchester in 1761. Some authorities regard the St. Helen's Canal as the commencement of the canal era as it was opened to traffic in 1757, but this claim is difficult to uphold as the St. Helen's Canal is in fact a canalised river navigation and not a wholly artificial cut like the Bridgewater Canal. Even today, certain items of historical interest survive at Worsley on the Bridgewater Canal such as the entrance to the extensive system of subterranean canals by which coal was carried from the face to the basin where it was transhipped into larger boats. One or two of the remarkable canal boats used on this underground system are still to be seen, together with other correspondingly miniature navigational appurtenances, also Old Warke Dam, the original canal reservoir. The third Duke of Bridgewater was the founder of the English canal system and much credit for the Bridgewater Canal belongs to John Gilbert his chief engineer. Credit is often given to James Brindley for much of Gilbert's work, but every student of the canal age should read 'The Canal Duke' by Hugh Malet.

The canal era, which commenced in 1761, lasted practically until the opening of the railway from London to Birmingham in 1838, and during this period over 300 Acts of Parliament were placed on the statute book relating to canals, and great engineering works were carried out by James Brindley, Thomas Telford, John Rennie, William Jessop and others. The canals made possible the Industrial Revolution, which was in its infancy when canals started and England was still to a great extent self-sufficient, that is to say depending very largely upon her own resources.

The English country town (and in the 18th century there were very few towns which might not be so described) was very closely linked with its surrounding rural area by ties of mutual dependency. The town depended upon the labours of the countryman, who, in turn, required the products of the town craftsman and also town wastes for his land; the canal, winding out from market towns through the countryside by many village wharves, conforms to this homogenous pattern. The Industrial Revolution, with its new conception of an England importing food and raw materials and exporting manufactured goods, brought about a complete transformation. The old trade map faded, on the new map the important routes were those linking the great industrial areas with the ports, and it was the waterways which conformed most closely to this new pattern and which enjoyed the best hope of survival.

Yet even these were threatened, for when the railways were built, conflict with the canals was inevitable. As the price for withdrawing their opposition to railway promotions, the canal companies would commonly force a railway company to buy out their canals and at an extortionate price. Parliament laid down an obligation which exists to this day that railway companies must fully maintain all canals thus acquired, but the circumstances of the acquisition, and the fact that the canal merely competed for traffic with the railway, led the latter owners to follow a systematic policy more or less of neglect, high tolls and the raising of all possible obstacles to trade (such as closing the waterways to traffic on Sundays, or prohibiting power-driven boats). Through working arrangements with independent canals was made difficult or impossible, while the most vital task of dredging was generally neglected. The objects were so to neglect the canal that trade fell away and ceased, whereupon a private bill for abandonment was promoted and usually passed by an overworked legislature wholly ignorant of what was going on. It should be emphasized that the diminution of canal trade is in great part the result not of scientific or economic progress but merely of a deliberate policy pursued by interested parties. The tradition and consequences of this long-standing policy have been inherited by the State now that most waterways have come into its hands; much will have to be done by the public, however, if the vast benefits to be derived from a well-run river and canal system are not to go by default. In the last 70 years, commission after commission has recommended the development of our canal system, but railway policy continued unchecked and as recently as 1943 one company obtained powers to abandon nearly 200 miles of waterway from which traffic had been driven by neglect.

Today the ancient life of the river has almost ceased to exist and consequently the river is threatened by disuse and dereliction on the one hand and ignorant and wanton exploitation on the other. Net fishing, instead of being controlled to allow for the interests of the the rod fisherman, has been virtually abolished. By a process very similar to that of the enclosures, the net fisherman has been deprived of a calling which his ancestors followed for countless generations; on some rivers, the fishing is strictly preserved for a few wealthy individuals and syndicates. As a result of the milling monopoly, thousands of country mills with their ponds, weirs and sluices, have become derelict, and due to the decay of agriculture in the years between the two world wars, the old systems of land drainage, irrigation and water conservation have become choked up and in many cases lost to memory. River towing-paths have become impassable because of erosion or enclosure, while withy beds have reverted to boggy wilderness owing to the eclipse of the craft of basket making. Rushes, once regularly cut back for use as baskets, thatch or litter have either grown up to choke water courses or been uprooted wholesale. Serious and uncontrollable flooding has often been the result.

Meanwhile, active forces of disruption have accelerated the process of decay and dissolution. The bitumen laden surface water from modern roads, and industrial pollution (the latter readily preventable), have been steadily and surely destroying the wild life of our rivers both above and below water. The ultimate result of this destruction upon natural ecology cannot be measured. The establishment of large riverside power stations has not only destroyed river amenities but, by discharging hot condensate, has raised the temperature of many rivers to such an extent that, in summer periods of low water, great fish mortality is caused. Finally, excessive pumping for urban and industrial purposes has, in some districts, so lowered the water-table that in periods of drought, the upper courses of rivers and tributaries dry up completely.

Beginning under the stress of wartime expediency, some attempt was made to remedy the effects of previous neglect. Unfortunately, however, such work has generally been undertaken with insufficient local knowledge and an eye to quick results with the consequence that in the majority of cases it has done more harm than good. Usually the aim has been to eliminate instead of control flooding, and to secure the quickest possible run-off with no regard to the question of water conservation. This policy is largely conditioned by the fact that owing to the loss of moisture-retaining humus in the soil, the rate of run-off from the land is more rapid than in the past, and consequently the risk of excessive floods in winter and drought in summer is much greater. So far from solving this fundamental problem, rapid drainage is a temporary expedient which, in the long run, merely aggravates it. Rivers have been dredged so deeply that flooding has been temporarily eliminated altogether with the result that riverside watermeadows, whose value depended on periodic flooding, have been rendered practically worthless. Also to obtain a quicker rate of flow, river banks have been stripped of vegetation which enormously accelerates bank erosion and thus causes increased silting in the lower reaches. Unless this silting up is checked by constant dredging, serious flooding recurs, thus the process of bank clearance ultimately defeats its own object.

The development of rivers and construction of canals began about the same time in Ireland and Scotland. The tidal portions of the Bann, Forth, Clyde, Tay and Foyle have been used for transport since the earliest times, but after the fall of the Roman Empire they were disused until revival of trade and commercial enterprise which came much later than in England. Some of the waterways in Northern Ireland and Scotland have been state-owned for many years, and although state-ownership is usually the subject of political controversy, it must be stated in all fairness that the waterways so owned have benefited. This experience is not uncommon, and some of the finest and most efficient canals on the continent are state-owned.

By far the most hopeful auguries for the future are the foundation and rapidly increasing influence of the Inland Waterways Association, which body is concerned to advocate the restoration and maintenance in good order of all British navigable waterways to their full use for both trade and pleasure traffic. A long series of public enquiries has unvaryingly advised that water transport is by far the cheapest for many categories of goods and recommended a new constructive national waterways policy as a matter of urgency. No notice has ever been taken. The increasing demand for waterborne recreation is a new factor with incalculable potentialities. All who wish for better conditions on the waterways of the future, should join this energetic organisation which is limited by guarantee and is run on a non-profit distributing basis. As well as helping in a vital struggle, members receive various advantages including the Association's Bulletin, the main national guide to current developments. The address of the Association is 114 Regent's Park Road, London, NW1 8UQ.

River Welland at Spalding showing the gasworks under reconstruction in 1901

Classical canal architecture at Sleaford Canal Wharf

Martin Chapman - Sleaford Canal Society

The Association in recent years has advocated a National Waterways Conservancy as a solution to the problems of the waterway system, a perusal of this volume showing the various authorities connected with navigation indicates that rationalisation of some sort is vital and overdue. Promoters of the National Waterways Conservancy point to the Thames Conservancy as a model, and no praise can be too high for the efficient way the latter body has restored the river from its neglect in the last century. The Bowes Committee which reported in July 1958 has actuated much of the thought regarding modern conditions of waterways. Modern pressures and changes have shown that a strong navigation authority unhindered by sectional pressures is necessary.

The Docks and Inland Waterways Executive, a section of the British Transport Commission was formed on the 1st January 1948, and the waterways passed to the British Waterways Board on the 1st January 1963. It was not until that date that the waterways were under an organisation freed from railway control. The Transport Act 1968 brought further changes, Section 104 and the 12th Schedule listed 'Commercial Waterways' and 'Cruising Waterways'.

The Annual Report and Accounts for 1968 gives the official statement of the present situation regarding the waterways under the heading 'Framework of Opportunity' from which the following is an extract:

1. The Transport Act 1968, which received Royal Assent on 25th October, provides the 'new charter for the waterways' which the White Paper 'British Waterways: Recreation and Amenity' envisaged in September 1967. After many years of uncertainty the Act resolves issues crucial to the future of the waterways and in particular their role for recreation and amenity which the Board have stressed in their previous reports.

2. Among the Act's many important new provisions relating to inland waterways, the most striking is the classification of the Board's Waterways into:

    (a) the Commercial Waterways, to be principally available for the commercial carriage of freight;

    (b) the Cruising Waterways, to be principally available for cruising, fishing and other recreational purposes; and

    (c) the remainder.

The Commercial and Cruising Waterways, as scheduled to the Act, are listed in Appendix 111. Subject to various safeguards the Minister may by Order alter the status of any of the Board's waterways.

3. To make possible the new amenity role, the Board's general powers are amended to include—for the first time—the power to provide services and facilities for the use for amenity or recreational purposes (including fishing) of the inland waterways or reservoirs owned or managed by them.

4. The Board's new maintenance duty is to maintain the Commercial Waterways in a suitable condition for use by commercial freight-carrying vessels and the Cruising Waterways in a suitable condition for use by cruising craft.

5. The 'Remainder' waterways are required to be dealt with in the most economical manner possible (consistent, in the case of a waterway which is retained, with the requirements of public health and the preservation of amenity and safety). At the same time, important new powers enable local authorities and certain other bodies to enter into agreements with the Board for the maintenance by or transfer to local authorities and other bodies of any 'Remainder' waterway, or of any part of or any works connected with any such waterway.

6. During the passage of the Bill, the Lord Chancellor announced an undertaking concerning certain canals in the 'Remainder' category. This was that for a period of three years no action would be taken by the Board, without the consent of the Minister of Transport, which would prevent their ultimate restoration.

The canals which are the subject of the undertaking are listed in the front of this book.

The Act also establishes the Inland Waterways Amenity Advisory Council whose main functions are:

(a) to advise the Board and the Ministers on any proposals to add to or reduce the Cruising Waterways;

(b) to consider any matter affecting the use or development for amenity or recreational purposes, including fishing, of the Cruising Waterways, and any matter with respect to the provision of services or facilities for those purposes on the Cruising Waterways or the Commercial Waterways and, where they think it desirable, to make recommendations on such matters to the Board or to the Minister after consulting the Board, and

(c) to be consulted by the Minister on certain proposed Orders to be made by the Minister.

The Advisory Council was established on an informal basis in May 1968 in advance of the Act, the chairman with 21 other members was appointed as a statutory body on 18th November 1968.

The Countryside Commission, in conjunction with the British Travel Authority, the Forestry Commission, the Nature Conservancy, the Sports Council, the Water Reserves Board and the British Waterways Board, have formed a Countryside Recreation Research Advisory Group (C.R.R.A.G.) to co-ordinate research in countryside recreation.

In spite of the many statements to the effect that the 1968 Act was a new deal for the Waterways, the slow withdrawal of trading boats which moved through in all weathers, has led to a serious decline in the depth of water available, and some of the so-called cruising waterways have become very shallow. The Board is woefully short of money for improvements, much of their trouble being caused by the fact that it carries out drainage functions in a number of areas for which it receives no payment; other similar functions are also implemented free of charge. Nevertheless, merging river authorities with navigation authorities is not always a satisfactory solution and the Bowes Committee did not recommend it in the case of the Broads when they considered this area. The drainage authorities, however, have done a superb restoration of the River Nene under the direction of the late Mr. George Dallas and restoration of the Great Ouse was completed under the Anglian Water Authority direction.

The tremendous rise of the voluntary spirit which has restored the Lower Avon, the Upper Avon, the Stratford Canal, Linton Lock, Buxworth Basin and other enterprises does not yet fit as much into the national pattern as it deserves, and a good deal of new thinking is needed in respect of this. The waterway movement has been a great force for good in this country's difficult post-war years and it deserves some better recognition than it receives from the nation which pours out large financial sums for the benefit of road haulage and a mere pittance to water transport. It is no mere coincidence that Britain's European industrial competitors treat their waterways as vital trade arteries.

Concern for the state of inland waterways has been expressed for a long time. In 1905 a Canals Trust Bill was introduced in Parliament, its object to acquire, develop, extend and administer in the public interest, canals and navigations in England and Wales. This Bill never reached the statute book but the thoughts behind it were remarkably like those that actuated the Inland Waterways Association when they brought forward their scheme for a National Waterways Conservancy, although at the time the Association was unaware of the 1905 proposals.

There are many local organisations now formed to deal with waterways many of which have voluntary working party groups. These are co-ordinated by a special group within the IWA called the Waterway Recovery Group Ltd who have vehicles, plant and equipment but need more voluntary labour and finance. Offers of plant and equipment are equally appreciated. The British Waterways Board publish *Digest* which lists the latest addresses of local societies and these do unfortunately change from time to time as they are run by volunteers. Close links are kept with other waterway organisations. Up to date addresses can

Douglas G. Russell

be obtained from the Inland Waterways Association and in many cases also from the local authority where the society operates. Many associations are affiliated to the IWA; some are recognised as clubs by the RYA but co-operation exists in practically all cases. Other bodies are in process of formation.

General   Inland Waterways Association Ltd., 114 Regents Park Road, London, NW1 8UQ
The East Anglian Waterways Association Ltd. , Wych House St. Ives, Huntingdon
The Scottish Inland Waterways Association.
Inland Waterways Protection Society:.
Railway and Canal Historical Society

Locks, Navigation weirs and Lifts

The inventor of the pound lock is not definitely known, but credit is generally given to Leonardo da Vinci for his six locks on the Milan Canal constructed in 1487. Credit for the construction of Britain's first lock is invariably given to John Trew who commenced building the Exeter Canal in 1563, although claims have been put forward that the Canterbury Stour Locks and the River Idle Locks, which are all derelict, were constructed prior to that date. Pound locks were built on the Thames in the 17th century at Iffley, Sandford and Swift Ditch, also on the Wey Navigation and other rivers.

Locks are usually constructed of masonry or brick or a combination of both, although there are several exceptions where the gates are of steel. Gates of the guillotine type are timber. Others have sloping turf sides with railway sleepers driven in the base of the slope to prevent boats settling down on the sides when the lock is being emptied, this type of lock can be found on the Kennet River section of the Kennet and Avon Navigation and also on the River Wey Navigation. Lock gates are usually made of timber, although there are a few exceptions where the gates are of cast iron. Gates of the guillotine type are ceasing to be rarities, formerly the only examples were the famous stop-lock at Kings Norton on the Stratford-on-Avon Canal and the old Shropshire Canal tub-boat locks, but recently locks have been constructed with gates rising vertically on the Rivers Nene, Great Ouse, Witham and elsewhere.

Locks are almost invariably rectangular, the only exception being the Gravesend No. 1 Lock on the now abandoned Gravesend and Rochester Canal, and some on the Oxford Canal and Lower Avon Navigation, which are diamond shaped. The rise of such locks is only small and this construction was adopted to equate the water of the lock with a small rise, with the ordinary deeper locks above it. On the original Upper Avon and River Lark Navigation there were circular and crescent shaped locks, the Waveney also had crescent shaped locks, now closed, and the abolished lock at Brantham on the Suffolk Stour was hexagonal shape.

Staircase locks or 'risers' are locks arranged in flights, with the lower gate of one lock acting as the upper gate of the next. The maximum number of locks arranged in this manner is eight on the Caledonian Canal at Banavie. The main disadvantage of such an arrangement is that boats cannot pass each other during the locking through unless they can actually pass in the lock chamber. At Foxton, on the Grand Union, the risers are in two sets so that craft can pass each other halfway through the flight of locks.

On the British canal system sluice paddles are usually worked manually by lock-keepers or boat crews using a portable windlass. Paddles are sometimes fitted to the gates and sometimes to the lock wall when they are named 'ground paddles'. Some locks have paddles on both the lock walls and gates, but it is more usual for both sets of paddles to be fitted at the upper end of the lock only. Although the rack and pinion paddles are generally operated by a windlass, there are still surviving examples of the old ratchet and crowbar system on the Calder and Hebble and elsewhere. The modern locks at Hatton on the Grand Union have enclosed gearing in a metal case and observation has to be made through a small window to check the position of the sluice valve mechanism. On the Lower Thames, Caledonian Canal and certain other waterways the locks have been mechanized.

Stop locks have gates to work in either direction and these usually occur at the junction of two navigations when the variation in level either way is small. The bulk of the water used by canals is consumed by locks. In an essay by Mr. W. O'Brien which won the Canal Association prize in 1858, he explains the water consumption during lockage as follows:

'The loss of water caused by the passage of a boat through a lock is as follows:

W equals L plus B, when the boat ascends.

W, loss of water; L, lockfull or prism of water having the area of lock for its basis and the total fall of the lock for its height;

B, volume of water displaced by the boat.

When the boat descends, the loss is:

W equals L minus B.

A boat going up or down takes W water, whatever be the number of locks, each lockful taken from the summit level going all the way down. If a boat goes up to the summit level and down again on the other side, it causes an expenditure equal to 2L, supposing the boat's load not to vary materially in the course of the journey.

If the descending boat is immediately followed by one ascending, or vice versa, the loss is still the same, or only L per boat.

Sometimes, in steep ascents, several locks are joined together without any intermediate pound; the cost of construction is lessened thereby: but in that case an ascending boat requires as many locksful as there are locks, in addition to the volume displaced by the boat, or

nL plus B,

n being the number of adjacent locks.

In descending, the loss of water is L minus B as before.'

There are several ways of saving water used during lockage, and in the report by the late Mr. L. T. C. Rolt to the Association for Planning and Regional Reconstruction on Inland Waterways they are given as follows:

1. *Waiting Turns.* The most economical use of water is secured if a boat moving up a flight of locks is succeeded by a boat travelling in the opposite direction. It leads to considerable delay unless traffic is heavy and regular but is sometimes enforced in time of drought.

2. *Side Ponds.* These consist of small reservoirs built beside each lock at a level midway between that of the upper and lower pounds and connected to the lock by means of a paddle or sluice. A descending boat entering a full lock first discharges the water from the lock into the side pond until lock and side pond equalise with the lock half empty. The sidepond paddle is then closed, and the remainder of the water in the lock is discharged into the canal below in the ordinary way. Similarly, an ascending boat entering the empty lock first fills the lock from the side pond before drawing the remainder from the canal above. In each case half a lock of water is saved. Many of the locks on the Grand Union Canal employ this system.

3. *Paired Locks.* In this case duplicate locks, side by side, employ the principle described above, one acting as a side pond to the other.

4. *Pumping Back*. The installation of pumping units at each lock or compact flight of locks which return lockage water from the lower to the higher levels.

Cossington Locks on the Leicester Section of the Grand Union Canal

Navigation Weirs or Flash Locks

These are primitive appliances for overcoming changes of level, which merely consist of a weir with gates that can be opened and closed by alteration of paddles or raising the sluice gate vertically. Water is held up in reaches by the weirs which have to be opened, and after the water in the reaches above and below the weir has run to a level, the craft can pass through.

Flash locks were to be found until recent years on the River Thames where they caused a nuisance to commercial barge traffic and did not help the Thames Severn Canal. They were also found on the Nene, Great Ouse and Fenland waterways and the Lower Avon but none are now in use except the single gate lock on the River Wey which used in conjunction with the nearby lock, renders it not strictly a 'flash lock'. They were also used on some very early navigations such as the Severn, Wye, Canterbury Stour. These weirs had to be set in advance of the boat and were dangerous if not carefully used.

Lock Operation

This varies from waterway to waterway, but the notes below will give the general principle on British waterways. Drainage navigations usually have a guillotine upper gate and those on the Leeds and Liverpool Canal and Staffordshire and Worcestershire Canal (Bratch Locks) have special instructions. Local enquiries are always advised.

Locks are often operated by boat crews, but on the Thames, Severn, Trent, Lee and Stort and many of the northern waterways, they are operated by lock-keepers. There is no guiding rule and prior information should be sought from the navigation authority.

British Waterways Board issue a detailed circular giving lock opening times, hours of manning, etc. Locks may be subject to closure at certain times and details should be obtained from the navigation authority before a cruise is commenced.

To operate locks a windlass is generally required; on the Trent and Thames and other waterways when the lock keeper is off duty observe instructions carefully. For windlass data see *Navigation Hints* page 24.

Rack and pinion mechanisms are being replaced by hydraulic paddle gear on many waterways. Some of the old mechanisms will be retained, usually if they are scheduled as ancient monuments. In an emergency, hydraulic gear does not permit paddles to be dropped quickly, therefore extra care must be taken.

The operation of a single lock

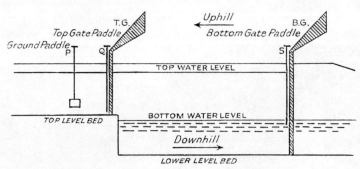

Going uphill—lock empty. Top gates will be shut and paddles (P) and (Q) closed.

A1   Enter lock.
A2   Close bottom gates (BG). See bottom gate paddles (S) are closed.
A3   Open ground paddles (P).
A4   Open top gate paddles (Q) when submerged.
A5   When lock is full open top gates (TG).
A6   Leave lock. Close top gates, close all top paddles.

Going uphill—lock full.

B1   Close top gates (TG). See top gate paddles (Q) and ground paddles (P) are closed.
B2   Open bottom gate paddles (S).
B3   When lock is empty open bottom gates (BG). Proceed as in A1—6.

Going downhill—lock full.

When locking downhill, keep vessel in lock clear of top-gate sill.
C1   Enter lock.
C2   Close top gates (TG). See top gate paddles (Q) and ground paddles (P) are closed.
C3   Open bottom gate paddles (S).
C4   When lock is empty, open bottom gates (BG).
C5   Leave lock. Close all bottom paddles.

Going downhill—lock empty.

D1   Close bottom gates (BG). See bottom gate paddles (S) are closed.
D2   Open ground paddles (P).
D3   Open top gate paddles (Q) when submerged.
D4   When lock is full open top gates (TG). Proceed as in C1—5.

Staircase Lock Flights.

The operation of staircase lock flights—in which the upper gates of one lock are also the lower gates of the one above—will not be found difficult if the procedure given below for the Leeds and Liverpool Canal is followed exactly.

The complete instructions are for working through the 5-rise staircase at Bingley Upper (Locks Nos. 25 to 29). For the 2-rise staircases at Oddy (4 and 5), Dobson (14 and 15) and Dowley Gap (20 and 21), and for the 3-rise staircase at Forge (8 to 10), Newlay (11 to 13), Field (16 to 18) and Bingley Lower (22 to 24), modifications of the instructions are set out under each section.

N.B. On staircase locks the top (No.1) lock is kept full at all times.

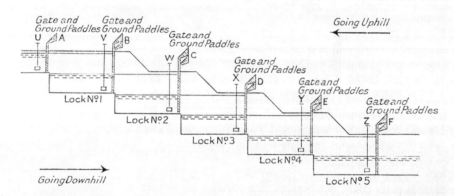

Going Uphill—Locks Empty.

A1   Open gates (F) and enter No. 5 Lock.
A2   Close gates (F). See gate and ground paddles (Z) are closed.
A3   Half-open ground paddles (UVWXY).
A4   When No. 5 Lock is full close ground paddles (X).
A5   Open gates (E) and enter No. 4 Lock.
A6   Close ground paddles (Y) and gates (E).
A7   Open ground and gate paddles (X).
A8   When No. 4 Lock is full, close ground paddles (W).
A9   Open gates (D) and enter No. 3 Lock.
A10 Close ground and gate paddles (X) and gates (D).
A11 Open ground and gate paddles (W).
A12 When No. 3 Lock is full, close ground paddles (V).
A13 Open gates (C) and enter No. 2 Lock.
A14 Close ground and gate paddles (W) and gates (C).
A15 Close ground paddles (U).
A16 Open ground and gate paddles (V).
A17 When No. 2 Lock is full, open gates (B) and enter No. 1 Lock.
A18 Close ground and gate paddles (V) and gates (B).
A19 Open ground and gate paddles (U).
A20 When No. 1 Lock is full open gates (A) and leave lock.
A21 Close gates (A) and close ground and gate paddles (U).

OPERATING 2-RISE STAIRCASES

Use the lettering given for Locks Nos. 2 and 1 in the diagram (No. 1 Lock full):

Carry out operations A13 and A14 followed by operations A16 to A21.

OPERATING 3-RISE STAIRCASES

Treating the flight as locks Nos. 3 to 1 in the diagram (No. 1 Lock full):

Carry out operations A9 and A10.

Half-open ground paddles (WVU).

When No. 3 Lock is full, close ground paddles (V) and (U).

Open gates (C) and enter No. 2 Lock.

Close ground paddles (W) and gates (C).

Carry out operations A16 to A21.

Going Uphill—Locks Full.

B1   Open ground and gate paddles (Z) and empty No. 5 Lock.
B2   Open gates (F) and enter No. 5 Lock.
B3   Close gates (F) and ground and gate paddles (Z).
B4   Open ground and gate paddles (Y).
B5   When No. 5 Lock is full, open gates (E) and enter No. 4 Lock.
B6   Close gates (E) and ground and gate paddles (Y).
B7   Open ground and gate paddles (X).
B8   When No. 4 Lock is full, open gates (D) and enter No. 3 Lock.
B9   Close gates (D) and ground and gate paddles (X).
B10 Open ground and gate paddles (W).
B11 When No. 3 Lock is full, open gates (C) and enter No. 2 Lock.
B12 Close gates (C) and ground and gate paddles (W).
B13 Open ground and gate paddles (V).
B14 When No. 2 Lock is full, open gates (B) and enter No. 1 Lock.
B15 Close gates (B) and ground and gate paddles (V).
B16 Open ground and gate paddles (U).
B17 When No. 1 Lock is full, open gates (A) and leave lock.
B18 Close gates (A) and ground and gate paddles (U).

OPERATING 2-RISE STAIRCASES:

Use the lettering for Locks Nos. 2 and 1 in the diagram:

Start with operation B10; when water level in No. 2 Lock has fallen to that of the pound below, open gates (C) and enter No. 2 Lock. Proceed from B12 and work through in sequence to B18.

OPERATING 3-RISE STAIRCASES:

Treating the flight as locks Nos. 3 to 1 in the diagram:

Start with operation B7; when water level in No. 3 Lock has fallen to that of the pound below, open gates (D) and enter No. 3 Lock. Proceed from B9 and work through in sequence to B18.

Going Downhill—Locks Empty.

C1   Open gates (A) and enter No. 1 Lock (No. 1 Lock full).
C2   Close gates (A). See ground and gate paddles (U) are fully closed.
C3   Open ground and gate paddles (V).
C4   When water level in No. 1 Lock has fallen to that of No. 2 Lock, open gates (B) and enter No. 2 Lock.
C5   Close gates (B) and ground and gate paddles (V).

C6   Return to No. 1 Lock and open one gate paddle (U).

C7   Open ground and gate paddles (W).

C8   When water level in No. 2 Lock has fallen to that of No. 3 Lock, open gates (C) and enter No. 3 Lock.

C9   Close gates (C) and ground and gate paddles (W).

C10 Open ground and gate paddles (X).

C11 When water level in No. 3 Lock has fallen to that of No. 4 Lock, open gates (D) and enter No. 4 Lock.

C12 Close gates (D) and ground and gate paddles (X).

C13 Open ground and gate paddles (Y).

C14 When water level in No. 4 Lock has fallen to that of No. 5 Lock, open gates (E) and enter No. 5 Lock.

C15 Close gates (E) and ground and gate paddles (Y).

C16 Open ground and gate paddles (Z).

C17 When water level in No. 5 Lock has fallen to that of the pound below, open gates (F) and leave lock.

C18 Close gates (F) and ground and gate paddles (Z).

OPERATING 2-RISE STAIRCASES:

Using the lettering for Locks Nos. 1 and 2 in the diagram (No. 1 Lock full):

    Carry out operations C1 to C7.

    When the water level in Lock No. 2 has fallen to that of the pound below, open gates (C) and leave lock.

    Close gates (C) and ground and gate paddles (W).

OPERATING 3-RISE STAIRCASES:

Treating the flight as Locks Nos. 1 to 3 in the diagram (No. 1 Lock full):

    Start with operation C1 and work through in sequence to C10.

    When the water level in Lock No. 3 has fallen to that of the pound below, open gates (D) and leave lock.

    Close gates (D) and ground and gate paddles (X).

Going Downhill—Locks Full.

D1   Open gates (A) and enter No. 1 Lock.

D2   Close gates (A). See ground and gate paddles (U) are closed.

D3   Walk down to Locks Nos. 5, 4 and 3 and half-open ground paddles (Z, Y and X).

D4   Proceed to Lock No. 2 and open ground and gate paddles (W).

D5   Return to No. 1 Lock and open ground and gate paddles (V).

D6   When water in No. 1 Lock has fallen to level of No. 2 Lock, close ground and gate paddles (W).

D7   Open gates (B) and enter No. 2 Lock.

D8   Close gates (B) and ground and gate paddles (V).

D9   Return to No. 1 Lock and open one gate paddle (U).

D10 Open ground and gate paddles (W).

D11 When water in No. 2 Lock has fallen to level of No. 3 Lock, close ground paddles (X).

D12 Open gates (C) and enter No. 3 Lock.

D13 Close gates (C) and ground and gate paddles (W).

D14 Open ground and gate paddles (X).

D15 When water in No. 3 Lock has fallen to level of No. 4 Lock, close ground paddles (Y).

D16 Open gates (D) and enter No. 4 Lock.

D17 Close gates (D) and ground and gate paddles (X).

D18 Close ground paddles (Z).

D19 Open ground and gate paddles (Y).

D20 When water in No. 4 Lock has fallen to level of No. 5 Lock, open gates (E) and enter No. 5 Lock.

D21 Close gates (E) and ground and gate paddles (Y).

D22 Open ground and gate paddles (Z).

D23 When water level in No. 5 Lock has fallen to that of the pound below, open gates (F) and leave lock.

D24 Close gates (F) and ground and gate paddles (Z).

OPERATING 2-RISE STAIRCASES:

Using the lettering given for locks Nos. 1 and 2 in the diagram:

Carry out operations D1 and D2.

Open ground and gate paddles (W).

When water level in No. 2 Lock falls to that of the pound below, close ground and gate paddles (W).

Open ground and gate paddles (V).

When water level in No. 1 Lock has fallen to that of No. 2 Lock, open gate (B) and enter No. 2 Lock.

Carry out operations D8 and D9.

Open ground and gate paddles (W).

When water level in No. 2 Lock has fallen to that of the pound below, open gates (C) and leave lock.

Close gates (C) and ground and gate paddles (W).

OPERATING 3-RISE STAIRCASES

Treating the flight as locks Nos. 1 to 3 in the diagram:

Carry out operations D1 and D2.

Walk down to No. 3 Lock and half-open ground paddles (X).

Walk back to No. 2 Lock and half-open ground paddles (W).

Carry out operations D5 to D9 in sequence.

Close ground paddles (X).

Open ground gate paddles (W).

When water level in No. 2 Lock has fallen to that of No. 3 Lock, open gates (C), and enter No. 3 Lock.

Carry out operations D13 and D14.

When water level in No. 3 Lock has fallen to that of the pound below, open gates (D) and leave lock.

Close gates (D) and ground and gate paddles (X).

Before leaving a lock see that all paddles are fully and securely closed. Failure to do so may result in serious flooding of property, stranding of craft through loss of water from the pound above and possible flooding of craft when the pound is refilled. When passing through a lock to a higher pound it is important to close top gates and paddles before leaving.

Lifts and Inclined Planes

There is only one lift of the vertical type in this country at present and that is at Anderton where vessels 72 feet by 14 feet 6 inches can be transferred from the River Weaver to Trent and Mersey Canal. This lift was opened in July 1875 and was worked hydraulically until 1908. It was then converted to the present method of electric operation.

Many lifts formerly constructed have gone out of use, these and inclined planes were to be found on the following canals:

Bude Canal
Chard Canal
Coalport Canal
Dorset and Somerset Canal
(canal was never completed)
Duke of Sutherland's Tub Boat Canal
Grand Union Canal (Foxton)
Grand Western Canal
(lifts from Taunton to Lowdwell)
Ketley Canal

Kidwelly and Llanelly Canal
Monkton Canal (Blackhill)
St. Columb Canal
Shrewsbury Canal
Shropshire Canal
Somerset Coal Canal
Tavistock Canal
Torrington Canal
Worcester and Birmingham Canal
(Tardebigge)

On the Continent of Europe where inland waterways are being developed there are many gigantic locks and inclined planes. A new inclined plane in Belgium rises 220 feet and takes 1,350 ton barges.

There has been a large boat slide erected on the River Leven a tributary of the River Clyde to expedite craft going from Loch Lomond to the Clyde. A number of rivers do have rollers or slides to help light craft change from one level to another. Some only deal with canoes etc. but others e.g. barrage on the Stour, can deal with small cruisers.

The boat slide on the river Leven

Tunnels

In order to overcome differences in levels, canal constructors often resorted to tunnelling. It will be noted that most tunnels are without tow-paths which were omitted for economy. Before the days of engines, boats were legged or shafted through tunnels, an exhausting method of propulsion and many of the early canal tunnels had their professional 'leggers'; the fee for a legger in Sapperton Tunnel on the Thames Severn was five shillings for a loaded boat. It is chiefly the later tunnels that have towing paths, but in the case of Harecastle it is no longer available. Some tunnels are wide enough for two narrow boats to pass, others have regulations governing entry at certain hours. In case of doubt enquiries should be made, particularly for those navigating with light craft. Dudley Tunnel is not continuous as Castle Mill and Shirt's Mill Basins divide into 3. The longest section is 2904 yards.

Canal Tunnels of Great Britain (over 50yds long)

Name	Waterway	Yards
Standedge	Huddersfield Narrow Canal (open for ventilation only)	5698
Strood	Gravesend and Rochester Canal (now used as a railway tunnel)	3946
Dudley	Birmingham Canal Navigations (Not continuous)	3154
Blisworth	Grand Union Canal	3075⅝
Netherton *	Birmingham Canal Navigations	3027
Harecastle	Trent and Mersey Canal	2919
West Hill (or Wast)	Worcester and Birmingham Canal	2726
Braunston	Grand Union Canal	2048
Foulridge	Leeds and Liverpool Canal	1640
Crick	Grand Union Canal	1528
Preston Brook	Trent and Mersey Canal	1239
Husbands Bosworth	Grand Union Canal	1166
Islington	Grand Union Canal	960
Saddington	Grand Union Canal	880
Shortwood	Worcester and Birmingham Canal	613
Tardebigge	Worcester and Birmingham Canal	580
Barnton	Trent and Mersey Canal	572
Gannow	Leeds and Liverpool Canal	559
Gosty Hill	Birmingham Canal Navigations	557
Savernake	Kennet and Avon Canal	502
Chirk *	Shropshire Union Canal	459
Shrewley	Grand Union Canal	433
Saltersford	Trent and Mersey Canal	424
Ashford	Brecon and Abergavenny Canal	375
Coseley *	Birmingham Canal Navigations	360
King's Norton	Stratford-on-Avon Canal (Brandwood)	352
Hyde Bank	Peak Forest Canal	308
Maida Hill	Grand Union Canal	272
Newbold *	Oxford Canal (2 tow-paths)	250
Snarestone	Ashby Canal	250
Dunhampstead	Worcester and Birmingham Canal	236
Whitehouses *	Shropshire Union Canal	191
Woodley *	Peak Forest Canal	167

* These canals have a towing-path

Name	Waterway	Yards
Drakeholes	Chesterfield Canal	154
Armitage *	Trent and Mersey Canal (opened out 1971)	130
Leek	Trent and Mersey Canal (Leek Branch)	130
Galton (opened 1974)	Birmingham Canal Navigation	122
Edgbaston *	Worcester and Birmingham Canal	105
Ashted *	Birmingham Canal Navigations	103
Summit Tunnel	Birmingham Canal Navigation	103
Ellesmere *	Shropshire Union Canal	87
Cwmbran	Monmouthshire Canal	87
Cowley *	Shropshire Union Canal	81
Knott Mill *	Rochdale Canal	78
Froghall	Trent and Mersey Canal (Caldon Branch)	76
Cookley *	Staffordshire and Worcester	65
Bath No. 1*	Kennet and Avon Canal	57⅔
Curdworth *	Birmingham Canal Navigations	57
Bath No. 2*	Kennet and Avon Canal	55

The following canal tunnels (over 50 yards long) are no longer in use being derelict or abandoned. (Some may be restored and re-opened):

Name	Waterway	Yards
Sapperton	Thames Severn Canal	3808
Pensax	Kington, Leominster & Stourport (uncompleted)Canal	3850
Lappal	Birmingham Canal	3795
Norwood	Chesterfield Canal	3102
Butterley	Cromford Canal	3063
Old Harecastle	Trent and Mersey Canal	2897
(Now replaced by New Harecastle Tunnel)		
Morwelldown	Tavistock Canal	2540
Oxenhall	Hereford & Gloucester Canal	2192
Crimson Hill	Chard Canal	1800
Southnet	Kington, Leominster & Stourport Canal (completed but never used)	1250
Greywell	Basingstoke Canal	1200
Berwick	Shropshire Union Canal	970
Southampton	Southampton & Salisbury Canal (never completed)	880
Falkirk	Union Canal	696
Manchester	Manchester & Salford Junction Canal	499
Aylestone	Hereford & Gloucester Canal	440
Wellow	Somerset Coal Canal (Radstock Arm)	405
Ashperton	Hereford & Gloucester Canal	400
Hincaster	Lancaster Canal	377
Hardham	Arun Navigation	375
Scout	Huddersfield Narrow Canal	220
Coombe Hay	Somerset Coal Canal	195½
Bury	Manchester Bolton and Bury Canal	141
Cardiff	Glamorganshire Canal	115
Cricklade	North Wilts Canal	100
Hag*	Cromford Canal	93
Cwmbran	Monmouthshire Canal	87
Knott Mill (Manchester)	Rochdale Canal	78
Gregory *	Cromford Canal	76
Salford (two short lengths)	Manchester, Bolton and Bury Canal	50
Buckland Hollow *	Cromford Canal	50

* These canals have a towing path.

Name	Waterway							Yards
Sowerby Long Bridge ...	Rochdale Canal ...	...	...	...	...	...	...	50
Little Tunnel ...	Basingstoke Canal	...	...	...	...	...	...	50

Broad Street Tunnel (Birmingham) has not been included as although it is 83 yards long, it is not a tunnel in the accepted sense. It must be emphasised that a number of these old tunnels are not sealed off and should not be explored without taking special precautions. The owner of the land must be approached for permission and expert advice sought. Roof falls regularly occur and exploration is highly dangerous. For this reason Standedge Tunnel can no longer be visited by arrangement. The underground canals at Worsley linked with the Bridgewater Canal are also closed. This underground mining network covered 46 miles. The Institute of Mining has detailed records.

There was a tunnel at Whittle Hills on the Walton Summit Branch of the Leeds and Liverpool Canal 259 yards long. A section fell in soon after completion and it became two short tunnels in a cutting.

Inside Sapperton Tunnel on the Thames and Severn Canal

Philip Weaver

Inside the Harecastle Tunnel on the Trent and Mersey Canal

British Waterways Board

Aqueducts

British canals have some very fine examples of this method of overcoming differences in levels, generally found when a canal has to be carried over a river.

The first British canal aqueduct to be constructed was Barton Aqueduct on the Bridgewater Canal in 1761, this was 600 feet long and built of stone. It is often incorrectly called Brindley's Aqueduct as at that time Brindley was a foreman/engineer serving under John Gilbert and the Duke of Bridgewater. Gilbert was the engineer who saved the structure from collapse. This astonishing feat of early engineering was replaced in 1893 by the present Barton Swing Aqueduct.

Two aqueducts are to be found on the Shropshire Union Canal, both constructed by Telford, Chirk aqueduct crossing the River Ceinog is 600 feet long and was opened for use in 1801; Pontcysyllte crosses the Dee Valley, is 1007 feet long and was opened two years after Chirk. Rennie's famous aqueduct crosses the Lune at Lancaster, 600 feet long, it was opened in 1796 and consists of five arches of 75 feet span each. Aqueducts will be found on many other canals and their construction is worthy of close examination as they form some of the finest examples of early civil engineering, notably: Brindley's Aqueducts over River Sow on the Staffordshire and Worcestershire Canal, Oldknow's monumental Marple Aqueduct on the Peak Forest Canal and Dundas Aqueduct (near Bath) on the Kennet and Avon Canal.

Scotland provides examples of aqueducts on the Union Canal where it crosses the Water of Leith, River Avon and River Almond, and also on the Forth and Clyde at Maryhill. Here the canal crosses the River Kelvin on an aqueduct 400 feet long. There is a new aqueduct at Hermiston on the Union Canal, 103 yds long.

In Northern Ireland a fine aqueduct will be found on the Lagan Navigation, which is carried on four masonry spans across the River Lagan, near Moira. It is being preserved though the Lagan is closed.

One of the best known aqueducts of recent construction is that carrying the Grand Union over the North Circular Road near Wembley Middlesex.

Stanley Ferry Aqueduct on the Aire and Calder Navigation is 164ft long. This is being preserved and a new aqueduct has been built alongside it.

Motorway construction has made the building of new aqueducts necessary. A typical example is the one at Burnley taking the M65 under the Leeds and Liverpool Canal.

Bridges

The hump-backed canal bridge is familiar to most road users. It is usually constructed of masonry and brick, although in the Midlands and the North, subsidences due to mining have often necessitated the use of bridges which can easily be raised when the headroom is less than that required by statute. Such bridges are generally constructed of steel girders.

The towing path alongside the waterway is often carried under the bridge, although on the River Nene and in the Fen District 'the haling way' does not continue underneath the bridges, and towing ropes have to be disconnected at each bridge and connected again on the other side. On the Stratford Canal and other narrow midland canals, are the famous 'split bridges' with a slot 1¼ inches wide in the centre of the bridge through which the towline can be passed. Bridges which carry the towing path from one side of the waterway to the other are termed 'roving bridges'.

Opening bridges are to be found on many waterways. There are three kinds: (1) revolving or swing bridges, (2) lifting or bascule bridges, (3) transporter bridges. Tower Bridge, London is an example of the hinged bascule type, in which a leaf is pivoted and counterbalanced at the back end. An example of a transporter bridge can be seen at Runcorn over the River Mersey. On canals and rivers the commonest opening bridges encountered are lifting bridges which open upwards and which, theoretically, should be easy to operate as they are generally counterbalanced, and 'turn bridges' pivoted in the centre or at one end to turn through an angle of 90 degrees and give a clear channel to traffic on the river or canal. Practically all types of hand-worked bridges are less easy to operate now, due to lack of maintenance. Some opening bridges have bridgekeepers as on the River Witham and Fossdyke Canal in the Lincoln area, but the majority have to be opened by the boatman, viz. Oxford Canal south of Napton, and many others.

When opening bridges, great care should be taken, particularly with the type opened with a windlass similar to that used for lock-gate operation, as the windlass can fly back and cause serious injury.

Care should be taken on rivers in flood time when negotiating bridges, as there are often dangerous eddies caused by the water heaping up on the side of the bridge facing upstream.

On rivers in particular, some of the bridges are very fine architecturally and form part of our national heritage of ancient monuments. The following four ancient bridges have chantry chapels; St. Ives Huntingdonshire, Bradford on Avon Wiltshire, Rotherham Yorkshire, and Wakefield Yorkshire, whilst two still have houses on them namely Pulteney Bridge Bath and High Bridge Lincoln. The structure on the famous Monnow Bridge at Monmouth is a fortified gatehouse.

Tidal Information

Craft in navigable waters which are influenced by the ebb and flow of the tide are usually conducted in the same direction as the tidal current. It should be noted that tides are influenced to a great extent by wind, water and the height of the rise and fall of the tide. In rivers, tides are also affected by the volume of land water coming down from the upper reaches, and in places such as the entrance to the Market Weighton Canal in the River Humber, the volume of land water is so great at some times of the year that craft cannot enter the canal from the tidal river for several days. On the River Thames during the rainy seasons the sluices are often kept raised for days at the Richmond half-tide lock to allow for easy discharge of the land water from the upper portion of the Thames Catchment area.

On some rivers the flood tide flowing up the river becomes heaped up and is termed a 'bore' or 'eagre'. The latter term is used in eastern England and the other in the west. This phenomena can be seen on the Rivers Parrett, Dee, Severn and Trent, as well as on other rivers whose estuaries contract to a narrow channel in a very short distance proceeding upstream from the sea.

As with all so called tidal constants, the times and heights of tides given in the body of this work must be regarded as approximate. Yachtsmen venturing onto tidal waters should first obtain a Nautical Almanac for reference and make careful enquiries locally as to prevailing conditions.

Navigation Hints

These notes include those printed in a leaflet compiled by the late L. T. C. Rolt and the author, for the Inland Waterways Association.

Commercial and pleasure traffic on canals.

It is sometimes suggested that conflict is likely to occur between the interests of these two categories of user. We believe that such conflict is unnecessary and opposed to the interests of both parties and to the future of the waterways themselves. The following brief notes have been compiled with a view to promoting understanding and goodwill in the future.

Some navigable inland waterways are first and foremost commercial highways and it is in the interest even of the pleasure boatman that they should remain so. Priority, therefore, should always be given to the working boat. Frequently every minute is of importance to the working boatman who is usually paid, not by the hour, but by the ton carried. If consideration is shown to the working boatman he will almost always reciprocate.

General Navigation Hints.

There is generally a shoal on the inside of turns. Boats should, therefore, as far as possible keep to the outside. If turns are not thus taken wide, boats are liable to run aground and possibly impede other traffic.

When approaching blind turns and especially turns under or near bridges, the boatman should slow down, sound his audible warning (with which every boat should be equipped) and listen attentively for a possible similar warning from an oncoming craft. If a boat is heard to be approaching a blind turn or a narrow bridge hole she should be given the right of way. The temptation to race to the bridge should be resisted; apart from other considerations, the oncoming boat is very probably the heavier.

The maritime passing rule of 'port to port', or 'Keep to the Right' obtains on waterways but horse-drawn boats must always be given the tow-path side. Other craft must always give way to loaded boats. If such boats seem to be occupying a disproportionate amount of the channel, it will probably be because their draught makes this unavoidable if they are to navigate at all. The steerer of an oncoming boat should be observed, possibly he may signal that his boat should be passed on the wrong side. (Such a signal will proceed from his knowledge of the channel).

Boats should never travel at such a speed that they are followed by a wave breaking on one bank or both banks of the waterway. A 'breaking wave' damages the banks and antagonises waterway officials. The boat which causes it is consuming extra fuel without any proportionate increase in speed.

Obey bye-laws and observe sound signals where applicable.

Sound Signals on B.W.B. Waterways:

One short blast (About 1 second)	I'm altering my course to starboard (to the right)
Two short blasts	I'm altering my course to port (to the left)
Three short blasts	My engine is going astern (in reverse)
Four short blasts	I'm about to manoeuvre (always followed by one or two short blasts)
One long blast	To be sounded every 20 seconds when approaching a bend.

Use of Locks (not manned by lock keepers)

A working boat should not be overtaken when approaching a lock or flight of locks as the consequence will be that a working boatman will then find the lock or locks against him. Similarly, when a pleasure boatman sees a working boat following him through a flight of locks, he should let the working boat pass him. The working boatman can usually work through the locks more quickly and for him time is money. Few things cause as much bad feeling among working boatmen as pleasure boats which insist on locking through first.

When descending in a lock, a boat should never be allowed to lie against or to float back towards the top gate or gates. There is a masonry sill projection into the lock chamber below the top gate. This sill uncovers as the lock empties. If the stern of a boat lodges on it the back of the boat may be broken and other catastrophies result.

On most canals the lock sluices are known colloquially as 'paddles'. Where there are both side and gate paddles the former should be drawn first. Where the lock is considerably wider than the boat, and there are side paddles on both sides of the lock, the paddle on the same side as the boat should be drawn first as this will help to prevent the boat cannoning about the lock.

Where side-ponds exist, they should always be used because they serve a vital function in economising water, always an important matter on an artificial waterway. With all other paddles closed, the side-pond should be drawn, and left until the water in the side-pond and the water in the lock chamber make a level. The side-pond paddle should then be dropped and the lock filled or emptied in the usual way. The same procedure is applicable to paired locks with an inter-connecting paddle. Operation of a side-pond may involve a small additional expenditure of time. For this reason working boatmen may sometimes be observed disregarding it. But, as already stated, it is good practice always to use a side-pond, provided it is in working order. It is in no one's interest to deplete a canal of water.

When a boat is descending a flight of locks with very short intervening pounds and an ascending boat is observed in the next lock down, the lower gate paddles of the upper lock should not be drawn before the crew of the ascending boat have drawn the upper gate paddles of the lower lock. If this rule is disregarded, the pound may flood and, flowing over the upper gates of the lower lock, swamp the boat below. Any stretch of water, however long or short, between the locks is termed a pound.

After leaving a lock through which his boat has ascended, the boatman should always close the top gate or gates. The lower gates should not be left to sustain the full weight of water in the pound.

Similarly, particular care should be taken to see that all paddles holding up water are left fully closed. Very serious wastage of water can be caused, even to the extent of rendering a canal unnavigable, by paddles being partly drawn. The risk is greatest with the enclosed worm-and-nut paddle gears used on the Grand Union Canal north of Braunston because, when released, these do not always run back to their full extent, particularly in cold weather. The paddles should not be left until the rubber seating washer is plainly visible through the peep-hole in the worm-casting.

Normally paddle gears should be wound down with the windlass and not permitted to descend with a crash under their own weight. The latter procedure   is fraught with danger to boatman and the gear itself.

*A windlass is required to open paddles on locks. These are not standard and there are at least four sizes. For instance, the Staffs. and Worcs. Canal, Shropshire Union and others use a 1″ spindle, the Kennet and Avon Canal 1⅛″ and the Grand Union, River Wey and Basingstoke use a 1½″, as also does the Trent and Mersey at their wide locks. However, the Trent and Mersey canal at its narrow locks uses a spindle only ⅞″. There are a number of curiosities like the hand spike used on the Calder and Hebble.

A check should be made before journeys are made with the authority or club. Membership of a cruising club is always recommended as they do extend hospitality to those away from home and offer useful advice of all sorts. Their advice as well as that of the navigation authority about windlasses can be invaluable. There are a number of shoddy windlasses offered for sale some even made in soft metal like aluminium. It is important that the size of hole is correct and also that of the taper. A square hole on a tapered spindle causes serious damage as many regular canal travellers know. Take extra care at the locks converted to the hydraulic system. These are a mixed blessing whilst liked by newcomers to the canals they have serious snags in as much as the paddles cannot be dropped quickly in emergency.

At locks with a lock keeper always obey his instructions.

*The terms 'paddle' and 'windlass' are not used on Scottish canals.

Mooring.

If there is an alternative, often there is not, it is bad practice to moor against the tow-path. This should never be done on a waterway which still has horse-drawn boats and even on other waterways the practice can be a source of danger to users of the tow-path.

Mooring lines should never be stretched across the tow-path, but attached to mooring rings when available or, in the absence of rings, to mooring spikes driven into the bank of canal. Mooring spikes should not be driven too deep lest they penetrate the 'puddle' or watertight lining of the waterway.

It is bad practice to moor on or near a turn or immediately at the head or tail of a lock. In both cases inconvenience and even danger would be likely to result both to the craft which is moored and to other craft on the waterway.

At a remote mooring a riding light should not be so bright as to dazzle approaching steerers.

Miscellaneous Observations.

Normally a towing path is not a public right of way, nor, while the waterway remains navigable (the proper condition of a waterway) is it desirable that it should be so. The tow-path serves many essential purposes connected with the operation of the waterway and it is important that there should be a legal right to exclude hooligans and other undesirables. The boatman benefits as much from this as the navigation authority. Generally, however, and outside large towns, pedestrians may use the tow-path by courtesy. Angling rights are usually reserved to some particular organisation which leases them. Cycling on the tow-path is usually permitted only in connection with the operation of boats ('lock-wheeling').

The crowding of locksides when the boats are passing through is not a passport to popularity with the boatman. Permits for cycling and walking towpaths are issued by several navigation authorities including the BWB.

Great care should be taken by inland waterway navigators in the tideways, the Wash, the Mersey, the Thames Estuary and other inland waterway tidal links needing expert seamanship and often the assistance of a pilot. It cannot be too strongly emphasised that 'International Regulations for Preventing Collisions at Sea' apply to many inland waterways where sea-going craft navigate.

An inaccurate statement is often made that sail has right of way over powered craft. On the Broads and many estuaries this fallacy has caused great nuisance. A vessel in a dredged channel cannot alter course in many instances and often has little room to manoeuvre. Regulations, general and local, should always be studied and obeyed. A full knowledge of them is necessary for all. Waterways, whether tidal or non-tidal, should be treated with respect and those venturing for the first time should take a few simple lessons in seamanship. A well handled boat is a credit to the skipper, a source of interest to the onlooker and a very good friend to its insurance company.

The Little Ship Club, amongst others, runs excellent navigation classes, the Royal Yachting Association gives invaluable advice to all yachtsmen and a course of instruction at one of the R.Y.A. listed sailing schools is well worth while for potential motor cruiser skippers and yachtsmen. Navigation problems should be referred to the local club and thence to the R.Y.A. In conclusion, wear a life jacket and take care.

The IWA has a number of books in their book list for sale dealing with navigation. Some boatyards run navigation courses in the off season. Those using BWB waterways should obtain a copy of *Boating on the Waterways*.

Any unusual happening on the canal or river should be reported. In the first instance to the navigation authority and then, if appropriate, to the IWA or the RYA. There are unfortunately an increasing number of cases of back-waters, little used canals and rivers which have been used without let or hindrance for generations being claimed for fishing only and boats obstructed. Happenings of this sort should be immediately reported.

Authorities

British Waterways

Sixty per cent of the waterways of England, Scotland and Wales are nationalised and controlled by the British Waterways Board, the headquarter offices of which are in Melbury House, Melbury Terrace, London, NW1 6JX   Telephone 01-262-6711

COMMERCIAL AND CRUISING WATERWAYS
(Transport Act 1968, Section 104 and 12th Schedule)

The Board's Freight Services Division is responsible for the promotion of freight traffic and facilities on the commercial waterways and for the management of the Board's warehouses and inland terminals, docks and carrying fleet. The modernisation of the Sheffield and South Yorkshire Navigation shows the way forward for improving our waterways system for commercial transport. The Board is constantly in touch with future developments, and has carried out specialised work for expanding traffic. All enquiries for commercial use of waterways should be addressed to the Freight Services Division at the London headquarters. The following is a list of the commercial waterways. It should be pointed out that there is limited commercial traffic on certain waterways not in this list and any freight enquiries involving waterways on the B.W.B. network should be sent in for study and consideration.

The main navigable channels of the following waterways are designated as commercial waterways:

The Aire and Calder Navigation from the tail of River Lock, Leeds, and from the Calder and Hebble Navigation at Wakefield, to its entrance to Goole Docks and to its junction with the River Ouse at Selby.

The Calder and Hebble Navigation from the tail of Greenwood Lock to its junction with the Aire and Calder Navigation at Wakefield.

The Caledonian Canal.

The Crinan Canal

The Sheffield and South Yorkshire Navigation from the tail of the bottom lock at Tinsley to its junction with the River Trent at Keadby.

The New Junction Canal connecting the Sheffield and South Yorkshire Navigation with the Aire and Calder Navigation.

The Trent Navigation from the tail of Meadow Lane Lock, Nottingham, to Gainsborough Bridge.

The Weaver Navigation and the Weston Canal from Winsford Bridge to the junctions with the Manchester Ship Canal at Marsh Lock and at Delamere Dock.

The River Severn from Stourport to its junction with the Gloucester and Sharpness Canal at Gloucester.

The Gloucester and Sharpness Canal.

The River Lee Navigation from Hertford to the River Thames at Limehouse and to the tail of Bow Locks.

WATERWAYS FOR PLEASURE CRAFT

1.   The Board's pleasure craft licensing system is related to the schedules of cruising and commercial waterways in the Transport Act 1968.   With a single licence, all the waterways in England and Wales in these schedules are available for cruising.   Separate arrangements apply in Scotland as indicated in paragraph 7.

2.   The waterways thus available are as follows:—

In Southern England and Wales and the South Midlands
The main navigable channels of the following waterways:

The River Severn from Stourport to its junction with the Gloucester and Sharpness Canal at Gloucester.*

The Gloucester and Sharpness Canal.

The River Lee Navigation from Hertford to the River Thames at Limehouse and to the tail of Bow Locks.*

The Ashby Canal from its junction with the Coventry Canal to Snarestone.   The Birmingham Canal from its junction with the Worcester and Birmingham Canal at Worcester Bar to its junction with the Staffordshire and Worcestershire Canal at Aldersley by way of the Birmingham level as far as the head of Factory Locks, Tipton, and thence by way of Wolverhampton Level, including the branch leading to its junction with the Stourbridge Canal at Black Delph by way of the Netherton Tunnel.

The Birmingham and Fazeley Canal from its junction with the Birmingham Canal at Farmer's Bridge to its junction with the Trent and Mersey Canal at Fradley, including the detached portion of the Coventry Canal between Huddlesford Junction and Fradley Junction and the Digbeth branch.

The Coventry Canal from its junction with the Birmingham and Fazeley Canal at Fazeley to Coventry.

The Grand Union Canal from its junction with the Birmingham and Fazeley Canal at Digbeth and Salford to its junction with the River Thames at Brentford and at Regent's Canal Dock, including the branches to Northampton and Aylesbury and the Hertford Union Canal leading to the River Lee at Old Ford.

The Grand Union Canal from Leicester to Norton Junction, including the branch to Market Harborough.

The Kennet and Avon Canal from High Bridge, Reading, to the tail of Tile Mill Lock, and from the head of Bull's Lock to the tail of Hamstead Lock, and from the tail of Hanham Lock to the tail of the bottom lock at Bath.

* See para. 5

The Oxford Canal from its junction with the Grand Union Canal at Braunston to its junction with the Coventry Canal at Hawkesbury and from its junction with the Grand Union Canal from Napton to Oxford.

The Staffordshire and Worcestershire Canal.

The River Stort Navigation.

The Stourbridge Canal from its junction with the Birmingham Canal at Black Delph to its junction with the Staffordshire and Worcestershire Canal at Stourton.

The Stratford-on-Avon Canal from its junction with the Worcester and Birmingham Canal at King's Norton to its junction with the Grand Union Canal at Kingswood.

The Worcester and Birmingham Canal.

In the North and East Midlands and Northern England and Wales
The main navigable channels of the following waterways:

The Aire and Calder Navigation from the tail of River Lock, Leeds, and from the Calder and Hebble navigation at Wakefield, to its entrance to Goole Docks and to its junction with the River Ouse at Selby.

The Calder and Hebble Navigation from the tail of Greenwood Lock to its junction with the Aire and Calder Navigation at Wakefield.

The Sheffield and South Yorkshire Navigation from the tail of the bottom lock at Tinsley to its junction with the River Trent at Keadby.

The New Junction Canal connecting the Sheffield and South Yorkshire Navigation with the Aire and Calder Navigation.

The Trent Navigation from the tail of Meadow Lane Lock, Nottingham to Gainsborough Bridge.*

The Weaver Navigation and the Weston Canal from Winsford Bridge to the junctions with Manchester Ship Canal at Marsh Lock and at Delamere Dock.

The Calder and Hebble Navigation from Sowerby Bridge to the tail of Greenwood Lock, including the Huddersfield Broad Canal to Aspley Basin. The Chesterfield Canal from the tail of Morse Lock, Worksop, to its junction with the River Trent.

The Erewash Canal from Tanworth Road Bridge to its junction with the River Trent.

The Fossdyke Navigation.*

The Lancaster Canal from Preston to Tewitfield, including the branch to Glasson Dock.

The Leeds and Liverpool Canal from Old Roan Bridge, Aintree, to Leeds, including the branches to Tarleton and Leigh.

The Macclesfield Canal.

The Peak Forest from the top of Marple Locks to Whaley Bridge.

* See para. 5

The Ripon Canal from its junction with the River Ure to the tail of Littlethorpe Lock.

The Shropshire Union Canal from its junction with the Manchester Ship Canal at Ellesmere Port to its junction with the Staffordshire and Worcestershire Canal at Autherley, including the branches to the River Dee at Chester, to Llantisilio and to Middlewich.

The River Soar Navigation from its junction with the River Trent to Leicester.*

The Trent and Mersey Canal including the branch to Hall Green.

The Trent Navigation from Shardlow to the tail of Meadow Lane Lock*, Nottingham, by way of the Beeston Canal and part of the Nottingham Canal and including the branch to the River Soar and the length of the River Trent from its junction with the Nottingham Canal to Beeston Weir. The River Ure Navigation from its junction with the Ripon Canal to Swale Nab.

The Witham Navigation from Lincoln to Boston.*

3. The use of pleasure craft is also permitted by the Board on certain of their other waterways not referred to in the Transport Act schedules. This permission may be revoked at any time according to circumstances on the individual waterway. To be on these waterways, craft must have a valid licence but the permission referred to may be revoked without affecting the terms of the licence in any way. The waterways to which these arrangements apply are as follows:

(A) *For cruising:*

Sheffield and South Yorkshire Navigation—from the tail of the bottom lock at Tinsley to Sheffield Basin.

The Birmingham Canal Navigations in addition to lengths mentioned in Para. 2 (but excluding Bentley Canal from Fibbersley Bridge; Anson Branch; Dudley Tunnel; Titford Canal from Langley Green). The Birmingham Canal from Smethwick Junction to the head of Smethwick Locks by way of the Birmingham Level and thence by way of the Wolverhampton Level to Tipton Factory Junction, including the Gower Branch and the Spon Lane Locks Branch.

The Cannock Extension Canal from its junction with the Wyrley and Essington Canal at Pelsall to its limit of navigation as at the date of the Transport Act 1968.

The Dudley No. 1 Canal from Wolverhampton level to Park Head Locks.

The Dudley No. 2 Canal from its junction with the Netherton Tunnel Branch at Windmill End to Halesowen Basin, being its limit of navigation as at the date of the Transport Act 1968.

The Rushall Canal.

Soho Branch from Winson Green to Eyre St. Junction.

The Tame Valley Canal.

The Titford Canal from its junction with the Birmingham Canal at Oldbury to its limit of navigation as at the date of the Transport Act 1968.

* See para. 5

The Walsall Canal, The Walsall Arm Canal, The Wednesbury Old Canal, Bradley Canal from Deepfields Junction to Tup Street Bridge.

The Wyrley and Essington Canal from its junction with the Birmingham Canal at Horsley Fields to the head of Ogley Locks, including the branch to Anglesey Basin and the Daw End Branch. Bentley Canal from junction with Wyrley and Essington Canal to Hills Bridge.

The Erewash Canal from Tamworth Road Bridge to its terminus at Langley Mill.

The Slough Arm of the Grand Union Canal.

The Leeds and Liverpool Canal from Old Roan Bridge, Aintree to Stanley Dock.

The Caldon Arm of the Trent and Mersey Canal from its junction with the main line of the Trent and Mersey Canal at Etruria to Hazelhurst Junction and the branch towards Leek to the limit of navigation as at the date of the Transport Act 1968.

(B) *On special terms for craft confined to them or on a limited basis (e.g. canoeing):*

Kennet and Avon Canal and the River Avon*.

Monmouthshire and Brecon Canal excluding south of Pontypool and Crumlin Branch.

Bridgwater and Taunton Canal.

River Tone Navigation.

Ripon Canal and River Ure Navigation.

4. The above list is an outline one, not intended to be comprehensive of all arms and branches or to give precise limits but indicates the general position as at 1st April 1969. Local notices indicating actual limits or temporary stoppages or hazards which will vary according to circumstances should always be observed, and detailed information obtained as necessary from the Board's local offices.

5. There were certain river waterways where a payment for lockage gave a passage without a licence. This has been altered by the British Waterways Act 1971 which licences craft on these river navigations. Full details can be obtained from the British Waterways Board. The waterways concerned are marked with an asterisk.

6. The use of the waterways listed above by pleasure craft is subject to compliance with the Board's Bye-Laws, licensing conditions, and other directions of the Board. Copies of the Bye-Laws may be obtained from any of the Board's main offices. The Pleasure Craft Conditions are set out on the licence application form.

The British Waterways Board have received the consent of the Secretary of State for the Environment to promote a Private Bill in the 1983 session of Parliament.

Among the provisions in the Bill will be a clause, the effect of which would be to re-classify certain lengths of remainder waterway which were restored in the 1970s with financial assistance from the riparian local authorities. The Board believe that re-classification would secure further investment by the private sector in these waterways and give confidence for the future.

* See para. 5

In 1970 the chairman of the Board embarked on a series of discussions with the then riparian local authorities having remainder waterways within their areas to ascertain their views as to the future role which these waterways might play in the environment. As a result of these discussions, agreements were reached with the local authorities whereby they contributed towards the cost of restoring the length of waterway concerned to cruising waterway standard, and undertook to pay for the additional maintenance cost over and above that which the Board are bound to finance under the Transport Act, 1968.

The waterways concerned are:-

The Ashton Canal (Ducie Street Junction,
Manchester to Dukinfield Junction, Ashton).

Lower Peak Forest Canal (Dukinfield Junction to Marple).

Caldon Canal (Etruria to Froghall).

Caldon Canal (Leek Branch).

Erewash Canal (Long Eaton to Langley Mill).

Monmouthshire and Brecon Canal (Brecon to Pontypool).

Grand Union Canal (Slough Arms).

These 82 miles of waterways were upgraded to Cruising Waterway Standard by the British Waterways Act 1983, receiving Royal Assent on February 8th, 1983.

The Board are obliged, under Section 107 of the Transport Act, 1968, to deal with retained lengths of remainder waterway as economically as possible, consistent with the requirements of public health and the preservation of amenity and safety.

There are provisions in the Transport Act, 1968, and the National Parks and Access to the Countryside Act, 1949, which empower local authorities to contribute to the improvement and maintenance of waterways for recreational purposes.

SCOTLAND

7. Information about the canals in Scotland may be obtained from the following:

Caledonian Canal: Manager and Engineer, Caledonian Canal Office, Clachnaharry, Inverness. Tel. Inverness (0463) 33140

Crinan Canal: Engineer-in-Charge, Old Basin Works, Applecross Street, Glasgow G4 9SP. Tel. 041-332-6936

The normal pleasure craft licence does not apply and separate charges are payable for use of these canals.

THE BOARD'S OFFICES

8. Information about the Board's pleasure craft arrangements can be provided most readily by the

Pleasure Craft Licensing Office, Willow Grange, Church Road, Watford, Herts WD1 3QA (Tel. Watford (0923) 26422).

Local offices will also do their best to help, particularly with details of temporary stoppages, lock opening times, etc.

Canalphone. Up-to-date information on waterway stoppages caused by engineering work can be obtained from:
  01-702-8486 Midlands and North
  01-723-8487 Midlands and South
  This is a recorded information service.

9. The addresses of the Board's Area Engineering Offices are set out below:
  Wigan Area: Swan Meadow Road, Wigan, Lancs.   Tel. Wigan (0942) 42239
  Castleford Area: Lock Lane, Castleford, WF10 2LH, Yorks. Tel. Castleford (0977) 554351
  Northwich Area: Navigation Road, Northwich, CW8 1BH. Cheshire. Tel. Northwich (0606) 74321
  Nottingham Area: 24 Meadow Lane, Nottingham NG2 3HL. Tel. Nottingham (0602) 862411
  Birmingham Area: Reservoir House, Icknield Port Road, Birmingham BI6 0AA. Tel. 021-454-7091
  Gloucester Area: Dock Office, Gloucester GL1 2EJ. Tel. Gloucester (0452) 25524
  London Area: 43 Clarendon Road, Watford, Herts. WD1 1JE. Tel. Watford (0923) 31363
  Scotland: Old Basin Works, Applecross Street, Glasgow G4 9SP. Tel. 041-332-6936
  Amenity Activities Officer (Operations) and the *Fisheries Officer:* Wynyard House, Langley Road, Watford, Herts. Tel. Watford (0923) 26422

MOORING SITES

The Board offer moorings at various places. Charges which vary according to classification are also liable to alteration and schedules are obtainable from British Waterways Board offices on application.
Moorings are scarce particularly near the densely populated towns and cities.

The following site is managed on behalf of the Board by the firm stated:

  Grand Union Canal, Blomfield Road, Paddington, London. W.2.
  Enquiries to Turner Marina Ltd. 57 Fitzroy Road, London NW1 (Tel: 01-722-9806)

The Board also has reciprocal toll arrangements with the Bridgewater Canal Authorities.

British Waterways Board headquarters telephone numbers:
Engineering Dept.	01-725 8049
Estates Dept.	01-725 8034
Freight Division	01-725 8084
Leisure and Tourism Division	01 725 8082
Legal Dept.	01-725 8029
Press and Publicity Dept.	01-725 8005
Waterways News	01-725 8006

Regional Water Authorities

These public bodies are an amalgamation of river authorities and various other bodies with related water functions. A number of them are the navigation authority for certain waterways. Listed below are the main offices, but the local office can be located in the appropriate local telephone directory.

North West Water Authority, P.O. Box No. 261, Dawson House, Great Sankey, Warrington, Lancs WA5 3LW. *Tel.* Penketh (092 572) 4321

Northumbrian Water Authority, Eldon House, Regent Centre, Gosforth, Newcastle-upon-Tyne, NE3 3PX. *Tel.* Gosforth (0632) 841211

Yorkshire Water Authority, West Riding House, 67 Albion Street, Leeds LS1 5AA. *Tel.* Leeds (0532) 448201

Anglian Water Authority, Ambury Road, Huntingdon PE18 6NZ. *Tel.* Huntingdon (0480) 56181

Thames Water Authority, Nugent House, Vastern Road, Reading, Berks, RG1 8DB. *Tel.* Reading 593387

Southern Water Authority, Guildbourne House, Worthing, Sussex BN11 1LD. *Tel.* Worthing (0903) 205252

Wessex Water Authority, Techno House, Redcliffe Way, Bristol BS1 6NY. *Tel.* Bristol (0272) 25491

South West Water Authority, Box 22, 3-5 Barnfield Crescent, Exeter EX1 1RE. *Tel.* Exeter (0392) 50861/3

Severn Trent Water Authority, Abelson House, 2297 Coventry Road, Sheldon, Birmingham B26 3PR. *Tel.* 021-743-4222.

Welsh Water Authority, The Barracks, Brecon, Powys. *Tel.* Brecon (0874) 3182

A number of rivers as will be noted from the text are controlled by the British Waterways Board as navigation authority. In such cases the regional water authority will have drainage, sewage and other functions under its control, but not navigation. Excellent liaison exists between the various bodies.

For the general public with any problem, reference should be made to: **The Water Authorities Association,** 1 Queen Anne's Gate, London, SW1H 9BT. *Tel.* 01-222-8111.

This organisation has been created by the water authorities to co-ordinate and act as the amenity arm of the water industry. They will also be able to supply information about the various water parks now being established in various parts of the country such as the Lee Valley Regional Park, the Colne Valley Park, Cotswold Water Park and Thorpe Water Park.

The present Government (1988) is proposing the privatisation of the regional water authorities which will mean a considerable amount of re-organisation.

Routes

The following are some of the routes which can be taken by craft navigating the rivers and canals of England. Reference should be made to the body of the work for particulars of each waterway.

Route 1. River Thames (Richmond) to Bristol Channel at Avonmouth.
Waterways
River Thames (Richmond).
Kennet and Avon Canal Navigation.
River Avon (Avonmouth)
Approximate distance 159 miles.
The through route can be used at present only by canoes.

Route 2. River Thames to River Severn (Sharpness Docks)
Waterways
Same as Route 1 to Avonmouth.
Thence Bristol Channel to Sharpness.

Route 3. River Thames (Brentford) to River Severn (Gloucester).
Waterways
Grand Union Canal (Brentford to Kingswood).
Stratford-on-Avon Canal.
Worcester and Birmingham Canal.
River Severn (Gloucester).
Approximate distance 190 miles.
Between Braunston and Napton Navigation is over the Oxford Canal.

Route 4. River Thames (Oxford) to River Severn (Gloucester).
Waterways
Oxford Canal.
Grand Union Canal.
Stratford-on-Avon Canal.
Worcester and Birmingham Canal.
River Severn (Gloucester).
Approximate distance 138 miles.

Route 5. River Thames (Brentford) to River Mersey.
Waterways
Grand Union Canal.
Birmingham Canal Navigation.
Staffordshire and Worcestershire Canal.
Shropshire Union Canal (Ellesmere Port).
Manchester Ship Canal.
Approximate distance 236 miles.

Route 6. River Thames (Brentford) to River Mersey (Runcorn).
Waterways
Grand Union Canal.
Oxford Canal.
Coventry Canal.
Birmingham Canal Navigation.
Trent and Mersey Canal.
Bridgewater Canal (Runcorn).
(Top of closed locks)
Approximate distance 221 miles.

Route 7. River Thames (Brentford) to Leicester
Waterways
Grand Union Canal.
Approximate distance 131 miles.

Route 8. River Thames (Brentford) to Birmingham.
Waterways
Grand Union Canal.
Approximate distance 137 miles.

Route 9. River Thames (Brentford) to Cambridge.
Waterways
Grand Union Canal.
River Nene.
Middle Level Navigation.
River Great Ouse.
River Cam.
Approximate distance 220 miles.

Route 10. River Thames (Brentford) to River Humber (Trent Falls).
Waterways
Grand Union Canal.
River Trent and Nottingham Canal.
Approximate distance 270 miles.

Route 11. River Thames (Brentford) to the Wash.
Waterways
Grand Union Canal.
River Nene.
Approximate distance 173 miles.

Route 12. River Severn (Gloucester) to the Wash.

Waterways
River Severn.
Worcester and Birmingham Canal.
Stratford-on-Avon Canal.
Grand Union Canal.
River Nene.
Approximate distance 210 miles.

Route 13. River Severn (Gloucester) to River Humber (Trent Falls).

Waterways
River Severn.
Worcester and Birmingham Canal.
Birmingham Canal Navigations.
Coventry Canal.
Trent and Mersey Canal.
River Trent and Nottingham Canal.
Approximate distance 215 miles.

Route 14. River Severn (Gloucester) to the River Mersey.

Waterways
River Severn.
Staffordshire and Worcestershire Canal.
Shropshire Union Canal.
Manchester Ship Canal.
Approximate distance 133 miles.

Route 15. River Severn (Gloucester) to River Mersey (Runcorn).

Waterways
River Severn.
Worcester and Birmingham Canal.
Birmingham Canal Navigations.
Staffordshire and Worcestershire Canal.
Trent and Mersey Canal.
Bridgewater Canal (Runcorn).
(Top of closed locks)
Approximate distance 155 miles

Route 16, River Humber (Goole) to River Mersey (Liverpool)

Waterways
Aire and Calder Navigation.
Leeds and Liverpool Canal.
Approximate distance 169 miles

Route 17, River Humber (Trent Falls) to River Mersey (Runcorn)

Waterways
River Trent and Nottingham Canal.
Trent and Mersey Canal.
Bridgewater Canal (Runcorn)
Approximate distance 214 miles.

MAINTENANCE STOPPAGES
Due to the heavy arrears of maintenance, stoppages for engineering work have increased in recent years, particularly on B.W.B. waterways. Always check with the local office before travelling. Waterway magazines do also list stoppages and clubs and societies do receive from B.W.B. a stoppage list.

LOCK OPENING HOURS
Boats operating in the Midlands have practically unrestricted cruising, during daylight hours. In some other areas locks close early and also opening bridges. Advance planning is advisable, particularly on the majority of Yorkshire Waterways.

RADIO COMMUNICATION
Anyone visiting the River Trent, River Ouse (Yorks.) Aire and Calder, or Sheffield and South Yorkshire Navigations should obtain a radio. Sound signals are now rarely used and communication can be made to lock-keepers. Full details from British Waterways Board.

Delph Locks on the Dudley Canal near Brierley Hill, Birmingham

Inland Waterways of England and Wales

ARRANGEMENT OF THIS WORK

The main canals and rivers of England, Wales, and Scotland including those that are nationalised, are listed alphabetically in the following pages. Tributaries are included immediately after the river or canal to which they connect. A number of tidal estuaries are included either because they have at one time or another been the subject of legislation or because of their importance as yachting centres. Only the basic details of these are, however, given and yachtsmen intending to cruise thereon are advised to consult coastal sailing directions and pilot books.

Figures given alongside the marginal headings Length, Beam, Draught and Headroom are to be regarded as maximum dimensions for craft using the particular waterway.

Unless otherwise stated, depths and heights are given at normal water level, the following abbreviations are used in connection with tidal waterways:

H.W.S.T.   High Water at Spring tides
or M.H.W.S.   Mean high water springs

H.W.N.T.   High Water at Neap tides
or M.H.W.N. Mean High Water Neaps

L.W.   Low water

METRICATION

For this 6th edition the author and publishers considered converting the distance tables to metric units but for various reasons imperial units are retained. The subject is of some complexity as the Metrication Board has been abolished and compulsory metrication halted. The Port of London Authority anticipate that for a number of years to come tidal height predictions will continue to be published in both feet and metres; their distance tables are listed in sea miles and land miles. The Thames Water Authority lists its River Thames section in miles.

The great bulk of canal literature and data is in miles and furlongs and this coupled with the fact that mileposts are being erected in new locations in miles and furlongs leaves us in no doubt that for the time being we must meet the wishes of those concerned with the inland waterways by continuing to use imperial units.

River Adur (1)

This is now an estuary navigation. The first work on this river was done under an Act of Parliament of 1807, it was extended through two locks to West Grinstead by a further Act of 1825, but the locks were derelict by 1870. At high tide it is a useful river to explore with light craft, in pleasant pastoral countryside. Dredging works have improved navigation in recent years. Shoreham Port Authority Revision Order 1968 and 1969, applies.

Authority	**From entrance to Old Shoreham Bridge and Southwick Canal**
	Shoreham Port Authority, Harbour Offices, Southwick, Sussex. Tel. Southwick (038 778) 592613. (For lock and tide times only: Southwick (038 778) 592366.
	Old Shoreham to Bines Bridge
	Southern Water Authority, Guildbourne House, Worthing, Sussex. Tel. Worthing (0903) 205252.

From and to	Bines Bridge to river mouth.
Distance	11⅛ miles.
Length	Unlimited
Beam	,,

Draught					
To Upper Beeding Bridge, H.W.S.T. ...	...	...	8ft. 6ins.
To Bines Bridge, H.W.S.T.	...	...	...	...	3ft. 0ins.

Headroom					
Through Upper Beeding Bridge, H.W.S.T. ...	...	6ft. 9ins.
To Bines Bridge, H.W.S.T.	...	...	...	...	5ft. 6ins.

Tow-path	From Bines Bridge to Old Shoreham Bridge.
Locks	None. The two locks on the upper reaches of the river at West Grinstead and Lock Farm are derelict. There were also 2 and possibly 3 'Flash Locks' used in the past.
Connections	The old River Adur forms a branch canal, from the eastern arm of the harbour to Portslade and Aldrington, a distance of 1¾ miles. The entrance locks to this canal (sometimes called Southwick Canal) will admit craft up to the following dimensions:
Length	374ft.
Beam	57ft.
Draught	22ft.
	No overhead obstructions in the canal or port.
	River Adur, Eastern Branch, is navigable to Mock Bridge (2 miles). (The dimensions of craft for the Canal section also apply to the river up to Tarmac Wharf.)

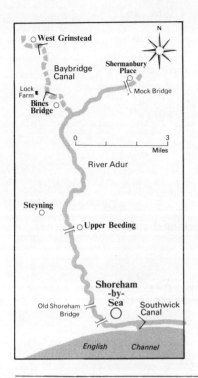

Navigation notes

The tide ebbs very quickly, and this leaves only a narrow channel in between the banks. Craft should, if possible, leave Shoreham at 4 hours flood, so as to go upstream with the tide. A guide to Shoreham Harbour is available and gives directions for craft entering from the sea. There is a Common Law right of navigation to Shermanbury. Local information can be obtained from the District Engineer, S. W. A. Henfield, Beeding, West Sussex. Tel. Steyning (0903) 813098.

High water at Beeding Bridge approximately one hour after Shoreham. High water at Shoreham about 10 minutes after Dover.

Speed limit   4 miles per hour.

Distance Table	Miles	Furlongs
Bines Bridge (Road Bridge, B. 2135) to:		
Junction with River Adur (Eastern Branch)	—	7
Footbridge	1	6
Upper Beeding Bridge	5	1
Old Shoreham Bridge	8	5
Railway Bridge (British Railways, S.R.)...	9	2
Norfolk Bridge, Shoreham-by-Sea ...	9	4
Kingston-by-Sea Wharf	10	5
Junction with Southwick Canal	11	—
Mouth of river	11	1

Aire and Calder Navigation and River Aire (2)

The Aire and Calder network of waterways were originally promoted by Acts passed in the years 1699, 1774, 1820 and 1828. They are mainly commercial waterways, a number of locks having been modernised to European standards where boatmen should observe coloured light signals. The locks to Leeds are approximately size 217ft. by 18ft, 6ins. and below Castleford 457ft. by 22ft. Maximum dimensions listed are those imposed by physical conditions of the waterway. The landscape is mainly industrial but the upper Calder valley and the western approaches to Wakefield are amenity areas of a distinct order.

Authority

British Waterways Board, Local office: Dock Street, Leeds 1. Tel. Leeds (0532) 36741/7.
Area Engineer's office: Lock Lane, Castleford, Yorkshire. Tel. Castleford (0977) 554351
Associated British Ports (Goole), Dock Office, Stanhope Street, Goole, North Humberside DN14 5BB. Tel. Goole (0405) 2691/5.

From and to
Main Canal: Goole Docks to Leeds Bridge and junction with Leeds and Liverpool Canal.
Wakefield Section: Castleford Junction to Fall Ing Lock and junction with Calder and Hebble Navigation.

The Barnsley section is now derelict and abandoned, although several pounds still hold water. Some restoration in progress. Barnsley (Dearne) Aqueduct, a fine specimen, has been demolished.

Selby Section: From main line at Knottingley to junction with the River Ouse at Selby.

Dewsbury Old Cut: Double Locks, junction with Calder and Hebble to Savile Town Wharf.

Main Line

Distance	Goole to Leeds—34 miles.	
Length	Up to Leeds Lock 185ft. 0ins.	Through Leeds Lock 142ft. 0ins.
Beam	18ft. 9ins.	17ft. 8ins.
Draught	8ft. 0ins.	7ft. 6ins.
Headroom	12ft. 3 ins.	12ft. 3ins.
Locks	13. Fall from Leeds. (Open during the usual working hours). (Lemonroyd Lock is now 258ft x 23ft 5ins)	

Wakefield Section

From and to Castleford Junction (main line Goole to Leeds) to Wakefield Fall Ing Lock (junction with Calder and Hebble Navigation).

Distance 7½ miles (Branch to Wakefield Old Wharf ½ mile).

Length	142ft.	*Draught*	7ft.
Beam	17ft. 6ins.	*Headroom*	12ft. 3ins.

Locks 4. Fall from Wakefield. (Branch to Old Wharf: One lock falling from Wakefield called Wakefield Old Lock).

Lock and bridge-keepers Usual working hours, Sundays by arrangement. Details available from the Area Engineer.

Selby Canal

From and to Bank Dole Junction, Knottingley (main Goole to Leeds Canal) to junction with the River Ouse at Selby.

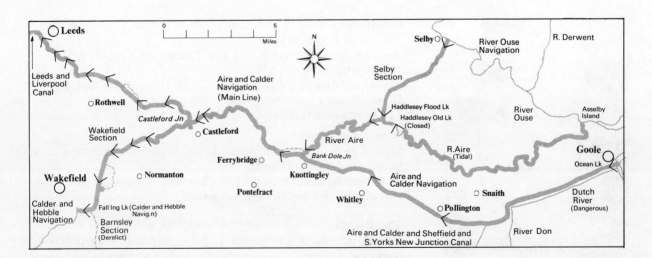

Distance	11¾ miles.
Length	78ft. 6ins.
Beam	16ft. 6ins.
Draught	6ft.
Headroom	10ft.
Locks	4. Lock gates worked by boat owners (lock-keepers operate Selby Lock which is tidal. Details on application to B.W.B.) Fall from Bank Dole.
Bridges	Numerous.

River Aire

From and to	The entrance from the River Ouse at Asselby Island, about 5 miles above Goole, to the junction with the Selby branch at Haddlesey.
Remarks	From the entrance to as far as Haddlesey Old Lock, now closed, the river is open navigation but at Haddlesey it comes under the jurisdiction of British Waterways. From its entrance to Haddlesey Old Lock the river is tidal.
Canoeing Note	The River Aire is unattractive for canoeing except above Leeds between Skipton and Kirkstall. In a rainy season it is canoeable to the source at Malham Cove.
Distance	From the entrance to Haddlesey Old Lock (closed), 16¾ miles. From Haddlesey Old Lock to the junction Selby Branch, ¾ mile.
Length	78ft. 6ins.
Beam	16ft. 6ins.
Draught	About 5ft. 6ins.
Headroom	11ft.
Locks	One. (Closed in 1937). Fall from junction with Selby Branch.
Tow-path	Only on the section under the jurisdiction of British Waterways.

Applicable to whole system

Tow-path Throughout navigation, except tidal portion of River Aire.

Lock and bridge-keepers Not on duty on six statutory holidays, Saturday afternoons and Sundays, except Bulholme, Ferrybridge, Whitley and Pollington all on main line, but craft can generally be passed on prior notification to the British Waterways Board, Area Engineer's Office.

Special note The commercial traffic on this waterway is generally dense and the greatest care should be taken by pleasure craft operators particularly when meeting and passing other craft.
Compartment boats (locally called 'Tom Puddings') were towed in trains of up to 19 boats at a time. These boats were withdrawn from service in 1986.

Speed limits 6 miles per hour on the Aire and Calder Navigation and 4 miles per hour on the Selby Canal and River Aire.

Facilities Limited. A boatyard at Goole and also just inside the adjoining Leeds and Liverpool Canal at Leeds.

Distance Table

Main Line (Places indented are off the main line of navigation).

Junction with Leeds and Liverpool Canal, Main Line, and Leeds Bridge to:

	Miles	Furlongs
Crown Point Bridge	—	4
Nether Mills Wharf	—	4
Island Wharf	—	4
New Dock Basin, Leeds Lock No. 1	—	4
Fearn's Island	—	6
Suspension Bridge	1	—
Goodman Street Wharf	1	2
Hunslet Wharf	1	4
Knostrop Turn Bridge, **Knostrop Flood Lock No. 2**	1	6
Knostrop Lock No. 3	1	7½
Fishpond Lock No. 4	4	—
Woodlesford Lock No. 5	5	2
Swillington Bridge Wharf	5	4
Fleet Mills	6	4
Lemonroyd Lock No. 6	6	4
Fleet Bridge	6	4
Savile Colliery Basin	7	—
Astley Cut Staiths	7	6
Kippax Lock No. 7	8	4
Allerton Wharf	9	—
Castleford*****Junction with Wakefield Section*	10	—
Castleford Flood Lock No. 8	10	—
Short Branch: Castleford Dam and Mills through		
Castleford Middle Lock (a sidelock 70ft. 8ins. wide)	10	2
Bulholme Lock No. 9	10	6
Fairburn	13	2
Ferrybridge Lock No. 10 *(Flood Lock)*	15	2
Mill Bridge Wharf	15	6

*Turn left, going downsteam here, when traffic lights are green. Avoid weir straight ahead.

Distance Table

	Miles	Furlongs
Cow Lane Bridge ...	16	6
Shepherd Bridge ...	16	6
Bank Dole Junction, *junction with Selby Branch*	17	—
Toll Bar Bridge ...	17	—
Whitley Lock No. 11 ...	21	—
Short Branch—Heck Basin ...	22	4
Pollington Lock No. 12 ...	24	4
Crowcroft Bridge ...	25	—
Junction with Aire and Calder and Sheffield and South Yorkshire		
Junction Canal ...	26	6
Beever's Bridge Wharf ...	27	4
Goole Old Waterworks Pumping Station ...	30	6
Goole Timber Pond (Dog and Duck) ...	33	2
South Dock Bridge ...	33	4
Entrance Locks to Goole Docks, *junction with River Ouse,* Ocean		
Lock No. 13 ...	34	—

Wakefield Section

Fall Ing, junction with Calder and Hebble Navigation to:

	Miles	Furlongs
Junction with Old Wharf Branch (one lock) ...	—	2
Junction with Barnsley Canal (derelict) ...	—	6
Short Branch—Kirkthorpe Dam ...	1	2
Broadreach Lock No. 1 ...	1	6
Stanley Aqueduct ...	2	5
Birkwood Lock No. 2 ...	3	2
King's Road Lock No. 3 ...	4	2
Foxholes Side Lock (to Foxholes Basin) ...	4	2
Woodnook Lock No. 4 ...	5	4
Short Branch—Altoft's Lock * ...	5	2
—Altoft's Basin ...	5	2
—Fairies Hill Lock ...	5	6
Pottery Bridge ...	7	4
Castleford Mere ...	7	2
Castleford Junction, *junction with Main Line* ...	7	4

* Now disused. Alternative route is via Fairies Hill Lock

Selby Section

Bank Dole Junction, Knottingley, to:

	Miles	Furlongs
Bank Dole Lock No. 1 ...	—	4
Beal Bridge Wharf ...	2	4
Beal Lock No. 2 ...	2	6
Birkin Wharf ...	3	6
Commencement of Selby Canal and Haddlesey Flood Lock No. 3,		
junction with River Aire ...	6	4
Paper House Bridge ...	7	2
Gateforth Landing ...	7	6
Burton Bridge ...	8	4
Burn Bridge Wharf ...	9	2
Selby Bridge Wharf ...	11	2
Selby Swing Bridge Wharf ...	11	4
Selby Lock No. 4, *junction with River Ouse* ...	11	6

Distance Table

	Miles	Furlongs
River Aire Section		
Junction with Selby Branch to:		
Haddlesey Old Lock (closed)	—	6
Temple Farm	2	2
Temple Hirst	4	—
Weeland	4	6
Snaith	8	2
Rawcliffe	12	—
Newland	13	4
Airmyn	15	6
Asselby Island, *junction with River Ouse*	16	6
Dewsbury Old Cut Section		
Double Locks, junction with Calder and Hebble Navigation to:		
Dewsbury Gas Works	—	2
Brown and Company's Chemical Works	—	4
Coal Wharf	—	6
Timber Yard	—	6
Savile Town Wharf	1	—

Aire and Calder and Sheffield and South Yorkshire New Junction Canal (3)

*See plan Sheffield and S Yorkshire Navigation p. 299

This short waterway serves to connect not only the Aire and Calder Main with the Sheffield and South Yorkshire Canal, but also Sheffield with the River Trent via the Sheffield and South Yorkshire Navigation. It was not opened until 1905, to increase the scope of the coal trade carried in 'Tom Puddings'.

Authority	British Waterways Board, Local Office: Dock Street, Leeds 1. Tel. Leeds 36741/7.
From and to	*Junction with the Aire and Calder main canal, about 7 miles west of Goole, to junction with the Sheffield and South Yorkshire Navigation, near Bramwith.
Distance	5½ miles.
Length	215ft.
Beam	22ft. 6ins.
Draught	9ft.
Headroom	Unlimited.
Locks	One. Sykehouse.

Tow-path	Throughout navigation.
Lock and bridge-keepers	Not on duty on six statutory holidays, Saturday afternoons and Sundays. Navigation at weekends can be arranged by prior notice.
Speed limit	6 miles per hour.

Distance Table

Bramwith, junction with Sheffield and South Yorkshire Navigation (River Dun Navigation) to:

	Miles	Furlongs
Sykehouse Lock (only lock on this canal)	3	4
Junction with Aire and Calder Navigation Main Line	5	4

River Alde (4)

The entrance to this river is most difficult and dangerous, due to the shifting shingle bar across the entrance. It is a lonely estuary and Shingle Street was a village destroyed in the war. Whilst its entrance is shingle, its banks are very muddy. The river is known as the Ore below Orford.

Authority	*None, an open navigation.
From and to	Snape Bridge to Shingle Street.
Distance	21 miles.
Length	Unlimited.
Beam	,,
Draught	To Slaughden Quay (near Aldeburgh) 10ft. To Iken, 4ft.† To Snape Bridge at H.W.S.T. 5ft.
Locks	None.
Tow-path	,,
Canoeing note	Only canoeable for about 2 miles, above Snape Bridge.
Tides	Mean rise and fall at Aldeburgh is 8 feet and the tidal stream runs at about 4 knots in the river, on the average. At the entrance it may run at up to 6 knots. It is high water at the bar 30 minutes before H.W. Harwich and at Slaughden Quay about 2 hours after H.W. at the bar.

*See Imray Chart C28

†It is possible to take a yacht to Iken and lie there in about 4 feet of water at all states of the tide. Location of the hole can easily be found by local enquiry.

River Ancholme (5)

The Ancholme Navigation was promoted under Acts of 1767, 1802 and 1825. John Rennie was extensively concerned with the navigation which carried mainly agricultural produce. A very old navigation, a patent was granted in 1287 for improving the river to Bishopbridge, to assist traffic from the Humber.

The main line is straight and the countryside is not easily observed over the high banks. At certain times, such as after very heavy rain, being a drain, the river may be used for sluicing off the land and craft cannot enter.

There is a Rase-Ancholme Trust which seeks to expand the waterway to Market Rasen. Above Harlam Hill is a new cut into the River Rase which can be used by small craft for some distance.

Authority	Anglian Water (Lincolnshire River Division), 50 Wide Bargate, Boston, Lincs. PB21 6SA.
From and to	South Ferriby Sluice on the River Humber to Bishopbridge.
Distance	19 miles.
Length	Above Harlam Hill Lock—69ft. Below Harlam Hill Lock—80ft.
Beam	Above Harlam Hill Lock—16ft. Below Harlam Hill Lock—19ft.
Draught	6ft. 6ins. for 9 miles up to Brigg, then gradually lessening to 3 feet at Harlam Hill Lock, 17 miles up from South Ferriby sluice.
Headroom	On New River Ancholme—11ft. 6ins. On Old River Ancholme at Brigg—11ft.
Locks	2. South Ferriby worked by lock-keeper. Harlam Hill by boat crews. Fall from Bishopbridge. (Harlam Hill Lock now has a guillotine gate and is very difficult to work).
Bridges	13.
Speed limit	4½ miles an hour.
Tow-path	Throughout navigation.
Facilities	These are scarce. There is a marina near the entrance and one at Ancholme Bridge which is an inn with comprehensive boatyard facilities.
Tides	High water at Ferriby Sluice 18 minutes after Hull.

Distance Table								*Miles*	*Furlongs*
Bishopbridge to:									
Owersby Landing ...	...	...	...	...	...	...	...	1	4
Atterby Landing ...	...	...	...	...	...	...	...	2	–
Harlam Hill Lock No. 1 ...	...	...	...	...	...	...	...	2	4

Distance Table

						Miles	Furlongs
Snitterby Bridge	...	...	...	...	...	2	6
Brandy Wharf	...	...	...	...	...	4	—
Redbourne Old River	...	...	...	...	...	6	2
North Kelsey Landing	...	...	...	...	...	6	4
Hibaldstow Bridge	...	...	...	...	...	6	6
Cadney Bridge	...	...	...	...	...	7	6
Southern junction with navigable loopline of							
Old River Ancholme through Brigg, 1¾ *miles long*			...	9	4		
Brigg, town and new bridge	...	...	...	...	10	2	
Northern junction with navigable loop line of							
Old River Ancholme through Brigg	...	...	...	10	6		
Castlethorpe Bridge	...	...	...	...	...	11	4
Broughton Bridge	...	...	...	...	...	12	4
Worlaby Landing	...	...	...	...	...	13	4
Bonby Landing	...	...	...	...	...	14	6
Appleby Landing	...	...	...	...	...	16	—
Saxby Bridge	...	...	...	...	...	16	2
Scabcroft	...	...	...	...	...	17	2
Horkstowe Bridge	...	...	...	...	...	17	6
Ferriby Sluice, Lock No. 2, *junction with River Humber*					19	—	

River Arun (6)

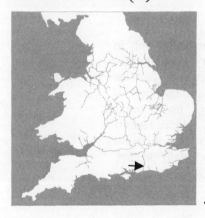

The River Arun was promoted as a navigation under Acts dated 1732 and 1793. The head of navigation was Newbridge, near Wisborough Green. The navigation, 6 locks and Hardham Tunnel, are now all derelict as the Arun Navigation was closed in 1896. The river in recent years, has been extensively dredged for land drainage purposes and under favourable conditions craft can reach Pallingham.

The scenery is dull until Arundel, where the castle dominates the river scene, thereafter through the South Downs it is very fine particularly by the Black Rabbit Inn, an old bargeman's inn that has now become a famed beauty spot and good mooring for the visitor. The Pulborough area has been dredged recently and this section is now much easier to navigate than it has been for many years. Famous and historic Stopham Bridge is usually the head of navigation for the average cruiser on a good tide. There is a Wildfowl Trust Centre by the River Arun just north of Arundel. Other Acts 1785 and 1821.

Authority	**From Entrance to Arundel Bridge** The Littlehampton Harbour Board, Paines Wharf, Littlehampton, Sussex. Tel. Littlehampton (090 64) 21215 **Above Arundel Bridge** Southern Water Authority, Guildbourne House, Worthing, Sussex. Tel. Worthing (0903) 205252. Craft from sea must stop and report to the Harbour Master at Littlehampton.
From and to	The entrance at Littlehampton to Pulborough.
Distance	Littlehampton to Pulborough, 22 miles. Littlehampton to Pallingham Lock, 25½ miles. (Small craft should be able to reach Pallingham Lock on a favourable tide).

Littlehampton to Arundel at low water

Length	95ft.
Beam	10ft.
Draught	3ft. At high water, larger size craft can navigate as there is a rise of about 20 feet of water.
Headroom	See bridges for headroom.

Arundel to Pulborough

Dimensions	Above Arundel Bridge to Pulborough the river is accessible only to small motor craft and boats. The depths vary considerably. At high tide there is about 8 feet of water to Amberley and 3 to 4 feet at Pulborough. Between Amberley and Greatham the river is shallow and requires some care to navigate through, and towards Pulborough weeds are likely to cause obstruction. Under favourable tidal conditions it is possible for small craft to reach the ruins of Pallingham Lock. The Canal above this lock is totally derelict. but restoration has commenced under the aegis of the Wey Arun 'Canal Trust Limited.
Tow-path	Exists in places only.
Locks	None.
Canoeing Note	Canoeable from Newbridge, near Billinghurst.
Bridges	Between Littlehampton and Pulborough, 8 bridges span the river as follows:

	Approximate Clearance at	
	H.W.S.T. ft. ins.	*Low water* ft. ins.
Littlehampton Swing Bridge ...	5 0	20 0
Ford Railway Fixed Bridge ...	11 0	21 0

				Approximate clearance at	
				H.W.S.T.	*Low water*
				ft. ins.	ft. ins.
Arundel Bridge	...	...	...	4 0	12 0
Offham Bridge	...	...	...	8 0	12 0
South Stoke Bridge		...	...	8 0	12 0
Houghton Bridge	...	...	...	3 0	9 0
Greatham Bridge	...	...	...	8 0	12 0
Pulborough Bridge		...	...	4 0	8 0

Great care should be taken in negotiating all bridges as the clearance may be materially affected by flood waters.

Speed Limit

6½ knots. Above Arundel 5½ knots. Speed limits are rigorously enforced for protection of river banks etc., by the Southern Water Authority under a bye-law but they have no responsibility for navigation.

Charges

There are no charges above Arundel Bridge or waters outside the jurisdiction of the Littlehampton Harbour Board.

Yachtsmen wishing to obtain further information with regard to the navigation of the river should apply to the Harbour Master, Littlehampton.

Facilities

Limited to Littlehampton, Arundel and Pulborough. No boatyards except for light craft.

Tides

The river is tidal and streams run from 4 to 6 knots.

At Littlehampton spring tides rise 16 feet, neaps about 12 feet. High water at Arundel about one hour after Littlehampton. Spring tides rise 10 feet, neaps about 8 feet.

The stream at the entrance and along the river is generally strong both on the flood and ebb.

Arun Navigation

This is at present derelict but the Wey Arun Canal Trust have already done some restoration work on a long term project to re-open the link from the River Wey to the sea. The Arun Navigation was separate from the Wey Arun Junction Canal and ran to Newbridge, on the Petworth – Billingshurst Road, from Pallingham Lock. Pallingham was a double staircase lock, and distances were as follows:

Newbridge Wharf to:	Miles	Furlongs
Orfold Aqueduct	1	2
Lordings Lock (sometimes called Orfold)	1	3
Lee Farm Lock	3	–
Pallingham Quay and Docks	4	3
Pallingham Lock (Double)	4	4

The navigation joined the river at Pallingham and left the Arun at Hardham to enter the River Rother and go via Hardham Lock to the canal running due south to cut off the bend in the river with two low bridges. The canal had a lock at the top end of the tunnel (Hardham Tunnel 375 yards) and also at the junction of the canal, at Coldwaltham with the Arun.

The navigation was legally abandoned in 1896, under the Railway and Canal Act 1888.

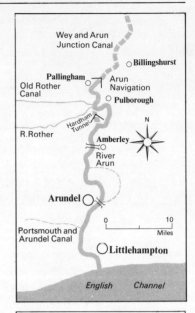

Distance Table

Pallingham Lock (derelict) to:

	Miles	Furlongs
Stopham Bridge (Inn)	2	2
Junction with River Rother (western)	2	4
Water's Edge Inn (mooring)	3	3
Pulborough Bridge (Swan Inn)	3	4
Greatham	5	6
Coldwaltham Bridge	6	5
Old Arun Canal junction (derelict)	7	3
Bury Wharf and Ferry	8	7
Houghton Bridge and Amberley Station	10	—
South Stoke	13	2
Offham Bridge	16	6
Black Rabbit Inn	17	6
Arundel Bridge (Bridge House Inn)	18	6
Railway Bridge (Southern Region)	21	6
Junction of Old Portsmouth and Arundel Canal	22	4
Littlehampton Ferry	24	6
Littlehampton Harbour mouth	25	4

Ashby de la Zouch Canal (7)

This waterway was promoted by an Act in 1794 and once carried heavy coal traffic. Attractive and historical countryside which includes Bosworth Field.

Authority
British Waterways Board.

From and to
Junction with Coventry Canal at Marston to Snarestone (originally continued to Moira, but this section has been abandoned by B.T.C. Act 1956.

Distance	22 miles.
Length	72ft.
Beam	7ft.
Draught	3ft. 6ins.
Headroom	6ft. 6ins.

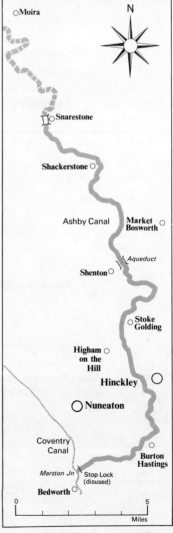

Locks	None. (Marston Junction stop lock is now converted stop gate)
Bridges	Numerous.
Tow-path	Throughout navigation, except Snarestone Tunnel.
Tunnels	Snarestone, 250 yards. No tow-path.
Remarks	Canal is ideal for pleasure craft.
Facilities	There is a boatyard at Stoke Golding and some limited facilities at Market Bosworth at the BWB mooring. Several inns near canal.

Distance Table

Marston Junction, junction with Coventry Canal and Marston stop lock to:

	Miles	Furlongs
Railway Bridge (London Midland Region, Trent Valley line) ...	—	6
Burton Hastings ... .` ...	3	—
Watling Street Bridge, boundary Warwickshire and Leicestershire ...	5	—
Hinckley brickyard (inn and village nearby)	5	5
Higham-on-the-Hill	7	4
Stoke Golding Wharf	8	6
Shenton Station (site of Bosworth Battle)	13	—
Market Bosworth Station (Market Bosworth, one mile)	14	7
Carlton Bridge and Sence Brook	15	6
Congerstone	17	1
Shackerstone	18	2
Snarestone village and tunnel	21	—
Head of Navigation (just above Bridge 61)	22	—

Ashton, Peak Forest and Macclesfield Canals (8)

These three canals have been, for many years, considered as one navigation. In the Great Central Railway days, it was the 'A.P.M.'.   Recently the importance of the canals has been emphasised as they are part of the Cheshire Canal Ring. This consists of:

The Peak Forest from Marple to Dukinfield (8 miles).
The Ashton Canal (6¾ miles).
The Rochdale Canal at Ducie Street (1¼ miles).
The Bridgewater Canal at Castleford to Preston Brook (24 miles).
The Trent and Mersey Canal, Kidsgrove to Hall Green (30 miles).
The Macclesfield Canal (28½ miles long, rejoining the Peak Forest Canal at Marple).

The Upper Peak Forest Canal runs from Marple to Buxworth Basin. The latter is being restored by the Inland Waterways Protection Society. This forms a useful branch of the Cheshire Ring, though not part of it. There are inns and boatyards on the three canals. shopping at Macclesfield, Congleton, Bollington and Marple, also facilities at Whaley Bridge and New Mills.

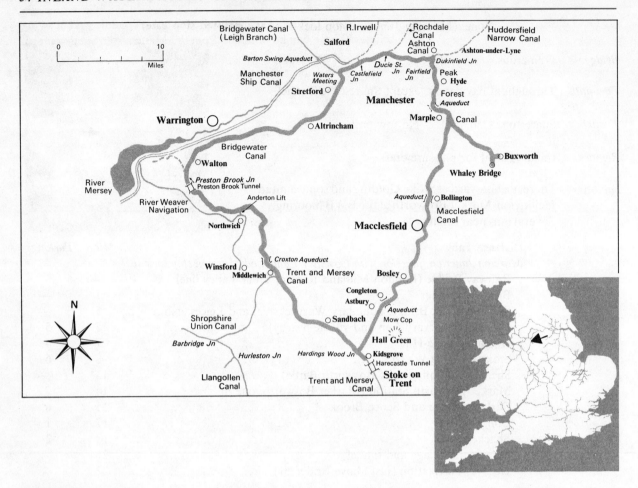

ASHTON CANAL

This Canal was promoted under Acts dated 1792, 1793, 1798, 1800 and 1805. It was the scene of one of the largest voluntary clearance operations called *Operation Ashton*. It is in a wholly industrial area but at the Manchester end it runs through a series of caverns. Now completely restored.

Authority	British Waterways Board.
From and to	Junction with Rochdale Canal at Manchester to junction with Peak Forest Canal at Ashton-under-Lyne.
Distance	Main Canal—6¼ miles.
Length	70ft.
Beam	7ft.
Draught	2ft. 9ins.
Headroom	5ft. 4ins.
Locks	18. Rise from Manchester. Lock gates worked by boat crews.

A Leeds and Liverpool key is required to unlock paddle gear at swing bridges. These can be obtained from the Manchester Section Yard, adjacent to Lock No. 2.

Tow-path	Throughout canal.
Bridges	82 (including moveable bridges).
Branches	Fairbottom, Hollinwood, Islington and Stockport branches are closed.

Distance Table

Manchester Ducie Street, junction with Rochdale Canal to:

	Miles	Furlongs
Lock No. 1 Ancoats junction with Islington Branch (Closed) ...	—	3
„ No. 3 Ancoats ...	—	4
„ No. 4 Beswick Locks 5, 6,* 7, follow in the Beswick flight ...	1	2
„ No. 8 Clayton Lock Nos. 9, 10, 11, 12, 13, follow in the Clayton flight ...	2	—
Clayton Junction, *junction with Stockport Branch* (Closed) ...	2	3½
Lock No. 13 Clayton (top lock) ...	2	5½
„ No. 14 Edge Lane ...	2	7
„ No. 16 Fairfield ...	3	4
„ No. 18 Fairfield Junction, *junction with Hollinwood Branch* (Closed). ...	3	5½
Guide Bridge Railway Station ...	5	3
Ashton-under-Lyne, Walk Mill Bridge ...	6	—
Dukinfield Junction, *junction with Peak Forest Canal* ...	6	2
Ashton-under-Lyne, junction with Huddersfield Narrow Canal ...	6	5½

PEAK FOREST CANAL

This canal was promoted under Acts dated 1794, 1800 and 1805. The scenery changes after leaving the Ashton Canal and Marple Locks are ascended. Very fine stone navigation works.

Authority	British Waterways Board.
From and to	Junction with the Ashton Canal at Dukinfield to Buxworth Basin.
Distance	Main Line—14¾ miles. Whaley Bridge Branch—½ mile.
Length	70ft.
Beam	7ft.
Draught	3ft. This is below standard and may be improved.
Headroom	6ft.

* Lock No. 6 is sometimes known as Bradford Lock.

Locks	16. Lock gates worked by boat crews. Rise from Dukinfield. The 16 locks are in one magnificent flight at Marple rising 209 feet.
Bridges	62 (including 8 swing bridges).
Tow-path	Throughout canal and branch, except Hyde Bank Tunnel.
Tunnels	2. Woodley:—Length, 167 yards Headroom 7ft. 6ins. Tow-path through tunnel. Hyde Bank:—Length 308 yards. Headroom 7ft. 0ins. No tow-path.

Distance Table

Dukinfield Junction, junction with Ashton Canal to:

	Miles	Furlongs
Dukinfield Hall	1	—
Hyde Gas Works	2	4
Apethorne Aqueduct over road	3	1
Woodley Tunnel	4	4
Leach Bridge	4	6
Hatherlow Aqueduct over road	5	4
North end of Hyde Bank tunnel	6	2
South end of Hyde Bank tunnel	6	3½
Marple, Aqueduct over River Etherow	6	6
Lock No. 1, Marple (commencement of flight) ...	7	—
Marple, head of Lock No. 16, *junction with Macclesfield Canal, Main Line*	8	0
Ridge End Bridge	8	4
Disley, Dryhurst Bridge	10	7
Bank End Bridge (Inn)	12	—
Wirksmoor, wharf and warehouse	12	—
Aqueduct over Furness Brook	13	1
Greensdeep Swing Bridge	13	7
Junction with Whaley Bridge Branch (½ mile long) ...	14	—
Aqueduct over River Goyt	14	1
Buxworth, termination of canal	14	6

(Restoration of complete Basin complex at Buxworth is being carried out by the Inland Waterways Protection Society)

Marple Aqueduct on the Peak Forest Canal

Dr Martin Whalley Inland Waterways Protection Society

Peak Forest Canal. The Upper Basin at Buxworth in 1982

MACCLESFIELD CANAL

The Macclesfield Canal was promoted by an Act in 1826 and is second only to the Welsh Canal in scenic beauty.   It runs on a high contour from Marple to Bosley giving unrivalled views over the countryside. There are fine views of Mow Cop with its folly, 1,000 feet up. As one proceeds north on the Trent and Mersey Canal it should be remembered that the entrance to the Macclesfield Canal is on the left, as the canal crosses over the Trent and Mersey to run north to Marple. Summit Level is 521ft above ordnance datum.

Authority	British Waterways Board.
From and to	Junction with the Peak Forest Canal at Marple to junction with Trent and Mersey Canal at Hall Green.
Distance	Main Canal—26¼ miles. High Lane Branch—¼ mile.
Length	70ft.
Beam	7ft.
Draught	3ft. (This is below standard and may be improved.)
Headroom	6ft.

Locks	13. Lock Gates worked by boat crews. 12 locks are at Bosley and the other is a stop lock at the southern end. Fall from Marple.
Bridges	104 (6 swing bridges). Lowest bridge, Poynton.
Tow-path	Throughout canal and branch.
Facilities	There are five boatyards on the canal. Several nearby inns and shopping at Macclesfield, Bollington, Marple and some villages.

Distance Table

Marple Junction, junction with Peak Forest Canal to:

	Miles	Furlongs
Windlehurst or Back Lane Bridge	1	6
Junction with High Lane Branch	2	2
Aqueduct over Railway	2	5
Bullock's Girder Bridge	2	7
Red Acre Aqueduct	4	4
Hibbert's Brow or Corner Bridge	6	1
Whiteley Green Bridge	7	—
Bollington Coal Wharves and Bollington Aqueduct	7	6
Clark's Change Bridge	8	7
Chapel-en-le-Frith Road Bridge	10	2
Macclesfield, Buxton Road, Wharf	10	7
Macclesfield, Holland's Bridge	11	2
Sutton Aqueduct	12	2
Leek New Road Bridge	12	6
Fool's Nook	14	2
Crow Hole Bridge	15	4
Bosley, Locks Nos. 1–10 commence	16	1
Bosley, Locks Nos. 11 and 12	17	1
Aqueduct over River Dane	17	3
Crossley Hall	18	3
Buglawton Road Bridge	18	7
Tall Ash (road bridge)	19	7½
Main Line Railway Bridge	20	3½
Biddulph Valley Railway Aqueduct	20	7
Dog Lane or Canal Road Aqueduct	21	5½
Congleton Wharf	21	6
Watery Lane Aqueduct	23	2
Astbury	24	—
Littler's Wharf	25	1
Hall Green, *junction with Trent and Mersey Canal, Hall Green Branch* and Hall Green Stop Lock No. 13	26	1

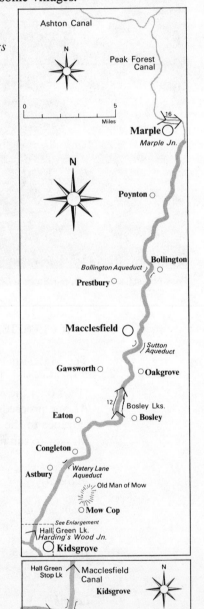

River Avon (Bristol) (9)

This section of the Avon with Bristol Docks was made navigable by Acts passed in 1700, 1749, 1803, 1806, 1808 and 1809. It is part of the through route from the Severn to the Thames and has the Avon Gorge with its fine suspension bridge in the tidal section. Considerable alterations to this route are proposed as the Bristol Authority is considering closing its docks. A new route is projected, but only to cruiseway standards.

Craft are required to register with the H.M. Coastguard yacht and boat safety scheme if travelling from Sharpness to Avonmouth or vice-versa. The scheme is administered from H.M. Coastguard, Mumbles, Swansea, West Glamorgan (Tel. Swansea (0792) 66534). Admiralty Chart No. 1166 is essential (River Severn to Sharpness). The passage is usually considered to be dangerous – and pilotage is advised. A pilot usually costs £50, and can be obtained via The British Waterways Board, Pierhead Offices, Sharpness. Copies of Tide Tables and information can be obtained by owners of pleasure craft from the Dock Master's Office. The passage is not advisable for some types of narrow boats, even in good weather.

A map of the Kennet and Avon Canal by Nicholas Hammond is obtainable from the publishers but a newcomer to the area should contact the Authority before his trip.

Authority	The Port of Bristol Authority, Dock Master's Office, Underfall Yard, Cumberland Road, Bristol, BS1 8XG. Tel. Bristol (0272) 2538.
From and to	Avonmouth to the junction with the Kennet and Avon Navigation at Hanham Lock, situated about 5 miles above Bristol (junction is 100yds seawards of Hanham Lock)
Remarks	The River Avon is navigable for sea-going vessels from Avonmouth as far as the docks at Bristol.
Distances	From the sea at Avonmouth to the junction with the Kennet and Avon Canal at Hanham Lock, 14¼ miles.

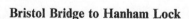

Bristol Bridge to Hanham Lock

Length	100ft.
Beam	17ft. 6ins.
Draught	6ft.
Headroom	10ft (7ft when Prince's Street bridge is closed).
Locks	2. Netham and Cumberland Basin Entrance Lock, Fall, Hanham to Avonmouth. (Totterdown Lock, Guinea Street Lock and Bathurst Locks are closed).
Bridges	Two opening and eleven fixed
Tow-path	There is a tow-path from Hanham Lock to Marsh Bridge, Bristol.
Approx. time to navigate	About 1½ hours from Cumberland Basin Inner Lock to Hanham Lock.

Speed limit and *Bye-laws*	4 to 6 miles an hour. The Bye-laws may be obtained on application to the General Manager, Port of Bristol Authority.
Connections	Cumberland Basin Lock to Bristol Floating Harbour.
Mooring	Visiting craft may not be moored in the City Docks for more than 30 days without a licence. St. Augustine's Reach and Wapping Wharf are reserved for visiting boats.
Navigation Notes	Netham Lock generally has its gates open to feed the City Docks locks and graving docks. It is generally only used against floods and tides that exceed the crest of Netham Dam. There is a fast ebb run down towards Netham Dam after the highest spring tides opposite the St. Annes Board Mills. Under the conditions it is essential to carry an anchor, so in emergency craft are not swept on to the Dam.
Facilities	Bristol has extensive shops, entertainment etc., and is the only available place to call en-route. There are boatyard facilities available.
Tides	High water at Cumberland Basin, Bristol, about 8 minutes after high water at Avonmouth. Tidal rise: Ordinary Spring tides 33ft., Neap tides 22ft. High water at Hanham, about ¾ hour after high water at Cumberland Basin. Springs rise about 3 feet.

Distance Table   *Miles   Furlongs*
Tail of Hanham Lock, junction with Kennet and Avon Navigation to:

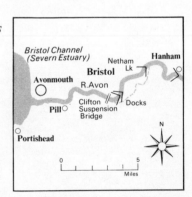

	Miles	Furlongs
Hanham Colliery Wharf	1	4
Conham	1	7
Netham Lock No. 1	3	4
Bristol, Cumberland Basin Entrance Lock No. 2 ...	6	4
Clifton Suspension Bridge...	6	7
Pill	11	1
Avonmouth, *junction with Avonmouth Docks and Estuary of River Severn*	13	1

River Avon (Warwick) (10)

The Upper Avon Navigation was acquired by the old Great Western Railway in 1859 and very shortly afterwards became derelict. Approximately 3½ miles of the Avon is navigable from the Memorial Theatre at Stratford upstream to Alveston Weir. The river was made navigable under Acts passed in 1751 and 1793, and in the past carried considerable barge traffic. The Lower Avon has been fully restored by one of the most remarkable voluntary efforts, similar work is now completed on the Upper Avon. The lower river winding round Bredon Hill now carries regular pleasure traffic and is open to Stratford. Evesham and Pershore are delightful country towns, and Stratford is at its best by the river where there are excellent moorings. The Upper Avon Navigation Act 1972 applies.

The Lower Avon until recent years, ceased at Workman Bridge, but in 1966, Collins Brothers donated Evesham Lock, main dam, sluice and weir to the Lower Avon Navigation Trust, the limit of whose jurisdiction is now just north of Evesham Lock. It is of interest to note that the Lower Avon was in the hands of the Perrott family of Craycombe, Fladbury, who continued to operate the navigation, albeit on a very decreasing income, until 1924 when William Fisher took it over and formed the Lower Avon Navigation Company. Later Mr. Fisher disposed of his controlling interest to John Whitehouse of Evesham and it was then purchased in 1949 by C. D. Barwell, who acted in concert with the Inland Waterways Association to establish the present Lower Avon Navigation Trust Limited, which is a registered charity. Mr. Barwell's leadership and campaign to restore the Lower Avon, for which he received a well merited O.B.E., has inspired numerous restoration schemes elsewhere.

The Upper Avon Navigation Trust Ltd has now canalised the river from above Evesham to Stratford by building new locks and weirs in a most remarkable voluntary effort under the direction of David Hutchings, M.B.E. who also led the restoration of the Stratford-on-Avon Canal. There are plans to continue the Upper Avon Navigation to the Grand Union Canal. The Higher Avon has always been navigable after a fashion to the Aqueduct at Warwick and canoeists have used the river from Rugby. However landowners at Charlecote Park and Warwick Castle have on occasion claimed the river although the Orders in Council made on the 9th March 1636 seem to indicate the river was a free one to Coventry. A distance table of the Upper Avon to the aqueduct at Warwick is listed below.

A guide *Gateway to the Avon* is available from Lower Avon Navigation Trust.

Authority	**Upper Avon. Stratford-on-Avon to Evesham** The Upper Avon Navigation Trust Ltd., Avon House, Harvington, Evesham, Worcs. Tel. Evesham (0386) 870526. **Lower Avon. Evesham to Tewkesbury** Lower Avon Navigation Trust Ltd., Mill Wharf, Mill Lane, Wyre Piddle, Pershore, Worcs. WR10 2JF. Tel. Pershore 552517. Although the L.A.N.T. own Evesham Lock, the navigation rights are owned by the U.A.N.T. Therefore use of the Evesham lock need U.A.N.T. tolls.
From and to	Stratford to junction with the River Severn at Tewkesbury.
Distance	Stratford to Evesham, 17½ miles. Evesham to Tewkesbury, 25½ miles.
Length	70ft.
Beam	13ft. 6ins.
Draught	4ft.
Headroom	10ft.
Locks	Lower Avon, (Tewkesbury to Evesham) 8. Upper Avon, (Evesham to Stratford) 9. Fall from Stratford. Lock-keepers at some locks. Standard 1″ windlass required.
Speed limit	6 miles per hour.
Tow-path	On some parts of the navigation.
Special note	The concerns now owning the waterway are non-profit companies with the status of charities. They are pledged to restore and

maintain the locks, weirs, dams and sluices, without which the river would revert to its natural state of a small mud-bound brook, inaccessible to the angler, unnavigable to craft and an offence to the eye. The work of restoration is carried out by the Trust's volunteer working parties, and the success of their work is dependent upon donations from the public for the purchase of essential materials. Being a non-profit-making concern, every penny subscribed is devoted to the restoration. Plenty of riverside facilities but moorings are in short supply.

Navigation notes

Full details for cruising on the river can be obtained from the Upper or Lower Avon Navigation Trusts. King John's Bridge, Tewkesbury gives the least clearance and is the gauge bridge for the navigation. Above Pershore Lock there is a low level power line 20ft. above the water-line, and masts must be kept lowered. Craft entering from the Severn should steer a course close to the Town Quay alongside the Mill to avoid the mud bank at Tewkesbury.

The Higher Avon has historically been the river above Stratford. The Higher Avon Navigation Trust Ltd is only concerned with the river above Alveston Weir to Warwick.

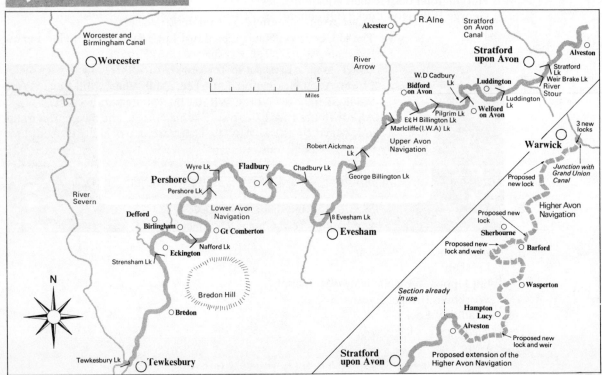

Distance Table
(Warwick Aqueduct to Stratford Bridge) (Higher Avon Navigation)

Warwick Aqueduct to	*Miles*	*Furlongs*
Warwick Mill	1	–
Barford Mill	3	7

Distance Table	*Miles*	*Furlongs*
Wasperton	6	5
Hampton Lucy Mill	8	4
Charlecote	9	–
Alveston Mill	11	–
Alveston Ferry	12	5
Stratford Bridge	15	–

(Small cruisers can go from Stratford to Hatton Rock, turning just below Alveston Weir)

(Stratford to Tewkesbury)

Stratford Bridge, junction with Stratford-on-Avon Canal to:

Stratford Lock	—	4
Weir Brake Lock	—	5
Luddington Lock	3	2
Binton Bridge	5	1
Welford Lock (W. A. Cadbury Lock)	6	2
Grange Lock (now called Pilgrim Lock after the Pilgrim Trust)	8	—
E & H Billington Lock (Barton)	8	7½
Bidford Bridge (Bidford-upon-Avon)	9	4
Marlcliffe Lock (I.W.A. Lock)	10	6½
Harvington Lock (Robert Aickman Lock)	13	5
George Billington Lock* (Offenham)	14	2

Upper river Avon. Memorial tablet to George Billington

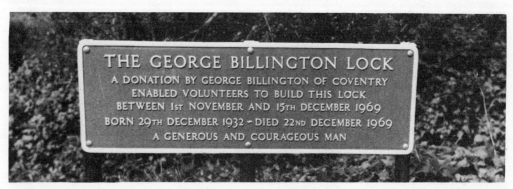

THE GEORGE BILLINGTON LOCK
A DONATION BY GEORGE BILLINGTON OF COVENTRY
ENABLED VOLUNTEERS TO BUILD THIS LOCK
BETWEEN 1ST NOVEMBER AND 15TH DECEMBER 1969
BORN 29TH DECEMBER 1932 - DIED 22ND DECEMBER 1969
A GENEROUS AND COURAGEOUS MAN

Offenham	16	—
Evesham Lock (this lock is the first lock on the Lower Avon Navigation but Upper Avon Navigation tolls apply.	18	2
Workman Bridge, Evesham	18	3
Chadbury Lock	20	1
Fladbury Lock	23	—
Wyre Lock	27	1
Pershore Lock	28	1
Nafford Lock	33	5
Eckington Bridge	35	1
Strensham Lock	38	1
Bredon	39	1
Twyning Fleet (Inn)	40	1

* George Billington was a young man who died of an incurable disease, two days after the lock was completed bearing his name on a commemorative plaque.

Upper river Avon . Upper Welford lock in 1971.
This lock has been disused since 1875

Upper river Avon. Pilgrim lock under construction

Distance Table

	Miles	*Furlongs*
Tewkesbury Lock (Avon Lock)	42	5
Tewkesbury, *junction with River Severn*	42	7

Basingstoke Canal (11)

A curious legal situation surrounds this waterway. No part of it has been abandoned by Act of Parliament. Its construction was promoted by an Act in 1777. Due to railway competition, the original company was wound up in 1869. In 1910 this winding up order was found invalid, and the responsibility for upkeep and the power to exact tolls remained vested in the ghost of the original company. There had been an order for the winding-up of the company in 1876 and there was a further order of the court in 1878 dissolving the Company of Proprietors of the Basingstoke Canal Navigation.

The effect of the Dissolution Order was that the lands forming part of the undertaking reverted to the original grantors freed from the obligations imposed by the original statute of 1777. As, however, the liquidator had purported to sell certain lands belonging to the Company of Proprietors before the company was dissolved in 1878, the present owners, who derived title from the liquidator's sale have acquired a title to the land by virtue of adverse proceedings and have not succeeded to any obligation imposed by the Act of 1777.

The canal is a 'green finger' through urban areas at Woking and Brookwood, but is surrounded by very fine trees throughout its length. The upper reaches are very lonely, particularly near Dogmersfield Park. The canal has the unique feature of flashes, which are small adjoining lakes, and if dredged, would form a fine linear park. Mitchet Lake is a good example of a flash that could well see better recreational use. A number of pounds are occupied by houseboats. The Surrey and Hampshire Canal Society are working with the two councils to restore the canal.

Authority

(a) Surrey. Surrey County Council, Surrey House, Eden Street, Kingston-upon-Thames, Surrey. Tel. 01-549-6111

(b) Hampshire. Hampshire County Council, The Castle, Winchester. Tel. Winchester (0962) 4411.

Boat licenses from Canal Manager, Ash Lock Cottage, Government Road, Aldershot, Hants. Tel. Aldershot (0252) 31380.

From and to	Woodham, junction with River Wey to Greywell.
Remarks	This canal is being restored. Originally it terminated at Basingstoke Wharf but the top 5 miles of the canal bed have been sold. Greywell Tunnel is now impassable and the length of canal now usable is 31 miles to the village of Greywell. It could technically be restored to Up Nateley if the tunnel is repaired. The canal may be re-opened by 1988 and the summit level is now dredged and in use.
Distance	31 miles.
Length	72ft. 6ins.
Width	13ft. 6ins.
Draught	3ft. 6ins.
Headroom	Woodham to Fleet, 7ft. 6ins. Fleet to Greywell, 5ft.
Locks	29. Rise from junction with River Wey.
Tunnels	One. Greywell, 1,200 yds., impassable due to fallen roof.
Bridges	Numerous. Two swing bridges at Greywell end, which need prior notice for opening. There is also a swing bridge near Woking.
Tow-path	Throughout navigation.
Facilities	No boatyards at present, a good sprinkling of inns throughout. Surrey and Hampshire Canal Society trip boat at Odiham. Slipways at Farnborough Wharf Bridge (A.325), and Barley Mow Bridge.

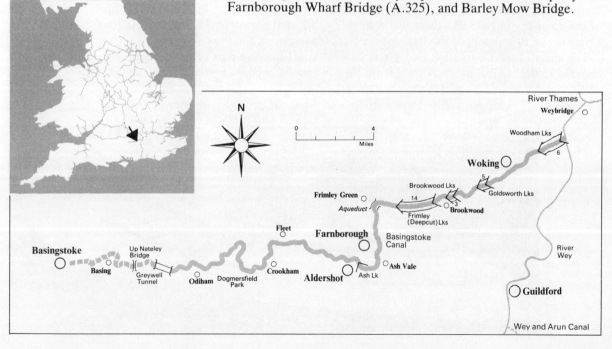

Dieter Jebens. Surrey and Hampshire Canal Society

Basingstoke Canal . Lock no. 25 being restored under a Manpower Services Commission scheme

Basingstoke Canal. Lock no.15 in its restored condition

Clive Durley. Surrey and Hampshire Canal Society

Distance Table

Woodham, junction with River Wey to:

	Miles	Furlongs
Woodham Bottom Lock No. 1 (2, 3, 4 and 5 follow at intervals)	—	2
Woodham Top Lock No. 6	1	4
Sheerwater	2	2
Maybury Hill	3	—
Woking, Wheatsheaf Bridge	3	7
Goldsworth Bottom Lock No. 7 (8, 9 and 10 follow at intervals). ...	5	2
Goldsworth Top Lock No. 11 (The Row Barge Inn).	5	5
Brookwood Bottom Lock No. 12	7	3
Brookwood, Lock No. 13	7	3½
Brookwood Top Lock No. 14	7	4
Pirbright, bottom of Frimley Locks, No. 15 (Frimley Locks Nos. 16, to 27 follow at regular intervals)	8	5
Frimley Top Lock No. 28	10	4
Frimley Green (The Kings Head Inn)	11	7
Mitchet Lake	13	2
North Camp Railway Station	13	6
Ash Lock No. 29 (Long Level Pound begins)	16	—
Aldershot, Main Road Bridge (Aldershot to Farnborough)	17	6
Pondtail Bridge	20	5
Fleet	21	5
Crookham (The Chequers Inn)	23	5
Crondall Bridge	24	2
Grubb's Farm Bridge (The Barley Mow)	25	4
(canal now enters and curves round Dogmersfield Park)		
Pilcot Bridge (Inn)	26	6
Winchfield	27	—
Odiham (The New Inn)	29	—
North Warnborough (The Swan Inn)	30	1
Greywell, and east end of Greywell Tunnel (The Fox and Goose Inn)	31	1
(Greywell Tunnel is impassable and canal terminates here. Ownership of the canal continues to Brickiln Bridge).		
Up Nateley	32	5

Beaulieu River (12)

The Beaulieu River flows through the Beaulieu Estate (8,000 acres, 5 miles long and 3 miles wide). This is one of the most beautiful parts of the New Forest with the enchanting villages of Beaulieu and Buckler's Hard. Many of Nelson's wooden men of war were built in the latter place. The ownership of the river is unique, in that it includes the bed of the tidal reaches and the foreshore down to the low water line. The area is designated one of outstanding natural beauty and contains the remains of Beaulieu Abbey. There is a Maritime Museum at Buckler's Hard.

Authority   Private property and all enquiries should be made to the Harbour Master, Buckler's Hard, Hampshire.

From and to   *Stone Point to Beaulieu.

Distance	8 miles.
Length	Unlimited.
Beam	,,
Draught	7ft. at high tide at Beaulieu Bridge.
Headroom	Unlimited.
Locks	None. Sluices at Beaulieu stop navigation to all but light craft.
Tow-path	None.
Bridges	,,
Tides	There is double high water in Beaulieu River, the first H.W. occurs about half an hour before H.W. Portsmouth, the second 2 hours after the first. Spring tides rise 10ft. Neaps 9ft.

Beverley Beck (13)

This canal or creek was promoted under Acts of Parliament dated 1726 and 1744. It was used for many years before that date being kept in repair by the Corporation. Beverley is a very pleasant country town with its fine Minster and a wealth of old domestic architecture dating back to the days when it was a wool town.

Authority	Beverley District Council, Lairgate Hall, Beverley, North Humberside, HU17 8HL. Tel. Hull (0482) 882255.
From and to	Beverley to River Hull at Grove Hill.
Distance	¾ miles.
Length	65ft.
Beam	17ft. 6ins.
Draught	6ft. 6ins.
Headroom	Unlimited.
Locks	One. Grove Hill. Fall to River Hull.
Tow-path	Throughout the canal.

Birmingham Canal Navigations (14)

The B.C.N. navigations were promoted by Acts dated 1768, 1769, 1783, 1784, 1785, 1794, 1806, 1811, 1815 and 1818. A very excellent guide has been produced by R. B. Manion and K. D. Dunham, and this should be used by all visitors to the system. We are grateful to quote from this document as follows:

'It is a story of four canals and three canal companies. The oldest of these was the Birmingham Canal Company whose canal was authorised in 1786 from the Staffordshire and Worcestershire Canal at Aldersley to run for 22½ miles to Birmingham via 29 locks. Engineered by James Brindley, the first section from Wednesbury to Birmingham was opened to trade in November 1769, with the whole line following by 1772. The vast mineral wealth along its route ensured that it was an immensely profitable concern.

In the early 1780's a great battle was fought, both inside and outside Parliament, between the Birmingham Company and a group of rival promoters, for the right to build a canal from Birmingham to Fazeley. The Birmingham Canal Company won, bought out the rival promoters and became 'The Birmingham and Birmingham & Fazeley Canal Company'. The name changed in 1794 to 'The Birmingham Canal Navigations'. The new canal was engineered by John Smeaton, of Eddystone Lighthouse fame, as were the contemporary improvements to the original canal at Smethwick and the first extensions which eventually built up to the system as we know it today, that towards Walsall. All were being completed by the early 1790's.

The second of the companies to make its appearance was the Dudley Canal Company who gained authorisation for its line on the same day in 1776 as the Stourbridge Canal to extend from that canal at Brierley Hill towards Dudley. Originally a modest affair 2¼ miles long with nine locks it was engineered by Thomas Dadford, senior. It was no sooner opened in 1779 than talk of an extension through Dudley Hill to join the Birmingham Canal began. Authorised in 1785 the extension rose by 5 locks before entering the 3,177 yards long Dudley Tunnel from which it emerged to join the Birmingham Canal at Tipton. No sooner was this completed in 1792, after a long struggle, than the idea of a further extension from the southern end of Dudley Tunnel to Selly Oak to join the Worcester and Birmingham Canal was mooted. At the time this latter canal was barred from joining the Birmingham Canal at Birmingham by the famous Worcester Bar. This extension was nearly 11 miles long and included two more tunnels, the longer, Lappal, was 3,795 yards long and the fifth longest canal tunnel to be built. Authorised in 1793, the extension was completed by 1798.

The last of the canal companies to come on the scene was that owning the Wyrley and Essington Canal which was authorised in 1792, from the Birmingham Canal at Wolverhampton to the mines around Wyrley, with branches to Essington and Walsall. The main line was about 8 miles long with 5 locks, and there were 5 in the short Essington branch, but the two mile long branch to Birchills, in Walsall, was level. Before the works were finished another Act of Parliament in 1794 authorised an extension from Birchills, mostly at the same level as the main line and the Birchills Branch, to Brownhills, then falling by 30 locks through Lichfield to join the Coventry Canal at Huddlesford, a distance of 15½ miles. There were also branches to Lord Hay's quarries near Little Bloxwich and to Daw End. By the turn of the century all were complete, as was the Cannock Chase Reservoir now better known as Chasewater.

For the next forty years all three companies were increasingly prosperous as the area they served developed into the industrial centre of the world. Branches were built and the old canal lines improved. The most ambitious of these was that of the Birmingham Canal Navigations which between 1825 and 1838, built a completely new main line, between Deepfields and Birmingham, under the guidance of Thomas Telford, thus reducing Brindley's

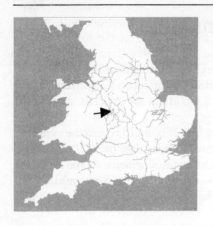

original 22½ miles to a little over 15. These improvements, plus connections with what is now the Grand Union Canal in Birmingham, added to congestion at the top end of the Birmingham and Fazeley Canal and to relieve this, the Tame Valley Canal was opened in 1844 from Wednesbury to the Birmingham and Fazeley Canal at Salford Bridge.

In 1840 the Birmingham and the Wyrley and Essington Companies amalgamated and in 1846 the Dudley Company also joined the B. C. N. Soon after, the concern came under railway control but internal traffic was encouraged and only the external trade suffered from the usual tactics of railway ownership. Trade continued to increase and the system to expand. Netherton Tunnel was built by 1858 to relieve the pressure on the old Dudley Tunnel, and by 1863 the Cannock Extension Canal, the last major work of the B. C. N., was finished. By the end of the 19th century goods carried had risen to over 8½ million tons annually, but thereafter it slowly fell away, though over a million were still moved in the early 1950's. Today the figure is very small indeed.

As traffic declines so branches have become disused and abandoned. The first to go was the Essington Branch and closures have continued steadily so that from the 160 odd navigable miles of 1865 only just over 100 now survive and many of these are threatened. In the 1968 Transport Act the Birmingham and Fazeley Canal, the Main Line together with the Netherton Tunnel Branch and the Dudley Canals giving access to the Stourbridge Canal, are designated as 'Cruising Waterways', all the rest, some 65 miles are in the class of 'remainder' whose future must be decided very shortly. To ensure their retention as navigable waterways so that all that has happened during the past 200 years has not been in vain, *they must be used.'*

There are plenty of winding holes and the canals are of an exceptionally generous cross section, but care must be taken, as these waterways are in an industrial area, to avoid 'foreign bodies', particularly at bridge holes. The B. C. N. Society and the Midlands branch of the I. W. A., are very active and should be contacted by strangers making an extensive cruise.

There are a number of features of interest. The system has canals at 3 levels, the Tame Valley (408ft), the Birmingham Level (453ft) and the Wolverhampton Level (473ft). Not all the waterways are industrial and a number of sections, while close to urban areas, have a fine amenity value.

The following features are of special interest:

Titford Pool. This is the highest part of the B. C. N. and to reach it you climb Oldbury Locks from the Wolverhampton Level up to 511 feet. The M5 crosses the pool on stilts, but it is very rural.

Farmers Bridge and the Aston Flight. These are examples of the Birmingham part of the B. C. N. as distinct from the Black Country. On foot or by boat, they are still spectacular and were once to the canal system what the escalator is today to London travellers at Piccadilly Circus.

Galton Cutting and Bridge, Smethwick. This is the B. C. N. at its best. The Birmingham Level passes through a deep cutting spanned by Telford's graceful iron bridge built in 1829, 70 feet above the canal. Twenty feet higher in a neighbouring cutting runs the Wolverhampton Level past the coaling stage where, until a few years ago, coal was still loaded from the Jubilee Colliery.

Dudley Old Tunnel. This is on the Wolverhampton Level and access is only possible from the east end. But if your boat draws about 18 inches, has a tough bottom and not too much top-hamper, and you have tough hands, you will get through. Castle Mill Basin, about a fifth of the way, is an extraordinary place, you emerge from one hole into the bottom of this quarry and then continue down another hole on your way back to Park Head; other holes lead off into the old limestone working similar to the mines at Worsley but these are impassable. The main tunnel is 3,154 yards long. (Netherton Tunnel (3,027 yards) which pierces the same ridge to the south, is less romantic). It is a wide waterway with tow-paths on either side and waterfalls coming through the roof which no zig-zagging can avoid. It is on the Birmingham Level. This tunnel is controlled by the Dudley Canal Trust. No power boats permitted in Singing Cavern now opened.

There were about 600 private basins with short lengths of canal on the B.C.N. A full coverage with data is at present impossible. A survey of the closed canals in the Birmingham area is published by the B.C.N. Society. It is invaluable to students.

Birmingham may be considered to be the centre of the canal system of England. The canals are numerous and for commercial use, the main lines however form a link for the passage of pleasure craft from the south and east to the west and north as follows:

Main Line. From Worcester Bar, Birmingham junction with the Worcester and Birmingham Canal, to junction with the Staffordshire and Worcestershire Canal at Aldersley.

Birmingham and Fazeley Canal. From junction with Main Line, near Worcester Bar, to the junction with the Coventry Canal at Fazeley and with the detached portion of the same canal at Whittington Brook. This waterway leads to the junction with the Trent and Mersey Canal at Fradley.

Along this Birmingham and Fazeley Canal are the two important junctions with the Grand Union Canal. The first at Ashted via the short Digbeth branch, and the second at Salford Junction where the old Birmingham and Warwick Junction Canal joins.

Wyrley and Essington Canal. From Horsley Fields Junction with Main Line to junction with the Anglesey Branch Canal. (It is closed from the junction with this Branch to Huddlesford and mostly filled in).

Dudley Canal. From junction with Old Main Loop Line to junction with Stourbridge Canal leading to Staffordshire and Worcestershire Canal at Stourton Bridge.

Authority	British Waterways Board.
Distance	In this list are all of the canals with branches

1. Main Line Worcester Bar to Aldersley Junction, 15½ miles
Branches:

Oozells Street Loop Line	¼ mile
Icknield Port Road Wharf Loop Line	¾ mile
Soho Branch Loop Line	1¼ miles
Parker Branch (closed and filled in)	¼ mile
Dunkirk Branch (closed and filled in)	¼ mile
Dixons Branch (closed and filled in)	1¼ miles

2. Wednesbury Oak Loop Line Originally 4¼ miles, now only 1⅞ miles are open.
Branch:

Ocker Hill Branch (closed)	⅜ mile

3. Old Main Loop Line From Smethwick Junction to Tipton Factory Junction, 6 miles 4 furlongs.
Branches:

Engine Branch	$\frac{5}{8}$ mile
Spon Lane Locks Branch	$\frac{3}{8}$,,
Titford Canal (Short length only now open)...	$1\frac{3}{4}$ miles
Oldbury Loop Line (closed)	1 mile

4. Gower Branch Canal ... ... $\frac{1}{2}$ mile

5. Netherton Tunnel Branch ... ... $2\frac{7}{8}$ miles

6. Dudley Canal Line No. 1 ... ... $4\frac{1}{2}$,,
Branches:
Dudley Canal Line No. 2 ... ... $5\frac{3}{4}$ miles
(Lappal Tunnel is closed, and there is no through traffic.
The section from Halesowen to Selly Oak is abandoned).
Withymoor Branch Canal (closed and filled in) ⅜ mile
Bumble Hole Branch Canal (partly filled in) $\frac{1}{2}$ mile

7. Bradley Locks Branch Canal (navigable to Bottom
Lock only) ... ... $\frac{7}{8}$,,

8. Tipton Green and Toll End Communication ... $1\frac{1}{2}$ miles
(closed)

9. Wednesbury Old Canal ... ... $2\frac{5}{8}$,,
Branches:
Ridgacre Branch Canal (Restorable but weedy) $\frac{3}{4}$ mile
Dartmouth Branch Canal (closed) ... ... $\frac{5}{8}$,,
Halford Branch Canal (closed) ... ... $\frac{1}{2}$,,

10. Walsall Canal ... ... 7 miles
Branches:
Haines Branch Canal (closed) ... ... $\frac{5}{8}$ mile
Danks Branch Canal (closed) ... ... $\frac{3}{8}$,,
Lower Ocker Hill Branch Canal (closed) ... $\frac{1}{8}$,,
Gospel Oak Branch Canal (closed) ... $\frac{1}{2}$,,
Monway Branch Canal (closed) ... ... $\frac{1}{4}$,,
Anson Branch Canal (Navigable to M6 culvert) ½ mile

11. Walsall Branch Canal ... ... $\frac{7}{8}$ mile

12. Bentley Canal (closed) $3\frac{3}{8}$ miles
Branch:
Neachells Branch Canal (closed) ... ... $\frac{1}{2}$ mile

13. Tame Valley Canal ... ... $8\frac{1}{2}$ miles

14. Rushall Canal ... ... $2\frac{3}{4}$,,

15. Birmingham and Fazeley Canal ... ... $20\frac{1}{2}$,,
Branches:
Newhall Branch (completely filled in) $\frac{1}{4}$ mile
Digbeth Branch Canal ... ... $\frac{7}{8}$,,

16. Wyrley and Essington Canal ... ... $23\frac{1}{2}$ miles
Branches:
Sneyd Branch Canal (The Wyrley Bank section

of 3¼ miles to Wyrley Wharf is closed)	...	¼ mile
Lord Hay's Branch Canal (closed)	...	...	⅞ ,,
Daw End Branch Canal	...	...	...	5¼ miles
Anglesey Branch Canal	...	...	...	1½ ,,

17. Cannock Extension Canal (closed except for ¼ mile) ,

18. Churchbridge Branch Canal (closed)

Locks

The number of locks on the canals listed above is as follows:

1. 24 locks. Nos. 1 to 3 rise from Birmingham. Nos. 4 to 24 fall from Birmingham.

2. None.

3. 3 locks. Rise from Smethwick Junction. On the Spon Lane Branch there are 3 locks which fall from Spon Lane Junction. There are also 6 locks on the Titford Canal which rise from Oldbury Locks Junction.

4. 3 locks. Fall from Brades Hall Junction.

5. None.

6. 12 locks. Fall from Tipton.

7. 9 locks. Fall from Bradley Locks Junction. (Closed)

8. 10 locks. Fall from Tipton Green Junction. (Closed)

9. None.

10. 8 locks. Fall from Riders Green Junction.

11. 8 locks. Fall from Birchills Junction.

12. None.

13. 13 locks. Fall from junction with Walsall Canal.

14. 9 locks. Fall from Longwood Junction.

15. 38 locks. Fall from Farmers Bridge. There are 6 locks on the Digbeth Branch which fall from Aston Junction.

16. 30 locks. Fall from junction with Anglesey Branch Canal. These locks are closed. There were 5 locks on the Sneyd and Wyrley Bank Branch Canal which rose from Sneyd Junction which are also closed.

17. None.

18. 13 locks. Fall from Rumour Hill Junction. These locks are obliterated due to colliery workings.

Main Line

Locks

24. Lock gates worked by boat crews.
Fall from Birmingham.

Bridges

Numerous.

Tunnels

Summit Tunnel 102yds (Tow path)
Coseley, 360 yards. Tow-path both sides.

Minimum height above water level	... ...	15ft. 3ins.
Minimum width at water level	... ...	15ft. 9ins.
Minimum width at water level, including both tow-paths		24ft. 9ins.

Galton Tunnel 123yds (Tow path)

There are long bridges over the canal at Broad Street, Birmingham and near Albion Wharf, Wolverhampton, though they are not usually regarded as tunnels.

Birmingham and Fazeley Canal

Salford Bridge Junction to Whittington Brook.

This canal is linked with the Grand Union Canal at Aston Junction, by the short Digbeth Branch Canal, which is only ⅞ miles long.

Locks	38. (14 locks Salford Junction to Whittington Brook). Fall from Farmers Bridge.
Bridges	Numerous.
Tunnels	Curdworth, 57 yards. Tow-path.

Digbeth Branch Canal

Locks	6. Lock gates worked by boat crews. Fall from Aston Junction.
Bridges	Numerous.
Tunnels	Ashted. 103 yards, Tow-path.

Wyrley and Essington Canal

Locks	30. There are 7 flights of locks at Ogley. These fall from Horseley Fields Junction, they are all closed.
Bridges	Numerous.
Tunnels	None.

Dudley Canal, Line No. 1

Locks	12. Lock gates worked by boat crews. Park Head locks are closed at present but under repair (1972). Fall from Tipton.
Bridges	Numerous.
Tunnels	Dudley, 3,154 yards. No tow-path. (Owned by the Dudley Canal Trust)

Minimum height above water level   ...   ...   5ft. 9ins.
Minimum width at water level   ...   .   8ft. 5ins.
Netherton, 3,027 yards. (Netherton Tunnel Branch). Tow-path both sides.
Gosty Hill, 557 yards. (Dudley Canal Line No. 2). No tow-path.
Lappal, 3,795 yards. (Dudley Canal Line No. 2). This tunnel is closed.
Note: The 80 yard structure at Broad Street, Birmingham, is not usually considered a tunnel. Do not go through Dudley Tunnel if the boat fouls the height gauge and also, due to restricted bore, engines must not be used. A new branch tunnel has been made to lead into the Singing Cavern, a tourist attraction. The 144' cavern is much larger but closed at present. The new tunnel is 65 yards long.

Applicable to whole system

Length	71ft.
Beam	7ft.
Draught	3ft. 6ins.
Headroom	Standard. 8ft. 6ins. (Birmingham and Fazeley Canal 7ft. 6 ins. and Salford to Whittington Brook 7ft. 6ins). But reduced in places to 6ft. 6ins. On the Dudley Canal the headroom through the 'legging' tunnel is 5ft. 9ins. and there is also a 'temporary' bridge at Riders Green Locks giving the same headroom.
Tow-path	Throughout navigation except for certain tunnels.

Distance Table

Main Line

Miles Furlongs

Birmingham, Worcester Bar, *junction with Worcester and Birmingham Canal to:*

	Miles	Furlongs
Farmer's Bridge, *junction with Birmingham and Fazeley Canal (N) and Junction with Oozells Street Loop (E)*	—	2½
Eastern Junction with Icknield Port Road, Wharf Loop Line	—	7
Western Junction with Icknield Port Road, Wharf Loop Line —left and Eastern Junction with Soho Branch Loop Line—right	1	0
Western Junction with Soho Branch Loop Line	1	6
Smethwick Junction, *junction with Old Main Loop Line* from Smethwick Junction to Tipton Factory Junction	2	6
Bromford Junction, *junction with Spon Lane Locks Branch*—right, and junction with Parker Branch (closed)—left	5	—
Pudding Green Junction, *junction with Wednesbury Old Canal* ...	5	6
Albion Junction, *junction with Gower Branch*	6	2½
Dunkirk Junction, junction with Dunkirk Branch (closed)	6	3
Dudley Port Junction, *junction with Netherton Tunnel Branch Canal*	7	—
Junction with Dixon's Branch (closed)	7	4
Watery Lane	8	—
Tipton Factory Junction, *junction with Old Main Loop Line* from Smethwick Junction to Tipton Factory Junction (Tipton Factory Lock Nos. 1 to 3)	8	4
Bloomfield	8	6
Coseley Tunnel, south end	9	3
Deepfields Junction, *northern junction with Wednesbury Oak Loop Line*	10	1
Parkfields Basins	10	7
Rough Hills	12	—
Horseley Fields, *junction with Wyrley and Essington Canal.*	13	1
Wolverhampton, Albion Wharf	13	2½
Wolverhampton, Lock No. 4 (top)	13	6
Aldersley Junction, *junction with Staffordshire and Worcestershire Canal—Main Line* and Wolverhampton Lock No. 24 (bottom) ...	15	4

Soho Branch Loop Line
Eastern Junction with Main Line to:

	Miles	Furlongs
Junction with Soho Branch, ½ mile to Soho Wharf*	—	5
Winson Green Wharf	—	7
Western Junction with Main Line	1	2

Distance Table

	Miles	Furlongs

Wednesbury Oak Loop Line
British Waterways Board Workshops to:

	Miles	Furlongs
Pothouse Bridge Wharf	—	5
Capponfield	1	—
Deepfields Junction, *northern junction with Main Line*	1	7

The rest of the canal is closed

Old Main Loop Line from Smethwick Junction to Tipton Factory
Smethwick Junction, junction with Main Line to:

	Miles	Furlongs
Junction with Engine Branch, Smethwick (Smethwick Lock Nos. 1, 2 and 3)	—	4
Spon Lane Wharf and Junction, *junction with Spon Lane Locks Branch* (Spon Lane, Lock Nos. 1, 2 and 3)	2	—
Oldbury Locks Junction, *junction with Titford Canal*	2	5
Junction with Houghton Branch Canal	2	6
Southern junction with Oldbury Loop Line ⎫ this loop is	2	7
Northern junction with Oldbury Loop Line ⎭ closed ...	3	2½
Brades Hall Junction, *junction with Gower Branch*	3	7
Aqueduct over Netherton Tunnel Branch Canal	4	3
Tipton Junction, *junction with Dudley Canal*	5	4
Tipton Green Junction, *junction with Tipton Green and Toll End Communication (closed)*	5	6
Tipton Factory Junction, *junction with Main Line*	6	4

Titford Canal
Oldbury Locks Junction with Old Main Loop Line, to:

	Miles	Furlongs
Oldbury Lock No. 6	—	1
Top of Oldbury Locks, *junction with Spon Lane Branch* (5 furlongs)		
Oldbury Lock No. 1 Spon Lane Branch can be navigated for about one furlong but there is no winding hole	—	3
Uncle Ben's Bridge	—	7
Junction with Portway Branch (100 yards)	1	2
Causeway Green	1	6

Gower Branch Canal
Brades Hall Junction, junction with Old Main Line, to:

	Miles	Furlongs
Brades Hall Lock No. 1 (top)	—	0½
Brades Hall Lock No. 3 (bottom)	—	2
Albion Junction, *junction with Main Line*	—	4

Netherton Tunnel Branch Canal
Dudley Port Junction, junction with Main Line, to:

	Miles	Furlongs
North End of Netherton Tunnel	—	4
Windmill End Junction, *junction with Dudley Canal*	2	7

*The remains of the Birmingham Heath Canal.

Distance Table	*Miles*	*Furlongs*

Dudley Canal Line No. 1

Tipton Junction, junction with Old Main Loop Line to:

	Miles	*Furlongs*
North End of Dudley Tunnel	—	3
Junction with Pensnett Canal* (closed) and Park Head Lock No. 1	2	1
Park Head Junction, *junction with Dudley Canal—Line No. 2*—Park Head Lock No. 3 and top of Blowers Green Lock No. 4	2	3
Woodside Junction, junction with Two Lock Line Canal (closed) ...	3	1
Brierley Hill, Delph Lock No. 5 (top)	4	1
Black Delph Wharf, Delph Lock No. 12 (bottom) and *junction with Stourbridge Canal—Main Line*	4	4

Dudley Canal Line No. 2

Park Head Junction, junction with Dudley Canal Line No. 1 to:

	Miles	*Furlongs*
Blackbrook Junction, junction with Two Lock Line Canal (closed)	—	6
Primrose Hill Wharf	1	5
Southern junction with Bumble Hole Branch Canal	2	3
Windmill End Junction, *junction with Netherton Tunnel Branch Canal* and northern junction with Bumble Hole Branch Canal (now closed)	2	5
Rowley Wharf	4	—
Old Hill and northern end of Gosty Hill Tunnel	4	3
Coombeswood	5	—

The Canal is abandoned from this point to Selly Oak
(Hawne Basin is owned by the Coombeswood Canal Trust)

Bradley Locks Branch Canal (derelict at present)

Bradley Branch Canal (derelict at present)

Bradley Locks Junction, junction with Wednesbury Oak Loop Line, and top of Bradley Locks to:

	Miles	*Furlongs*
Moorcroft Junction, *junction with Walsall Canal*	—	7

(Bradley Lock Nos. 1 to 9 are in this section)

Tipton Green and Toll End Communication

Tipton Green Locks are closed and it is no longer possible to reach the bottom of Tipton Locks from the Walsall Canal.

Wednesbury Old Canal

Pudding Green Junction, junction with Main Line, to:

	Miles	*Furlongs*
Riders Green Junction, *junction with Walsall Canal*	—	
Junction with Ridgacre Branch Canal (the rest of the canal is closed)	1	2

Ridgacre Branch Canal (unnavigable but restorable)

Junction with Wednesbury Old Canal to:

	Miles	*Furlongs*
Junction with Dartmouth Branch Canal (closed)	4½	
Junction with Halford Branch Canal (closed)	5½	
Termination of Canal	6	

Walsall Canal

Ryders Green Junction, junction with Wednesbury Old Canal and top of Ryders Green Locks No. 1 to:

Great Bridge, *junction with Haines Branch,* and bottom of Ryders Green

Distance Table	Miles	Furlongs
Locks No. 8	—	6
Junction with Danks Branch (closed)	1	—
Toll End	1	1
Junction with Lower Ocker Hill Branch (closed)	1	2
Junction with Tame Valley Canal	1	3
Junction with Gospel Oak Branch (closed)	2	0½
Junction with Monway Branch (closed)	2	1½
Moorcroft Junction, *junction with Bradley Branch Canal*	2	3
Moxley Stop	3	—
Junction with Bilston Branch (now closed)	3	2½
Junction with Willenhall Branch (now closed)	3	4
Bug Hole Wharf	4	2
Darlaston Green Wharf	4	6
Junction with Anson Branch	5	1
Walsall Junction, *junction with Walsall Branch Canal*	6	7
Walsall, Public Wharf	7	—

Anson Branch

Junction with Walsall Canal, junction with Bentley Canal to:

	Miles	Furlongs
End of Branch (motorway culvert)	1	3

Walsall Branch Canal

Birchills Junction, junction with Wyrley and Essington Canal to: ...

	Miles	Furlongs
Birchills Wharf, and top of Walsall Locks No. 1	—	2
Walsall Junction, *junction with Walsall Canal* and bottom of Walsall Locks No. 8	—	7

Bentley Canal (closure imminent)

Tame Valley Canal

Junction with Walsall Canal to:

	Miles	Furlongs
Golds Hill Wharf	—	3
Holloway Bank Wharf	1	0
Rushall Junction, *junction with Rushall Canal*	3	4
Hamstead Wharf	4	3
Barr Top Lock Wharf, and top of Perry Barr Locks, 1st Flight, Lock No. 1	5	4
Perry Barr, 1st Flight, Lock No. 7	6	—
Perry Barr, 2nd Flight, Lock Nos. 8, 9, 10 and 11	6	2
Perry Barr Wharf	6	4
Perry Barr, 3rd Flight, Lock Nos. 12 and 13	7	7
Salford Junction, *junction with Birmingham and Fazeley Canal* right and left, and *junction with Birmingham and Warwick Section of the Grand Union*	8	4

Rushall Canal

Longwood Junction, junction with Daw End Branch of Wyrley and Essington Canal, and Rushall Lock No. 1 (top) and No. 2, to:

Distance Table

	Miles	Furlongs
Bell Wharf and Rushall Lock Nos. 3 to 9	1	4
Rushall Junction, *junction with Tame Valley Canal*	2	6

Birmingham and Fazeley Canal

Farmers Bridge, junction with Main Line to:

	Miles	Furlongs
Junction with Newhall Branch Canal, and Farmers Bridge Lock No. 1 (top)	—	1
Farmers Bridge Lock No. 13	1	—
Aston Junction, *junction with Digbeth Branch*, and Aston Lock No. 14 (top)	1	4
Aston Lock No. 24 (bottom)	2	4
Salford Junction, *junction with Grand Union*—right, and *junction with Tame Valley Canal*—left	3	2
Erdington Wharf	5	1
Minworth Top Lock, No. 25	6	2
Minworth 2nd Lock, No. 26	6	4½
Minworth Bottom Lock, No. 27	7	1
Jeffrey's Dock Wharf	7	6
Dunton Wharf, Curdworth Lock, No. 28	9	4
Curdworth Lock, No. 29	9	7½
,, ,, ,, 32	10	1
,, ,, ,, 33	10	2½
,, ,, ,, 34	10	5
,, ,, ,, 35	11	1
,, ,, ,, 36	11	2
,, ,, ,, 37	11	5½
Curdworth Bottom Lock, No. 38	12	1
Fazeley Junction, *junction with Coventry Canal*	15	—
Hopwas	17	6
Whittington Brook, *junction with Coventry Canal*—detached portion	20	4

Digbeth Branch Canal

Aston Junction, junction, with Birmingham and Fazeley Canal to:

	Miles	Furlongs
Junction with Grand Union Canal	—	6
Bordesley Basin	—	7

Wyrley and Essington Canal.

Horseley Fields Junction, junction with Main Line to:

	Miles	Furlongs
Heath Town Wharf	—	7
Wednesfield Junction, *junction with Bentley Canal*	1	2
Sneyd Junction, junction with Sneyd and Wyrley Bank Branch Canal (closed)	6	2
Birchills Junction, *junction with Walsall Branch Canal*	8	—
Junction with Lord Hay's Branch Canal, near Little Bloxwich (now closed)	11	7
Pelsall Junction, *junction with Cannock Extension Canal* ...	12	7
Catshill Junction, *junction with Daw End Branch Canal* ...	15	3
Junction with Anglesey Branch and Ogley Lock No. 1 (not usable)...	16	3

The Canal from **Ogley** to **Huddlesford** is closed.

Distance Table *Miles Furlongs*

Daw End Branch Canal
Catshill Junction, junction with Wyrley and Essington Canal to:

								Miles	Furlongs
Clayhanger Wharf ...	...	...	...	...	...	...	...	—	1
Black Cock Wharf	...	...	...	...	...	...	...	—	6
Aldridge Wharf ...	...	...	...	...	...	...	...	2	4
Daw End Wharf ...	...	...	...	...	...	...	...	4	—
Longwood Junction and Wharf, *junction with Rushall Canal*						...		5	2

Cannock Extension Canal
Pelsall Junction, junction with Wyrley and Essington Canal to:

								Miles	Furlongs
Wyrley Grove Wharf	...	...	...	...	...	...	...	—	5
Norton Canes Docks	...	...	...	...	...	...	...	1	6

River Blyth(15)

This river was made navigable by an Act of Parliament dated 1757, but the locks were closed in 1934 by an order made under the Land Drainage Act, 1930.

Authority	Waveney District Council, Southwold, Suffolk. Tel. Southwold (0502) 722366
From and to	River mouth to Blythburgh.
Distance	5½ miles
Length	Unlimited.
Beam	Unlimited
Draught	4ft. at high water to Blythburgh.
Headroom	6ft. at H.W.S.T.
Locks	(There were 4 on the navigation to Halesworth, now derelict.)
Tow-path	None.
Tides	Once craft have entered the river, there is an average depth of 7 feet at L.W.O.S., the rise and fall being about 4ft. 6ins. Neaps and 6ft. 6ins. Springs. River is navigable with decreasing depths to Blythburgh. High water at the entrance is about 35 minutes after H. W. at Lowestoft.
Canoeing	Of very limited use apart from the tideway, except to Halesworth.
Moorings	No responsibility can be accepted for craft mooring alongside the

main Southwold Harbour quay owing to tidal conditions. Moorings are sited mid-stream from the ferry to Bailey Bridge, but the accommodation is extremely limited and advance enquiries should be made of the Harbour Master concerning availability before any visit is made.

Special note	The drainage authority who is in complete charge of the river above Southwold is Anglian Water, The Cedars, Albemarle Road, Norwich. Tel. Norwich (0606) 21257/8.

BRECON AND ABERGAVENNY CANAL.

(This has now been amalgamated with the Monmouthshire Canal, and renamed Monmouthshire and Brecon Canal. See page 218)

Bridgewater Canal(16)

The Acts relating to this canal were dated 1737, 1759, 1760, 1762, 1766 and 1795. This canal was promoted to success by Francis Egerton, 3rd Duke of Bridgewater, who is often called the Father of the Canal System. This canal was famous as the first of the 'canal age' and incorporated the Barton Aqueduct. John Gilbert was the engineer who constructed this early masterpiece. James Brindley served under Gilbert for part of the canal's construction, though it is widely asserted that this waterway was Brindley's Canal. Barton Aqueduct was widely and incorrectly called Brindley's Aqueduct, although it was saved just in time by Gilbert from collapse! Barton Swing Aqueduct replaces it.

At Worsley there remains a network of underground canals, long disused, though the entrance is still to be seen. The underground main line of the canal was 4 miles long, the upper canal 2 miles and the side branches totalled 40 miles. Canals are now closed as they are unsafe. The canal is a commercial waterway but the authorities licence pleasure craft on an annual basis. There is a reciprocal arrangement with the British Waterways Board.

Authority	Manchester Ship Canal Company, Estates Office, Dock Office, Trafford Road, Salford, M52 2XB. Tel. 061 872 2411.
From and to	Junction with the Rochdale Canal at Castlefield, Manchester to junction with the Manchester Ship Canal at Manchester, and the Trent and Mersey Canal at Preston Brook and to Runcorn *(see connections)*.
Connections	Besides having junctions with the Rochdale Canal and Manchester Ship Canal, this waterway has the following branches and junctions: Stretford and Leigh branch, joining the Leeds-Liverpool Canal at Leigh.

The Preston Brook branch from Waters Meeting-Main Canal to junction with the Trent and Mersey Canal at Preston Brook.
Hulme Lock branch to River Irwell, Upper Reach.

Distance

From junction with the Rochdale Canal at Manchester to Runcorn, 28 miles 1 furlong.
From junction with the Rochdale Canal to Preston Brook junction with the Trent and Mersey Canal, 23½ miles.
Preston Brook branch from Main Canal to junction with Trent and Mersey Canal, three quarters of a mile.

Length

70ft.

Beam

14ft. 9ins.

Draught

Castlefield, Manchester, to Cornbrook Bridge, 5ft.
Cornbrook Bridge to Preston Brook, Waters Meeting, 4ft.
Waters Meeting, Preston Brook, to Runcorn 4ft.

Headroom

11ft.

Locks

One. Hulme Lock (Manchester). Fall to Ship Canal.

Bridges

Numerous.

Tow-path

Throughout Canal and branches except Manchester to Cornbrook.

Charges

There is a scale of charges for pleasure craft and application must be made to the Bridgewater Canal Manager.

Speed limit and bye-laws

Copies of bye-laws are obtainable on application to the authority. Small craft owners are advised to consult the manager before navigating.

Facilities

Several boatyards and the marina at Preston Brook holds 420 boats and has a village complex.

Stretford and Leigh Branch

(For particulars of Leigh Branch of Leeds and Liverpool Canal, see page 181)

From and to

Junction with Main Canal at Stretford, 2½ miles below Manchester to junction with the Leigh branch of the Leeds and Liverpool Canal at Leigh.

Distance

10¾ miles.

Length

70ft.

Beam

14ft. 9ins.

Draught

4ft. (normal)

Headroom

8ft. 6ins.

Locks	None.	*Beam*	14ft. 9ins.	*Headroom*	8ft. 6ins.
Bridges	Numerous.	*Draught*	4ft. (normal)		

Hulme Lock Branch

From and to	Manchester, Egerton Street Bridge to River Irwell Upper Reach.
Distance	⅛ mile.
Length	70ft.
Beam	14ft. 9ins.
Draught	5ft.
Headroom	10ft. 6ins.
Locks	One. Fall to Ship Canal.

Preston Brook Branch

From and to	Preston Brook Junction on the Bridgewater Canal to Preston Brook.

Distance	¾ mile.	*Draught*	4ft.
Length	70ft.	*Headroom*	11ft.
Beam	14ft. 9ins.	*Locks*	None.

Special note — The canal at Runcorn is now severed from the Manchester Ship Canal, and the flight of 10 locks have been dismantled. The Runcorn and Weston Canal that ran from the junction with the Runcorn Locks and Runcorn Docks through to Weston Point where it joined the River Weaver has also been closed.

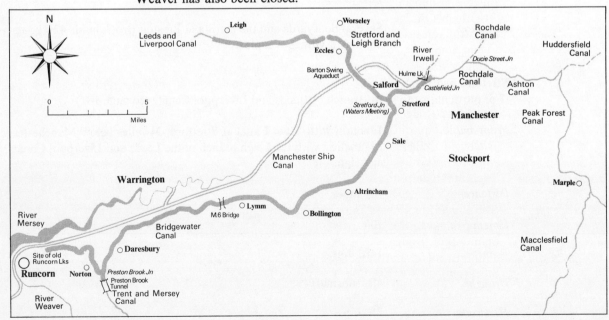

Distance Table
Main Line.

Manchester, Castlefield, junction with Rochdale Canal—Main Line to:

	Miles	Furlongs
Manchester, Egerton Street Bridge, *junction with Hulme Locks Branch*	—	2
Manchester Docks, Cornbrook Bridge	1	0
Throstle Nest Bridge	1	3
Trafford Road Bridge and Coal Wharves	1	4
Stretford—Waters Meeting *junction with Stretford and Leigh Branch*	2	6
Stretford Gas Works	3	0
Longford Bridge	3	2
Rathbone's Boat Yard	3	4
Stretford Wharf, Edge Lane Bridge	3	6
Stretford Watch House	4	0
River Mersey Aqueduct (Barfoot)	4	3
Dane Road Wharf and Dr. White's Bridge	4	6
Sale Warehouse and Wharf	5	1
Coal Wharf and Sale Bridge	5	2
Roebuck Lane Wharf	5	5
Marsland's Bridge	5	7
Timperley Bridge	6	7
Railway Bridge (Stockport Line)	7	1
Railway Bridge	7	3
Broadheath Wharves	7	4
Broadheath Warehouse, Bridge and Coal Wharf	7	5
Seamon's Moss Bridge	8	4
Dunham School Bridge	9	3
Dunham Town Bridge	9	6
Dunham Underbridge (Woodhouse Lane Aqueduct)	10	1
River Bollin Aqueduct	10	2
Bollington Warehouse and Wharf	10	5
Agden Bridge and Wharf	11	3
Burford Lane Warehouse and Wharf	12	1
Burford Lane Underbridge	12	2
Grantham's Bridge	12	3
Oughtrington Bridge	12	6
Lymm Stables	13	—
Lymm Warehouse	13	4
Lymm Bridge	13	5
Whitborough Aqueduct	13	6
Brookfield Bridge	13	7
Barsbank Aqueduct	14	2
Ditchfield Bridge and Wharf	14	5
M6 Motorway Bridge	15	—
Thelwall Underbridge	15	4
Pickering's Bridge	15	6
Cliff Lane Bridge Wharf and Underbridge	16	2
Grappenhall Bridge	16	5
Stanny Lunt Bridge	17	—
Lumb Brook Underbridge	18	
Stockton Quay, Warehouse, Wharf and Bridge	18	4

Distance Table

	Miles	Furlongs
Red Lane Bridge	18	7
Hough's Bridge, Walton	19	3
Walton Lea Bridge	19	5
Walton Wharf	19	6
Walton Bridge	19	7
Chester Road Underbridge and Wharf	20	1
Thomason's Bridge	20	2
Acton Grange Bridge	20	4
Moore Bridge	21	—
Moorefield Bridge	21	4
Keckwick Bridge	21	6
Keckwick Hill Bridge	22	2
George Cleave's Bridge	22	3
Red Brow Underbridge	23	—
Preston Brook, Waters Meeting, *junction with Preston Brook Branch*	23	3
Norton Warehouse, Canal Arm and Railway Aqueduct	23	4
Cawley's Bridge	23	6
Borrow's Bridge	23	7
Railway Bridge	24	—
Norton Town Bridge	24	2
Norton Bridge	24	5
Norton Townfield Bridge	25	—
Green Bridge	25	4
Astmoor Bridge and Wharf	26	1
Astmoor Tannery	26	3
Bates' Bridge	26	6
Highfield Tannery, Astmoor Wharf and Basin	26	7
Gas Works, Halton Road	27	—
Halton Road Wharf	27	1
Runcorn Delph Bridge and Bridgewater Foundry	27	4
Runcorn Dock Yard (The Sprinch)	27	5
Camden Tannery	27	6
Doctor's Bridge and Top Locks Warehouse	28	—
Runcorn, top of Locks, Waterloo Bridge and Railway Arches. ...	28	1

(Flight of 10 locks leading to Manchester Ship Canal have been closed and dismantled).

Hulme Lock Branch

Length from junction with Main Line to *junction with Irwell*

Upper Reach (Hulme Deep Lock) (This lock built in 1962 replaces the 3 old locks).	—	1

Preston Brook Branch

Preston Brook, junction with Main Line to:

Preston Brook. Bridge (Chester Road)	—	2
Preston Brook, *junction with Trent and Mersey Canal—Main Line* ...	—	6

Stretford and Leigh Branch

Stretford, Waters Meeting, junction with Main Line, to:

Taylor's Bridge	—	1

Distance Table

	Miles	Furlongs
Barton Swing Aqueduct over Manchester Ship Canal	2	2
Patricroft Basin and Warehouse	2	5
Patricroft Bridge	2	6
Patricroft Railway Bridge	3	1
Monton Green Bridge	3	5
Worsley Coke Ovens	4	2
Worsley Warehouse and Wharf	4	4
Worsley Bridge	4	6
Keeper's Turnbridge	5	6
Bridgewater Colliery Tips and Boothstown Bridge	6	4
Vicar's Hall Bridge...	7	—
Whitehead Hall Bridge	7	4
Astley Bridge	7	6
Lingard's Bridge	8	3
Morley's Bridge	8	4
Marsland Green Bridge	8	7
Great Fold Bridge	9	1
Hall House Bridge	9	3
Butt's Basin and Wharf and Toll Office	9	6
Butt's Bridge	9	7
Dick Mather's Bridge	10	2
Railway Bridge	10	4
Junction with Leigh Branch of Leeds and Liverpool Canal	10	6

Bridgwater & Taunton Canal (17)

This canal was built under Acts passed in 1811 and 1824. It formed a feeder and distributor to Bridgwater Dock. It has been out of use since the war as the swing bridges have not been reinstated. Running through rolling Somerset countryside, its condition is deplorable as inland water recreation in the West Country is hard to find. Bridgwater is an ideal centre for canoeists and light craft users to explore this and adjoining waterways.

Authority	British Waterways Board.
From and to	Taunton, junction with River Tone Navigation, to Bridgwater.
Distance	14½ miles.
Length	54ft.
Width	13ft.
Draught	3ft.
Headroom	8ft. (At the time of going to press the swing bridges are still fixed)
Locks	6. Fall from Taunton. 1 Barge lock to River Parrett from Dock.

Bridges	Numerous. At present swing bridges do not work.
Tow-path	Throughout navigation.
Remarks	River Tone Navigation is now derelict from Taunton to Ham Mill. The short section at Taunton is three quarters of a mile long. The section below Ham Mill is tidal and is navigable to Burrow Bridge. No boatyard facilities but several inns nearby.
Special note	Part of this navigation has been re-opened. At present there are several bridges across the canal which obstruct the navigation and restrict the statutory headroom. The canal is open from Taunton to Bridgwater Dock. Locks Nos. 1 - 6 have been restored.

Bridgwater

Depth of water in Bridgwater Dock, 15 to 16ft.
Available length for vessels in Tidal Basin, 180ft.
Width of opening of gates from Dock to Tidal Basin, 32ft.
Width of opening of gates from Tidal Basin to River Parrett, 42ft.

Bridgwater and Taunton Canal. Lock with unusual gate mechanism

Distance Table   *Miles   Furlongs*
Firepool Lock No. 1, Taunton, junction with River Tone
Navigation,* to:

									Miles	Furlongs
Bathpool	...	...	...	...	...	...	...	...	1	6
Creech St. Michael		...	...	...	...	...	...	...	3	—

Maunsell, Top Lock No. 2	...	...	...	...	...	6	6
Maunsell, Bottom Lock No. 3	...	...	...	...	...	7	—
North Newton	...	...	...	...	...	7	1
Kings Lock No. 4 ...	...	...	...	...	...	8	2
Standards Lock No. 5	...	...	...	...	...	9	—
Ford Gate ...	...	...	...	...	...	9	6
Entrance Lock to Bridgwater Dock and Termination of Canal (Bridgwater Lock No. 6) ...	...	...	...	...	...	14	—
Outlet from Bridgwater Dock to River Parrett (Lock) .	...	...	14	$1\frac{1}{2}$

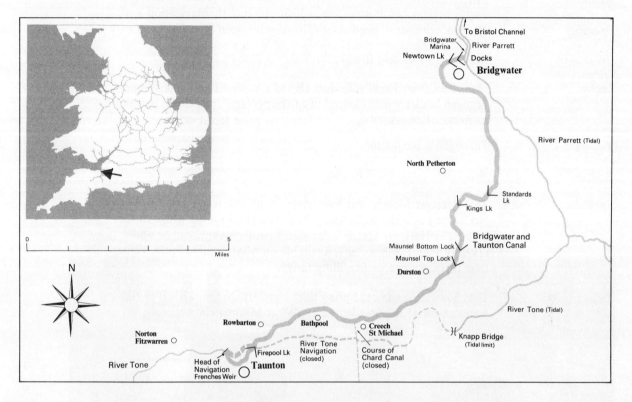

Bude Canal (18)

This canal was navigable throughout until it was closed by Act of Parliament in 1891.

The canal network was originally promoted under Acts dated 1774 and 1819. For some years the swing bridge has been inoperative, and this unauthorised fixing continued until an Act was passed in 1960, promoted by the Bude-Stratton U. D. C. which legally fixed the bridge now known as Falcon Bridge. A headroom of at least 3ft. 6ins. is provided to let light craft proceed to the head of the navigation at Rodd's Bridge. There are many remains of the tub boat canal for inspection. Bude is a pleasant seaside resort but the coast can be a dangerous place for boats in rough weather.

Authority   North Cornwall District Council, The Castle, Bude, Cornwall.
Tel. Bude (0288) 3111

* River Tone is navigable from the gas works to Firepool Lock, a distance of three quarters of a mile.

Controlling Officer: The Harbour Master, The Wharf, Bude. Cornwall.

From and to	Bude Sea Lock to Rodd's Bridge.
Distance	1¼ miles
Length	85ft.
Beam	24ft.
Draught	9ft. 6ins.
Headroom	Unlimited to Falcon Bridge. 3ft. 6ins. to Rodd's Bridge
Locks	One. Fall from Rodd's Bridge. (Rodd's Bridge Lock and Whalesborough Lock are now closed but can be portaged, as canal is in water to Rodd's Bridge).
Tow-path	Throughout navigation.
Bridges	None over section still in use.
Facilities	The Harbour Master will lock ships in or out whenever possible. No locking is undertaken until 7ft. is registered on the gauge at the locks. The Harbour Master's decision whether locking can be undertaken is final. Fresh water is available on wharf, daily requirements free, there is a charge for filling tanks.
Tides	Tide flows to Sea Lock. Spring tides rise 23ft. Neaps, 17ft. It is high water about 45 minutes before H. W. at Milford Haven.

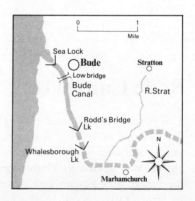

Special note   The Tub Boat Canal was closed in 1891, the works being finally abandoned in 1901. There were six inclined planes at Marhamchurch, Hobbacott Down (Thurlibeer), Vealand, Merrifield, Tamerton and Werrington (Bridgetown). Tub Boats 20ft x 5ft 6ins. had a draught of 1ft 8ins and carried 4 tons. The canal ran from Rodd's Bridge inland up the Tamar valley to Druxton Wharf, near Launceston. There were branches at Tamar Lake and towards Holsworthy to Balgonmoor Wharf. There are numerous remains to be inspected and sections have been retained in water for water supply.

Calder and Hebble Navigation (19)

This waterway has a delightfully rugged appearance matching the area it approaches, namely the Pennines. The locks match the stone buildings of the older industrial premises.

The navigation was promoted by Acts dated 1758, 1769 and 1825. The waterway was never as successful as the Aire and Calder to which it fed the bulk of its traffic. The smaller locks always restricted a good deal of possible trade. The waterway has a number of unique features such as the hand spike to operate locks above Wakefield. These spikes can be purchased from the yard at Shepley Bridge or at Castleford Lock.

The waterway now has no commercial traffic but care is needed on the lower reaches. These reaches are frankly industrial but above Mirfield there are some beautiful stretches of scenery, particularly Wakefield Bridge to broadcut, past Lupset Hall. The banks are well wooded here as they are in many other surprising places. The waterway drains the Calder Valley and the section can carry heavy flood water, hence the additional flood lock at the ends of the cuts. Dewsbury Basin is popular for winter moorings.

Authority   British Waterways Board.

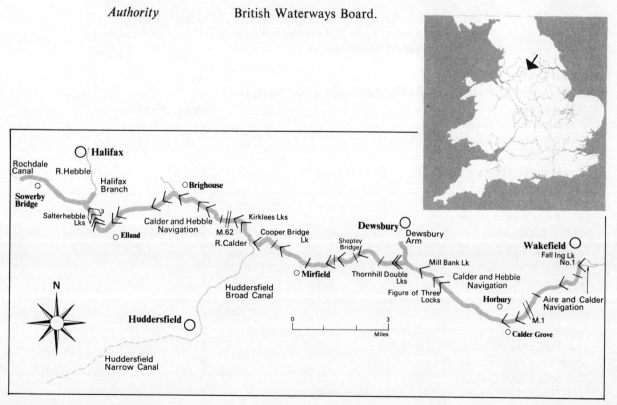

	Broadcut Top Lock to Sowerby Bridge	Fall Ing Lock, Wakefield to Broadcut Top Lock
Length	57ft. 6ins.	120ft. 0ins.
Beam	14ft. 2ins.	17ft. 6ins.
Draught	5ft. 0ins.	6ft. 6ins.
Headroom	9ft. 0ins.	11ft. 0ins.

From and to Junction with the Aire and Calder Canal at Wakefield to Sowerby Bridge. There are several short branches in use which are part of the old navigation.

Sections of the Rochdale Canal have been restored. Through navigation projected. Connection with the Calder and Hebble in progress.

Distances 21½ miles. (Wakefield Weir Stream ½ mile, Dewsbury Old Cut ¾ mile)

Locks 27 locks, (8 Flood gates). Rise from Fall Ing, Wakefield.
Lock gates worked by boat crews.
Thornes, Broadcut Low and Shepley Bridge Lock are double length locks with intermediate gates. Additionally Thornes has also a parallel lock as well but this is not used.

Tow-path Throughout Main Line navigation.

Facilities Numerous boatyards and inns.

Branch Horbury Branch is now closed, there were 2 locks in this branch. There were also 14 locks on the Halifax Branch and one on Tag Cut, these locks are all now closed to navigation.

Distance Table

Fall Ing Lock No. 1, junction with the Aire and Calder Navigation

Main Line to:	Miles	Furlongs
Wakefield Flood Gates	–	4
British Waterways Board Wharf (on Short Branch of River Calder)	–	4½
Lupset Park, Thornes Locks No. 2 (Double Locks)	1	–
Thornes Flood Gates	2	–
M.1. Road Bridge	2	4
Broad Cut Low Lock No. 3	2	7
Waller Bridge	3	–
Broad Cut Top Lock No. 4	3	2½
Horbury Bridge, Bingley Arms Hotel (Flood control point)	5	–
Junction with Horbury Cut (Closed)	5	5
Figure of Three Locks Nos. 5 and 6	6	–
Mill Bank Lock No. 7	6	5
Junction with Dewsbury Arm (Dewsbury Basin 6 Furlongs)	7	–
Thornhill Double Locks Nos. 8 and 9	7	0½
Thornhill Power Station Wharf	7	6
Thornhill Flood Gates (The River Calder is navigable to Dewsbury Mills Weir)	8	–

Distance Table	*Miles*	*Furlongs*
Ravensthorpe Village, Greenwood Lock No. 10	8	7
Greenwood Flood Gates	9	1
Shepley Bridge, The Ship Inn, Shepley Bridge Lock Nos 11	9	4
British Waterways Board Yard, Dry Dock, Section Inspectors Office	9	5
Mirfield Boatyard	10	–
Ledgard Flood Gates	10	6
Battye Lock No. 12	11	6
Battye Flood Gates	12	2
Cooper Bridge Lock No. 13	12	6
Cooper Bridge Flood Gates	13	–
Junction with River Calder, leading to the Huddersfield Broad Canal	13	0½
Kirklees Low Lock No. 14	13	4½
Kirklees Top Lock No. 15	13	5½
Anchor Pit Flood Gates (Kirklees)	14	2
Brighouse Locks Nos. 16 and 17	15	1
Brighouse Basin Entrance (Superb moorings in a landscaped basin, close to town facilities)	15	2½
Ganny Lock No. 18	15	6
Brookfoot Lock No. 19 (flood control point)	16	–
Cromwell Lock No. 20	16	3
Park Nook Lock No. 21	16	7
Elland Lock No. 22	17	1
Woodside Mills Lock No. 23	18	–
Longleas Lock No. 24	18	3
Salterhebble Locks Nos. 25, 26 and 27. (The first lock has an electrically operated guillotine gate, operated by lock-keeper at top lock).	19	–
Junction with closed Halifax Branch (open for 600 yards)	19	0½
Sowerby Bridge. Basin, moorings and facilities.	21	4

River Cam (20)

This navigation was promoted by Acts dated 1702 and 1813. The navigation is wide and open at the commencement of the Cam, at Pope's Corner, and continues as a Fenland river to the first lock. Upstream from here the river resembles the Thames, even to having lock-keepers at all locks. The last section through 'The Backs' is congested in the season with punts and oarsmen, the cruisers should not go above Jesus Green Lock. The journey past the colleges in early morning, in spring, is an experience not to be missed. The trip on the last section should be made by dinghy, as the wealth of architecture needs close and detailed observation. It is possible to portage a light craft at the Mill Pool and proceed upstream to above Grantchester. Canoeable to Guilden Morden (Cam) and Audley End (Granta) (semi-private).

Wicken Fen with its museum is on the Wicken Lode and is a unique National Trust property preserving a section of Fenland before drainage.

Authority	**From Silver Street, Cambridge to Bottisham Lock** Conservators of the River Cam, the Guildhall, Cambridge. CB2 3QJ. Tel. Cambridge (0223) 58977 **From Bottisham Lock to junction with the River Ouse** Anglian Water, Great Ouse House, Clarendon Road, Cambridge. Tel. Cambridge (0223) 61561.
From and to	Cambridge to the junction with the River Ouse at Popes Corner.
Distance	Cambridge to the junction with the River Ouse, 14⅜ miles.
Length	100ft.
Beam	14ft.
Draught	4ft.
Headroom	9ft.
Locks	3. Lock gates worked by lock-keepers except Bottisham Lock. Fall from Cambridge.
Bridges	Numerous.
Connections	Reach Lode and Burwell Lode can be reached from Upware. Connection is also made with Swaffham Lode, and the Great Ouse. Soham Lode is only suitable for light craft as the depth of water is only 1ft. 6ins.

Reach Lode and Burwell Lode

Authority	Anglian Water, Great Ouse House, Clarendon Road, Cambridge. Tel. Cambridge (0223) 61561.
From and to	Upware, junction with River Cam to Burwell and Reach village.
Distance	3¾ miles to Burwell, 3 miles to Reach.
Length	50ft.
Beam	13ft. 6ins.
Draught	Burwell Lode, 4ft. Reach Lode, 2ft. 6ins.
Headroom	9ft.
Locks	One. Reach Lode Sluice. Generally the lock falls from Reach but the lock is provided with two sets of bottom gates that open either way. The top guillotine gate is electrically operated.
Tow-path	Throughout navigation, and termed locally 'Haling Way'.
Remarks	These navigations were formerly used by fen lighters, now these Lodes are used by pleasure craft only. At Burwell village there are

two arms to the Lode and this gives several good moorings. Wicken Lode is shallow and can only be navigated with care. Inns at Burwell, Wicken. No boatyards. Inn near entrance from Cam. Except for local inhabitants navigation of Wicken Lode ceases at junction with Monks Lode.

Swaffham Lode

Authority　　　The same as for Reach and Burwell Lodes.

From and to　　Junction with River Cam to Slade Farm.*

Distance　　　2 miles.

Length　　　　96ft.

Beam　　　　　15ft.

Draught　　　　For the first two miles 2ft. but after this the Lode gets shallower.

Headroom　　　9ft.

Locks　　　　　There is one entrance lock, Swaffham Lode Sluice. Fall from Swaffham.

Tow-path　　　Throughout navigation.

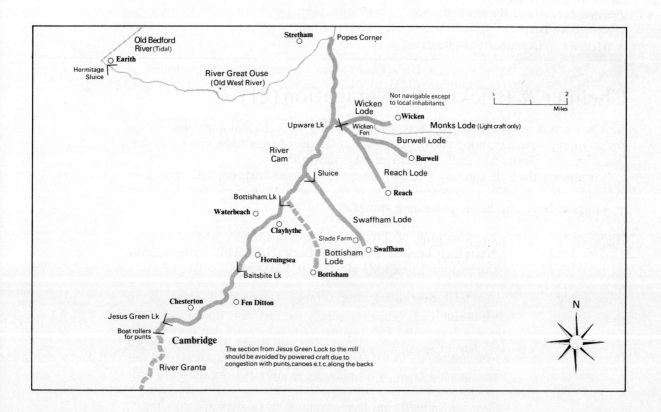

* Low bridges and lack of depth prevent craft reaching Swaffham.

Distance Table
River Cam.

Kings Mill, Cambridge, to:

	Miles	Furlongs
Jesus Green Lock, Cambridge	—	6
Chesterton Ferry	2	4
Fen Ditton	3	4
Baitsbite Lock No. 2	4	5
Horningsea	5	2
Clayhythe Bridge — *Waterbeach Station and village distance half a mile*	6	5
Bottisham Lock No. 3	7	5
Mouth of Bottisham Lode* (unnavigable)	7	6
Junction with Swaffham Lode	9	—
Upware, *junction with Reach and Burwell Lodes*	11	2
Popes Corner, *junction with Great River Ouse*	14	3

Burwell Lode

Upware, junction with River Cam, to:

	Miles	Furlongs
Reach Lode Sluice (lock)	—	$0\frac{1}{2}$
Junction with Wicken Lode	—	3
Pout Hall, *junction with Reach Lode leading to Reach village, $2\frac{1}{8}$ miles*	—	7
Manure works	2	6
Burwell village	3	6

Wicken Lode (not navigable beyond junction with Monks Lode,
except for local residents)
Junction Burwell and Wicken Lodes, to:

	Miles	Furlongs
New River Drain	1	1
Wicken Fen (National Trust Reserve)	1	4

Chelmer & Blackwater Navigation (21)

This navigation was promoted by Acts dated 1766 and 1793. Its statutory depth is the lowest of any waterway, being only 2 feet. This has led river barges to be unusual in size, being broader, shorter and shallower than on other navigations.

It is a pretty river, though very unknown except to the local boatmen. Like other East Anglian waterways, mills are a prominent part of the scenery. Visitors can find temporary moorings at Heybridge before proceeding upstream.

Authority	The Company of Proprietors of the Chelmer and Blackwater Navigation Limited, Paper Mill Lock, North Hill, Little Baddow, Chelmsford, Essex CM3 4F. Tel. (024 541) 2025.
From and to	The tidal river Blackwater through Heybridge Basin Lock to Chelmsford.
General remarks	At Heybridge Basin, entered from the River Blackwater by sea locks, vessels up to 107 feet long, 26 feet beam and drawing 12 feet can enter the basin. A considerable number of large and small craft moor here.
	Commercial traffic has now ceased on this waterway.

* Bottisham Lode is unnavigable but enthusiasts have navigated short sections at Cottenham Lode.

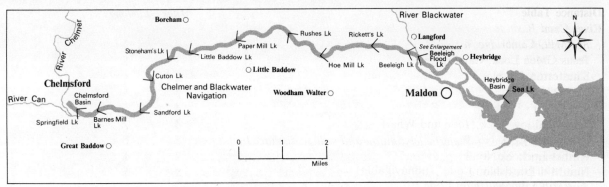

Distance	13¾ miles.
Length	60ft.
Beam	16ft.
Draught	2ft 6ins
Headroom	6ft 5ins

Locks	13. Lock gates worked by boat crews, except Heybridge Sea Lock. Fall from Chelmsford.
Bridges	Several. Low headroom at most bridges.
Navigation notes	In dry seasons the supply of water is very limited and the company is strict with regard to unauthorised opening of locks. The use of the locks in summer is often discouraged but pleasure craft licences are issued if the boat is in responsible hands and the company are satisfied with the bona-fides of the applicant.
Facilities	Apart from small boathouses, no boatyards, refreshments at Chelmsford, Little Baddow and Heybridge.
Tow-path	Throughout navigation.
Tides	The River Blackwater is tidal to Heybridge Sea Lock. High water 1¼ hours after Dover. Spring tides rise 12ft., Neaps 8ft.
Special note	A navigable link in the form of boat rollers has been constructed at Chelmsford to link the Chelmer and River Can. Light craft can go approximately 8 miles. Several proposals for extensions have been made for the river at Chelmsford. Canoeable from Little Waltham.

Distance Table

Chelmsford Basin to:

	Miles	Furlongs
Springfield Lock No. 1	—	3
Barnes Mill Lock No.2	1	1
Sandford Lock No. 3	2	1
Cuton Lock No. 4	3	1
Stoneham's Lock No. 5	4	--
Little Baddow Lock No. 6 and Wharf	4	7
Paper Mill Lock No. 7	6	1
Rushes Lock No. 8	7	4
Hoe Mill Lock. No. 9	8	6
Rickett's Lock No. 10	10	1
Beeleigh Lock No. 11	11	---
Beeleigh Flood Lock No. 12	11	4
Heybridge village	12	2
Heybridge Sea Lock No. 13	13	7

Chesterfield Canal (22)

This canal was promoted originally by an Act passed in 1771. It commences at Stockwith Basin and then runs through pleasant agricultural country, after Drakeholes Tunnel, it enters wooded country, and at Retford the canal basin is in the town centre. The canal goes to Worksop through Babworth Forest and Osberton Park to the 'Gateway to the Dukeries'. The Retford and Worksop (Chesterfield Canal) Boat Club are very helpful to visitors and issue a useful handbook. The organisation is in fact a canal society who have done a great deal to re-open part of the canal. The tunnel at Norwood collapsed in 1908 and has never been repaired. The present head of navigation is Morse Lock and the rest of the canal above it has an uncertain future. Restoration to Chesterfield is virtually impossible but some sections may be restored for recreation. The Retford and Worksop Boat Club who have helped re-open the canal, greatly assist visitors, their headquarters is at Clayworth. The long term plan is to re-open the canal to Norwood Tunnel, but B.W.B. have sold some sections. A section near Killamarsh has been re-opened for fishing, and another also, at the Chesterfield end.

Authority　　　British Waterways Board.

From and to　　Junction with the River Trent at West Stockwith to Worksop. The canal is not now navigable between Worksop and Chesterfield.

Distances　　　West Stockwith to Worksop, 26 miles.
　　　　　　　　West Stockwith to Chesterfield, 45½ miles.

Length　　　　72ft.

Beam　　　　　Stockwith to Retford 14ft. 6ins. Above Retford 6ft. 11ins.

Headroom　　　7ft.

Locks　　　　　16. Locks worked by boat crews except Stockwith Trent Lock which is opened by lock-keeper. Locks 1—49 inclusive are derelict.

Bridges	Numerous.
Tunnels	2. Drakeholes, 154 yards. Headroom, 10ft. Norwood, 3,102 yards. (Closed through colliery subsidence).
Speed limit	4 miles per hour.
Moorings	Available from tidal section of River Trent at West Stockwith Basin. Standard charges payable to British Waterways Board, Wilford Street, Nottingham, or local representative. Club moorings at Top Middle Lock 55.
Tow-path	Tow-path throughout navigation, except Drakeholes Tunnel.
Facilities	Canalside inns and boatyards at West Stockwith and Retford.

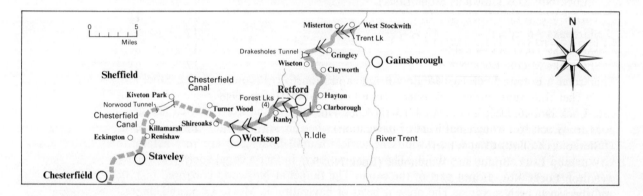

Navigation note

The only approach to the canal is through West Stockwith Lock from the Trent. Great care is needed on the Trent and the West Stockwith Yacht Club are helpful to visitors. Visitors are advised to ring the lock-keeper at Gainsborough (0427) 890204 for advice as to time of arrival as the tides can be inconvenient. There is an aegre on the Trent and this must be considered when planning a trip. Usually 5 hours after high water is the time limit for getting into West Stockwith Lock, but this varies considerably, and the lock-keeper's advice should be followed closely. Great care must be taken to conserve water and reporting any damage or leaks is something that must be done at once. Water levels are maintained by pumping.

Tides	It is high water at West Stockwith 2 to 2½ hours after Hull.

Distance Table
Chesterfield to:

								Miles	Furlongs
Ford Lane Lock No. 1	...	...	...	...	...	...	...	—	7
New Bridge Lock No. 2	...	...	...	...	...	...	...	1	6
Blue Bank Lock No. 3	...	...	...	...	...	...	...	2	3
Dixon's Lock No. 4	...	...	...	...	...	...	...	2	7

Distance Table	*Miles*	*Furlongs*
Staveley Works Lock No. 5	3	4
Hartington Colliery	4	7½
Belk Lane Lock No. 6	10	5
(Then follows Norwood Locks Nos. 7 to 29)		
Norwood Tunnel, West End	12	0½
Norwood Tunnel, East End	13	7
Top Treble or Summit Locks Nos. 20, 21 and 22 (Thorpe Locks) ...	16	1
Thorpe Locks Nos. 23 ,24 and 25	16	2
Thorpe Locks Nos. 26 27 and 28 (Low Treble Locks)	16	3
Thorpe Locks Nos. 29 30 and 31	16	3½
Brown's Lock Nos. 32 (Part of the Thorpe flight)	16	4½
(Then follows Locks Nos. 33 and 34 of the Thorpe flight)		
Turner Wood Lock No. 35 (sometimes called Quarry Lock) and Wharf	16	6½
(Then follows Turner Wood Locks Nos. 36 37 38 39 40 and 41. Lock No. 39 is known as Stone Lock).		
Turner Wood Low Lock No. 41	17	1½
Shireoaks Aqueduct	17	2
Shireoaks Top Lock No. 42	17	6
Shireoaks Middle Lock No. 43	17	6½
Shireoaks Bottom Lock No. 44 Low Bridge and Wharf	17	7
(Then follows at intervals: Doefield Dunn Lock No. 45 Haggonfield Lock No. 46, Deep Lock No. 47, Stret Lock No. 48)		
Morse Lock No. 49 (present head of navigation)*	19	4
Shireoaks Colliery Coal Wharf	19	7
Worksop Lock, Bridge and Warehouse (Lock No. 50)	20	—
Kilton Locks Nos. 51 and 52	21	—
Osberton Lock No. 53	23	2
Ranby, Chequers Inn	25	1½
Forest Top Lock No. 54 (then follow Forest Locks Nos. 55, 56 and 57)	26	2
West Retford, Wharf Bridge and Lock No. 58	29	7
Aqueduct over River Idle	30	1
Retford Lock No. 59	30	2½
Whitsunday Pie Lock (Hop Pole Inn) No. 60	31	6
Clarborough Bridge, (St. John's)	32	2
Clarborough Bridge (Gate Inn)	33	—
Hayton (Boat Inn)	34	6
Clayworth Wharf and Top Bridge	35	7
Drakeholes Wharf and West End of Drakeholes Tunnel (White Swan Inn)	39	—
Gringley Top Wharf and Top Lock No. 61	40	6
Gringley Low Lock No. 62 and Low Lock Bridge	41	4
Walkeringham Bridge and Wharf	42	5
Misterton, Cooper's Bridge	43	6½
Misterton Top Lock No. 63	44	5½
Misterton Low Lock No. 64	44	6
Railway Bridge (British Railways, Eastern Region) (Packet Inn) ...	44	7
Stockwith Bridge	45	3½
West Stockwith, Trent Lock No. 65, *junction with River Trent* ...	45	4

*The foregoing derelict section is included for completeness in case any portion is reopened for amenity and recreation.

Chichester Canal (23)

This canal was originally part of the old Portsmouth—Arundel route, linking London with Portsmouth via the Wey—Arun Junction Canal, a route derelict for nearly a century. The lower reaches of the canal are still used for the purposes of mooring yachts and houseboats. The Chichester Yacht Basin Ltd lease this section from the county council. The fairway to the lock gates is in places marked by perches and should not be confused with the dredged fairway to the Chichester Yacht Basin which is marked by piles and lies just to the north. It almost dries at low water springs. The canal was originally promoted by an Act passed in 1817. Details of the Chichester Channel are given on Chart No Y33 by the publishers. Two swing bridges have been abolished and the canal culverted. The decision to close part of the canal was taken by the Chichester City Council on the 6th June 1928 under Section 7 of the Chichester Canal Transfer Act 1892. Canal leased to the Chichester Canal Society (1984). Chichester Harbour Conservancy Act 1971 applies.

Authority	West Sussex County Council, County Hall, Chichester. Tel. Chichester (0243) 785100
From and to	Birdham Pool to Chichester Basin.
Distance	4½ miles. (Only navigable from Chichester Harbour to Birdham Lock. The rest is for light craft that can be portaged).
Length	85ft.
Beam	18ft.
Draught	7ft.
Headroom	Unlimited.
Locks	One. Saltern's Lock. Fall from Chichester. Casher Lock is not workable and the rest of the canal to Chichester is unusable except for light craft that can be portaged round obstructions.
Tow-path	Throughout navigation.

Distance Table:

Chichester Basin to:	*Miles*	*Furlongs*
Hunston. *Junction with Portsmouth and Arundel Canal.*		
(Closed at present)	1	3
Donnington	2	1
Birdham Lock (derelict)	3	2
Salterns Lock (Entrance to Canal)	4	–
Low Water Channel Chichester Harbour	4	4

River Colne (24)

This estuary navigation was the subject of six Acts, dated 1623, 1689, 1718, 1740, 1750 and 1781. Mainly used for coasting trade, it has played a part in the export of oysters from the river below Wivenhoe. There are excellent yachting facilities in the estuary.

Authority	Colchester Borough Council, The Harbour Master. Tel. Colchester (0206) 5858. After hours: Colchester (0206) 76725
From and to	†East Mill, Colchester to Colne Point.
Distance	11 miles.
Length	195ft.
Beam	28ft.
Draught	Maximum to The Hythe on Spring tides, 11ft. Maximum to The Hythe on Neap tides, 9ft.
Headroom	Unlimited*
Remarks	The river is practically dry at low water above Wivenhoe. The Borough Council of Colchester are the harbour authority for the navigable channel, except Brightlingsea Creek. Not practicable for canoeists above Colchester.
Tow-path	On both banks to Wivenhoe from Colchester.
Tides	High water at Brightlingsea half an hour after Dover. Spring tides rise 10ft. 6ins., Neaps rise 7ft. 6ins.

Distance Table

East Mill, Colchester and East Bridge (tidal limit) to:	*Miles*	*Furlongs*
Railway Bridge – line into Colchester St. Botolph's station	–	1
Site of railway bridge – former harbour branch	–	5
Hythe Bridges – present effective head of navigation	–	6½
The Hythe – start of main commercial wharves	–	7
Colchester Borough Council Harbour Depot and Swinging Berth	–	7½
End of wharves on east bank	1	–
End of commercial wharves on west bank	1	5
Dredging disposal site	1	6
Rowhedge Wharf	3	4
Junction with Roman River leading to		
Fingringhoe Mill and Quay	3	5
Wivenhoe Port	3	5½
Wivenhoe Shipyard – James W. Cook & Co. (Wivenhoe) Ltd.	3	7
Fingringhoe Ballast Quay	4	–
Arlesford Creek leading to Thorrington Mill and quay	5	2
Northern junction with Greedon Creek		
(upstream of Rat Island)	7	–

* There is a bridge at Hythe, headroom 4ft. at Spring tides.
† See Imray Chart No Y17 River Colne to Blackwater and Crouch.

Distance Table	*Miles*	*Furlongs*
Southern junction with Geedon Creek (downstream of Rat Island)	7	3
Junction with Pyefleet Channel leading to The Strood, West Mersea	8	–
Westmarsh Point, leading to Brightlingsea and St. Osyth Creeks	8	3
Mersea Point (west bank) and St. Osyth Point (east bank)	8	4
Colne Point, limit of Colchester Borough Council's jurisdiction	11	–

Coombe Hill Canal(25)

This waterway originally constructed to shorten the haulage distance for coal and other goods to Cheltenham. Several suggestions were made to extend the waterway. It was constructed under an Act in 1792 and closed by an Act in 1876. Some progress has already been made in its restoration.

Authority	Coombe Hill Canal Trust, Sec., N.Q. Grazebrook Esq., 43 Cannon Street, Birmingham, B2 5EQ. Tel. (021 632) 4199.
From and To	*Junction with the Severn at Wainlode, to Coombe Hill.
Distance	2¾ miles.
Length	64ft
Beam	14ft 6ins
Draught, Headroom	Canal under reconstruction.
Locks	Two. There was a double lock at the entrance, but this will need to be completely rebuilt.
Remarks	This is a private venture, and the owners have a large amount of material stored to start a museum. They are restoring the basin and ancillary buildings. At first the aim is to re-open the canal, and possibly use a trip boat on it. The problem of connection with the Severn, is that the land connecting the canal to the river is not under the same ownership.

*See plan R. Severn page 292.

Coventry Canal(26)

This canal was promoted by Acts passed in 1768, 1786 and 1819. It originally carried heavy coal traffic but now is used by pleasure craft, being particularly well situated with lock-free sections and linked with the Ashby Canal and Oxford Canal. Apart from stop locks at Marston Junction and Hawkesbury Junction (Sutton Stop), there is a level network of waterways totalling 53¾ miles very close to urban areas yet rural in many places. The lonely area between Fradley and Fazeley was the setting for the ghost story 'Three Miles Up'. The country in this section is well wooded. Tamworth and Atherstone are useful ports of call and Coventry Cathedral and the partly rebuilt city are interesting to visit. The route via Braunston Junction, Hawkesbury Junction and Fradley Junction is popular for a through way as it avoids Birmingham, particularly when going from the Grand Union and Oxford to the northwestern area.

Authority	British Waterways Board.
From and to	Junction with Oxford Canal at Hawkesbury Junction to junction with the Trent and Mersey Canal at Fradley.
Connections	The Coventry Canal has junction with the Ashby Canal at Marston about 3 miles north of Hawkesbury, and junction with the Wyrley and Essington Canal at Huddlesford, about 4 miles short of the junction with the Trent and Mersey Canal. This canal is closed except for a short length for mooring. The waterway leading to Coventry has junction with the Main Line at Hawkesbury.
Distances	Junction with Oxford Canal at Hawkesbury to junction with Trent and Mersey Canal at Fradley, 32½ miles. Coventry Basin to junction with Birmingham and Fazeley Canal at Fazeley, 27 miles. Hawkesbury Junction to Coventry, 5½ miles. The detached portion of the canal from Whittington to junction with the Trent and Mersey Canal, 5½ miles.
Length	72ft.
Beam	7ft.
Draught	3ft. 6ins.
Headroom	6ft. 6ins.
Branches	Griff Colliery Canal, three quarters of a mile.
Locks	13. Hawkesbury Stop Lock is on the Oxford Canal. Rise 6 inches. Fall from Coventry.
Bridges	Numerous. One swing bridge
Tow-path	Throughout navigation.

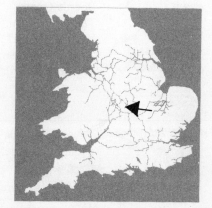

Facilities   Several boatyards and inns.

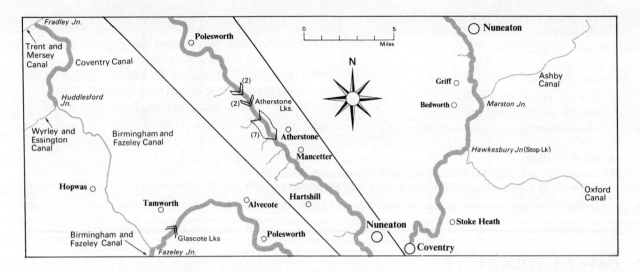

Distance Table

Coventry Basin, to:

	Miles	Furlongs
Stoke Basin ...	2	—
Navigation Wharf ...	2	6
New Inn Wharf ...	4	—
Longford Wharf ...	4	4
Hawkesbury Junction, *junction with Oxford Canal—Main Line* (Stop Lock) (Greyhound Inn) ...	5	4
Newdigate Colliery...	6	4
Bulkington Lane ...	7	2
Charity Basin ...	8	—
Marston Junction, *junction with Ashby Canal* ...	8	2
Griff ...	9	2
Coton Old Wharf ...	10	—
Coton Boot Wharf ...	10	2
Wash Lane Wharf ...	11	—
Midland Quarry ...	11	6
Nuneaton Wharf ...	11	6
Judkin Quarry ...	11	6
Boon's Quarry ...	12	6
The Anchor Inn ...	13	6
Hartshill Wharf ...	14	2
Wide Hole Wharf ...	14	6
Mancetter Wharf ...	15	6
Atherstone, Top Lock No. 1 ...	16	4
Atherstone Lock No. 5 ...	16	7
Atherstone Lock No. 6 ...	17	$3\frac{1}{2}$
Atherstone Lock No. 7 ...	17	4
Baddesley Colliery Basin ...	17	4
Atherstone Lock No. 8 ...	17	7
Atherstone Lock No. 9 ...	17	$7\frac{1}{2}$

Distance Table

	Miles	Furlongs
Atherstone Lock No. 10	18	3
Atherstone Bottom Lock No. 11	18	4
Polesworth	21	4
Pooley	22	2
Alvecote	23	2
Amington	23	4
Glascote Top Lock No. 12	25	4
Glascote Bottom Lock No. 13	25	5
Fazeley Junction, *junction with Birmingham and Fazeley Canal* ...	27	—

Detached Portion

Whittington Brook, junction with Birmingham and Fazeley Canal to:

	Miles	Furlongs
Huddlesford Junction, *junction with Wyrley and Essington Canal* ...	1	4
Fradley Junction, *junction with Trent and Mersey Canal—Main Line*	5	4

River Crouch (27)

Navigation up to Battlesbridge is difficult due to shoals and sandbanks. Barges regularly trade to the mill at Battlesbridge. This is a very popular yachting centre, particularly in the area near Burnham-on-Crouch. The Crouch Harbour Authority 1974 applies.

Authority	Crouch Harbour Authority, Harbour Office, Belvedere Rd., Burnham on Crouch, Essex. Tel. (0621) 783602
From and to	*Battlesbridge to Holliwell Point.
Distance	17½ miles.
Length	Unlimited.
Beam	,,
Draught	7ft. High water spring tides to Battlesbridge.
Headroom	Unlimited.
Connections	River Roach.
Locks	None. There were previously tidal doors at Battlesbridge to enable craft to proceed upstream. These are now disused.
Tow-path	None of use to navigation. Sections of the river have a footpath alongside.
Bridges	None.
Tides	The rise and fall at Burnham is about 10 feet on the average and the stream runs there at some 5 knots. High water at Burnham about 50 minutes after Dover.

*See Imray Chart No Y7 Thames Estuary — Southern Part.

Distance Table   *Miles* *Furlongs*
Holliwell Point to:

								Miles	Furlongs
Junction with River Roach	...	...	...	...	...	...		2	5
Burnham-on-Crouch	...	...	...	...	...	...	...	4	1
Ferry and Timber Yard	...	...	...	...	...	...	...	6	4
Bridgemarsh Island (eastern end)		...	...	...	...	...	...	7	7
Bridgemarsh Island (western end)			...	...	...	...	...	10	3
Ferry (foot passengers) from north to south Fambridge					...	...	12	—
Hullbridge Ferry (foot passengers)		...	...	...	...	...	15	—
Battlesbridge Mill ...	...	...	...	...	...	...	...	17	4

River Dart(28)

An extremely beautiful Devon river, popular with yachtsmen, due to its renowned scenery. Care is needed in navigation. Dart Harbour and Navigation Act 1975 applies.

Authority	Dart Harbour and Navigation Authority, Old Post Office, South Bank, Dartmouth, Devon. Tel. Dartmouth (080 43) 2337.
From and to	*Totnes to Kingswear.
Distance	$10\frac{1}{4}$ miles.
Length	Unlimited.
Beam	"
Draught	High water: Spring tides 9ft. 6ins., Neap tides 7ft. 6ins., to Totnes. (There is liable to be considerable variation in these figures).
Headroom	Unlimited. Small steamers go on a regular service to Totnes from Dartmouth.
Connections	Bow Creek and Old Mill Creek for craft drawing less than 5 feet.
Port charges	Harbour Dues, etc., According to a scale available on application.
Navigation notes	Bow Creek and Old Mill Creek dry out at low water and it is therefore advisable to go up near high water and leave about an hour later. Canoeable from Buckfastleigh but a very rocky boulder strewn trip.
Tides	High water at Totnes 30 minutes after Dartmouth.

*See Imray Chart No Y47 River Dart

Dartford & Crayford Navigation (29)

A commercial waterway promoted by Act of Parliament in 1840. It is entered on the south side of Long Reach, opposite Purfleet. This navigation is a portion of the River Darenth with its tributary the River Cray made navigable. Below Dartford Lock navigation is tidal.

Authority	Clerk to the Commissioners, Commissioners of the Dartford and Crayford Navigation, 27 High Street, Dartford, Kent. Tel. Dartford (0322) 21157.
	Creek Superintendent, Lock Cottages, Dartford Creek, Dartford, Kent. Tel. Dartford (0322) 24039
From and to	*Dartford to River Thames, and Branch from Crayford Mill to River Darenth.
Distance	2¾ miles. Branch three quarters of a mile (tidal).
Length	165ft.
Beam	23ft.
Draught	From River Thames to the wharves above Dartford Lock, about 7ft., rising to 11ft. on spring tides. Head of navigation and River Cray is about 6ft.
Headroom	28ft.
Tow-path	None.
Locks	One. Fall from Dartford. (Operated up to 2 hours either side of high tide).
Tides	High water at the junction with River Thames about 37 minutes before London Bridge. High water at Dartford Lock about 40 minutes before London Bridge. Spring tides rise 18ft. 6ins. Neap tides 15ft. High water at the entrance about 40 minutes after London Bridge.
Bridges	One. This is a lifting bridge.

*See Imray Chart No C2 River Thames.

River Deben (30)

This is an estuary navigation that has not been promoted by statute. A popular yachting centre with excellent facilities. There is a shifting shingle bar at the entrance. *There is a chart for this river available from the publishers of this book. Canoeable from Melton, not above.

Authority	None, an open navigation.
Distance	11 miles.
Length	Unlimited.
Beam	,,
Draught	To Waldringfield, 8ft., To Woodbridge, 7ft. 6ins. at high water only. To Melton Bridge, 4ft. at high water only.
Headroom	Unlimited.
Locks	None.
Tow-path	None.
Tides	The rise and fall of the tide is about 12ft., while the stream runs at up to 6 knots in the entrance and 4 knots elsewhere in the river.

River Dee (31)

The estuary of the Dee is a very old navigation. The original Acts were dated 1734, 1744 and 1791. The river below Chester is industrial and can be treacherous to navigate. The journey past the weir upstream is worth the trouble of waiting for a convenient tide. Wide open but attractive country particularly near Eaton Hall. It is possible to pass Chester Weir on an ordinary spring tide with boats drawing not more than 3 feet of water and craft can proceed 10 miles upstream to Almere Ferry. Beyond Almere Ferry there is a shoal at the confluence of the Rivers Dee and Alyn which renders further navigation upstream very difficult, particularly after a period of very dry weather. In certain conditions boats drawing 3 feet can get as far as Farndon Bridge, which is about 12 miles above Chester. Very light craft drawing only one foot can reach Bangor-on-Dee.

Authority	**Chester Weir to Point of Air** Welsh National Water Development Authority, Dee and Clwyd Division, Chester Road, Flint. CH6 5DX. Tel. Flint (035 26) 2383. **Chester Weir to Almere Ferry** Chester City Council, Town Hall, Chester, CH1 2HN. Tel. Chester (0244) 40144. (B.W.B. Local Office: Chester (0244) 372620)
From and to	Almere Ferry to Point of Air.

*Imray Chart No Y16 Walton Backwaters to Ipswich and Woodbridge.

Distance	33 miles.
Length	Unlimited.
Beam	,,
Draught	To Chester at H.W.S.T. 8ft. To Almere Ferry, 3ft.
Headroom	To Chester, 10ft. Above Chester, 9ft. 6ins.

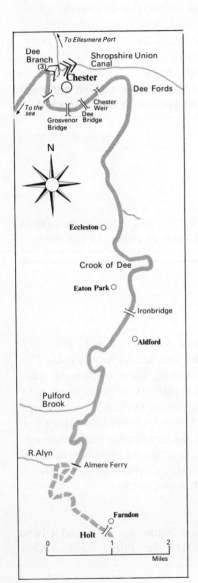

River Dee at Chester

G.H. Pursell

Locks	None. There is an adjustable gate in Chester Weir. This is controlled by North West Water Authority, Wirral Water Supply Unit, 69 Allport Road, Bromborough, Wirral, Cheshire. To use this gate prior notice must be given of at least 72 hours. Tel. 051 608 8521.
Tow-path	None.
Connections	Shropshire Union Canal at Crane Wharf, Chester. Entry to and from the Dee, approximately one hour each side of HW.
Charges	Anchorage Toll is not levied on pleasure craft in the River Dee. Tolls on ships using the navigation are payable at Connah's Quay to the Collector of Customs and Excise. Anchorage tolls at Mostyn are collected by the Harbour Master on behalf of the River Board. Tolls are payable to the local authority and water authority.
Bridges	Within the tideway there are four bridges, viz: the Wrexham to Seacombe Railway Bridge, two bridges on the main roads from Birkenhead to North Wales and a footbridge at Higher Ferry. At Chester is the railway bridge, and between Chester and Handbridge there is an old Roman Bridge, the Grosvenor Bridge. Above Chester Weir is a suspension bridge.
Licence details	These may be obtained from the City of Chester Environmental Health Department, Tarvin House, Tower Wharf, Raymond Street, Chester. Tel. Chester (0244) 40144 Ext. 2300
Tides	High water at Connah's Quay is at approximately the same time as high water at Liverpool. At Crane Wharf, Chester, Spring tides rise 9ft. The phenomenon of the bore will be encountered at spring tides between Connah's Quay and Chester.

Distance Table

Almere Ferry to:

	Miles	Furlongs
Pulford Brook	1	4
Ironbridge, Eaton Park and Hall	3	4
Crook of Dee	5	—
Eccleston Ferry	6	—
Chester, Dee Bridge (a weir here stops craft, except by special arrangement)	10	—
Chester Gas Works (Site)	11	—
Chester, Crane Wharf, *junction with Shropshire Union Canal*	12	2
Saltney	12	6
Sandycroft	15	5
Queensferry Bridge	16	7
Railway Bridge	17	5
Connah's Quay	18	6
Point of Air	33	—

River Derwent (32)

The river was originally constructed by powers granted by an Act of 1701. Though a popular river for boating, the statutory navigation rights above Sutton Lock were revoked in 1935 by the London and North-Eastern Railway, who were then in control. The upper reaches, at present closed, pass through very fine country including the Castle Howard area. Navigation in the lower reaches is improved now a new lock in the barrage is constructed, which is situated near the outfall of the Derwent into the Ouse. The size of the lock is 60ft by 14¾ft wide. There is a Derwent Trust which hopes to restore the river to navigation. Navigation enquiries to the Trust. Navigation rights by prescription appear to still exist to Malton and possibly above.

Drainage Authority	Yorkshire Water Authority, West Riding House, 67 Albion Street, Leeds, LS1 5AA. Tel. Leeds (0532) 448201
From and to	Junction with the River Ouse at Barmby-on-the-Marsh to Sutton Lock. There is a plan to re-open the river to Malton by means of a Trust.
Distance	15½ miles, to Sutton Lock and 38 miles to Malton. It is possible to reach Malton only by small craft that can be portaged round the locks.
Length	54½ft
Beam	13¾ft
Draught	4ft
Headroom	About 10ft. 6ins. From Barmby-on-the-Marsh to Sutton Lock.
Locks	6. (Only 2 are in use at present.) Fall from Malton. The first lock is through the barrage, and the second lock is at Sutton (or Elvington) and these are now in use. The barrage lock-keeper will advise re a windlass to open Sutton Lock which is non-standard. The third lock at Stamford Bridge is now rebuilt but has lacked bottom gates for some time. The fourth lock at Buttercrambe and the fifth at Howsham are awaiting rebuilding. The last lock at Kirkham has been replaced with a weir and will need a completely new lock. Stamford Bridge originally had an extra pair of gates for use at low water.

Tow-path	Unusable along many sections.
Bridges	Numerous.
Speed limit	No vessels to be navigated at such a speed as to do injury to the banks or cause inconvenience, etc.
Navigation notes	Visitors to the river are advised to write to the River Derwent Trust, 69A Park Road, Guiseley, Leeds LS20 8EW for information.
	It is advisable to notify Barmby Barrage lock-keeper before entering river. (Tel. Selby (0757) 638579)
	The Yorkshire Water Authority issue 3 keys, and require a fee for an inspection certificate. Contact the Y.W.A. before your voyage.
Tides	High water at Barmby-on-the-Marsh about one hour and 40 minutes after Hull. Springs rise about 11ft, Neaps 6ft. 9ins.

Distance Table

Barmby-on-the-Marsh Junction with River Ouse to:

	Miles	Furlongs
Barmby-on-the-Marsh Village	—	4
Loftsome Bridge	2	1
Wressel	3	—
Breighton	4	7
Menthorpe	5	2
Bubwith, Derwent Bridge	6	7
Ellerton Landing	9	7
Thorganby	10	4
Cottingwith Ferry, *junction with Pocklington Canal*	11	4
Ings Bridge	13	—
Sutton Lock No. 1	15	4
Bridge between Elvington (right bank) and Sutton-on-Derwent (left bank)	15	5
Kexby Bridge	18	3
Stamford Bridge Lock No. 2 (double staircase)	21	7
Buttercrambe Bridge	24	6
Buttercrambe Lock No. 3	25	—
Scrayingham	26	—
Howsham Lock No. 4 (site of)	28	4
Kirkham Abbey Lock No. 5 (now abolished), (double staircase)	31	2
Castle Howard Station. (site of)	32	1
Hattons Ambo Station (site of)	34	7
Cherry Islands	35	3
Malton (County Bridge.) Termination (originally navigable to Yedingham)	38	—

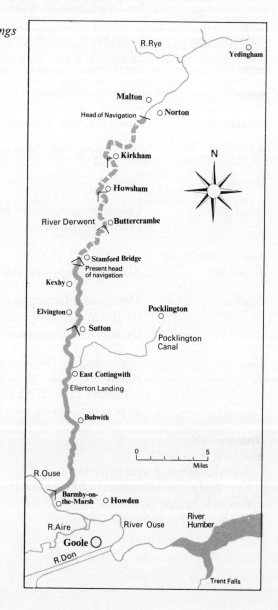

River Don(33)

This navigation is mainly the 'Dutch River' constructed by Vermuyden, the Netherlands engineer, in 1625. The straight cut experiences very fast tidal currents and the river is usually considered dangerous for pleasure craft unless exceptional care is taken. The river at Fishlake was diverted in 1943 and no longer passes Fishlake Ferry.

Authority	Yorkshire Water Authority, West Riding House, 67 Albion Street, Leeds. LS1 5AA. Tel. Leeds (0532) 448201.
From and to	*Junction with River Ouse at Goole to junction with River Don (under jurisdiction of Sheffield and South Yorkshire Navigation) at Fishlake Old Ferry.
General remarks	Three miles below Fishlake Old Ferry this waterway is known as the Dutch river. It is tidal throughout.
Distances	From Goole to Bramwith Aqueduct, about 12¼ miles.
Length	Unlimited.
Beam	"
Draught	About 6ft. 6ins. Depends on tide.
Headroom	Varies up to 15ft. Depends on tide.
Tow-path	None.
Speed limit	Vessels to be navigated in such a manner and at such speed as not to damage banks, etc. For special speed limits see Notices.
Approx. time taken to navigate	About one hour with tide.
Caution	The above information refers only to normal conditions. The river is liable to exceptional high tides and fresh water floods, thus making the information unreliable.
Tides	High water at Goole one hour after Hull. Spring tides rise 13ft., Neaps 9ft. Tide flows past Fishlake Old Ferry to the tail of Stainforth Lock. High water at Stainforth Lock one hour 20 mins. after Goole. Spring tides rise 7ft. 6ins.

Distance Table

Bramwith Aqueduct to:

	Miles	Furlongs
Fishlake, junction with River Don.	3	—
New Bridge, commencement of Dutch River	6	6
Rawcliffe Bridge	8	7
Goole, *junction with River Ouse*	12	2

Driffield Navigation (34)

This waterway is in an isolated condition. Struncheon Hill Lock is workable, but Snakeholme Locks are derelict. It is possible to reach Brigham, but Wansford, Whin Hill and Driffield Locks are also derelict, although this waterway was in use to Driffield as late as 1947. The lock at Struncheon Hill was rebuilt recently by the Hull Water Authority who abstract water from West Beck; it was previously a double lock (staircase) which gave the original total lockage on the waterway as seven — it is now six. The navigation can be traversed to Hempholme; Bethel's Bridge, which has been fixed, giving only 4 feet 6 inches headroom. The waterway is a 'main river' for land drainage purposes of the Yorkshire River Authority (up to the confluence with Nefferton Beck) who have no control over the navigation.

The Commissioners had in the past slowly disappeared, and had not been replaced, and the situation came about that there was only an acting clerk and no Commissioners although there were still some funds in the navigation account. In spite of this in 1966 a warrant to abandon the navigation a short distance either side of the bridge at Wansford was issued by the Ministry of Transport. It appeared that the acting clerk, who did not appear to have the authority, and without a quorum of the Commissioners, took steps with the authorities to allow the bridge at Wansford to be lowered. The Charity Commission have taken steps, after consultation with the Driffield Navigation Amenities Association, and the Inland Waterways Association, to reform the Commissioners and sort the problems of the navigation out. There is water in the cut throughout and light craft should be encouraged to use it as it is a delightful waterway through attractive countryside. Restoration of the locks should present few problems.

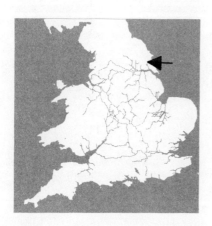

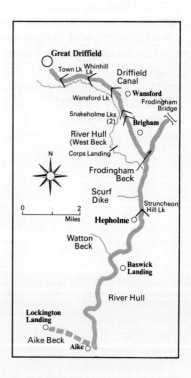

Authority	Driffield Navigation Commissioners, 18 Exchange Street, Great Driffield, North Humberside. YO25 7LD. Tel. (0377) 47377.
From and to	*Great Driffield to River Hull, at Aike.

Distance	11 miles.
Length	61ft.
Beam	14ft. 6ins.
Draught	4ft.
Headroom	9ft. 6ins.
Branches	Corps Landing 1¾ miles, Frodingham Beck 1¾ miles. This branch is only open to Frodingham Bridge which no longer swings open and restricts navigation. Distance to bridge one mile.
Locks	6, (5 out of order). Fall from Great Driffield.
Tow-path	Throughout Main Line, but there is no tow-path on the Frodingham Beck Branch.
Tides	High water at Struncheon Hill Lock approximately 3 hours after Hull. At H.W.S.T. the rise will be sometimes as much as 6 to 7 feet in winter and in summer the rise is 3 to 4 feet.

Distance Table

Driffield Wharves to:

	Miles	Furlongs
Driffield Lock No. 1	—	3
Whin Hill Lock No. 2	1	5
Wansford Lock and village (Lock No. 3)	2	4
Snakeholme Locks (Nos. 4 and 5, staircase)	3	—
Junction with Frodingham Beck	5	—
Junction with Branch to Corps Landing (unnavigable)	5	6
Struncheon Hill Locks Nos. 6 and 7. junction with River Hull ...	7	—
Tophill Low Landing	8	2
Baswick Landing	8	4
Aike	11	—

* See River Hull p.160

Droitwich Canals (35)

(a) Droitwich Canal (sometimes called Droitwich Barge Canal)

This 5¾ mile long canal was opened in 1771, and after many years of disuse it was abandoned in 1939. The Droitwich Canals Trust Ltd. was formed in 1973 to restore it and create a 22 mile cruising ring.

Authority	Droitwich Canals Trust Ltd., 1 Hampton Road, Droitwich, Worcestershire WR9 9PA. (The Trust lease the canal from the Wychavon District Council). Tel: Worcester (0905) 774225. Bye-laws are enforced by the Trust.
From and to	River Severn to Droitwich.
Distance	5¾ miles.
Length	71 ft 6 ins
Beam	15 ft
Draught	5 ft
Headroom	8 ft
Locks	8. Lock gates worked by boat crews. Rise from River Severn.
Bridges	Several, including swing bridges. The first bridge up the canal from Hawford is exactly as built by Brindley and has not been touched since construction.

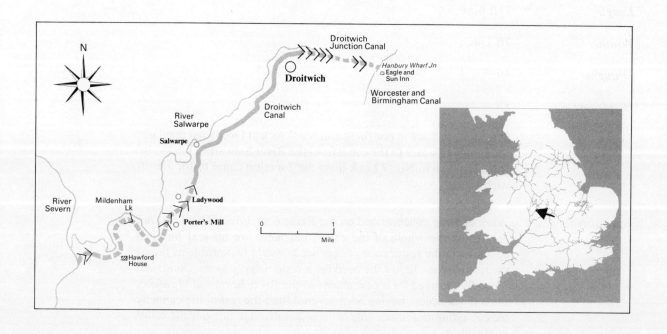

Towpath	Throughout the canal.
Facilities	A marina is projected for the centre of Droitwich. A mooring area and slipway is available in the town centre.
Remarks	This canal is under a restoration project and needs voluntary help and finance from anyone nearby. Already 3 miles are open between Ladywood and Droitwich. Projected opening date 1992/3.

Distance Table

Droitwich, junction with Droitwich Junction Canal to:	*Miles*	*Furlongs*
Droitwich Canal Basin and Marina Site	–	2
Siding Lane Wharf	1	–
Salwarpe Bridge	2	2
Ladywood Lock No. 1	3	–
Ladywood Lock No. 2		
Ladywood Lock No. 3		
Ladywood Lock No. 4		
Porter's Mill Lock No. 5	3	4
Mildenham Mill Lock No. 6	4	4
Hawford Lock No. 7	5	4
Hawford Lock No. 8	5	6
Junction with River Severn.		

(b) Droitwich Junction Canal

Authority	As above
From and to	Droitwich to Hanbury Wharf Junction with the Worcester and Birmingham Canal.
Distance	1½ miles.
Length	71ft 6ins
Width	7ft 1ins
Draught	4ft
Headroom	8ft
Locks	7. Locks 1 to 5 are in one flight and No. 7 lock at Droitwich regulates the supply of water to the canal from the River Salwarpe. Locks rise from Droitwich. No. 7 Lock links the Junction canal to the Droitwich Canal.
Special Note	Work is being concentrated on the Barge Canal first. The Trust not only owns the whole of the canal, but there are no real physical obstacles to the restoration. There are however two problems facing the restoration – firstly the need for a water supply to the canal, and secondly the need for a new access to the River Severn at Hawford; the original access having been severed from the rest of the canal by the culverting and embanking of the original bridge carrying the A449 at Hawford.

Water is available from the River Salwarpe, either in Droitwich as originally, or further down the river below Ladywood, or a combination of the two. In any event, the Severn-Trent Water Authority have stated that a supply of water can be made available and the Trust is at the stage of detailed negotiations with the authority as to the precise point and method of abstraction. There is also an indeterminate supply of water available from several springs and it is quite possible that this will make up a substantial proportion of the estimated 2 million gallons per day required for proper operation of the canal.

Access to the Severn can be effected by utilising the course of the River Salwarpe from Hawford Mill to its junction with the Severn. As this section of the Salwarpe is already navigable by most river craft, it provides a neat solution to the problem. A study is being made to see if most of the original route can be re-opened with a tunnel under the A449 road, using part of the River Salwarpe as a diversion into Droitwich. A towpath guide booklet is available.

Exeter Ship Canal (36)

The first canal cut in England since the Roman occupation, was commenced in 1563 under powers granted by an Act passed in 1539. A further Act was passed in 1829. This is a busy waterway. There are two entrances from the Exe Estuary, one at Turf Lock and one at Topsham Lock. The River Exe is also navigable through King's Arms flood gates to Exe Bridge, the latter can only be passed when the tide makes a level.

Authority	The Corporation of the City of Exeter, Municipal Offices, Exeter. Harbour Master and Wharfinger, and Canal Superintendent, Mr. R. Thomas, City Basin, Exeter. Tel. Exeter 74306.
From and to	Turf Lock, River Exe Estuary to Exeter.
Distance	5 miles, 1½ furlongs.

Main Line

Length	122ft.
Beam	25ft.
Draught	10ft. 6ins.
Headroom	33ft. (3ft when closed).

Through King's Arms Flood Gates

Beam	25ft.

Through Topsham Lock (Derelict at present)

Length	88ft. 5ins.

Beam	25ft.
Locks	2. Turf and Double Locks. Lock gates worked by lock-keepers. There is a side lock at Topsham, to the River Exe which falls from Canal to River Exe. Fall from Exeter.
Tow-path	Throughout navigation.
Bridges	4 swing. headroom 3ft when closed. Notice is required to open swing bridges.
Speed limit	4 miles per hour.
Navigation notes	It takes approximately 2 hours to navigate from Turf Lock to Exeter. Cost of opening lifting bridges is so high that craft seldom use the canal.
Tides	High tide at Turf Lock 15 minutes after Exmouth. Spring tides rise 15ft. Neap tides rise 10ft.

Distance Table

	Miles	Furlongs
Head of Canal Basin, Exeter to:		
Junction with River Exe through Kings Arms Flood Gates	—	1½
Double Locks No. 1	1	3½
Topsham, *junction with River Exe Estuary* through Topsham Lock ...	3	6
Turf Lock, No. 2 entrance lock to canal from River Exe Estuary ...	5	—
Pier head, entrance to Turf Gutway from River Exe estuary ...	5	1½

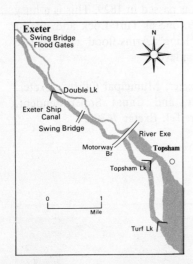

River Foss (37)

The River Foss was promoted by Acts dated 1793 and 1801. The navigation originally commenced at Sheriff Hutton Bridge, but in recent years it has extended only to Monk Bridge.

Authority	Ouse and Foss Navigation Trustees, Guildhall, York. Tel. York (0904) 54544.
From and to	*Monk Bridge to Blue Bridge, junction with River Ouse at York.
Distance	1¼ miles.
Length	82ft.
Beam	18ft. 6ins.
Draught	6ft. 6ins.
Headroom	10ft.
Locks	One. Fall to River Ouse.
Tow-path	None.
Bridges	5.
Canoeing note	In high water canoeable from Sheriff Hutton.

Distance Table
Monk Bridge to:

	Miles	Furlongs
Laverthorpe Bridge	—	2
Foss Bridge	—	6
Castle Mills Bridge and Lock	1	—
Blue Bridge, *junction with River Ouse*	1	2

Fossdyke Canal (38)

This is a very ancient navigation originally contructed by the Romans about A. D. 120 and deepened by Henry I in 1121. It is still a well used and broad waterway through flat open country. Saxilby is well worth visiting. The Fossdyke makes an 'open confluence' on the west side of Brayford Mere. The authorities are statutably obliged to keep a channel 5 feet deep, 35 feet wide across the Brayford Mere—due west to east—entering the Witham at Brayford Mere open confluence. The short distance of the River Witham from Brayford Mere to High Bridge is disputed water and all tolls are listed from High Bridge to Boston Grand Sluice Lock. Brayford Mere belongs to the city of Lincoln, but is controlled by the Anglia Water Authority, 50 Wide Bargate, Boston, Lincs. The River Till is navigable for light craft for 6¼ miles to Squire's Bridge and also the Upper Witham from Lincoln to Grantham.

The Fossdyke and Witham Navigations had a variety of owners from the Middle Ages onwards, culminating in their being owned by the Company of Proprietors of the Witham Navigation. Under a 999 year lease of 1850, the navigation rights were leased to the Great Northern Railway and the Great Eastern Joint Railway. When the waterways were nationalised in 1948 the proprietors were not taken over and the British Waterways Board as the navigation authority continued to make payments to them of over £20,000 per annum.

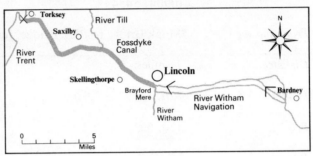

Authority	British Waterways Board.
From and to	Junction with River Trent at Torksey to junction with River Witham at High Bridge, Lincoln.
Distance	11¼ miles.
Length	74ft. 6ins.
Beam	15ft. 2ins.
Draught	5ft.
Headroom	12ft. If proceeding through Lincoln into River Witham under High Bridge, Lincoln, 8ft. 10ins.
Locks	One. Lock gates worked by lock-keeper. Rise from River Trent. this lock has four pairs of gates, two being flood gates.
Bridges	Numerous. One lifting bridge, power operated.
Speed limit	4 miles per hour.
Tow-path	Throughout navigation.
Tides	Torksey Lock cannot be opened for several hours before and after low water. Boats which cannot 'lock in' due to the tide should beware of going aground when the tide drops, and of the effects of the bore or aegre which can be felt at Torksey. Yachtsmen should not leave their boats unattended as mooring ropes may be snapped and craft swamped. High water at Torksey 2½ to 3 hours after Hull.

Distance Table

Torksey Lock, junction with River Trent to:

								Miles	Furlongs
Torksey Wharf	...	...	...	...	...	...	...	—	2
Hardwick Ferry	...	...	...	...	...	...	...	3	0½
Drinsey Nook	...	...	...	...	...	...	...	3	6
Saxilby	...	...	...	...	...	...	...	5	3
Mill Lane	...	...	...	...	...	...	...	5	5
Chemical Works	...	...	...	...	...	...	...	6	2
Burton Lane	...	...	...	...	...	...	...	8	1
Skellingthorpe	...	...	...	...	...	...	...	8	7
Lincoln, west end of Brayford Mere	...	...	...	...	...	10	6½
Lincoln, *junction with upper portion of River Witham* ...	...	...	11	1
Lincoln, High Bridge, *junction with River Witham Navigation*	...	11	1½

River Fowey (39)

This river is fairly well sheltered. A considerable number of vessels transporting china clay will be found on the river as there is deep water at high tide up to Fowey jetties.

Authority	Fowey Harbour Commissioners, Harbour Master's Office, Albert Quay, Fowey, Cornwall. Tel. Fowey (072 683) 2471.
From and to	St. Catherine's Point to Lostwithiel.
Distance	7 miles.
Length	Unlimited.
Beam	„
Draught	4ft. This applies only to high water at Lostwithiel.
Headroom	Unlimited.
Locks	None. Tidal throughout.
Tow-path	None.
Tides	High water at the entrance about 5 hours before Dover. Spring tides rise 16ft. 6ins. Neap tides rise 12ft. 9ins.

River Frome (40)

The river is narrow and winding with high rushes on both banks. It is advisable to give signals frequently. The entrance is marked with stakes. Poole Harbour includes the Dorset Lakes which are extensively used by pleasure craft. Light craft can proceed a short distance above Wareham. It is sometimes canoeable from Dorchester.

Authority	Wessex Water Authority, Nuffield Road, Poole, Dorset. Tel. Poole (020 13) 71144.
Note	At the mouth of the river is Poole Harbour. This is controlled by the Poole Harbour Commissioners, Harbour Office, Poole, Dorset. Tel. Poole (020 13) 85261.
	The jurisdiction of the Commissioners ends at Giggers Island.
From and to	*Poole Harbour to Wareham.
Distance	7¾ miles.
Length	Unlimited but a vessel of more than 25ft. will have difficulty in turning at Wareham.
Beam	Unlimited.
Draught	High water, 5ft. 6ins.
Headroom	Unlimited to Wareham Bridge. Wareham Bridge 8ft. L.W.S.T., 3ft. H.W.S.T.
Locks	None. Tidal throughout.
Tow-path	Along approximately 2 miles only, commencing at Wareham.
Tides	High water at Wareham is approximately one hour after Poole.

*See Imray Chart No. Y23 Poole Harbour.

River Glen (41)

Entrance to the river depends on the state of the tide in the River Welland. The tidal gates are operative only at times when the tidal water coincides with the water level of the river. Small boats that can be portaged round the sluices can ascend Bourne Eau to Bourne. The Bourne Eau junction with the River Glen is the last and only turning point above Pinchbeck Bars Bridge. Craft can proceed for another 2 miles above the junction but there is no turning. This river flows through flat but pleasant country which, in bulb time, is enchanting. Surfleet's leaning church is of interest.

Authority	Anglia Water Authority, Welland and Nene Division, Oundle, Peterborough. Tel. Oundle (083 22) 3366.
From and to	Junction with the River Welland to Tongue End (Spalding— Bourne road bridge)
Distance	11½ miles.
Length	Unlimited but craft over 30ft. will find turning difficult.
Beam	14ft. 6ins.
Draught	2ft. to 3ft.

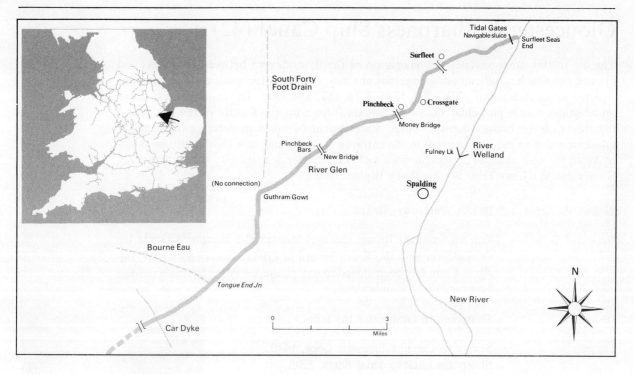

Headroom	6ft. above ordinary summer water level.
	Headroom at the Sluice Bridge at the entrance depends upon the tidal level.
Locks	Tidal gates at entrance. Boats can pass the sluice either on the first level or back level of the tide.
Bridges	12. None restricts the water width.
Speed limit	Craft must be navigated at such a speed as not to cause damage or inconvenience.
Tides	High water at the junction with the River Welland about 15 to 20 minutes after high water at Fosdyke Bridge. High water at Boston, Clay Hole about 20 minutes before Kings Lynn.

Distance Table

Junction with River Welland to:

	Miles	Furlongs
Entrance Sluices	—	1
Railway Bridge	1	2
Road bridge, Surfleet village	2	3
Crossgate Bridge	3	5
Railway Bridge	4	1
Money Bridge	5	4
Pinchbeck Bars, New Bridge	6	4
Guthram Gowt (There is no connection with the South Forty Foot Drain, now closed)	8	7
Railway Bridge	9	7
Tongue End (junction with Bourne Eau, not navigable except to craft that can be portaged)	11	4

Gloucester & Sharpness Ship Canal (42)

The use of this canal obviates the navigation of the River Severn between Sharpness and Gloucester, which is difficult and dangerous at times, especially for small craft. It was constructed under Acts dated 1793, 1797, 1805, 1818, 1822 and 1825. The canal has distinctive architecture, and in particular the swing bridges form a unique feature of the navigation together with the bridge-keepers' houses. Care should be taken in entering the canal at Gloucester due to the swift current in the entrance channel, and care should also be taken to avoid the weir channel by the entrance lock. Gloucester is a fine city with a cathedral. Slimbridge Wildfowl Trust is near Patch Bridge.

Authority	British Waterways Board.
From and to	Entered from the Bristol Channel through the Sharpness Docks to the junction with the River Severn at Gloucester. (The feeder, the River Cam, has been closed to navigation for years but once carried barge traffic to Cambridge).
Distance	Sharpness to Gloucester 16¾ miles.
Length	Severn to Canal, Gloucester Lock, 144ft. Sharpness Lock to Tidal Basin, 320ft. Gloucester and Sharpness Canal, 190ft.
Beam	Severn to Canal, Gloucester Lock, 22ft. Sharpness Lock to Tidal Basin, 55ft. Gloucester and Sharpness Canal, 29ft.
Draught	Severn to Canal, Gloucester Lock, 10ft. Sharpness Lock to Tidal Basin, 21ft. 6ins. Gloucester and Sharpness Canal, 11ft
Headroom	Unlimited.
Locks	2. There are entrance locks at Sharpness and a lock connecting the canal with the River Severn at Gloucester. Lock gates worked by lock-keepers. Gloucester Lock rises from the river, and Sharpness Lock falls to Tidal Basin. Side locks to River Severn are closed to navigation.
Bridges	13 swing bridges. Ample warning should be given to the bridge-keepers to open the bridges, and craft must not approach too closely until it is seen that the bridge is actually opened. The signal for request to open is generally two long blasts. Width between swing bridge abutments 34ft 6ins. (There is a new lifting bridge at the exit from Gloucester Docks).
Speed limit	6 miles per hour.
Approx. time to navigate	About 4 to 5 hours.
Tow-path	Throughout navigation.

Sharpness Lock. This operates from 2½hrs before H.W. until ½hr after H.W. (approx.)
V.H.F. Channel 16, 14 (24 hours)
Call *Sharpness Central*

Canal pilotage

Pilotage is available for whole length of canal, details on application to British Waterways Board. For pilotage to Bristol, see River Avon (Bristol) section

Towage charges can be obtained on application.

Special remarks

Boats must not attempt to moor on the tow-path side. There is a considerable amount of traffic up and down the canal, and the general rule is to give the tow-path side to all commercial traffic unless they signal otherwise.

The traffic on the canal can set up a surge when it passes and therefore under no circumstance leave craft unattended particularly in the narrow sections unless advice has been obtained. B.W.B. staff are helpful but advance notice of using the canal is a great help to all concerned. Severn lock-keepers can phone ahead with arrival times. Care should be taken when passing commercial craft due to the surge that these craft create. There are a number of sea going craft moored in the canal. Care should be taken with the anglers as the deep unpolluted waters make very good fishing.

If proceeding out to the Bristol Channel, craft should be at the Sharpness Sea Lock well before locking out time which is generally about 2 hours before high water.

Care should be taken by yachtsmen as the Ship Canal is used by large commercial craft which cannot give way to small craft. Bye-laws controlling this canal and the River Severn should be obtained from British Waterways Board.

Facilities

Boatyards at Gloucester and Sharpness. Several inns by canal. Marina at Sharpness in Canal.

Gloucester and Sharpness Ship Canal. Purton Lower Bridge

Tides

High tide at Sharpness about one hour after Avonmouth. Spring tides rise about 25ft. Neap tides rise about 15ft.

Distance Table

Gloucester, entrance lock and junction with River Severn to:

	Miles	Furlongs
Gloucester Lock (Bascule Bridge over lock)		
Gloucester Docks (water area 14 acres)		
Llanthony Road Bridge	—	3
Monk Meadow Dock	—	5
Monk Meadow Wharf	—	7
Hempstead Bridge	1	4
Sims Bridge	2	2
Rea Bridge	2	6½
Quedgeley Oil Depot	4	—
Sellars Bridge and the Pilot Inn	4	1
Hardwicke Bridge	4	7
Parkend Bridge	6	1
Site of Pegthorne Bridge (removed)	6	6
Saul Junction	7	6
Sandfield Bridge and Grain Silos	8	1
Fretherne Bridge and Cadbury's Factory	8	7
Splatt Bridge	9	6½
Cambridge Feeder Branch	11	—
Ryalls Bridge	11	1
Patch Bridge	11	7
Purton Upper Bridge	14	2½
Purton Lower Bridge	14	3½
Purton Timber Pond	15	—
Site of Severn Bridge	15	2
Junction with Old Line	15	3½
High and Low Level Swing Bridges*	15	4½
Sharpness Lock	15	7½
Tidal Basin Gates	16	2

Grand Union Canal (43)

The Grand Union Canal was formed by amalgamation in 1929, and further extended in 1932 when the following canals were acquired and the whole system became known under the one name, the Grand Union Canal. The date of the original Acts is given after the waterway.

Regents Canal and Limehouse Docks, 1812, 1813, 1816, 1819 and 1821.
Hertford Union Canal (also known as Duckett's Canal), 1824.
Grand Junction Canal, 1793, 1794, 1795, 1798, 1801, 1803, 1805, 1812, 1818, and 1819.
Warwick and Napton Canal, 1794, 1796 and 1809.
Warwick and Birmingham Canal, 1793 and 1796.
Birmingham and Warwick Junction Canal, 1840.
Leicester Navigation, 1791.
Lougborough Navigation, 1776.
Erewash Canal, 1777.
Leicestershire and Northamptonshire Union Canal, 1793 and 1805.
Old Grand Union Canal, 1810.

* Entrance to Sharpness Docks, water area 20 acres.

Also within the Grand Union group is 5½ miles of the Oxford Canal, between Braunston and Napton. Tolls for London—Birmingham traffic are collected over this portion.

This is Britain's longest canal. Traffic, apart from the London area, is mainly pleasure craft, although the canal links the London Docks to Birmingham and Nottingham. The Limehouse Basin is disused apart from some lighterage traffic. The Canal climbs over the Chiltern Hills and passes the canal museum at Stoke Bruerne. Throughout, the scenery on the canal is very fine, particularly over the Chiltern summit level and the Foxton summit on the Leicester section. The latter is 412ft. and is therefore one of the highest canals in the country. Warwick, Leicester, Loughborough, Aylesbury and Nottingham are some of the interesting places en route. Ample facilities for boats and refreshment throughout.

The route is heavily locked, but pleasant scenery through the 'shires' more than compensates for this, as it is pleasantly diversified. Facilities for pleasure craft have sprung up all along the canal and a very comprehensive marina has been established at Braunston Junction and there are others. Limehouse Basin was previously called Regents Canal Dock. A short section of the canal in Leicester with 2 locks is owned by the Leicester City Council. Transfer under an Act passed in 1890.

Authority   British Waterways Board.

Connections   Besides having junction with the River Thames at Brentford and Limehouse, and the River Lee through the old Hertford Union Canal, the Grand Union Canal connects with the following waterways:

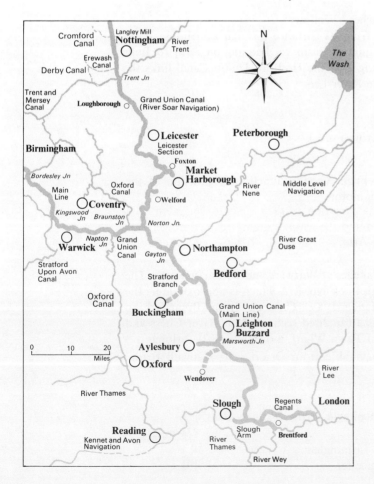

At Braunston and Napton with the Oxford Canal.

At Kingswood Junction with the Stratford-on-Avon Canal.

At Birmingham with the Birmingham Canal Navigations.

At Trent junction with the River Trent.

At Langley Mill with the Cromford Canal (now derelict).

At Northampton with the River Nene.

From and to

Main Line. From Brentford Lock, junction with the River Thames to Norton Junction where it divides:

To junction with the Birmingham Canal Navigation at Digbeth Junction or at Salford Bridge Junction. Birmingham (the latter via the old Birmingham and Warwick Junction Canal). On this route the Oxford Canal used the same waterway between Braunston and Napton.

To Leicester, Loughborough, junction with the River Trent at Trent Junction Long Eaton, thence running to Langley Mill and having junction with the derelict Cromford Canal. The Derby Canal is now derelict.

There are several branches as follows:

The Regents Canal from its entrance through Limehouse Basin at Limehouse to Paddington Basin via Paddington Arm to Bulls Bridge. Along this navigation the Hertford Union Canal links the Regents Canal with the River Lee.

Slough Arm.

Wendover Arm to Tring Ford Lock

Aylesbury Arm.

Northampton Arm. From Gayton Junction to junction of the River Nene at Northampton.

Welford Arm.

Market Harborough Arm.

There are also short branches at Warwick and Rickmansworth. The latter is entered through Lock No. 81A which is approximately the same size as the standard G. U. lock from Brentford to Berkhampstead. This is a canalised section of the River Chess and it runs from the lock to Town Wharf, a distance of $2\frac{1}{2}$ furlongs.

The River Brent is navigable from Osterley to Hanwell Bridge (max. length 60ft).

Distances

Main Line

Brentford Lock Junction with River Thames to
Braunston Junction ...   . $93\frac{1}{2}$ miles

Braunston Junction to Birmingham   ...   ... $43\frac{1}{2}$,,

Norton Junction to Leicester   ...   . $40\frac{1}{8}$,,

Grand Union Canal. Narrow boats near Braunston in 1958

,,	,,	,, *junction with River Trent* ...	$66\frac{1}{8}$	,,
,,	,,	,, Langley Mill	$77\frac{5}{8}$	,,

Total Distances Main Line

Brentford to Birmingham	$137\frac{1}{4}$	,,
,, ,, Leicester	$130\frac{7}{8}$	,,
,, ,, *junction with River Trent*	$155\frac{5}{8}$	,,
,, ,, Langley Mill...	$167\frac{3}{8}$	,,

Main Line

Length
72ft. Brentford to Berkhamstead, 77ft. (78ft. to Watford).
Thames Lock and one of the two Brentford Locks is 95ft. long.

Beam
London to Berkhampstead, 14ft.
London to Birmingham, Camp Hill Locks, 7ft.
Leicester to Langley Mill 10ft.
Market Harborough to Leicester 7ft.
Norton Junction to Foxton, 7ft.
Thames Lock and one of the two Brentford Locks is 18ft. 6ins. wide.

Draught
3ft. 6ins.

Headroom
7ft. 6ins. except for Regents Canal and Hertford Union.
The locks from London to Birmingham (Sampson Road) are 14ft. wide. The section from Sampson Road to Salford Junction has narrow 7ft. locks. Although the locks are 14ft. wide, Sandy Lane Bridge (1 mile south of Birmingham) is only 13ft wide. British Waterways Board do not permit craft over 7ft beam to go beyond Berkhampstead. From Leicester South, craft over 7ft beam are not permitted (*vide* 1968 Transport Act).

Locks	**Main Line**

Main Line

From Brentford to Braunston Junction, 102 locks.

Locks No. 1 to No. 6 rise from Braunston.

Locks No. 7 to No. 21 fall from Braunston.

Locks No. 22 to No. 45 rise from Braunston.

Locks No. 46 to No. 101 fall from Braunston.

(Lock No. 69A was renumbered in 1819 when as extra lock was constructed at Nash Mills.)

Braunston Junction to Birmingham, 64 locks.

Locks No. 64 to No. 52 rise from Salford Junction.

Locks No. 52 to No. 24 fall from Salford Junction.

Locks No. 23 to No. 1 rise from Salford Junction.

(Lock No. 58 is a stop lock on the branch to Digbeth Junction.)

Norton Junction to Langley Mill, 73 locks.

Locks No. 1 to No. 7 rise from Norton Junction.

Locks No. 8 to No. 59 fall from Norton Junction.

Locks No. 60 to No. 73 rise from River Trent.

Lock gates worked in places by lock-keepers, otherwise by boat crews.

A few locks are closed on Sundays and after working hours in the London and Birmingham areas, and also the Northampton Arm. In many cases a passage can be arranged by giving prior notice to the Area Engineers Office nearest the locks in question.

Special Note River Soar Navigation

Alterations are projected for the River Soar Navigation which between Leicester and the Trent has been subject to severe flooding. A Bill was presented to Parliament by the Severn-Trent Water Authority in 1982 and work started in 1983. Redhill Lock will have a lowered sill, and the levels altered up to Ratcliffe. Here the lock will be rebuilt nearby to accommodate different levels created. Alteration of levels to improve water retention will necessitate the abolition of Kegworth Shallow Flood Lock. Just North of Kegworth Deep Lock, a new lock will be built, which is part of the new structure in Kegworth Weir. A new aqueduct and canal section will be constructed in the Mountsorrel area. Some minor alterations will also take place on the Soar and new automatic sluices will be built in several places. The flood scheme improvements will greatly improve navigation by reducing the length of closures due to flooding which makes navigation impossible.

Bridges **Main Line** Numerous

Flood warnings Flood warning lights are installed on the sections affected by flooding of the River Soar. (Leicester Section).

Tunnels **Main Line**

Between Brentford and Norton Junction:

Blisworth, 3075⅝ yards. No tow-path. (Keep right in the tunnel).

Norton Junction to Birmingham:

Braunston, 2048⅝ yards. No tow-path. (Keep right in the tunnel).

Shrewley, 433 yards. No tow-path. (Keep right in the tunnel).
(Shrewley Tunnel has a special separate tunnel for the towing path)

Norton Junction to Langley Mill:
Crick, 1527½ yards. No tow-path. (Keep right in the tunnel).
Husbands Bosworth, 1170¾ yards. No tow-path. (Keep right in the tunnel).
Saddington, 881¾ yards. No tow-path. (Keep right in the tunnel).
Saddington is sometimes known as Fleckney Tunnel.

Tides   High water spring tides flow into the canal at the Brentford end from the Thames for the first three-quarters of a mile to Brentford Lock. High water at Brentford one hour after London Bridge.

Regents Canal

From and to   Limehouse Basin, Limehouse, to junction with Paddington Arm of Grand Junction, at Warwick Avenue, Paddington.

Distance   8 miles, 5 furlongs.

Length   78ft. Ship Lock from Thames, 350ft.

Beam   14ft. 6ins. Ship Lock from Thames, 60ft.

Draught   4ft. 6ins. Ship Lock from Thames, 20ft.

Headroom   9ft. Ship Lock from Thames, unlimited.

Locks   13, including Regents Canal Dock River Ship Lock.
Locks No. 1 to No. 12. Fall to Regents Canal Dock.
Lock No. 13. Fall to River Thames from Dock at low tide, level at high tide.

Regent's Canal. Hampstead Road Locks

Chris Cove-Smith

Regents Canal

Bridges	Numerous.
Tunnels	Islington, 960 yards. No tow-path. Maida Hill, 272 yards. No tow-path.

Hertford Union Canal

From and to From junction with Regents Canal at Bethnal Green to Old Ford   Junction with River Lee.

Distance	Approximately 1¼ miles.
Length	78ft.
Beam	14ft. 6ins.
Draught	4ft. 6ins.
Headroom	8ft. 6ins.
Locks	3. Fall to junction with River Lee at Old Ford.
Bridges	Two.
Tunnels	None.

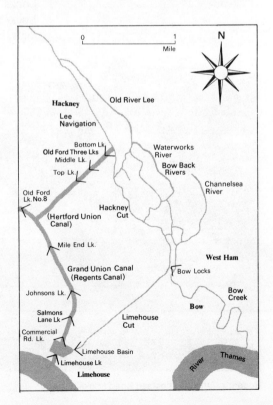

Paddington Arm

From and to	Paddington to Bulls Bridge, join Main Line.
Distance	13½ miles level.
Length	Same as Regents Canal.
Beam	,, ,, ,, ,,
Draught	,, ,, ,, ,,
Headroom	,, ,, ,, ,,
Bridges	6

Slough Arm

From and to	Junction with Main Line at Cowley Peachey Junction, 9 miles above Brentford to Slough.
Distance	4 miles 7½ furlongs.
Length	Same as Brentford to Berkhamstead.
Beam	Same as Brentford to Berkhamstead
Draught	,, ,, ,, ,, ,,
Headroom	,, ,, ,, ,, ,,
Locks	None.
Tunnels	None.
Bridges	12.

Wendover Arm

From and to	Junction with Main Line at Lock 45 to site of Tring Ford Stop Lock.
Distance	One and a half miles level.
Locks	Tring Ford Stop Lock. Fall from Bulbourne Junction.
General remarks	Remainder of the Branch to Wendover has been abandoned but it still serves as a feeder. Restoration is under consideration.

Aylesbury Arm

From and to	Junction with Main Canal at Marsworth Junction, 38½ miles above Brentford, to Aylesbury.
Distance	6¼ miles.
Length	72ft.
Beam	7ft. 3ins.

Draught	3ft.
Locks	16. Fall from Marsworth.
Bridges	19.
Tunnels	None.

Old Stratford and Buckingham Arms (derelict)
Originally ran to Buckingham through 2 locks. A distance of 10¾ miles, these two arms were separate, the Old Stratford being wide and the Buckingham Arm narrow.

Northampton Arm

From and to	Junction with Main Canal at Gayton, 77¼ miles above Brentford, to junction with the River Nene at Northampton.
Distance	4 miles, 6 furlongs.
Length	72ft.
Beam	7ft.
Draught	3ft. 6ins.
Locks	17. Fall from Gayton junction.
Bridges	14 (including 4 drawbridges and 3 railway bridges).

Welford Arm

From and to	Junction with Main Canal to Welford Basin.
Distance	1⅝ miles.
Length	72ft.
Beam	7ft.
Draught	3ft. 6ins.
Locks	One. Fall from Welford.
Bridges	3.

Market Harborough Arm

From and to	Junction with Main Canal to Leicester at Foxton, 112½ miles above Brentford, to Market Harborough.
Distance	5½ miles
Length	Same as Foxton to Leicester.
Beam	,, ,, ,, ,, ,,
Draught	,, ,, ,, ,, ,,

Headroom	,, ,, ,, ,, ,,
Locks	None.
Bridges	13.

Private Arms

There are numerous private branches to the Grand Union Canal in the London area. The most important are:

Weedon Military Dock (now obstructed by low railway bridge). ...	$\frac{5}{8}$ mile
Otter Dock, Yiewsley	1 mile
Cowley Hall Dock	$\frac{1}{6}$,,
Liddall's	$\frac{1}{6}$,,
Cooper's, Yiewsley	$\frac{1}{8}$,,
Stockley, Yiewsley	$\frac{1}{8}$,,
Pocock's, West Drayton	$\frac{1}{4}$,,
Dawley, Yiewsley	$\frac{1}{4}$,,
Hanwell Loop, North Hyde	$\frac{1}{4}$,,
Victoria Dock, Southall	$\frac{1}{3}$,,
Passmore's Dock, Southall	$\frac{1}{4}$,,
Maypole Dock, Southall	$\frac{1}{6}$,,
Troy Cut, Harefield	$\frac{1}{4}$,,

(Some of these have now been filled in. This list has been included for historical interest).

Grand Union Canal. Bulbourne maintenance yard near Tring

Applicable to whole system

Speed limit and bye-laws	Speed limit 5 miles per hour. Notices and Regulations are given on Notice Boards along the canal.
Approx. time to navigate	From London to Birmingham, if continuous, about 65 hours.
Tow-path	Throughout navigation except certain tunnels.
Navigation notes	There is barge traffic in the London area up to Berkhampstead, therefore care should be taken by pleasure craft and every co-operation given to the working boatman. Special note should be made of the locks that are closed after working hours. Full details can be obtained from British Waterways.

Distance Table
Main Line.   Braunston to Brentford

Braunston Junction, junction with the Oxford Canal, Braunston Branch and Braunston Stop to:

	Miles	Furlongs
Braunston Bottom Lock No. 1 and Bridge No. 2	—	3
Braunston Top Lock No. 6 and Bridge No. 5 ...	—	7½
Braunston Tunnel, north end	1	1¾
Braunston Tunnel, south end	2	3¼
Welton Bridge No. 6	2	4¾
Water Lane Bridge No. 9, Norton	3	7¼
Norton Junction, *junction with the Leicester Line* and Norton Wharf	4	1½
Buckby Top Lock No. 7 and Bridge No. 11 ...	4	3
Daventry Road Bridge No. 13, Long Buckby ...	4	7
Long Buckby Lock No. 9 and Railway Bridge	5	—
Buckby Bottom Lock No. 13	5	5¼
Muscot Mill Bridge No. 18	6	3
Brockhall Bridge No. 19	6	6½
Watling Street Bridge No. 22	7	5¼
Dodford Road Bridge No. 23	8	1
Weedon Station Bridge No. 24	8	7
Junction with Weedon Military Dock	9	0½
Stowe Hill Bridge No. 26	9	7
Flore Lane Bridge No. 27	10	1¾
High House Bridge No. 29	10	5
Heyford Bridge No. 32	11	4¾
Bugbrooke Bridge No. 36	13	—
Bugbrooke Valley Aqueduct	13	2
Banbury Lane Bridge No. 43	14	7¾
Wright's Lane Bridge No. 45	15	3½
Gayton Junction, *junction with the Northampton Branch*	16	4½
Railway Bridge, Blisworth (Euston to Crewe main line)	17	—
Blisworth Bridge No. 51 and Blisworth Mill	17	5½

Distance Table	*Miles*	*Furlongs*
Blisworth Tunnel, north end	18	1½
Blisworth Tunnel, south end	19	7½
Stoke Bruerne Top Lock No. 14, Bridge No. 53 and the Waterways Museum	20	2¾
Stoke Bruerne Lock No. 18 and Stratford Road Bridge No. 54	20	7¼
Stoke Bruerne Bottom Lock No. 20 and Bridge No. 54A	21	0¾
Grafton Bridge No. 57 and Grafton Wharf	22	5
Yardley Bridge No. 60 and Yardley Wharf	23	7¾
Castlethorpe Bridge No. 64 and Thrup Wharf	25	7
Cosgrove Ornamental Bridge No. 65	26	4¾
Cosgrove Junction, *junction with the Old Stratford Branch,* and Cosgrove Lock No. 21	26	7½
Wolverton Aqueduct	17	3¼
Galleon Bridge No. 68, Old Wolverton	27	6¾
Wolverton Bridge No. 71 and Wolverton Station	28	6½
Bradwell Bridge No. 72 and Bradwell Wharf	29	6¼
Newport Pagnell Road Bridge No. 74	30	1¾
Stantonbury Bridge No. 75	30	6¾
Newport Pagnell Road Bridge No. 76	31	2¾
Linford Bridge No. 77 and former junction with Newport Pagnell Canal	31	7¼
Willen Road Bridge No. 79	32	6¼
Willen Bridge No. 81	33	5¾
Little Woolstone Bridge No. 83	34	6¾
Simpson Road Bridge No. 94, Fenny Stratford	38	1¼
Fenny Stratford Lock No. 22 and Fenny Stratford Wharves	38	3¼
Watling Street Bridge No. 96, Fenny Stratford	38	5
Water Eaton Bridge No. 98	39	3
Orchard Mill Bridge No. 102 Great Brickhill	40	5½
Stoke Hammond Lock No. 23 and Bridge No. 104	41	3¼
Soulbury Bottom Lock No. 24	42	4
Soulbury Top Lock No. 26 and Three Locks Bridge No. 107	42	4¾
Old Linslade Bridge No. 110 and Old Linslade Wharf	44	0¾
Leighton Lock No. 27	42	3¼
Leighton Buzzard Bridge No. 114 and Leighton Buzzard Wharves	46	1½
Grove Lock No. 28	47	4½
Church Lock No. 29 and Bridge No. 116	48	0¾
Slapton Lock No. 30	49	6½
Slapton Bridge No. 120	49	7¼
Horton Lock No. 31 and Bridge No. 121	50	2¾
Ivinghoe Bottom Lock No. 32	50	7¾
Ivinghoe Top Lock No. 33 and Bridge No. 122	51	1
Ivinghoe Road Bridge No. 123 and Ivinghoe Wharf	51	4¾
Seabrook Bottom Lock No. 34	51	6½
Seabrook Top Lock No. 36	52	2¾
Cheddington Bridge No. 126 and Cheddington Wharf	52	5¾
Marsworth Lock No. 37	53	3

Distance Table

	Miles	*Furlongs*
Marsworth Lock No. 38	53	$3\frac{1}{2}$
Marsworth Junction, *junction with the Aylesbury Branch,*		
Startopsend Lock No. 39 and Marsworth Bridge No. 132	54	$2\frac{3}{4}$
Marsworth Lock No. 40	54	5
Marsworth Top Lock No. 45 and Bulbourne Junction, *junction with the Wendover Feeder Branch*	55	$0\frac{3}{4}$
Bulbourne Bridge No. 133 and Bulbourne Depot ...	55	$3\frac{1}{4}$
Tring Cutting Bridge No. 134	56	$0\frac{1}{4}$
Bridge No. 135, Tring Station Pendley ...	56	$6\frac{1}{2}$
New Ground Bridge No. 136 ...	57	$5\frac{1}{2}$
Cowroast Lock No. 46 (Summit Lock) and Bridge No. 137	58	$1\frac{1}{2}$
Dudswell Top Lock No. 47	58	$4\frac{3}{4}$
Dudswell Bottom Lock No. 48 and Bridge No. 138 ...	58	$6\frac{1}{4}$
Northchurch Top Lock No. 49 and Bridge No. 139 ...	59	$4\frac{1}{4}$
Bushes Lock No. 50, Northchurch	59	$7\frac{1}{4}$
Northchurch Bottom Lock No. 52	60	$3\frac{1}{4}$
Berkhamstead Top Lock No. 53 and Berkhamstead Station	60	$6\frac{1}{4}$
Berkhamstead Bottom Lock No. 55	61	2
Topside Lock No. 56 Northchurch	61	$6\frac{3}{4}$
Bottomside Lock No. 57	62	1
Sewerage Lock No. 58, Bourne End	62	$3\frac{1}{4}$
Bourne End Bottom Lock No. 59, and Bridge No. 146	62	$7\frac{3}{4}$
Bourne End Mill	63	$0\frac{1}{2}$
Winkwell Top Lock No. 60	63	2
Winkwell Bridge No. 147	63	3
Winkwell Bottom Lock No. 61	63	$3\frac{1}{2}$
Boxmoor Top Lock No. 62	63	$7\frac{3}{4}$
Fishery Lock No. 63, Boxmoor and Fishery Bridge No. 149	64	3
Station Road Bridge No. 150, Hemel Hempstead ...	64	$6\frac{1}{2}$
Boxmoor Bottom Lock No. 64	65	$0\frac{1}{2}$
Two Waters Road Bridge No. 151	65	$1\frac{1}{4}$
Apsley Top Lock No. 65 and Bridge No. 153	65	5
Apsley Lock No. 66	65	$6\frac{1}{2}$
Apsley Bottom Lock No. 67 and Apsley Mill	65	$7\frac{3}{4}$
Nash Mill Top Lock No. 68 and Nash Mill	66	$3\frac{1}{2}$
Nash Mill Bottom Lock No. 69 and Red Lion Lane Bridge No. 155	66	$4\frac{3}{4}$
Kings Langley Lock No. 69A and Kings Langley Mill	67	$5\frac{1}{4}$
Home Park Mill Lock No. 70 and Bridge No. 159 ...	68	$1\frac{1}{4}$
Home Park Farm Lock No. 71	68	$5\frac{3}{4}$
Hunton Bridge Top Lock No. 72 and Hunton Bridge Mill	69	$3\frac{1}{4}$
Hunton Bridge Bottom Lock No. 73	69	$4\frac{1}{4}$
Lady Capel's Lock No. 74 Watford	70	1
Grove Ornamental Bridge No. 164	70	$3\frac{1}{2}$
Grove Mill, Watford	70	$4\frac{1}{2}$
Cassiobury Park Top Lock No. 75	70	$7\frac{3}{4}$
Cassiobury Park Lock No. 76	71	$0\frac{3}{4}$
Ironbridge Lock No. 77 and Bridge No. 167	71	$4\frac{1}{4}$
Cassiobridge Lock No. 78	72	2

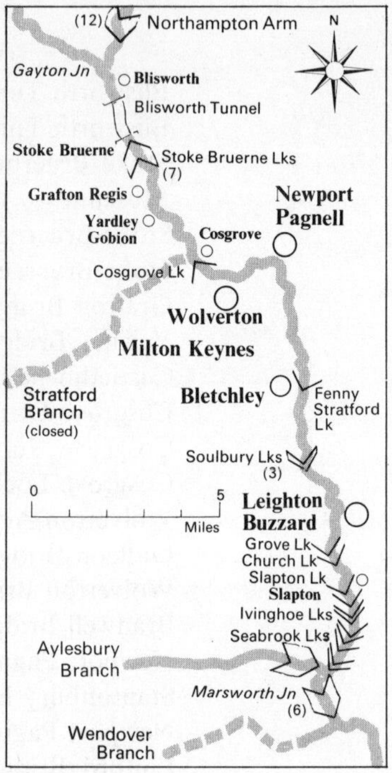

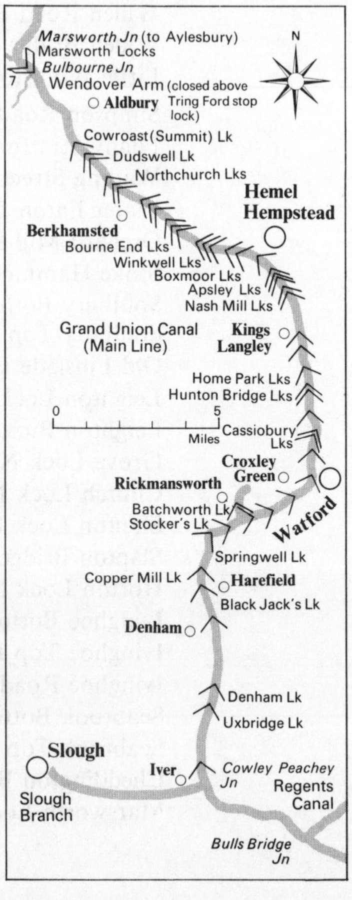

Distance Table

	Miles	Furlongs
Cassiobridge No. 169, Watford	72	3¼
Croxley Mill	72	6¾
Common Moor Lock No. 79, Croxley and Bridge No. 170	73	1
Lot Mead Lock No. 80	73	7
Batchworth Lock No. 81, Rickmansworth, Batchworth Bridge No. 173 and Batchworth Junction, *junction with the Rickmansworth Branch*	74	5
Stockers Lock No. 82 and Bridge No. 175	75	3
Springwell Lock No. 83 and Bridge No. 176	76	0¾
Harefield Lime Works	76	7½
Copper Mill Lock No. 84, Harefield	77	1¼
Troy Junction, junction with the Troy Branch (private)	77	3¾
Black Jack's Lock No. 85 and Troy Mill	77	6¼
Harefield Brick and Cement Works (St. Ann's Dock)	78	1½
Harefield Moor Lock No. 86	78	7
Denham Lock No. 87 and Aqueduct over Frays River	80	3½
Oxford Road Bridge	80	6¼
Uxbridge Lock No. 88 and King's Mill	81	2¾
Bridge No. 185, Uxbridge	81	4½
Dolphin Bridge No. 186 and Dock, Uxbridge	82	0¼
Cowley Lock No. 89 and Cowley Road Bridge No. 188	85	0¼
Packet Boat Dock, and Bridge No. 190	83	5¾
Cowley Peachey Junction, *junction with the Slough Branch*	83	7¼
Trout Bridge No. 191 Yiewsley	84	1¼
Yiewsley High Street Bridge No. 192, West Drayton Station	84	3¾
Stockley Road Bridge No. 195	85	3¾
Broad's Dock (disused)	85	5½
Dawley Bridge No. 197	86	0¾
Woolpack Bridge No. 198	86	2¼
Workhouse Bridge No. 199	86	4¾
Station Road Bridge No. 200, Hayes	86	7¼
Chair Dock, Hayes	87	0¼
Bulls Bridge Junction, *junction with the Paddington Branch,* and Bulls Bridge Depot	87	4½
Western Road Bridge No. 201 Southall ..	87	7¾
North Hyde Bridge No. 202	88	3¾
Adelaide Dock	88	6½
Wolf Bridge No. 203 Norwood	89	—
Maypole Dock	89	4
Norwood Top Lock No. 90 and Glade Lane Bridge No. 204	89	5
Norwood Lock No. 91	89	6½
Windmill Lane Bridge No. 205 (Three Bridges)	90	—
Hanwell Top Lock No. 92	90	1¼
Hanwell Bottom Lock No. 97 and River Brent	90	4¼
Osterley Lock No. 98	91	3
M. 4 Motorway Bridge	91	4¼
Gallows Bridge No. 207 Brentford	91	7
Clitheroe's Lock No. 99, Brentford	92	1½
Great West Road Bridge No. 208 Brentford	92	4
Brentford Gauging Lock No. 100, Brentford Wharves and Warehouses	92	6¾
Brentford High Street Bridge	92	7¼

Distance Table   *Miles*   *Furlongs*

	Miles	Furlongs
Ham Wharf and Dock	93	1¼
Thames Locks No. 101 and Dock Road Bridge, Brentford	93	2¾
Junction with the River Thames	93	4½

Regents Canal

Paddington, junction with Paddington Arm to:

	Miles	Furlongs
Maida Hill Tunnel	—	3
Finchley Road Bridge	—	7

Regent's Canal

British Waterways Board

	Miles	Furlongs
Avenue Road Bridge	1	2
Junction with Cumberland Market Branch (now mostly filled in)	1	5
Hampstead Road Lock No. 1 and Chalk Farm Road Bridge ...	2	2
Hawley Lock No. 2	2	3
Kentish Town Lock No. 3 and Kentish Town Road Bridge	2	3½
St. Pancras Locks No. 4	3	1
York Road Bridge	3	3
Caledonian Road Bridge	3	5
West end of Islington Tunnel	3	6
East end of Islington Tunnel	4	2
City Road Lock No. 5	4	2½
Junction with City Basin Branch (partly filled in)	4	3

Regent's Canal near Camden Lock

	Miles	Furlongs
Sturts Lock No. 6	4	7
Kingsland Road Bridge	5	3½
Acton's Lock No. 7	5	7
Cambridge Road Bridge	6	2
Old Ford Lock No. 8	6	5½
Junction with Hertford Union Canal	6	7
Devonshire Street Goods Station (E. R.)	7	1
Mile End Lock No. 9	7	3
Mile End Road Bridge	7	3½
Johnson's Lock No. 10	7	6
Salmon's Lane Lock No. 11	8	0½
Commercial Road Lock No. 12 and entrance to Limehouse Basin	8	3
Limehouse Basin, Limehouse Lock, *junction with River Thames* (Lock 13)	8	5

Hertford Union Canal

Junction with Main Line to:

	Miles	Furlongs
Top of Old Ford Three Locks (Nos. 1, 2 and 3). These three locks are known as Upper, Middle and Lower	—	7½
Junction with River Lee—Main Line	1	1½

Paddington Branch

Bulls Bridge Junction, junction with the Main Line to:

	Miles	Furlongs
Hayes Road Bridge No. 20 Southall	1	1¾

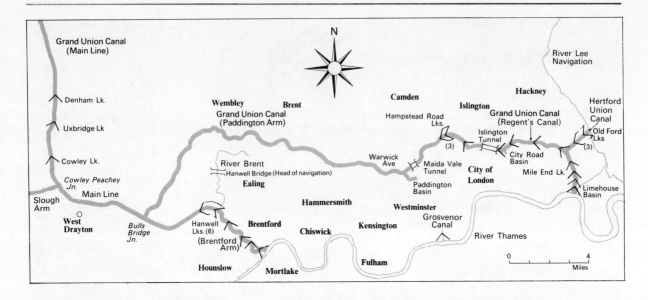

Distance Table

	Miles	Furlongs
West End Bridge No. 18 Greenford	2	6½
Northolt Road Bridge No. 17	3	—
Oxford Road Bridge (Western Avenue) Greenford	3	4½
Lyons Dock, Greenford	4	2¾
Oldfield Lane Bridge No. 15 and Greenford	4	5¾
Greenford Road Bridge	4	7½
Ballot Box Bridge No. 13 and Horsendon	5	6¼
Piggery Bridge No. 12 Alperton	6	7¼
Ealing Road Bridge No. 11 Alperton	7	0¾
Aqueduct over River Brent	8	—
Aqueduct over North Circular Road	8	0½
Willing's Bridge No. 10, Twyford	8	3½
Bridge No. 8, Lower Place	9	2
Old Oak Bridge No. 7, Willesden and Old Oak Wharf	9	5½
Mitre Wharves and Dock	10	2½
Scrubbs Lane Bridge No 6 Kensal Green	10	3½
Kensal Green Docks (renamed Port A Bella Dock)	11	1½
Kensal Green Bridge No 4	11	2½
Wedlake Street Footbridge, and Harrow Road Wharves	11	5¼
Carlton Bridge	12	0¼
Harrow Road Bridge No. 3 Paddington	12	3½
Ranelagh Road footbridge	12	5½
Westbourne Terrace Bridge Paddington	12	7
Little Venice, *junction with the Regent's Canal*	12	7½
Harrow Road Bridge No. 2	12	7¾
Western Avenue Motorway Extension	13	0¼
Bishops Road Bridge No. 1	13	1¼

Distance Table	*Miles*	*Furlongs*
Paddington Basin and Wharves	13	$4\frac{1}{2}$

Slough Branch
Cowley Peachey Junction, junction with the Main Line to:

	Miles	*Furlongs*
Fray's Aqueduct	—	$1\frac{1}{4}$
River Colne Aqueduct	—	4
Colne Brook Aqueduct	—	$5\frac{3}{4}$
Thorney Lane Bridge, Iver	1	$0\frac{1}{2}$
Meeking's Bridge	1	$7\frac{1}{2}$
Hollow Hill Lane Bridge	2	$1\frac{1}{4}$
Langley Station Bridge	2	6
Trenches Bridge, Langley	3	$1\frac{1}{4}$
Langley Schools Bridge	3	3
Middle Green Bridge	3	$5\frac{1}{2}$
Uxbridge Road Bridge	4	$1\frac{1}{4}$
Wexham Road Bridge	4	$3\frac{3}{4}$
Slough Basin and Wharves	4	$7\frac{1}{2}$

Rickmansworth Branch
Batchworth Junction, junction with the Main Line to:

	Miles	*Furlongs*
Batchworth Lock No. 81A	—	$0\frac{1}{4}$
Drawbridge and Rickmansworth Basin	—	$0\frac{3}{4}$
Head of Branch by Rickmansworth Gas Works (site of)	—	$2\frac{1}{2}$

Wendover Branch
Bulbourne Junction, junction with the Main Line to:

	Miles	*Furlongs*
Gammel Bridge No. 2 and New Mill Wharf	—	$5\frac{1}{4}$
Tring Ford Pumping Station and Tring Ford Stop Lock	1	2

(The rest of the branch to Wendover is closed but restoration under consideration)

Aylesbury Branch
Marsworth Junction, junction with the Main Line to:

	Miles	*Furlongs*
Marsworth Locks Nos. 1 and 2 (staircase) and Marsworth Bridge No. 1	—	$0\frac{1}{2}$
Marsworth Lock No. 6 and Long Marston Bridge No. 2	—	$4\frac{1}{4}$
Marsworth Bottom Lock No. 8 and Wilstone Bridge No. 3	—	$6\frac{3}{4}$
Wilstone Lock No. 9 and Bridge No. 5	1	$0\frac{1}{2}$
Puttenham Lock No. 10	1	$5\frac{1}{4}$
Puttenham Lock No. 11 and Puttenham Bridge No. 7	1	$6\frac{3}{4}$
Buckland Bridge No. 8	2	$3\frac{3}{4}$
Buckland Lock No. 12	2	$4\frac{3}{4}$
Aston Clinton Lock No. 13 and College Road Bridge No. 9 ...	2	$7\frac{1}{4}$
Broughton Lock No. 14 and Broughton Road Bridge No. 15 ...	4	6
Oakfield Bridge (Aylesbury ring road)	5	2
Aylesbury Lock No. 15	5	$3\frac{3}{4}$
Walton Mill...	5	6
Aylesbury Bottom Lock No. 16 and Bridge No. 17 ...	5	$6\frac{1}{2}$
Walton Bridge No. 18	5	$7\frac{1}{4}$
Aylesbury Basin and Wharves	6	$1\frac{1}{2}$

Distance Table

	Miles	Furlongs
Northampton Branch		
Gayton Junction, junction with the Main Line to:		
Milton Road Bridge No. 2, Gayton	—	0¾
Milton Road Bridge No. 3	—	4¼
Rothersthorpe Top Lock No. 1	—	5¾
Rothersthorpe Lock No. 2 and Milton Road Bridge No. 4	—	6½
Rothersthorpe Lock No. 12 and Motorway Bridge	1	3¾
Rothersthorpe Bottom Lock No. 13 and Bridge No. 7	1	5¼
Wootton Lock No. 14 and Rothersthorpe Road Bridge No. 9 ...	2	0¾
Hardingstone Lock No. 15	3	0¼
Duston Mill Bridge No. 13 and Hunsbury Hill Ironworks	3	2½
Northampton Lock No. 16	4	0½
Cotton End Wharf and Bridge No. 17	4	5¼
Northampton Lock No. 17, *junction with River Nene*	4	6
Market Harborough Branch		
Foxton Junction, junction with the Leicester Line to:		
Foxton Main Street Bridge No.2	—	4½
Foxton Bridge No. 3	—	5½
Clarkes Bridge No. 4	—	7
Johnson's Bridge No. 6	1	2¾
Gallow's Hill Bridge	2	0¼
Great Bowden Hall Bridge No. 9	3	3½
Uncle Tom's Bridge No. 11	4	0¾
Market Harborough Wharves and Basin	5	4
Birmingham to Braunston. Main Line		
Salford Bridge, junction with the Tame Valley Canal and the Birmingham and Fazeley Canal, to:		
Salford Shallow Lock No. 64	0	1¼
Nechells Power Station	0	2
Aston Church Road Bridge No. 109	0	5½
Saltley Viaduct No. 108	1	1½
Garrison Bottom Lock No. 63	1	3
Duddeston Mill Road Bridge No. 106	1	4
Garrison Fourth Lock No. 62	1	5
Garrison Third Lock No. 61	1	6
Landor Street Bridge No. 105 and Garrison Second Lock No. 60	1	7
Garrison Top Lock No. 59	2	0
Garrison Lane Bridge No. 103	2	1¾
Watery Lane Bridge No. 99	2	4
Bordesley, *junction with branch (3½ furlongs*) to the Digbeth Branch of the Birmingham Canal Navigations*	2	5
Camphill Bottom Lock No. 57		
Camphill Bottom Lock No. 57 and Adderley Street Bridge No. 94	2	5¼
Camphill Fifth Lock No. 56	2	6
Coventry Road Bridge No. 93 and Camphill Fourth Lock No. 55	2	6½
Sandy Lane Bridge No. 92 and Camphill Third Lock No. 54	2	7½

* and includes Warwick Bar Stop Lock No. 58

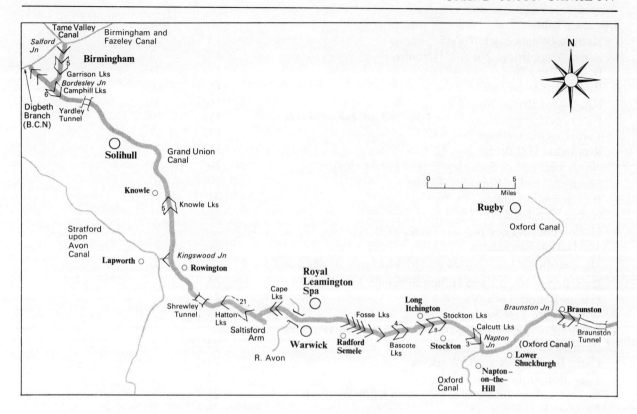

Distance Table

	Miles	Furlongs
Camphill Second Lock No. 53	3	0
Camphill Top Lock No. 52	3	0¾
Sampson Road wharves (British Waterways Baord)	3	1½
Golden Hillock Bridge No. 89	3	7
Hay Mills Refuse Destructor and Bridge	4	5¾
Tyseley Wharves (British Waterways Board)	5	2¼
Yardley Tunnel No. 86a	5	6½
Lincoln Road Bridge No. 85, Acocks Green	6	6
Richmond Road Bridge No. 84, Olton	7	1¼
Dove House Lane Bridge No. 82, Ulverley Green	8	0½
Rowood Bridge No. 80, Solihull	8	5¼
Elmdon Heath Iron Bridge No. 79	9	1½
Catherine de Barnes Bridge No. 78	10	3½
Henwood Bridge No. 77	11	1
Barston Lane Bridge No. 76, Copt Heath	11	4¾
Motorway Bridge (M42)	11	5¼
Copt Heath Bridge No. 75	12	0
Waterfield Bridge No. 73	12	4¾
Kixley Bridge No. 72	13	0¼
Kenilworth Road Bridge No. 71, Knowle	13	3
Knowle Top Lock No. 51	13	3¾

Distance Table	*Miles*	*Furlongs*
Knowle Bottom Lock No. 47	13	5¾
Kings Arms Bridge No. 70, Heronfield	14	2
Baker's Lane Bridge No. 68	14	7½
Rising Bridge No. 66	16	0½
Kingswood Bridge No. 65	16	7¼
Kingswood, *junction with the Stratford on Avon Canal*	17	0¾
Turner's Green Bridge No. 63	17	7
Rowington Hill Bridge No. 62	18	3¾
North west end of Shrewley Tunnel (433 yards)	20	1½
South east end of Shrewley Tunnel	20	3½
Hatton Station Bridge No. 56	21	0¾
Hatton Top Lock No. 46	22	1
Hatton Fourth Lock No. 43, Turnover Bridge No. 54 and Hatton Workshops	22	2½
Hatton Middle Lock No. 36 and Middle Lock Bridge No. 53	22	6
Ugly Bridge No. 52 and Hatton Sixteenth Lock No. 31	23	1½
Hatton Bottom Lock No. 26	24	0½
Warwick By-pass Bridge	24	1
Budbrooke, *junction with branch to Saltisford, Warwick* (formerly 3¾ furlongs, but now only 2½ furlongs)	24	2¾
Cape Top Lock No. 25, Warwick	24	7
Cape Bottom Lock No. 24	25	0
Coventry Road Bridge No. 49, Guy's Cliff, Warwick	25	4¾
Emscote Bridge No. 46	26	1½
Avon Aqueduct	26	3½
Leam Bridge No. 44	26	6½
Bishop's Tachbrook Road Bridge No. 41, Leamington	27	5¼
Clemens Street Bridge No. 40, Leamington	27	6¾
Radford Road Bridge No. 35	29	0¾
Radford Bottom Lock No. 23	29	6¾
Fosse Bottom Lock No. 22	30	3½
Fosse Middle Lock No. 21	30	5
Fosse Top Lock No. 20	30	7½
Wood Lock No. 19	31	4¾
Welsh Road Bridge No. 30 and Welsh Road Lock No. 18	32	1¼
Bascote Bottom Lock No. 17	32	5
Bascote Top Lock (Staircase pair Nos. 15 and 14)	32	6½
Cuttle Bridge No. 25, Long Itchington	34	2½
Itchington Bottom Lock No. 13 (Stockton flight)	34	3¾
Stockton Ninth Lock No. 12 and junction with Kaye's Arm	34	6
Stockton Bridge No. 23 and Stockton Eighth Lock No. 11	34	7½
Stockton Top Lock No. 4	35	3¼
Birdingbury Bridge No. 21	35	5¾
Gibraltar Bridge No. 20	36	3
Calcutt Bottom Lock No. 3	37	7
Calcutt Top Lock No. 1	37	7¾
Napton, *junction with the Oxford Canal*	38	4¼

(The through route to London now continues over the Oxford Canal to Braunston Junction, from where the bridge numbering starts)

Distance Table

									Miles	Furlongs
Flecknoe	...	...	...	...	...	...	...	...	41	2
Nethercote	...	...	...	...	...	...	...	...	41	4
Wolfhamcote	...	...	...	...	...	...	...	42	6
Braunston *(junction with Oxford Canal, Northern section)*	...	...	43	4

Grand Union Canal near Braunston

The Leicester Line

Norton Junction, junction with the Main Line to:

							Miles	Furlongs
Watling Street Bridge No. 5	...	...	...	...	...	...	1	$2\frac{1}{2}$
Welton Station Bridge No. 6 and Welton		...	...	...	1	$6\frac{1}{2}$
Watford Bottom Lock No. 1	...	...	...	...	...	...	2	$1\frac{1}{2}$
Watford Lock No.2	...	...	...	...	...	...	2	2
Watford Lock No. 3 (staircase)	...	...	...	...	...	2	$2\frac{1}{2}$
Watford Top Lock No. 7	...	...	...	...	...	...	2	3
Motorway Bridge	...	...	...	...	...	...	...	2	$3\frac{1}{2}$
Crick Tunnel, south end	...	...	...	...	...	...	3	$6\frac{1}{4}$
Crick Tunnel, north end	...	...	...	...	...	...	4	$5\frac{1}{4}$
West Haddon Road Bridge No. 12 and Crick		...	...	...	4	$7\frac{1}{2}$
Yelvertoft Bridge No. 19 and Yelvertoft		...	...	...	7	$1\frac{1}{2}$
Haddon Road Bridge No. 22 and West Haddon		.	...	...	7	$7\frac{1}{2}$
Darkers Bridge No. 23 Winwick Grange		...	...	...	8	$2\frac{1}{4}$
Elkington Bridge No. 28 and Elkington		...	...	...	10	$3\frac{1}{4}$
Stokleys Bridge No. 31 Stanford		...	...	...	...	11	$4\frac{3}{4}$

Distance Table

	Miles	Furlongs
Halfway Bridge No. 35 Stanford … …	13	—
South Kilworth Road Bridge No. 37 … …	13	$5\frac{3}{4}$
Aqueduct over River Avon … … …	15	$3\frac{1}{2}$
Junction with the Welford Branch	15	$4\frac{1}{4}$
North Kilworth Bridge No. 45 and North Kilworth	16	$2\frac{1}{2}$
Husbands Bosworth Tunnel, south end … …	17	$0\frac{3}{4}$
Husbands Bosworth Tunnel, north end … …	17	6
Theddingworth Road Bridge No. 50 … …	19	$5\frac{1}{2}$
Morton's Bridge No. 56 and Lubenham	21	6
Gumley Road Bridge No. 60 … … …	22	$5\frac{3}{4}$
Foxton Top Lock No. 8 (staircase) … …	22	$7\frac{1}{2}$
Foxton Lock No. 13 (staircase) … … …	23	$0\frac{1}{4}$
Foxton Bottom Lock No. 17 and Bridge No. 61	23	$0\frac{3}{4}$
Foxton Junction, *junction with the*		
Market Harborough Branch …	23	1
Debdale Wharf Bridge No. 65 and Debdale	24	3
Gumley Bridge No. 69 and Gumley …	25	$3\frac{1}{2}$
Smeeton Hills Bridge No. 70 … … …	25	$5\frac{1}{4}$
Smeeton Road Bridge No. 72 … … …	26	$5\frac{1}{2}$
Saddington Tunnel, south end … … …	26	$6\frac{3}{4}$
Saddington Tunnel, north end … … …	27	$2\frac{3}{4}$
Kibworth Top Lock No. 18 … … …	28	$1\frac{1}{2}$
Kibworth Second Lock No. 19 … … …	28	$3\frac{1}{2}$
Kibworth Lock No. 20 and Kibworth Bridge No. 75	28	$4\frac{1}{4}$
Kibworth Bottom Lock No. 21 … …	28	$5\frac{1}{4}$
Crane's Lock No. 22 and Bridge No. 76 …	29	$0\frac{3}{4}$
Great Glen Station Bridge No. 77 … …	29	$6\frac{1}{4}$
Newton Church Bridge No. 80 … … …	30	5
Newton Top Lock No. 23 … … …	30	6
Newton Middle Lock No. 24 … … …	30	$7\frac{3}{4}$
Wain Bridge No. 81 Newton Harcourt …	31	—
Newton Bottom Lock No. 25 … … …	31	$1\frac{1}{4}$
Wigston Top Lock No. 26 … … …	31	$5\frac{1}{4}$
Wigston Lock No. 27 and Bridge No. 82 …	31	6
Wigston Lock No. 28 and Langham's Bridge No. 83	31	$7\frac{3}{4}$
Wigston Bottom Lock No. 29 and		
Tythorn Bridge No. 84 … …	32	$1\frac{1}{2}$
Kilby Bridge No. 87 … …	32	$7\frac{1}{4}$
Kilby Bridge Lock No. 30 and Bridge No. 88 …	33	$2\frac{1}{4}$
Double Rail Lock No. 31 … … …	33	$5\frac{1}{4}$
Irving's Lock No. 32 … … … …	34	1
Crow Mill Bridge No. 92 South Wigston …	34	$4\frac{1}{4}$
Bush Lock No. 33 … … … … …	34	7
Little Glen Bridge No. 94 … … …	35	$2\frac{1}{2}$
Little Glen Lock No. 34 … … … …	35	6
Blaby Bridge No. 98 … … …	36	$0\frac{1}{4}$
Whetstone Lane Lock No. 35 and Whetstone		
Lane Bridge No. 99 …	36	$1\frac{3}{4}$
Gee's Lock No. 36 and Bridge No. 101 …	37	$0\frac{1}{4}$
Blue Bank Lock No. 37 and Blue Bank		
Bridge No. 102	37	$3\frac{1}{2}$

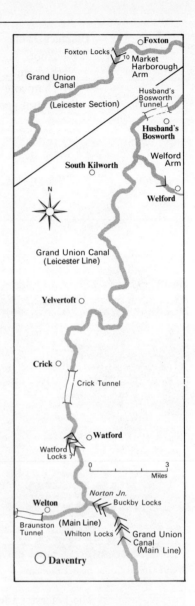

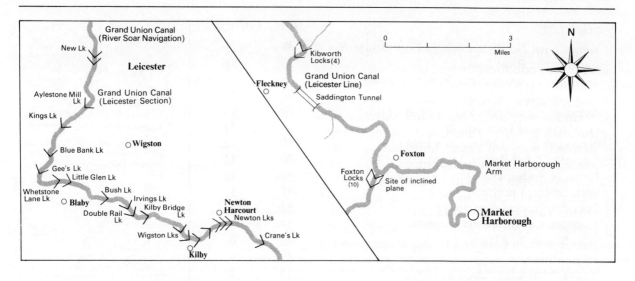

British Waterways Board

Grand Union Canal (Leicester Section) at Foxton Locks

Distance Table

	Miles	Furlongs
King's Lock No. 38 and King's Lock Bridge No. 104.	38	$2\frac{1}{2}$
Canal enters River Soar	38	$3\frac{3}{4}$
Aylestone Bridge No. 106 (Freestone Bridge) ...	38	5
Aylestone Mill Lock No. 39	39	2
Aylestone Gas Works and St. Marys Mills ...	39	$7\frac{1}{2}$
St. Marys Mill Lock No. 40	39	$7\frac{3}{4}$
New Lock No. 41 (Freeman's Lock)	40	$2\frac{1}{4}$
Upperton Road Bridge, Leicester	40	$4\frac{3}{4}$
Newarke Bridge, Leicester	40	$7\frac{3}{4}$
West Bridge, Leicester	41	1
Leicester, North Lock No. 42	42	—
Leicester, Canal Carriers Wharves, Warehouses, and Public Wharf.	42	4
Limekiln Lock No. 43	42	6
Belgrave Lock No. 44	43	3
Belgrave Wharf	43	6
Birstall Lock No. 45 and Wharf	45	1
Thurmaston Lock No. 46 and Wharf	46	1
Barkby Wharf	47	2
Junction Lock No. 47	48	2
Cossington Lock No. 48	49	—
Sileby Lock No. 49	50	3
Mountsorrel Lock No. 50	51	3
Mountsorrel Wharf	51	5
Barrow-on-Soar Wharf	53	—
Barrow-on-Soar Lock No. 51	53	3
Pilling's Flood Lock No. 52	55	—
Loughborough Wharf	56	2
Loughborough, *junction Branch*, one eighth of a mile long to Loughborough Basin ...	57	—
Loughborough Lock No. 53	57	2
Bishops Meadow Lock No. 54	58	—
Normanton-on-Soar Wharf	59	3
Zouch Mills	60	—
Zouch Lock No. 55	61	1
Kegworth Old Lock No. 56	63	1
Kegworth Wharf	63	4
Kegworth New Lock (Flood Lock) No. 57 ...	63	5
Kingston-on-Soar Plaster Wharf	63	7
Ratcliffe-on-Soar Lock No. 58	65	—
Redhill Lock No.59	65	6
Junction with River Trent	66	1

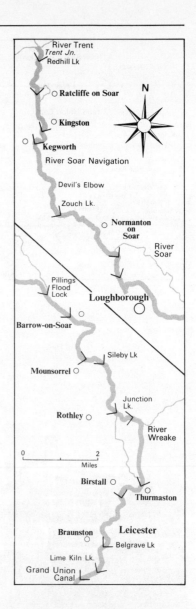

This section of the Grand Union Canal joins the River Trent in the Soar Mouth or Red Hill branch of the Navigation. On leaving the Grand Union Canal (Old Loughborough Navigation Section) all boats must turn upstream to the left until the head of Cranfleet Cut is reached. Downstream leads to Thrumpton Weir only.

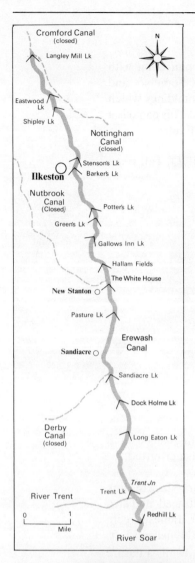

Distance Table — Erewash Canal   *Miles   Furlongs*

	Miles	Furlongs
Trent Lock No. 60 and Toll Office (Erewash Section of the Grand Union Canal)	66	1
Long Eaton No. 61	67	7
Dock Holme Lock No.62	68	1
Sandiacre Lock No.63	69	3
Sandiacre Junction, *junction with Derby Canal,* Sandiacre Pasture No. 64	69	4
Sandiacre Village	70	3
Junction Lock No. 65 and Toll Office	71	5
The White House, junction with Nutbrook Canal (now derelict and abandoned)	71	6
Hallam Fields Lock No. 66	72	1
Gallows Inn Lock No.67	72	7
Green's Lock No. 68	73	3½
Potter's Lock No. 69	73	6
Barker's Lock No. 70	74	5½
Stenson's Lock No. 71	75	7½
Shipley Lock No. 72	76	2½
Eastwood Lock No. 73	76	5
Langley Mill, junction with Cromford Canal. (closed except for ⅛ mile at this end) ...	77	7

(Lock No. 14 of the Cromford Canal has been restored and it is now possible to go through this to the Great Northern Basin at the top end of the closed Nottingham Canal).

Welford Branch

Welford Junction, junction with the Leicester Line to:

	Miles	Furlongs
Bosworth Mill Bridge No. 1	—	2
Gilberts Bridge No. 2	—	6½
Welford Lock No. 1 and Bridge No. 3	1	1¾
Welford Wharf and Basin	1	5

Erewash Canal. Trent Lock

Grand Western Canal (44)

This canal was promoted under Acts dated 1796, 1811 and 1812, its connection with Taunton has long been abandoned. The navigation passes through rural Somerset and Tiverton in Devon, where there is a fine 15th century church and ancient buildings which remain from the time when this town was a centre of the wool and lace trades. This canal is a remnant of a project ship canal from Bristol to the English Channel near Exeter.

Authority	Devon County Council, County Hall, Exeter EX2 4QQ. Tel. Exeter (0392) 77977.
From and to	Lowdwells to Tiverton
Distance	10½ miles.
Length	Unlimited, except by width of the canal.
Beam	7ft.
Draught	3ft. 6ins.
Headroom	7ft. 3ins.
Locks	None.
Tow-path	Throughout navigation.

Facilities   A horse-drawn boat operates on the canal and light craft can be hired at Tiverton. Several inns on the route. Electric boats permitted.

General remarks   This canal has always operated as an isolated navigation since the link with Taunton became derelict. The route can still be traced, and also the sites of the old lifts erected by that early engineer, James Green. Of particular interest is the Tone Aqueduct and the Nynehead Lift.

The top two miles lead to the derelict lock at Lowdwells a nature reserve. Unpowered craft may use the canal on application to the D.C.C. at Exeter. The D.C.C. have designated the canal as a country park and issue literature about it. Prices on application. The closed section is mainly on private property but part can be explored from public footpaths.

Distance Table

Lowdwells to:

	Miles	Furlongs
Whipcott Wharf	—	7
Burlescombe Wharf	1	6
Ayshford	2	7
Sampford Peverell	5	2
Rock House Wharf	6	4
Halberton	7	1
Road Bridge (A. 373 road)	8	6
Tiverton	10	6

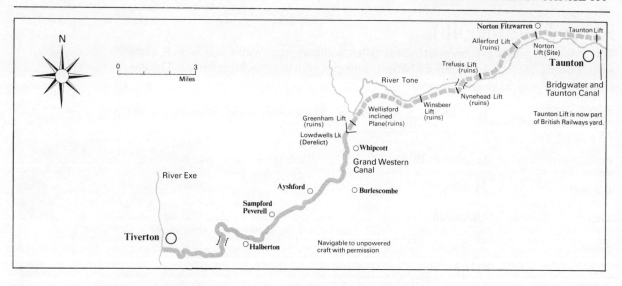

Grosvenor Canal (45)

Originally built to supply water to Chelsea, this cut was three-quarters of a mile long and ran to a basin now occupied by Victoria Station. It was converted to a navigable canal in 1823. In 1866 it became used for barging away refuse. It was extensively reconstructed in 1929 and at present 650 tons of refuse is collected by barges every week. Commercial, for use by the Council only.

Authority	Westminster City Council, City Engineer's Department, Grosvenor Canal Depot, Gatcliff Road, London, SW1 Tel. 01-730 1540.
From and to	*Chelsea Bridge to near Ebury Bridge.
Distance	Nearly half a mile.
Length	90ft.
Beam	18ft. 6ins.
Draught	7ft.
Headroom	8ft. 6ins.
Locks	One, equipped with extra gates to keep out very high tides Rise from River Thames.
Tides	High water at the entrance approximately 30 minutes after London Bridge.

*See plan page 133.

River Hamble (46)

This tidal navigation extends northwards from Southampton Water and is well marked with beacons. Moorings are difficult to find as the river is a busy yachting centre. The River Hamble Harbour Revision Act applies.

Authority	Hampshire County Council, The Castle, Winchester, Hants. SO23 8UJ Tel. Winchester (0962) 4411
From and to	*Hamble to Botley.
Distance	7½ miles.
Length	Unlimited.
Beam	Unlimited
Draught	At high water to Botley, 5ft. At high water to Bursledon, 8ft. 6ins.
Headroom	Unlimited to Bursledon. Bursledon to Botley: 13ft. at High water Springs. 25ft. at Low water Springs.
Locks	None. Tidal throughout.
Tow-path	None.
Tides	Double High water, at the entrance, 10 minutes before and one hour 51 minutes after High water at Dover. Spring tides rise 13ft. Neap tides rise 10ft. 3ins.

*See Imray Chart
No. C3 Isle of Wight

Huddersfield Broad Canal (47)

This waterway was constructed under an Act passed in 1774. It is often known as Sir John Ramsden's Canal, after its promoter. It linked the Huddersfield Narrow Canal now closed to the Calder and Hebble Navigation. Commercial traffic on the canal ceased in 1953 but the canal has been used by cruisers and its cruising potential is being explored. Unlike the adjoining Calder and Hebble Navigation, standard British Waterway windlasses can be used. Aspley Basin at the head of the canal at Huddersfield is now a very useful mooring close to the town centre.

Authority	British Waterways Board.
From and to	Junction with the Main Line of the Calder and Hebble Navigation at Cooper Bridge, to junction with the Huddersfield Narrow Canal at Huddersfield. The head of the canal is Aspley Basin.
Distance	3¼ miles.

Length	57ft. 6ins.
Beam	14ft. 2ins.
Draught	4ft. 6ins.
Headroom	8ft 9ins
Locks	9. Lock gates worked by boat crews. Rise from Cooper Bridge.
Bridges	Numerous. Keys for Turnbridge Lifting Bridge can be obtained at Lock No. 9 Lockhouse. The Leeds and Liverpool 'T' shaped key will operate the bridge. These can be obtained from B.W.B. at Leeds.
Tow-path	Throughout navigation.
Speed limit	3½ miles per hour.

Distance Table

Cooper Bridge, Lock No. 1 junction with Calder and Hebble Navigation to:

	Miles	Furlongs
Lock No. 2 Colne Bridge	—	1½
Bradley	—	4
Lock No. 3 Ladgrave	—	6
Lock No. 4 Longlands	1	0½
Deighton	1	2
Lock No. 5 Turnpike Road	1	5
Lock No. 6 Reading	1	6
Lock No. 7 Fieldhouse Green	1	7½
Lock No. 8 Falls	2	0½
Fartown Green Lock No. 9 (Red Doles) ...	2	2
Turnbridge Lifting Bridge	3	—
Huddersfield, *junction with Huddersfield Narrow Canal*	3	4

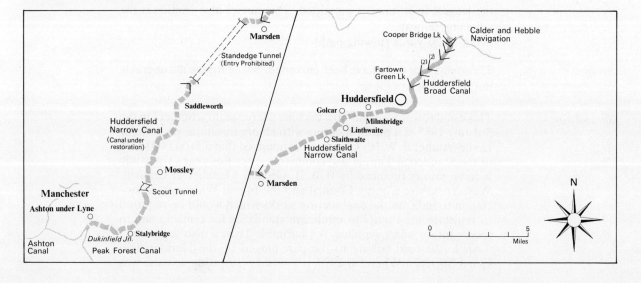

Huddersfield Narrow Canal (48)

An ex-Railway Canal (L.N.W. Rly) authorised in 1794 but not completed until 1811. It was closed in 1944 by the L.M.S. Rly Act that destroyed so many canals. It was out of use for many years before its closure and was not a commercial success due to the number of locks. It goes across the Pennines, in some very fine scenery and some of the summit reservoirs are in the Peak District National Park. It passes through a region of wild moors that is likely to be designated a Country Park. Standedge Tunnel on the summit level is the longest and highest tunnel in Britain being 645 feet above Ordnance Datum. The Huddersfield Canal Society has commenced active restoration of the Canal.

Authority	British Waterways Board.
From and to	A junction with the Huddersfield Broad Canal in Huddersfield to Ashton-under-Lyne junction with the Ashton Canal.
Distance	19 miles 7 furlongs
Length	70ft
Beam	6ft 10ins
Draught	3ft 6ins
Headroom	6ft 8ins
Locks	74. Lock Nos. 1 to 42 rise from Huddersfield. Lock Nos. 43 to 74 fall to Ashton-under-Lyne. Lock Nos. 22, 23, and 32 restored. Work commenced restoring 27 other locks (1985)
Towpath	Throughout the navigation
Tunnels	Standedge 5698 yards (No towing path). Apart from maintenance groups of B.W.B. no access to the Tunnel, the longest in Britain, is permitted. This tunnel also ventilates the adjoining railway. Scout 220 yards (towing path)
Bridges	75, a number of these have been culverted. Swing Bridge not operable but restorable at Golcar.
Special note	This canal restoration has now become a large scale scheme. On the 3rd July 1985 at a public meeting with all organisations present Sir Leslie Young, B.W.B's Chairman announced that a £100,000 study of the Standedge Tunnel will commence later this year. The study is to be jointly financed by B.W.B, Greater Manchester Council, West Yorkshire County Council and the Inland Waterways Association to indicate the engineering works which would be required to reinstate the tunnel to minimum standards for cruising and to secure future water supplies. A Charitable Trust is also suggested. Sir Leslie paid tribute to the part played by the Huddersfield Canal Society. 'When, in 1980, a modest restoration scheme was

Lock numbers

East of Summit (E)

1 First Lock
2 - 3 2 Locks
4 Longroyd Bridge Lock
5 Paddock Foot Lock
6 Mark Bottom Lock
7-11 Milnsbridge Flight
12 Rough Holme Lock
13-14 Ramsden Locks
15 Golcar Brook Lock
16-17 Westwood Locks
18 Can Lock
19 Holme Lock
20 Spot Lock
21 Waterside Lock
22 Pickle Lock
23 Dartmouth Lock
24 Shuttle Lock
25 Shaker Wood Lock
26-30 5 Locks
31 Booth Lock
32-33 Pig Tail Locks
34-42 Francis Locks

West of Summit (W)

32 Summit Lock
31 Ward Lane
30-25 Diggle Flight
24 Woolroad Lock
23 Limekiln Lock
22 Dungebooth Lock
21 Wade Lock (Uppermill Lock)
20 Hall Lock
19-18 Royal George Locks
17-16 Two Locks
15 Roaches Lock
14 Fourteenth Lock
13 Thirteenth Lock
12 Whitehead's First Lock
11 Eleventh Lock
10-9 Two Locks
8 Straley Hall Lock
7 Top Lock
6 Castle Hall Lock
5-2 Four Locks
1 Ashton Lock

undertaken at Uppermill, the prime mover was the Society. Since that time the Society's members have continued to be active, with the assistance of those bodies now represented on the Huddersfield Narrow Canal Joint Committee.'

He added: 'A great deal of money has to be found and many possible sources, including the EEC, will be explored. I am confident that the right level of co-operation is there together with a strong desire to see this trans-Pennine waterway link re-established.'

In 1951 the top gates of locks were replaced by concrete weir planks, and by 1956 the canal through Slaithwaite had been filled and piped. Between the mid 1950s and the Transport Act of 1968, further sections of this canal were infilled and piped and the land sold off to developers. Local Authorities carried out improvement works like the A670 at Uppermill effectively splitting the canal. It was fortuitous that provision for a continuous water supply was maintained, otherwise the restoration of the Ashton Canal in 1972 may not have been possible.

Since 1968 the canal has been a Remainder Waterway under the provisions of the 1968 Transport Act, however, supplies of water equating to 2 million gallons per day have been available from the Water Authority sources.

Following the scheme at Uppermill involving two locks and nearly a mile of canal undertaken by the Canal Society in collaboration with the Greater Manchester Council, in 1983/84, West Yorkshire County Council and Kirklees Metropolitan Council initiated a Manpower Services Commission Scheme for the restoration works between Slaithwaite and Marsden, a distance of some three miles of canal passing through 19 locks, followed by the proposal to reconnect the Broad and Narrow canals at Aspley Basin in Huddersfield and restore the first two lock lengths from Wakefield Road to Queen Street South.

The Tameside Canals Development Association are proposing to restore the first three locks and approximately one mile of canal from Portland Basin to Bailey Street in Stalybridge, meanwhile the Huddersfield Canal Society have commenced restoration works at Locks 31 and 32 at Diggle (owned by Oldham Metropolitan District Council) and initiated a survey of the canal through Stalybridge by the Consultants Atkins & Partners (about two miles of canal from Bailey Street to Bank Lane).

Several M.S.C. Schemes involving towing path improvements in the Oldham and Tameside areas are being co-ordinated by B.W.B. Standedge Tunnel has been closed since 1948. There were irregular structural failures in the unlined section of the tunnel. These failures involve the B.W.B. in removing debris from time to time to ensure a continued water supply, particularly to the Ashton Canal. At the Tunnel End Cottages is an excellent information and exhibition centre.

Distance Table

Huddersfield, junction with Huddersfield Broad Canal to:

	Miles	Furlongs
Milnsbridge	2	5
Golcar	3	2
Linthwaite	3	7
Slaithwaite	5	0
Head of Lock No. 42E Marsden and north-east end of summit level	7	2
Marsden Railway Station	7	6

Distance Table	Miles	Furlongs
North-east end of Standedge Tunnel	8	2
South-west end of Standedge Tunnel, and Diggle Railway Station	11	3
Head of Lock No. 32W, Diggle, and south-west end of summit level	11	4
Saddleworth	13	6
Upper Mill	14	0
Greenfield	14	7
Mossley	16	0
Scout Mill	16	5
Millbrook	17	3
Stalybridge	18	6
Ashton-under-Lyne, *junction with Ashton Canal* (Lock No. 1 nearby)	19	7

River Hull (49)

A portion of this river comes under the jurisdiction of the Driffield Navigation promoted by Acts in 1767, 1801 and 1817. The lower section forms the port of Hull.

Authority	**Struncheon Hill Lock to Aike*** Driffield Navigation Commissioners, 18 Exchange Street, Driffield, North Humberside, YO25 7LD.
	Aike to Sculcoates Goate. A free navigation.
	Sculcoates Goate to the River Humber Hull Corporation, Guildhall, Hull. Tel. Hull 36880.
From and to	Tail of Struncheon Hill Lock, and junction with Driffield Navigation to Hull, junction with River Humber.
Distance	20 miles. Arram Beck, quarter of a mile.
Headroom 9ft.	*Beam/Length* Unlimited.
Draught	Hull to Grove Hill, 6ft. Grove Hill to Struncheon Hill Lock, 5ft. Arram Beck, 3ft.
Locks	None. Tidal throughout. A barrier has been created at Hull to keep out exceptionally high tides.
Connections	At Aike with Driffield Navigation.
	With Leven Canal, near Aike. (Not now navigable. Used for fishing only.)
	With Beverley Beck at Grove Hill.
General remarks	The tide flows very strongly at river mouth and for a considerable distance upstream.
Tow-path	Throughout navigation, except from mouth of river to Hull Bridge.

*See Driffield Navigation page 115.

Tides　　　　　　High water at Struncheon Hill 3 hours after Hull.

Distance Table

Tail of Struncheon Hill Lock and junction with Driffield Navigation to:

	Miles	Furlongs
Tophill Low Landing	1	2
Baswick Landing	1	4
Aike, *junction with River Hull Navigation*	4	—
Junction with Leven Canal (closed to traffic, and is now only used for fishing)	4	4
Junction with Arram Beck	5	5
Tickton, Hull Bridge (formerly a rolling bridge – now fixed)	7	2
Grove Hill, *junction with Beverley Beck*	9	—
Wawne Ferry	11	6
Stone Ferry	17	4
Hull, Sculcoates Goate	19	1
Hull, *junction with Queen's Dock*	19	1½
Hull, *junction with Drypool Basin,* leading to Victoria Dock	19	4
Hull, *junction with River Humber*	20	—

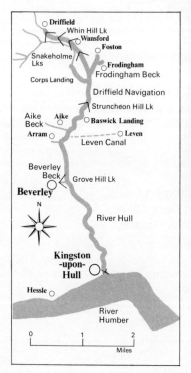

River Humber (50)

This navigation although not strictly within the category of an inland waterway is one that should be traversed only by those fully acquainted with its shifting sandbanks and strong tides. Navigation is very difficult, but pilotage can be arranged, special rates being in operation for the Humber, Goole and Trent pilotage waters. Owing to the variation of the navigable channel in the Upper Humber, there are no recognized anchorage grounds. There are no public mooring berths, but usually very little objection is offered to yachts mooring temporarily to private jetties. Anchorage is not allowed in the fairway of the river. Compulsory pilotage may be in operation in certain areas.

Authority	Associated British Ports, P.O. Box 1, Kingston House Tower, Bond St, Hull. HU1 3ER. Tel. Hull (0482) 52251.
From and to	Humber Entrance to Trent Falls.
Distance	36½ miles.
Length	Unlimited
Beam	„
Draught	Sea to King George V Dock at Hull, 28ft. to 34ft. Hull Roads to Trent Falls, governed by the tidal rise and the least depth in the channel. (On occasions as little as 6 inches at Mean Low Water Springs.)
Headroom	Unlimited.
Tow-path	None.
Connections	Rivers Ouse, Trent and Hull are connected with each other by this tidal waterway as well as the River Ancholme and Market Weighton Canal.
Locks	None. Tidal throughout.
Docks	All docks on the Humber are owned by the British Transport Dock Board. (All communications to Chief Docks Manager, Dock Office, Hull; Port Master, Grimsby and Immingham Dock Office, Grimsby; or Docks Manager, Dock Office, Goole.
Navigation guides	The Associated British Ports publish in convenient form, the Rules and Humber Bye-laws and publish monthly copies of their latest surveys between Burton Stather on the Trent and Barton Haven (a short distance westward of Hull, but on the Lincolnshire side of the Humber). They also publish annual copies of a chart showing the latest soundings in the Humber between Barton Haven and Spurn Head. Copies of the Survey and chart can be obtained from the offices. Admiralty charts cover the Humber Estuary from Hull to Spurn Point.
Tides	It is high water at Hull at about 5 hours before H. W. Dover. High water at Ferriby Sluice about 18 minutes after Hull. Spring tides rise 22ft. 4ins. Neap tides rise 15ft. 3ins. High water at Trent Falls about 30 minutes after Hull. Spring tides rise 19ft. 8ins. Neap tides rise 12ft. 5ins.

Distance Table

Left Bank			Right Bank	
Miles	*Furlongs*		*Miles*	*Furlongs*
		Trent Falls, junction with River Ouse and River Trent to:		
1	4	*Junction with Market Weighton Canal*		
2	4	Broomfleet		
		Whitton	2	6
5	4	Brough		
		Winteringham Haven	5	4
		Ferriby Sluice, *junction with River Ancholme Drainage and Navigation*	8	4
		South Ferriby	9	2
9	—	North Ferriby		
		Chalderness	11	—
		Barton-upon-Humber	12	2
12	—	Hessle		
		New Holland	15	4
17	—	Hull, *junction with River Hull*		

River Idle (51)

The river is little used for navigation as the depth of the water particularly near Misson is unlikely to be more than eighteen inches. Bawtry is a pleasant town and worth a visit. The navigation was originally promoted by an Act in 1720. Due to the artificial cut made near Bawtry, by the old Great Northern Railway Company, the river wharf at Bawtry has become silted and useless. Craft with a very shallow draught can proceed another 8 miles upstream from Bawtry.

Authority	Severn-Trent Water Authority, Abelson House, 2297 Coventry Road, Sheldon, Birmingham, B26 3PS. Tel. 021-743 4222.
From and to	Stockwith to Bawtry Bridge.
Distance	$10\frac{7}{8}$ miles.
Length	Unlimited.
Beam	18ft.
Draught	To Idle Stop, 2ft. 6ins. Above, 1ft. 6ins.
Headroom	9ft.
Tow-path	Original path is unusable in most places.

Special note	Navigation rights were extinguished by the Trent River Authority (General Powers) Act 1972, Section 10, but the river can be used for boats. Conditions do vary considerably as land drainage is regarded as the paramount function.

Locks	Sluice-gate at West Stockwith. (Sluice-keeper raises gate). This is a sluice, the gates being raised vertically. Boats can only pass twice daily when there is low water in the tidal Trent. This is done to facilitate drainage.
Connections	Joins the River Trent at Stockwith.
Tides	High water at Stockwith about 2 to 2½ hours after Hull.

Distance Table

Bawtry to:

	Miles	Furlongs
Misson	3	4
Idle Stop	6	1
Misterton and Haxey Road Bridge	9	—
Misterton Soss	10	—
Stockwith, *junction with River Trent*	10	7

Kennet and Avon Canal and Navigation (52)

This canal is under reconstruction and since 1951 it has not been possible to navigate it throughout. Other sections may be opened as repairs are effected and therefore local enquiries are advised.

The navigation was promoted by Acts in 1794, 1796, 1798, 1801, 1805, 1809 and 1813. There are a number of special features of the canal which are as follows:

Crofton Pumping Station contains two engines, one being a James Watt Condensing engine. Recent research has disclosed that the other, previously thought to have been of Watt vintage, is a rebuild of a Sims Combined engine of 1844. The existing Watt engine dates from 1810.

Bruce Tunnel with a fine inscription over its eastern portico and through which the canal passes at Savernake. Length 502 yards, and of exceptionally large bore.

The famous flight of 29 locks at Devizes—the second longest flight in Great Britain—with its regularly laid out side pounds over the middle 17 locks—and said to be the best designed flight of locks in the country.

The aqueducts at Dundas and Avoncliffe, near Limpley Stoke, twice carrying the beautiful 10 mile Bath-Bradford pound from side to side of the Avon Valley, and across river and railway.

Claverton Pumping Station, near Bath. The design of this plant is attributed to John Rennie. Restoration work has been undertaken by the Engineering Department of Bath University with the approval of The British Waterways Board. Until recently prior application for permission to view had to be made to B.W.B. Dock Office, Gloucester, but this arrangement may change with the restoration.

The canal provides a wide through route across Britain. It has great amenity value throughout its length, climbing through Great and Little Bedwyn to a summit of over 400 feet. Newbury, Devizes and Bradford-on-Avon are very attractive market towns and from Bradford-on-Avon some of the finest scenery in England is found and it can be truly said to rival the Welsh section of the Shropshire Union Canal. The aqueducts at Avoncliffe and Dundas near Monkton Coombe, mentioned above, are in a good state of preservation after over 150 years and are a fine tribute to the sound design and building of our forefathers but there are some arrears of maintenance.

The approach to Bath is delightful through the pretty Avon Valley and once the City of Bath is reached a unique journey through short tunnels takes one to the top of the six locks at Bath. Here again the lay-out of the locks is a wonder of engineering, as they climb down the hill round very tight corners. There are numerous places to launch trailed craft in the canal, and already the opened sections are busy with cruisers. The country round the Vale of the White Horse and Savernake Forest make the restoration of this canal an urgent necessity.

Local information can be obtained from the Kennet and Avon Canal Trust Ltd., The Wharf, Couch Lane, Devizes, Wiltshire, SN10 1EB, or from the Section Inspectors of B.W.B. (Mr. C. Rogers) at Lower Wharf, Padworth Reading, RG7 4JS. Tel. Woolhampton (073 521) 2277; and Mr. S. Miles, Devizes Workshops, Devizes, Wilts. Tel. Devizes (0380) 2859.

There is water in most of the canal and it can be used by canoes, dinghies, etc. for most of its length providing that they can be portaged around unusable locks.

At the present moment three sections of the canal have been designated as 'cruiseways'. These are from Reading to the tail of Tile Mill Lock No. 99, from the head of Bulls Lock No. 88, to the tail of Hamstead Lock No. 81 (in the Newbury area) and from the tail of Bath Botton Lock No. 7 to the tail of Hanham Lock No. 1 (junction with River Avon under jurisdiction of Bristol Corporation). B.W.B. will doubtless in due course wish to upgrade the waterway to cruiseway status when it is re-opened throughout.

The Kennet and Avon Canal Trust Ltd. raise funds for restoration and their efforts are linked to local authorities and others who have subscribed to the funds to restore the navigation. Restoration commenced in 1964 with the repair of Sulhampstead Lock, 8 miles west of Reading, and now navigation extends to Padworth Lock No. 96. Ufton Lock No. 98 has been de-gated and is not now used. Padworth Lock No. 96 and Aldermaston Lock No. 95 are scheduled to be restored by 1985, but further progress from Reading is delayed by the need to repair turf sided locks which are costly to re-build.

Aldermaston Bridge was re-opened in October 1981 with a new electrically operated lifting bridge. Two other serious problems were the Devizes flight of 29 locks and the two mile length of canal from Limpley Stoke to Avoncliff Aqueduct. The former has benefited from a job creation scheme backed by the financial help of the Kennet District Council. The Devizes flight is now awaiting more finance to fit the gates to the remaining 21 locks. The latter section of canal has always had a serious leakage problem and has been dry for years. A job creation scheme has dealt with this problem and finance for materials was provided by the Trust, work was sponsored by the Wiltshire County Council. All three of these projects had the expert advice and help of B.W.B.

Navigation is now possible from Greenham Lock No. 86, through Hungerford and Frox-field, to Crofton Pump. Crofton Locks (9) have still be be restored, but from the top of, Lock No. 55 the summit level and Bruce Tunnel, can be used to the top of Devizes Locks. Parts of the waterway are coming into use on the next sction to Bath but problems have been overcome at the two aqueducts. Locks are in order throughout this section but at Bath, a major rebuild has been necessary and in the Bath flight lock Nos 8 and 9 have been combined into one deep lock. This merging of two locks and the abolition of Ufton Lock has reduced the total lockage to 104.

The Trust have an office and canal shop at Devizes Wharf and donations are warmly welcomed. This is the biggest restoration project in the country, and finance is now the only obstacle remaining to re-opening this navigation.

For navigation from Bristol, to the sea and up to Sharpness, see the River Avon (Bristol) section, as this journey needs an experienced skipper and the right sort of sea going boat.

Authority	British Waterways Board.
From and to	Junction with the River Thames at Reading to junction with the River Avon at Hanham.

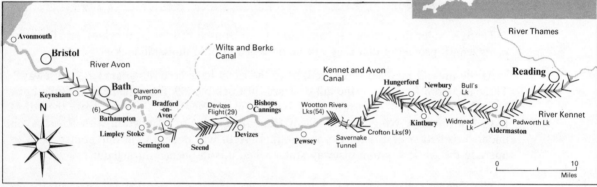

General remarks	This navigation consists of the River Kennet Navigation, Kennet and Avon Canal and the River Avon Navigation. It is the southern-most of the three which may be termed 'Across England Waterways' and links the River Thames with the Bristol Channel through Bristol and Avonmouth. Blakes Lock at Reading is controlled by the Thames Water Authority. 117ft 6ins x 18ft x 3ft.
Distance	86½ miles.

Kennet River

Length	Inside of lock top mitre to inside of lower mitre, 79ft. Usable length (inside lower mitre to top end sill), 71ft. 6ins.
Width	Between quion faces, 15ft. The size of craft which can negotiate the locks depends upon the shape. A craft of 14ft. beam would be limited to about 67ft. in length, but a narrow boat say 6ft. 10ins. × 71ft. 10ins. would be able to pass through.

Kennet and Avon Canal

Length	73ft.
Beam	13ft. 10ins.
Draught	3ft. 6ins.
Headroom	8ft. 10ins.*

* An obstruction at Newbury gives less than this headroom.

Avon River

Length	75ft.
Beam	16ft.
Draught	3ft. 6ins.
Headroom	8ft. 9ins.*
Locks	104 Locks Nos. 1–6 on the River Avon rise from Hanham. Locks Nos. 7 to 54 rise, on the canal section, from Bath. Locks. Nos. 55 to 85 fall to Newbury where the canal section ends. Locks Nos. 86 to 106 on the River Kennet section fall to Reading. (Locks have not been renumbered to allow for the two deletions.)
Bridges	Numerous. (Some are swing bridges). Aldermaston (Electrically operated lift bridge) Some hand operated bridges are being mechanised.
Tunnels	Savernake, 502 yards. No tow-path. Boats hauled through by means of chains fixed to side wall. Two short tunnels in Bath.
Tow-path	Throughout navigation except Savernake Tunnel.
Obstruction	The Newbury obstruction is a wartime temporary bridge still in place, underside about 6ft. 6ins. above normal water level. The Southern Electricity Board Station at Greenham Mill, Newbury, will on request, adjust the water level to give greater headway. If coming from the west there is a telephone box on Newbury Wharf, near the bridge. If approaching from the east, a personal call at the Electricity Station, which is near Greenham Lock will be preferable.

Distance Table

High Bridge, Reading, commencement of River Kennet Section and junction with portion of River Kennet under jurisdiction of the Thames Water Authority to:

	Miles	Furlongs
County Lock No. 106	—	4
Fobney Lock No. 105	1	4
Southcote Lock No. 104	2	4
Burghfield Village	3	4
Burghfield Lock No. 103	4	—
Garston Lock No. 102	5	2
Shenfield Lock No. 101	6	—
Sulhamstead Lock No. 100	6	5
Tile Mill Lock No. 99	8	—
Ufton Lock No. 98 (now disused and degated)	8	6
Towney Lock No. 97	8	3
Padworth Lock No. 96	10	—
Aldermaston Lock No. 95	10	2
Woolhampton Mill and Lock No. 94	12	—
Heals Lock No. 93 (also called Hales)	13	2
Midgham Lock No. 92	13	6
Colthrop Lock No. 91	14	4
Monkey Marsh Lock No. 90	15	—

Distance Table

	Miles	Furlongs
Widmead Lock No. 89	16	—
Bulls Lock No. 88	16	2
Ham Mills Lock No. 87	17	—
Greenham Lock No. 86	18	—
Newbury Wharf, commencement of Kennet and Avon Canal Section		
(Newbury Lock No. 85)	18	4
Guyers Lock No. 84	19	4
Higg's Lock No. 83	20	—
Benham Lock No. 82	20	5
Hamstead Lock No. 81	22	—
Copse Lock No. 80	22	3
Drewitts Lock No. 79	22	7
Kintbury Lock No. 78	24	4
Brunsden Lock No. 77	26	1
Wire Lock No. 76	26	7
Dunn Mill Lock No. 75	27	—
Hungerford Lock No. 74	27	4
Hungerford Marsh Lock No. 73	28	1
Cobbler's Lock No. 72	28	4
Picketfield Lock No. 71	29	4

Kennet and Avon Canal at Newbury

Distance Table

	Miles	Furlongs
Froxfield Bottom Lock No. 70	30	—
Froxfield Middle Lock No. 69	30	$1\frac{1}{2}$
Oakfield Down Lock No. 68	30	3
Little Bedwyn Lock No. 67	31	2
Little Bedwyn Field Lock No. 66	31	5
Burnt Mill (or Knight's Mill) Lock No. 65	32	1
Great Bedwyn Church Lock No. 64	32	6
Crofton Bottom Lock No. 63	33	5
Crofton Top Lock No. 55	35	1
Savernake Tunnel, East End (also called Bruce Tunnel)	36	—
Burbage Wharf	37	—
Wootton Rivers Top Lock No. 54	37	1
Wootton Rivers Bottom Lock No. 51	37	7
Brimslade	38	—
Wootton Rivers	38	4
New Mill	39	4
Pewsey Wharf	41	4
Wilcot	43	—
Honey Street Wharf	45	4
Horton Bridge	49	4
*Devizes Top Lock of 29 Locks, No. 50 (Kennet Lock)	53	4
Devizes Bottom Lock No. 22	55	4
Foxhangers	56	—
Wragg's Wharf	56	4
Scott's Wharf	56	6
Seend Lock No. 21 (top)	57	7
Seend Lock No. 17	58	4
Semington Top Lock No. 16	60	3
Tail of Semington Bottom Lock No. 15, junction with Wilts. and Berks. Canal (abandoned) and Semington Wharf	60	4
Hilperton Wharf	63	—
Bradford-on-Avon and Lock No. 14	65	4
Avoncliffe Wharf	67	—
Murhill Quarry	68	—
Limpley Stoke	69	—
Dundas	70	—
Hampton Quarry	72	4
Bathampton Mill	73	—
Darlington Old Wharf	74	—
Sydney Wharf and Pinche's Wharf	74	4
Bath, Top Lock No. 13	74	5
(Bath Locks 8 & 9 have been combined to form a deep lock)		
Bath, Bottom Lock No. 7, *junction with River Avon*	75	2
Bath, River Avon, centre of Bath Old Bridge and commencement of River Avon section	75	4
Weston Lock No. 6	77	6
Railway Bridge	78	2
Railway Bridge	79	4
Kelston Lock No. 5	80	6
Saltford Lock No. 4	81	4
Opposite Golden Valley Wharf	82	—

*Lock No. 49 in the flights is now called Maton Lock. Other locks will be named later.

Distance Table

	Miles	Furlongs
Swinford Lock No. 3	82	2
Centre of Avon and Gloucester Railway Wharf	84	—
Opposite Shellard's Lime Quarry	84	2
Keynsham Lock No. 2	84	4
Londonderry Wharf	85	—
Tail of Hanham Lock No. 1, *junction with River Avon, under jurisdiction of Bristol Corporation*	86	4

Kennet and Avon Canal at Bath

Kyme Eau - Sleaford Canal (53)

This navigation was abandoned by Act of Parliament in 1878. The lower portion was open to navigation from Ewerby Waithe Common to the River Witham until recently, when the lock at Lower Kyme was replaced by a sluice gate. Craft 70ft by 14ft by 3ft can navigate up to Lower Kyme Sluice, a distance of one mile and 5 furlongs. The original Act was passed in 1794. As we go to press we are advised that Lower Kyme Lock is to be repaired. The section below South Kyme village is called Kyme Eau and the navigation is carried through high embankments.

Authority	Anglian Water Authority, 50, Wide Bargate, Boston, Lincs. Tel. Boston (0205) 5661.
From and to	Chapel Hill, junction with River Witham to Sleaford.
Distance	12¼ miles.
Length	72ft
Beam	14ft 6ins
Draught	3ft
Headroom	7ft 6ins
Bridges	7
Locks	7. (The small craft that might attempt a passage have to be manhandled over the sluices which have been placed across the old locks as the locks are closed at present).
Tow-path	Throughout the navigation, but certain sections are private. Enquiries advised.
Special note	There is a Sleaford Navigation Society and enquiries should be sent to Mr. M. Chapman, 8 Kirkby Close, Southwell, Notts. Telephone: Southwell (0636) 812572. They are anxious to restore the navigation and preserve certain navigation properties. Although closed in 1878, over half survived in use until the 1940s. This is a delightful waterway in an area short of this type of navigation with attractive stretches.

Distance Table
Sleaford (Carre Street Wharf) to:

	Miles	Furlongs
Cogglesford Lock and Mill	–	5
Dyers Mill or Bone Mill Lock	1	4
Corn Mill Lock (This is the only mill working)	2	3
Paper Mill Lock	2	5
Haverholme Lock (Haverholme Priory)	3	4
Cobblers Lock	4	5
Ewerby Waithe Common	5	6
South Kyme	8	–
Lower Kyme Lock	10	5
Chapel Hill, *junction with River Witham*	12	2

(Corn Mill Lock and Haverholme Lock are on private property, and permission is needed to inspect.)

Lake District (54)

An area of great beauty, it is possible to canoe from Derwentwater to Lake Bassenthwaite, but otherwise the lakes are not connected. Launching advice can be obtained from The National Trust (N.W. Area), Broadland, Ambleside, Cumbria.

The principal lakes are as follows:
Power boating is permitted on Windermere, Ullswater and Coniston Water.

Buttermere (National Trust)	$1\frac{1}{2} \times \frac{1}{2}$ miles. Private, but can be used with permission.
Crummock Water (National Trust)	$2\frac{1}{2} \times \frac{3}{4}$ miles. Private, but can be used with permission.
Thirlmere	$3\frac{3}{4} \times \frac{1}{2}$ miles. Private, Manchester Corporation reservoir. No access.
Ullswater	$7\frac{1}{2} \times \frac{3}{4}$ miles. No permission required.
Derwentwater	$3 \times 1\frac{1}{4}$ miles. Private, but permission to navigate can be obtained.
Bassenthwaite	$4 \times \frac{3}{4}$ miles. As for Derwentwater.
Coniston	$5 \times \frac{1}{2}$ miles.
Wastwater	$3 \times \frac{1}{2}$ miles.
Haweswater	$4 \times \frac{1}{2}$ miles. Reservoir, private.
Windermere	$10\frac{1}{2} \times 1\frac{1}{4}$ miles. No permission required.

Lake Windermere

The most popular lake is Windermere being the biggest, and fuller details are listed below.

Authority	South Lakeland District Council, P.O. 18 Stricklandgate House, Kendal, Cumbria LA9 4QQ. Tel. Kendal (0539) 24007.
From and to	Waterhead Public Pier to Lakeside.
Distance	$10\frac{1}{2}$ miles.
Dimensions	There is no restriction on size.
Locks	None.
Regulations	The Lake is controlled by the Lake Windermere (Collision Rules) Order 1961 (Statutory Instrument 1961 No. 343). There are Lake Wardens and Police Patrols in boats equipped with two-way radio equipment. (Lake Patrol telephone: Windermere 2353).
Facilities	There are facilities for all water sports on the Lake and a number of pleasure boats giving transport services. Free access is provided at Bellman Landing, Storrs Park at Windermere, and at the Promenade, Waterhead, Ambleside. A slipway is provided by the Council's Boathaven at Parsonage Bay.
Navigation notes	A chart of the Lake is published in an information booklet issued by the authority on application. Visitors are strongly urged to obtain a copy.
Moorings	The authority provides moorings as well as private boatyards. Mooring overnight on the lake is prohibited.

Lancaster Canal(55)

This waterway was promoted under Acts passed in 1792, 1793, 1796, 1800, 1807 and 1819. A large scale undertaking, it commenced at Kendal 144 feet nine inches above sea level and ran due south through Hincaster Tunnel to Tewitfield through eight locks. This section is now closed and the navigation commences at the foot of the locks and runs over the Lancaster Aqueduct, a very fine structure built by John Rennie, to Preston. The canal has beautiful scenery throughout but is isolated, apart from an entrance from the sea via the Glasson Dock branch. Its fame rests in some degree on the wonderful views of Morecambe Bay obtained from the canal. Lancaster and Preston are both tourist centres worthy of closer inspection. Glasson Dock has a Scottish quality and numerous facilities are available, and lovely Cockermouth Abbey is nearby. The district is full of surprises particularly to a visitor from the south.

The canal was planned to proceed from Preston across an aqueduct to the Leeds and Liverpool Canal, but this route was never opened, though a tramroad linking the two canals was in use until its closure by the London and North-Western Railway in 1879.

Over two miles of the canal in Preston have been closed; it used to terminate at South Basin Wharf. The aqueduct over the River Lune is 600 feet long and was completed in 1797, its five arches are each of 70 feet span, the canal being approximately 62 feet above the river. The River Wyre aqueduct is smaller and spans the river by one arch 54 feet long.

The waterway was closed to navigation above Tewitfield, by the Transport Act 1955 but the B.W.B. still owns the canal to Stainton and Hincaster Tunnel above that point, the rest of the canal has been sold. The problem of water shortage has been solved in some degree by the disposal of the canal north of Crowpart Bridge. Prolonged rain caused rises in the water table and the pressure build up under the canal caused blow outs.

The circumstances of the loss of the canal through Tewitfield Locks to Kendal are very regrettable as the locks could easily have been repaired; however the M. 6. motorway was placed over the canal, with culverts that would obstruct boats on the canal. At no great cost the M. 6 could have been taken over the canal without obstructing the navigation and the Lancaster Canal Trust, who fought hard to retain the upper section, are now maintaining a constructive and watchful eye on the rest of the navigation, particularly its structures scheduled as ancient monuments.

The Holme to Killington Section must be kept open for water from Killington Reservoir. Usually light craft that can be portaged can reach Stainton. 8½ miles. (B.W.B. control this section).

Authority	British Waterways Board.
From and to	Preston to Tewitfield (branch to Glasson).
Distance	42½ miles. Glasson Branch, 2⅞ miles long.
Length	70ft.
Beam	14ft.
Draught	3ft. 10ins.
Headroom	7ft.
Locks	Main Canal. None. Tewitfield locks are closed. Glasson Branch. 7. Fall from Lodge Hill.

Tow-path	Throughout navigation.
Bridges	Numerous. There are some swing bridges, approx. 140.
Tunnels	None in use. Hincaster Tunnel 377 yds. long is on the isolated and closed section.
Facilities	Five boatyards and several inns. Railway Museum at Carnforth, Garstang best for 'en-route' shopping.

Distance Table

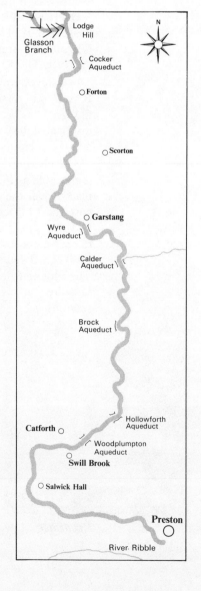

Preston (near Old Ashton Basin) to:

	Miles	Furlongs
Bridge 12 (B. 5411 Road)	—	4
Savick Aqueduct (over Savick Brook)	—	7
Cottam Mill House Bridge	1	4
Salwick Hall Bridge	4	3
Salwick Wharf	4	5
Kirkham Bridge	5	—
Swill Brook Basin	7	4
Woodplumpton Aqueduct (Woodplumpton Brook)	7	6
Hollowforth Aqueduct (Barton Brook)	9	1½
Roebuck Bridge	11	4
Myerscough Hall Bridge (Myerscough Hall one mile)	11	6
Brock Aqueduct (River Brook)	12	3
Preston—Lancaster Road Bridge (A.6) ...	12	5
Calder Aqueduct (River Calder)	14	4
Greenhalgh Castle and Bridge	15	6
Wyre Aqueduct (River Wyre)	16	4
Garstang	16	7
Richmond Bridge and Basin	22	6
Cocker Aqueduct (River Cocker)	23	2
Lodge Hill, *junction with Glasson Dock Branch*	24	1
Galgate Basin Wharf	24	2
Conder Aqueduct (River Conder)	24	6
Scotforth Bridge (commencement at Burrow Heights cutting)	26	3
British Waterways Board Depot	29	2
Lancaster Basin	29	4
River Lune Aqueduct	31	7
Hest Bank	34	4
Bolton-le-Sands (Packet Boat Hotel) ...	35	6
Carnforth	38	2
Motorway M. 6	38	7
Keer Aqueduct (River Keer)	40	4
Disused Quarry Branch (Lovers Creek)	41	—
Berwick Hall and Bridge	41	4
Tewitfield, Old Turnpike Bridge	42	—
Tewitfield (bottom of closed locks)	42	2

Glasson Dock Branch

Lodge Hill, junction with Main Line to:

	Miles	Furlongs
Lock No. 1	—	0½

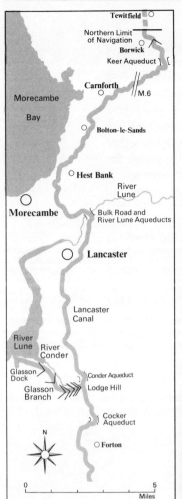

Distance Table						Miles	Furlongs
Lock No. 2 ...	...	...	...	...	...	—	3
Lock No. 3 ...	...	...	...	...	...	—	4
Lock No. 4 ...	...	...	...	...	...	1	0
Lock No. 5 ...	...	...	...	...	...	1	4
Lock No. 6 (Thurnham Mill)		...	...	...	1	6
Lancaster—Cockerham Road (A. 588) ...		...		1	7
Entrance to Glasson Dock		...	...	...	2	5
Glasson Basin Lock. No. 7, *junction with Glasson*							
Dock, belonging to Lancaster Port Commissioners				2	7

Lancaster Canal. Rennie's aqueduct over
the river Lune at Lancaster

River Lee (56)

The river can be entered either through Limehouse Basin, $3\frac{1}{2}$ miles below Tower Bridge, or through Bow Creek. Below Lee Bridge there are several subsidiary canalised waterways, the most important being Bow Creek, the Old River Lee, the City Mills River and Waterworks River, St. Thomas's Creek, Abbey Creek and Channelsea River.

The Hertford Union (or Ducketts) Canal connects the waterway with the Regents (now Grand Union) Canal about 3 miles above the entrance. The River Stort joins the River Lee at Fieldes Weir, Hoddesdon, 7 miles below Hertford. Previously the river had its own lock at Limehouse, but this has been filled in and a short canal has been cut to join the river at Limehouse Basin. The entrance lock can handle 30 wide barges per hour and is fully mechanized. (350ft. $\times$ 60ft. $\times$ 20ft.) The bridge over the entrance lock is an opening one. The original Acts for this waterway were passed in 1425, 1430, 1561, 1767, 1779, 1805 and 1824. The route is industrial in the lower reaches, but the Lee Valley has been a keen talking point for preservationists. The section from the junction with the Stort to Hertford is very fine and includes Great Amwell, the beginning of the famous New River. Sir Hugh Myddleton's water supply channel is maintained as an ornamental waterway that should be inspected by all canal enthusiasts. The Stort is probably the prettiest navigation in the south, has many mills and lock houses, and was originally promoted under Acts dated 1759 and 1766. Hunsdon Lock, with its adjoining mill, mentioned in the Domesday Book, is the loveliest of many attractive river places. The short cut nearby the lock is navigable for very small craft only.

The Lee and Stort both carry a large amount of land drainage water at flood times, and after heavy rains the headroom under the bridges is greatly reduced.

A new channel and lock to replace Hard Mead No. 3 has been completed.

Authority	British Waterways Board.
From and to	River Thames to Hertford.
Distance	From the entrance to Hertford Town Mill, $27\frac{3}{4}$ miles.
Tow-path	Throughout navigation, except Old River Lee section. St. Thomas's Creek, Bow Creek, Abbey Creek and Channelsea River.

Main Line Limehouse to Hertford

Length	88ft.
Beam	From Limehouse to any point short of Old Ford Locks, 19ft. From Old Ford Locks to any point short of Ponders End Lock, 18ft. From Ponders End Lock to Hertford, 15ft. 9ins.
Draught	From Limehouse to Enfield Lock, 5ft. From Waltham Common Lock to Hertford, 4ft. 9ins.
Headroom	6ft. 9ins. at ordinary water level.

Bow Creek. From junction with Main Line to Barking Road Bridge, about $1\frac{1}{4}$ miles.

Length	90ft.
Beam	19ft. 6ins.
Draught	5ft.

Old River Lee, City Mills River and Waterworks River

Length	88ft.
Beam	19ft.
Headroom	7ft 4ins (High tides can reduce this considerably).
Draught	5ft.

Locks

21 along main river, Limehouse to Hertford. Fall from Hertford.
Bow Creek—Bow Tidal Lock. Fall to Bow Creek, level at high tide.
Bow Back River—City Mills Lock. Fall to Stratford.
Old River Lee—Carpenters Road Lock. (Disused).
Fall from Carpenters Road.
(Marsh Gate Lock has been disused for many years).
Channelsea River—Abbey Mill Lock (was closed in 1946).
Fall from Stratford.
Ware Lock is controlled by the Thames Water Authority.

Tides
As far as Old Ford Locks, all branches of the river are tidal.
High water at Limehouse about 10 minutes before London Bridge.
Spring tides rise 20ft., Neap tides rise 16ft.
Old Ford Locks about 3 minutes after London Bridge.

Bridges	60.
Approx. time to navigate	From River Thames to Hertford, approximately one day. From River Thames to Bishops Stortford (via Rivers Lee and Stort), one and a half days.
Speed limit	3 miles per hour in artificial cuts and 4 miles per hour in old Navigation channels.
Sunday navigation	The locks are open on Sundays in the summer season. Owners of licensed craft can operate the locks themselves if they pass a lock operating test. The Traffic Supervisor, Bow Locks, can arrange such a test.
Facilities	At least four boatyards and riverside inns.

Bow Back Rivers

In the area of Bow, London, adjoining the River Lee, are the Bow Back Rivers. It was said that King Alfred had them dug as a defence measure against the Danes to draw off water from the main river. In the industrial revolution these channels were used to drive mills such as Three Mills, City Mills, etc., and they were improved for navigation about 1870, but some of the waterways now carry little traffic. West Ham Corporation greatly improved the drainage of the area and improved the navigation channels in 1933–35. Abbey Mill Lock was eliminated after the last war and a number of channels have fallen into disuse. The jurisdiction of the B.W.B. on these back rivers relates to certain improvement works (including Prescott Channel and Sluices) carried out in the 1930's, mainly for flood prevention purposes, and the jurisdiction of the B.W.B. does not extend up the Channelsea River.

At the present moment City Mills Lock and Carpenters Road Lock are disused. The latter lock has radial gates.

This network of waterways with a number of disused channels has an enormous recreational potential in East London and they should be incorporated into the Lee Valley Scheme.

RIVER STORT *(Tributary of the River Lee.)*

Authority	As River Lee.
From and to	Junction with the River Lee at Hoddesdon to Bishops Stortford.
Distance	13¾ miles.
Length	88ft.
Beam	13ft. 4ins.
Draught	4ft.
Headroom	6ft. 3ins. at ordinary water level.
Locks	15.
Bridges	Numerous.
Speed limit	3 miles per hour in artificial cuts. 4 miles per hour in Old River Navigation channels.
Tow-path	Throughout navigation.
Sunday navigation	The same as the River Lee.

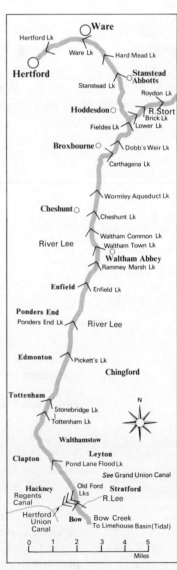

Distance Table

Hertford Town Mill to:

	Miles	Furlongs
Hertford, Dicker Mill Bridge	—	4
Hertford Lock No. 1	—	6
Balance Engine House, New River Water	1	2
Company's Intake Ware Lock No. 2 ...	2	2
Ware Bridge	2	7
Amwell, Hard Mead Lock No. 3 ...	3	6
Amwell Marsh Bridge	4	2
Stanstead Lock No. 4	4	6
Stanstead Bridge	5	1
Rye House Bridge	6	5
Junction with River Stort	7	1
Fieldes Weir Lock No. 5	7	2
Dobbs Weir Lock No. 6	8	—
Carthagena Lock No. 7	8	6
Broxbourne Bridge	9	2
Wormley, Aqueduct Lock No. 8 ...	10	6
Holy Field Marsh Bridge	11	2
Cheshunt Lock No. 9	11	6

								Miles	Fur.
Cheshunt Dock								12	4
Waltham Common Lock No. 10								12	6
Waltham, Town Bridge and Lock No. 11								13	6
Rammey Marsh Lock No. 12								14	—
Enfield Lock, Engineer's Office, Toll Office and British Waterways Board Workshops								14	6
Ponder's End Lock No. 14								16	6
Pickett's Lock No. 15								17	6
Bleak Hall Bridge								18	6
Stonebridge Lock No. 16								20	—
Tottenham Lock No. 17								20	6
Spring Hill Footbridge								21	7
Lee Bridge								23	—
Pond Lane Flood Lock No. 18								23	2
Junction with Hertford Union Canal								24	7
Old Ford Locks No. 19 and Toll Office (Duplicate Locks)								25	—
Junction with Old River Lee through Old Ford Tide Gates ...								25	—
Junction with St. Thomas's Creek								25	6
Bow Bridge								25	6
Bow Toll Office, and *junction with Bow Creek through Bow Tidal Lock*								26	2
Bromley Stop Lock No. 20								27	1
Britannia Stop Lock No. 21								27	4
Limehouse, Limehouse Basin								27	5

Navigation of Old River Lee through Old Ford Tide Gates
Old Ford Tide Gates, junction with Main Line of river to:

Junction with Pudding Mill River							—	1
Junction with City Mills River							—	2
Carpenters Road Lock (disused)							—	2½
Junction with Waterworks River							—	3

Pudding Mill River is navigable for 4 furlongs
City Mills River is navigable for 5 furlongs to City Mill
Waterworks River is navigable to West Ham Waterworks also for 5 furlongs

Bow Creek
Head of Bow Creek at tail of Three Mills to:

Junction with Abbey Creek							—	0½
Junction with Main Line of River through Bow Tidal Lock					—	2½
Barking Road Bridge, limit of jurisdiction of British Waterways, and *junction with portion of Bow Creek* under jurisdiction of the Port of London Authority							1	2½

Abbey Creek
Distance from junction with Bow Creek to Abbey Mills, junction with Channelsea River ... ... — 4

Channelsea River
Abbey Mills, junction with Abbey Creek to Phoenix Wharf ... ... — 3½

Distance Table   *Miles   Furlongs*

River Stort

Bishop's Stortford to:

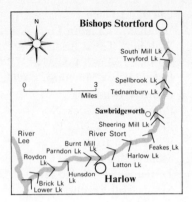

	Miles	Furlongs
South Mill Lock No. 1 ...	1	—
Twyford Lock No. 2 ...	2	—
Spellbrook Lock No. 3 ...	3	—
Tednambury Lock No. 4 ...	4	6
Sawbridgeworth Lock No. 5	5	—
Sheering Mill Lock No. 6	5	4
Feakes Lock No. 7... ...	6	—
Harlow Lock No. 8 ...	7	—
Latton Lock No. 9 ...	8	—
Burnt Mill Lock No. 10 ...	9	2
Parndon Lock No. 11 ...	9	6
Hunsdon Lock No. 12 ...	11	—
Roydon Lock No. 13 ...	12	1
Roydon Brick Lock No. 14	12	6
Roydon Lower Lock No. 15	13	3½
Junction with River Lee ...	13	6

Leeds and Liverpool Canal (57)

The canal was originally constructed under Acts in 1720, 1770, 1783, 1790, 1794 and 1819. A very fine, majestic waterway with outstanding engineering work to be seen and traversed, e.g. Bingley 5 Rise Locks with a rise of 60 feet, and the Burnley Embankment which takes the canal through the spires and chimney pots of Burnley, 60 feet up, and 1256 yards long. A good deal of the canal runs on a high contour over moorland made famous by Charlotte Bronte, in fact Haworth is not far from the canal. The summit pound is 487 feet above sea level.

This canal is the last of the three cross-Pennine canals as the Huddersfield Narrow and the Rochdale Canals are now closed to navigation. As we go to press restoration of these two canals is in progress. At both ends the canal climbs rapidly away from the industrial areas and quickly runs into open country, the high contour it occupies through a considerable section of its length adds to the enjoyment of the visitor. The canal is a wide one, the works on a grand scale, and even in the industrial areas many of the older premises have over the years acquired a mellowed flavour of their own. The views are very fine, with a lock-free pound 17 miles long, with Skipton and its short but unique Springs Branch, leading to Skipton Castle, waiting to be explored.

bird sanctuary country to the River Douglas. Sea-going craft can proceed from the Douglas to the River Ribble and thence by sea to Glasson Dock where they can enter the Lancaster Canal. Such a trip should only be made by experienced navigators.

The Stanley Dock Cut gives access to the Liverpool Docks and the Mersey Estuary but only experienced navigators with suitable craft should enter the Estuary. The Leigh Branch links this canal to the Bridgewater Canal thus avoiding use of the Mersey Estuary. Visitors to the canal will find a remarkable number of places to visit near the canal and a local guidebook is advised for an extended visit.

Authority	British Waterways Board.
From and to	Leeds to Liverpool.
Connections	The most important branches are:
	Rufford Branch to the River Douglas and Ribble Estuary.
	Leigh Branch from Wigan to the northern end of the Bridgewater Canal.
	Stanley Dock Branch to Liverpool Docks.
Distance	Leeds to Liverpool, 127 miles.
Length	From Leeds to tail of 21st lock at Wigan, 62ft.
	From tail of 21st lock to Liverpool, 72ft.
Beam	14ft.
Draught	3ft. 9ins.
Headroom	8ft.
Locks	There are 91 locks in all, 44 on the Leeds side of the summit and 47 on the Liverpool side. Lock gates worked by boat crews. Locks Nos. 1 to 44, rise from Leeds.
	Locks Nos. 45 to 91, fall to Liverpool.
	Special key and large windlass required for this canal. Obtainable from B.W.B. Area Office. Coming from the Bridgewater Canal these can be obtained at Plank Lane Bridge.
Bridges	Numerous. Many of these are swing bridges and care must be taken in operating them, particularly the older wooden bridges.
Tunnels	Foulridge, near Colne. 1,640 yards. No tow-path.
	Gannow, near Burnley. 559 yards. No tow-path.
	Do not enter tunnel if someone is coming towards you.
Facilities	A fair number of boatyards and a number of wayside inns, even on remote sections. Skipton and Keighley (for Bronte Country) are the best overnight stops.

Leigh Branch

From and to	Junction with the Main Leeds and Liverpool Canal at Wigan to junction with the Bridgewater Canal at Leigh
Distance	7½ miles
Length	72ft.
Beam	14ft. 3ins.
Draught	4ft.
Headroom	8ft.

Locks	2. Lock gates worked by boat crews. Fall from Wigan.
Bridges	Numerous. Plank Lane Bridge is electrically operated and prior notice must be given for a passage after normal working hours. B.W.B. licence holders are usually given priority.

Stanley Dock Cut Branch

From and to	Liverpool, junction with Main Line to Stanley Dock.
Distance	Quarter of a mile to Stanley Dock. (It is a further three eights of a mile to the Mersey through Salisbury and Colingwood Locks. Permission is required from the Mersey Docks and Harbour Board.
Dimensions	Same as Leigh Branch.
Locks	Stanley Dock Cut Lock Nos. 1, 2, 3 and 4. Fall from junction with Main Line.

Rufford Branch

From and to	Junction with Main Line at Lathom to junction with River Douglas at Tarleton. The River Douglas is a tributary of the River Ribble. The River Ribble is controlled by Port of Preston Authority, Dock Offices, Preston, Lancs. Tel. Preston (0772) 726711. (They also control the tidal Douglas).
Navigation	River Ribble is navigable to Penwortham Bridge, Preston, but at H.W.S.T. it is possible to go about 2 miles upstream with a small cruiser.
Distance	7¼ miles.
Length	62ft.
Beam	14ft.
Draught	3ft. 6ins.
Headroom	8ft.
Locks	8. Fall from junction with Main Line at Lathom.
Bridges	Numerous.

Springs Branch

From and to	Junction with Main Line to Skipton Rock Staithes.
Distance	Half a mile.

Walton Summit Branch

	Closed and filled in. This branch used to be linked by tramway with the Lancaster Canal at Preston.

Applicable to whole system

Speed Limit	4 miles per hour.

Tow-path   Throughout navigation except through Foulridge and Gannow Tunnels.

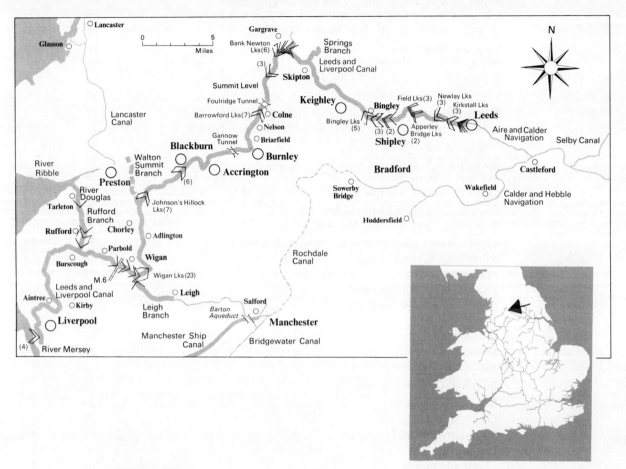

Distance Table

Leeds, River Lock No. 1 and junction with Aire and Calder Navigation to:

	Miles	Furlongs
Leeds Wharf and Office Lock No. 2		2
St. Anne's Ing Lock No. 3	—	4
Oddy Locks Nos. 4 and 5 (staircase)	—	6
Spring Garden's Locks No. 6	1	—
Armley Wharf	1	4
Kirkstall Wharf	3	—
Kirkstall Lock No. 7 (Kirkstall Brewery nearby)	3	4
Kirkstall Forge Locks Nos. 8, 9 and 10 (staircase)	4	—
Newlay Locks Nos. 11, 12 and 13 (staircase)	4	4
Rodley Wharf	6	2
Apperley Bridge, Wharf and Dobson Lock Nos. 14 and 15 (staircase)	9	—
Strangford Basin	9	7
Field Locks Nos. 16, 17 and 18 (staircase)	10	2
Junction with Bradford Canal (abandoned)	12	4
Shipley Warehouses	12	6
Hirst Lock No. 19	14	—
Dowley Gap Locks Nos. 20 and 21 (staircase)	14	3

Distance Table	Miles	Furlongs
Bingley, Dubb Wharf	15	2
Bingley 3 Rise LocksNos. 22, 23 and 24 (staircase)	15	3
Bingley 5 Rise Lock(Nos. 25, 26, 27, 28 and 29 (staircase)	16	4
Marquis of Granby (Granby Bridge) Riddlesden	18	—
Keighley Warehouses	18	3
Silsden	22	4
Kildwick	24	2
Snaygill Bridge	27	6
Skipton Wharf and *junction with Springs Branch*	29	2
Bottom Lock, Gargrave and Holme Bridge Lock Nos. 30*	33	2
Top Gargrave Lock No. 35	35	—
Bottom Lock, Bank Newton No. 36	35	2
Top Lock, Bank Newton No. 41	35	6
Cross Keys Inn, East Marton	38	—
Bottom Lock, Greenberfield No. 42	40	4
Top Lock, Greenberfield No. 44	40	6
Coates Wharf (Barnoldswick distant half a mile)	41	4
Salterforth Wharves	43	4
Foulridge Wharf	45	—
Foulridge Tunnel (east end)	45	1
Foulridge Tunnel (west end)	46	1
Top Lock, Barrowford No. 45	46	6
Bottom Lock, Barrowford No. 51	47	4
Nelson	48	6
Brierfield	50	2
Bankhall Colliery	53	—
Burnley Wharf	54	4
Gannow Tunnel	56	—
Rose Grove Wharf	56	4
Hapton Bridge	58	2
Clayton-le-moors	62	4
Church Kirk Warehouses (Accrington distant one mile)	63	6
Rishton	66	—
Whitebirk Power Station	68	4
Whitebirk Bridge	68	6
Blackburn, Eanam Warehouses	70	2
Blackburn Top Lock No. 52	71	—
Blackburn, Nova Scotia Wharf and Blackburn Bottom Lock No. 57	71	4
Cherry Tree Wharf	73	—
Stamworth Bridge and Quarries	75	—
Riley Green	76	—
Wheelton Wharves	78	6
Top Lock, Johnson's Hillock Lock No. 58	79	2
Tail of Bottom Lock, Johnson's Hillock Lock No. 64 and *junction with Walton Summit Branch (now closed)*	79	6
Botany Wharf (Chorley distant one mile)	81	—
Cowling Bridge	82	2
Adlington	85	—

* The Gargrave Locks 30—35 are sometimes named as follows:
   30, Holme Bridge. 31, Eshton Road. 32, Higherland. 33, Anchor. 34, Scarland. 35, Stegneck.

Distance Table

	Miles	Furlongs
Red Rock Bridge ...	87	4
Wigan Top Lock No. 65 ...	90	—
Rose Bridge ...	91	—
Branch to Ince Hall Collieries ...	91	4
Junction with Leigh Branch, between Locks Nos. 85 and 86 ...	92	—
Wigan Bottom Lock No. 87 ...	92	2
Wigan Warehouses...	92	4
Pagefield New Lock No. 88 ...	93	3
Ell Meadow Lock No. 89 ...	94	—
M.6 Motorway ...	95	—
Dean Lock No. 90, Gathurst (two locks side by side) ...	96	—
Appley Bridge ...	97	4
Appley Lock No. 91 (use deep lock) ...	98	—
Parbold ...	99	4
Junction with Rufford Branch ...	102	4
Burscough Bridge Wharf ...	103	2
Burscough, New Lane Bridge ...	104	2
Scarisbrook, Heaton's Bridge ...	106	—
Scarisbrook Bridge (Southport distance 4 miles) ...	107	—
Halsall Bridge ...	108	4
Dawn Holland Cross Bridge ...	110	6
Lydiate, Hill Bridge ...	112	6
Lollies Bridge (nearby Scotch Pipers Inn, Lancashire's oldest inn) ...	112	7
Maghull, Red Lion Bridge ...	114	2
Maghull Hall Bridge ...	114	6
Pye's Bridge, Melling ...	116	6
Blue Anchor Bridge and Aintree Racecourse ...	118	—
Old Roan Bridge ...	118	6
Netherton Bridge ...	119	—
Gorsey Lane Bridge ...	121	—
Litherland Bridge ...	122	6
Linacre ...	123	6
Bootle Wharf and Coffee House Bridge ...	124	4
Bankhall Wharf ...	125	4
Sandhills Tip ...	125	6
Sandhills, Commercial Road Wharves ...	126	—
Liverpool, *junction with Stanley Dock Cut* ...	126	4
Liverpool, Wharves ...	127	—

Springs Branch

Junction with Main Line to:

	Miles	Furlongs
Mill Bridge ...	—	2
Skipton Rock Stone Staithes ...	—	4

Leigh Branch

Junction with Main Line to:

	Miles	Furlongs
Poolstock Lock No. 1 and 2 ...	—	1½
Park Lane ...	1	6
Bamfurlong Bridge ...	3	1
Dover Bridge ...	4	—

Distance Table

	Miles	Furlongs
Edge Green Basin	4	4
Plank Lane Bridge	5	4
Bickershaw Colliery Tip	5	6
Leigh Warehouses	7	—
Junction with Stretford and Leigh Branch of Manchester Ship Canal Company's Bridgewater Canal	7	2

Rufford Branch or Lower Douglas Navigation

Junction with Main Line to:

(Lathom Top Lock No. 1, Lathom Bottom Lock No. 2, and Runnel Brow Lock No. 3 follow immediately after canal entrance).

	Miles	Furlongs
Moss Lock No. 4 (Nearby is the Ship Inn, locally called 'The Blood Tub').	—	6
German's Lock No. 5	1	1
Baldwin's Lock No. 6	1	4
Marsh Moss Bridge and Wharves	2	4
Rufford Lock No. 7	3	—
Rufford Canal Warehouse	3	1
Sollom (disused lock)	5	2
Bank Bridge and Wharves	6	2
Town End Bridge and Wharf	6	6
Railway Sidings	7	—
Tarleton Lock No. 8, *junction with tidal River Douglas* ...	7	2
River Ribble, Estuary and *junction with River Douglas*	11	2

(Entry to navigation controlled by the Port of Preston Authority).

Leeds and Liverpool Canal. Swing bridge at Riddlesden

Louth Navigation (58)

This navigation commences in the town of Louth and proceeds through attractive Lincolnshire countryside to the Humber at Tetney. It has been long out of use though it is canoeable and has water in it throughout. It was legally abandoned in 1924. It has been included here as there are proposals to open the canal up to navigation.

Authority	Anglia Water Authority, 50, Wide Bargate, Boston, Lincolnshire. Tel. Boston (0205) 5661.
From and to	Louth to the Humber at Tetney.
Distance	11¾ miles
Length	72ft
Width	15ft
Draught	5ft 6ins
Headroom	Not limited.
Locks	8 (None in use)
Towpath	Throughout waterway.
Remarks	This waterway has been included as there have been a number of suggestions that in the long term this canal would be restored. The AWA is understood to be in favour of its restoration. The problem with this canal was that it was not possible to enter the canal from the Humber at all states of the tide. Entry was limited to one week at HWOST. This gave a draught of 5ft 6ins. For pleasure craft a longer range of tides would suffice. The dimensions listed above are those that applied when the canal was in use.

Distance Table

Louth, River Head to:	*Miles*	*Furlongs*
Louth Top Lock No. 1	–	2
Keddington Lock No. 2	–	5
Ticklepenny Lock No. 3	1	–
Willows Lock No. 4	1	3
Salter Fen Lock No. 5	2	1
Alvingham, Alvingham Lock No. 6	2	4
High Bridge	3	4
Out Fen Lock No. 7	4	–
Austen Fen	5	–
Beargate Bridge	6	–
Firebeacon First Wharf	6	6
Firebeacon Second Wharf	7	–
Fulstow Bridge	7	6
Thoresby Bridge	8	6

Tetney Lock (site)	10	6
Tetney Warehouse	11	–
Sea Bank or White Gate, *end of canal*	11	6

(There is a channel from this point to the Humber, a distance of 3½ miles through the sand flats. The channel was marked by beacons).

Lydney Canal and Harbour (59)

This canal was promoted under an Act dated 1810 and originally connected with Pidcock's Canal which has long been derelict.

Authority	Severn-Trent Water Authority, Lower Severn Division, Southwick Park, Gloucester Road, Tewkesbury, Gloucestershire. Tel. Tewkesbury (0684) 294516.
From and to	Lydney Station to River Severn.
Distance	One mile.

Length	100ft.	
Beam	24ft.	
Draught	12ft.	
Headroom	Unlimited.	
Locks	One. There is one lock between the tidal basin and canal and one pair of tidal gates from tidal basin to Severn Estuary.	
Tow-path	Throughout waterway.	

Accommodation

	Measurements in feet				Average depth of water on outer sill	
	Normal depth	*Length*	*Width*	*Entrance*	*M.H.W.S.*	*M.H.W.N.*
Tidal Basin	24	270	75			
Lower Dock	13½	780	105	33	24*	12*
Upper Dock	12	850	88			

Tolls and charges   On application to Dock Manager.

Manchester Ship Canal (60)

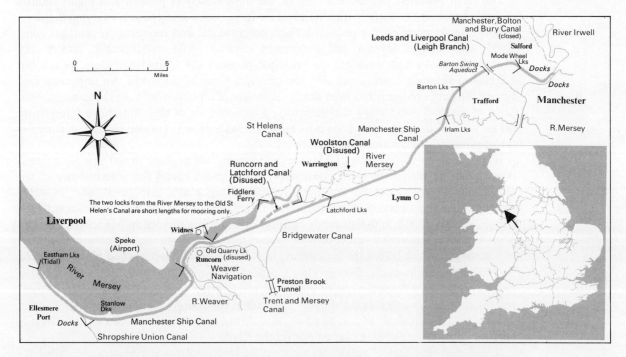

* The sand banks (in the river Severn) over which vessels must pass in approaching or leaving Lydney Harbour vary in level, and are sometimes two feet higher than the level of the sill of the Sea Entrance Gate.

The Port of Manchester, which comprises the Manchester Ship Canal, the great terminal docks at Manchester and other dock systems along the waterway, is controlled by the Manchester Ship Canal Company, which is both proprietor and port authority. The powers of the undertaking are embodied in the Manchester Ship Canal Act, 1885, which constitutes it a statutory company. Later Acts, concerned with financial aid afforded by the municipality of Manchester to the Ship Canal Company during the construction of the canal, accord the corporation an important representation upon the board of directors, and consequently a share in the direction of the undertaking. This combination of municipal and private interests is unique in this country, although not unknown in the case of public utility concerns abroad, and in view of this the following extra historical data has been included for the student by courtesy of the company.

The composition of the board is almost equally divided between the representatives of the shareholders and those of the corporation: there being ten directors elected by the shareholders and eleven appointed by the corporation, constituting a directorship of twenty-one, of which the chairman is elected by the shareholders' directors, while the deputy chairmanship is held by a corporation director. Corporation representatives are necessarily members of the city council, and they automatically retire from the board of the company at the end of their period on the council. On re-election to the council the appointment to the Ship Canal Company's board must be renewed if the re-elected alderman or councillor is to continue to be a director of the company. The influence of the corporation upon the conduct of the company's affairs is solely through its appointed representatives who act upon their own judgment.

Manchester as a port was brought into existence by the construction of the Ship Canal, which was commenced in November 1887 and opened for through traffic on 1st January 1894. The canal which is 36 miles long, was partly achieved by canalising short stretches of the rivers Irwell and Mersey, but for the greater part of its length was a new cutting unrelated to the course of any previous waterway.

The canal provided Manchester, one of the most closely populated and highly industrialised areas in the country, with a terminal for large ocean-going vessels enjoying the same freight rates as ports on the seaboard. Such geographical and economic advantages combined with modern lay-out and equipment ensured rapid development, and to-day Manchester ranks high amongst the principal ports of the United Kingdom, possessing established shipping connections with the principal ports of the world. An important feature of the port's progress has been the development of an industrial zone in the neighbourhood of the docks and along the waterway, a consequence of their enterprise foreseen by the pioneers of the canal and made possible by the wide powers granted to the company for the acquisition of land along the waterway.

It is difficult to-day, in view of Manchester's established position in our maritime transport system, to realise the acute controversy which raged round the practicability of the Ship Canal when the scheme was first advanced. In spite of a traditional belief in water transport and the success of the Bridgewater Canal, constructed to link the town with the Mersey estuary in the mid-eighteenth century, opinion was divided in Manchester on the possible outcome of such a vast enterprise as the Ship Canal. Even the Manchester Chamber of Commerce, which held a special meeting in 1877 to consider reports and plans advanced by two private individuals, George Hicks, a Scotsman, and Hamilton Fulton, a London engineer, approved the scheme with great caution. Outside Manchester it was for the most part held to be an extravagant dream. The public exhibition of Fulton's model aroused some popular enthusiasm which, however, died down, to be revived in 1881 by encouraging news of improvements being carried out on the Clyde.

It was then that Daniel Adamson assumed leadership of the movement and called together the mayors of Manchester and surrounding towns, commercial magnates and capitalists and leaders in the co-operative and labour movements. Thirteen representatives of

Lancashire towns and fifty-five leading merchants and manufacturers attended, a provisional committee was appointed and engineers briefed. Both Hamilton Fulton and Leader Williams prepared plans and reports, and that of the latter for a canal with several levels maintained by locks was the one laid before Parliament. It underwent many modifications in the several Bills which Parliament considered, but the plans finally passed adhered to the principles he originally laid down.

In July, 1882, on the motion of Councillor Bosdin Leech, who became historian of the canal, the Manchester Corporation resolved 'to take up the question of the canal with the vigour and earnestness which its importance demanded', and towards the end of the year a guarantee fund of £25,000 was assured, many Manchester aldermen and councillors subscribed as individuals, but nothing contributed from the public purse. When the promoters later turned to the raising of a fund of £100,000 to meet Parliamentary expenses and deposits, the corporation was approached on the ground that the issue was one of wide local importance. Public opinion was, however, scarcely solid enough to encourage the corporation to respond, although the General Purposes Committee unanimously passed a resolution to the effect that the widening and improving of the rivers Irwell and Mersey and the making of them navigable as a Ship Canal be referred to the Parliamentary sub-committee.

The close of the year saw a great deal of enthusiasm. Public meetings were constantly held, at which the aid of Manchester and adjoining corporations was invoked and M.P.'s were called upon to support the Bill. In November the mayor moved the resolution which had been passed by the General Purposes Committee, that the undertaking and administration of the canal should be vested in a trust for the benefit of the public in general and that Manchester and other local authorities in the neighbourhood of the proposed canal should to authorised to contribute to the cost of, and to take part in, the supervising and the execution of the work and its general management. The press generally held that the council had gone too far, but there was some support for the corporation's contributing towards an undertaking 'which should be of such benefit to the city'. A conference of municipal corporations went to the length of investigating the engineering details and reviewing the economic arguments.

December, 1882, saw the first Bill deposited unaided by any official grants. This provided for the creation of a trust on the application to Parliament of local authorities representing a rateable value of £4,000,000. The principles governing a possible transfer to a public trust are embodied in the Act of 1885. On technical grounds the Examiner refused the Bill as it failed to comply with standing orders. Mammoth petitions were presented and an appeal made to a special committee. Standing orders were conditionally suspended. The Bill passed the Commons, but was rejected by the Lords.

Another effort to obtain Parliamentary powers demanded more money. Undeterred, the promoters completed their arrangements for depositing a second Bill, which provided for a capital of £8,000,000, and Adamson applied to the corporations of Manchester, Salford and the surrounding boroughs to contribute one penny in the pound on their rateable value in order to strengthen the subscription list and emphasize the reality of their support. When Adamson, with his colleagues, set out for London in January to make arrangements for the Parliamentary deposit he left Manchester acutely divided on the propriety of the municipality acceding to his request, but opinion in favour of municipal aid was apparently stiffening, for in May the corporation decided to contribute £10,000 in the event of the Bill being passed.

Pealing of bells and great jubilation in Manchester and Oldham marked the passage of the second Bill through the Lords, but joy was premature, for the Commons, who had passed the first Bill, rejected the second. The committee met immediately and unanimously resolved to persevere in their efforts to make Manchester a port.

Parliament, as if to make amends, handled the third Bill with great celerity. It passed the Lords' committee in May, the Commons' committee on 3rd August, and was referred to the House the same day, obtained its third reading on 5th August and received the royal assent next day, and, according to critical opinion, Manchester was at last fully authorised to start throwing its millions into the 'big ditch'.

The method of raising capital was as acutely debated as the question of finding money for legal expenses. The opinion was advanced, on the one hand, that the workers should not be allowed to risk their savings, and, on the other, that corporations had no right to support private enterprise. Some favoured the local corporations taking shares on the ground that the canal would be a great highway upon which the prosperity of Lancashire would depend; and that the corporation should obtain influence and voting power in order to prevent the canal becoming a money-making concern or passing into the hands of mono-polist railway companies.

The response to the first prospectus was disappointing and the issue was withdrawn and powers sought and obtained for payment of interest out of capital. Adamson, than whom no man deserved better the gratitude of Manchester for his devotion, energy and pluck, re-signed, to be succeeded in the chairmanship by Lord Egerton, an appropriate choice, for his kinsman, the Duke of Bridgewater, had by his perseverance secured the success of what was deemed to be one of the foundations of Manchester's prosperity, and in Lord Egerton's words, 'had to beg every shilling for the Bridgewater Canal'. The difficulties of flotation and the consequent misgivings as to the company's prospects brought into being a consul-tative committee composed of representative citizens—some known critics of the canal were included—which was charged, under the chairmanship of the Mayor of Manchester, to advise on the best methods of raising funds.

In July, 1887, a new prospectus was issued and by 4th August the Board of Trade certifi-cate was signed to the effect that the statutory requirements regarding the issue and accep-tance of capital had been fulfilled. A list of shareholders published in December, 1887, was close upon 39,000. Money difficulties disposed of, the contract was let, and in November Lord Egerton cut the first sod on the site of Eastham Locks. Labour streamed up from all parts of the country and the neighbourhood was dotted with finger-posts directing labourers to the works.

It might be thought that the leaders of this great adventure were now heading along the primrose path with their trials and disappointments behind them, but not so. Landslides occurred, quicksands were encountered and, most costly in time and money of all, unprece-dented floods on several occasions broke through the earthworks, submerging large sections of the works and plant and laying thousands of hands idle.

The cumulative effect of such adversities, the growing bill of legal costs and rising labour charges were making demands upon capital which were unprovided for, and by the end of the year, it was found that additional funds, estimated at not less that £1,700,000 would be required. Encouraged by popular opinion, which now strongly favoured municipal aid, the Special Committee of the Council, recommended assistance to the extent of £3,000,000. The general tenor of the report was to the effect that the work could not be postponed without affecting its efficiency and that funds could not be raised by public appeal in a reasonable time. The committee were of the opinion that the company's estimate of the funds required was too low and that even if the obligation to pay interest out of capital was cancelled, it would take approximately £2,500,000 to complete the work, but that it would be prudent that £3,000,000 should be provided.

This eminently practical report was moved by the mayor, Alderman John Mark, and carried unanimously. Manchester approved it but there were mixed views on the decision to cease interest payments out of capital on the existing share capital. Salford Corporation came forward with an offer of £1,000,000 but the Manchester Bill had already been deposited. It was passed in July, 1891. The corporation raised the money by issues of 3 per cent deben-ture stock and elected five directors by ballot to serve on the board of the company. In

November there were assurances given that progress was according to plan and funds adequate, but the Special Works Committee, which had recently been set up, was divided and there was some criticism of the estimates, with the result that a representative committee was set up and harmony restored.

Whatever doubts there may have been about the adequacy of the available funds were settled in December by the combined efforts of the Mersey and Irwell, which broke into the Irlam section and submerged it to a depth of 20 feet. During the same flood period the Bollin broke in, flooding over 2 miles of cutting. The close of 1891 saw the canal opened as far as the Weaver, the new port of Saltport created, and altogether about half the waterway completed.

By the summer of 1892 disquieting rumours were current again, the canal could not be opened till January, 1894—the first reliable prophesy in this direction! About the same time it became apparent that another £1,250,000 was thought necessary to finish the work. In August the shareholders considered the supplementary estimates and agreed to further borrowing, thereby earning the sympathy and admiration of the whole country. The wary Special Committee recommended £2,000,000 and the City Council again carried the report unanimously. Salford again proposed to contribute, but a borough funds meeting, which had supported the proposal before, rejected it on this occasion. A poll, demanded by the mayor, disclosed a large majority in favour. A poll of Oldham ratepayers also favoured a loan.

The Manchester, Salford and Oldham Bills were taken together before a Select Committee of the Lords, which found itself in the unusual position of having to decide between 'various claimants to the honour of lending money'. The Lords decided to confine themselves to the Manchester Corporation Canal Bill and Oldham and Salford withdrew with the credit of having offered to assist the canal undertaking over its difficulties.

The city's representation on the Board of the company, which has already been described, was provided for in this Bill of 1892.

The spirit with which the city came to the company's aid was admirably expressed by Alderman Sir John Harwood in seconding the motion to accept the first report of the Special Committee. 'If the Council wished to maintain the character of their city', he said, 'they would never suffer so much money subscribed by so many needy people to lie there as a monument of a want of fidelity to their trust as public servants and of loyalty to the cause, the trade and the interests of a great city'. The spirit and fortitude of the original shareholders is beyond praise. As to the promoters, the canal is their imperishable monument. When capital was first being sought, the view was widely held that the canal would benefit the workers greatly, even were no dividends earned for the investors. Certainly the benefit of the undertaking to the community from its earliest days is undisputed, although incalculable. Dividends were first paid for the year 1915 and have since been paid without intermission. Traffic on the Upper Reaches has declined and the canal's future is threatened.

Authority	The Manchester Ship Canal Company, Estates Dept., Dock Office, Trafford Road, Salford M52 2XB. Tel. 061-872 2411.
From and to	Eastham Locks on the left bank of the River Mersey, 6 miles above Liverpool, to Manchester (Woden Street Footbridge above Manchester Docks).
Movement of pleasure craft on the Ship Canal	The movement of pleasure craft on the Ship Canal is, generally speaking, regulated so that pleasure craft do not meet any deep sea vessels. However, should a pleasure craft meet a larger vessel, deep sea or otherwise, they should make appropriate sound signals as indicated in Schedule 1 of the Company's General Bye-laws and act

as required by the International Regulations for Preventing Collisions at Sea and the Company's Bye-laws so far as they are applicable.

Whilst passing another vessel, pleasure craft should avoid getting close in to the canal bank as displacement of water from the passing vessel might cause the pleasure craft to ground.

Naked lights of any kind must not be produced on deck of pleasure craft whilst navigating between Stanlow and Ince.

No pleasure craft should leave any section or berth without first obtaining permission, and information as to traffic movement. It is advisable not to leave until the next section is clear of traffic.

At all times pleasure craft must be alert to receive instructions when passing Hailing Stations, viz. Old Quay Swingbridge, Weston Mersey Lock, Stanlow and Ellesmere Port.

No pleasure craft shall enter the canal without first contacting the nearest control point and obtaining final permission to proceed. Such craft must have written permission of the Harbour Master to enter the canal.

All pleasure craft owners should be familiar with the Company's General Bye-laws with special regard to the rules of navigation and signals.

Canal narrow boats are considered to be unsuitable for navigation on the Manchester Ship Canal.

Distance	36 miles.
Depth	28ft. to Manchester, 30ft. to Ince Oil Berth.
Headroom	70ft.
Locks	5. Mode Wheel, Barton, Irlam, Latchford, Eastham. Fall from Manchester.

Mode Wheel, Barton, Irlam and Latchford Large Locks

Length	600ft. These locks are further divided by an intermediate pair of gates so that alternative locks of 450ft. and 150ft. in length respectively, can be made.
Width	65ft.

Mode Wheel, Barton, Irlam and Latchford Small Locks

Length	350ft. Locks can be sub-divided by intermediate gates giving lengths of 120ft. and 250ft. respectively.

Eastham Large Lock

Length	600ft.
Width	80ft.

Eastham Medium Lock

Length	350ft.
Width	50ft.

Side locks giving access to the Canal from the Tidal River Mersey:

Runcorn Old Quay

Length	250ft.
Beam	45ft.

Weston. Mersey

Length	600ft.
Beam	45ft.

Tow-path   There is a tow-path only from Trafford Mills Ltd., Ordsall Lane, Salford to Woden Street Footbridge, Manchester, at the head of the Canal.

Tides   When the tide in the River Mersey rises to a level of 28ft. 2ins. above Liverpool Bay Datum, which takes place on about 7 or 8 days in a fortnight, it enters the Ship Canal at Eastham and affects the level of the water in the bottom pond of the canal, between Eastham and Latchford Locks.
High water at Eastham 20 minutes after Liverpool.
High water in the Ship Canal Latchford Locks about one hour 15 minutes after Liverpool.
Ordinary Spring tides rise 3ft. 6ins. High Spring tides rise 5ft. 6ins.

Tidal levels above Liverpool Bay Datum at Eastham Locks:

	ft.	ins.
High water at Equinoctial Spring tides ...	31	9
Average High water Spring tides	29	3
Average High water at Neap tides	23	3
Average Low water of Neap tides	7	0
Average Low water of Spring tides	0	11

The levels of the upper sills of the 80ft. and 50ft. locks at Eastham are 32ft. and 29ft. respectively below statutory level. The outer or lower sill of each lock is 13ft. below Liverpool Bay Datum.

Bridges   Provided the height of the masts or funnels is not more than 70ft. 9ins. from the water-line, vessels can pass under the fixed bridges under normal conditions. During floods or high tides only 70ft. is available. Equipment is available at Eastham for removing the tops of masts and/or funnels.

Connections   River Mersey at Eastham.
Shropshire Union Canal at Ellesmere Port.
River Weaver and Weaver Navigation at Western Point. Weston Marsh Lock 229ft. long by 42ft. 8ins. wide.
River Mersey at Warrington. Walton Lock 150ft. by 30ft.

River Irwell, Upper Reach.
Side Locks giving access from the Ship Canal to the tidal River Mersey are situated at Runcorn, Old Quay, and Weston Mersey.

Warning

Small craft owners navigating the canal must obtain the written permission of the Harbour Master. The provisions of the Company's General Bye-law No. 42 in relation to vessels leaving berth must be strictly complied with. Before proceeding on passage, owners of small craft should ascertain from the Harbour Master or his nearest assistant what traffic is moving on the Canal. If there is heavy sluicing at the locks it is not safe for small craft to attempt a passage. Permission to use the canal must be made at least 48 hours before entering the harbour.

Inter-communication between locks

The locks and swing bridges are all connected by private telephone with each other and with the head office and dock office.

General notes

The waterway is only used by small craft as a through route, and care should be taken at all stages of the journey. The slope of the canal bank varies in different sections of the canal and small craft should not navigate too close in to the banks when approaching and passing larger vessels, but in accordance with the provisions of Bye-law 18 small craft should keep out of the track of ocean-going vessels. Those in charge of small craft should familiarise themselves with the Schedule of Signals and Bye-laws relating to navigation contained in the General Bye-law. The entrance to the Ship Canal at Eastham is 25 miles from the Mersey Bar, and the access is from the sea via the lower estuary. The access channel has been excavated to a depth of 13ft. below Liverpool Bay Datum.

The Manchester Ship Canal Act, 1960

Pleasure Craft.

1 Section 52 of the Harbours Clauses Act 1847 as incorporated with the Manchester Ship Canal Acts 1885 to 1960 in its application to the Company and the Harbour Master shall notwithstanding the provisions of section 33 of the Harbours Clauses Act 1847 as also so incorporated extend so as to empower the Harbour Master unless the following conditions have been or will be complied with:
(a) notice in writing of the date and time on which it is proposed to enter the Harbour and of the intended movement of the pleasure craft in the Harbour has been given to the Harbour Master not less than forty-eight hours before the time of entry;
(b) on or before the giving of the said notice there has been produced to the Harbour Master—
(i) (A) a passenger steamer's certificate issued by the Ministry of Transport under Part III of the Merchant Shipping Act 1894 or a certificate showing that the pleasure craft is for the time being classed by Lloyds Register of Shipping or some other classification society approved by the Company; or (B) a certificate given within the previous

twelve months by a surveyor of shipping who is either a member or an associate member of the Institute of Naval Architects or is approved by the Company or by a boat builder who is either a member of the Ship and Boat Builders' National Federation or is approved by the Company that the pleasure craft is seaworthy and suitable for navigation on the Canal; and
(ii) a certificate that the owner is insured in respect of the pleasure craft with an insurer approved by the Company against third party liability in a sum of not less than fifty thousand pounds;
(c) during such time as the pleasure craft is in the Harbour it is—
(i) equipped with the articles specified in the Third Schedule to this Act; and
(ii) in charge of a person over twenty-one years of age who has such experience of navigation as will enable him to navigate in the Harbour with reasonable competence.

2 Notwithstanding the provisions of subsection (1) of this section if the Harbour Master is of the opinion that the entry into or movement of the pleasure craft in the Harbour at the date and time specified in a notice given under paragraph (a) of subsection (1) of this section would or would be likely to cause such interference with commercial traffic in the Harbour as to make it necessary for such entry or movement not to take place at the date and time so specified he may postpone such entry or movement for such period as he considers to be necessary to avoid interference with commercial traffic and shall thereupon notify the Master of the pleasure craft of a date and time as soon thereafter as is reasonably practicable when the pleasure craft may enter the Harbour or move within it.

3 Subsection (1) of this section shall not apply to a pleasure craft requiring to enter the Harbour from the River Mersey owing to stress of weather or other emergency.

Schedule
1 An adequate anchor and cable.
2 At least two warps each being not less than fifty feet in length and of sufficient strength.

3 Such navigation lights and equipment for signalling by sound as will enable the pleasure craft to comply with the International Regulations for Preventing Collisions at Sea and with the Company's Bye-laws.
4 At least two fire extinguishers of a foam type approved by the Ministry of Transport and maintained in accordance with the Ministry's recommendations.
5 Sufficient life-saving apparatus for as many passengers and crew as the pleasure craft is designed to carry.
6 An Admiralty chart or other chart approved by the Company for the Harbour and adjacent waters.
7 A copy of the Company's Bye-laws for the time being in force.
8 A current tidal almanac.

Enquiries should be made to The Harbour Master, Trafford Park 2411, extension 232.
Address: Manchester Ship Canal Company, Dock Office, Trafford Park, Manchester 17.

Mersey and Irwell Navigation
Howley and Woolston Locks together with the Woolston Canal (New Cut) are closed. This only leaves a short section east of Warrington Bridge open to the closed Howley Lock.

River Irwell—Upper Reach

From and to	Manchester, Woden Street Footbridge and junction with Manchester Ship Canal to Hunt's Bank.
Distance	1⅜ miles.
Length	Unlimited.
Beam	25ft.
Draught	Woden Street to Water Street Warehouse, 5ft. 6ins. Water Street Warehouse to Bonded Warehouse, 4ft. 6ins.
Headroom	15ft.
Locks	None.
Tow-path	There is a tow-path from Woden Street Footbridge to Albert Bridge only.

Walton Lock Branch

From and to	Connects Mersey and Irwell Navigation near Arpley with Manchester Ship Canal.
Distance	3½ furlongs.
Length	150ft.
Beam	30ft.

Draught	8ft.
Headroom	14ft. at high water.
Locks	One. Walton. This lock has double gates and the fall may be either way depending on the tide.
Tow-path	None.

Runcorn and Latchford Canal (locally known as The Black Bear Canal)
Closed by virtue of the Manchester Ship Canal (Black Bear Canal Local Enactment) Order 1976 (S.I. 1976 No. 1084) operative from 6th August 1976. Canal site sold to the Warrington Borough Council in 1977.

Tides	High water on spring tides will flow to Woolston Weir on the weir stream of the River Mersey, just below Woolston Lock (now closed). High water at Bank Quay, Warrington, on spring tide sabout 1 hour 15 minutes after Liverpool. Spring tides rise 8ft. to 9ft. High water at Howley Lock on spring tides about 1 hour 20 minutes after Liverpool. Spring tides flow from the River Mersey to the west end of Walton Lock. High water at Walton Lock about 1 hour 20 minutes after Liverpool. Spring tides rise 8ft. to 9ft.

Distance Table

	Side of Canal	Distance from Eastham Locks *Miles*	Distance from Manchester *Miles*
Eastham Locks	—	—	36
Eastham Lay-by	E and W	$\frac{1}{4}$	$35\frac{3}{4}$
Eastham Crane Berth	W	$\frac{1}{2}$	$35\frac{1}{2}$
Bankfield Wharf	W	$\frac{5}{8}$	$35\frac{3}{8}$
Hooton Wharf	W	$1\frac{3}{8}$	$34\frac{5}{8}$
Mount Manisty	E	$1\frac{3}{4}$–$2\frac{3}{8}$	$34\frac{1}{4}$–$33\frac{5}{8}$
Bowaters U. K. Pulp & Paper Mills	W	2	34
Pool Hall Wharf	W	$2\frac{1}{2}$	$33\frac{1}{2}$
Ellesmere Port Wharf *(entrance to Shropshire Union Canal)*	W	$2\frac{7}{8}$	$33\frac{1}{8}$
Ellesmere Port (Grain Warehouse)	W	$3\frac{1}{8}$	$32\frac{7}{8}$
Stuart Wharf	S	$3\frac{1}{2}$	$32\frac{1}{2}$
Manchester Dry Docks Co. Ellesmere Port ...	S	$3\frac{3}{4}$	$32\frac{1}{4}$
Stanlow Wharf	S	$3\frac{7}{8}$	$32\frac{1}{8}$
Associated Ethyl Wharf	S	4	32
I.C.I. (Dyestuffs) Wharf	S	$4\frac{1}{8}$	$31\frac{7}{8}$
Esso Petroleum Co. Barge Wharf	S	$4\frac{3}{8}$	$31\frac{5}{8}$
Stanlow Oil Docks and Turning Basin	N	$4\frac{1}{2}$	$31\frac{1}{2}$
Stanlow Lay-by	S	$4\frac{5}{8}$	$31\frac{3}{8}$
Ince Coaster Berth	S	$5\frac{1}{4}$	$30\frac{7}{8}$
Ince Oil Berth	S	$5\frac{3}{8}$	$30\frac{5}{8}$

Ince Tying-up Berth	S	$5\frac{5}{8}$	$30\frac{3}{8}$
Ince Wharf	S	$6\frac{5}{8}$	$29\frac{3}{8}$
Holpool Gutter	S	$7\frac{3}{4}$	$28\frac{1}{4}$
Frodsham Pumping Stage	S	$8\frac{1}{2}$	$27\frac{1}{2}$
Weaver Mouth	—	$9\frac{7}{8}$	$26\frac{1}{8}$
Weston Marsh Lock, *entrance to Weaver Navigation*	E	$9\frac{7}{8}$	$26\frac{1}{8}$
Weaver Sluices	W	$10\frac{1}{8}$	$25\frac{7}{8}$
Weston Mersey Lock (entrance)	W	$10\frac{7}{8}$	$25\frac{1}{8}$
Weston Point Docks	E	11	25
Delamere Dock, *entrance to Weaver Navigation*	E	$11\frac{1}{8}$	$24\frac{7}{8}$
Weston Point Salt Works (I. C. I.) (Tip)	E	$11\frac{1}{4}$	$24\frac{3}{4}$
Runcorn Lay-by	E	$11\frac{1}{2}$	$24\frac{1}{2}$
Bridgewater Lock (closed)	N	$11\frac{3}{4}$	$24\frac{1}{4}$
Runcorn Docks	S	$12\frac{1}{4}$	$23\frac{3}{4}$
Runcorn Railway Bridge	—	$12\frac{1}{2}$	$23\frac{1}{2}$
Widnes Bridge	—	$12\frac{5}{8}$	$23\frac{3}{8}$
Old Quay Lock	N	13	23
Old Quay Swing Bridge	—	$13\frac{1}{4}$	$22\frac{3}{4}$
I.C.I. (General Chemicals) Wharf	N	$13\frac{1}{2}$	$22\frac{1}{4}$
I.C.I. (Chem. and Met.), Astmoor Wharf	N	14	22
I.C.I. (Chem. and Met.) Works	N	$14\frac{1}{4}$	$21\frac{3}{4}$
Stone Delph	S	$15\frac{1}{8}$	$20\frac{7}{8}$
Randles Sluices	N	$15\frac{3}{8}$	$20\frac{5}{8}$
Moore Lane Lay-by	N	$16\frac{3}{8}$	$19\frac{5}{8}$
Moore Lane Swing Bridge	—	$17\frac{1}{8}$	$18\frac{7}{8}$
Acton Grange Wharf	N	$17\frac{1}{2}$	$18\frac{1}{2}$
Acton Grange Viaduct	—	$17\frac{7}{8}$	$18\frac{1}{8}$
Chester Road Swing Bridge	—	$18\frac{3}{4}$	$17\frac{1}{4}$
Warrington Wharf and Walton Lock	N	19	17
Northwich Road Swing Bridge and Twenty-Steps Lock	—	$19\frac{3}{8}$	$16\frac{5}{8}$
Latchford High Level Bridge	—	$20\frac{1}{8}$	$15\frac{7}{8}$
Knutsford Road Swing Bridge	—	$20\frac{3}{8}$	$15\frac{5}{8}$
Latchford Viaduct	—	$20\frac{3}{4}$	$15\frac{1}{4}$
Latchford Locks	—	21	15
Thelwall Pumping Stage	N	$21\frac{1}{2}$	$14\frac{1}{2}$
Thelwall Ferry	—	$21\frac{3}{4}$	$14\frac{1}{4}$
Statham Pumping Station No. 3 (disused)	N	$22\frac{1}{2}$	$13\frac{1}{2}$
Statham Pumping Station No. 2 ,,	N	$22\frac{3}{4}$	$13\frac{1}{4}$
Statham Pumping Station No. 1 ,,	N	$23\frac{1}{8}$	$12\frac{7}{8}$
Rixton Junction	N	24	12
Warburton High Level Bridge	—	$25\frac{5}{8}$	$10\frac{3}{8}$
Millbank Wharf	S	26	10
Cadishead Ferry	—	$26\frac{5}{8}$	$9\frac{3}{8}$
Cadishead Viaduct	—	$26\frac{7}{8}$	$9\frac{1}{8}$
Partington Coaling Basin	N and S	27–$27\frac{3}{8}$	9–$8\frac{5}{8}$
Irlam Wharf (Lancs. Steel Corpn.)	N	$27\frac{3}{4}$	$8\frac{1}{4}$
Mersey Weir	S	28	8
Irlam Viaduct	—	$28\frac{1}{8}$	$7\frac{7}{8}$
Irlam Wharf (C.W.S.)	N	$28\frac{1}{8}$	$7\frac{7}{8}$

Irlam Locks	—	28⅜	7⅝
Irlam Ferry	—	28⅝	7⅜
Hulmes Bridge Ferry	—	29⅝	6⅜
Barton Locks	—	30⅜	5⅝
Barton Road Swing Bridge	—	31¾	4¼
Barton Swing Aqueduct	—	31¾	4¼
Barton Oil Berth	S	31⅞	4⅛
Irwell Park Lay-by	N	32⅛	3⅞
Irwell Park Wharf	N	32¼	3¾
Eccles Oil Wharf	N	32½	3½
Brown and Polson's Wharf	S	32¾	3¼
Corn Products Ltd	S	32⅞	3⅛
Weaste Oil Wharf	N	33¼	2¾
Weaste Lay-by	N	33½	2½
Weaste Wharf	N	33½	2½
Southern Oil Wharf	N	33⅝	2⅜
Esso Oil Wharf	S	33¾	2¼
Mode Wheel Locks	—	33⅞	2⅛
Manchester Dry Docks Co.	S	34	2
Salford Quay	N	34–34¼	2–1¾
British Oil and Cake Mills	S	34¼	1¾
No. 9 Dock Entrance	N	34¼	1¾
Trafford Wharf	S	34⅜–34⅝	1⅝¾–1⅜
Turning Basin, Nos. 8, 7 and 9 Docks	—	34⅝	1⅜
C.W.S. Sun Mills	S	34¾	1¼
Dock Railway Swing Bridge	—	34⅞	1⅛
Trafford Road Swing Bridge	—	35	1
English and Scottish C.W.S.	N	35⅛	⅞
R. and W. Paul Ltd	N	35¼	¾
Colgate-Palmolive Co.	N	35¼	¾
Spillers Ltd. (J. Jackson and Sons)	N	35⅜	⅝
Trafford Mills	N	35⅜	⅝
Pomona Docks, Nos. 4, 3, 2 and 1	S	35⅜–35⅝	⅝–⅜
Cornbrook Wharf	S	35¾	¼
Woden Street Bridge	—	36	—

Mersey and Irwell Navigation

Main Line, Rixton Junction to Bank Quay, Warrington.

(Woolston New Cut is closed to navigation. Woolston Lock and Howley Lock are closed).

River Irwell Upper Reach

Manchester, Woden Street Footbridge, and junction with Manchester Ship Canal to:

Junction with Hulme Locks Branch of Bridgewater Canal	—	1
Regent Road Bridge	—	2
Prince's Bridge, junction with Manchester, Bolton and Bury Canal (now closed)	—	4
Junction with Manchester and Salford Junction Canal (now closed)	—	5
Manchester Ship Canal Company's Bridgewater Warehouses, Water Street and Irwell Street Bridge	—	6
Albert Bridge	—	7
Bonded Warehouse	1	—

Distance Table								*Miles*	*Furlongs*
Blackfriars Bridge ...	...	...	...	...	...	...	...	1	1
Victoria Bridge and Station Approach ...		...	...	...	...	...	...	1	2
Hunt's Bank	...	...	...	...	...	...	...	1	3

Walton Lock Branch
Junction with Mersey and Irwell Navigation—Main Line—to:

Walton Lock No. 1	...	...	...	...	...	...	...	—	2¼
Junction with Manchester Ship Canal	...	...	...	...	...	—	3¼

Market Weighton Canal (61)

This canal was promoted by an Act of Parliament in 1772 and originally ran nearly to Market Weighton, a distance of 9½ miles. The London and North-Eastern Railway relinquished their interest in the canal by the Market Weighton Drainage Act in 1900, which also authorised abandonment of the upper 3½ mile section. A large drainage scheme has been carried out on the canal which has improved navigation. The entrance lock has now been re-gated following a campaign by the local society, this lock was scheduled as an ancient monument and is usable under certain conditions (owners: Yorkshire River Authority). The navigation right through the entrance lock was abandoned in 1971 under Section 112 of the Transport Act 1968. Visitors to the canal should contact the Market Weighton Canal Society, at 47 Market Place, Market Weighton, York, YO4 3AJ. The short canal at Canal Head to the road has been long derelict. Holme Canal or (Vasasour's Canal).

Authority Market Weighton Drainage Board, Waterloo Buildings, Pocklington, Yorkshire. Tel. Pocklington (075 92) 2115.

From and to Canal Head to the River Humber.

Distance 9½ miles

Length 70ft.

Width 14ft. 10ins.

Draught 4ft. 3ins.

Headroom 9ft. Minimum depending on water level under Newport Bridge (A63)

Locks One. This lock has two pairs of sea-gates and two pairs of navigation gates. Usually fall from Humber, but locks work either way. (2 locks are derelict and another one under reconstruction).

Tow-path Throughout navigation. (East side)

Navigation notes The canal is navigable at present only to Sod Houses Lock from the Humber but work has been carried out on the rest on the canal by the Canal Society. Their Hon. Secretary, Mr. G. B. Miles points out that difficulties in getting into the canal from the Humber have been exaggerated. The best way is to come in from the west and the channel is a straight line from Trent falls but dries out at LW. The channel from the east is deeper and gives a depth of 3ft 3ins at LW but is variable and moves making an up to date chart essential. The entry to the channel off Brough is very variable and the tidal flow is such that it is possible to go aground on the east end of Whitton Sand even on a rising tide. Only suitable craft for a tidal estuary, properly equipped, under the right weather conditions should make the passage.

Small boats, canoes etc., may be launched at Newport, Broomfleet, or Landing Lane.

Keep well clear of land drainage outfalls and in very rainy conditions levels can vary considerably.

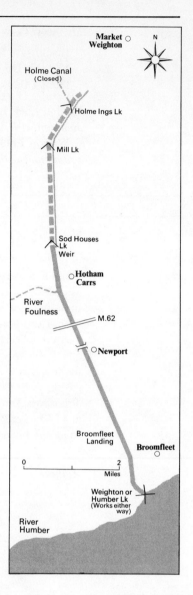

Distance Table

Weighton Lock, junction with Humber to:

	Miles	Furlong
Lantern Lane (Public Footpath to Broomfleet)	–	5
Broomfleet Landing (overnight mooring)	1	–
Brickyard Bridge	1	4
Railway Bridge (Main Line to Hull)	1	6
Landing Lane (Road access to canal, not suitable in wet weather)	2	1
Newport (Dead slow here, in view of numerous obstructions). 3 Inns and Shops. A63 Road Bridge	3	1
Motorway Bridge M62	3	5
Sandholme Landing Bridge	3	7
Sod Houses Lock	5	7
Land of Nod Farm	7	2
Mill Lock	8	–
Holme Ings Lock	8	7½
Canal Head	9	4

River Medway (62)

This river was made navigable by Acts passed in 1664, 1740, 1792, 1802 and 1824. This river is a surprise inasmuch as it is close to London and industrial North Kent, but carries little pleasure traffic. From the commencement at Tonbridge it is flat country to Hampstead, but not by any means dreary since it runs through the 'garden of England' with its orchards and hop fields. It is hilly country from Hampstead to Maidstone, particularly near Teston (pronounced Teeston). There is an ancient bridge near the latter place and also at East Farleigh. Near Branbridges Wharf is a very fine selection of oast houses at Beltring. There are a number of National Trust properties nearby. Tonbridge and Maidstone are fine towns with a number of places of interest to the visitor, e.g., Tonbridge Castle and public school, and at Maidstone the Archbishop's Palace with Leeds Castle nearby. Within the port of Rochester it is possible to embark and disembark at Ship Pier or Blue Boar Pier in the Limehouse Reach or at Strood Pier in Bridge Reach. In Tower Reach, Esplanade Pier may be used. There are other public landing places in the estuary at Commodore Hard, Gillingham, and also nearby at Pier Steps downstream of the dockyard entrance. Upnor Causeway

Sun Pier, Chatham and Town Quay Steps, Rochester, also are available but Strood Esplanade Steps is suitable for dinghies only.

The Medway Lower Navigation Company, a statutory undertaking, was transferred to Medway Ports Authority under the Medway Ports Reorganisation Scheme, 1968, made under the Harbours Act, 1964, as extended by the Docks and Harbours Act, 1966.

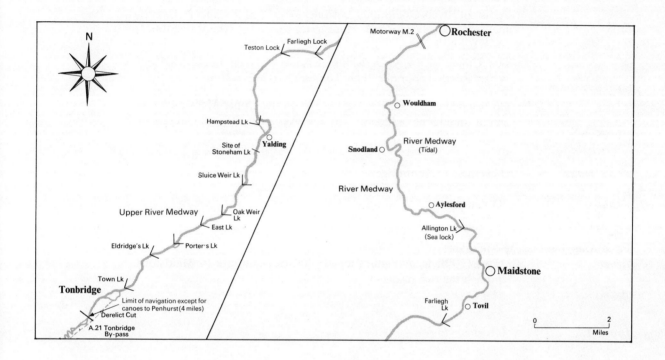

Authority

From Sheerness to Allington Lock

Medway Ports Authority, The Secretary, Sheerness Docks, Sheerness, Kent. ME12 1RX. Tel. Sheerness (0795) 662211.

The chief executive and the Harbour Master are located at this address and have the same telephone number,

The port limits are now from Garrison Point at Sheerness to Allington Lock, and in addition navigational control extends seawards from Sheerness to Medway buoy including the tributaries and creeks thereon of the River Medway. The river between Allington Lock and College Gardens, Maidstone, is now under the jurisdiction of the Southern Water Authority. The Swale, from a line from Shellness on the Isle of Sheppey across the estuary to a point east of The Sportsman Inn at Seasalter thence to the junction with the River Medway opposite Westminster Pier, Sheerness, with the tributaries and creeks thereon.

Resident Engineer, Allington Lock, Nr. Maidstone Kent.
Tel. Maidstone (0622) 52864

From Allington Lock to Tonbridge: Upper Medway Navigation
The Southern Water Authority Kent River and Water Division, Miller House, Lowes Stone Street, Maidstone, Kent. Tel. Maidstone (0622) 55211

Engineer's Department, 76/78, College Road, Maidstone, Kent. Tel. Maidstone (0622) 55211.

Assistant Rivers Operation Controller (Western). Engineer's Department, 76/78 College Road, Maidstone, Kent. Tel. Maidstone (0622) 55211.

The Upper Medway Divisional Engineer, Town Lock, Medway Wharf Road, Tonbridge. Tel. Tonbridge (0732) 4466.

Correspondence regarding navigation on the Upper Medway Navigation should be addressed to the Assistant Rivers Operations Controller (Western)

From and to	Sheerness to Tonbridge.
Distance	43 miles.

From Allington Lock to Maidstone

Length	175ft (100ft in maximum length that can navigate to Maidstone, through the two bridges)
Beam	21ft 6ins
Draught	6ft. 6ins.
Headroom	10ft. 6ins. at Maidstone. Headroom of bridges: Rochester Bridge provides a clearance of 10ft. at the centre of the middle arch at high water ordinary spring tide. At low water the clearance is 39ft., but with a depth of only 2ft. 6ins. in places. Passage under Rochester Bridge should not be attempted by vessels of over 2ft. draught at low water spring tides. Aylesford Bridge, 10ft. Maidstone Bridge, 10ft. 6ins.

Maidstone to Tonbridge

Length	80ft.
Beam	18ft. 6ins.
Draught	Must not exceed 5ft. 6ins, below Hampstead Lock and 4ft. above.
Headroom	*To Tonbridge,* 8ft. 6ins. normal. (Tonbridge, 6ft. 6ins. through the Great Bridge). *Above Tonbridge*, the recognised navigation ceases at the Great Bridge but it is possible to proceed for nearly 2 miles upstream. Barges

used to trade to Leigh as late as 1907. There was an attempt to extend the navigation to Penshurst but this was a failure. Above the Great Bridge there are two channels, the one on the port side going upstream is best, if a headroom of 5ft 3ins is sufficient. The other twisting and narrow route has a headroom of 6ft. The two arms encircle the sports ground and unite at the railway bridge. It is possible to go as far as Long Reach (one of the old river navigation cuts) to Lucifer footbridge but the headroom is only 4ft 8ins. There is a good depth of water under this bridge to the end of Long Reach where navigation ceases at the footbridge in the New Cut below Leigh Sluices.

There is a barrage above Tonbridge but this is usually open.

Locks	One, (Allington Lock) between Rochester and Maidstone, worked by by lock-keepers and open on Sundays and Bank Holidays. Nine locks between Maidstone and Tonbridge worked by boat crews subject to Southern Water Authority's regulations and the purchase of a lock pass which must be obtained before passing through locks. These are generally obtainable at East Farleigh Lock, Yalding Depot and at the Authority's Offices at Maidstone and Leigh.
Tow-path	From New Hythe to Tonbridge, except in Maidstone between Maidstone Bridge and High Level Bridge.
Bridges	Numerous.
Information	A booklet entitled *Boating on the Upper Medway Navigation* is available free from the Southern Water Authority at the addresses given above and should be read before navigating above Allington Lock.
Discharge of polluting matter and litter	The Southern Water Authority, as rivers pollution prevention authority for the whole of the River Medway and its tributaries, look to people who use the river for pleasure purposes for help in keeping both tidal and non-tidal waters as clean as possible by refraining from discharging into them any foul or polluting matter or any refuse or litter. Pollution of non-tidal waters is an offence and, by virtue of a special statutory order, the tidal waters of the River Medway above Millhall, Aylesford, are classed as non-tidal for the purposes of the River (Prevention of Pollution) Act, 1951.
* Navigation notes	The tidal section contains many shoals and it is very shallow at low tide. Proceeding upstream yachtsmen should proceed on the flood tide leaving Rochester Bridge about 2 hours after low water. Coming downstream it is advisable to leave Allington at High Water so as to reach Rochester not later than 4 hours ahead. A useful booklet is published by the Medway Ports Authority.

*See Imray Chart No. Y18 River Medway.

Tides

High Water at Allington Lock about 50 minutes after Sheerness Downstream of Allington Lock there is less than 2 feet of water at low tide, with about 10 feet at high water springs and 7 feet at high water neaps.
The lock is open to traffic 3 hours before and 2 hours after high tide, depth of water permitting.

Medway port operation service

The Medway Ports Authority maintain a Port Operation and Information Service at Garrison Point, Sheerness (Tel. Sheerness (0795) 663025/6) for the purpose of providing radio and radar assistance to all vessels navigating in the River Medway and the Thames Estuary. The Station (Call Sign 'Medway Radio') is manned on a 24 hour basis and keeps a continuous radio watch on the following International V.H.F. Channels: Channels 16, 14, 11, 9 and 22.

Port Operations Headquarters will, on request, pass information relating to shipping movements, navigational information, meteorological and tidal conditions.

SURVEYS Frequent hydrographic surveys of the Channels of the River Medway are carried out, and such surveys can be inspected or purchased from the Port Authority's Offices.

CASUALTIES Should a vessel become stranded or sink, the matter should be immediately reported to the Harbour Master, who can be contacted any time of the day or night by telephoning the Medway Port Operation Service (Sheerness 3025/6), giving the following particulars:
Name and description of vessel. Position and nature of casualty. Whether visible.
Should any craft be observed to be in need of assistance, such assistance may be obtained by telephoning the above Port Operation Service.

PILOTAGE The main navigable channel from the seaward approaches to Upnor is clearly marked by buoys, and is easy to follow. However, the middle reaches of the river are bounded by extensive mud flats and saltings which are covered at high water and provide many secondary channels to the Hoo and Rainham areas.
These channels should not be attempted without reference to large scale charts, a number of which are generally available, and the stranger should beware of straying too far from the main navigable channel for fear of grounding on a falling tide.

Facilities

There are several boatyards and clubs with facilities for visitors. There are a number of riverside inns plus a number very near the river. Excellent shopping at Maidstone and Tonbridge. village shops are close to the river in many places.

Launching sites

Launching of craft is possible at several boatyards at Allington, Maidstone, East Farleigh, Yalding, East Peckam and Tonbridge. A launching ramp at Hampstead Lock is controlled by a lock-keeper.

River Medway. Bridge and lock at East Farleigh

G.H. Pursell

Distance Table

Tonbridge Wharf and Bridge to:

	Miles	Furlongs
Tonbridge Town Lock No. 1	—	2
Eldridge's Lock No.. 2	1	5
Hartlake Wharf and Porter's Lock No. 3	2	5
East Lock No. 4	3	6
Ford Green Bridge	4	2
Oak Weir Lock No. 5	4	5
Norwood Bridge	5	—
Arnold's Mill Head	6	—
Branbridge's Wharf and Arnold's Mills and Sluice Weir Lock No. 6	6	—
Railway Bridge and Stoneham (Stoneham Lock is disused)	7	—
Hutson's Yard	7	2
Mouse Bay	7	4
Yalding Wharf and Anchor Sluice (Anchor Inn)	8	—
Hampstead Lock No. 7	8	2
Wateringbury Bridge	10	—
Teston Bridge	11	4
Teston Lock No. 8	11	1
Barming Bridge	12	6
Farleigh Lock No. 9	13	2
Ellis's Wharf	13	4
Point Shoot	14	2
Tovil Paper Mills and Benstead's and Constable's Wharves	14	4
Maidstone, College Gardens, boundary of the Kent River Authority	15	2
Medway Mill	16	6

Allington Lock No. 10 (sea lock with intermediate pair of gates) (The

Malta Inn) ...	...	...	...	...	...	...	...	...	17	6
Forstal ...	...	...	...	...	...	...	...	...	18	6
Preston ...	...	...	...	...	...	...	...	...	19	—
Aylesford ...	...	...	...	...	...	...	...	...	19	—
Mill Hall ...	...	...	...	...	...	...	...	...	20	—
New Hythe ...	...	...	...	...	...	...	...	...	20	6
Hawkwood, Rochester City Stone		...	...	...	...	...	...	22	—
Snodland ...	...	...	...	...	...	...	...	...	22	6
Halling ...	...	...	...	...	...	...	...	...	24	—
Wouldham ...	...	...	...	...	...	...	...	...	24	6
Cuxton ...	...	...	...	...	...	...	...	...	26	4
Rochester Bridge ...	...	...	...	...	...	...	...	29	—
Chatham ...	...	...	...	...	...	...	...	...	30	2
Brompton and Gillingham		...	...	...	...	...	...	33	6
Port Victoria ...	...	...	...	...	...	...	...	40	6
Mouth of Swale and Queenborough Pier			...	...	...	...	42	—
Sheerness, *junction with the estuary of the River Thames*				...	...	42	6

River Mersey (63)

The river below Garston is only suitable for seagoing vessels as the tides of the Mersey are very dangerous. The navigation channel above Garston is marked by lightbuoys as far as Runcorn Railway Bridge, there are no buoys above Runcorn. This is a tidal navigation though an Act of Parliament was passed in 1805 to enable tolls to be collected.

Authority   **Lower Mersey.** Garston to Liverpool.
Mersey Docks and Harbour Board, Dock Office, Liverpool. L3 1B2. Tel. 051–236–6010.

Upper Mersey. Bank Quay, Warrington, to Garston.
The Upper Mersey Navigation Commissioners have ceased to exist.

From and to   Bank Quay, Warrington, to Liverpool.

Distance   (1) 6½ miles. (2) 18¾ miles.

Length   Unlimited.

Beam   ,,

Draught   At spring tides to Warrington, 9ft.

Headroom   82ft.

Locks   None.

Tow-path   ,,

			Right Bank	

Connections	Weaver Navigation at Weston Point (via The Manchester Ship Canal).
	Leeds and Liverpool (via Liverpool Docks).
	Mersey and Irwell Navigation at Warrington.
	Manchester Ship Canal at Weston and Eastham. (Runcorn Lock to M.S.C. was closed in 1970).
Caution	Due to dangerous tides and, in the Upper Mersey, constantly shifting sandbanks, navigation in the River Mersey should not be attempted by any craft without up to date advice from the navigation authorities.
Tides	High water at Garston 13 minutes after Liverpool.
	High water at Weston Point 25 minutes after Liverpool.
	High water at Runcorn 30 minutes after Liverpool.
	High water at Bank Quay, Warrington, 1 hour and 12 minutes after Liverpool.
	At Warrington spring tides rise 8ft. to 9ft.

Distance Table

Left Bank			Right Bank	
Miles	Furlongs		Miles	Furlongs
		Bank Quay, Warrington to:		
7	2	Runcorn, *junction with Manchester Ship Canal through Old Quay Lock,* Runcorn Runcorn Bridge.		
7	4	Widnes, West Bank Dock	7	5
8	4	Runcorn (Bridgewater Lock was closed in 1920)		
9	4	Weston Point, *junction with Manchester Ship Canal through Weston Mersey Lock*		
18	2	*Eastham, junction with main entrance to Manchester Ship Canal*		
		Garston	18	6
		Dingle Point	21	3
		Birkenhead		
24	0	Liverpool, Prince's Landing Stage	24	3
		Liverpool, Salisbury Dock, giving access, through Collingwood and Stanley Docks to the Stanley Dock Cut, Branch of the Leeds and Liverpool Canal	25	3
43	1	Mersey Bar Light vessel	43	1

Middle Level Navigation(64)

Middle Level is the name given to the area containing the network of waterways lying between and connecting the River Nene with the Great Ouse. All are artificial cuts or old streams improved and intended mainly for drainage of the Fens, but also for transporting agricultural produce etc. in the districts. As will be noted from the Table of Dimensions, these waterways can only be navigated by small craft. The name of the drain has no reference to the width of the channel.

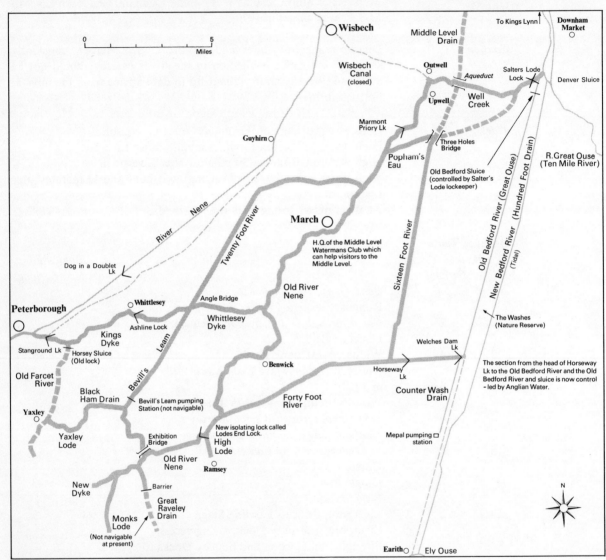

A full list of the drains is as follows:

Kings Dyke	Black Ham Drain	Pophams Eau
Whittlesey Dyke	New Dyke	Sixteen Foot River
Bevills Leam	Yaxley Lode	Forty Foot River
Old River Nene	Ramsey High Lode	Middle Level Drain
Old Farcet River (not now navigable)	Well Creek	Monks Lode
	Twenty Foot River	Great Raveley Drain (Not a statutory navigation)

Excluding Well Creek from Salter's Lode to Marmont Priory and the Old Popham's Eau from Nordelph to Three Holes, the majority of the remaining navigation channels are maintained in reasonable order. Navigation is not permitted in the Commissioners' Main Drain between the aqueduct and the St. Germans pumping station.

Weed growth in the channels is rapid during the late spring and early summer and the process of cutting takes several months, so that, unavoidably, there will be lengths with fairly heavy weed growth. All persons using the rivers are requested to keep a careful look-out for weed ropes which are placed across the river adjacent to cutting operations, and navigators are requested to carefully remove these ropes and replace them immediately after passing by. It is essential to anyone requiring to navigate, to advise the Middle Level Commissioners.

Navigation Bye-laws concerning the use of craft on Middle Level waterways apply. The Bye-laws provide (inter alia) that no lock may be navigated between the hours of 10 a.m. and 4 p.m. on Sundays or Christmas Day. No navigation toll is payable in respect of pleasure craft.

In view of the very complicated nature of the area the following information may assist students as well as navigators of the area.

The state of the navigations is as follows*:

Old Bedford Tidal Sluice	Length 15ft. Width 13' 6" Sill Level 98·15 Head (soffit) 115·0	Under jurisdiction of Anglian Water Authority. Sluice keeper's Tel. Downham Marker 2292. Normal water level 103·5. Old Bedford can only be entered at level water in tidal river.
Old Bedford River	No restriction.	Well maintained.
Welches Dam Sluice (Lock)	Length approx 40ft. Width 10' 9" Sill level 97·0 Head 6' 10"	Unattended. Two low bridges at this sluice restrict the headroom. If the water level in the channel is high, the headroom is further restricted. Key at Welches Dam Farm.
Forty Foot River to Horseway	No structural restrictions.	Heavy weedgrowth. Under jurisdiction of the Anglian Water Authority.
Horseway Lock	Length approx. 40ft. Width 11' 9" Sill level 94·5 Head unrestricted.	Unattended. Screw to work lock kept at nearest cottage to site and this should be returned immediately after locking through.
Lodes End Lock	Length approx 65ft 12ft wide	New lock to avoid obstruction by New Bevill's Leam pumping station.

* (Note. All levels are givern to datum 100ft. below Ordnance, i.e.—100 O.D.N.)

Forty Foot River	All bridges 7ft. headroom.	¾ mile to junction with Sixteen Foot River contains shoals, depth not exceeding 2' 6". Remainder of river to Wells Bridge is a drainage channel and well maintained. Draught 4ft.
River Nene to Floods Ferry	ditto	Drainage channel well maintained. Route passes through village of Benwick.
Whittlesey Dyke	ditto	Drainage channel well maintained. No telephone.
Ashline Lock, Whittlesey	Length 53ft. Width 11' 6" Sill level 100·45 Head unrestricted.	
King's Dyke	All bridges 7ft headroom.	Depth of water 3' 10". Draught not exceeding 2' 6". Water levels are normally below navigation level and notice must be given 48 hours prior to locking through at Ashline or Stanground, to permit adjustment of water levels. During very dry periods this cannot be given. Restricted length through Briggate, Whittlesey: maximum length of craft which can negotiate sharp bend, 35ft., and there is a length of 330 yds. where the width is restricted to 14ft. and depth to 3' 10". Craft should proceed at not more than 1 m.p.h. to prevent grounding.
Stanground Sluice (Lock)	Length 49ft 7ins Width 11' 6" Sill level 102·34 Head 16' 3" (with level of 104·34).	Lock unattended. Mr. Rootham. Tel. Peterborough 66413
Well Creek Route		
Marmont Priory Sluice (Lock)	Width 12' 0" 5ft. of water over sill.	Officially attended. Owner of sluice cottage keeps key.
Well Creek	6ft. headroom at normal water level.	Several low bridges through the villages of Upwell, Outwell and Nordelph. Sharp turn in Outwell. Proceed with caution.
Salters Lode Sluice (Lock)	Width 12' 6" 6' 6" of water over sill. Length 63ft Ample headroom.	Exit to the tidal Ouse, made on level water. Lock attended. Tel. Downham Market (0366) 2292. Apply to him for tidal information and times of exit and entrance.

The Middle Level is partly flat and uninteresting but the area in Outwell and Upwell in particular is very similar to Holland and the river through March is full of delightful surprises, particularly the north bank of the river. The East Anglian Waterways Association have a number of local members who will assist visitors.

Acts passed in 1753, 1793/4, 1810, 1844, 1848, 1852 1862, and 1874 deal with the Middle Level in some measure. Bye-laws were made under powers granted by the 1874 Act.

Authority	**All drains except the Forty Foot River from Welches Dam to Horseway Sluice.** Middle Level Commissioners, March, Cambridgeshire. Tel. March (035 42) 53232. (Horseway Sluice is owned by the Middle Level Commissioners.) *Welches Dam Sluice to Horseway Slice.* Anglian Water Authority, District Office, Ely, Cambs. Tel. Ely (0353) 2958/9. The waterway from the top of Horseway Sluice to the Old Bedford River was transferred from the M.L.C. in 1974. (Reference No. 199. Land Drainage Transfer 1974 – 1st February 1974).
The Main Route	From Peterborough (Stanground Lock): Kings Dyke. Whittlesey Dyke (part of). Old River Nene (part of) or the Twenty Foot River: Well Creek. Salters Lode.
The alternative route is the lower route:	Whittlesey Dyke. River Nene. Forty Foot River. Horseway Lock. Welches Dam Lock. Old Bedford River. Old Bedford Sluice (Tidal Doors).
Distance	From Peterborough (Stanground Lock), River Nene, to Salters Lode Sluice, River Ouse about 30 miles.
Length	46ft. Craft over 35ft. in length may find some difficulty in negotiating the sharp bend in Briggate, Whittlesey (King's Dyke).
Beam	This should be 11ft., but at Welches Dam it is only 10ft. 9ins
*Draught**	3ft. 6ins. for craft passing from the Nene to the Ouse.
Headroom	This should be 8ft. by statute, but at several bridges it is only 6ft. and at Exhibition Bridge it is only 5ft 4ins.
Locks (Locally termed Sluices)	King's Dyke—One Stanground Lock entrance and exit from system. Farcet River—One was at Horsey (now converted to drainage sluice). Whittlesey Dyke—One at Whittlesey. Fall from Stanground.

* Most of the channels have a depth from 5ft. to 9ft.

Old River Nene—One Marmont Priory, Upwell. Fall from Stanground
Well Creek—One Salters Lode (entrance to and exit from system.) Lock falls either way depending on tide.
Forty Foot River—One at Welches Dam, entrance to Old Bedford (under jurisdiction of the Anglia Water Authority). Fall from Welches Dam.
Forty Foot River—One Horseway Lock. Fall from Welches Dam. Lodes End Lock is on the old River Nene to the west of the junction with Ramsey High Lode rises from junction to Nightingales Corner.
Lock-gates worked by lock-keepers and boat crews jointly. (Craft can only pass Old Bedford Sluice on the back level, that is, on the level of the ebb tide. This section is controlled by the Anglia Water Authority and is used to enter the Middle Level).

Special note   As we go to press we understand certain changes will be made in the Middle Level system. This is due to the fact that the shrinkage of the Fens in the western section is varying so much that some isolating mechanism must be installed. A pumping station which will completely obstruct navigation, is now built on Bevill's Leam, near to Tebbitts Bridge. So as not to isolate the western navigations, a new lock is built at Middlemoore Bridge, near Ramsey. Lock dimensions will be the same as ruling size for the Middle Level.

Bridges   Numerous.

Speed limit and by-laws   4 miles per hour. Copies can be obtained at Middle Level Offices, March.

Charges   Canal Dues. On application, payable at the Locks—Stanground and Salters Lode.

Tow-path   Throughout navigation. This is called locally a 'haling way'. Path does not go under bridges, and frequently changes from one side of the navigation to the other without a roving bridge.

Tides   Ebb Tide on the Great Ouse at Salters Lode on the back level is from 2 to 3 knots. Due to weather conditions the tide varies considerably. Due allowance should be made. High water at Salters Lode is one hour 5 minutes after King's Lynn.

Distance Table
King's Dyke
Head of Stanground Sluice (lock) and junction with Stanground Branch of River Nene, called 'Broadwater', to

	Miles	Furlongs
Junction with Farcet River (not navigable)	1	1
Fields End Bridge	2	2
Whittlesey, *junction with Whittlesey Dyke*	4	2

Whittlesey Dyke
Whittlesey Village, junction with Kings Dyke to:

Whittlesey or Ashline Sluice (lock)	—	$3\frac{1}{2}$

Distance Table

	Miles	Furlongs
Angle Corner, *junction with Twenty-foot River and Bevils Leam.* ...	2	6
Floods Ferry, junction with old River Nene	6	1

Bevill's Leam (obstructed by Pumping Station)

Angle Corner, junction with Whittlesey Dyke and Twenty Foot River to:

Chapelbridge	1	4½
Pondersbridge	3	5
Tebbitts Bridge	4	4
Bevill's Leam Pumping Station (not passable)...	4	7
Mere Mouth, *junction with Old River Nene and Black Ham Drain* ...	5	—

Black Ham Drain

Mere Mouth, junction with Bevills Leam, and Old River Nene to: ...

British Railways (E.R.) Main Line Bridge, ¾ miles southwest of Yaxley village	3	5

Old River Nene

Mere Mouth, junction with Bevills Leam and Black Ham Drain to:

Exhibition Bridge (Lowest in system 5ft 4ins)	2	4
Nightingale's Corner, *junction with New Dyke* (not navigable) ...	2	6
St. Mary's Village and Bridge	3	4
Saunders Bridge, *junction with Ramsey High Lode*	5	6
Wells Bridge, *junction with Forty Foot River*	6	5
Benwick Village and Bridge	10	5
Floods Ferry, *junction with Whittlesey Dyke*	13	2
Staffurth's Bridge	14	2
March	18	2

Distance Table				*Miles*	*Furlongs*
Twenty Foot End, *junction with Twenty Foot River*				20	3½
Popham's Eau End, *junction with Popham's Eau*				22	3
Marmont Priory Sluice (Lock)				24	1
Upwell				25	3
Outwell, *junction with Well Creek* and Wisbech Canal (Not navigable—abandoned)				26	1

New Dyke
Nightingale's Corner, junction with Old River Nene to:

Holme Village				3	2

There are two branches from New Dyke, viz. Monks Lode and Great
Raveley Drain. The latter is a route to the Woodwalton Fen Nature
Reserve which can be visited by appointment. This is not a
navigation and is obstructed near the nature reserve.

Ramsey High Lode
Saunder's Bridge, junction with Old River Nene to:

Ramsey				1	1

Well Creek
Outwell, junction with Old River Nene and Wisbech Canal (not navigable—abandoned) to:

Aqueduct over Middle Level Drain				1	2
Nordelph				3	3
Salter's Lode Sluice (lock) and *junction with River Ouse*				5	3

Twenty Foot River
Angle Corner, junction with Whittlesey Dyke and Bevills Leam to:

Poplar Tree Bridge				—	5
Beggars Bridge				1	2
Infields Bridge				4	2
Goosetree Farm				5	6
Hobb's—Lots Bridge				6	6
Twenty Foot End, *junction with Old River Nene*				10	3

Popham's Eau
Popham's Eau End, junction with Old River Nene to:

Three Holes Bridge, *junction with Sixteen Foot River*				2	2
Middle Level Drain (no junction is made with this drain)				2	4

Middle Level Drain (No connection with Popham's Eau)
Popham's Eau to:

Pingle Bridge				1	3
Aqueduct carrying Well Creek over the Middle Level Drain ...				2	—

Sixteen Foot River
Three Holes Bridge, junction with Popham's Eau to:

Cottons Corner				—	6
Bedlam Bridge				4	1
Stonea Railway Station				5	1
Boots Bridge				6	6
Junction with Forty Foot River (Sixteen Foot Corner)				9	5

Distance Table

Forty Foot River, or Vermuyden's Drain

Wells Bridge, junction with Old River Nene to:

	Miles	Furlongs
Forty Foot Bridge	—	4
Puddock Bridge	3	2
Leonard Child's Bridge	5	2
Chatteris Dock (Chatteris distant 1 mile)	6	—
Junction with Sixteen Foot River (Sixteen Foot Corner)	7	6
Horseway Village	8	7
Horseway Sluice (lock)	8	1
Welches Dam Sluice* (lock), and *junction with the Old Bedford River and* Counter Wash Drain	10	4

Salter's Lode lock

* Welches Dam Sluice is also know as Black Sluice.

Monmouthshire and Brecon Canal (65)
(incorporating the Brecon and Abergavenny and Monmouthshire Canals).

The first section is navigable throughout. This is the old Brecon Canal. The scenery on this canal is exquisite and the canal has one level pound 25 miles long. It lies within the Brecon Beacons National Park and is a contour canal which takes it along the sides of mountains and hills bordering the lovely Usk valley. The Brecon National Park Authority have co-operated in the re-opening of this canal which is not connected to the national canal system, however trailer boats can be put in the water at many places and there is an official slipway at Govilon. Features of the canal include magnificent views of the Black Mountains, Crickhowell with its 13th century bridge across the river, the Gilwern aqueduct with its one massive arch, and the four arched aqueduct near Brynich Lock. All around the canal is magnificent walking country, and Torpanton is a particularly good centre to start from. Abergavenny is a charming market town. Nearby is Patrishow with its hidden church with rood loft and not far away is the ruined abbey of Llanthony. The canal takes its water supply from the Usk at Brecon, the gateway to rural Wales, and this is crystal clear water in which fish abound.

The canal was promoted originally by Acts of Parliament in 1793 and 1804. For administration it is merged with the Monmouthshire Canal which originally commenced at Pontymoyle. This canal is, at present, in a derelict condition, some locks being unworkable; weed and years of general neglect making it only canoeable, though it leads to extremely attractive country. It was closed from Newport to the docks in 1879, and a further section in Newport closed in 1930. In 1954 the canal in the vicinity of Cwmbran New Town was closed and now the whole canal south of Cwmbran has been subject to redevelopment.

The Monmouthshire canal was promoted under Acts dated 1792, 1797 and 1862. Certain sections are very attractive. There is a scheme to preserve the canal from Sebastopol to the northern boundary of Newport Borough and also a section of the Crumlin Arm from Mill Street to the M4 motorway. This arm will be kept in water for amenity but locks will not be restored. Of the old Monmouthshire Canal, only the section from Sebastopol north is navigable and the two restored locks are isolated. Restoration south through the Pontnewydd Five Locks is projected and if Cwmbran New Town can be reached enthusiasm for the restoration will take a leap forward. The canal navigation works have a number of features of interest.

The Brecon and Abergavenny section was helped by National Parks legislation designed to benefit the Norfolk and Suffolk Broads. The Broads were not scheduled as a National Park but the Brecon Beacon were, so funds were available to assist restoration.

Authority	(a) British Waterways Board. (Brecon to immediately south of Solomon's Bridge, Sebastopol, Bridge 47).
	(b) Local authorities and others. (Sebastopol to Newport and Crumlin Branch).
	South of Sebastopol the owners of the canal are obliged to allow passage of water for industrial use in the southern area of the canal. B.W.B. still own several bridges south of Sebastopol.
From and to	Brecon to Newport (Crumlin Branch closed by Act in 1949)
Distance	42⅜ miles.
*Length	64ft. 9ins.
*Beam	9ft. 2ins.

*Lock sizes but a bridge restricts dimensions to 50ft x 8ft. 6ins.

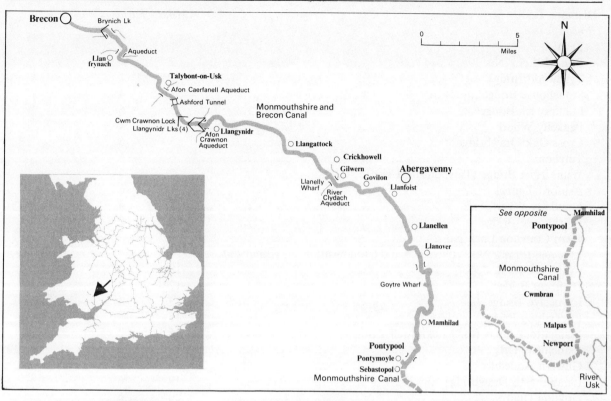

Headroom	5ft. 7ins.	*Draught*	3ft.

Locks	6. Fall from Brecon (Brecon and Abergavenny)
	31. Fall from Pontymoyle (Monmouthshire) 2 locks restored.

Bridges	Numerous. Several lift bridge, one electrically operated using B.W.B. toilet key.

Special note	Considerable restoration work has been carried out by the local authorities and the Torfaen Canal Society. The phase projected is to go from Crown Bridge due south to the five locks at Pontnewydd. Further south, Malpas Lock No. 29 and Gwastad Lock No. 30 have been put into working order but are isolated at present. No winding in Brecon. Wind ¼ mile before terminus.

Tunnels	Ashford, 375 yards. Height 8ft. 4ins.
	Width 10ft. 9ins.
	Cwmbran 87 yards.

Tow-path	Throughout canal except Ashford and Cwmbran Tunnels.

Facilities	There are 3 boatyards and a sprinkling of inns, but the canal is a lovely rural one.

Distance Table

Brecon to:

	Miles	Furlongs
Brynich Bridge	1	4
Brynich Lock No. 1	2	—
Tynewydd Bridge	3	2
Stonehouse Bridge	3	4
Llanfrynach Bridge	3	6
Penkelly Wharf	4	4
Cross Oak Drawbridge	5	6
Talybont	6	6
White Hart Bridge (Talybont-on-Usk)	7	5
Ashford Tunnel	7	6
Llandetty Wharf	8	4
Workhouse Bridge	9	2
Cwm Crawnon Lock No. 2	10	—
Llangynidr Lock No. 3 (Nos. 4, 5 and 6 follow after this within 400 yards) (B. W. B. depot)	10	2
Dwffrant Bridge	12	2
Llwncelyn Bridge	13	4
Ffawyddog Bridge	15	—
Llangattock Quay (for Crickhowell 1 mile)	15	2
Llanelly Wharf	18	2
Gilwern Aqueduct	18	6
Llanwenarth Drawbridge	19	6
Govilon Quarry	20	6
Llanfoist, Incline Bridge (Abergavenny, 1 mile)	21	6
Llanellen Bridge	23	6
Twynglas Bridge	24	2
Halls and Llanover Wharves (almost extinct)	25	6
National Park southern boundary	24	5
Parkybrain Wharf	28	2
Keepers Bridge	31	—
Typoeth and Llanvihangel Bridges	32	2
Pontymoyle, junction with Monmouthshire Canal	33	2
Crown Bridge, Limit of navigation. (8ft. wide diameter bridge near Sebastopol)	34	2
Pontrhydyyn Wharf	34	4
Cwmbran Tunnel	35	–
Pontnewydd Locks No. 1 to 5	35	4
Cwmbran Locks Nos. 6 to 15	36	4
Cwmbran Siding	36	6
Oakfield Wharf	37	2
Oakfield Locks Nos. 16 and 17	37	4
Tycock Locks Nos. 18 to 27	38	4
Tycock Wharf and Brickyard	38	6
Tynyffynon Lock No. 28	39	2
Malpas Wharf	40	2
Malpas Lock No. 29 (restored)	40	4
Malpas Junction, junction with Crumlin Branch (abandoned) ...	40	6
Gwastad Lock No. 30 (restored)	40	6½
Crindau Bridge	41	–
Tunnel Wharf	41	2

Distance Table

						Miles	Furlongs
Newport Corporation Wharf	...	...	...	...	...	42	–
Mill Street (or town) Lock No. 31	...	...	...	...	42	1
Newport, Llanarth Street ...	...	...	...	...	...	42	3

The whole of the Distance Table has been included as certain sections are likely to be preserved for amenity, though the canal as a navigation is closed below Sebastopol.

Monmouthshire
and Brecon Canal.
Brynich
lock outside Brecon

British Waterways Board

Monmouthshire
and Brecon Canal
Talybont
lifting bridge

British Waterways Board

River Nene (66)

From its entrance from the Wash to the Dog-in-a-Doublet lock about 5 miles below Peterborough, the river is tidal. From the Wash to Bevis Hall, a distance of about 13 miles, the river is under the jurisdiction of the Port of Wisbech Authority, above Bevis Hall to Northampton, to the Anglia Water Authority. Vessels of 2,000 tons navigate to just below Wisbech Bridge. The navigation was promoted by Acts dating 1714, 1725, 1754, 1756, 1794, 1827 and 1829. The old route of the Nene was through Salter's Lode Sluice, Well Creek, and Ramsey, Uig and Whittlesea Meres, a tedious and difficult navigation to which extensive alterations have been made. The cut from Guyhirne to Stanground was made as late as 1726/8. Cardinal Morton was responsible for much early work on the river.

The river became almost derelict in the late 1920's and was difficult to navigate due to eight navigation weirs and an obstruction from a gravel shoal below Peterborough. Due to the initiative of the late George Dallas, the river was restored by the Catchment Board and is now a model navigation. The numerous locks each needing approximately 95 turns of the handle are the deterrent to the larger use of the river.

The valley of the Nene, from Northampton to Peterborough, is renowned for its quiet loveliness. The river in its leisurely course to the sea passes many delightful and historic stone built villages. Castle Ashby and Elton Hall are famous stately homes, also Fotheringhay with its lantern towered collegiate church and remains of the 12th century castle where Richard II was born and Mary Queen of Scots, executed. Wansford village and Peterborough Cathedral are also of particular interest.

The area falls in the limestone belt and the villages are remarkably like Cotswold England. Elton is a fine example, and the bridges are, in several cases, old and very fine

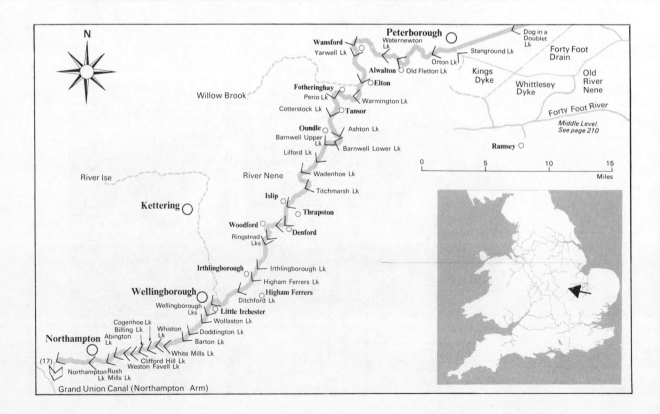

specimens of the mason's art. In an area of high amenity value, particularly below Irthling-borough to Alwalton, there is an almost complete lack of tourists, and the inns and river, as well as other amenities have not been spoiled and remain unsophisticated.

The river carries a large volume of water and must be treated with respect, care also is necessary at the ancient bridges. Called the Nen from Northampton to Wellingborough, and Nene from here to the sea.

Authority	**River mouth to Bevis Hall** Fenland District Council, Harbour Master's Office, Nene Parade, Wisbech, Cambs. Tel. Wisbech (0945) 61369. **From Bevis Hall to Northampton** AnglianWater Authority, Engineer's Office, North Street, Oundle, Peterborough, PE8 4AS. Enquiries should be addressed to the Engineer, Tel. Oundle (093 22) 3366/7.
From and to	The Wash* to Northampton.
Distance	From the Wash to Northampton, 91½ miles. Stanground Branch (5 furlongs in length) from Peterborough to Stanground Lock. West Bridge Branch (Northampton) 5½ furlongs.
Connections	With the Middle Level Navigation (for the River Ouse, etc.) at Peterborough. With the Grand Union Canal (Northampton Branch) at Northampton. The connection to the Thorney River, via 2 locks (staircase) at Dog-in-a-Doublet has been closed and converted to a fixed sluice. West Bridge Branch is navigable with some difficulty, though not legally abandoned, at the Northampton end.
Warning to yachtsmen	It is sometimes necessary to moor large cargo vessels at any point between Wisbech and the river end, all fours, i.e., with wires fore and aft and to both banks. Yachtsmen are, therefore, warned to stem the tide and wait till the vessel is able to slack away wires. Also large vessels when under way, cannot get out of the centre of the fairway. There is a proper mooring place for yachtsmen at Wisbech, further details from the Harbour Master. Chester House Bridge, Wellingborough. The ancient monument bridge at Irthlingborough restricts beam to 13ft., although the locks are 14ft. wide. The tidal lock at Dog-in-a-Doublet is closed at night, unless special arrangements are made with A.W.A. No moorings downstream.
Tides	Tides are much influenced by winds both as regards times and heights. Strong winds from W.N.W. through north to N.E., usually cause the flood tide to flow earlier, and raise the height of water as much as 2 to 3 feet above that predicted. Strong winds from the east through south to W.S.W., produce the opposite effects. Times and depths are also influenced by the amount of fresh water in the river.

*See page 382

Run of Tides

Wisbech	Springs	Flood 3 hours. Ebb 9 „
	Neaps	Flood 4 hours. Ebb 8 „
Sutton Bridge	Springs	Flood 4 hours. Ebb 8 „
	Neaps	Flood 5 hours. Ebb 7 „

Tides run strongly for several miles above Wisbech and often exceed 4 knots, even at neaps. (Care should be taken on this section as the bed is stoned and the sides piled with concrete, there is also a strong run on the ebb.)

Conditions in the tidal compartment of the river are liable to variation and those who intend to use the river should make application to the Anglia Water Authority, Oundle, or to the Port Manager, Wisbech, if they are near the limits of draught, beam etc., although information cannot be guaranteed.

There is a shoal downstream from Dog-in-a-Doublet Lock over which there is about 5 to 6ft. of water at high water neaps, and 1ft. 6ins. at low water neaps under adverse conditions, when the sluices are not discharging fresh water from upstream. The highest part of the shoal is on the Whittlesey to Thorney Road. Seasonal variations in shoaling arise and when navigating east at Dog-in-a-Doublet Lock, enquiries to the authorities is essential. Care should be taken at some of the bridges on the river.

High water at Wisbech about 10 minutes before H.W at Kings Lynn.

Wash to Wisbech

Length   260ft.

Beam   40ft.

Draught   17ft.

Headroom   Unlimited.

Wisbech to Peterborough

Length   130ft.

Beam   20ft.

Draught   6—7ft.

Headroom   Guyhirne Bridge: At H.W. Springs, 4ft. At H.W. Neaps, 10ft.
                        At L.W. Springs, 12ft. At L.W. Neaps, 13ft.

Peterborough to Northampton

Length	78ft.
Beam	13ft.
Draught	4ft.
Headroom	7ft. above L.W.

Tow-path This changes from one side of the river to the other without a roving bridge. There is no tow-path on the West Bridge and Stanground branches. The bulk of the path is usable though some of the bridges across weir channels have been removed.

Locks **Wisbech to Peterborough.** One at Dog-in-a-Doublet (power operated). Tel. Peterborough (0733) 202219. Resident lock-keeper. Advance notification of passage through lock is advisable.

Peterborough to Northampton. 37 locks. Locks worked by boat crews. (See *Special note* below). The 38 locks fall from Northampton.

Bridges From the Wash to Bevis Hall, 2. One swing bridge at Sutton, and one fixed bridge at Wisbech. From Bevis Hall to Northampton, 69 fixed.

Speed limit and bye-laws In that part of the river under the jurisdiction of the Wisbech Port Authority, the speed limit must be such as not to damage river banks or cause inconvenience. For that part of the river under the jurisdiction of the Anglia Water Authority, bye-laws for pleasure craft can be obtained on application to the Engineer, North Street, Oundle.

Charges From the sea to Bevis Hall, by arrangement with the Harbour Master, Nene Parade, Wisbech.
From Bevis Hall to Northampton, application should be made to the Anglia Water Authority. No toll is charged for passing through Dog-in-a-Doublet Lock. Other charges on application.

Facilities There are three marinas: at Billing, Cogenhoe and Oundle. Numerous inns near to river and a 2,000 acre Nene Country Park at Ferry Meadows near Peterborough. The Wildfowl Trust have a centre at Peakirk.

Canoeing note No satisfactory canoeing above Northampton.

Pilotage For pilotage upstream from Wisbech contact should be made with Pilot B. H. Locke. Tel. Wisbech (0945) 62870.

Special note All Nene Locks have pointing doors on the upstream side, but the bottom gates are usually of the guillotine variety. Radial top gates (up and over), were fitted at Northampton, Rush Mills and Ditchford. Rush Mills and Northampton have been replaced by ordinary mitre gates and Ditchford is due for replacement. Abington new lock has all mitre doors and as repairs and replacement become necessary it seems all Nene gates will have pointing doors. The Grand Union key will fit the 1¼ inch square spindle, but a key is needed to unlock the bottom gates and these can be obtained from the Anglia Water Authority at Oundle who will also supply full details of lock operation and any other navigational details required. A fee of £5 is required for loan of lock keys.

The locks are used for regulating the discharge of water in the river and if lock paddles are found in an open or partly open position they should be reset to the same opening after the lock has been used.

The course of the river navigation channel has been altered at Northampton. Abington Lock is moved further south in connection with a flood relief scheme. Care should be taken to keep to the correct channel.

Distance Table

Northampton, junction with Northampton
Branch of the Grand Union Canal to (via Grand Union Canal Lock):

	Miles	Furlongs
Northampton, South Bridge	—	1
Northampton Lock No. 1	—	3
Rush Mills Lock No. 2	1	7
Abington Lock No. 3	2	7
Weston Favell Lock No. 4	3	4
Clifford Hill Lock No. 5	4	3
Billing Lock No. 6	4	7
Cogenhoe Lock No. 7	6	2
Whiston Lock No. 8	7	4
White Mills Lock No. 9	8	3
Barton Locks No. 10	9	1
Doddington Lock No. 11	10	1
Wollaston Lock No. 12	11	1½
Upper Wellingborough Lock No. 13	12	4
Wellingborough Bridge	12	7
Lower Wellingborough Lock No. 14	13	4
Ditchford Lock No. 15	15	3½
Higham Lock No. 16	17	5
Irthlingborough Bridge	18	1
Irthlingborough Lock No. 17	18	5
Upper Ringstead Lock No. 18	21	1
Lower Ringstead Lock No. 19	21	5
Woodford Lock No. 20	24	—
Denford Lock No. 21	24	7
Thrapston Bridge	26	1
Islip Lock No. 22	26	3½
Titchmarsh Lock No. 23	28	5
Wadenhoe Lock No. 24	31	1½
Lilford Lock No. 25	32	3
Upper Barnwell Lock No. 26	34	5
Lower Barnwell Lock No. 27	35	—

Titchmarsh Mill
on the River Nene

Distance Table

	Miles	Furlongs
Ashton Lock No. 28	37	—
Oundle Bridge	38	—
Cotterstock Lock No. 29	39	1
Perio Lock No. 30	40	7
Warmington Lock No. 31	43	3
Elton Lock No. 32	44	7
Yarwell Lock No. 33	47	7
Wansford Lock No. 34	49	1
Wansford Bridge	49	5
Waternewton Lock No. 35	52	7
Alwalton Lock No. 36	54	7
Orton Lock No. 37	58	5
Peterborough Bridge	60	5
Peterborough, *junction with Branch to Stanground and Middle Level Navigations*	61	1
Dog-in-a-Doublet Lock No. 38 (power-operated, with emergency hand operation) (Inn)	65	5
Popeley's Gull	67	4
Cross Guns	70	4
Guyhirne	73	7
Bevis Hall	77	2
Wisbech Town Bridge	79	6
Wisbech	79	7
Horse Shoe Bend	80	4
Osborne House	80	7
West Walton Ferry	82	6
Junction with South Holland Main Drain (sluice entrance is only opened at flood times)	86	5
Sutton Bridge	87	3
The Wash at Crabs Hole, Mouth of River	91	4

North Walsham and Dilham Canal (67)

This is a canalisation of the River Ant, and was promoted by Act of Parliament in 1812. The bottom 3 locks were in use until 1935. The section from Antingham to Swafield Bridge was closed in 1927 by warrant of the Ministry of Transport. This canal traverses some beautiful woodland and passes 2 mills, its restoration is long overdue. The legal position of this waterway is the same as the Basingstoke Canal in that the 1812 Act does not relate to the present company, though this Act has never been rescinded. The public right of navigation exists throughout, to Swafield Bridge.

Authority	(a) North Walsham Canal Co. Ltd., Ebridge Mills, North Walsham, Norfolk (Swafield Bridge to Honing Lock) (b) Honing Lock South, now in private ownership.
From and to	Junction with River Ant to Honing Lock. (Honing Lock to Swafield Bridge is now impassable due to lack of maintenance.)
Distance	2¼ miles only available for navigation. Boatyards at Wayford Bridge will give advice to visitors.
Length	50ft.
Beam	12ft. 4ins.
Draught	3ft.
Headroom	7ft.
Locks	4. None in use. In the last century the total was 6, but 2 went out of use in 1892. Fall from Swafield.
Branches	East Ruston Branch, 3½ furlongs. Honing Staithe Cut, 110 yards. Meeting Hill Branch, 2 furlongs. There was never a branch of the canal to Dilham Village. The route to Dilham is from Smallburgh River to Swan's Nest Corner and thence via a canal, Dilham Dyke. The Dyke is owned by the East Anglian Waterways Association Limited, who also own the staithe. The dyke was previously a private canal serving the brickworks, now closed, and the Association, have declared a public right of way so that boats can go to Dilham Staithe. The Yarmouth Port and Haven Commissioners bye-laws apply to the river and dyke section. The river was originally navigable to The Rookery, but this section is silted up. There are no mooring fees for the use of Dilham Staithe but public use is restricted to 48 hours for each visit.

Distance Table   *Miles   Furlongs*

Junction with Smallburgh River (leading to Dilham Dyke) to:

	Miles	Furlongs
Junction with North Walsham Canal* (Commissioners jurisdiction ceases here)	—	2½
Tonnage Bridge	—	6½

* The North Walsham Canal commenced above the junction with the Smallburgh River as when it was constructed the river section above the junction was in fact, Broad Fen, a Broad that has now disappeared.

Distance Table

	Miles	Furlongs
Junction with East Ruston Branch	1	1½
Honing Lock No. 1	2	1
Honing Common Bridge, and *junction with Honing Staithe Cut* ...	2	3
Briggate Lock No. 2 and Mill	3	2
Junction with Meeting Hill Branch (Parish Staithe)	4	1
Ebridge Lock No. 3 and Mill (Staithe)	5	—
Spa Common Bridge (North Walsham one mile distant) (Staithe) ...	5	7½
Bacton Wood Lock No. 4 (Staithe)	6	0
Austin Bridge	6	3½
Swafield Bridge and Mills (Staithe)	7	2½

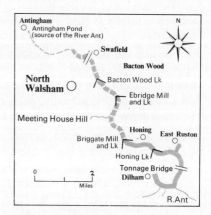

The Norfolk and Suffolk Broads(68)

The Bure, Yare and Waveney Rivers and Great Yarmouth Haven were the subject of Acts passed in 1670, 1722, 1747 and 1772. The main acts controlling the navigation on the Broads were passed in 1866, 1907 and 1963 and these cover the powers of the Commissioners. There was an Act in 1827 to promote the navigation between Norwich and Lowestoft when, due to the shallow condition of the River Yare, Haddiscoe Cut was constructed and Oulton Dyke was enlarged to Oulton Broad. A cut was made into Lake Lothing which became a tidal harbour and a lock was constructed with gates working either way at Mutford. This navigation was a failure although it is still in use today by pleasure craft, but sea-going vessels have reverted to using the River Yare.

The River Bure was a navigation to Aylsham, but the navigation rights of the original Act passed in 1773 were abandoned by Warrant of the Minister of Transport dated 22nd September 1926 and the Order was dated 24th February 1927. The locks have been disused and derelict since 1912 when they were seriously damaged by floods. There is a good depth of water all the way to Aylsham at present as the water level is held up by weirs and light craft that can be portaged still use the river.

The navigation to Bungay on the River Waveney was in use until a later date. It was possible to use Ellingham and Geldeston Locks as late as 1929, although Wainford went out of use in 1928. Navigation under the original Act passed in 1670 was rescinded by an order of the Minister of Agriculture and Fisheries under Section 41 of the Land Drainage Act 1930, on the 26th April 1934.

The North Walsham and Dilham Canal is listed separately. This waterway is still controlled to some extent by the original 1812 Act which has not been rescinded but a section above Swafield is now closed. Although the Bure and Waveney Acts have been legally rescinded both waterways have been extensively used by light craft. The Bure has been navigated to Ingworth Mill above Aylsham for many years and regattas were held in it over 100 years ago. The Waveney is regularly used by light craft to Bungay and on occasions to Diss. There are records of a canoe trip from Lopham Ford to the sea before the turn of the century.

The Broads are a unique area and there is no comparable inland waterway network. Their origin has been the subject of much conjecture, but the serious student could well read *The Making of the Broads* issued by the Royal Geographical Society, which contains a good deal of material by Dr. J. M. Lambert and others. There have been a number of theories about certain sections of the Broads and their early history, but the Broads as we know them today, are substantially as they were 150 years ago, with the exception of the fact that until recent years, they have in most cases been seriously reduced in area. The large scale dredging carried out by the Bure and Waveney Commissioners now amalgamated with the Yare Commissioners, who removed one million tons of silt from the Broads between 1954 and 1970, has had the effect of arresting the silting up process, and in several parts has enlarged the area of water. Undoubtedly, parts of the Broads were dug for peat as long ago as the time of King John and the area is rich in history.

Like all popular resorts, certain sections have been subject to overcrowding at the peak holiday season, but it is still possible at these crowded times to find many deserted corners of Broadland with their unique heritage of flora and fauna. Beccles, on the Waveney, has a charter from Queen Elizabeth 1. The church has a very fine separate bell tower and in the church at Ranworth, the rood screen, dating from 1485, is superb. At Norwich the yacht station has excellent facilities and moorings are being extended at the present station to give access into the city which has a cathedral and many fine parish churches. Norwich has one of the finest open air markets in the country as well as a mediaeval street, Elm Hill.

Horning one of the prettiest Broadland villages, has a very fine church with its own private staithe. The wealth of books about the area give details of places to be visited, but the inland waterway enthusiasts should particularly visit the wind pump on Horsey Mere owned by the National Trust. A number of these wind pumps have been restored and give character to the area, although in bygone days early Broadland holidaymakers claimed that the cranking and creaking of them disturbed their sleep.

Wroxham, Hickling and Barton Broad are particularly good for sailing, and hydroplane and speed boat races are held on Oulton Broad. Care is necessary in navigating from the Bure to the Waveney and the instructions regarding Breydon Water should be strictly followed, although cruising Breydon can be a very exciting experience. Care is also necessary navigating from the Bure to the Yare.

The Norfolk Wherry Trust owns *Albion*, the only Norfolk wherry left in a state similar to the days when it was trading with cargoes to village staithes. The wherry is now based at Womack Water at its own base and is seen frequently on the Broads with organised parties. This wherry was used for many years to take the Bishop of Norwich, who is the Lord Abbot of St. Benet's, to the annual open air service at the ruins of St. Benet's Abbey on the first Sunday in August. The wherry yacht *Olive*, also preserved (by Peter Bower, a private conservationist), is also used for the annual service. Both these vessels are the sole survivors of their type and local enquiries may lead to a private viewing when they are not afloat. *Olive* is based at Wroxham and St. Benet's Abbey is located on the Bure downstream of Ant mouth.

The many village churches are extremely interesting, particularly those with round towers and there seems to be a connection between the round towers of Ireland and those of Norfolk and Suffolk as regards their original function. Somerleyton Hall on the Waveney

The Bishop of Norwich talking to Peter Bower, owner and restorer of the wherry *Olive* which conveyed him to the annual open air service at St Benet's Abbey in August 1979

Eastern Daily Press

is one of a number of places open to the public, and Howe Hill, an imposing thatched mansion of Edwardian interest whose grounds contain one of the finest water gardens with many miniature canals, adjoins Crome's Broad.

The Bure above Wroxham to Coltishall and the Waveney at Beccles both give the lie to Broadland's detractors who dismiss the area as being flat. The Nature Reserves and Nature Trails of the Norfolk Naturalists Trust and details of their work are recorded elsewhere in the section. Like the Fen country, the sunsets in Broadland are remarkable and are partly due to the dry climate. The area is lucky in its weather, particularly early and late in the year and these form ideal times for exploration, especially for the enthusiast.

There are two special Broadland problems, namely parish staithes, and navigation rights on the closed Broads. A note has been included on the former problem but the latter is a very involved legal tangle. Wherries regularly used Hoveton Great Broad as a short cut to Wroxham, thus there would appear to be a prescriptive right of navigation at least across the Broad, several other cases are noted in the Distance Tables. The Law Journal of the 4th December 1953, gives a considered opinion on the matter in an article by E. W. H. Christie who raises many points of interest.

Commercial traffic has virtually ceased on the Bure and the Waveney, but coasters trading to Norwich are still encountered. Special care must be taken when meeting these sea-going boats as they cannot move out of the narrow dredged channel and strict observation of signals must be made. On the Bure and Waveney, sugar beet transported by motorised wherry was the last traffic carried and this ceased in recent years. The sole remnant of trade is the rare small barge carrying reeds, as reed cutting for house thatching is a thriving industry, and Norfolk reeds are much sought after.

Before mooring to banks or elsewhere, yachtsmen should always ascertain whether there will be sufficient water to lie afloat at low tide. Generally moorings are free but a small fee is levied in some places.

Authorities

The rivers are managed by the following authorities.
Rivers Yare, Bure and Waveney Commissioners.
This body is under the control and general superintendence of the Great Yarmouth Port and Haven Commissioners, 21 South Quay, Great Yarmouth. Tel. (0493) 855151.

Oulton Broad, Waveney District Council
New or Haddiscoe Cut is under the jurisdiction of the Anglia Water
Authority. Commissioners bye-laws apply.
The Broads Authority
This body was formally constituted in March 1979. Address:
Thorpe Lodge, Yarmouth Road, Norwich, NR7 0DU. Tel. Nor-
wich (0603) 37273. Bill is in progress through Parliament to vest
overall powers in Broadland in a new Authority (1988).

History
The idea of a 'Broads Authority' came from the Norfolk branch of the Association of
District Councils at the time when consultations were taking place regarding the
possibility of designating the Broads as a National Park. The district councils affected
(5 in Norfolk and 1 in Suffolk) were joined by the two county councils, the Anglian
Water Authority, and the Great Yarmouth Port and Haven Commissioners and after
consultation it was agreed that a locally controlled body of this nature could achieve a
great deal for the Broads area. The local enthusiasm for this new authority and the
determination for its success have been evident from the beginning. The Countryside
Commission have been (and still are) a major interested party in the Authority and are
of great assistance.

Constitution and Powers
Six district councils and two county councils namely, Broadland District Council,
Great Yarmouth Borough Council, North Norfolk District Council, Norwich City
Council, South Norfolk District Council, Waveney District Council, Suffolk County
Council, Norfolk County Council form the Broads Authority under Sections 101 and
102 of the Local Government Act 1972, with executive powers – the Countryside
Commission, the Anglian Water Authority and the Great Yarmouth Port and Haven
River Commissioners are, however, co-opted members as of right. The Broads
Authority has powers delegated by the constituent local authorities and decides its own
budget. Proposals affecting the functions of the Anglian Water Authority and Port and
Haven Commissioners are recommendations to the respective authorities.

Objectives
"Recognising the national importance of the area for its landscape, nature conservation
and recreational value, the overriding consideration is to conserve and enhance the
natural beauty and amenity of the area as a whole including its wildlife, while protecting
the economic and social interest of those who live and work in the area and preserving
its natural resources and, having regard to those interests and resources, facilitating the
use of the Broads for recreational holiday purposes both waterborne and land-based
and for the pursuit of scientific research education and nature study."

Area
a) The boundary of the area within which the Broads Authority exercises its executive powers is related to the Broads themselves and the adjacent rivers and marsh-
lands. (Shown on the map following these notes.)
b) The Broads Authority acts in an advisory capacity in relation to a larger area as
circumscribed by the hydrometric catchment of the Rivers Bure, Waveney, Wensum
and Yare and their tributaries so far as they lie within the Districts of Broadland,
Great Yarmouth, North Norfolk, Norwich, South Norfolk and Waveney.

Finance
The Broads Authority is financed through contributions from the constituent local
authorities.
  The Anglian Water Authority's and the Port and Haven Commissioners' contributions are in the form of capital works carried out together with an annual subscription
from each of them of one tenth of administrative costs. The contribution from the
Countryside Commission is in the form of grants to specific projects and payment of a
proportion of the Authority's administrative costs.

Staff
In addition to a permanent administrative staff, officer advice is provided by
constituent bodies of the Authority. Also advice is obtainable from a technical panel
and specialists advisers from the bodies forming the authority.

The Broads Authority area

Terms of Reference to the Authority

(a) To define the problems of Broadland, solutions to them, and to secure the implementation of those solutions by making recommendations to the constituent statutory authorities in so far as implementation cannot be achieved by the use of executive powers of the Broads Authority.

(b) To formulate, and from time to time to review, a Management Plan for Broadland which shall include the updating of the Broadland Study and Plan.

(c) To secure the implementation of the Management Plan by making recommendations to the constituent statutory authorities in so far as implementation cannot be achieved by the use of the executive powers of the Broads Authority.

(d) To co-ordinate the activities of the constituent District and County Councils, the Countryside Commission, the Anglian Water Authority and the Great Yarmouth Port and Haven Commissioners and for this purpose, to make recommendations to those authorities in so far as co-ordination cannot be achieved by the use of the executive powers of the Broads Authority.

(e) To act as the forum of communication between the District and County Councils, the Countryside Commission, the Anglian Water Authority, and the Great Yarmouth Port and Haven Commissioners and other interested bodies in all matters relating to Broadland.

(f) To publish an annual report for submission to the constituent authorities, the appropriate Government Department and for public information.

(g) To undertake any other activities arising from or relating to Broadland in furtherance of the Broads Authority's objectives.

(h) To exercise the functions of the constituent District and County Councils in relation to:

A (i) Strategic and local recreation planning and provision.

(ii) The provision, management, and improvement of country parks, camping, caravan and picnic sites.

(iii) Nature conservation, access to open country, open spaces, and inland waterways excluding navigation and existing yacht stations and moorings. The Broads Authority to review the situation in due course.

(iv) The creation, diversion, extinguishment and maintenance of footpaths and bridleways.

(v) Tourism including interpretation, information and associated visitor services, but excluding the provision of gypsy caravan sites and formal parks and gardens.

B (i) Areas of outstanding natural beauty.

(ii) Conservation areas.

(iii) Trees.

(iv) Derelict land.

(v) Advertisements.

(vi) Buildings of architectural or historic interest.

(vii) Ancient monuments.

(viii) Development control (including enforcement, revocation and discontinuance orders) compensation resulting from planning decisions and deemed consent applications.

(ix) Local plans and all other planning policy documents (whether satutory or not) excluding structure plans.

(xi) Litter.

(xii) Traffic management.

(xiii) Car Parking.

(xiv) Licensing of pleasure boats and vessels let for hire or carrying passengers for hire and boatmen in charge of such vessels (Public Health Acts Amendment Act 1907 (Part X).

For the purpose of the above functions to exercise the functions of the constituent District and County Council relating to:

(a) Research

(b) The acquisition and development of land.

(c) Bye-laws

(d) Institution and defence of legal proceedings.

General remarks

The Norfolk and Suffolk Rivers cover 120 miles of waterways, most of which are navigable. The three main rivers are the Yare, Bure and Waveney, all of which are tidal and may be entered either via Lowestoft or Yarmouth.

Speed limits

Speed limits, which are strictly enforced by patrol launches and electronic equipment, are in force on the rivers and are marked by notices on the banks, similar to road signs. Maximum penalty for exceeding the limits £50.

Motor-launch bye-laws

On application to the Commissioners at South Quay, Great Yarmouth.

The Oulton Broad Joint Committee no longer exists and the Broad is now controlled by the Waveney District Council, but the Commissioners still carry out dredging, which was very substantial in the years 1976/1978. Bye-laws for Oulton Broad are similar to those of the Commissioners.

Bridge warning signs

There are warning boards lettered red on white at certain bridges, and the commissioners have erected gauges which are clearly visible as you approach. The figures on the post show the maximum height in feet under the bridge, reading it off at water level. The clearance figure applies to the peak of the arch over the navigable channel. The least easy bridge to negotiate is Potter Heigham road bridge. Great care is necessary here. The centre height is only 6ft. 8ins. at average high-water, and the sides fall away sharply to the water in a half circle.

Just inside the Herbert Woods basin there is a bridge gauge with a swing-arm where you can test the clearance of your boat as for the bridge itself. This service is operated by Blakes Ltd., but by arrangement they will assist anybody requiring a passage with Pilot. Hoseason's pilots are nearby.

Parish staithes

The problem of parish staithes has been for many years a very difficult one. The East Anglian Waterways Association commenced a study of the problems in 1960 which could take years to complete as the legal difficulties in a number of cases are extremely involved and it would need a lifetime of work to ascertain the basic facts. The title 'parish staithe' has been interpreted very liberally as any staithe where a boat may moor whether it belongs to a parish, the A.W.A., Commissioners or privately.

It has become very obvious to those of us who have studied the subject that a large number of 'public' staithes were in fact, privately owned, frequently by the local lord of the manor, who permitted their use commercially without restraint. As the wherry traffic decayed these staithes were gradually assimilated into the adjacent landholding and public access by land or water was lost. It is possible that in a number of cases these staithes could be recovered, leased from their owners and brought back into use if sufficient funds were available. These staithes have been included in the list although there is no trace of their being other than privately owned. Parishioners do not have the right to moor permanently or obstruct a staithe.

In a few cases public staithes appear to have been unwanted, Fritton on the Waveney is an example, and in this case there would seem to be no requirement to, or advantage in recovering the staithe. It no longer has agricultural use.

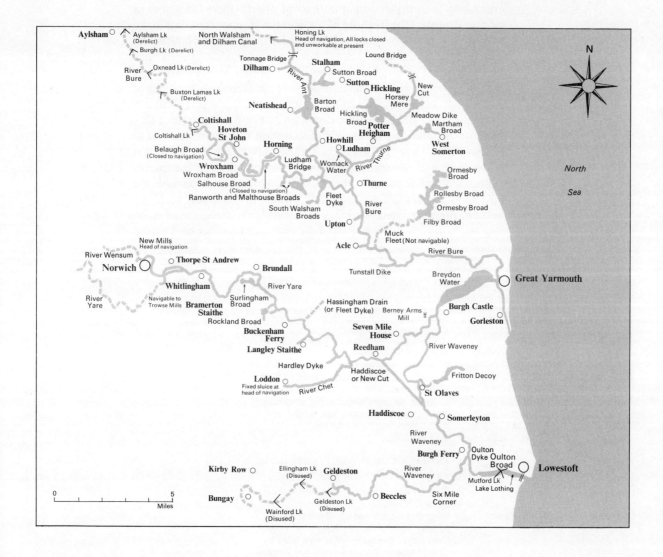

A number of staithes have been registered under the Common Registration Act 1965.

A by-product of the inquiries into the various staithes has been the re-discovery of some riverside land, usually poor land, which might also be procurable for use as additional mooring space. In certain cases, finance being available, this could be a more advantageous method of procuring mooring space than the rehabilitation of disused staithes.

The authorities in a number of instances have had to deal with commercial use of staithes and other obstructions such as car parking and mobile refreshment vans. Obstruction and nuisance has also been caused by the use of parish staithes by commercial hire firms for boat letting. As a general principle, except where there has been a specific stransfer, the freehold of some of the staithes is vested in the A.W.A. or the Smallburgh Internal Drainage Board, although neither of these bodies has a direct interest in maintaining the staithes for the general public for mooring. The author belives that it is impossible for the public, and here the public means the inhabitants of each parish, to lose the use of the staithes since the legal position is that the Awards have the authority of an Act of Parliament and that therefore no one can obtain by prescription a right which would derogate from the proper use of the staithes. Under ideal conditions it seems that the commissioners could best administer the parish staithes with the assistance of the local authorities. It is possible for the commissioners to act as they have powers in this matter under an Act of Parliament dated 1886. The following list is intended as a guide only and is not comprehensive. Comments will be welcomed by the author.

Parish	Situation	Conditions and Comments
Acle	S.W. of bridge Top of Boat Dyke	Owned by local boatyard.
Barton Turf	Barton Broad	Satisfactory condition. Owned by Parish Council. Piled by Commissioners.
Belaugh	Belaugh	Staithe owned by Trafford. Estate leased to and piled by Commissioners.
Bramerton	Bramerton Common.	In use and piled by Commissioners.
Burgh St. Peter	Below Waveney Inn.	Satisfactory. Unclassified 6296. Leadingl to river edge.
Burgh Castle	W. of Church.	Is noted as parish staithe in Enclosure Award. Shallow water – not in use.
Catfield	Catfield Common	Fair condition. Owned by parish.
Catfield	Wood End (Barton Broad.)	Fair condition.
Catfield	Catfield.	Owned by Catfield Poor Trustees and is rented by the Parish Council.
Chedgrove	Chedgrove	Piled by Commissioners. Possibly owned by local Trust.
Coltishall	The Common	River bank on common administered by parish. Rented from King's College. Cambridge. Practially all is now piled by Commissioners except a small bay downstream.
Dilham	By Brick Kiln Bridge.	Owned by East Anglian Waterways Assoc. Leased to and piled by Commissioners.
East Ruston	By old M. & G. N. railway track site in village.	Ownership unknown. Canal branch is mainly weeded up.
Fritton	Opposite 7 mile house.	Noted in Parish Award. Staithe not now required.
Geldeston	Geldeston Dyke	No record of public ownership. A former staithe reported in the river, below the dyke, now disappeared.
Hickling	Behind Pleasure Boat Inn.	Fair condition. Owned by Smallburgh Internal Drainage Board. Managed by the Parish Council.
Horning	3 staithes.	Satisfactory. Owned by the Parish Council.
Horsey	E corner of Horsey Mere	Satisfactory. Owned by the Parish Council.
Irstead	Near Church.	Piled by Commissioners.
Irstead	Gay's Staithe	Located by Barton Angler Hotel, fairly recent Award indicated no owner but Parish and District Councils can act to stop improper usage.

Parish	Situation	Condition and Comments
Langley	Langley Dyke.	No record of public ownership.
Loddon	Town staithe.	Owned by South Norfolk District Council. New basin cut in 1971.
Ludham	S of bridge on River Ant.	Satisfactory. Owned by the A.W.A.
Ludham	Opposite Reedham Marsh (How Hill).	Staithe receding and becoming shallow. Owned by the A.W.A.
Ludham	Top of Womack.	Satisfactory. Owned by the A.W.A.
Martham	1. End of Damgate 2. Beside Ferry Dyke 3. Upstream of Martham Boat-building and Development Co.	All three owned by the A.W.A.
Neatishead	Village staithe.	In use.
North Cove	Cove Staithe.	Noted in Navigation Book of Reference as public road and staithe. No other details available.
Oulton	Near Mutford Bridge.	Small public jetty.
Potter Heigham	N.W. of bridge.	Owned by the A.W.A. or Parish Council.
Ranworth	Malthouse Broad.	Owned by Blakes.
Reedham		Satisfactory. Part owned by Broadland District Council.
Rockland St. Mary	Rockland Broad	In use. Owned by Poor Trustees, and leased to and piled by Commissioners.
Repps	SW of Heigham Bridge.	Poor condition. Owned by parish.
Repps	Repps Lower (Pug Street)	Owned and repaired by the A.W.A.
Smallburgh	Wayford Bridge	Piece S.E. of bridge. Belongs to the Norfolk C.C.
Somerleyton		Common staithe at end of road below Dukes Head Inn, (site of old ferry), noted in Award. Adjacent land to S. is Poor Land.
Stokesby	The Green	Owned by parish council.
West Somerton		In use. Small craft only due to shallow water.
South Walsham	S. Walsham-Outer Broad	Small strip owned by parish with access over private land.
Stalham	Stalham Dyke	Satisfactory, although a portion is used as coal dump.
Sutton	Sutton Staithe	In use. Owned by Smallburgh Internal Drainage Board.
Thorpe	Village green staithe.	In use. Piled by Commissioners.
Thurne	Thurne Dyke	Satisfactory. Owned by the A.W.A. Surveyor of Highways holds end of Dyke as public cattle watering.
Upton	Upton Dyke	Ownership vested in the A.W.A.
Woodbastwick		End of Horning Ferry only.
Woodbastwick	By Decoy Broad	Owned by Woodbastwick Estate.
Worlingham	Near old mill	Noted in 1823 and four road orders as village staithe.
Wroxham	No trace of village staithe	
Wroxham	Castle staithe	In use.

In recent years the Commissioners have created moorings for a 24 hour stay at the following places:

Somerleyton	Duke's Head moorings.
Hoveton	Immediately upstream of The Three Horseshoes public house.
Hoveton	Viaduct moorings.

Wroxham	On the newly opened section of Bridge Broad.
Potter Heigham	A stretch of bank 150ft long, on the left bank of the River Thurne has been reserved as a short stay mooring for yachts raising/lowering gear. This is located below the old bridge at Potter Heigham. Motor cruisers should not moor here.

Registration certificates

Under the River Bye-laws, 1946, all pleasure boats using the rivers are required, before being used, to exhibit a Certificate in a holder (supplied by the Commissioners upon payment of toll) renewable each year.

Scale of charges

On application to the Great Yarmouth Port and Haven Commissioners.

Norfolk Naturalists' Trust

Norfolk has long been recognized as outstanding for its wealth of wild life and its great variety of natural beauty. The county is most fortunate in that it contains the beautiful Breckland as well as the unique Broads system, in addition to which it has a delightful coastline.

Norfolk was the first county in Great Britain to organise nature conservation. This was effected by the establishment of the Norfolk Naturalists' Trust which is an independent body and a registered charity. The Trust was founded in 1926 for the purpose of acquiring properties in Norfolk and on its borders which require protection as nature reserves, and holding these in perpetuity. The principal concern of the Trust is conservation, and it is now responsible for over thirty properties covering some 6,000 acres of the county.

The Norfolk Naturalists' Trust now owns or leases seven areas in Broadland. By acquiring these properties and managing them as nature reserves, the Trust has been able to conserve the natural habitats and has succeeded in encouraging several of the now comparatively rare species of birds to return and nest in Broadland. Much has been achieved by restoring reed and sedge beds in areas which before their acquisition by the Trust were derelict but had once been the primary source of reed for thatching and other uses. The nine Broadland reserves are as follows:

Martham and Starch Grass. 147 acres, part purchased 1928 and part leased 1971; designated as a Site of International Importance for Waterfowl.

Alderfen Broad. 72 acres purchased in 1930; designated as a Site of Special Scientific Interest.

Hickling Broad and Heigham Sound. 1361 acres, part purchased and part leased in 1945; designated as a National Nature Reserve and Site of International Importance for wildfowl.

Barton Broad. 365 acres, half gift and half purchased in 1945, 1952 and 1974; designated as a Site of Special Scientific Interest.

Surlingham Broad. 253 acres, purchased in 1948; designated as a Site of Special Scientific Interest.

Ranworth and Cockshoot Broads. 144 acres given to the Trust in 1949; forms part of the Bure Marshes National Nature Reserve.

Firs Marsh, Burgh St. Peter. 2½ acres leased in 1964.

Hardley Flood and Chedgrave Common. 100 acres leased in 1972; designated as a Site of Special Scientific Interest.

Upton Fen. 120 acres purchased in 1979; designated as a Site of Special Scientific Interest.

Of these reserves those at Hickling, Martham, Barton and Surlingham Broads are directly accessible to river craft.

The Trust provides facilities for a limited number of visitors to some of the reserves where observation hides and nature trails are provided such as Hickling. There is a Broadland Conservation Centre at Ranworth which highlights some of the problems in the Broads and provides viewing facilities over Ranworth Broad. The Trust always welcomes new members who have the satisfaction of knowing that they are playing a constructive part in saving at least some areas of the rapidly changing Norfolk landscape.

Further details of membership and the nature reserves may be obtained from The Secretary, The Norfolk Naturalists Trust, 72 Cathedral Close, Norwich, NR1 4DZ. Telephone Norwich (0603) 25540.

(These notes on the Trust and its reserves have been prepared by the director, Moira Warland M.Sc, whose assitance is gratefully acknowledged.

OULTON BROAD AND DYKE

General remarks	This waterway connects the River Waveney through Mutford Lock with Lake Lothing, Lowestoft Harbour and the sea. Navigation lights must be shown at night, by moving craft.
Distance	From Lowestoft Harbour to River Waveney, 4½ miles.
Length	86ft.
Beam	20ft.
Draught	9ft.
Headroom	Unlimited.
Locks	Mutford or Oulton Lock. This lock has double gates so that the lock can work either way depending on the tide.
Bridges	All swing bridges. Proceeding through Lake Lothing from Lowestoft Harbour, care must be taken in navigating Lowestoft Swing Bridge. Its height is rather deceptive and numerous craft find trouble owing to this. Attention must also be given to the tides here.

Tow-path	None.
Tolls	Scale of charges of the Great Yarmouth Port and Haven Commissioners apply. The controlling authority for the collection of tolls other than mooring tolls, is the Rivers Yare, Bure and Waveney Commissioners.
Tides	Oulton Broad and Dyke are tidal. High water at Lowestoft 42 minutes after Yarmouth Bar. Spring tides rise 6ft. 6ins. Neap tides rise 5ft. 3ins. Mutford Bridge Lock, east end has high water at the same time as Lowestoft. The west end of the lock has high water 3 hours later than the east end. Water at both ends of the lock makes a level 2 hours after high water, and 2 hours after low water, at Lowestoft.
Moorings	There are numerous facilities for mooring on Oulton Broad at the yachting station and elsewhere. Rates for Oulton Broad are available on application.

Oulton Broad Yachting Station

The station is under the control of the Waveney District Council and is situated at the eastern end of the Broad within 100 yards of the main road. There is a harbour master and full facilities are available for yachtsmen.

The station comprises 700 feet of quay, protected by piers. Depths of water alongside quay about 5 feet.

Distance Table								**Miles**	**Furlongs**

Junction with River Waveney at north end of Oulton Dyke to:

								Miles	Furlongs
Oulton Dyke South	...	...	...	...	...	...	...	1	2
West end of Oulton Broad	...	...	...	...	...	...	1	4
'Wherry Inn' and staithe ...	...	...	...	...	...	...	2	1½
Mutford Bridge Lock, staithe, east end of Oulton Broad, and entrance to Lake Lothing	...	...	...	...	...	...	...	2	2
Lowestoft Bridge	...	...	...	...	...	...	...	4	1
Mouth of Lowestoft Harbour	...	...	...	...	...	...	4	3½

RIVER WAVENEY

General remarks	The southernmost of the three main rivers of the Broads has a common entrance with the River Yare at the west end of Breydon Water near Great Yarmouth. It may also be entered from Lowestoft Harbour via Lake Lothing, Oulton Broad and Dyke. From its entrance to Bungay it is 25¾ miles long, and is tidal to Geldeston Lock. The section from Geldeston to Bungay is closed except for light craft that can be portaged around sluices. Navigation lights must be shown at night, by moving craft.
Distance	From junction with River Yare at west end of Breydon Water to Bungay, 25¾ miles. Junction with River Yare to Geldeston Lock, 21½ miles.

Tides	It is high water at St. Olave's Bridge about 2½ hours after Yarmouth. High water at Yarmouth Bar is 1¾ hours before Dover. Beccles about 4 hours after Yarmouth Bar. The tide usually flows up to Beccles where there is an average rise of 2½ feet. Above this to Shipmeadow (or Geldeston) Lock the tidal limit, there is a rise of about one foot nine inches. The stream is very strong from the entrance to Somerleyton.

From Junction with River Yare to Geldeston Lock

Length	Unlimited.
Beam	,,
Draught	At H.W.S.T. about 5ft. 6ins.
Headroom	8ft. 4ins. (see Bridges).
Locks	The navigation above Geldeston (or Shipmeadow) Lock is now discontinued except for light craft. Beyond Shipmeadow there are two other locks, Ellingham and Wainford, but the gates have been removed and fixed sluices installed.
Tow-path	None.
Bridges	Between the entrance and Geldeston are the following bridges:

		Approximate Headroom at H.W.	Channel width
St. Olaves	Fixed	8ft.	78ft. 6ins.
Somerleyton	Swing	Unlimited	54ft. 4ins.
Beccles Road	Fixed	6ft. 6ins.	41ft.

Tolls	Payable to the Collector, Yare, Bure and Waveney Commissioners, 21 South Quay, Great Yarmouth. The rates are the same as those ruling on the other rivers.
Moorings	Along the River Waveney, there is free mooring and landing at the following yachting centres: Beccles. Burgh St. Peter Staithe, St. Olaves, Geldeston, Worlingham, Somerleyton, Burgh Castle. For mooring along the banks and elsewhere a charge may be made. Beccles: At the Yacht Station, at the Quay at the north end of the town. The station is maintained by the Town Council. Charges are made on a sliding scale. St. Olaves: At Bell Inn Quay also along the quay below the bridge.
Connections	**River Waveney Broad** Known as Fritton Decoy. This is land locked as Blocka Run connecting the Broad with the river is not navigable. **Geldeston Dyke** Is ½ mile long but very shallow after the site of the Railway Bridge.

Somerleyton Dyke

110 yards long, is available for mooring.

Distance Table

Bungay Staithe to:

	Miles	Furlongs
Wainford Mill and Lock (disused)	—	5
Ellingham Mill and Lock (disused)	2	—
Geldeston Lock (or Shipmeadow Lock) (disused)	4	1½
Nine Poplars	6	1½
Beccles Town Bridge	7	3½
Stanley Brickyard Staithe	8	7½
Aldeby Staithe	10	1
Worlingham Staithe	10	4
Six Mile Corner Short Reach	11	6
Seven Mile Corner	12	5
Carlton Share Mill	14	0½
Burgh St. Peter Staithe and Ferry	14	3½
Junction with Oulton Broad and Dyke	15	2
Somerleyton Dyke	18	1½
Somerleyton Staithe	18	2
St. Olave's Railway Bridge	19	6
Haddiscoe, Staithe and *junction with Haddiscoe Cut*	20	1
St. Olave's Bridge and Staithes	20	3½
Burgh Staithe and Brickyard	25	1
Burgh Castle	25	3
Junction with River Yare at West End of Breydon Water	25	6

NEW OR HADDISCOE CUT

This artificial cut is part of the old Norwich and Lowestoft Navigation. The route was authorised in 1827 and opened in 1833. It was a failure but the route is still used by pleasure craft.

Authority	Anglian Water Authority, Norfolk and Suffolk Division, The Cedars, Albemarle Road, Norwich, NOR 81 E. Tel. Norwich (0603) 53257/8. The Commissioners Tolls and Bye-laws apply to the cut.
From and to	This cut links the Rivers Waveney and Yare.
Distance	2½ miles.
Tides and depths	The cut is tidal throughout and has a rise of 2 to 3 feet. There is a depth of 5 feet of water in the centre of the channel at mean low water.
Width	Of the cut: 70ft. Of the channel: 40ft.
Depth	5ft. at low tide.
Headroom	24ft.
Locks	None.

Bridges	A fixed bridge has replaced old lift bridge.
Warning	Craft must not moor in the Cut except at the quay at the Queens Head Inn.
Tolls	Commissioners tolls and bye-laws apply.
Tow-path	None.

Distance Table   Miles   Furlongs
Reedham, junction with River Yare to:

	Miles	Furlongs
Road Bridge, Queens Head Inn	2	0
Haddiscoe, *junction with River Waveney*...	2	1½

RIVER YARE

(The River Wensum forms the first 2¾ miles of this navigation)

From and to and general remarks	The centre river of the Broads is entered from the sea at Yarmouth Haven and, running through Breydon Water, is navigable as far as Norwich, a distance of 30 miles. The river is tidal throughout. Navigation lights must be shown at night by moving craft. Chain Ferry at Reedham for cars and lorries.
Distance	Yarmouth Haven entrance to Norwich Foundry Bridge, 30 miles.
Tides	It is high water at: Reedham, about 2½ hours after Yarmouth Bar. Cantley, about 3 hours after Yarmouth Bar. Buckenham, about 3½ hours after Yarmouth Bar. Norwich, about 4½ hours after Yarmouth Bar. At Reedham springs rise about 3 feet and at Norwich 1 foot 9 inches (average). The tide runs very strongly at Yarmouth and across Breydon Water as far as Reedham, requiring great care in navigation.
Length	Not restricted but the maximum length for turning in the basin at Norwich is 170 feet.
Beam	30ft. on high tide.
Draught	10ft 6ins on high tide.
Headroom	(See bridges) Unlimited as far as Norwich.
Locks	None.
Bridges	The approximate dimension are as follows

		Headroom at H.W. *(when closed)*	Channel *width*
Yarmouth Haven Bridge	Bascule	9ft. 6ins.	90ft.
Reedham Railway	Swing	10ft.	54ft. 6ins.
Norwich, Trowse Railway	Swing	9ft. 5ins.	54ft
Norwich, Carrow Road	Bascule	14ft.	54ft

Norwich, Foundry Road	Fixed	7ft.	54ft.
East End Thorpe. Old River	Fixed	6ft. 2ins.	—
West End Thorpe. Old River	Fixed	6ft. 2ins.	—

The river Wensum is navigable for 1½ miles above the yacht station to Norwich New Mills. There are several bridges, all fixed, in the following order from the yacht station:

	Approximate Headroom at H.W.
Bishop Bridge	10ft. 6ins.
Whitefriars Bridge	9ft. 6ins.
Fye Bridge	9ft. 6ins.
St. George's Bridge	10ft. 2ins.
Duke's Palace Bridge	12ft. 9ins.
St. Mile's Bridge	9ft. 9ins.

Tolls

Payable to the Rivers Yare, Bure and Waveney Commissioners. The tolls are the same as those ruling on the other rivers.

Tow-path

None.

Moorings

Yarmouth and Norwich at the Yacht Stations.
Along the River Yare, there is free mooring and landing at the following yachting centres:
Reedham, Buckenham, Coldham Hall Inn, Brundall, Surlingham, Bramerton Woods End Inn, Norwich, Cantley Red House. A small charge may be made for moorings along the banks and elsewhere overnight. e.g. at Berney Arms.

It is dangerous to moor on bends. Moor at recognized mooring places only. The River Yare is used extensively by coastal and sea-going craft which due to their relatively large size and the restricted size of the channel, are not always able to observe the right of way. Pleasure craft are, therefore, advised to give trading boats the right of way at all times.

Yarmouth Yacht Station. This station is now leased to J. King. It is situated towards the northern end of the town on the River Bure above its junction with the River Yare
Length of quay is about 1,500 feet and there is a depth of about 5 feet of water alongside.

An attendant is on duty throughout daylight hours during the yachting season.

The station is suitable and available for yachts of the inland type with not more than 9ft. 6ins. height of superstructure above water level, to negotiate fixed bridges. Facilities at station.

Sailing yachts approaching the station from the direction of Acle must do so on an ebb tide. 200 yards or so before reaching the site of the old railway bridge, turn into the wind, lower sails and drop a weight over the bow, first making sure that the line attached to the weight is secured to the ring on the foredeck. The tide will then carry the craft stern first. Use the weight over the bow as a break and steer with the tiller but keep it within the well. If a stay at the yacht station is intended there is no need to lower the mast as the moorings are reached before the bridge. If no stay is intended, the mast must be lowered to permit passage under the two bridges.

Approaching the yacht station from the direction of Breydon Water, arrange to arrive at the mouth of the River Bure at slack tide. Moor to one of the three posts on the left or at the wharf on the right of the River Bure before reaching the first of the two bridges. Lower the mast and proceed to the yacht station on the flood tide—not before.

Norwich Yacht Station. The Yacht Station is under the control of the Norwich Corporation and is situated near Thorpe Station, just above the Foundry Bridge. Attendants are on duty throughout daylight hours.

At Thorpe. Moorings available in the old river, and at Village Green Quay, also at the boatyard. This is an excellent mooring for Norwich in the high season as there is a good bus service.

RIVER YARE BROADS AND BRANCHES

River Chet	Branch river from River Yare.
Authority	Rivers Yare, Bure and Waveney Commissioners.
From and to	Junction with River Yare to Loddon.
Distance	3½ miles.
Length	Unlimited.
Beam	About 16ft.
Draught	3ft.
Locks	None.
General remarks	Turning is easy at Loddon, where there is an excellent staithe. This neglected river has been dredged and cleaned out and boat yards have been opened at Loddon.
Breydon Water	
General remarks and navigational warning	This large inland lake is situated westward of Yarmouth. It is generally shallow, except for the channel of the River Yare which is towards its southern shore, and which is marked by green stakes on its northern and red stakes on its southern side. These stakes should not be approached too closely, as the mud extends right up to them. At the Yarmouth end of Breydon, the Knowle an extensive shoal, must be avoided, it is however well marked with posts and dolphins.

Through the Yarmouth bridges and across Breydon Water, the tide runs with considerable strength, and on this account the approach to Yarmouth from Breydon, and the navigation through the bridges, especially from the Yare to the Bure and vice versa is difficult, especially for strangers with sailing craft. Knowledge and judgement are required as to the right moment for lowering canvas and masts, bearing in mind the necessity for keeping sufficient way on to negotiate the bridges.

Proceeding through Vauxhall Bridge, yachtsmen should time their arrival in order to negotiate it at slack tide about 1½ hours after low water, when there are generally depths of 6 to 7 feet in the fairway.

The best time to start to cross Breydon Water is about 3 hours before high water, and up the River Bure at 2 hours before high water.

In navigating through for the first time, strangers are advised to seek local assistance.

There are no licensed pilots for this navigation, and as there are no fixed charges, yachtsmen should make arrangements as to price before accepting assistance. In this respect, the Yarmouth attendant, on duty at the Yacht Station, will always be pleased to give advice. Tel. Great Yarmouth 2794.

Rockland Broad
About 66 acres. Depth about 3 feet.
Craft must be kept to channel up Fleet Dyke, marked by black posts with white tops until near marker buoys' notice board, thence across the Broad in line with the red marker buoys.

Entrance to the dyke leading from Train Reach to the Broad is marked by a large sign.

An alternative entrance is from Rockland Reach up Short Dyke and across the Broad by the reverse procedure.
Rockland Dyke is 3 furlongs in length and The Fleet 5 furlongs long.

Surlingham Broad
Near Brundall. A small Broad suitable for light craft only. Distance navigable about 3 furlongs.
Depth about 3 feet at low tide in the channel across the Broad.
Bargate Water has sufficient draught for cruisers. This section of Surlingham Broad provides an alternative route to the main river and is sometimes confused with the main Broad itself.

Hardley Dyke
Length 2½ furlongs. Depth 2 to 3 feet.

Langley Dyke
Length 2½ furlongs. Depth 2 to 3 feet.

Loop Line of Old River round Thorpe Village
Length 5½ furlongs. Depth 3 feet.

Trowse Mills Cut (River Yare)
Length nearly one mile. Depth 3 feet.

River Yare. *(The first 2¾ miles of the Navigation is the River Wensum).*

Distance Table   *Miles   Furlongs*
Norwich, New Mills, to:
  Norwich, Fye Bridge ... ... — 4½

Distance Table

	Miles	Furlongs
Norwich, Bishop Bridge ...	1	1½
Norwich, Foundry Bridge and Thorpe Railway Station	1	4
Norwich, New Carrow Bridge and Toll Office	2	0½
Norwich, east end of Colman's Works, and *junction with Branch to Trowse Mills (River Yare)*	2	6½
West end of Thorpe New Cut, and western *junction of loop line of old river round Thorpe Village*	3	1
East end of Thorpe New Cut, and eastern *junction of loop line of river round Thorpe Village*	3	6
Whitlingham	4	1
Thorpe Hospital	4	7
Postwick Hall	6	—
Bramerton Staithe	6	4
Surlingham, Brickyard Staithe	7	3
Surlingham Ferry and Staithe	8	2
Entrance to Surlingham Broad	9	3
Brundall Railway Station	9	6
Exit from Surlingham Broad	10	—
Coldham Hall Ferry and Staithe (Coldham Hall Inn)	10	2½
Junction with Strumpshaw Dyke (unnavigable)	10	5¼
Junction with Rockland Dyke, leading to Rockland Broad	11	4½
Buckenham Staithe	12	5
Buckenham Ferry	12	7
Junction with Hassingham Dyke (unnavigable)	13	5
Junction with Langley Dyke	14	6½
Cantley Ferry and Railway Station	15	6½
Hardley Brickyard Staithe	17	0½
Junction with Hardley Dyke	17	2½
Hardley Cross, *junction with River Chet*	18	3
Norton Staithe	18	5
Reedham Ferry (Reedham Ferry Inn)	18	7
Reedham, *junction with New Cut*	20	2
Upper Seven Mile House	21	7
Six Mile House	22	7
Berney Arms Staithe and Railway Station	24	4
Western Extremity of Breydon Water and *junction with River Waveney*	24	6
Yarmouth, eastern extremity of Breydon water, and *junction with River Bure*	28	5
Haven Bridge, Great Yarmouth	28	7
Gorleston Ferry	30	2
Gorleston, mouth of River	31	5

Branch to Trowse Mills (River Yare)
Junction with Main Line of Navigation to:

Trowse Mills (unnavigable to here at present due to weeds)	—	7½

Loop Line of Old River round Thorpe Village
Western junction with Main Line of Navigation to:

Thorpe Railway Station (now closed)	—	4½
Eastern junction with Main Line of Navigation	—	5½

Rockland Dyke and Rockland Broad
Junction with Main Line of Navigation to:

Commencement of Rockland Broad*	—	5
Rockland Staithe on Rockland Broad	—	7

Langley Dyke
From junction with Main Line of Navigation to:

Staithe at upper end	—	2½

Hardley Dyke
From junction with Main Line of Navigation to:

Hardley Staithe	—	2½

RIVER BURE

From and to and general remarks

The northernmost of the three main Broads rivers, is entered from the River Yare close by Vauxhall Station, Yarmouth, and is navigable to Coltishall. Above this point the locks are closed to head of navigation at Aylsham.

The Bure has several tributaries, the most important of which are the Rivers Thurne and Ant. The river is tidal to Wroxham.

Navigation lights must be shown at night by moving craft.

Distances

Entrance Junction with the River Yare to Coltishall, 31½ miles. Coltishall to Aylsham, 9¼ miles, (light craft that can be portaged only).

Tides

It is high water (according to winds) at Acle Bridge about 2½ hours after Yarmouth Bar. Horning about 4 hours after Yarmouth Bar. The tide usually runs strongly between Yarmouth and Acle.

Tow-path

None.

Length†

75ft.

Beam†

16ft.

Draught

6ft. below Wroxham, 5ft. above Wroxham.

Headroom

See Bridges.

Bridges

The following bridges span the river from the entrance to Wroxham.

			Approximate Headroom at H.W.	Channel Width
Vauxhall	Fixed		7ft.	100ft.
Runham Suspension	"		6ft.	64ft.
Yarmouth Railway	"		15ft.	98ft. 10ins.
Acle Road	"		12ft.	78ft.
Wroxham Road	"		7ft. 3ins.	26ft. 5ins.
" Railway	"		10ft.	47ft.

* A line of posts marks the navigation channel across the Broad.

Locks	None. The 5 locks on the old Aylsham Navigation are closed. Buxton Lock is completely filled in and Burgh Lock is virtually non-existent. A portage ramp for light craft has been installed at Coltishall Lock.
Tolls	Payable to the Collector, Rivers Yare, Bure and Waveney Commissioners.
Moorings	For Yarmouth Yachting Station (see page 242).

Along the River Bure, there is free mooring and landing at the following yachting centres:

Stokesby, Acle, Horning, Wroxham, Coltishall.

For mooring along the banks and elsewhere, a small charge may be made.

Unless compelled to do so, do not moor anywhere between Stracey Arms on the River Bure and Great Yarmouth Yacht Station.

Wroxham Regatta 1910

RIVER BURE BROADS AND BRANCHES

Belaugh Broad,   Private – restored by Broads Authority.

Bridge Broad   A section opened recently by the Commissioners after having
(Wroxham)   closed for many years.

South Walsham Broad, reached by Fleet Dyke, $\frac{7}{8}$ mile long.
        At western end is Common Broad, which is private, but the owner allows cruising and sailing. Draught available is 4ft. at L.W. springs in most places but there are small portions under this figure.

Ranworth Broad,   reached by Ranworth Dam, $\frac{3}{8}$ mile long.
        Not available for navigation, but the eastern end, popularly known as Malthouse Broad, is open. Depth is about 5ft.

Cockshoot Broad and Dyke. Chained and private except for a short section of the dyke used for moorings.

Great Salhouse Broad, adjoins river. Depth of water, 4 to 5ft.

Little Salhouse Broad, adjoins river. Depth of water, 4 to 5ft.

Wroxham Broad,   adjoins river. 112 acres in extent.
        There is no public staithe on the Broad.

Little Switzerland   This was an area of local canals connecting with the Bure. They were located on the western side of the Bure between Belaugh and Wroxham. These canals were cut into the hillside to enable wherries to go up to the marl workings and load. One canal was over half a mile long. There would appear to be scope for some aquatic development on this site.

Hoveton Great Broad, 105 acres, chained and private.
        Visitors are cordially invited to walk round the Nature Trail which has recently been laid out at Hoveton Great Broad by the Nature Conservancy. The purpose of the trail is to demonstrate in simple, non-technical language, the natural history of this part of Broadland and the reasons why Hoveton Great Broad is included in the Bure Marshes National Nature Reserve.
        Starting and ending on the banks of the River Bure at a point just upstream from the entrance to Salhouse Broad, the Trail consists of a path about half a mile long which can be walked without getting wet feet, admission is free and a descriptive leaflet, obtainable from the Trail Warden, costs only a few pence.
        During the summer months, the Trail is usually open from 10 a.m. until 5 p.m. on Mondays to Fridays inclusive, and from 2 p.m. until 5 p.m. on Sundays, it is closed on Saturdays. The Trail can only be reached by boat—access by land is impossible. Those visiting can moor their boats alongside the Trail Quay free of charge. In the interests of the birdlife, dogs may not be taken round the trail.

Little Hoveton Broad, popularly known as Black Horse Broad.
        Depth of water 3 to 4ft. Open from Easter to 1st September each year.

Upton Dyke,	$\frac{3}{8}$ of a mile long.
Acle Dyke,	$\frac{1}{4}$ of a mile long.

The following Broads are land locked, as Muck Fleet, which connects them to the River Bure is not navigable even for rowing boats: **Filby, Ormesby, Rollesby, Lily.** Rowing boats and dinghies may be hired to navigate these Broads.

Distance Table	Miles	Furlongs
Aylsham Bridge and Staithes to:		
Aylsham Lock (closed)	1	—
Burgh Bridge	2	3
Burgh Lock (totally derelict)	3	—
Oxnead Lock (closed)	3	6
Lamas Church	5	3
Buxton Lamas (site of Buxton Lock)	5	7
Coltishall Bridge	9	$0\frac{1}{2}$
Coltishall Lock (closed there is a portage ramp for light craft) ...	9	2
Boundary of Aylsham Navigation*	9	4
Coltishall Staithe (Rising Sun and King's Head Inns)	10	—
Coltishall Anchor Inn	10	4
Belaugh Village	11	3
Castle Staithe, Castle Inn	13	1½
Entrance to Bridge Broad (reopened recently)	14	3½
Wroxham Railway Bridge...	14	$5\frac{1}{2}$
Wroxham Bridge	14	7
Junction with North Entrance to Wroxham Broad	16	—
Junction with South Entrance to Wroxham Broad	16	4
Junction with entrance to Little Salhouse Broad	17	$0\frac{1}{2}$
Junction with western entrance to Great Salhouse Broad	17	2
Junction with eastern entrance to Great Salhouse Broad	17	4
Entrance to Hoveton Great Broad, private (the entrance is chained)	18	—
Entrance to Hoveton Little Broad	19	1
Lower Street, Horning, Swan Hotel	19	6
New Inn, Horning	19	$7\frac{1}{2}$
Horning Ferry and Ferry Inn (Ferry now closed)	20	4
Cockshoot Dyke, leading to Cockshoot Broad (this is private, and the entrance is chained) Staithe at entrance	20	7
Junction with Ranworth Dam, leading to Malthouse Broad and Ranworth Broad. (Ranworth is chained and private).	22	2
Junction with River Ant	23	4
Junction with Fleet Dyke	24	1
St. Benedict's Abbey	24	$6\frac{1}{2}$
Thurne Mouth, *junction with River Thurne*	26	$2\frac{1}{2}$
Junction with Upton Dyke	27	7
Acle Bridge	29	1
Junction with Acle Dyke	29	7
Muck Fleet Dyke, not navigable. (Communicates with Lily, Filby, Rollesby and Ormesby Broads)	30	4
Stokesby Staithe	31	—
Tunstall Dyke, not navigable at present	31	$6\frac{1}{2}$

* Aylsham to Coltishall is not navigable except for light craft as the locks are derelict.

Distance Table

							Miles	Furlongs
Stracey Arms Inn and Staithe	...	...	...	...	...	...	32	3
Herringby Staithe	...	...	...	...	...	...	33	5
Six Mile House	...	...	...	...	...	...	34	2
Runham Staithe	...	...	...	...	...	...	34	5
Runham Swim Ferry and Five Mile House	...	...	...	...	35		.3
Mautby Swim Ferry	...	...	...	...	...	...	36	2½
Three Mile House	...	...	...	...	...	...	37	6
Two Mile House	...	...	...	...	...	...	38	7
Yarmouth Yacht Station	...	...	...	...	...	...	40	2
Yarmouth Public Staithe and Suspension Bridge	...	...	...	40		3
Yarmouth, *junction with River Yare and eastern extremity of Breydon Water*	...	...	...	...	...	...	40	5

RIVER ANT

From and to	This tributary of the Bure is entered 6 miles above Acle, and about 1½ miles beyond the River Thurne, runs northward through Barton Broad to Antingham Pond.
Distance	Junction with River Bure to Junction with North Walsham Canal, 8 miles.
Tides	The tidal effect is not felt very much beyond Ludham Bridge, the rise and fall being about 7 inches.
Length	Up to about 60ft.
Beam	Up to about 17ft.
Draught	Approximately 5ft. at L.W. springs.
Headroom	See Bridges.
Locks	None.

				Approximate Headroom at H.W.	Width of Channel
Bridges					
	Ludham Bridge	... ...	Fixed	8ft.	17ft. 10ins.
	Wayford Bridge	... ...	„	7ft.	13ft. 10ins.

Tow-path	None.
Tolls	Payable to the Collector, Yare, Bure and Waveney Commissioners. The tolls are the same as ruling on the other rivers.
Moorings	Along the River Ant there is free mooring and landing at the following yachting centres: Ludham, Stalham, Wayford and on Barton Broad. For mooring along the banks or elsewhere, a small charge may be made.

RIVER ANT BROADS AND BRANCHES

Barton Broad About 365 acres in extent.
Depth about 3ft. 6ins. to 4ft. In navigation channels it is about 5ft. to 5ft. 6ins.
Craft should leave black posts with white tops on the starboard hand and the red posts on the port hand when proceeding to the head of the navigation. Junctions of channels are now marked by black and yellow posts. (New I.A.L.A. system – 4 different varieties according to cardinal points). Some black posts have been repainted green.
There are two staithes on Barton Broad:
Catfield Wood End Staithe. Eastern shore of the Broad, ⅜ mile from southern entrance of river into the Broad. Barton Turf Staithe. North-west corner of the Broad and about ¼ mile from northern entrance of the river.

Sutton Broad Depths about 5ft. This Broad is full of reeds and only the channel is available for navigation.

Crome's Broad Chained and private.

Stalham Dyke Depth about 5ft. 6ins.
Length 1 mile 1 furlong.

Old Lime Kiln Dyke Depth about 5ft. 6ins.
Length about ½ mile.
Staithe at end of Neatishead Village.

Distance Table

Junction with River Bure to:

	Miles	Furlongs
Ludham Bridge	—	7
Irstead Church	4	1
Southern entrance of River to Barton Broad*	4	4
Northern entrance of River to Barton Broad	5	6
Junction with Stalham Dyke	6	2½
Wayford Bridge, Staithes	7	7
Junction with Smallburgh River, leading to Dilham Dyke	8	—
Junction with North Walsham and Dilham Canal	8	2½

Stalham Dyke

Junction with River Ant to:

	Miles	Furlongs
Junction with Sutton Dyke (leading to Sutton Staithe Country Club)	—	4
Stalham Staithes	1	1

RIVER THURNE

From and to This tributary of the Bure is entered about 3½ miles above Acle, and connects Hickling Broad, Horsey Mere and Martham Broad with the main waterway.

* For Sutton, Stalham, Wayford and Honing, craft should keep to the right passing Pleasure Hill Island on the left.

Distance	Entrance to head of River (Martham Broad), 6 miles.
Tides	The river is tidal, the average rise and fall being about 8 inches.
Length	About 60ft.
Beam	7ft. 6ins.
Draught	5ft. 6ins.
Headroom	See Bridges. 6ft. 6ins. at mean H.W.
Locks	None.

Bridges			*Approximate* Headroom at H.W.	Channel Width
	Potter Heigham Old Road	Fixed	6ft. 6ins.	21ft.
	„ „ New Road	„	7ft. 6ins.	70ft.

Take great care navigating through the old road bridge which is very narrow. Pilotage through the bridge can be obtained from Herbert Wood's Boatyard. Special enquiries are advised.

Tow-path	None.
Tolls	Payable to the Yare, Bure & Waveney Commissioners. The tolls are the same as those ruling on the other rivers.
Moorings	Along the River Thurne there is free mooring and landing at the following yachting centres: Potter Heigham, Martham Staithe. For mooring along the banks of elsewhere, a small charge may be made.

RIVER THURNE BROADS AND BRANCHES

Heigham Sound Depth about 5ft. 6ins. in navigation channel, elsewhere about 3ft. Navigation channel is marked the same way as Barton Broad.

Hickling Broad Reached through Candle Dyke, Heigham Sound and White Slea Meres. The largest Broad with the exception of Breydon Water. Depths about 3ft. Catfield Dyke is navigable to Catfield Staithe. Generally shallow. Keep near posts where water is the best. Excellent mooring at Pleasure Boat Inn.

On this Broad the channel is marked on the starboard (right) hand only when proceeding towards Hickling Staithe. Keep within 100ft. of these Hickling posts and keep them on the port side returning towards Potter Heigham.

To find the entrance to Catfield Dyke off Hickling Broad, and Waxham New Cut off Horsey Mere, look for the leading marks. These are two posts each surmounted by a triangle, all painted white. By bringing these in line and steering towards them, you will arrive at the entrance to the Dyke or the New Cut.

There is a water trail on Hickling Broad operated by the Norfolk Naturalists' Trust during the summer months. The reed-lighter operating the trail runs from the Pleasure Boat Inn. Other trails are available from the Warden's House, Stubb Rd, Hickling.

Moorings	There are three staithes, namely Hickling Staithe, Catfield Staithe, and a private staithe near Hickling Staithe. Lines of posts mark the navigation channel across the Broads to the staithes. A short branch off Catfield Dyke leads to Catfield Common Staithe.
Horsey Mere	Depth from 2 to 6ft. There is one staithe on Horsey Mere situated at its eastern end, distant about 7 furlongs from the southern extremity of the Mere. The Nelson Head ½ mile from the Staithe is the only inn in the area.
Martham Broad	Depth from 2 to 3ft. Sock Drain is not navigable.
White Slea Broad	Depths about 5ft. 6ins. in the navigation channel. Elsewhere about 3ft.
Womack Water	Depth about 4ft. Length ⅞ mile.
Blackfleet Broad	Silted up, unnavigable.
Thurne Dyke	Depth about 3ft. Length ⅛ mile.

Distance Table
River Thurne

Thurne Mouth, junction with River Bure to:	Miles	Furlongs
Junction with Thurne Dyke	—	3
Junction with Womack Water	1	2½
Pug Street Staithe	2	2
Potter Heigham Bridge	3	—
Junction with Candle Dyke (leading to Hickling Broad, Horsey Mere and New Cut)	4	4
Martham Staithe and Ferry	4	6½
Head of the navigation of the River, and *junction with navigation across* *Martham Broad to West Somerton*	5	5½

Navigation through Candle Dyke, Heigham Sound and White Slea Mere to Hickling Broad

South end of Candle Dyke and junction with River Thurne to:		
North end of Candle Dyke and southern extremity of Heigham Sound	—	3
North-western extremity of Heigham Sound and *junction of Dyke leading to White Slea Mere*	1	1½
Southern extremity of White Slea Mere	1	2½

Distance Table

	Miles	Furlongs
North-western extremity of White Slea Mere and *junction of Dyke leading to Hickling Broad*	1	4½
South-eastern extremity of Hickling Broad	1	5

Navigation through Candle Dyke, Heigham Sound, Meadow Dyke and Horsey Mere to Lound Bridge, Palling, on Waxham Cut

South end of Candle Dyke, and junction with River Thurne to:

	Miles	Furlongs
North end of Candle Dyke and southern extremity of Heigham Sound	—	3
North-eastern extremity of Heigham Sound and *junction with Meadow Dyke*	1	1½
Southern extremity of Horsey Mere	2	1
Northern extremity of Horsey Mere and *junction with Waxham New Cut*	2	6
Waxham Bridge (navigation ceases here)	4	—
The right of navigation may still exist to:		
Lound Bridge, 1 mile from Palling Village	6	2
Waxham to Lound is totally weeded up.		

Navigation across Martham Broad to West Somerton

Junction with River Thurne to:

	Miles	Furlongs
Western extremity of Martham Broad	—	1
Eastern extremity of Martham Broad, and *junction of Dyke leading to West Somerton* ... ... —	—	4
West Somerton Staithes ... ... —	—	7

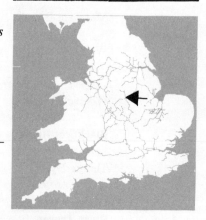

Nottingham Canal (69)

This Canal was constructed under powers granted by an Act of 1792 and originally joined the Erewash Canal at Langley Mill to the Trent Navigation at Nottingham. Most of the navigation is, however, now abandoned, the short remaining section between Lenton Chain and Nottingham forming a by-pass of an unnavigable section of the River Trent and is thus incorporated in the latter navigation. † The Canal from Lenton Chain to Langley Mill was 12⅜ miles long and there were 18 locks. The top end of the canal is navigable from the Great Northern basin to the bottom of the Cromford Canal. The bottom lock of the Cromford is restored linking the Basin to the Erewash.

Authority	British Waterways Board.
Length	2½ miles.
Branches	One. Nottingham from near Boots Warehouse to Manvers Street, length ¼ mile. There is a short arm of 200 yards from this branch known as Poplar Cut.
Dimensions	As for River Trent, Nottingham Section.
Locks	2. Meadow Lane and Castle. Fall from Lenton Chain. (82ft x 14ft 6 ins x 8ft headroom).

*See plan River Trent page 367

River Great Ouse (70)

This river and its tributaries was originally promoted as a navigation by Acts passed in the following years, 1670, 1751, 1795, 1796, 1805, 1810, 1816, 1818, 1819, 1827 and 1830. The Hundred Foot River (sometimes called the New Bedford River) was constructed in about 1650.

There have been many disputes and much litigation regarding river rights in the past as, for many years, the Great Ouse Catchment Board, followed by its successor, the Great Ouse River Board, and now the Anglian Water Authority, has been the drainage authority but has had no powers to expend monies on navigation, and bye-laws have been made under Section 79 of the Water Resources Act 1963 so that the river can be restored throughout to navigable conditions. Boats must be registered with the A.W.A. and charges are available on application.

The Great Ouse is the biggest of the Fenland rivers; Fenland is a very wide expression, but is generally considered to be that area of 2,500 square miles which extends from south of Lincoln to Suffolk, and from St. Ives to King's Lynn. This area is, in the main, a shallow basin consisting on its eastern side of clay and silt beds close to the sea, which in former times came much further inland. It is a very ancient area and for a study of its formation, one must go back at least as far as the last ice age. Numerous forests once covered part of the area, but in the course of time the trees died off sinking into the peat to become bog oak.

Certain of the fringe areas have been inhabited since Roman times, but after 400 A. D., it seems likely that the Fen country was for all practical purposes uninhabited until Christianity came to England when some of the Holy Fathers took to the Fens to establish their religious institutions at, for example, Ely and Crowland. Areas of reed and swamp formed a natural defence against marauders of various kinds who invaded the country.

But Fenland has changed out of all recognition since the Middle Ages; now tamed by vast drainage works, it contains some of the richest farming land in Britain and although often represented as flat and uninteresting country, there are, within it, areas of amenity value on a par with the River Thames, for example between St. Ives and Huntingdon. Most of the waterways in the Fens are navigable but, unlike cruising on other parts of the canal system, it must be remembered that they are all predominantly drainage channels and authorities who control them are primarily concerned with drainage. In the past, navigation was indeed the main function of the rivers as, in early times, roads were bad and few and far between.

The most important name connected with the drainage of the Fens is that of Cornelius Vermuyden who pioneered the work for the Duke of Bedford in the middle of the 17th century. The inhabitants of the area who earned their livelihood by fishing, wild fowling, etc. hated the drainage experts who sought to turn the Fens into agricultural land. Over the years vast lakes known as meres—Whittlesea, Ramsey, Trundle and Ugg Meres— were drained; Whittlesea, the largest mere, covering over 1600 acres, was drained during the last century increasing the value of the land tenfold.

There is a longstanding tradition in some quarters to show Cornelius Vermuyden in an unfavourable light, this is due to the undoubted injustice caused by his drainage works, but it is doubtful whether this social upheaval was as great as that caused by the Enclosure Act of later years which certainly caused more hardship.

Since early drainage works were completed there have been a number of disastrous floods, but none so bad as that of 1947 when damage was estimated at £20 million. Great gaps were torn in the river walls and in the neighbourhood of Ely 15,000 acres of land were flooded. Further trouble occurred in 1953 but gigantic works carried out by the Great Ouse River Authority followed by the Anglian Water Authority since should cure most of the drainage problems. Far reaching proposals made to Vermuyden in 1638 were the same in principle as those made to and adopted by the River Board in recent years. Allowing for the fact that the

Fen level in Vermuyden's day was 15ft higher than at present, it is probably fair to say that had his ideas been accepted then, the more recent flooding disasters would have been greatly minimised.

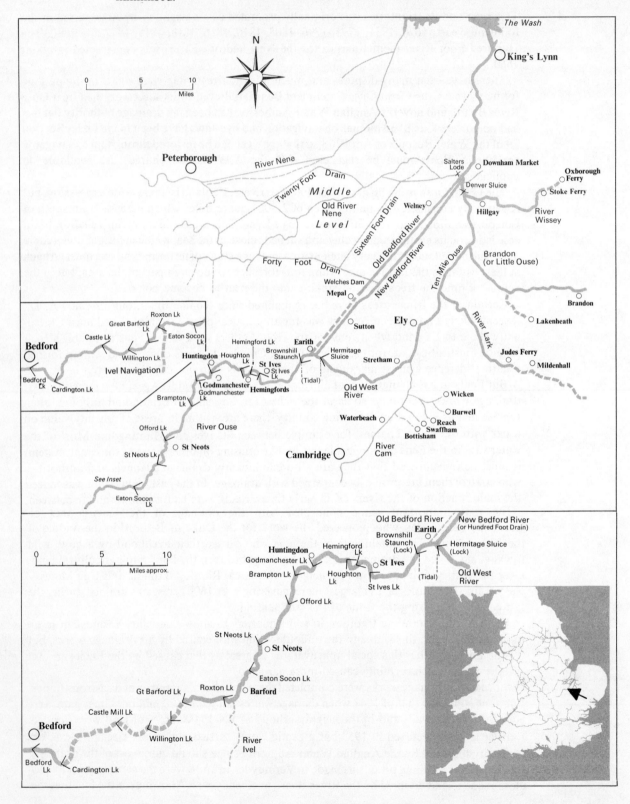

The river flows through attractive towns, Bedford which has associations with John Bunyan, St. Neots, Huntingdon and Godmanchester, St. Ives and Ely with its magnificent cathedral. Much of the cruising area is deserted even at peak holiday times, particularly the tributaries of which the Wissey is probably the prettiest. Wicken Fen (National Trust) has a museum and is a section of Fen country kept in its original state. A problem of navigation in recent years was the extensive shallowing of the Old West River which serves no drainage function. At the instigation of the East Anglian Waterways Association this was dredged in 1965–8 by the Royal Engineers in co-operation with the river authority. This operation on over 11 miles of river is the largest to date by the Services on any waterway and has been invaluable in maintaining trouble free navigation. On the Old West River is the famous pumping engine at Stretham which should be visited.

Authority	Anglian Water Authority, Great Ouse Division, Clarendon Road, Cambridge. Tel. Cambridge (0223) 61561. (The waterways within an are of the Anglian Water Authority running south-west from Denver Sluice along the New Bedford River or Hundred Foot River to Over, then south-east to Stow-cum-Quy, then north-east to Methwold. Norfolk and then back north-west to Denver are known as the South Level Rivers. Such rivers as the Old West, the Lark, Little Ouse and Great Ouse and their tributaries are in this area).
From and to and General remarks	Kempston Mill (near Bedford) to King's Lynn and The Wash. There appears to be a public right of navigation from Bedford to the Grand Union Canal but no locks were ever erected on this section of the river. The Great Ouse Restoration Society was formed to campaign and assist lock reconstruction to Bedford, a task now achieved. At Earith, the Ouse becomes tidal and is continued along a 21 mile artificial cut, known as the Hundred Foot or New Bedford River. Also at Earith the Old River under the names, Old West, Ely Ouse and Ten Mile, branches off and eventually rejoins the main river at Denver. The Old River has junction with the River Cam and three tributaries, the Lark, the Little Ouse (or Brandon River) and the Wissey.
Distance	Bedford to The Wash, 75 miles.
Special note	The Old Bedford River is in two sections, and the northern portion from Welches Dam is navigable, but the lower detached section is not navigable.
Length	Great Barford to Earith, Brownshill Staunch Lock, 100ft. Earith to Denver and the Wash, unlimited but maximum length at Denver Lock, 70ft.
Beam	Kempston Mill to Great Barford 10ft 2 ins Great Barford to Earith, 10ft. 10ins. Earith to Denver, 12ft. 6ins. Denver to the Wash, 17ft. 6ins.

Width of channel	Tempsford Bridge to Earith, about 30ft. Earith to Denver, 30ft. to 40ft. Denver to the Wash, 50ft. to 70ft.

Draught

Tempsford Bridge to Earith. At minimum water level there is, generally speaking, a minimum draught of 4ft. 6ins. on this section of river with the exception of a length approximately two miles below St. Neots Mill where the draught is only 3ft. Above Brownshill Staunch for ¾ mile is also only 3ft.

Earith to Denver Sluice. The depth available from Earith to Denver via the Hundred Foot River is considerably influenced by the amount of fluvial water, but under dry weather conditions the minimum draught is only about one foot at low water, spring or neap tides. During a high neap tide draught would be about 2ft. and on a high spring tide about 3ft. to 3ft. 6ins.

Denver to King's Lynn. The depth of water from Denver Sluice to King's Lynn varies according to the tide and river discharges. The minimum depth at low water spring tides is approximately one foot and on neap tides about 2ft. 6ins. For purposes of navigation, the maximum permissible draught on spring tides may be taken as 10ft. and on neaps about 6ft.

Canoeing note

Canoeable from Buckingham.
The Felmersham Reach of the Upper Ouse approximately 2 miles has been dealt with under Section 10 A.W.A. Act 1977 creating a public right of navigation to manual propelled, and sailing craft.

Tides

King's Lynn to the Wash. Rise: Springs, 23ft. 6ins. Neaps, 19ft. 6ins.

Locks

15. Fall from Bedford.

Dimensions

	Draught ft. ins.	Width ft. ins.	Length ft. ins.	Approx. Headroom under gates ft. ins.
Roxton	4 3	13 0	81 6	9 0
Eaton Socon ...	4 0	11 2	103 6	8 3
St. Neots	3 7	11 6	108 0	12 4
Buckden	4 6	11 2	100 0	8 3
Brampton	5 6	11 9	104 0	8 6
Godmanchester ...	4 0	13 2	100 0	8 6
Houghton	5 3	11 6	91 0	8 6
Hemingford ...	5 6	12 6	92 0	8 6
St. Ives Staunch ...	4 10	10 10	102 9	10 0
Brownshill Staunch	4 8	13 3	100 0	10 0

Bridges

Tempsford Bridge to Earith. 12 bridges and 2 footbridges. Minimum headroom 7ft. 6ins.

Earith to Denver. Headroom under bridges at high water:

			Spring Tides		Neap Tides	
Earith Bridge	...	...	11ft.	9ins.	14ft.	8ins.
Sutton Gault	...	...	9ft.	6ins.	13ft.	4ins.
Mepal	...	...	10ft.	9ins.	14ft.	2ins.
Railway Bridge	...	...	8ft.	9ins.	13ft.	6ins.
Welney	...	...	7ft.	10ins.	12ft.	8ins.

(There is a new bridge at Mepal 360 yards upstream of the old one).

Denver to Wash. Headroom under bridges at high water:

			Spring Tides		Neap Tides	
Downham	...	...	8ft.	2ins.	12ft.	9ins.
Stow	...	...	7ft.	9ins.	12ft.	4ins.
Railway	...	...	12ft.	2ins.	16ft.	9ins.
Magdalen	...	...	7ft.	8ins.	12ft.	2ins.
St. Germans	...	...	8ft.	2ins.	12ft.	9ins.
Railway	...	...	15ft.	8ins.	20ft.	3ins.
Free Bridge	...	...	9ft.	4ins.	13ft.	11ins.

The headroom given is for average tides.

Tow-path	Throughout the navigation to King's Lynn except at certain bridges.
Bye-laws	On application to the A.W.A.

Old Bedford River and Counter Wash Drain

The Old Bedford River is in two parts, the southern portion from Earith to Welches Dam being only a flood channel for filling the Hundred Foot wash lands in times of flood. The Old Bedford commences to be navigable at Welches Dam where it forms a junction with Counter Wash Drain and Forty Foot Drain on the Middle Level. It proceeds via Welney to Old Bedford Sluice, near Salters Lode which is a single tide door that can be opened only when the tide makes a level. As the tide rises rapidly this sluice must be passed rapidly. The Wildfowl Trust has a centre at Welney near Hundred Foot Bank.

From and to	(1) Welches Dam to Salters Lode (Old Bedford River). (2) Welches Dam to Mepal Pumping Station (Counter Wash Drain).
Distance	(1) 12¼ miles. (2) 3 miles.
Length	Unlimited, but craft over 46ft. long cannot go through Welches Dam Lock into Forty Foot Drain.
Beam	15ft. Entrance Lock to Forty Foot is 10ft. 9ins.
Draught	3ft. 6ins.
Headroom	8ft.
Locks	One flood gate at Salters Lode. (This can only be passed when the tide makes a level).

Old River

General remarks	The Old River comprises the following:
	Old West River from Earith to junction with River Cam.
	Ely Ouse, junction with River Cam to Littleport.
	Ten Mile River, Littleport to Denver.

Distance

Earith to Denver, approx. 31⅛ miles.

Old West River	"	11⅝	"
Ely Ouse	"	9¼	"
Ten Mile River	"	10¼	"

Length

Governed by Hermitage and Denver Locks, 90 and 70ft. respectively. Length is not limited through Denver Sluice if passing through when the tide makes a level.

Beam

Hermitage Lock, 12ft. 6ins. Denver Sluice, 16ft. 6ins.

Draught

Hermitage Lock, 5ft.
Old West River.
   Hermitage Lock to Flat Bridge, approx. 4ft.
   Flat Bridge to Aldreth Cause way, 4ft. 6ins.
   Aldreth Causeway to junction River Cam, 5ft.
Ely Ouse, min. 8ft.
Ten Mile River. 9ft. 6ins.
Denver Lock, Upstream 14ft. Downstream 8ft.—9ft. (at L.W.).

Locks

2. Hermitage and Denver. Fall from Earith at Hermitage. Denver has gates that open either end depending on the state of the tide. Guillotine gates have been installed.

Bridges

Headroom under Bridges:

Old West.		*ft.*	*ins.*
Willingham Flat Bridge		9	4
Aldreth		10	6
Twenty-Pence		10	4
Stretham Ferry		10	3
Stretham Wooden Bridge		11	1
Military Road Bridge		10	6
Wooden Bridge		11	4
Railway		11	4
Ely Ouse			
Newmarket Railway		10	10
Ely High Bridge		10	8
Cutter Railway Bridge		10	7
Muckhill Railway Bridge		10	9
Beet Factory Footbridge		11	8
Beet Factory Pipe Line		11	10
Adelaide Railway Bridge		10	10
Adelaide Road Bridge		13	11
Sandhill Bridge		11	4
Ten Mile			
Littleport Bridge		11	2
Hilgay Toll Bridge		10	3

Railway Bridge	...	...	...	...	...	12	3
Denver Sluice Foot Bridge		...	...	...		13	10
Denver Sluice Road Bridge		...	...	...		15	2

Headroom downstream water levels *ft. ins.*

Denver Sluice Foot Bridge	M.H.W.S.	7	7
	M.H.W.N.	11	7
Denver Sluice Road Bridge	M.H.W.S.	8	11
	M.H.W.N.	12	11

Tides

Levels in the Hundred Foot River are affected as far as Mepal on neap tides and up to Earith on spring tides. The tidal effect on the old course of the river is slight but some reduction in level occurs at low water when Denver Sluice is opened for discharge purposes. Apart from this, the old course is maintained at a normal navigation level of 13ft. 8ins. above Denver Lock sill. High water at Denver Sluice is approximately one hour after King's Lynn.
At Earith spring tides rise about 1ft. 6ins.
At Denver Sluice spring tides rise about 11ft. 6ins.
Neaps rise about 8ft.

Navigation notes

Care should be taken to ensure that the guillotine gates are raised sufficiently high to allow boat to pass underneath.

Distance Table *Miles Furlongs*

(Part of the Upper Great Ouse to Kempston Mill can be navigated 2½ miles from Bedford.)

Bedford to:

							Miles	Furlongs
Bedford, Duck Mill Lock (Town Lock)	...	...	...	...	...		—	2
Cardington Lock No. 2	...	...	...	...	...	...	2	—
Castle Lock No. (also known as Castle Mills Lock)	...		...	...		3	5
Willington Lock No. 4*	...	...	...	...	...	...	5	6
Old Mills Lock Site (now abolished)	...	...	...	...		6	4
Great Barford and Great Barford Lock (Archer Inn)	...		...	...	7	2
Roxton Lock No. 7	...	...	...	...	...	...	9	5
Tempsford Bridge (Anchor Inn)	...	...	...	...	...		10	2
Little Barford	...	...	...	...	...	...	12	5
Eaton Socon and Eaton Socon Lock No. 8	...	...	...		13	7
St. Neots	...	...	...	...	...	...	15	—
St. Neots Lock No. 9	...	...	...	...	...	...	16	2
Great Paxton	...	...	...	...	...	...	18	—
Offord No. 10	...	...	...	...	...	...	20	1
Brampton and Brampton Lock No. 11	...	...	...	...		23	1
Godmanchester Lock No. 12	...	...	...	...	...		24	3
Huntingdon	...	...	...	...	...	...	25	1
Hartford	...	...	...	...	...	...	26	2
Houghton Lock No. 13	...	...	...	...	...		27	7
Hemingford Lock No. 14	...	...	...	...	...		29	3
St. Ives Bridge (an ancient and beautiful structure)	...	...	...	30	6
St. Ives Staunch (lock)	...	...	...	...	...		31	1
Holywell	...	...	...	...	...	...	33	4

Distance Table

	Miles	Furlongs
*Brownshill (or Over) Staunch (lock)	36	2
Earith Village (The Crown)	38	—
Earith, commencement of New Bedford River and *junction with old course of river*—Earith to Denver—and Earith Bridge	38	4
Sutton Bridge	42	1
Mepal Bridge	43	3
Oxlode	47	4
Welney Suspension Bridge	52	6
Termination of Hundred Foot River and junction with old course of river —Earith to Denver—at the tail of Denver Sluice	58	6
Salter's Lode, *junction with Old Bedford River and junction with Well Creek*	59	1
Downham Bridge (Downham Market distant 1 mile)	60	1
Stow Bridge	62	7
Magdalen Bridge	66	—
Wiggenhall Bridge	68	—
Commencement of Eau Brink Cut	68	3
The Free Bridge and termination of Eau Brink Cut	71	3
King's Lynn, entrance to King's Lynn Docks	72	6
The Wash, mouth of the river	74	6

*Below the Staunch it is tidal, but one can again leave the tideway by entering Hermitage Lock and going to Denver via the Old West River.

River Great Ouse. Tidal gates at Denver about 1907. The barge *Charles* had to to wait for the tide to make level before passing through the gates. The sluice was partly rebuilt in the 1920's

Distance Table   *Miles   Furlongs*

Old Course of River—Earith to Denver (Old West).

Earith, junction with Main Line of river and Hermitage Sluice Lock No. 1
to:

	Miles	Furlongs
Aldreth Bridge	3	3
Twenty Pence Ferry	7	1
Stretham Ferry	8	6
Popes Corner, *junction with River Cam*	11	5
Junction with Soham Lode (navigable by light craft only)	12	7
Ely Station Dock (closed)	14	7
Cutter Inn	15	0
Junction with River Lark	18	7
Littleport Bridge	20	7
Brandon Creek, *junction with Little Ouse*	24	2
Southery Ferry	25	3
Hilgay Bridge	28	—
Junction with River Wissey	30	—
Denver Sluice, and *junction with Main Line of river Lock No. 2* ...	31	1

Old Bedford River (The Old Bedford from Earith to Welches Dam is unnavigable).

Welches Dam, junction with Forty Foot River and Counter Wash Drain to:

	Miles	Furlongs
Purls Bridge...	—	6
Railway Bridge (E.R.).	2	5
Welney Village and Bridge	6	—
Old Bedford Sluice, Salters Lode and *junction with River Ouse* ...	12	2

Counter Wash Drain

Welches Dam, junction with Forty Foot River and Old Bedford River to:

	Miles	Furlongs
Mepal Pumping Engine	3	—

GREAT OUSE TRIBUTARIES

Little Ouse or Brandon River

General remarks	Navigation to Thetford is not possible due to fixed sluices, except for a dinghy. Lakenheath Lode is navigable only for a short distance to the sluice at the railway bridge. It is well worth while taking a dinghy above Brandon Staunch as the scenery to Thetford is exceptional. Navigation rights were vested in the old Thetford Corporation but are now vested in the A.W.A.
From and to	Junction with the Old River at Brandon Creek to Brandon Staunch. (light craft to Thetford.) (Branch to Lakenheath)
Distance	22½ miles Lakenheath Lode 3¼ miles.
Length	Unlimited.
Beam	Unrestricted.
Draught	Min. 4ft. 6ins. near Wilton Ferry. There is 2ft. 6ins. to Brandon under favourable conditions.

Headroom	See Bridges.	
Locks	None. There were 8 navigation weirs on this river. Sheepwash Staunch and Crosswater Staunch have been abolished and some of the others have been converted to sluices which obstruct navigation. Distance table shows exact locations. Most of the fixed sluices have boat rollers.	
Tow-path	Throughout navigation.	

Bridges

Headroom under Bridges:	*ft.*	*ins.*
Brandon Creek Bridge	10	6
St. John's Road Bridge	10	4
St. John's Foot Bridge	9	9
Wilton Bridge	10	6

Distance Table:

	Miles	*Furlongs*
Thetford Town Bridge (former London to Norwich Road) and wharves	0	0
Thetford New Bridge (present main Norwich Road A11)	0	1
Thetford Staunch No. 1	0	4
Thetford Middle Staunch No. 2	1	7
Turfpool Staunch No. 3	2	6
Fison's fertiliser factory, Two Mile Bottom	3	3
Croxton Staunch No. 4	3	6
Santon Staunch No. 5	5	2
Santon Downham Bridge	5	7
Brandon Bridge (Swaffham Road) and wharves	8	6
Brandon Staunch No. 6. (Present head of navigation)	9	1
Railway Bridge (Ely to Norwich line)	10	0
Sheepwash Staunch No. 7 (site of)	10	5
Junction with Cut-Off channel	12	4
Cut-Off channel syphon	12	5
Wilton Bridge (Lakenheath to Feltwell Road)	13	0
Crosswater Staunch No. 8 (site of)	16	4
Junction with Lakenheath Lode, Botany Bay	17	0
Little Ouse Bridge	20	4
Brandon Creek Bridge and junction with river Great Ouse	22	4
Lakenheath Lode:		
Lakenheath Quayside and Dumpling Bridge (track to Turf Fen)	0	0
High Bridge (Shippea Hill Road)	0	6
High Bridge Staunch	0	6
Railway Bridge (Ely to Norwich line)	2	7
Accommodation Bridge	3	1
Junction with Little Ouse	3	2

River Lark

General remarks	This river was formerly navigable to Bury St. Edmunds, but is now only navigable above Judes Ferry by small craft that can be portaged round the sluices. The navigation rights under the original Acts still remain (1700 and 1817). In view of the interest in this river we have included a detailed Distance Table showing positions of the old navigation works. Most

of the staunches have gone, Kings Staunch (Cow Gravel) is the best for inspection. Chimney Mills Lock was rebuilt after the last war but no gates were ever fitted.

From and to	Junction with the Ely Ouse at Branch Bridge near Littleport to Judes Ferry.
Distance	13⅛ miles.
Length	88ft.
Beam	14ft. 6ins.
Draught	Min. 4ft. 6ins. to Isleham. Min. 2ft. 6ins. upstream of Isleham.
Headroom*	See Bridges.
Tow-path	Throughout navigation.
Locks	One at Isleham. Draught 2ft. 9ins, Length 88ft., Width 15ft. Fall from Mildenhall. There is another lock at Icklingham in working order but this is totally isolated by derelict navigation works on either side of it.

Bridges	Headroom under Bridges:				*ft.*	*ins.*
	Prickwillow Railway Bridge	...	...	...	10	3
	Prickwillow Road Bridge	...	...	...	10	3
	Judes Ferry Bridge	...	...	...	10	7

Distance Table

	Miles	Furlongs
Northgate Dock, Bury St. Edmunds (ultimate terminus)	0	0
Bury St. Edmunds By-pass Bridge (A45 Ipswich to Cambridge Road)	0	1
Tollgate Lock No. 1	0	5
Tollgate Bridge, Bury St. Edmunds (A134 Thetford Road)	0	5
Junction with short branch to Fornham Dock (original terminus basin)	0	6
Bury St. Edmunds Staunch No. 2 (Canal Staunch, or Babwell Clough)	0	7
Fornham Staunch No. 3 (Mill Farm Staunch)	1	5½
Fornham Park Lock No. 4 (just above road bridge)	1	7½
Causeway Bridge, Fornham All Saints (B1106 road)	2	0
Ducksluice Farm Lock No. 5 (Duck's Lock)	2	5½
Hengrave Bridge (Hengrave to Culford Road)	3	1½
Hengrave Lock No. 6 (Grange Farm Lock)	3	3
Chimney Mill Lock No. 7	3	7
Flempton Lock No. 8 (West Stow Lock) (just above road bridge)	4	4
West Stow Bridge (Flempton to West Stow Road)	4	4
West Stow Staunch with accommodation bridge over (Boyton Staunch) (No 9)	4	6½
Fulling Mill Lock No. 10 (West Stow Heath Lock)	5	2
Fulling Staunch No. 11 (Lackford Staunch)	5	4½
Cherry Ground Lock No. 12, Lackford	6	1
Lackford Bridge (A110 Mildenhall to Bury St. Edmunds Road)	6	2
Mill Heath Upper Staunch No. 13) Cavenham	6	6½

*The main A11 road at Barton Mills has been lowered and the river put through a siphon. There is usually 5 feet headroom for light craft.

Distance Table

	Miles	Furlongs
Mill Heath Lower Staunch No. 14) Lock	6	7
Farthing Bridge, Icklingham (Cavenham to Icklingham Road)	7	6
Icklingham Lock No. 15 and Icklingham Mill Bridge	8	0
Temple Bridge	8	5½
Temple Bridge Staunch No. 16	8	6
Jack Tree Staunch No. 17	9	0
Junction with Tuddenham Mill Stream	10	4
Junction with Cut-Off Channel	10	5
Barton Mills New Bridge (A11 Norwich to London Road)	10	7½
Barton Mills Lock No. 18	11	0
Barton Mills Old Bridge (former main road)	11	0
Barton Hall Staunch No. 19 (Jeffries Halt Staunch)	11	3
Mildenhall Gas Works Lock No. 20 (Old Lock)	12	1
Mildenhall Bridge (B1102 Fordham Road)	12	1½
Mildenhall Turf Lock No. 21 (New Lock – staunch until 1890s)	12	2
Mildenhall West Upper Staunch No 22 (eliminated 1890s)	12	7
Mildenhall West Lower Staunch No. 23 (eliminated 1890s)	12	7½
Wamil Hall Bridge, Worlington (accommodation)	13	2
King's Staunch No. 24 (Cow Gravel Staunch)	13	5
West Row Bridge, Judes Ferry (Freckenham Road)	14	4
Freckenham Gravel Staunch No. 25 (West Row Staunch or New Staunch)	15	0
Junction with Lee Brook	15	4
Isleham Staunch No. 26 (replaced by Isleham Lock)	16	6
Isleham Lock No. 26	16	4
Prickwillow Bridge (B1382 Ely Road) (former junction with Great Ouse)	22	4
Railway Bridge (Ely to Norwich line)	22	6
Junction with River Great Ouse and bridge (Littleport to Ely back road)	24	5
Tuddenham Mill Stream:		
Junction with the river Lark	0	0
Tuddenham Mill Stream Staunch No. 1	0	6
Tuddenham Mill (terminus of branch)	1	2

River Wissey

From and to   Junction with Great Ouse to Oxborough Ferry.

Distance   10½ miles.

Length   Unlimited.

Beam   Unrestricted.

Draught   Min. about 3ft. 6ins.

Width of channel   30ft. to 40ft.

Headroom   See Bridges.

Locks   None.

						ft.	ins.
Tow-path	Throughout navigation.						

						ft.	**ins.**
Bridges	Headroom under Bridges:						
	Hilgay Railway Bridge ...	...	...	...		10	4
	Hilgay Road Bridge ...	...	...	...		8	2
	Beet Factory Railway Bridge ...	...	...			8	7
	Beet Factory Pipe lines (2) ...	...	...			10	1
	Stoke Ferry Bridge ...	...	...	...		9	4

Distance Table:

	Miles	*Furlongs*
Oxborough Ferry and wharf	0	0
Whittington	1	0
Stoke Ferry Bridge (A134) and wharf	1	4
Branch to Cut-Off Channel	2	0
Accommodation Bridge into Stoke Ferry Fen	2	0½
Siphon over Cut-Off Channel	2	2
Lode to Northwold Fen	2	5
Methwold Lode (To Methwold Village)	3	2
Lode to Stoke Ferry Fen	3	5
Lode into Methwold Common	3	7
Wissington New Road Bridge (B1160)	5	2
Wissington Sugar Beet Factory Wharf	5	3
Wissington Light Railway Bridge	5	5
Hilgay Old Road Bridge (ex A10) and wharf	8	3
Hilgay New Road Bridge (A10 By-pass)	8	3½
Hilgay Railway Bridge	10	2
Junction with Great Ouse	10	4

Soham Lode

From and to   River Ouse to Soham Railway Bridge.

Distance   3½ miles. Only for shallow draught craft up to 1ft. 6ins..

Cottenham Lode

Navigable for light craft from the Old West to Cottenham.

River Kym

Navigable for small cruisers for about one mile from the main river at St. Neots.

River Ouse (Sussex) (71)

The river was promoted as a navigation by Acts dated 1790, 1791, 1800, 1806 and 1814. Thames sailing barges traded to Eastwood's Cement Works until 1956. The section above Lewes through the South Downs is very attractive but through navigation ceases at Hamsey Lock (near a very fine church), as this structure is derelict. Craft can, however, navigate round the old river section thus avoiding a portage at Hamsey Lock. Other locks in the section above are also derelict, but the river is canoeable to a short distance above the ruins of the double staircase lock at Barcombe. A section above the Anchor House Inn near Isfield is used for pleasure boating as far as the 'Waterfalls'. Below Hamsey Lock the banks are pitched with chalk for most of the river's length and craft can only make a landing at Newhaven, Piddinghoe and Lewes.

Authority	Southern Water Authority, Guildbourne House, Worthing, Sussex. BN11 1LD. Tel. Worthing (0903) 205252.
	The Upper Ouse Navigation Company set up under the 1814 Act ceased to exist many years ago. The original Acts do not appear to have been subject of any extinguishing Order or Act.
Distance	Newhaven Harbour entrance to ruins of Hamsey Lock, 9½ miles. Originally navigable to Linfield.
Length	Unlimited.
Beam	16ft. to Lewes, 10ft. above Lewes.
Draught	3ft. to Hamsey.
Headroom	See Bridges.
Locks	None. All are derelict – total was 18.
Tow-path	Throughout navigation.

Bridges The approximate depths and headroom at H.W.S.T. are as follows:

	depth	clearance
Newhaven Swing Bridge	18ft.	17ft.
Southease Bridge (Swing bridge)	14ft.	10ft.
2 Railway Bridges over Glynde Reach (not over main river)	8ft.	5ft.
Southerham Railway Bridge	14ft.	10ft.
Lewes Town Bridge	10ft.	7ft. to crown of arch.
Lewes Railway Bridge	6ft.	8ft.

Facilities	Four miles above Lewes, there is a stretch of river three miles long and that is used by a small boat yard which hires out canoes and light craft. This section is of exceptional beauty and the craft are based on The Anchor Inn. This was an original inn for bargemen using the river.
Tides and navigation	The river is tidal and navigable at high water to Lewes Bridge for craft drawing up to 6ft. at their own risk.
	Above Lewes it is only possible for small craft to navigate up to the ruins of Hamsey Lock. High water at Lewes about one hour after Newhaven. Spring tides rise 9ft. to 10ft. High water at Newhaven, about 5 minutes before Dover. At half-tide the stream near to Southease Bridge runs at about 7 to 8 knots.

Distance Table

Ruins of Hamsey Lock to:

	Miles	Furlongs
Lewes Corporation Wharf and Phoenix Foundry	1	2
Lewes Bridge	1	4

Distance Table						Miles	Furlongs
Lewes Portland Cement and Line Works	...	...	...	...		2	—
Southerham Swing Bridge (British Railways. S.R.)		...	...	...		2	2
Southease Bridge (swing bridge) ...	...	...	...	...	...	5	2
Piddinghoe ...	...	...	...	...	...	...	6	7
Newhaven Bridge (swing bridge)		...	...	...	...	...	8	4
Newhaven Harbour Mouth	...	...	...	...	...	...	9	4

River Ouse (Yorkshire) (72)

The river navigation was originally promoted by Acts of Parliament in the years 1642, 1657, 1727, 1732 and 1767 forming part of the through route to the Ripon Canal. It still carries heavy commercial traffic and sea-going coasters regularly use the river as far inland as Selby. The country across the plain to York is flat and there are only two locks on the Ouse, the next lock being above Swale Nab on the Ure. The river is prettiest in the upper reaches above Linton Lock.

York is a famous old city with its fine Minster and three miles of ancient walls with four large gates. It was once a Roman station and there are many old buildings to be visited. There is also a railway museum here. The lower reaches (Selby and below) are dull, whilst navigation below Goole is only for the experienced as it can be very dangerous. Moorings in York present a problem, for a brief visit the public quay is excellent but for anything longer, moorings are not easily found, though the York Motor Boat Club is helpful to strangers. Visitors can use Foss Basin which is reached from the main river a short distance from Foss junction near Skeldergate.

The Ouse has a serious, but interesting series of obstructions called 'clay huts' which are mostly situated downstream from Linton Lock. These are mounds of clay that slip down from the high banks, mainly in an area between Newton-on-Ouse and Nun Monkton. Local enquiries are advised and local charts are available from Naburn Marina.

The levels in the non-tidal sections are fairly constant but sudden floods do occur in wet weather and a rise of 12 feet is not unknown, though such flooding is not often experienced during the summer.

Authority

Between Trent Falls and Swale Nab, the river is under the jurisdiction of three Authorities:

Trent Falls to Skelton Railway Bridge, Goole. Associated British Ports, P.O. Box 1, Kingston House Tower, Bond St., Hull HU1 3ER. Tel. Hull (0482) 52251.

Skelton Railway Bridge, Goole to Widdington Ings
Ouse and Foss Navigation Trust, Secretary, Town Clerk of York, Guildhall, York. Tel. York (0904) 54544.

Naburn Lock. Tel. Escrick (090 487) 229.
(Transfer of navigation for this section is under discussion with the B.W.B.)

Widdington Ings to Swale Nab Linton Lock Navigation Commissioners, 1/3 Wheelgate, Malton, Yorks. (For continuation of waterway see River Ure which is owned by the British Waterways Board.)

From and to and general remarks	Trent Falls junction with River Humber, River Trent, River Ouse and Swale Nab junction with River Ure Navigation. This waterway is tidal as far as Naburn Locks. The Linton Lock Navigation Commissioners include 2 members of the Inland Waterways Association.
Connections	The river has junctions with Goole Docks and the Aire and Calder Navigation, the River Aire at Asselby Island, the River Derwent at Barmby-on-the-Marsh (17 miles above Trent Falls), Selby Canal at Selby and River Wharfe at Cawood.
Pilotage	100ft downstream of Skelton Railway Bridge to Goole pilotage is compulsory. This situation also applies to the Selby area.

Distances

Trent Falls to Swale Nab	61¾ miles.
Goole to Swale Nab	52½ ,,
Trent Falls to Naburn Locks	37¼ ,,
Trent Falls to Goole	8 ,,

Trent Falls to Naburn Locks

Length   Unlimited.

Beam   ,,

Draught

Between Trent Falls and Goole:	Spring tides ...	18ft.
	Neap ,, ...	12ft.
Between Goole and Selby:	Spring tides ...	13ft.
	Neap ,, ...	8ft.
Between Selby and Naburn Locks:	Spring tides ...	8ft. 6ins.
	Neap ,, ...	6ft.

Naburn Locks to York

Length 150ft.   *Beam* 25ft. 6ins.   *Draught* 8ft. 6ins.

Headroom   From Trent Falls to Ouse Bridge, York, all bridges movable, except Naburn railway bridge fixed at 25ft. 6ins. above normal summer level.

York to Swale Nab

Length 60ft.   *Beam* 15ft. 4ins.   *Draught* 4ft.

Headroom   16ft. 4ins.

Locks   2. Linton Lock and Naburn Locks. Twin Lock at Naburn, Large Lock 150ft. × 24ft. 6ins. × 8ft. 6ins., Small Lock 82ft. × 19ft. × 6ft. 6ins.
Naburn Locks closed on Sunday night. Lock gates at Naburn worked by lock-keepers. Fall from Swale Nab.

Tow-path   There is a tow-path from Swale Nab to the junction with River Wharfe, except for a short distance in York.

Bridges   6 Swing bridges between Goole and York. 3 bridges above York. Six short and one long blast is the recognised signal for opening bridges. Maximum headroom, 16ft. 4ins.

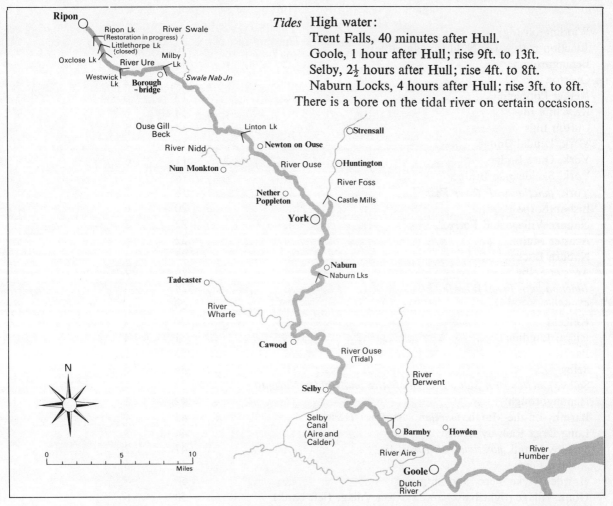

Tides High water:
Trent Falls, 40 minutes after Hull.
Goole, 1 hour after Hull; rise 9ft. to 13ft.
Selby, 2½ hours after Hull; rise 4ft. to 8ft.
Naburn Locks, 4 hours after Hull; rise 3ft. to 8ft.
There is a bore on the tidal river on certain occasions.

Navigation notes

From Trent Falls to Goole there are lighted beacons, those on the right bank showing a green light and a red light from the left bank. At Goole it is advisable to go inside the Docks for mooring as the tide runs very strongly at this point. Before going upstream from Goole it is advisable to make local enquiries about Howden Dyke which is difficult at certain states of the tide. Excellent advice on navigating the river can be obtained from the Ripon Motor Boat Club whose handbook is available for sale to visitors. Naburn Marina gives advice to visitors.

Ouse Gill Beck is the boundary between the River Ouse and River Ure.

Facilities

A lonely river above York. Two boatyards at York but inns and shopping facilities are sparse apart from York.

Distance Table

Swale Nab, junction with River Ure Navigation, and junction with River Swale (unnavigable) to:

	Miles	Furlongs
Aldwark Bridge	4	2
Junction with Ouseburn, or Ouse Gill Beck (unnavigable)	5	5
Linton Lock	7	6
Newton-on-Ouse	8	6

Widdington Ings	9	6
Junction with River Nidd (unnavigable)	10	—
Beningbrough	11	2
Overton	13	2
Nether Poppleton	13	6
Rawcliffe Ings	14	6
Clifton Ings	15	6
York, Lendal Bridge	17	4
York, Ouse Bridge	17	6
York, Skeldergate Bridge	18	—
York, *junction with River Foss*	18	2
Bishopthorpe	20	6
Naburn Village and Ferry...	22	2
Acaster Malbis	22	6
Naburn Locks	23	4
Acaster Selby	26	2
Junction with River Wharfe	28	—
Cawood	29	—
Kelfield	30	2
Riccal Landing	31	4
Barlby	35	2
Selby	36	6
Selby, *junction with Selby Branch of Aire and Calder Navigation* ...	37	—
Hemingbrough	42	2
Barmby-on-the-Marsh, *junction with River Derwent*	43	4
Long Drax Railway Bridge	44	1
Asselby Island, *junction with River Aire*	47	2
Airmyn Ferry	47	6
Howden Dyke, Ferry and Shipyard	50	—
Hook Village (right bank) and Skelton Village (left bank) ...	50	6
Goole, entrance to Docks, and *junction with Aire and Calder Navigation Main Line* (via Ocean Lock)	52	6
Goole, *junction with portion of the River Don known as the Dutch River*	52	7
Swinefleet	54	6
Saltmarshe	56	6
Whitgift	57	6
Blacktoft	59	6
Trent Falls, *junction with Rivers Humber and Trent*	60	6

Oxford Canal (73)

Originally promoted by Acts in 1769, 1775, 1786, 1794, 1799, 1807, 1808 and 1829, this is one of the most popular cruising canals. It originally commenced in Oxford at the basin, now alas filled in, but it still commences very close to the city centre. The section from Oxford to Banbury is through delightful pastoral country very like the scenery on the lost Thames Severn Canal. The Cherwell section is wide, well wooded and a haunt of wild life.

The canal is never far from rail or road, yet achieves an air of remoteness that is rare on a canal so situated, the buildings and swing bridges all combine to give the Oxford an air of its own. The summit level, Claydon to Napton, is probably as interesting and attractive as the Grand Union (Leicester Section) except that the Oxford's route twists and bends to give constantly changing scenery which feature is part of the canal's charm being an early waterway constructed by James Brindley. Some of the windings of the canal in northern parts were shortened by Thomas Telford.

Oxford and its University are world famous, but the river view in many places does not do it justice. The canal passes many villages including such gems as Aynho, Cropredy, Wormleighton and Marston Doles. Banbury is pleasant but unremarkable, though the yellow stone gives it an air of its own.

The entrance via Duke's Cut, is so called as this short cut to the backwater of the Thames. It is a better entrance to the canal than at Oxford. The old tunnel at Fenny Compton, 1,188 yards long, was opened out in 1868 to save rebuilding but this narrow section is still called The Tunnel.

This is an attractive canal but one of the busiest in the country carrying pleasure traffic in the cruising season.

Authority	British Waterways Board.
From and to	Junction with the River Thames at Oxford (above Osney Lock) to junction of the Coventry Canal at Hawkesbury. Alternative route from the Thames is via Duke's Cut Branch. To enter this proceed upstream, through Kings Lock and bear right into a backwater of the Thames a mile above the lock. This leads to Duke's Cut. Louse Lock connects with a Thames Backwater Sheepwash Channel.
Connections	The Oxford Canal has also junction with the Grand Union Canal at Napton Junction and shares the same waterway from there to Braunston Junction.
Distances	77 miles. (A number of arms, originating from the straightening of the canal, number 8. The Wyken and Rugby Arms are used for moorings and the rest are derelict apart from Brownsover Arm. This is used as a water feeder from the River Swift).
Length	72ft.
Beam	7ft.
Draught	3ft. 6ins. Napton to Oxford 3ft. 3ins.
Headroom	7ft.
Locks	Main Line, 46. Lock gates worked by boat crews, except the lock at the beginning of Duke's Cut. Locks Nos. 1—16 rise from Hawkesbury. Locks Nos. 17—46 fall to Oxford. Duke's cut Branch, 1 lock, falls either way. When the locks at Hillmorton were duplicated in 1840, they were renumbered 2—7 inclusive. This gives 46 locks on the canal, though there are only 43 changes of level. (Lock No. 44 on the Main Line (Shuttleworth's) is incorrectly

referred to as Duke's Lock. Duke's Lock is nearby on the cut leading from the canal to the Thames at King's Lock. This cut was owned by the Duke of Marlborough who leased it in 1798 to the Oxford Canal Company for 200 years).

Bridges	73. Maximum headroom as above. There are a number of swing bridges on this waterway that have to be opened by boat crews. There is a railway swing bridge across the entrance to Louse Lock at the beginning of the canal. This bridge is fixed open and the railway is closed. Electric drawbridge upstream from Isis Lock (1¼ miles) operated by local factory.
Tow-path	Throughout navigation.
Tunnels	One at Newbold, 250 yards long. Tow-path.
Speed limit	5 miles per hour.
Facilities	Numerous boatyards and canal side inns.

Distance Table

Hawkesbury Junction (Sutton Stop) and Stop Lock No. 1, junction with Coventry Canal to:

	Miles	Furlongs
Tushes Bridge	1	—
Junction with branch to Wyken Old Colliery (Coventry Canal Society moorings)	1	4
Ansty Bridge	3	6
Hopsford Valley Aqueduct	5	—
Lord Craven's	5	2
Grime's Bridge. Combe	6	4
Stretton Stop Lock and Toll Office, *junction with Stretton Wharf Branch*	7	2
North end of Brinklow Hill, *junction with Brinklow Wharf Branch*	7	6
Easenhall Lane Bridge	8	—
Hall Oaks Corner	8	2
Hungerfield	9	—
North end of Walton's Hill, junction branch to Fennis Field Lime Works (unnavigable)	9	4
Cathiron Lane Bridge	10	2
Newbold and Harborough Road Bridge, junction with branch to Norman's and Walker's Lime Works (unnavigable)	11	—
Newbold Wharf	11	4
Junction with Rugby Wharf Branch	12	4
Brownsover Wharf	13	—
Brownsover Mill	13	4
Clifton New Wharf, junction with branch to Clifton Mill (unnavigable)	14	—
Hillmorton Locks Nos. 2, 3, 4, 5, 6, 7 (Duplicate locks side by side)	15	2
Hillmorton	15	4
Kilsby Road Bridge	16	6
Barby Road Bridge	17	4
Barby Wood Bridge	18	4

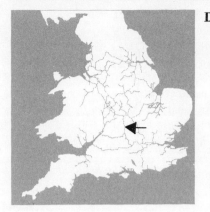

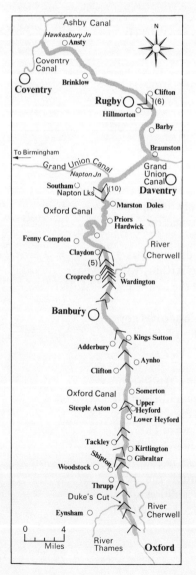

Distance Table	Miles	Furlongs
Willoughby Wharf	21	—
Braunston Turn, *junction with Braunston Branch*	22	6
Wolfhampcote	23	4
Nethercote	24	6
Flecknoe	25	—
Shuckburgh Wharf	26	2
Napton Junction, *junction with Birmingham—London Main Line of the Grand Union Canal*	27	6
Coventry Road Bridge	28	2
Napton Wharf	28	6
Napton Brickyard	29	—
Napton Bottom Lock No. 8. Then follows Nos. 9, 10, 11, 12, 13 Napton Flight, then Green's Lock No. 14 and also Napton Lock No. 15	30	—
Marston Doles and top of Napton Locks (No. 16)	31	6
Griffin's Bridge, Wormleighton	37	—
Sherne Hill Bridge	39	—
Fenny Compton	39	2
Claydon Lock Nos. 17, 18, 19, 20, 21	42	6
Elkington's Lock No. 22	43	2
Varney's Lock No. 23	43	7
Broadmoor Bridge (Broadmoor Lock No. 24) ...	44	4
Cropredy Lock No. 25	45	4
Slat Mill Lock No. 26	46	7
Jobson's Lock No. 27	47	6
Salmon's Lock No. 28	48	5
Grimsbury Mill	49	2
Banbury, Toll Office, Lock No. 29 and Wharves	50	—
Grant's Lock No. 30	52	1
Twyford Wharf (Kings Sutton distant one mile)	52	6
King's Sutton Lock No. 31	53	5
Adderbury	55	—
Nell Bridge Wharf (Nell Bridge Lock No. 32) ...	55	4
Weir Lock No. 33	56	2
Aynho Wharf (Aynho distant one mile) Inn ...	56	6
Souldern Wharf	57	2
Somerton Wharf (Somerton Deep Lock No. 34)	59	—
Upper Heyford (Heyford Common Lock No. 35)	60	7
Lower Heyford Lock No. 36	62	2
Lower Heyford	62	6
Dashwood's Lock No. 37	64	2
North Brook Lock No. 38	64	6
Washford Hill Stone Quarries	66	2
Kirklington, Enser's Mill Lock No. 39 (also known as Pigeon's Lock)	66	6
Enslow	68	—
Canal enters River Cherwell, Gibraltar Lock No. 40 ..	68	3½
Weir, or Cherwell Lock No. 41, Canal leaves Cherwell	69	3
Thrupp	70	4

Distance Table

	Miles	Furlongs
Langford Lane Wharf	71	—
Kidlington Bridge and Round Ham Lock No. 42	71	6
Yarnton Lane Bridge	72	2
Kidlington Green Lock No. 43	72	5
King's Bridge Wharf	73	4
Tail of Shuttleworth's Lock No. 44 and *junction with Duke's Cut Branch*, leading to River Thames...	74	—
Wolvercote Bridge and Lock No. 45	74	6
Summertown.	75	6
Heyfield Road Wharf	76	—
Oxford, Walton Well Bridge	76	4
Oxford, *junction with River Thames* through Louse or as it is sometimes called, Isis Lock No. 46	77	—

(A short length of the closed route to the old basin has been re-opened, it is called Hythe Bridge Arm and is used for moorings.)

Braunston Branch
Length from junction with Main Line to:

	Miles	Furlongs
Braunston, Toll Office, Wharf and *junction with Grand Union Canal— Main Line*	—	4

River Parrett(74)

The Parrett was promoted by Acts 1699, 1707 and 1804. These Acts were mainly to improve the nearby River Tone. An Act was promoted in 1795 to improve the navigation from Langport to Ilchester.

The Parrett runs through pleasant but unremarkable countryside, but Bridgwater has a charm of its own. The town is rich in history having associations with King Arthur, with the Monmouth Rising and it was also here that Charles Stuart lost hope when the castle fell, but little remains of the castle today.

Langport once a thriving river trading town, has a decayed air—all the river trade has now departed. The intrepid boatman in a craft that can be portaged could spend an interesting week exploring the Parrett and its adjoining waterways many of which are strongly reminiscent of the Fens.

The area is ripe for waterway development. A new barrage is projected for the Parrett downstream from Bridgwater and this will be located probably 1 mile upstream of Dunball Wharf. This would raise the water level and make a connection possible with the waterways north of the Parrett. Long term resotration of the locks at Langport, Midelney, and at Thorney Mills should be considered. Possibly the Parrett flood relief channel could be merged into an overall scheme which could connect with King's Sedgemoor drain. There is a need for an overall study of this area and a plan prepared to deal with drainage, navigation and there also seems to be a strong case for an approach for E.E.C. funds to do this. In addition to the local IWA there is a Somerset Waterways Association which can give advice and help on local waterways.

Authority   **Sea to Bridgwater Bridge**
Sedgemoor District Council, The Priory, St. Mary Street, Bridgwater, Somerset. TA6 3EJ. Tel. Bridgwater (0278) 4391.

Bridgwater to Thorney Mills
Wessex Water Authority, Somerset Rivers Division, The Watergate, West Quay, Bridgwater, Somerset. Tel. Bridgwater (0278) 8271.

From and to	Thorney Mills to Bridgwater Bar.
Distance	34¼ miles.
Length	54ft.
Beam	14ft.

Draught	To Bridgwater, Spring tides, 17ft. Neap tides, 8ft. To Dunwear, Spring tides, 3ft.
Headroom	Unlimited to Bridgwater Telescopic Bridge.
Locks	Three (out of use). Flood Gates at Oath. Fall from Thorney Mills.
Tow-path	None below Bridgwater. Above Bridgwater tow-path to Thorney Mills.
Connections	Rivers Isle and Yeo, also Westport Canal.
	Tributary River Brue is navigable for 1½ miles to Highbridge. The River Tone is navigable to Knapp Bridge a distance of 5¾ miles. The Tone from here to Taunton can only be used by light craft that can be portaged.
Navigation notes	The tidal sluice at Oath can be passed once a fortnight when tide makes a level. Langport lock is derelict. Light craft can ascend the Isle River for about 2 miles but craft have to be portaged past Midleney Lock, which generally has stop planks fitted in position. Light craft can reach Ilchester on the Yeo, though large boats can ascend to Pibsbury under favourable conditions. The Westport Canal has been dredged throughout by the W.W.A. and is usable by light craft.
Tides	The tides are strong below Bridgwater and with the exception of the lowest tides, they form a bore below Combwich which varies in height from 2 to 4ft.
	High water at Bridgwater town 1 hour 10 minutes after Bridgwater Bar. Spring tides rise 15ft. Neap tides rise 6ft.
Facilities	There are a few inns nearby but very little boatyard facilities.

Distance Table

Thorney Mills Bridge Lock (disused) to:

	Miles	Furlongs
Junction with Rive Isle (leading to Westport Canal) ...	—	6
Junction with River Yeo	3	—
Langport Bridge	3	6
Langport Lock	3	7½
Oath Flood Gates	6	4
Stathe	7	4
Burrow Bridge, *junction with River Tone*	9	—
Dunwear Brick Works	13	6
Bridgwater, Town Bridge	15	2
Bridgwater, entrance to Dock and Bridgwater and Taunton Canal	15	5
Dunball	18	6
Combwich	23	6
Stert Point	27	7
Junction with River Brue, forming Branch to Highbridge	28	3
Burnham-on-Sea	29	2
Bridgwater Bar, mouth of river	34	2

River Brue

	Miles	Furlongs
Length from *junction with River Parrett to Highbridge*	1	4

River Yeo

Junction with River Parrett to:

	Miles	Furlongs
Pibsbury *(Weir)*	1	—
Little Load Bridge	4	—
Ilchester	8	—

River Isle and Westport Canal

Junction with River Parrett to:

	Miles	Furlongs
Midelney Lock (out of use)	–	0½
Entrance, to Westport Canal	1	–
Westmoor Bridge (Lowered)	1	5
Westport Canal Basin and Wharves	3	2

Pocklington Canal(75)

This canal was originally promoted by Act of Parliament in 1815, and was mainly an agricultural waterway, but carried quite heavy loads. Recently, as this canal is in an area with strong boating interests, Pocklington Canal Amenity Society has been formed to re-open the canal in co-operation with the British Waterways Board. Already Cottingwith Lock has been restored together with Gardham Lock. Navigation open to Melbourne (Summer 1983) Financial aid has been given by the Humberside County Council.

Authority   British Waterways Board.

From and to   Cottingwith Ferry to Junction with River Derwent to Canal Head, Pocklington. There are three very small arms at Bielby, Melbourne and Cottingwith.

Distance	9½ miles.
Length	57ft.
Beam	14ft. 3ins.
Draught	4ft.
Headroom	9ft.
Tow-path	Throughout navigation.
Locks	9. (7 out of use at present). Rise from Cottingwith.
Bridges	Three fixed and eight swing bridges.
Tides	High water at Cottingwith 4 hours 20 minutes after Hull. Neap tides are not felt above Cottingwith.
Facilities	A boatyard is projected at Melbourne and there are inns in the villages near the canal.

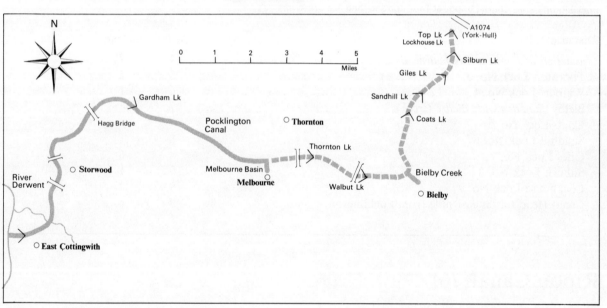

Distance Table

Cottingwith Ferry Junction with River Derwent, and commencement of Pocklington Canal to:

	Miles	Furlongs
Cottingwith Lock No. 1	—	2
East Cottingwith	—	4
Storwood	1	4
Hagg Bridge	2	2
Gardham Lock No. 2 (locally called 'Bramleys')	3	—
Melbourne	4	7

Pocklington Canal. Church bridge at Thornton showing fine brickwork

Distance Table

						Miles	Furlongs
Junction with arm to Melbourne Basin ...	...	...	...	...		4	7½
Thornton Lock No. 3 ...	...	...	...	...	...	5	2
Walbut Lock No. 4 ...	...	...	...	...	...	6	1
Bielby (*junction with Bielby Creek*) ...	...	...	...	...		7	—
Coats Lock No. 5 ...	...	...	...	...	...	7	6
Sandhill Lock No. 6 ...	...	...	...	...	...	8	1
Giles Lock No. 7 ...	...	...	...	...	...	8	6
Silburn Lock No. 8 ...	...	...	...	...	...	9	1
Lockhouse Lock No. 9 ...	...	...	...	...	...	9	3
Canal Head (distance 1 mile from Pocklington)	...	...	...			9	4

Ripon Canal(76)

This short waterway is in a beautiful well wooded area and the rural surroundings of the Ripon Motor Boat club are very close to the ancient town with its fine cathedral. The navigation was originally promoted under Acts passed in 1767 and 1820. Navigation on the Ure above the junction with Oxclose Lock is only possible for light craft but the river can sometimes be canoed for just over 40 miles to Hestholme Farm. Care should be taken by cruisers going to Oxclose Lock as the entrance cut is easily missed. The canal holds water all the way to Ripon Wharf and the two locks have been re-built.

Authority   British Waterways Board.

General remarks   Open for small pleasure craft and motor launches only. Draught not to exceed 2ft. 6ins. Navigation rights on this waterway were extinguished by British Transport Act 1955. The canal was leased to the Ripon Motor Boat Club after this date, but in 1968 it reverted to the B.W.B.

From and to	Junction with River Ure at Oxclose Lock to Ripon.
Distance	1¼ miles.
Length	57ft.
Beam	14ft. 6ins.
Draught	2ft. 6ins.
Headroom	8ft. 6ins.
Locks	One. Littlethorpe and Ripon Locks have been abolished.
Bridges	2.

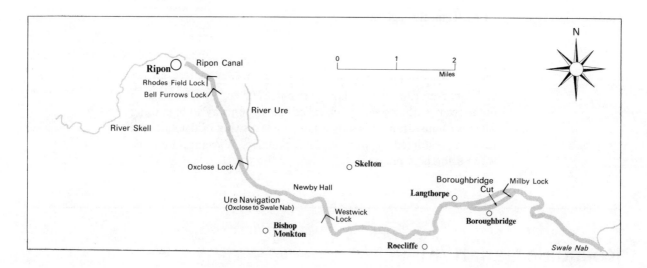

Tow-path	Throughout navigation.

Distance Table

Oxclose Lock and junction with Ripon Canal to:

					Miles	Furlongs
Bell Furrows Lock	...	...	...	...	1	2
Rhodes Field Lock	...	...	...	...	1	4
Ripon Wharf	...	...	...	...	2	1

River Roach (77)

Rather a muddy creek with a swift current but famous for wildfowl. Havengore Creek can only be used at high water and the 3 mile width of Maplin Sands is only covered by a few feet of water at ordinary spring tides.

Authority	Crouch Harbour Authority, Harbour Office, Belvedere Road, Burnham on Crouch, Essex. Tel. Maldon (0621) 783602.
From and to	*Junction with River Crouch at Wallingsea Ness to near Rochford.
Distance	9¼ miles.
Length	Unlimited.
Beam	,,
Draught	6ft. at H.W.S.T. to Great Stambridge Mill.
Headroom	Unlimited.
Locks	None. Tidal throughout.
Tow-path	None.

Branches	There is deep water half-way round Potton Island on its west side and light craft can use this channel to enter Havengore Creek and go out to sea near the ancient track called 'the Broomway' at high water. The maximum draught is only 3ft. There is a swing bridge but navigation is restricted by army artillery practice. Warnings are issued when firing is in progress.

Rochdale Canal (78)

Originally promoted by Acts 1794, 1800, 1804, 1806 and 1807. It was closed to navigation in 1952 except the section from a little above the Ashton Canal junction to Bridgewater Canal. The re-opening of the Ashton Canal and the rise of pleasure cruising in the area saved the canal from complete closure. This broad waterway substantially built by Jessop is remarkable climbing to 600ft and down to Yorkshire through 92 locks in 33 miles. The canal, after leaving Manchester, enters open country at Chadderton and climbs over the summit to the Calder valley through Todmorden to Sowerby Bridge.

The Rochdale is seen to be a major feature of the proposed Pennine Park. In spite of 36 obstructions, restoration work is being carried out. A list of restoration sites and authorities who are working on the canal is at the end of the distance table. Brian Holden, secretary of the Rochdale Canal Society, 24 Passmonds Crescent, Rochdale, Lancs, has enabled this section to have a complete distance table and restoration survey to date. The Rochdale Canal Company works continuously on maintenance of banks, aqueducts, reservoirs, etc. as the canal is a water supply feeder. The nine locks in Manchester have always been in use linking the Bridgewater and Ashton Canals, part of the Cheshire Ring.

*See Imray Chart No Y17

Authority	Rochdale Canal Company, 75 Dale Street, Manchester M1 2HG. Tel: 061 236 2456
From and to	Bridgewater Canal (Manchester) to Sowerby Bridge.
Distance	32 miles. Branches: Heywood 1½ miles, Rochdale 5½ furlongs.
Length	74ft.
Beam	14ft 2ins.
Draught	4ft.
Headroom	9ft.
Locks	92 Locks 1 to 36 Rise from Sowerby Bridge Locks 37 to 92 Fall to Manchester.
Bridges	Numerous.
Tunnel	Knott Mill, Manchester 78yds. No towpath. Sowerby Long Bridge 43yds. Towing path.
Special note	Restoration work is either complete or in progress at 39 locks.

Distance Table

Sowerby Bridge, junction with Calder and Hebble Navigation to:

	Miles	Furlongs
First Sowerby Bridge Lock No. 1	–	1½
Second Sowerby Bridge Lock No. 2	–	2
Third Sowerby Bridge Lock No. 3	–	3
Tim Bates' Lock No. 4	–	4
Brearley Lower Lock No. 5	2	7
Brearley Upper Lock No. 6	3	1
Broadbottom Lock No. 7	4	2
Mayroyd Mill Lock No. 8	5	2
Blackpit Lock No. 9	5	4
Stubbing Lower Lock No. 10	5	7
Stubbing Upper Lock No. 11	6	–
Rawden Mill Lock No. 12	6	6
Callis Lock No. 13	7	–
Holmcoat Lock No. 14	7	6
Shawplains Lock No. 15	8	3
Lob Mill Lock No. 16	8	5
Old Royd Lock No. 17	9	1
Shop Lock No. 18	9	6
Todmorden Lock No. 19	9	7
Wadsworth Mill No. 20	10	2
Shade Lock No. 21	10	3
Gauxholme Lowest Lock No. 22	10	4
Gauxholme Middle Lock No. 23	10	5
Gauxholme Highest Lock No. 24	10	6
Smithyholm Lock No. 25	11	–

Distance Table

	Miles	Furlongs
Pinnel Lock No. 26	11	1
Hollings Lock No. 27	11	2
Travis Mill Lock No. 28	11	4
Nip Square Lock No. 29	11	5
Winterbutlee Lock No. 30	11	6
Lightbank Lock No. 31	12	–
Sands Lock No. 32	12	2
Bottomley Lock No. 33	12	3
Warland Lower Lock No. 34	12	6
Warland Upper Lock No. 35	12	7
Longlees Lock No. 36	13	–
West Summit Lock No. 37	13	6
First Lock below W. Summit Lock No. 38	13	7
Second Lock below W. Summit Lock No. 39	14	–
Punchbowl Lock No. 40	14	1
First below Punchbowl	14	2
Second below Punchbowl	14	2½
Thickone Lock No. 43	14	3
Sladen Lock No. 44	14	4
Pike House Lock No. 45	14	5
Bent House Lock No. 46	15	–
Littleborough Higher Lock No. 47	15	2
Littleborough Lower Lock No. 48	15	3
Moss Upper Lock No. 49	19	–
Moss Lower Lock No. 50	19	1
Junction with Rochdale Branch	19	6
Blue Pits Highest Lock No. 51	20	6
Blue Pits Middle Lock No. 52	21	–
Blue Pits Lowest Lock No. 53	21	0½
Maden Fold, *junction with Heywood Branch*	21	1
Laneside (1st) Lock No. 54	22	1½
Laneside (2nd) Lock No. 55	22	2
Laneside (3rd) Lock No. 56	22	2½
Laneside (4th) Lock No. 57	22	3
Laneside (5th) Lock No. 58	22	4
Laneside (6th) Lock No. 59	22	5
Boarshaw Lock No. 60	23	1
Scowcroft Lock No. 61	23	3
Coneygreen Lock No. 62	23	4
Walk Mill Lock No. 63	23	5
Kay Lane Lock No. 64	24	6
Failsworth Lock No. 65	26	7
Tannersfield Highest Lock No. 66	27	5
Tannersfield Middle Lock No. 67	27	6
Tannersfield Lowest Lock No. 68	27	7
Newton Heath Lock No. 69	28	2
Pinfold Lock No. 70	28	4
Shears Lock No. 71	28	5
Scotchman's Lock No. 72	28	6
Ten Acres Lock No. 73	28	7
Drunken Bridge No. 74	29	–

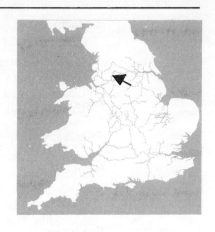

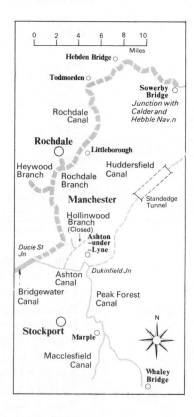

Distance Table

	Miles	Furlongs
Slater's High Lock No. 75	29	1
Slater's Lower Lock No. 76	29	2
Anthony Lock No. 77	29	4
Coalpit Higher Lock No. 78	29	6
Coalpit Middle Lock No. 79	29	7
Coalpit Lower Lock No. 80	30	–
Butler Lane Lock No. 81	30	0½
Ancoat's Lane Lock No. 82	30	5
Brownsfield Lock No. 83	30	6
Ducie Street. *Junction with Ashton Canal*	30	6½
Dale Street Lock No. 84	30	7
Piccadilly Lock No. 85	30	7½
Chorlton Street Lock No. 86	31	1
David Street Lock No. 87	31	2
Oxford Road Lock No. 88	31	3
Tib Lock Lock No. 89	31	5
Albion Mills Lock No. 90	31	6
Tunnel Lock No. 91	31	7
Duke's Lock No. 92. *Junction with Bridgewater Canal*	32	–

Special note   Locks 84-92 linking the Ashton to the Bridgewater Canal have always been open. Restoration work on this canal is being carried on at the following places:

Lock No.	Restoration Agency
6	Rochdale Canal Society.
10-19	West Yorkshire Metropolitan County Council, Calderdale (Halifax) Metropolitan Borough Council with M.S.C.
36	Rochdale Canal Society (now restored).
47, 48	Rochdale Metropolitan Borough Council with M.S.C.
49, 50	Now restored by Rochdale Metropolitan Borough Council with M.S.C.
51–61	Rochdale Metropolitan Borough Council with M.S.C.
64	Site of big dig – Oldham Metropolitan Borough Council, Waterway Recovery Group, the I.W.A. and Rochdale Canal Society.
65	Environmental improvement by Rochdale Canal Society and Waterway Recovery Group.
82, 83	Environmental improvement by City of Manchester, Rochdale Canal Society and Ashton Canal Society.

Note: M.S.C. – Manpower Services Commission.

River Roding (79)

From Barking Creek to the River Thames, this river is under the jurisdiction of the Port of London Authority. An arterial road bridge crosses the creek which contains many wharves. A commercial waterway, it is well used by lighterage companies. Promoted by Act of Parliament 1737.

Authority	Barking and Ilford Navigation Co. (1961) Ltd., c/o Younghusband and Stephens and Co. Ltd., London Road, Barking, Essex. Tel. 01-594-5393.
From and to	Ilford Bridge to Barking Creek.
Distance	1¾ miles.
Length	87ft. 6ins.
Beam	16ft. 9ins.
Draught	5ft.
Headroom	7ft. 6ins.
Locks	None. Tidal doors only, and vessels can therefore only pass when the tide makes a level and doors can be opened. (These are inoperative at present/1984.)
Bridges	Low bridge at Barking near tidal doors.
Tow-path	None.
Tides	High water at Barking 25 minutes before London Bridge. High water at Ilford the same time as London Bridge.

Distance Table

Ilford Bridge to:									Miles	Furlongs
Barking Bridge	...	...	...	...	...	...	...	...	1	4
Tail of Barking Lock and *junction with head of Barking Creek—River Thames*	...	...	...	...	...	...	...	...	1	6

River Rother (Eastern) (80)

Mainly used for land drainage, this navigation is little known though it was a popular place in Edwardian days for early motor launch trips from 'Star' lock (now called Scot's Float Sluice) to Bodiam Castle. The river joins the Royal Military Canal and restoration of the Iden Lock linking the Rother to Hythe has been mooted on several occasions as the Royal Military Canal is part owned by the National Trust. It was originally promoted by Acts of Parliament in 1826 and 1830. Rye is one of the most interesting towns in Great Britain: and with Winchelsea it is part of England's heritage handed down from the days of fortresses and castles. Its cobbled streets, hidden squares and old red roofs with delightful gables make it a tourist mecca.

The River Rother below Scots Float Sluice (Playden), the River Tillingham below Tillingham Sluice, Rye and Rock Channel connecting the Rother and Tillingham round the southern side of the town of Rye are part of the harbour of Rye for which the Southern Water Authority are also the harbour authority. All these waters are tidal and navigable. The harbourmaster's house (Tel: Camber (079 75) 225) is on the east bank of the river near its mouth (the harbour entrance). The Harbour of Rye Revision Order applies, 1976.

Reading Sewer is navigable after a fashion to Smallhythe but permission may be required.

Authority	Assistant Rivers Operations Controller (Southern), Southern Water Authority, Scots Float Depot, Military Rd., Playden, Rye, Sussex. TN31 7PH. Tel. Rye (0797) 3256. Sluice Keeper, Scots Float Sluice. Tel. Iden (079 78) 255.
From and to	*Rye Harbour to Bodiam. The sluice at Newenden has been abolished.
Distance	16⅜ miles.
Length	56ft.
Beam	13ft. 9ins.
Draught	3ft.
Headroom	9ft. 9ins.
Locks	One. Scot's Float Sluice, known previously as Star Lock rises or falls to Rye Harbour. This is equipped with double doors opening either way according to water level. Prior notice to sluice-keeper is essential. The reason for this being that land drainage interests are paramount and there are occasions when there is insufficient water above Scot's Float Sluice for navigation. The Rother and Jury's Cut Catchment Board (Variation of Local Acts) Order 1933, made under Section 4 of the Land Drainage Act 1930. Rise and fall to Rye Harbour.
Tow-path	This exists only on a portion of the navigation.
Tides	High water at Rye Bay is about H.W. Dover.
Connections	River Brede at Rye. The entrance lock has double doors opening either way. It will admit craft 40ft. long by 12ft. beam. There is varying headroom at the entrance due to tidal changes but craft drawing 3ft. could go under the bridge at the entrance with about 8ft. of headroom. The River Brede was navigable to Brede Village and Winchelsea, above Winchelsea only, light craft can make the trip. The situation regarding the River Brede needs clarification. The river navigation rights were abolished by regulation in 1934. The river is still navigable in the winter months, however during the summer the sluice at Udimore is used to retain water in the upper reaches of the river and therefore this stops the river being navigable there.

The Royal Military Canal used to connect at Iden Lock but this lock is out of use and the first 3¼ miles are overgrown. |

Distance Table

Bodiam Bridge (adjoining Bodiam Castle) to:

	Miles	Furlongs
Newenden	4	1
Junction with Newmill Channel	6	7
Kitchenham Road Bridge	8	—
Road Bridge (B. 2082)	10	—

*See plan page 291

Junction with Royal Military Canal (Iden Lock closed)	11	4
Scot's Float Sluice (lock)	12	4
Railway Bridge (S.R.)	13	6
Rye (*Junction with River Brede*)	14	—
Rye Harbour	15	3
East Pier	16	3

River Brede
Brede Sluice (Brede Village 1 mile distant) to:

Langford's Bridge	2	4
Railway Bridge (S.R.)	4	—
Railway Bridge	5	2
Winchelsea (junction with Dimsdale Sewer—unnavigable)	5	6
Entrance Lock	7	7

Royal Military Canal(81)

This canal was originally constructed as a work of defence, but after the invasion threat by Napoleon had passed, an Act was passed in 1807 to convert it to a navigation. It is unique in that it was not originally promoted by Act of Parliament but for military purposes. The Canal was leased in 1877 by the Secretary of State for War to the Lords Bailiff and Jurats of the Level of Romney Marsh for one shilling per annum. The Authority now lease the canal for the remainder of the 999 years term. It runs in a broad sweep behind Romney Marsh and is at present the subject of a campaign to effect its restoration. Restoration of Iden Lock, plus dredging would give the area non-tidal cruising for many miles. The short length of canal from West Hythe Dam to Seabrooks Outfall at Hythe is under the control of the Shepway District Council for pleasure and amenity. This section is not now connected to the main line of the canal.

Authority — a) Southern Waterway Authority, Miller House, Lower Stone Street, Maidstone, Kent, ME15 6NE. Tel Maidstone (0622) 55211.
b) (West Hythe Section). Apply to The Treasurer, Civic Centre, Folkestone, Kent. Tel. Folkestone (0303) 57388.

From and to — West Hythe Sluice to Iden Lock, near Rye. Junction with River Rother.

Distance — 19 miles.

Dimensions — Rowing boats, canoes and light craft only. Headroom 6ft.

Locks — None. Iden Lock, 2½ miles northward of Rye is not usable for navigation purposes.

Tow-path — Throughout the canal but very overgrown in places.

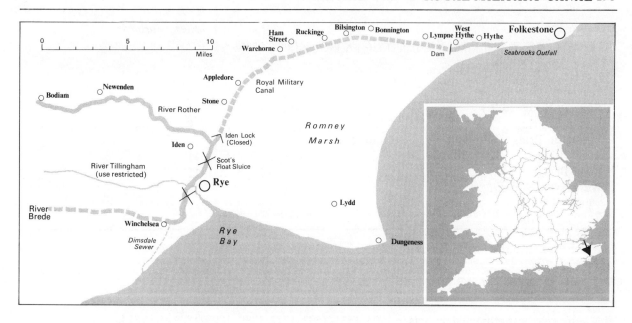

Navigation note For the lengths from West Hythe Dam to Iden Lock (closed). Consult Assistant River Operations Controller (Southern), Southern Water Authority, Kent River and Water Division, Scots Float Depot, Military Road, Playden, Rye, Sussex TN31 7PH. Tel. Rye (079 73) 3256.

River Rother. Scots Float sluice

Distance Table

Iden Lock, junction with River Rother (Iden Lock does not now operate, except for drainage) to:

	Miles	Furlongs
Appledore Bridge	3	2
Heigham Farm Bridge	5	4
Railway Bridge (S.R.)	6	2
Ruckinge Bridge	9	—
Bilsington Bridge (Bilsington Village distant 1 mile)	10	—
Road Bridge	11	1
Road Bridge	11	7½
West Hythe Sluice	19	—

River Severn (82)

This noble river was promoted by Acts in 1503, 1531, 1532, 1772, 1799, 1803, 1809 and 1814. Now navigable from Stourport to the sea, it was originally navigable after a fashion, to above Shrewsbury, and at very high water, to Welshpool. The old navigation above Stourport was by flash locks.

The Severn is a beautiful river, although the surrounding countryside is not spectacular, and it is only near Ironbridge that industrialisation does in any way spoil the scene. Shrewsbury, Bridgnorth, Bewdley, Gloucester, Worcester and Tewkesbury are delightful places to visit and are not so large as to lose their river setting. The fine cathedrals of Gloucester and Worcester and Tewkesbury Abbey compensate for the high banks that mar a good deal of the view from Stourport to Gloucester. The Ship Canal rather than the main river is always used by craft, and although less attractive is a work of art in itself and is referred to elsewhere.* The lower reaches of the Severn are dangerous and expert advice should be sought, but the arrival time of the bore can usually be ascertained locally.

The entrance to the river from the Bristol Channel to the disused Llanthony lock at Gloucester is rarely used for navigation, being difficult and dangerous, especially for small craft. A little way above Gloucester the river is canalised for a short distance, these portions being known as The Parting and Upper Parting, where the navigable channel suitable for the largest craft at low summer level is approximately 50 feet. This applies chiefly to the Rock Fords, Gloucester Parting and Lock Cuttings, the river itself is in most places of considerably greater width.

Maisemore Channel is closed and the lock is derelict, this used to link with the old Gloucester and Hereford Canal, now abandoned. Above Stourport Bridge the river continues for 9 miles to Arley Quarry, but is not navigable except for dinghies. Canoeable from Llanidloes in Wales. Restoration of the Upper Severn to Bridgnorth and possibly above is projected.

Authority	British Waterways Board.
From and to	Gloucester, junction with the Gloucester and Sharpness Ship Canal, to ½ mile above the junction with the Staffordshire and Worcestershire Canal at Stourport.
Connections	Besides having junction with the Gloucester and Sharpness Ship Canal, and the Staffordshire and Worcestershire Canal, the River

*See p. 126

Severn has junction with the River Avon at Tewkesbury and the Worcestershire and Birmingham Canal at Worcester.

Distance	Gloucester to Stourport, 42 miles.
Length	Gloucester to Worcester 135ft. Worcester to Stourport 89ft.
Beam	,, ,, 22ft. ,, ,, 18ft. 11ins
Draught	,, ,, 8ft. ,, ,, 5ft. 9ins
Headroom	,, ,, 23ft. 6ins. ,, ,, 20ft.

These dimensions relate only to cargo vessels

Locks

6. Including Gloucester and Sharpness Ship Canal Lock. Lock gates worked by lock-keepers. Light signals control navigation. Llanthony lock is closed. Fall from Stourport.

Tow-path

None.

Bridges

There are several bridges. The main ones are as follows:

	Headroom
Westgate Road, Gloucester	23ft. 6ins.
British Railways Bridge, Gloucester	23ft. 6ins.
Haw Bridge (take left hand arch)	24ft. 6ins.
Mythe Bridge, Tewkesbury	25ft. 3ins.
Upton	25ft.
Worcester	20ft.

The best channel is through the centre arch, marked by a red light.
Channel on the port side.

Holt Fleet Bridge	28ft. 7ins.

A new bridge carries the M50 just south of Upton on Severn.

Speed limit and bye-laws

8 miles an hour up-stream, 10 miles an hour down-stream. Bye-laws for the river are published by British Waterways Board and yachtsmen are recommended to obtain a copy from the Authority.

Approx. time taken to navigate

A vessel travelling at 8 miles an hour can reach Stourport from Gloucester in approximately 7 to 8 hours including passage through the various locks and assuming that there is a clear run. This is at low summer level; in times of fresh water, the journey would take longer against the stream.

Warning

Below Worcester there is some commercial traffic, most of which is large power driven barges, tugs, etc. which make a big wash and cannot give way to small craft.

Tides

High spring tides flow to Upton-on-Severn and the level of the river is affected up to the tail of Diglis Lock. Neap tides flow to between Framilode and Gloucester.
On Spring tides the first of the flood tides runs up the lower part of the river to Gloucester with a bore which attains its greatest height about Stone Bench. A tide giving from 15ft. to 16ft. of water on the sill of Bathurst Basin Lock, Bristol which is about midway be-

tween the lowest and highest tides, will set up a bore in the river. Only Sharpness tides of 24ft. and over affect the navigable part of the river at Gloucester. Tide tables can be obtained from Sharpness. High water at Framilode 1 hour 45 minutes after Avonmouth. Spring tides rise about 10ft.

High water at Gloucester on spring tides about 2 hours 45 minutes after Avonmouth. Spring tides rise 4ft. to 7ft. A tide giving 17ft. of water on the sill of Bathurst Basin Lock at Bristol will flow above the weir of Llanthony Lock, Gloucester.

High water at Tewkesbury on spring tides about 3 hours 45 minutes after Avonmouth.

High water at Upton-on-Severn on spring tides about 4 hours, 30 minutes after Avonmouth.

High water at the tail of Diglis Locks on spring tides about 5 hours 10 minutes after Avonmouth. Spring tides rise up to 1ft.

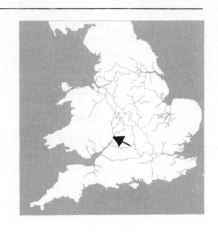

Distance Table

Arley Quarry Landing to:

	Miles	Furlongs
Upper Arley	1	4
Bewdley Bridge	5	2
Gladder or Whitehouse Brook enters river	8	3
Stourport Bridge (effective head of navigation)	9	—
Stourport, *junction with Staffordshire and Worcestershire Canal* ...	9	1
Lincomb Lock No. 1	10	3
Hampstall Ferry	11	4
Lenchford Ferry	13	6
Holt Lock No. 2	14	5
Holt Village	15	4
Grimley	17	—
Hawford, junction with Droitwich Barge Canal	17	5
Bevere Lock No. 3 (sometimes called Camp Lock) ...	18	1
Hallow	19	—
Pope Iron	20	3
Worcester Quay	21	4
Diglis, *junction with Worcester and Birmingham Canal*	22	—
Diglis Locks No. 4 (two locks side by side)	22	3
Teme Junction (River Teme is unnavigable) ...	23	1
Kempsey	25	1
Pixham	25	5
Clevelode	27	2
Rhydd	28	3
Severn Stoke	29	2
Hanley	31	—
Upton-on-Severn	32	—
Sexton's Lode	33	4
Barley House	34	4
Dowdeswell's Elms...	36	4
Tewkesbury Bridge (Bushley distant 1½ miles)	37	5
Tewkesbury, *junction with River Avon*	38	—
Tewkesbury Lock No. 5	38	4
Tewkesbury, Lower Lode and Ferry	39	3

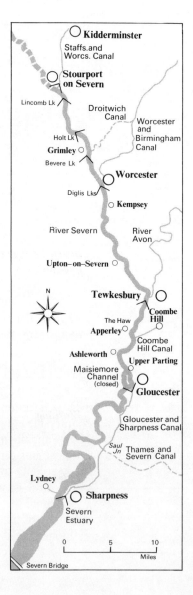

Distance Table

	Miles	Furlongs
Chaceley (right bank), Deerhurst (left bank)	40	7
Apperley	42	—
Haw Bridge	42	6
Coombe Hill	43	7
Wainlode	44	1
Ashleworth	46	1
Upper Parting, junction with Maisemore Channel from Upper Parting to Lower Parting (now closed)	48	4
Gloucester, Westgate Bridge	50	5
Gloucester, *junction with Gloucester and Berkley Ship Canal*	51	—
Gloucester, Llanthony Lock No. 6 (closed)	51	3
Gloucester, Upper Parting to Lower Parting (now closed)	52	—

Left Bank			Right Bank	
Miles	Furlongs		Miles	Furlongs
55	3	Stone Bench		
55	6	Elmore		
		Minsterworth	57	—
63	6	Framilode (junction with Stroudwater Canal (closed at present)		
		Newnham	68	4
		Bullo Pill	69	4
72	2	Fretherne		
78	4	Severn Bridge	78	4
79	1	Sharpness Point, *junction with old entrance to the Gloucester and Berkley Ship Canal.*		
79	6	*Sharpness Junction,* with entrance to Sharpness Docks and Gloucester and Berkley Ship Canal.		
		Junction with Lydney Canal and Harbour ...	81	—
91	—	Aust Cliff.		
		Beachy Point, and *junction with River Wye* ...	92	—
94	4	Severn Tunnel	94	4
100	4	Avonmouth, *junction with River Avon*		

Sheffield & South Yorkshire Navigation (83)

This is a commercial waterway in industrial England. There are some brief sections of countryside notably in a deep valley in the vicinity of Sprotbrough Lock near Doncaster and Long Sandall which had for some years a lock-keeper who vied with the Thames for floral displays, but generally the area this navigation traverses is flat 'wire-scaped' country with many cooling towers and much evidence of heavy industry. Students who wish to feel the pulse of the great industrial north should cruise this waterway.

Although the canal to Sheffield could do much to relieve road congestion it has actually lost most of its traffic and there are fears for its future; superbly built, it stands as a fine monument to the pioneers of the steel industry. The lower sections of the navigation with large locks still carry some heavy commercial traffic.

The original Act promoting the navigation was passed in 1815. Acts dealing with the Stainforth and Keadby Canal were passed in 1793, 1798 and 1809.

Authority	British Waterways Board.
From and to	From junction with the River Trent at Keadby near Scunthorpe, Lincs, passing through Thorne, Stainforth, Doncaster, Mexborough, Swinton and Rotherham to the centre of Sheffield. The Dearne and Dove Canal and branches are derelict except for the bottom four locks
Connections	The New Junction Canal from Bramwith near Doncaster to Sykehouse near Goole connects the Sheffield and South Yorkshire Navigation with the Aire and Calder Navigation and Goole Docks.

Distances

From junction with River Trent at Keadby to:

Doncaster ... ... $21\frac{1}{2}$ miles.
Rotherham ... ... $36\frac{1}{2}$,,
Sheffield ... ... $42\frac{3}{4}$,,

Dimensions

Sheffield to Hexthorpe:

Length	61 ft 6 ins	
Beam	15 ft 6 ins	
Draught	Sheffield to Lock No. 11	6 ft 0 ins
	Lock No. 11 to Hexthorpe	6 ft 10 ins
Headroom	10 ft 0 ins	

Hexthorpe to Bramwith:

Length	185 ft 0 ins
Beam	17 ft 3 ins
Draught	7 ft 6 ins
Headroom	11 ft 3 ins

Bramwith to Keadby

Length	61 ft 6 ins
Beam	16 ft 6 ins
Draught	7 ft 0 ins
Headroom	10 ft 9 ins

(Sheffield and South Yorkshire Improvement Scheme is completed and aims to improve the navigation so that craft up to 400 tons capacity can reach Rotherham and 700 tons capacity craft can reach Mexborough. Eastwood Top and Low Locks were replaced by one new lock, and Kilnhurst Forge Lock was abolished.
New lock sizes 22¾ft (7m) x 252½ft (77m).

Locks

Sheffield to River Dun Navigation, 11 locks, fall from Sheffield.
River Dun Navigation to Stainforth, 15 locks, fall from Tinsley.
Stainforth to Keadby, 2 locks, fall from Stainforth. Entrance lock at

Keadby has sea doors and navigation gates as River Trent rises above canal level. Dearne and Dove canal, only 4 are in use.

Stainforth Side Lock was closed in 1939, preventing entry into the continuation of the River Don.

There is a total of 28 locks at present (1982) from Sheffield to Keadby. This total includes two flood locks, which are generally open, on the River Dun Navigation. The locks on the Sheffield Canal, a total of eleven are not easy to work and have worn spindles so that ordinary windlasses are useless. Help can sometimes be obtained by ringing Sheffield (0742) 441981. With care a small metal object such as a 1p piece, or wire nail, can be inserted into the windlass aperture, so that the windlass fits tightly on the spindle. Below Tinsley locks are operated by lock keepers.

Bridges	Numerous, with many swing bridges. There may be a little delay at the railway swing bridges.
Facilities	There is a boatyard in Sheffield Basin, and very close by is a vast shopping market on several tiers. An IWA plaque is available to intrepid boatmen who reach Sheffield from the boatyard. There are three boatyards at Thorne and good moorings and local shops nearby. Mexborough, Doncaster and Rotherham are not easy places for moorings but a unique shop is by the waterside at Barnby Dun in a difficult area.
Tow-path	Throughout Main Line and Dearne and Dove Canal.
Sunday navigation	Sunday navigation on prior notification to The British Waterways Board, Area Engineer, Lock Lane, Castleford.
Navigation note	This is a commercial navigation and care must be taken in navigation particularly when passing large craft, who must keep to the deep channel.
	The entrance from the River Trent at Keadby needs very careful timing due to tidal conditions and it is essential to contact the lock-keeper beforehand by ringing Scunthorpe (0742) 782205. There is sometimes difficulty due to moored craft. It is generally recommended that craft turn round upstream of the lock, near to the bank at slack water, and drift back to the lock until it is opened. There is a sliding railway bridge at the beginning of the canal and eleven swing bridges. For bridge information ring Mexborough (0709) 582770. See also note under 'Lock's' Sheffield section.
Tides	High water at Stainforth Lock, 1 hour 20 minutes after Goole. Spring tides rise 7ft. 6ins.
	High water at Goole, about 1 hour 10 minutes after Hull.

Dearne and Dove Canal at Swinton (Closed except for locks 1 to 4 to Brown's Yard, Dale.)

Length	58ft.

Beam	14ft. 10ins.
Draught	5ft. 6ins.
Headroom	9ft. 3ins.

Distance Table

	Miles	Furlongs
Sheffield, Basin and Warehouses, to:		
Corporation Wharf	—	6½
Blagden Bridge	1	—
Stainforth Road Bridge	1	2½
Shirland Lane Bridge	1	4
Coleridge Road Bridge	2	0½
Broughton Lane Bridge	2	2
Top Lock of Tinsley Locks, No. 1	2	5½
Tinsley Top Wharf	2	7
Bottom Lock of Tinsley Top Locks, No. 7	3	1½
Turnpike Bridge Lock, No. 8 and Road Bridge	3	3½
Tinsley Low Wharf	3	4
Top Lock of Tinsley Low Locks, No. 9	3	5½
Bottom Lock of Tinsley Low Locks, No. 11 and *commencement of River Dun Navigation*	3	7
Jordan Lock No. 1	4	4
Holmes Wharf	4	7
Holmes Lock No. 2 and Bridge	5	—
Ickles Wharf and Ickles Lock No. 3	5	4
Rotherham, junction with River Rother, navigable for 1 furlong	5	7½
Rotherham, Flood Lock No. 4 and Top Wharf	6	2
Rotherham Wharf	6	3
Parkgate Railway Station and junction with Parkgate Branch Canal (derelict)	7	1
Eastwood Lock No. 5	7	5
Aldwarke Wharf	8	2
Aldwarke Lock No. 6	8	3
Dalton Main Colliery	9	5
Kilnhurst Flood Lock No. 7	10	3
Thrybergh Colliery	10	4
Kilnhurst Pottery and Colliery	10	5
Kilnhurst Road Bridge	10	7
Kilnhurst Forge Lock	11	3
Burton Ings Bridge	11	5
Swinton Wharf and *junction with Dearne and Dove Canal* and Lock No. 8 (Waddington Lock)	11	7
Swinton Road Bridge	12	1
Mexborough Railway Station and Road Bridge	12	5½
Mexborough Top Lock No. 9	13	2
Mexborough Local Board Wharf	13	6½
Mexborough Low Lock No. 10	14	5
Denaby Main Colliery	14	6½
River Dearne Bridge and Road to Cadeby	15	1
Conisbrough Wharf (Lock abolished)	15	6
Warmsworth Lime Kilns	17	4

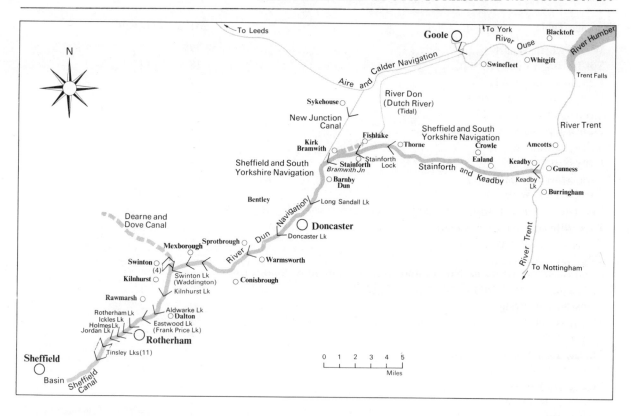

Sheffield Canal basin in 1959

R. Frost F.R.P.S.

Distance Table									*Miles*	*Furlongs*
Warmsworth Wharf	...	...	...	...	...	...	...	...	17	7½
Sprotbrough Lock No. 11	...	...	...	...	...	...	...	18	1½
Hexthorpe Sand Wharf	...	...	...	...	...	...	...	19	7
Doncaster Railway Workshops	...	...	...	...	...	...	20	7½
Doncaster Lock No. 12	...	...	...	...	...	...	...	21	2½
Doncaster Corporation Wharf	...	...	...	...	...	...	21	5
Arksey Landing	...	...	...	...	...	...	...	...	24	3
Long Sandall Lock No. 13	...	...	...	...	...	...	...	24	7
Kirk Sandall Wharf	...	...	...	...	...	...	...	25	7½
Barnby Dun Wharf	...	...	...	...	...	...	...	26	6½
Bramwith *junction with Aire and Calder and Sheffield and South Yorkshire New Junction Canal*	...	...	...	...	...	28	0½
Bramwith Lock No. 14	...	...	...	...	...	...	...	28	1
Stainforth Wharf	...	...	...	...	...	...	...	30	—
Head of Stainforth Lock No. 15 and commencement of *Stainforth and Keadby Canal* (Stainforth lock to Fishlake, closed).	...	...	30	1
Dunston Hill Bridge	...	...	...	...	...	...	...	30	3½
Thorne Lock No. 16	...	...	...	...	...	...	...	32	5
Thorne Wharf	...	...	...	...	...	...	...	33	—
Thorne Low Wharf	...	...	...	...	...	...	...	33	1
Wike Well Wharf	...	...	...	...	...	...	...	33	6½
Medge Hall Wharf	...	...	...	...	...	...	...	37	1
Godnow Bridge Wharf	...	...	...	...	...	...	...	38	1½
Crowle Wharf	...	...	...	...	...	...	...	39	5
Keadby Railway Station (Sliding Railway Bridge)	...	...	...	42	2
Keadby Lock No. 17 and *junction with River Tent Main Line*	...	42	7

Dearne and Dove Canal
(closed from Swinton Top Lock No. 4 to Barnsley Junction.)

Swinton junction with River Dun Navigation to:-
| | | | | | | | Miles | Furlongs
---|---|---|---|---|---|---|---|---|---
Swinton Bottom Lock No. 1 | ... | ... | ... | ... | ... | ... | — | ½
Swinton Top Lock No. 4 | ... | ... | ... | ... | ... | ... | — | 4

Continuation of River Dun Navigation from Stainforth Side Lock
Head of Stainforth Side Lock (closed) and junction with Stainforth and Keadby Canal to:-
| | | | | | | | Miles | Furlongs
---|---|---|---|---|---|---|---|---|---
Fishlake Wharf | ... | ... | ... | ... | ... | ... | ... | — | 6½
Thorne Waterside Wharf | ... | ... | ... | ... | ... | ... | 2 | 3
Fishlake, *junction with River Don* | ... | ... | ... | ... | ... | 2 | 6

Shropshire Union Canal (84)

The first section of the canal was constructed under an Act passed in 1772, and ran from Chester to Nantwich. The next section from Ellesmere Port to Chester was constructed by authority of an Act passed in 1793. The connection between Nantwich and Autherley Junction was later built under an Act of 1826 by the Birmingham and Liverpool Junction Canal Company and the branch from Barbridge Junction to Middlewich was brought into being by an Act of 1827 by the Chester and Ellesmere Canals Company. In 1846 these canals were all grouped together and called the Shropshire Union Canal Company.

The Welsh Canal which became grouped with the canals to Ellesmere Port, Chester and Autherley Junction, was built under an Act dated 1793, and another in 1796. Further Acts relating to the Shropshire Union canal were passed in 1801 and 1804, the latter authorised the building of the canal from Pontcysyllte to the Horseshoe Falls on the Dee. The Montgomeryshire Canal was constructed under an Act passed in 1794. There was a considerable difference in the Ellesmere Canal's route as planned and as constructed.

The Shropshire Union Canal is famous for its aqueducts. Thomas Telford's Pontcysyllte Aqueduct, a wrought iron structure 1007 feet long and 121 feet above the river Dee is the largest, followed by Chirk which is 600 feet long and 69 feet above the River Ceiriog. These fine aqueducts give much character to the Welsh Canal and avoid excessive lockage in hilly areas. There are also two aqueducts on the Montgomeryshire Canal, Vrnwy and Berriew, and at Nantwich and Stretton there are two of cast iron with original balustrades still in position. Whereas early canals followed the contours of the land, the Shropshire Union Main Line mostly follows a straight line across the country with cuttings and embankments like the modern railway. The fine views from this embankment south of Norbury Junction are typical of the Main Line and typical of the work of Telford, the engineer who carried out most of the work.

The canal passes many places of interest; the City of Chester with its cathedral walls and famous 'Rows' which are unique first floor shopping arcades. Amid a wealth of old half timbered houses are Bishop Lloyd's Palace, the Falcon Inn and God's Providence House. The Dee Bridge dates from 1282 and there are extensive Roman remains. South of Chester there are few towns on the Main Line, but Market Drayton and Audlem are old and of interest. Gnosall, an ancient village has good moorings particularly at the Boat Inn, and Norbury Junction with its inn The Junction Arms also has excellent moorings. Nantwich and Middlewich have a fine collection of old black and white buildings which characterizes many other ports of call on this canal.

The Welsh Canal too has many places of interest, Whitchurch with its old Town Hall, the Ellesmere Lake district, Chirk Castle, and the Vale of Llangollen. This last contains the famous abbey at Valle Crucis and Plas Newydd, the home of the Ladies of Llangollen. Llangollen has an Austrian air with its mountains and fine bridges over the River Dee which plunges among the rocks in the centre of the town; from these bridges salmon can be watched leaping. This town is the home of the International Eisteddfod, a mecca for the canal traveller. The lock-free trip over the aqueducts for a distance of twelve miles along the sides of the hills from New Marton to Llangollen is a wonderful experience.

Visitors to Llangollen will find the canal narrows for the last 5 miles and care should be taken if a trip is made on to Llantisilio as there is only one winding hole at Bridge 48a. The Horseshoe Falls near here should be visited even though they are man made, they form a semicircular weir and the canal is fed from the River Dee at these falls.

The lovely Newtown Arm (Old Montgomeryshire Canal) was closed in 1944 and the circumstances under which it was abandoned of no little interest. There was regular trade on this section until 1936 when, owing to general neglect, a burst occurred in the banks near Frankton as a result of which trade on the waterway ceased. One trader, who was discharging coal at Welshpool Wharf at the time, found himself trapped there and forced out of business because the company had failed to fulfill their obligations to make good the break and keep the waterway maintained to statutory standards. Powers of abandonment were obtained upon the ironic grounds that 'there had been no traffic on the canal for some years past.' Nowadays a large portion of the canal near Frankton Locks to Welshpool can be used by light craft that can be portaged past locks and around lowered bridges. Restoration of the canal is planned and progress so far is recorded under Montgomeryshire Canal.

Authority	British Waterways Board, except Whitby Locks Ellesmere Port operated by Manchester Ship Canal.
From and to	**Main Line** Autherley (near Wolverhampton) Junction with Staffordshire and Worcestershire Canal to Ellesmere Port, junction with the Manchester Ship Canal. There are several branches as follows: Middlewich branch connecting with the Trent and Mersey Canal. River Dee Branch to River Dee at Chester. Welsh Canal. Hurleston, near Nantwich to Llantisilio. Ellesmere Branch. Prees Branch.
Connections	Besides the above connections the Canal has junction with the River Dee at Chester.
Special note	Ellesmere Port has been refurbished and is now the National Waterways Museum, with inside and outside exhibits.

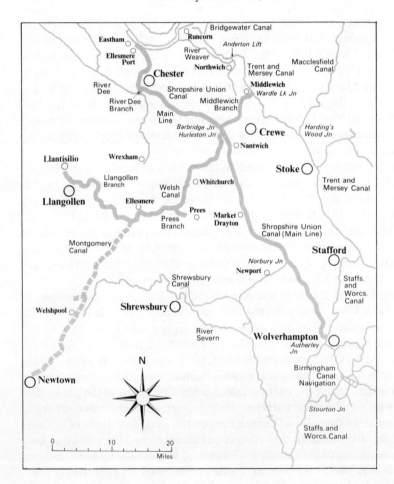

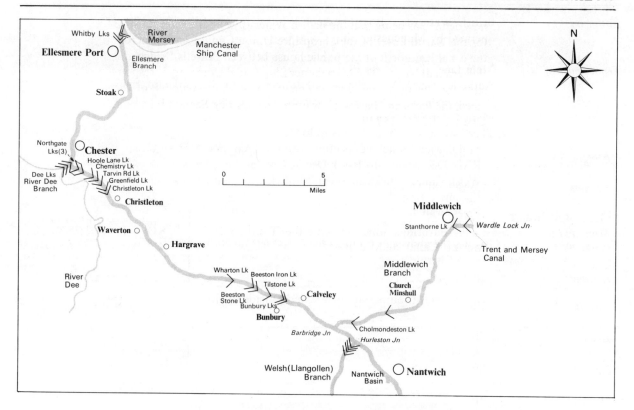

Distances	Main Line—66½ miles. River Dee Branch ⅛ mile. Middlewich Branch 10 miles. Welsh Canal 46 miles. Prees Branch 3¾ miles. Ellesmere Branch ¼ mile.

	From Autherley Junction to Nantwich exclusive	*From Nantwich inclusive to Ellesmere Port*
Length	70ft.	72ft.
Beam	7ft.	13ft. 3ins.
Draught	3ft.	2ft. 6ins.
Headroom	8ft.	8ft.

Tow-path	Throughout navigation.

Locks	46. Lock gates worked by boat crews.

Locks 1, 2 and 3 at Ellesmere Port are in pairs. Locks 1 and 2 have one lock for boats and one lock for 'flats'. Lock No. 3 has one ship lock and one lock for 'flats' both giving access to Ellesmere Port Docks.

Lock No. 1 at Autherley to Lock No. 28 at Hack Green, locks fall from Autherley. Lock No. 30, Bunbury to Lock No. 43 at Chester, locks fall from Nantwich. The three Ellesmere Port locks fall from Ellesmere Port to Ship Canal.

Whitby Locks, Ellesmere Port: It has not been made clear whether it is the British Waterway Board or the Manchester Ship Canal Company who are responsible for Whitby Locks, but the position is now defined as being that the British Waterways Board is responsible for the Wirral Level of the Shropshire Union Canal to a line across the canal just north of the public house between Powells Bridge and the terminal basins. The Manchester Ship Canal Company is responsible for the operation and maintenance of the remainder of the canal, the locks and basins. (For further details ring Section Inspector, Chester (0244) 25732).

Bridges	Numerous.
Tunnels	Cowley. 81 yards.

Middlewich Branch

From and to	From Barbridge junction with the Trent and Mersey Canal at Middlewich.
Distance	10 miles.
Length	70ft.
Beam	7ft.
Draught	3ft. 4ins.
Headroom	8ft.
Locks	3. Lock gates worked by boat crews. Fall from Barbridge Junction.
Bridges	Numerous.
Tunnels	None.

Welsh Canal

This branch is a waterway supply channel and all applications to use it by pleasure craft should be accompanied by full particulars and dimensions of the craft. The authority in fact encourages boats to use this lovely waterway and will assist where necessary. Cruising out of high season is advised due to congestion on this popular canal.

From and to	Hurleston Junction near Nantwich to Llantisilio near Llangollen.
Distance	46 miles.
Length	70ft.
Beam	6ft. 10ins.
Draught	To Trevor, 2ft. 6ins. To Llantisilio, 2ft.
Headroom	7ft. 6ins.
Locks	21. Lock gates worked by boat crews. Rise from Hurleston.
Bridges	Numerous. There is a number of lifting bridges which are opened by boat crews.

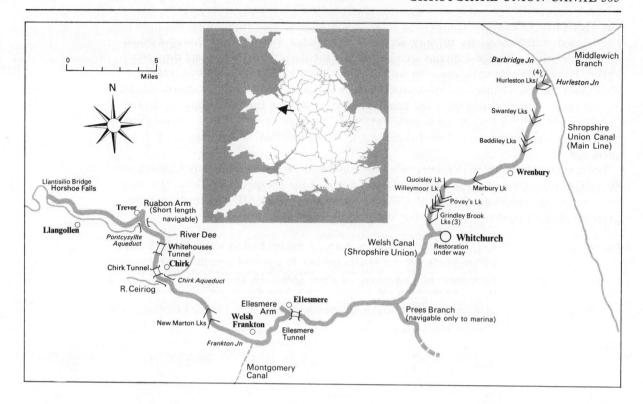

Tunnels	Ellesmere. 87 yards. Tow-path.
	Whitehouses. 191 yards. Tow-path.
	Chirk. 459 yards. Tow-path.
Aqueducts.	Pontcysyllte and Chirk.
	Boats cannot pass on the aqueducts.

Prees Branch

This branch is mainly in a peat area which is very similar to those in Ireland. It is navigable only to Waterloo Bridge and the marina.

From and to	Whixall to Quina Brook and the marina.
Distance	3¾ miles. (1½ miles only open to the marina).
Locks	None.

Ellesmere Branch

Distance	¼ mile.

Branch to River Dee

Distance	¼ mile.
Locks	3, called Dee Locks. Fall to river Dee.
Facilities	There are numerous inns and boatyards on the S.U. network.

The Montgomery Canal

This closed waterway winds its way through magnificent scenery from Shropshire to Montgomeryshire, through Llanymynech and across the River Vyrnwy to meet the Severn Valley. There is no physical connection with the latter river, but the canal follows it through Welshpool, and then climbs to Newtown. The basin is now filled in and the canal ceases at the pumping station, a mile from the basin. A canal clearance by the Shropshire Union Canal Society with the help of the Inland Waterways Association, has brought about plans for its long term restoration. The distance table is included for the assistance of those interested.

The first section Frankton to Carreghofa was considered part of the Ellesmere Canal, and the section from Carreghofa to Garthmyl was known as the Montgomery Canal (Eastern Branch) and the remainder formed the Western Branch of this canal. The route contains water throughout most of its length, but some bridges have been lowered.

Locks	1, 2, 3 and 4 Frankton, 5, 6 and 7 Aston, Fall to Carreghofa. 8 and 9 Carreghofa, 10 and 11 Burgeddon, Fall from Carreghofa. 12 Bank, 13 Cabin, 14 Crowther, 15 Pool Quay, 16 Welshpool, 17 and 18 Belan, 19 Brithdin, 20 Berriew, Rise from Carthmyl.
	21 Brynderwyn, 22 Byles, 23 Newhouse, 24 Freestone, 25 Dolfor, 26 Rock, Rise to Newtown.

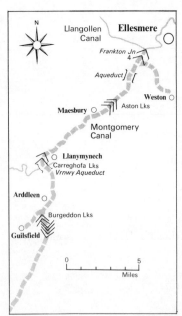
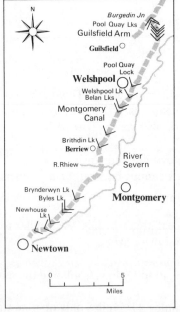

Restoration note	This canal is in a very neglected condition after 35 years of disuse. The Shropshire Union Canal Society Ltd have planned a restoration scheme for this lovely waterway. Already Welshpool Lock and the pound either side of it have been restored together with the section nearby. This section runs from near Welshpool to near Arddleen, through restored lock Nos. 15 to 10. The two locks at Carreghofa are under restoration at present. Much of this work has been carried out under the auspices of the Prince of Wales Committee financed by the Variety Club of Great Britain. Boats specially built to carry handicapped children, will use this section. A separate scheme to restore the section from Frankton Junction through four locks to the Queen Head (Inn) has been commenced by the I.W.A. and is completed.

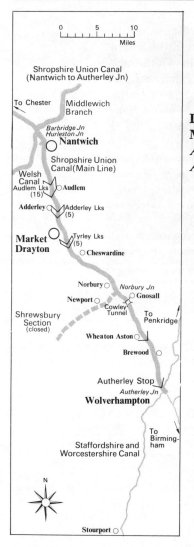

Freestone Lock No. 24, Dolfor Lock No. 25 and Rock Lock No. 26 have been sold together with the canal from Lock 24 to Newtown Wharf to the Newtown Development Corporation and since taken over by the Severn-Trent Water Authority. Whether any of this section can be re-opened is a matter for conjecture.

Distance Table	Miles	Furlongs
Main Line		
Autherley Junction, junction with Staffordshire and Worcestershire Canal, Autherley Lock No. 1 to:		
Pendeford Bridge	1	3
Chillington	3	5
Brewood	5	—
Watling Street Aqueduct	6	1
Wheaton Aston Lock No. 2	7	6
Church Eaton: High Onn	10	6
Gnosall	13	—
Norbury Yard and Dry Dock Junction with Branch to Shrewsbury now derelict. The Junction Inn	15	4
Shebdon	19	—
Knighton Factory	20	—
Park Heath	21	—
Goldstone Common: Cheswardine	23	—
Tyrley Top Lock No. 3	25	2
Tyrley Bottom Lock No. 7	25	5
Market Drayton Wharf (Market Drayton distant ½ mile)	26	5
Adderley Wharf and Adderley Top Lock No. 8 ...	29	7
Adderley Bottom Lock No. 12	30	1
Audlem Top Lock No. 13	31	4
(Locks Nos. 13 and 14 form the 1st Flight and Nos. 15 to 27 the 2nd Flight.)		
Audlem Wharf and Warehouse	32	6
Audlem Bottom Lock No. 27	33	1
Hack Green Lock Nos. 28 and 29	36	5
Nantwich Basin (Nantwich distant ½ mile)	38	7
Hurleston Junction, *junction with Welsh Canal*	40	6
Barbridge Junction, *junction with Middlewich Branch*	42	1
Wardle	43	3
Calveley	43	7
Bunbury Lock Nos. 30 and 31	44	7
Tilstone Mill, Bridge and Lock No. 32	45	5
Beeston, Lock Nos. 33 and 34	46	5
Wharton Lock No. 35	47	4
Bate's Mill	47	7
Crow Nest	50	2
Egg Bridge, Waverton	53	6
Christleton, Locks Nos. 36 and 37	55	3
Tarvin Lock No. 38	56	2
Hoole Lane Locks Nos. 39 and 40	57	—
Cow Lane, North Gate, Chester, Lock Nos. 41, 42 and 43 (staircase)	57	3
Chester, Tower Wharf	57	7
Chester, *junction with Branch to River Dee* (1 furlong)	58	—

Montgomery Canal. Vyrnwy Aqueduct in 1982

Restored Pool Quay top lock Montgomery Canal

Distance Table	Miles	Furlongs
Mollington ...	59	7
Backford ...	61	7
Caughall ...	62	7
Stoak ...	63	3
Stanney ...	64	3
Ellesmere Port Docks, and *junction with Manchester Ship Canal,* Locks Nos. 44, 45 and 46 ...	66	4

Middlewich Branch

Barbridge Junction, junction with Main Line, to:

	Miles	Furlongs
Cholmondeston Lock No. 1 ...	1	3
Egerton's Bridge ...	2	7
Minshull Lock No. 2 ...	3	—
Weaver Aqueduct ...	3	6
Church Minshull ...	4	7
Clive Green ...	8	—
Stanthorne Lock No. 3 ...	9	1
Middlewich, *junction with Wardle Lock Branch—Trent and Mersey Canal* ...	10	—

Welsh Canal

Hurleston Junction with Main Line, to:

	Miles	Furlongs
Hurleston Locks Nos. 1, 2, 3 and 4 ...	—	2
Ravensmoor ...	1	5
Swanley, Locks Nos. 5 and 6 ...	2	2
Baddiley, Locks Nos. 7, 8 and 9 ...	4	3
Wrenbury ...	6	2
Marbury Lock No. 10 ...	8	2
Steer Brook ...	8	7
Quoisley Lock No. 11 ...	9	7
Willymoor Lock No. 12 ...	10	7
Povey's Lock No. 13 ...	11	2
Grindley Brook, Lower Lock Nos. 14 to 16 ...	12	2
Grindley Brook, Upper Lock Nos. 17 to 19 (Staircase) ...	12	4
Junction with Whitchurch Branch. Closed and filled in ...	13	3
New Mill ...	13	5
Wrexham Road ...	14	—
Tilstock ...	16	7
Platt Lane ...	17	3
Whixall Moss Roving Bridge, *junction with Prees Branch* ...	19	—
Bettisfield ...	20	7
Hampton Bank ...	21	7
Little Mill ...	23	5
Junction with Ellesmere Branch 1/4 mile, Ellesmere Depot and Yard ...	25	5
Tetchill ...	27	1
Frankton, top of Frankton Locks and *junction with Montgomery Canal* to Newport (closed) ..	29	—
Maesterfyn ...	30	2
Hindford ...	31	4
New Marton Bottom Lock No. 1 (sometimes 'Martin') ...	32	3½
New Marton Top Lock No. 2 Level to Llantisilio ...	32	5

Distance Table *Miles   Furlongs*

	Miles	Furlongs
St. Martin's	33	6
Lovett's Wharf	34	3
Rhoswiel	35	—
Gledryd	35	2
Chirk Bank	36	—
Chirk Aqueduct	36	—
Chirk, north end of Chirk Tunnel	36	3
Black Park	37	2
Whitehouses Tunnel	37	6
Irish Bridge	38	5
Vron	39	—
Pontcysyllte Aqueduct (southern side)	39	3
Short Arm (remainder of closed Ruabon Branch)	40	—
Plas Isaf	41	5
Trevor	42	5
Llangollen	44	2
Pentrevelin	45	3
Berwyn Chain Bridge	45	3
Llantisilio Bridge	46	—

Prees Branch
Whixall Moss Roving Bridge, junction with Ellesmere Canal to:

	Miles	Furlongs
Minshull or Rodenhurst's Bridge	—	5
Boodle's Bridge or Waterloo (limit of navigation)	1	5
Sydney Bridge or Edstaston	3	—
Quina Brook	3	6

Montgomery Canal
Frankton, junction with Welsh Canal to:

	Miles	Furlongs
Lockgate Bridge, junction with Weston Branch 6 miles bottom of Frankton Locks 1 to 4	—	4
Rednal	3	1
Queens Head (Inn)	4	1
Aston Locks 5, 6 & 7	4	7
Maesbury	6	1
Redwith	7	3
Crickheath	8	1
Waen Wen	9	—
Pant	9	3
Llanymynech	10	4
Wall's Bridge, Wharf & Warehouse	10	7
Carreghofa Locks 8 & 9	11	4
Newbridge	12	—
Clopton's Wharf	13	—
Mardu	14	1
Arddleen	15	2
Burgeddon, top of Burgeddon Locks, and junction with Guilsfield Branch (2 miles) a nature Reserve	15	6
Burgeddon Locks 10 & 11	15	6½

Distance Table

									Miles	Furlongs
Gwernfelen ...	...	...	...	...	...	...	...	...	16	2
Bank Lock No. 12 ..	...	...	...	...	...	...	...	...	17	2
Cabin Lock No. 13									17	4
Crowther Lock No. 14									17	7
Pool Quay Lock No. 15	...	...	...	...	...	...	...	...	18	2
Buttington ...	...	...	...	...	...	...	...	...	20	1
Welshpool Lock No. 16	...	...	...	...	...	...	...	...	21	5
Whitehouse ...	...	...	...	...	...	...	...	...	22	4
Belan Locks 17 & 18	...	...	...	...	...	...	...	...	23	—
Brithdair Lock No. 19	...	...	...	...	...	...	...	...	25	6
Berriew Lock No. 20	...	...	...	...	...	...	...	...	26	2
Berriew Aqueduct									26	6
Evelvach	...	...	...	...	...	...	...	...	26	7
Redgate	...	...	...	...	...	...	...	...	27	3
Garthmyl	...	...	...	...	...	...	...	...	27	6
Bunker's Hill	...	...	...	...	...	...	...	...	29	1
Pennant Dingle	...	...	...	...	...	...	...	...	29	7
Brynderwyn Lock No. 21	...	...	...	...	...	...	...	...	30	6
Byles Lock No. 22									31	2
Newhouse Lock No. 23	...	...	...	...	...	...	...	...	31	6
Aberbechan	...	...	...	...	...	...	...	...	32	5
Newtown Pumping Station (present head of navigation)							...	...	33	

(The Canal to Newtown Basin and the three last locks have been sold)

Staffordshire and Worcestershire Canal (85)

The Act that promoted this canal was passed in 1766, a second Act was passed in 1790. One of the most prosperous of our waterways at the peak of its career, the owning company once paid a dividend of thirty eight per cent. From its junction with the Trent and Mersey Canal it soon runs through a man-made lake called Tixall Wide, originally constructed to make the canal more pleasing to the eye of the estate owner. This stretch of water is a natural habitat for wild life and looks very much like a Norfolk Broad.

After crossing the River Sow by an aqueduct it follows the Sow valley to Stafford, thence skirting Wolverhampton where, at only 2½ miles from that town, it follows the Stour Valley through Stourton and Kinver. The section above Wolverley where the canal is cut through red sandstone above the river valley is very fine and well engineered.

Stourport was the first real canal town of any size, its wharves, basins and warehouses surrounded by Georgian houses look very much as they did in Brindley's day, in fact much of the charm of this waterway derives from the fact that much of Brindley's work survives. The bell weirs of his design are particularly interesting and his aqueduct over the Trent is still in use. The section of canal at Stourton Junction is a good example of the 'green finger' near the town. Wightwick Manor (N.T.) is situated close to the waterway.

The canal is a busy one and the Staffordshire and Worcestershire Canal Society is one of the most vigorous in the country.

Authority   British Waterways Board.

From and to	The junction with the River Severn at Stourport to junction with the Trent and Mersey Canal at Great Haywood.
Connections	The canal has junction with the following waterways: At Stourton Bridge, 12 miles from Stourport, with the Stourbridge Canal. At Aldersley Junction, 25 miles from Stourport, with the Main Line Canal Birmingham Canal Navigations. At Autherley Junction, 25½ miles from Stourport, with the Shropshire Union Canal. At Hatherton Junction, 31 miles from Stourport, the Hatherton Branch Canal ran through the Churchbridge Locks to the Northern Section of the Birmingham Canal Navigations but this is now closed and the route in part is no longer visible. Two locks Nos. 1 & 2 survive in the Calf-Heath Marina which uses a short section of the closed canal.
Distance	46⅛ miles.
Length	70ft.
Beam	7ft. Through barge locks to Stourport Basin via locks 1 and 2: 15ft.
Draught	2ft. 6ins.
Headroom	6ft. 6ins.
Locks	43. Lock Nos. 1 to 31, rise from River Severn at Stourport. Lock Nos. 32 to 43, fall to Great Haywood. Pratt's Wharf Lock leading to the River Stour from the Canal to the river is closed at present. Stourport river locks are double locks. One set is 15ft. beam and the other is only 7ft. Special care should be taken at Bratch Locks where a special locking procedure applies.
Tow-path	Throughout navigation.
Bridges	119.
Tunnels	2. Cookley, length 65 yards. Towing path. Dunsley, length 25 yards. Towing path.
Speed limit	3 miles per hour.
General remarks	Stafford Branch formed by River Sow Navigation is now converted into a drain and no navigation is possible. It was originally one mile long with one lock. The River Stour branch is closed at present. It was 1¼ miles long. The river navigation of the River Stour was never completed through to the Severn and was replaced by this canal.

Facilities　　　　　There are 15 boatyards and numerous inns by the canal also facilities nearby as well.

Distance Table

Stourport, junction with River Severn Main Line and entrance locks (Stourport Lock Nos. 1 and 2) to Stourport Basin, to:

	Miles	Furlongs
York Street Lock No. 3	—	1
Lower Mitton Bridge	—	3
Gilgal Bridge and Wharf	—	5
Mitton Chapel Bridge	—	6
Upper Mitton Bridge and Wharf...	1	—
Bullock's Lane Wharf	1	4
Oldington Bridge	2	—
Junction with River Stour, through Pratt's Wharf Side Lock (closed at present)	2	3
Falling Sands Lock No. 4 or Oldington Lock	2	6
Falling Sands Bridge	3	1
Caldwell Lock No. 5 and Bridge	3	4
Round Hill Bridge	3	6
Caldwell Mill Bridge	3	6
Caldwell Hall Bridge and Public Wharf	4	—
Kidderminster Lock, No. 6, Wharf and Warehouse ...	4	3
Lime Kiln Bridge and Wharf	4	5
Stour Vale Iron Works	5	4
Wolverley Court Bridge and Lock No. 7	5	5
Wolverley Mill Wharf	5	7
Wolverley Bridge, Lock No. 8, and Wharf, The Lock Inn	6	1
Wolverley Forge Bridge	6	3
Debdale Bridge and Lock No. 9	7	2
Cookley Tunnel and Iron Works...	7	4
Austcliffe Bridge and Wharf	8	—
Clay House Bridge	8	2
Whittington Bridge, Lock No. 10	9	4
Whittington Horse Bridge...	9	6
Kinver Bridge, Lock No. 11 and Wharf...	10	3
Hyde Bridge, Lock No. 12 and Iron Works	11	—
Dunsley Tunnel	11	5
Stewponey Wharf, Lock No. 13	12	—
Stourton Bridge and Junction, *junction with Stourbridge Canal-Main Line* between Locks Nos. 13 and 14	12	2
Round House Wharf	13	5
Gothersley Bridge and Lock No. 14	14	—
Rocky or Hockley Lock No. 15	14	3
Green's Forge Bridge, Lock No. 16 and Wharf ...	15	1
Hincksford Bridge and Lock No. 17	16	2
Swindon Forge Bridge, Wharf, Iron Works and Lock 18	16	5
Marsh Lock No. 19	16	7
Botterham Bridge and Two Locks, Nos. 20 and 21 ...	17	2
Wombourn Common Bridge and Wharf	17	5
Heath Forge Wharf	17	7
Bumble Hole Bridge and Lock No. 22	18	4

Distance Table

	Miles	Furlongs
Bratch Bridge and Three Locks, Nos. 23, 24 and 25	18	7
Awebridge and Lock No. 26	19	6
Ebstree Lock No. 27	20	2
Dimmingsdale Lock No. 28 and Reservoir ...	20	4
Dimmingsdale Bridge	20	6
Mops Farm Bridge...	21	3
Castle Croft Bridge	21	6
Wightwick Bridge and Lock No. 29	22	4
Wightwick Mill Bridge and Lock No. 30 ...	22	5
Compton Wharf Lock No. 31 and Bridge ...	23	2
Tettenhall Bridge and Wharf	24	—
Dunstall Water Bridge	24	5
Aldersley Junction, *junction with Birmingham Canal Navigations-Main Line*	25	1
Autherley Junction, junction with *Shropshire Union Canal-Main Line*	25	5
Marsh Lane Bridge	26	3
Coven Heath Bridge	27	4
Cross Green Bridge and Wharf	28	3
Slade Heath Bridge and Railway Bridge ...	29	—
Laches Bridge	29	6
Moat House Bridge	30	2
Deepmore Bridge	30	6
The Cross Bridge, Hatherton, junction with Hatherton Branch (closed)	31	0
Calf Heath Bridge and Wharf	32	1
Four Ashes	32	—
Gailey Wharf, Bridge and Lock No. 32 ...	33	3
Brick-kiln Lock No. 33	33	4
Boggs Lock No. 34	33	6
Rodbaston Bridge and Lock No. 35	34	4
Otherton Lane Bridge	34	6
Otherton Lock No. 36	35	—
Line Hill Bridge	35	3
Filance Lock No. 37	35	7
Penkridge Bridge, Wharf, Lock No. 38	36	1
Longford Bridge and Lock No. 39	36	5
Longford Bridge	36	7
Teddesley Bridge	37	1
Park Gate Bridge, Lock No. 40	37	4
Shutt Hill Bridge and Lock No. 41	38	2
Acton Bridge and Wharf	38	6
Roseford Bridge	39	5
Deptmore Lock No. 42	40	—
Hazelestrine Bridge	40	3
Radford Bridge, Wharf and Warehouse Inn ...	41	2
Baswich Bridge and Salt Works	41	6
Lodgfield Bridge	42	4
Stoneford Bridge	43	—
Milford Bridge	43	6

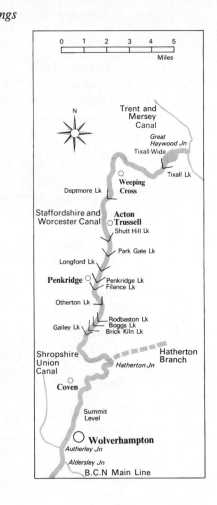

Cactus just below Wolverley lock on the Staffordshire and Worcestershire Canal in 1967

Distance Table									Miles	Furlongs
Tixall Bridge	...	...	...	...	...	...	...	...	44	4
Old Hill Bridge, Tixall Lock No. 43		...	...	...	...	...		44	6	
Great Haywood Wharf and Junction, *junction with Trent and Mersey*										
Canal	...	...	...	...	...	...	...	...	46	1

River Stour (Kent) (86)

This is a very old navigation, originally running to Canterbury through 2 flash locks above Fordwich. It was promoted by an Act in 1514 and there was a subsequent Act in 1825.

Fordwich is a pleasant old town, famous for its tiny town hall, ducking stool and a wealth of domestic architecture dating mainly from the Middle Ages. For centuries it was the Port of Canterbury when the adjoining Little Stour was also partly navigable.

Pleasant pastureland surrounds the Stour but care must be taken by boatmen at Stonar as the sluices here in times of heavy rain are opened and there is a dangerous cross current. Ancient Richborough Castle is on the river with large scale Roman remains and Sandwich, one of the five Cinque Ports, is still a port of call for coasters.

Above Fordwich, craft that can be portaged can reach Canterbury. Rights of navigation above Fordwich are somewhat obscure, but it seems likely that a right still exists though it may be limited to the inhabitants of the City of Canterbury. Those who venture above Fordwich should note there are portages at Sturry, and one mile above at the flour mills, also at Old Mills, Canterbury. The trip is one that should be made by the intrepid, particularly in view of the sights Canterbury has to offer to visitors.

Authority

From the sea to Poulders Sluice about three-quarters of a mile above Sandwich, the river is under the jurisdiction of the Sandwich Port and Haven Commissioners, Clerk's Office, 1 Potter Street, Sandwich, Kent CT13 9DR. Tel. Sandwich (0304) 612444. There is no navigation authority for the rest of the river.

Distance

From the entrance to Sandwich, about 4 miles. Sandwich to Fordwich, 15 miles.

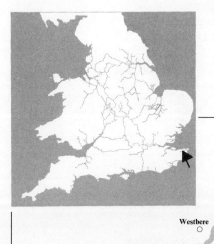

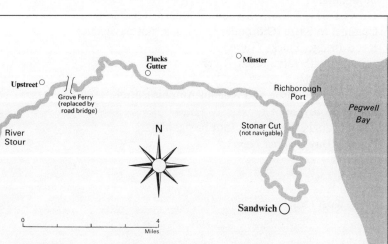

General remarks and navigation

From the entrance of the river at Pegwell Bay to Richborough, springs rise 12ft. and neaps 9ft. At Sandwich deduct about 2ft. 6ins. At low tide there is very little water in the lower reaches of the river. *River Stour above Sandwich:* The river is tidal to Fordwich near Canterbury, where further progress is stopped by a mill dam. Small craft up to about 4 feet draught can navigate to Fordwich. Care should be taken, however, of weeds above Sandwich, and also a look-out kept for weed booms, particularly near Chislet Colliery. Vessels for Richborough should not exceed 190ft. in length and vessels for Sandwich 115ft. Stonar Cut at Richborough can be very dangerous, particularly for small craft when the sluices are open. The river authority maintain a 50ft. high flagstaff at the upstream entrance of the Cut from which, when the sluices are being run, i.e. open, a red flag is flown by day and a red fixed light exhibited by night, visible for at least 600 yards. There are warning notices, illuminated at night, situated approximately 600 yards upstream and downstream of the Cut. There does not appear to be any rights of navigation above Canterbury.

Bridges

At Sandwich there is the Barbican bridge which can be opened on application to the toll collector at the bridge house.
There are 4 bridges above this point, the clearance of which is not more than 20 feet above high water spring.

Locks

None.

Tow-path

None.

Moorings

At the Wharf, Sandwich.

Tides

High water at Sandwich 30 minutes after Ramsgate.
Spring tides rise 8ft. and neap tides rise 7ft. at Sandwich.
High water at Ramsgate, about 20 minutes after Dover.

Distance Table
Fordwich Mill to:

	Miles	Furlongs
Stodmarsh	2	5
Grove Ferry, Railway Station, Southern Region	5	1
Channel to Sarre (Old outlet to the sea, not navigable)	8	2
Road Bridge, Plucks Gutter	8	3
Junction with Little Stour River	8	5
Railway Bridge	11	7
Richborough Castle and Roman Amphitheatre	13	—
Sandwich Bridge	15	2
Richborough, Stonar Cut (not navigable)	18	3
*Pegwell Bay, Pepper Ness	19	2

*See Imray Chart No. C8

River Stour (Suffolk) (87)

This waterway, has been included as there appears to be a prescriptive right of navigation and also the position of the locks above the barrage is uncertain. It can be canoed from Sudbury.

The original navigation was promoted by Acts passed in 1705 and 1781 though these Acts were not rescinded by Abandonment Acts or Closure orders.

The river is very lovely, made famous by the paintings of John Constable who lived and worked for a time at Flatford Mill, and of Gainsborough whose birthplace was Sudbury.

Four locks were rebuilt in 1933 in the same style as the original locks depicted in Constable's paintings; these were at Stratford St. Mary, Dedham, Flatford and Brantham. The rebuilt locks were hardly ever used and by 1939 became virtually unusable. Schemes were put forward to re-open them but the barrage at Brantham has since effectively closed the river to all but dinghies and canoes. The rebuilt locks were 95ft. by 10ft. with a draught of 2ft. 9ins.

The Stour Trust has been formed to encourage general interest in the river. This Trust can provide helpful information on navigation. Rollers to assist light craft are being installed at the old locks. The Trust has carried out restoration work on the river.

Sudbury Basin and nearby cuts have been restored with a good deal of assistance from the U.S. forces stationed in East Anglia. The terminal buildings are to be restored and will have amongst other things a theatre. The Ballingdon Cut and basin have been restored and with the restoration projected of Cornard Lock there should be a length of river available for cruising from Sudbury to Henny Lock. There have been considerable pressures to restrict cruising on this river in spite of the fact that the navigation acts have not been repealed. No attempt appears to have been made to alter the navigation acts by using Section 106 of the Transport Act 1968.

The river throughout is surprisingly wide with no large towns en route. There are some fine examples of East Anglian mills, notably Wissington and Flatford and the villages of Nayland, Bures, Flatford and Dedham are particularly attractive,.

Authority	Anglian Water Authority, Essex River Division, River House, Springfield Road, Chelmsford, Essex. Tel. Chelmsford (0245) 64721. (The area below Brantham is tidal and is controlled by the Harwich Harbour Conservancy Board.)
From and to	Junction with the tidal river at Brantham Lock near Manningtree, to Sudbury.
Special Note	Bye-Laws regulating the River were published early in 1983. These have the effect of banning power boats from Henny Lock to Brantham with very limited exceptions. Visitors to the river should consult the River Stour Trust for advice.

Distance	23½ miles.
Dimensions	Limited to light craft that can be portaged.
Locks	Originally 15 but most are now derelict and some have vanished. Fall from Sudbury. Flatford lock is usable.
Tow-path	From Sudbury to Brantham Barrage.
Bridges	Numerous.
Facilities	An excellent selection of village inns and village shops. Small boatyard facilities at Dedham and Flatford. Sudbury Terminus has been dredged and re-furbished.
Tides	Spring tides flow to the tail of Flatford Lock.
	Neap tides flow to the tail of Brantham Lock.
	High tide at Mistley, 42 minutes after Harwich. Spring tides rise 11ft. 6ins.
	High tide at Cattawade Bridge, 1 hour 2 minutes after Harwich. Spring tides rise 4ft. 3ins.
	The river is tidal from Brantham Lock to Orwell Haven and is used by sea-going vessels. The River Orwell joins the Stour near Orwell Haven and is a tidal navigation to Ipswich, a distance of 9½ miles. This channel to Ipswich is dredged to 17ft. Due to the tidal currents the tidal portions of the Orwell and Stour should not be attempted without local knowledge,.

Distance Table

Sudbury, Ballingdon Bridge, near boathouse, to:
(the original cut to the terminal Basin is now open)

	Miles	Furlongs
*Cornard Sluice (site of Cornard Lock) ...	1	—
Henny Street Sluices (site of Henny Lock) ...	2	6
Ruins of Pitmine Lock	3	6
Bures Mill and Sluice (site of Bures Lock) ...	6	6
Wormingford Mill and Wormingford Lock ...	9	1
Swan Lock (derelict)	9	3
Wissington Mill and Weir (site of Wissington Lock)	11	3
Nayland Weir (Nayland Lock site)	12	5
Nayland Bridge A. 134	12	6½
Horkesley Lock Site	13	1
Boxted Weir (site of Boxted Lock)	16	1
Langham Weir (site of Langham Lock) ...	17	1
Langham Bridge	17	4
Higham Hall, junction with River Brett ...	18	0½
Stratford re-built lock(disused)	18	7
Stratford St. Mary Bridge	19	5

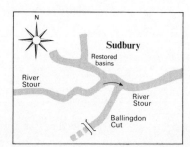

*Reconstruction planned

Distance Table

							Miles	Furlongs
Dedham re-built lock (disused) ...	...	...	...	...	...	...	20	4
Dedham Bridge ...	...	...	...	...	...	...	20	0½
Flatford Bridge ...	...	...	...	...	...	...	22	0½
Flatford re-built lock and Constable's Mill			...	...	...	...	22	1
Brantham Lock (not in use)* ...	...	...	...	...	...	...	23	·5
Cattawade Bridge ...	...	...	...	...	...	...	24	3
Brantham Barrage and Sluices							24	3½
Manningtree ...	...	...	...	...	...	...	25	1
Mistley ...	...	...	...	...	...	...	26	0½
Parkeston ...	...	...	...	...	...	...	34	—
Harwich ...	...	...	...	...	...	...	35	4

*Reconstruction planned

Stourbridge Canal(88)

This canal is in an area famous for its glass making wherein the furnaces looking like up-turned funnels, a feature of the industry, give this short waterway a character all of its own. In 1776 an Act was promoted to construct this canal which links the B.C.N. to the Staffordshire and Worcestershire Canal at Stourton. The latter place is in well wooded countryside, and the canal rises through Stourton Locks over the aqueduct (River Stour), and up the 'sixteen locks' to Brockmoor Junction. Another feature of the canal is the split bridges designed to avoid the towing rope being disconnected.

The Stourbridge 'sixteen locks' were restored to navigability in a three year rescue operation by the Staffordshire and Worcestershire Canal Society working in conjunction with the British Waterways Board. This unique operation by volunteers and B.W.B. staff working together restored the canal which was re-opened on 27th May 1967, by Mr. John Morris, Joint Parliamentary Secretary to the Ministry of Transport.

Authority	British Waterways Board.
From and to	Stourton Junction, junction with Staffordshire and Worcestershire Canal to Black Delph, junction with Birmingham Canal Navigations. Branches to Stourbridge and the Fens on Pensnett Chase.
Distance	5¾ miles. Stourbridge Branch, 1¼ miles. Fens Branch, ¾ mile, is now a canal feeder.
Length	70ft. *Draught* 3ft.
Beam	7ft. *Headroom* 8ft. 6ins.
Locks	20. Lock gates worked by boat crews. Flights of 16 and 4. Rise from Stourton Junction.
Tow-path	Throughout navigation.
Bridges	Several—see Headroom.

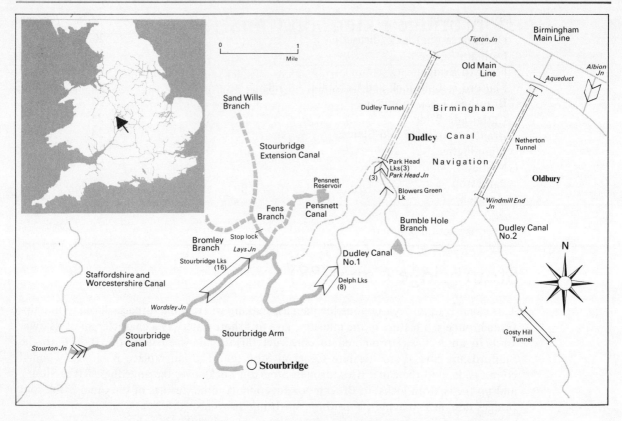

General remarks   The Branch to The Fens on Pensnett Chase connects at Blackmoor Junction with the Stourbridge Extension Canal.

Distance Table

Stourton Junction, junction with Staffordshire and Worcestershire–Main Line–and tail of Stourton Lock No. 1 to:

	Miles	Furlongs
Head of Stourton Top Lock No. 4	—	2
Wordsley Junction, *junction with Stourbridge Branch* and bottom of the sixteen locks No. 5	2	—
Buckpool	2	7
Lays Junction, *junction with Branch to the Fens on Pensnett* Chase, and top of sixteen locks No. 20	3	2
Brettell Lane	4	3
Black Delph, *junction with Birmingham Canal Navigations–Dudley Canal Line No. 1*	5	1

Stourbridge Branch

Wordsley Junction, junction with Main Line, to:

	Miles	Furlongs
Holloway End	—	7
Stourbridge	1	2

Branch to The Fens on Pensnett Chase

Lays Junction, junction with Main Line, to:

	Miles	Furlongs
Brockmoor Junction, *junction with Stourbridge Extension Canal* ...	—	2
The Fens, Pensnett Chase	—	$6\frac{1}{2}$

Stourbridge Extension Canal (89)

The canal is mostly closed but it still acts as a feeder to the Stourbridge Canal. This canal is in a very weedy state and can only be navigated from junction with Stourbridge Canal to the stop lock which is at present out of order. The head of the Canal was Shutend brickworks.

Authority	British Waterways Board.
From and to	Brockmoor to Bromley Branch.
Distance	2 miles (Bromley Branch ¼ mile, Sandhills Branch ¾ mile closed).

Length	72ft.	*Draught*	4ft.
Beam	7ft.	*Headroom*	6ft. 6ins.
Locks	1. Stop Lock. Level.		
Tow-path	Throughout navigation.		

Distance Table

	Miles	Furlongs
Brockmoor Junction, junction with Stourbridge Canal to:		
Stop Lock, and *junction with Bromley Branch*	—	1½

Stratford upon Avon Canal (90)

The Stratford-upon-Avon Canal was authorised in 1793, and was completed to the junction with the Grand Union, originally the Warwick and Birmingham Canal, at Kingswood in 1802. The southern section to Stratford was completed in 1816. Apart from the original Act of 1793, others concerning this canal were passed in 1795, 1799, 1809, 1815, 1817 and 1821.

The canal has a guillotine stop lock at its commencement at King's Norton which canal enthusiasts, unfamiliar with East Anglia, find a novelty. The canal is famous for one of the first battles for the waterways fought by the Inland Waterways Association when the Great Western Railway tried to fix the opening bridge at Lifford Lane; after 2 years of agitation however, they were forced to concede the right of navigation. The countryside is pleasant, open and rolling and the summit level has many pleasant surrounding walks, particularly near Earlswood and Waring's Green. The northern section has generally a greater wealth of interest than many more popular canals. Packwood House and nearby, Packwood Hall, are famous. Other noted country houses in the area are Baddesley Clinton, Chadwick Manor Wroxhall Abbey, Broom Hall, Bushwood Hall and Knowle.

The southern section from Kingswood is now owned by the National Trust and has been restored by volunteers of the Inland Waterway Association, prison labour was also used to the advantage of all concerned. The project was directed by David Hutchings, A.R.I.B.A. M.B.E. and the experience gained is being used in the restoration of the Upper Avon which is now completed. The canal from Kingswood to Stratford was re-opened by Her Majesty Queen Elizabeth the Queen Mother in July 1964.

The southern section has always suffered from a water shortage and though recently new arrangements have been made to improve matters, it is still essential that boatowners are exceptionally careful in seeing that all paddles are properly closed and to leave both gates closed when leaving every lock; it is irksome to have to close both upper and lower gates, but it does save water. This section goes through the Forest of Arden country, and there are good views from the two aqueducts, Wootton Wawen and Edstone, sometimes called Bearley.

Facilities are available at nearby villages and the canal is not one to be hurried through. Stratford has several good moorings, but for an overnight stay it is better to lock through into the Avon and moor opposite the theatre. For an extended stay at Stratford there is a mooring threequarters of a mile upstream which is run by the Town Council. The centre of the 'Shakespeare Industry', Stratford has much to offer the visitor. The birthplace of the Bard in Henley Street, Holy Trinity Church containing his grave, and the old Guildhall should all be seen as well as the Guild Chapel, the Town Hall, the 14 arch Clopton Bridge and a number of inns.

The re-opening of the canal was a wonderful achievement bearing in mind the derelict state into which it had sunk. Most of the locks had to be re-built apart from dredging and regating the others.

Authority	**Northern Section** British Waterways Board.
	Southern Section, Kingswood to Stratford The National Trust, Canal Office, Lapworth, Warwickshire. Tel. Lapworth (056 43) 3370. (The National Trust have given notice that they wish to relinquish control of the navigation).
From and to	King's Norton to Stratford-on-Avon.
Distance	25½ miles. Branch to Grand Union Canal is ⅛ mile
Length	71ft. 8ins.
Beam	7ft.
Draught	3ft.
Headroom	6ft.
Locks	56. Lock No. 1 at King's Norton, level. Locks 2 to 56, fall from King's Norton. Kingswood to Grand Union Canal Branch, 1 lock No. 20, fall to Grand Union Canal.
Bridges	70. Mostly fixed. A number of these have a small opening in the centre to pass the towrope through. The cottage at entrance has a key for the swing bridge near King's Norton Stop Lock.
Tunnels	King's Norton. 352 yards. No tow-path.
Connections	To Grand Union Canal at Kingswood via Short Branch ¼ mile long. Worcester and Birmingham Canal at King's Norton.
Tow-path	Throughout navigation, except King's Norton Tunnel, Preston Bagot road bridge and bridge into terminal basin.
Facilities	There are four boatyards on the waterway with good village inns and shops.

Distance Table

King's Norton, junction with Worcester and Birmingham Canal to:

	Miles	Furlongs
King's Norton Stop Lock No. 1	—	1
King's Norton Tunnel	1	—
Yardley Wood	3	—
Warings Green	7	6
Hockley Heath	9	6
Lapworth Top Lock No. 2	10	6
Lapworth Lock No. 6	11	4
Kingswood, head of Lapworth Lock No. 21 *and junction with Branch to Grand Union Canal* (Lock on branch, No. 20)	12	4
Dick's Lane Wharf and Lapworth Lock No. 26 ...	13	1
Lapworth Bottom Lock No. 27	13	1½
Rowington Lock No. 28	13	6
Rowington Lock No. 29	13	7½
Lowsonford (Post Office), Rowington Lock No. 30 ...	14	2
Lowsonford (Fleur de Lys) Lock No. 31	14	4
Lowsonford Lock No. 32	14	7
Yarningale Aqueduct and Claverdon Lock Nos. 33, 34 and 35.	15	5
Preston Bagot Locks Nos. 36, 37 and 38	16	2
Wootton Wawen Aqueduct over A. 34 Road	18	4
Bearley, Lock No. 39, commencement of Old Stratford Flight ...	19	5
Bearley Aqueduct Northern End	19	7
Wilmcote Railway Station	21	7
Old Stratford Lock No. 40, Locks 41, 42 and 43 follow at intervals	22	4
Old Stratford Lock No. 44, Locks 45–50 follow at intervals, Bishopton Lock No. 51	23	7
Bishopton and Stratford on-Avon-Town Boundary, then follows the flight of Stratford Locks 52 to 55	23	6
Stratford-on-Avon, Lock No. 56, and junction with Upper Avon Navigation.	25	4

Kingswood Branch

Kingswood Junction to:

	Miles	Furlongs
Lock No. 20	0	0½
Kingswood, *junction with Grand Union Canal*	0	2

Stroudwater Canal (91)

The waterway links the Thames and Severn Canal at Stroud with the Severn and the Gloucester and Berkeley Ship Canal. There is a Stroudwater and Thames Severn Canal Trust which has working parties on both navigations. The canal was first planned in 1720 and this makes it one of the oldest successful canal schemes in the country. The canal is still owned by its original promoters. It was promoted under Acts of Parliament 1730, 1759 and 1776. The proprietors are hoping to re-open the canal closed by Act of Parliament in 1954. An attractive canal in the Cotswold country.

Authority	The Company of Proprietors of the Stroudwater Navigation, 4/7 Rowcroft, Stroud, Gloucestershire GL5 3BJ. Tel. Stroud (045 36) 3381.
From and to	Wallbridge, Stroud to the River Severn.
Distance	8 miles
Length	70ft
Width	15ft 6ins
Draught	5ft
Headroom	11ft 6ins These do not apply at present but applied up to 1939
Locks	13 (including one staircase lock).
Remarks	The canal is canoeable east of Saul but a lot of work is needed to restore the navigation which is a long term project. The canal was parallel to and not a canalisation of the River Frome. Proposals to re-open this waterway from Wallbridge to Saul have been made. Dimensions for this lock will be 70 x 16 x 6 x 8ft.

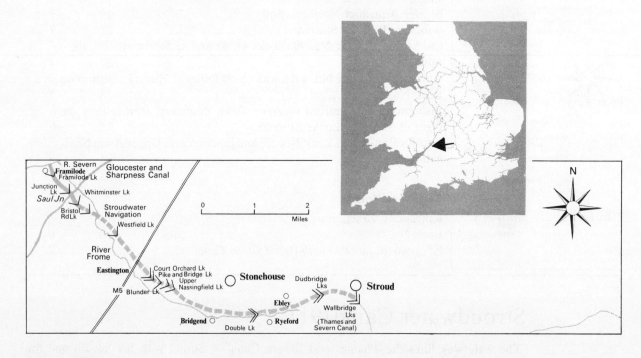

Distance Table

Wallbridge, Stroud junction with the Thames and Severn Canal to:

	Miles	Furlongs
Dudbridge Top Lock No. 1 (Franklin's Upper Lock)	–	4
Dudbridge Bottom Lock No. 2 (Franklin's Lower Lock)	–	4½
Ryeford Double Locks Nos. 3 and 4 (Staircase)	1	6
Upper Nassfield Lock No. 5 (Top of Five)	3	5

Distance Table	Miles	Furlongs
Blunder (or Lower Nassfield) Lock No. 6	4	–
(Turn) Pike or Eastington Lock No. 7	4	1
Court Orchard (or Dock) Lock No. 8	4	2½
Westfield Lock No. 9	4	4
Bristol Road Lock No. 10	5	3
Whitminster Lock No. 11	6	5
Saul, *junction with Gloucester and Berkeley Ship Canal*	7	–
Junction Lock No. 12	7	1
Tail of Framilode Lock No. 13, *junction with Severn Estuary*	8	–

Restoration work has commenced between Eastington and Stonehouse. The Stroudwater and Thames Severn Canal Trust are responsible for the restoration.

River Tamar (92)

This is one of the beautiful rivers that discharge into Plymouth Harbour, and very popular sailing water. The lock at Weir Head is no longer workable and thus navigation to Gunnislake as of old, is now impossible.

Authority	Queen's Harbour Master, H.M. Naval Base, Devonport, Devon. Tel. (0752) 53740.
From and to	Saltash Railway Bridge to Weir Head Lock.
Distance	19 miles. (If Weir Head Lock is restored the navigation will be 1 mile longer).
Length	Unlimited.
Beam	,,
Draught	At high water vessels drawing 5ft. can reach Weir Head.
Headroom	100ft.
Locks	None. Tidal throughout. (The I.W.A. (SW Branch) have done some clearance of Weir Head Locks and hope to restore it).
Tow-path	None.
Connections	The Lynher or St. Germans River joins the Hamoaze, as the Tamar is called below Saltash Bridge, this is navigable for light craft at high tide to Tideford, a distance of 6½ miles. Maximum draught is 6ft. at high water. The River Tavy joins the Tamar 1½ miles above Saltash Bridge. This is navigable to about 1½ miles above Maristow Quay at high tides, a distance of about 5 miles. Maximum draught to Maristow Quay is 8 to 10ft. and 5ft. to head of navigation. Both of these rivers are under the same authority as the Tamar.

Bridges	There are bridges at Saltash and Calstock. Electricity cables restrict headroom to 40ft. on the Tavy.
Tides	High tide at Weir Head 40 minutes after Plymouth. Spring tides rise about 5 feet, neaps about 1 foot.

Distance Table

Weir Head, to:

	Miles	Furlongs
Morwellham Quay, Morwell Rocks		
New Quay 1	1	6
Okeltor 2	2	4
Calstock 3	3	2
Halton Quay 4	4	5
Pentillie 7	7	7
Weirquay 8	8	4
Cargreen 10	10	4
Tavy Junction, *junction with River Tavy, tidal to Lapwell* 12	12	—
Saltash Railway Bridge 13	13	1
Junction with St. Germans River 14	14	5
Devonport 15	15	3
Plymouth 17	17	4
	19	—

River Tees (93)

The navigation is mainly used by sea-going vessels and is not generally used for pleasure boating. Commercial barges use the navigation.

Authority	Tees and Hartlepools Port Authority, Queens Square, Middlesbrough.
	Tel. Middlesbrough (0642) 241121
	Telegrams. 'Teescom, Middlesbrough.'
From and to	Fardean Side Ford to River Mouth.
Distance	24 miles.
Length	Unlimited
Beam	,,
Draught	Average available depth of water from mouth of river to Middlesbrough: High Water Spring Tides 34ft. High Water Neap Tides 29ft. Middlesbrough to Stockton: High Water Spring Tides 25ft. High Water Neap Tides 20ft. Depth Stockton to Yarm, not dredged or sounded, is: High Water Spring Tides 9ft. High Water Neap Tides 6ft. Depth available to Fardean Side Ford is approximately 4ft. 6ins, but even on some high tides there is sometimes a draught of only 6in.

Headroom	16ft.
Tow-path	None.
Locks	None. River tidal throughout.
Charges	None for pleasure craft.
Canoeing note	Although there are records that the river has been canoed from Barnard Castle, the general head of navigation seems to be from the village of Middleton-One-Row, which is nine miles above Yarm Bridge. It is a river for experts, as in dry weather it is too shallow to be practical, but in high water it is very fast with a few deep stretches. It is extremely rocky and is a very tricky river.
Tides	High Water at Yarm 55 minutes after Middlesbrough. Spring tides rise 8ft. Neap tides rise 3ft. High Water at Stockton 15 minutes after Middlesbrough. Spring tides rise 17ft. Neap tides rise 12ft.

Distance Table

Fardean Side Ford to:

	Miles	Furlongs
Yarm Bridge	3	2
Stockton and Thornaby	10	5
Newport	13	2
Ferry, Middlesbrough to Port Clarence	15	7
Mouth of river at low water	24	—

Tennant and Neath Canals (94)

These canals are separate entities but have been grouped together as they are the subject of a joint restoration campaign by the Neath and Tennant Canals Preservation Society. The Tennant Canal was a private venture completed in 1824; the Neath Canal was promoted by Act of Parliament in 1791 and was completed in 1795. The latter canal was extended in 1799 and for this a second Act was passed in 1798. The canals in recent years have formed water supply routes but are coming back into their own for recreation and amenity use. The variety of scenery is exceptional: mountain, woodland and estuarial with a sprinkling of fenland, old industrial sites and canal side architecture.

Authority	(a) Neath Canal Navigation, Bankide, The Green, Neath, W. Glamorgan. (From Glyn Neath to Neath and junction with Earl of Jersey's Canals). Telephone: Neath (0639) 55282 (b) Port Tennant Co. Ltd., 49 Mansel Street, Swansea SA1 5TB. Tel. (0792) 55891.
Neath Canal	
From and to	Swansea to Aberdulais. Branch: Red Jacket Pill to Neath Estuary.

Distance	13 miles
Length	60ft
Beam	9ft
Draught	2ft 9ins
Headroom	6ft
Locks	17 (originally 19 locks – top two locks now under the A465 trunk road). Fall from Glyn Neath.
Towpath	Throughout navigation.
Bridge	Numerous.
Remarks	The canal is privately owned by the major industrial concerns that extract water from it e.g. B.P. Baglan Bay. Sections of the canal at Resolven, Rheola and Aberpergwn have been restored by the Neath and Tennant Canal Preservation Society Ltd and the c.1795 canal workshops at Tonna are being re-built as a visitor centre under a Manpower Services Commission scheme. They are leased by the Neath and Tennant Canal Preservation Society.

Distance Table:

Glyn Neath, Canal Head to:	*Miles*	*Furlongs*
Maesmarchog Lock No. 1) Now buried below	–	–
Lamb Lock No. 2) A465 Trunk Road	1	–
(Canal is only intact from this point, Mill Terrace, near Lamb and Flag public house, the locks follow at intervals		
Foxes Lock No. 3		
Chain Lock No. 4		
Granery Lock No. 5		
Bwllfa'r Onn Lock No. 6		
Maes-gwyn Lock No. 7	2	–
Ynisultor Lock No. 8	2	2
Aber-clwyd Lock No. 9	2	4
Rheola Lock No. 10	3	1
Crugiau Lock No. 11	3	5
Resolven Lock No. 12	4	2
Farmer's Lock No. 13	4	3
Abergarwed Lock No. 14	4	6
Ynysarwed Lock No. 15	5	2
Gitto Lock No. 16	6	–
Witworth Lock No. 17	6	7
Lock Machine No. 18	7	4
Aberdulais, *junction with Tennant Canal*	8	5
Lock House Lock No. 19	9	1
Neath, Main Road Bridge over Canal and *junction with Earl of Jersey's Grave and Briton Ferry Canal* (This canal is ½ mile in length and is only used for water supply)	13	–

Tennant Canal

From and to	Swansea to Aberdulais. Branch: Red Jacket Pill to Estuary (Now closed)
Distance	8 miles 3½ furlongs.
Length	60ft
Beam	9ft (Through Red Jacket Lock 15ft)
Draught	2ft 9ins
Headroom	6ft (more than this is usually available)
Locks	1 (Aberdulais). Swansea Lock is now buried beneath railway sidings. Fall to Swansea.
Bridges	Numerous. (Rail, road and accommodation)
Remarks	The Tennant Canal (previously Neath & Swansea Junction Canal) is still privately owned by the Coombe-Tennant family and is used mainly as industrial water supply for B.P. Llandarey and B.P. Raglan Bay. Aberdulais aqueduct and basin have been restored by N. & T.C.P. Ltd. and received a Prince of Wales Award 1979 and Civic Trust (Wales) Award 1978 to recognise this achievement. The basin is now leased by the society and a public access agreement has been negotiated with the society, owners and West Glamorgan County Council.

Distance Table

Aberdulais, *junction with Neath Canal to:*

	Miles	Furlong
Aberdulais Lock and south end of aqueduct over River Neath	–	1
Neath, Main Road Bridge over canal	1	6½
Neath Abbey	3	–
Junction with Red Jacket Pill Branch (now infilled)	4	7
Briton Ferry Road, Railway Station	5	6
Junction with Glan-y-Wern Canal (closed)	6	3
Junction with Tir-isaf Branch Canal (closed)	7	5
Vale of Neath (Inn), Port Tennant	8	–

(Canal from this point to the Docks is now infilled and so also are locks)

General note	The navigation structures are of great interest, particularly the aqueduct at Aberdulais, 340ft long, (Tennant Canal) and the Ynysbwllog Aqueduct (Neath Canal). The potential recreational value of this waterway is very high. The canal route passes the walls of the 12th century Cistercian Neath Abbey, old iron works, Clydach and Aberdulais waterfalls and Penscynor Wildlife Park. The Neath valley is exceptionally beautiful and was painted by J. M. W. Turner. The Hon. Secretary of the N. & T.C.P., Ian Milne, 16 Gower Road, Sketty, Swansea, West Glamorgan who has given invaluable help

with this section, will be glad to receive offers of help; the task here is assisted by local authority assistance and the Welsh Office.

The River Neath is tidal to Tonna and carries some traffic. There were two river locks at Aberdulais to assist navigation to the mills with barges up to 100 tons but these have been long derelict. The Neath Canal Company own most of the canal except for a short section above Resolven, and from above Yscwrfa Bridge which are now owned by the Welsh Office. A short section above Abergarwed is privately owned.

River Thames (95)

The Thames has long been an ancient highway and possibly more books have been written about it than any other waterway, but its history is of great interest and for the following notes we are indebted to the Port of London Authority and the Thames Conservancy Board. These bodies can supply more detailed information to the serious enquirer, but in view of the complexity of the subject, a reasonable length of time should be allowed for reply.

Port of London Authority

The history of London as a port is naturally linked with the history of London as a great city. This can be divided into three main periods—the first period before the building of the commercial docks; the second, of just over a century, covering the years during which the private dock companies held sway; and finally the era of the Port of London Authority which started in 1909.

The first period lasted from early Roman times until the closing years of the 18th century and was highlighted by the great development in trade in Tudor times and the subsequent establishment of legal quays and sufferance wharves. Legal quays were 20 selected quays where, by authority of the Crown, all foreign goods were to be landed between sunrise and sunset. When these became inadequate for the volume of trade, sufferance wharves with restricted privileges were introduced. Situated within a mile or two of London Bridge and the Custom House on the north bank of the Upper Pool, these quays and wharves enjoyed a virtual monopoly until the end of the 18th century.

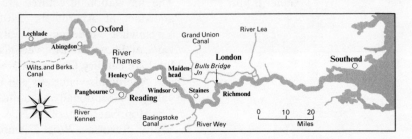

By this time the trade of the country had shown a marked increase and London, in spite of its congested river and shortage of berths, handled some 65 per cent by value of the country's total imports and exports. It can, therefore, be seen that the lack of accommodation at the quays and wharves led to cargoes remaining in lighters for weeks at a time before they could be dealt with, during which time they were exposed not only to the weather but to well-organised bands of thieves who profited from these chaotic conditions.

The wharf proprietors resisted every effort to provide additional facilities to remedy the crowded and overburdened condition of the port, a condition which led finally to the appointment of a parliamentary committee to inquire into the provision of adequate and efficient accommodation to cater for the increase in trade and shipping. No real action was taken as a result of this committee and it was left to the West India Merchants in conjunction with the Corporation of London to promote a Bill for the construction of enclosed docks on the Isle of Dogs.

The Bill was authorised by Parliament in 1799 and the West India Docks were formally opened on 22nd August, 1802. They had high brick walls and were patrolled and guarded by armed militia and special constables.

Incorporated into the Act of Parliament were two provisions—one granting the dock company a monopoly of the West Indian trade into and out of London for 21 years, and the other giving to the craft of wharfingers and lightermen the right to enter and leave the docks without payment of dues. This latter provision became known as the 'Free Water Clause' and was incorporated into all the subsequent Acts of Parliament relating to construction of further docks on the Thames.

The success of the West India Dock Company was such that other docks followed in quick succession. The London Docks were opened in 1805, the East India Docks in 1806, the St. Katharine Docks in 1828 and the Surrey Commercial Docks emerged haphazardly during the early years of the 19th century. The Victoria Dock was opened in 1855, Millwall Docks in 1868, and the Royal Albert Dock in 1880. The construction of the Tilbury Docks in 1886 marked the end of the surge of dock building spanning most of the 19th century.

If, at the beginning of the century, accommodation had been inadequate then at the end the reverse was true. The three dock companies then in existence, the London and India Docks Company, the Surrey Commercial Dock Company and the Millwall Dock Company, were faced with an excess of accommodation which, in part, led to the ruinous competition between these companies and the wharfingers.

The financial state of the dock companies now began to affect their ability to provide for the increasing size and draught of merchant ships. The London and India Docks Company —which had been formed by the amalgamation of the London and St. Katharine Dock Companies in 1864 when they incorporated the Victoria Dock Company, the merging of the East and West India Dock Companies in 1838 and the subsequent link-up of the two main bodies in 1900—now sought to remedy the situation. The Bill which would have revoked the Free Water Clause and allowed a charge to be levied on barges entering the control of the docks company, aroused great opposition and was rejected, but the continuance of the serious situation resulted in the setting up of a royal commission in 1900 to inquire fully into conditions within the port. Two years later, the commission issued a report calling for the control of the port by a new central authority.

The first Bill which sought to implement this recommendation was presented to Parliament in 1903 but failed to find favour, and it was not until 1908 that the Port of London Act was passed. Briefly, it transferred the undertakings and powers of the existing dock companies and the control of the tidal waters of the River Thames to a new body to be called The Port of London Authority.

Thus March 1909 saw the start of the third era in the history of the port with the newly constituted authority taking over its responsibilities. These responsibilities were many—to make good deficiencies in port accommodation, equipment and services for both shipowner and merchant, and to ensure the maintenance of a deep water channel leading from the estuary into the heart of the city.

A large element of competition still remained within the port; the riverside wharves were outside the jurisdiction of the new body, except for certain conservancy matters, and the Free Water Clause remained. Yet the authority by the way it set about putting its newly acquired house in order, soon fostered a feeling of confidence in its administration.

The present-day Port of London extends 90 miles upstream from the Thames Estuary to Teddington, the limit of the tidal waters.

Behind the river banks are the five enclosed dock groups, owned and controlled by the Port of London Authority, which afford all the facilities of a modern port, while on both sides of the river are situated many hundreds of public and privately owned wharves, factories, power stations, gasworks, oil installations, sugar refineries, etc., which play an important part in the trade of the port. Cold stores, granaries, barge building yards and dry-docking facilities for ship repair are also features of the riverside.

London is the largest port in the United Kingdom. In 1967, 60 million tons of goods passed through the Port of London and the net registered tonnage of vessels using the port totalled 89 million.

The original board of the Port of London Authority consisted of up to 30 members but under the Port of London Revision Order 1967, a new constitution of the board came into effect as from 1st October 1967. It was further revised in 1976.

Under the constitution which came into effect on 1st February 1976, the board must comprise not less than 9 and not more than 17 members. The Secretary of State for the Environment is required to appoint a chairman and not less than 7 or more than 10 other members not being officers of the PLA. Members are selected from amongst persons appearing to the Secretary of State to have wide experience of and to have shown capacity in one or more of the following: business management, financial matters, sea transport, inland transport, international commerce, the organisation of workers, riverside activities, environmental matters and navigation.

The chairman and other members appointed by the Secretary of State are required to appoint at least 1 but not more than 6 officers of the PLA to serve as members of the PLA.

The Authority is responsible for the control of some 90 miles of one of the busiest waterways in the world and the maintenance and operation of an estate of nearly 4,000 acres of which docks and warehouses comprise over 3,000 acres.

The conservancy duties of the port authority include all matters relating to navigation, the maintenance of adequate river channels, the regulation of river traffic, the provision and upkeep of a number of public ship and barge moorings, and the licensing of wharves and structures which extend into the river below the high water mark. The Authority, in addition, is responsible for surveying and charting the tideway, the removal of wrecks and obstructions, the prevention of pollution, and the registration of certain craft employed exclusively within the limits of the port as well as for the licensing of lightermen and watermen.

The capital of the undertaking is in the form of port stock bearing fixed rates of interest and loans under the Harbours Act 1964. Financially, therefore, the Port Authority is concerned only to collect sufficient revenue to provide efficient services and accommodation and to pay the annual interest to the stockholders and on the Harbour Act loans; any excess of revenue over expenditure being available for port improvements or for the reduction of port dues and charges.

The principal sources of revenue of the Authority are derived from the dues charged on ships entering the river and the docks and from charges rendered to merchants for services performed in connection with the handling and storage of import and export cargoes which pass over the quays of the five dock groups.

Although the Port of London Authority is the overriding body for the control of London's tidal waterway and its docks, there are many other services whose functions are an integral part of the everyday working of the port. A synopsis of the activities of these various associations is set out below:

Her Majesty's Customs and Excise

Officials of H.M. Customs administer and collect the revenue from duties levied on the various cargoes passing through the Port of London. Customs officers stationed at the docks or at wharves on the riverside examine all goods, whether imported or awaiting shipment. In respect of goods stored in bonded warehouses, i.e., awaiting payment of duty, the officers control the receiving and delivery of the cargo and supervise any operations, e.g., sampling, weighing, etc., which may be required by the merchant while the goods are still in store.

The Waterguard and Preventive branch of the service is concerned with the travelling public and the defence against smuggling in all its forms.

Fire Services

The River Service of the London Fire Brigade operates fire floats, which in case of fire at riverside premises, work in conjunction with the land forces.

The land services have stations strategically sited adjacent to dock and wharf areas. The Port of London Authority, in common with other operators in the port, relies on the London Fire Brigade and the Essex and Kent Fire Services further down-river for the control of any outbreak within the port.

Pleasure Traffic

During the summer months a number of companies operate passenger launches from West End piers at Charing Cross and Westminster. Services connect the piers with the up-river resorts at Richmond, Kew and beyond the landward limit of the port to Hampton Court, etc. Down-river services link the piers with Tower Pier and Greenwich.

The River Police

The Thames Division of the Metropolitan Police or, as they are more familiarly known, the River Police, patrol the Thames from Staines to Erith, below which point the lower reaches are policed by the Essex and Kent Constabulary.

The primary duty of the force is, of course, the prevention of crime, but the patrol launches work in close co-operation with the Authority in the matter of enforcing river bye-laws.

The launches of the River Police are normally manned by a sergeant and two constables, all of whom are fully trained in first aid.

Ship and Craft Towage

With the concentrated movement of ships and barges on the Thames highway, tugs plays an important part in the handling of ships in and out of the dock entrances and in the berthing of large liners at deep-water wharves.

Some 130 tugs are employed throughout the port for ship towage and the towage of lighters and floating equipment such as grain elevators, etc.

Port Health Authority

The Port Health Authority, under the Corporation of the City of London, is responsible for the health clearance of all ships entering the port, with a view to preventing the berthing or working of any ships where either passenger or crew are suffering from a communicable disease.

A second responsibility of the Health Authority is the control of food imports, again from the point of view of the satisfactory condition of the foodstuffs.

In addition, the Health Authority includes in its many duties the control of vermin within dock warehouses or premises, health conditions on houseboats moored within the port, etc.

Lighterage

With some 1,350 barges or lighters in daily use in the port, the lighterage business plays an important part in the transport of cargoes to and from the ship's side. Imports are discharged overside from the holds of the ship to barges and are distributed to warehouse or factory on the riverside. Exports are brought to the ship's side for loading.

Barges carry varying loads up to 750 tons and, as the majority are 'dumb' barges, i.e., without means of powered propulsion, they are towed to their destination by tug. Barges on tow are linked up to six in number, not more than three abreast and a full tow may easily be capable of moving up to 1,000 tons deadweight of cargo. Barges are usually flat bottomed so that they can sit on the river bed at low water alongside the point of collection or delivery.

Oil Wharves

Oil, with its by-products, is in tonnage the largest single commodity to be imported into London. Purfleet, 16 miles below London Bridge, is the up-river limit for ocean-going tankers and from Purfleet down to the estuary are the many oil installations of the Thames.

The Thames Conservancy

Priestley lists 38 Acts relating to the Thames from 1423 to 1829, but the main provisions relating to the Thames above Teddington which is controlled by the Thames Water Authority and contained in the following notes, part of which have been supplied by the original Thames Conservancy.

The Conservators of the River Thames, Thames Conservancy, were originally incorporated by the Thames Conservancy Act, 1857, and their jurisdiction as successors of the Corporation of the City of London then extended from Staines to Yantlet Creek, in the County of Kent. By the Thames Navigation Act, 1866, the river from Staines upwards to Cricklade, in the County of Wiltshire, formerly under the control of the Thames Navigation Commissioners, was added to the Conservators' jurisdiction. Very limited pollution prevention powers were conferred on the Conservators by the Act of 1857, and these were extended by an Act of 1866. Their powers as navigation and river purification authority were further extended and enlarged by various Acts passed in 1867, 1870, 1878, 1883 and 1885, and were eventually consolidated in the Thames Conservancy Act, 1894, which also reconstituted the Conservators. By the Port of London Act, 1908, the rights, powers and duties of the Conservators in the tidal waters, i.e., below an imaginary line about 165 yards below Teddington Lock, were, as from 31st March, 1909, transferred to the Port of London Authority, but above that limit the Thames remained under the jurisdiction of the Conservators, who were reconstituted by the Act. Since that date their powers and duties have been further amended by the Thames Conservancy Acts of 1910, 1911, 1921 and 1924, and consolidated in the Thames Conservancy Act, 1932, which latter Act was itself amended by the Thames Conservancy Acts, 1950 and 1959.

By the Land Drainage Act, 1930, the Conservators were constituted the Drainage Board of the Thames (above Teddington Lock) catchment area, in addition to their other functions, and exercise jurisdiction over some 2,402 miles of 'main river' as determined by Section 5 of the Land Drainage Act, 1930, comprising the Thames proper above Teddington and the whole or part of certain tributaries, indicated on the statutory map.

The Rivers, Prevention of Pollution, Acts, 1951 and 1961, also conferred further powers in respect of the prevention of pollution upon the Conservators.

By Orders made under the Water Resources Act, 1963, the Conservators were further reconstituted and were given the new water resources functions of river authorities within the Thames catchment area. In addition, they were granted certain functions of river authorities restricted to the control of abstractions of water from, and discharges of effluent and other matters into, underground strata in the London Excluded Area, which comprises the former administrative County of London and any adjoining areas not falling within the Thames or Lee catchment areas or in a river board area.

After 1963 there were a number of changes, culminating in the Water Act of 1973 by which all the Thames Conservancy functions were taken over by the Thames Water Authority. The Thames Conservancy Acts and Orders from 1932 to 1974 still apply, in the Water Act 1973 and in the following bye-laws, Thames Navigation and General Bye-laws 1957, Thames Launch Bye-laws 1952, Thames Registration Bye-laws 1953.

Thames Water's navigational jurisdiction extends over the River Thames between the town bridge at Cricklade, and the boundary obelisk approximately 293 yards downstream of Teddington Lock and also over the tributary River Kennet from its mouth upstream to a limit 70 yards eastwards of the High Bridge at Reading. Thames Water control the Thames Flood Barrier, just above Woolwich.

The river, for the purposes of inspection and control of navigation, is divided into four districts each with an inspector and an assistant inspector under a chief navigation inspector stationed at Reading, all responsible to the secretary. Their work includes the supervision of the operation of the locks and weirs.

The statutory powers and duties of the T.W.A. as a navigation authority include:

The construction and maintenance of locks, weirs and all other works necessary for the carrying on of the navigation;

appointment of water bailiffs for the protection of the fisheries;

regulation of the water level;

removal of sunken vessels;

removal of obstructions from the river and towpaths;

dredging for the purpose of maintaining and improving the navigation;

maintenance of the flow;

granting of licences for works in the river;

registration of motor launches, house boats and pleasure boats, and the regulation of these vessels;

levying of tolls on vessels;

making of byelaws for a number of purposes;

regulation of the navigation;

prevention of pollution from vessels.

The jurisdiction of the T.W.A. for the purposes of preventing pollution extends to all rivers, streams and ditches within the Thames catchment area of approximately 3,845 square miles and covering portions of some fifteen counties including part of the area under the jurisdiction of the Greater London Council. The T.W.A. also exercises control over discharges of trade or sewage effluent and other matter by means of wells, boreholes and pipes into all underground strata both within the catchment area and in the London excluded area. Effluents from sewage treatment works, factories and other premises which are discharged into streams or to underground strata must comply strictly with conditions laid down by the T.W.A. and in many cases stringent standards of quality have been imposed in respect of such discharges to rivers in order to ensure adequate purity of the rivers.

For administrative purposes as respects river purification the Thames watershed is divided into seven districts with an inspecting staff under the direction of the secretary or two chief inspectors with inspectors whose duties are to detect and report upon cases of pollution, and to take samples of sewage and other effluents and of the water in the Thames and its tributaries which are analysed by the T.W.A. analyst. In addition there is an inspector with an assistant whose main duty is the inspection of sanitary arrangements on vessels.

All towns and other places where works for the treatment and purification of sewage have been installed, as well as factories, farms and various premises, are kept under observation by the secretary's river purification staff to ensure that the various systems are efficiently maintained. In instances where adverse reports are received upon samples of effluent or other discharges, the responsible authority or person is called upon to discontinue the pollution; the general procedure in cases of a more serious nature is to serve a notice on the person causing or suffering the pollution, requiring discontinuance of the pollution within a stated time, not being less than three months, and in the event of the notice not being complied with, the person responsible becomes liable on conviction to a penalty. The T.W.A. endeavour, as far as possible, to procure the abatement of causes of complaint by persuasion and to have recourse to legal proceedings only when other measures have failed. The powers and duties of the T.W.A. under the Land Drainage Acts 1930 and 1961, are concerned with the general supervision with respect to the drainage of the Thames catchment area; exclusive permissive powers and jurisdiction with respect to the 'main river' and the banks thereof, and with respect to drainage works in connection therewith, improving of existing works, and construction of new works, the cleansing, repairing, deepening, widening and straightening of the 'main river' and generally maintaining it in a due state of efficiency; the making of bye-laws to secure the efficient working of the system of drainage; the appropriation and disposal of dredged material.

The daily gauging and recording of the river flow is one of the duties of the Conservators, and the quantities passing Teddington Weir each twenty-four hours are shown to be extremely variable. The maximum daily discharge ever recorded was 20,236 million gallons in the great flood of 1894. Subsequent investigations show that this maximum discharge was probably lower and probably that the correct figure is about 15,000 m.g.d. When bank high, the daily rate is about 4,500 million gallons. The statutory minimum gauged discharge at Teddington Weir is 170 million gallons, which must not be reduced by water abstraction below this figure except in special circumstances.

There are 48 pound locks on the Thames, one of these being in the River Kennet at Reading, and 138 weirs consisting of 44 main weirs, 43 subsidiary weirs and 51 overfalls. The uppermost lock is at Lechlade, and the lowermost at Teddington, where the system consists of three parallel locks, the largest being 650 feet long, 25 feet wide and fitted with three sets of gates capable of taking a tug and its tow of six barges at one time.

The number of places of interest on the river is a subject too large for this reference work and the many guide books published provide useful information. The Thames has a quality of its own, Robert Aickman in his book 'Know your Waterways', a concise mine of information, very aptly refers to the architecture and design of the locks, lock-keepers' houses, etc., as 'a continuous Edwardian picnic'. The river is full of variations and the difference between Lechlade and the great estuary has to be seen to be believed. But of the many lovely stretches of river there are few that would disagree with the claim that the most beautiful section is between Boulter's Lock and Cookham. This includes Cliveden which, on a sunny and misty morning has a magnificence that is breathtaking, but it is sad at the end to find the derelict Thames and Severn Canal whose state is largely due to that of the Upper Thames in the middle of the last century which restricted its development. Alas, we take the present state of the Thames for granted, but it has taken many years to bring the river to its present fine condition. Bradshaw's Guide in 1918 listed 'flash locks' (navigation weirs) on the river namely Eaton Weir, Eynsham Weir, King's Weir and Medley Weir; these old single gate locks were very wasteful in time and water and greatly hampered the useful development of the river.

Authorities	**Below Teddington** The Port of London Authority, London Dock House, Thomas More Street, London E1 9AZ. Tel. 01-481 4887. **Above Teddington** The Thames Water Authority, Nugent House, Vastern Road, Reading RG1 8DB. Tel. Reading (0734) 593387
From and to	**The Sea to Lechlade** The river continues to Cricklade about 10 miles above Lechlade, but above the latter place navigation is only possible at times for the smallest class of boat. As far as the tail of Richmond half tidal lock, the river is tidal.

Distances	London Bridge to Teddington Lock, 16 miles
	   ,, ,, ,, Lechlade Bridge, 140 miles
	   ,, '' Shivering Sand Tower P.L.A. Limit 59¼ miles

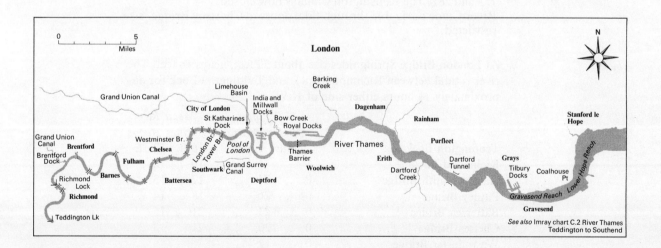

See also Imray chart C.2 River Thames
Teddington to Southend

Port of London Authority Section

P.L.A. Harbour service

The River Thames under the jurisdiction of the P.L.A. is divided into sections each in charge of an Assistant Harbour Master:

Upper Section	Teddington to Erith
Lower Section	Erith to the sea

All enquiries can be made of the Harbour Masters listed below or to the Pier Office in each section. Advice can also be obtained direct from the P.L.A. Harbour Service launches patrolling in all sections.

Upper Section

Harbour Service Office, The Toll House, Kew, Richmond, Surrey. Telephones (day or night) 01-940 8288/9
Cadogan Pier: 01–352–4604,

Assistant Harbour Master (Upper), Thames House, Gallions Entrance, London E16. Telephones (day) 01-481 5005

Lower Section

Assistant Harbour Master, T.N.S. Building, Royal Pier Road, Gravesend, Kent.
Telephones: Duty Officer, Thames Navigation Service: Gravesend 57724 (Day or night). Holehaven Landing Canvey Island (Day only). Canvey (0268) 683041.

Branches

The following Creeks are under the jurisdiction of the Port of London Authority:

Wandsworth Creek	$\frac{1}{4}$ mile	Barking Creek	2 miles
Bow Creek	1 ,,	Rainham Creek	$1\frac{1}{4}$,,
Deptford Creek	$\frac{3}{4}$,,	(now dammed)	

The Grosvenor Canal and the River Roding are detailed on pages 155 and 287. The Kensington Canal is now closed.
River Crane navigable through tidal doors to Chertsey Bridge, size restricted.

Tides

At London Bridge Spring tides rise about 22 feet, neaps 18 feet. The river is tidal between Richmond Lock and Teddington Lock for approximately $1\frac{1}{2}$ hours either side of H.W.

	H.W. after London Bridge		Mean Rise Springs Neaps	
Teddington Lock	1 hour	1 mins.	16 ft.	12 ft.
Richmond Lock	1 ,,	1 ,,	16 ,,	12 ,,
Hammersmith Bridge ...	0 ,,	31 ,,	17 ,,	13 ,,
Putney Bridge	0 ,,	26 ,,	18 ,,	14 ,,
Battersea Bridge	0 ,,	21 ,,	21 ,,	15 ,,
Chelsea Bridge	0 ,,	20 ,,	21 ,,	17 ,,
Westminster Bridge ...	0 ,,	12 ,,		

The following is the approximate duration of the tidal streams under normal conditions.

	Ebb Hours Mins.		Flood Hours Mins.	
Teddington Lock to Kew	8	0	4	0
Kew to Chelsea	7	30	4	30
Chelsea to London Bridge ...	7	15	4	45

The normal rate of the flood is 2 knots, and the ebb 2 to $2\frac{1}{4}$ knots in the upper reaches.

Effect of flood water

Following prolonged rainfall, particularly during the winter months, a large volume of flood water passes down the river from the upper reaches. Its effect is evident on the surface of the stream as far down river as Wandsworth and Chelsea, upsetting all tidal predictions and causing the stream to run seawards continuously for days at a time.

Coincident with an ebb tide the velocity of the flow at springs can attain a speed of as much as 5 knots; under these conditions it is dangerous to attempt navigation. At Richmond Bridge during flood time, the water runs through the arches like a mill race, standing on the upstream side of the buttresses up to 2 feet higher than on the lower side. The eddy effect on the downstream side of the bridge is also very dangerous, and navigation against the stream through the arches should not be attempted without due regard to this danger.

Headroom

See Bridges. The minimum Hammersmith Bridge is 14ft. 3ins., the maximum Tower Bridge is 29ft. 9ins.

Depths

The following are the approximate depths of water in each section:

	High water	Low water
London Bridge to Vauxhall ...	19ft. to 20ft.	6ft.

There are few patches of 5ft. at low tide near Waterloo Bridge, some of 4ft. at Westminster Bridge and just below Vauxhall Bridge there is a patch of 5ft.

	High water	Low water
Vauxhall Bridge to Battersea Bridge	22ft. 0ins.	6ft. 6ins.
Battersea Bridge to Hammersmith Bridge	19ft. to 20ft.	4ft. 6ins.
Hammersmith Bridge to Kew Bridge.	18ft. 6ins,	4ft. to 5ft.

Patches of 3ft. below Kew Bridge at low tide in dry periods.

Kew Bridge to Richmond Bridge	16ft. 0ins.	3ft. to 4ft.

Richmond Lock to Teddington Lock—5ft. 6ins. of water at a maintained level, 12ft. at high water ordinary tides.

Locks

Richmond Lock. The first lock on the river is half tidal.

Length	250ft. 0ins.
Maximum Breadth	26ft. 8ins.

Signals: The following are displayed from the lock and weir footbridge.

	By Day	By Night
(1) When the weir is down, i.e., No through navigation.	A red disc suspended from the centre of each arch.	A red light over the top centre of each arch.
(2) When weir is up, i.e., All clear for through navigation.	Disc removed.	2 orange red lights in each navigation arch.

Vessels wishing to pass through the lock should proceed slowly to within hailing distance of the lock entrance, and await the lock-keeper's instructions. (Telephone 01–940–0634).

Bridges

Richmond to Tower Bridge

The following table showing number of spans across the river, those generally used for navigation, the approx. maximum headway available above H.W.S.T. and depth of water under the central arch at dead low water.

Name of Bridge	Construction	Spans across Tideway	Navigation Arches numbered from left bank going down	Max. Headway above H.W.S.T. centre		Depth L.W. datum	
				ft.	ins.	ft.	ins.
Richmond	Stone	5	3	18	0*	6	6*
Richmond Rly.	Iron	3	2	18	0*	7	6*
Twickenham (New)	Concrete	3	2	20	0*	8	3*
Richmond Lock and Weir (P.L.A.)	Iron	5	2, 3, 4	18	6	4	3
Kew	Stone	3	2	18	0	4	3
Kew Rly.	Iron	5	3, 4	18	3	5	3
Chiswick (New)	Concrete	3	2	23	3	4	0
Barnes Rly.	Iron	3	3	18	3	4	6
Hammersmith	Suspension	3	Centre	14	3	4	6
Putney	Stone	5	2, 3, 4	18	6	4	6
Fulham Rly.	Iron	5	2, 3, 4	23	0	5	3
Wandsworth	Steel	3	Centre	20	0	6	0
Battersea Rly.	Iron	5	2, 3	20	9	7	6
Battersea	Iron	5	2, 3	18	6	7	6
Albert	Suspension	3	Centre	18	9	6	3
Chelsea	Suspension	3	Centre	22	3	6	9
Victoria Rly.	Iron	4	2, 3	20	3	5	9
Vauxhall	Stone	5	2, 3, 4	19	0	5	3
Lambeth	Stone	5	2 3 4	21	9	7	0
Westminster	Stone	7	2, 3, 4, 5	18	6	3	6
Charing Cross	Iron	6	2, 3	23	6	6	6
Waterloo	Stone	5	2, 3	18	9	7	6
Blackfriars	Iron	5	2, 3	23	9	7	6
Blackfriars Rly.	Iron	5	2, 3	23	6	8	6
Southwark	Steel	5	2, 3	24	9	8	6
Cannon Street Rly.	Iron	5	2, 3	23	9	8	0
London	Stone	3	2, 3	29	2	5	0
Tower Bridge	Stone and Iron	3	Centre	28	6	17	0
				Bascules up 140 ft.			

* At maintained level.

Lights. At night two *orange red* lights horizontally are exhibited in each navigation arch of the above bridges.

Bye-laws

Port of London river bye-laws can be obtained on application. However the P.L.A. publication *Pleasure craft users' guide to the tidal River Thames* is more appropriate for small boat users and is also obtainable from the P.L.A. The following are extracts from the regulations governing navigation and explain the essential rules. These should be learned by all users of the Thames whether in cabin cruisers, sailing yachts or dinghies, rowing craft or canoes.

General Navigation: It is the practice and always advisable to keep clear of commercial traffic. Barges towed by tugs are difficult to manoeuvre through bridges and they cannot stop if you get in their way. Passenger service vessels should also be watched for, they can only alter course slowly, or may not be able to at all. Coxswains and launch drivers should always look ahead and astern for commercial traffic and take appropriate avoiding action in plenty of time.

While the need to keep clear of commercial traffic is important in the more confined upper reaches of the River, there is a need to do so over the whole length of the Thames.

Ships of today are of such a size and so deep in the water that they are frequently confined to the deep water part of the channel. On the other hand, yachts with their small draught normally have no requirement to navigate in the main channel and generally can safely remain in the water to one side.

If it becomes necessary to cross the main channel, yachts should do so in the quickest manner possible, and give all commercial vessels a wide berth.

Power driven craft when proceeding up or down river should keep over to the starboard (right hand) side of the mid-channel when it is safe and practicable to do. If following a rowing crew and the river is crowded, then remain astern of them and give way to oncoming traffic.

Rowing craft when going against the tide, keep inshore as close as possible. Rowing when going with the tide, keep out of the stream, but make due allowance for commercial vessels which may be confined to the middle and deep water part of the channel.

Right of Way: When approaching a bridge or a bend in the river, vessels going against the stream must give way to any vessel that is coming along with the tide. This is particularly important at nearly low tide when eights going with the stream must go through Hammersmith Bridge or the centre arch of Chiswick Bridge because it is too shallow elsewhere to be safe.

Overtaking: A vessel which is overtaking must keep clear of the vessel which she is going to overtake until she is finally past and clear. There are sound signals associated with this manoeuvre—see below.

Crossing River: In order to take advantage of the set of the tidal stream and to navigate the many bends of the various reaches vessels crossing from one side of the river to the other shall do so at a proper time having regard to other vessels navigating up or down the river and shall be navigated so as not to cause obstruction, injury, or damage to any other vessel. Generally speaking a vessel crossing the river has no right of way over a vessel proceeding up or down.

Speed: There is no precise speed limit on the river below Wandsworth. Above Wandsworth it is 8 knots. Because vessels, particularly those with hard chines, can set up a heavy wash, they must navigate at such a speed that there is no likelihood of the wash causing any damage, injury or danger to persons, vessel or property.

Navigation without care and speeding likely to cause damage as mentioned above are offences making the owner or master liable to prosecution.

Silencers: Attention is drawn to the necessity of fitting engines with efficient silencers.

Water Ski-ing: Water ski-ing or aquaplaning behind speed boats is entirely prohibited on the River Thames within two hundred yards of any public beach, bathing place or residential property.

Sound Signals: Power driven craft which includes tugs, steamers, etc., make the following signals to indicate to other people what they are doing, or intend to do, with their own craft.

1 short blast means 'I am altering my course to starboard'
2 short blasts means 'I am altering my course to port'
3 short blasts means 'My engines are going astern'
5 or more short blasts mean 'I do not think you are taking sufficient action to keep clear of me'
4 short blasts followed by 1 short blast means 'I am turning round with my head swinging to starboard'
4 short blasts followed by 2 short blasts means 'I am turning round with my head swinging to port'
1 prolonged blast means 'I am about to get underway' i.e., leave the moorings or jetty where the craft is secured.
1 long blast followed by 1 short blast means 'I am about to overtake on your starboard side'. The vessel being overtaken will answer with a similar sound signal to indicate that she is ready to be overtaken.
1 long blast followed by 2 short blasts means 'I am about to overtake on your port side'. The vessel being overtaken will answer with a similar sound signal to indicate that she is ready to be overtaken.

Directions to be observed by persons in charge of vessels on the River Thames above and below London Bridge: There are certain regulations additional to the International Regulations for Preventing Collisions which require to be observed. Because of the different 'searoom' available, these regulations vary depending on whether navigating above or below London Bridge.

Above London Bridge:
'Fairway' means 'the central channel used for navigation up and down the river'.
'Small craft' means yachts, launches, rowing craft and other small vessels howsoever propelled of less than 65 feet in length.
'Vessels' means vessels over 65 feet in length.
'High speed craft' means vessel of any length howsoever propelled capable of proceeding at speeds of over 15 knots.

Directions:

In the fairway, small craft shall not hamper the passage of vessels which can navigate only inside such fairway.

Small craft and vessels shall not enter into or cross the fairway so as to obstruct another vessel proceeding along the fairway.

High speed craft shall keep out of the way of all vessels and craft.

Vessels in doubt that sufficient action is being taken to avoid collision may indicate this doubt by sounding five or more short and rapid blasts on the whistle.

Below London Bridge:

'Fairway' means (a) The one thousand foot wide channel from No. 1 Sea Reach Buoy to Gravesend and the main navigational channel from thence to London Bridge.

(b) The normal approach to the deep water anchorages of The Warp and Southend-on-Sea.

'Craft' means yachts, self-propelled craft and small vessels of any type, howsoever propelled.

Directions:

In the fairway craft of less than 65 feet in length shall not hamper the passage of a vessel which can navigate only inside such fairway.

Craft and vessels shall not enter into or cross the fairway between No. 1 Sea Reach Buoy and London Bridge so as to obstruct another vessel proceeding along the fairway.

Outside the fairway, the steering and sailing rules of the International Regulations for Preventing Collisions at Sea and of the Port of London Bye-Laws shall apply, but all craft shall keep well clear of vessels and their attendant tugs which are about to berth or moor.

Vessels in doubt that sufficient action is being taken to avoid collision may indicate this doubt by sounding five or more short and rapid blasts on the whistle.

Wrecks and Obstructions: A green spherical buoy usually with the word WRECK painted on the top is used to indicate a submerged obstruction. All boats should keep well clear. Where possible a wreck is marked by a boat or post by day with a green flag, and 2 green ball shapes, horizontally disposed. By night: 2 green lights similarly placed.

A vessel engaged in underwater work will exhibit by day, 3 shapes in a vertical line, the highest and lowest of these are red balls and the middle one is a white diamond. By night: 3 lights in a vertical line, red, white, red. The nature of the work performed by these craft usually necessitates that breast wires extend outwards from the sides of the vessel and therefore they should be given a wide berth.

A red flag means that divers are down—keep well clear and go slowly to avoid making any wash which might endanger the diver.

Obstructions not totally under water are marked by a post showing 2 red balls horizontally placed.

The triangle of shapes by day or lights by night, exhibited by a dredger on the tideway, gives no indication of the side on which to pass the dredger. In consequence they should be given a wide berth.

A triangle of three red discs or three red lights hanging from the arch of a bridge indicates it is closed to navigation.

Sunken craft—owners liability: Should any craft be unfortunate enough to sink in or near the channel, the P.L.A. have, under statutory powers, the right to remove the same by means of salvage craft. All expenses are recoverable from the owner at the time of sinking.

If a vessel in trying to avoid another runs aground or into a jetty the owner of the craft avoided may find himself sued for heavy damages.

Owners are strongly recommended to take insurance cover against these possibilities and are reminded that when a boat is loaned the owner is still legally responsible whether he is on board or not.

Public health, Pollution, etc: Owners and persons in charge of pleasure craft are reminded that it is an offence punishable on summary conviction by a fine of up to £100 to throw tins, bottles, cartons, paper, vegetable peelings and other forms of rubbish into the River Thames.

Oil, petrol and contents of chemical closets must not be spilt, discharged or allowed to flow into the River Thames. Offences of this nature are subject on summary conviction of fines of up to £1,000.

Safety rules

For the guidance of people afloat in rowing and sailing craft:

Do not cross the river in front of oncoming vessels. Always give commercial vessels a wide berth.

When going against the tide keep as close inshore as possible.

When going with the tide, remember that it is difficult to stop until you have turned round to stem the tide.

When casting off, look both ways before you proceed out into the stream, and wait until the fairway is clear.

When it is necessary to change places in the boat make sure you do this close inshore and don't stand up.

Keep clear of racing boats, whether sailing or rowing.

Beware of driving across the bows of barges moored at the buoys in the river or being carried against the pier of a bridge.

In strong winds crews of sailing craft should wear life jackets.

At all times, in all craft, life saving equipment should be readily available.

For Canoeists. The canoeist should particularly study all the foregoing rules and furthermore realise that in view of the frailty of his craft he must act with extreme care.

On long trips the canoeist who is responsible for his own safety should wear a life jacket and should be able to swim. It is advisable to have buoyancy bags or flotation units in his canoe. In the lower reaches this is the first essential.

Canoeists should:

Keep away from moored vessels, especially swim-headed barges.

Keep clear and as far away as possible from commercial traffic under way.

Cross the main channel, when this is necessary, as far as possible at right angles.

In the lower reaches, or in bad weather, use efficient spray covers.

Do not attempt to go below Putney unless in company.

Rowing Clubs. Numerous rowing clubs have their headquarters between Isleworth and Putney, and a large number of racing eights, fours and single scullers, are out daily. The greatest possible care is required in navigating power craft through this area, and on no account must wash be made.

It may be added that there are special bye-laws favouring rowing craft, but it will hardly be necessary to mention that in common courtesy, power craft should give all rowing boats the widest possible berth, consistent with their own safety.

Special arrangements are made for regattas, etc., particulars of which will be found in printed notices issued by the P.L.A. On such occasions all craft must keep clear of the course.

Requirements of H.M. Customs and Excise

Owners and masters of British yachts and other private craft and similarly owners of foreign yachts and other private craft arriving in, or departing from, United Kingdom waters, are subject in general to the same regulations as other foreign going ships. As many yacht owners appear to be quite uninformed of the essential requirements of the Commissioners of Customs and Excise, it is desirable that they become fully acquainted with the correct departure and arrival procedures as laid down in Notices.

Anchorages and moorings

All anchorages and public moorings within the limits of the Port of London, between Teddington and London Bridge are the property of the Authority. Numerous private firms, however, have berthing space along this part of the river which are held by licence from the P.L.A.

No private moorings may be laid down without the permission of the Authority. Subject to suitable sites, such permission may be granted on application to the Director of Marine Operations, Port of

London Authority, London, E1 9A2. The completed application must be returned to the Authority with plan in triplicate, showing the location of the proposed moorings. The key plan must be on a scale of 6 inches to one mile, and show both banks of the river half a mile below and above the site, with a general plan on a scale of 60 inches to the mile, showing the immediate locality with the moorings located in red. The P.L.A. drawing office can provide facilities for making tracings from special river charts.

When the application has been approved, the moorings are assessed according to their value to the applicant who has to pay a fee in addition to the Assessor's fee.

Houseboats which are defined as vessels used for residential purposes are not permitted to moor in that part of the river within the jurisdiction of the Port Authority, (i.e. downstream from Teddington Lock) and further the regulations do not allow such craft to berth in any of the Authority's docks or basins.

Houseboats may be permitted alongside frontages above Chelsea Bridge and on certain creeks in the Canvey Island area providing always that there is direct access from the shore.

It is necessary in such cases to obtain permission of the person or firm owning the river frontage stating that access over this property and the mooring of the vessel at their frontage will be permitted. The agreement of adjacent frontagers is also necessary. The vessel (which it is inadvisable to purchase in anticipation of such permission) must be inspected to ensure that it is in all respects suitable and riverworthy before proceeding to the site. Additionally it may also be necessary to obtain planning permission.

Upper Section
The following yacht and launch moorings belong to the Port of London Authority, and permission to use them must be sought from the Assistant Harbour Master, Upper Section.

OFF NORTH BANK *Access from Kew Pier*	OFF SOUTH BANK *Access from Cadogan Pier or Battersea Garden Pier*
No. 16 Strand on the Green 2nd	No. 23 Battersea Park 1st Yacht
„ 17 „ „ „ „ 3rd	„ 24 „ „ 2nd „
„ 18 „ „ „ „ 4th	*Access from Westminster Pier*
„ 19 „ „ „ „ 1st	„ 45 St. Thomas's 1st Yacht
„ 20 „ „ „ „ 2nd	„ 46 „ „ 2nd „
	„ 47 „ „ 3rd „
	Access from Charing Cross Pier or Festival Hall Pier
	„ 58 Charing Cross 1st Yacht
	„ 59 „ „ 2nd „
	„ 60 „ „ 3rd „
	„ 62 „ „ 4th „

There is a charge for mooring payable to the pierman.

The following bases are maintained in liaison with recognised youth groups:

Thames Young Mariners' Centre, Ham Dock, Richmond.
Built by the Surrey County Council. Consists of an inland basin with a private lock into the tidal Thames just below Teddington Lock.

Barn Elms Boathouse, Putney Reach.
Storage space for pulling boats and specialist rowing craft, eights, fours and pairs.

Riverside Base, Isleworth.
Operated by the Boy Scouts Association. Camping is possible here.

The Navy League T.S. 'Neptune'—Ravens Ait, Surbiton.
Here everything is run in naval fashion with visitors carrying out watch and mess duty turns.

Middle Section
Owing to the constant movement of commercial craft, there are very few suitable places considered safe enough for yachts to lay at anchor A reasonably safe anchorage is in Bugsby's Reach, just off the premises of Redpath Brown Ltd. and the Greenwich Yacht Club. Sometimes it is possible to arrange to moor alongside a barge road for the night, but this must be arranged direct with the owners or their roadsman who is usually in a cabin aboard the collar barge.

Lower Section
For berths in the river apply to the Assistant Harbour Master (Lower) Gravesend, via the Thames Navigation Service or the Harbour Service Patrol Launch for an anchorage or mooring. Anchorages are below Denton.

The Assistant Harbour Master may be able to give you a buoy or allow you to lie alongside one of the P.L.A. craft for the night on application.

Launching and Landing Sites

Motorists with boats on trailers or boats carried on the roofs of their cars can launch boats at the following sites:

Upper Section

Name of Site	Location	Road Approach
Teddington	Toughs' Boatyard	
Twickenham Draw Dock	Twickenham Embankment	via Twickenham Junction thence to Parish Church down Church Road.
Ham Landing (Public Car Park available)	Ham Fields	via Ham Road off Kingston Road.
Petersham Draw Dock	Petersham Meadow	via River Lane.

Richmond Bridge Draw Dock	Twickenham side of bridge	Over Richmond Bridge towards Twickenham turn sharp left at foot of bridge.
Water Lane Draw Dock	Richmond	Bottom of Water Lane.
Isleworth Draw Dock*	Isleworth Parish Church	via Church Street or down Syon Lane
Kew Bridge Draw Dock	Chiswick side of river	via Chiswick High Rd. to foot of Kew Bridge.
Ship Draw Dock, Mortlake	Mortlake Brewery	Down Ship Lane off Lower Mortlake Road.
Small Profits Draw Dock	Barnes	Cross Hammersmith Bridge via Lonsdale Road, Barnes.
Chiswick Draw Dock	Chiswick	via Dukes Avenue off Chiswick High Road.
Putney Draw Dock	Putney Bridge	Turn right over Putney Bridge.
Battersea Church Draw Dock	Battersea	Over Battersea. Bridge turn right.

Middle Section

The availability of launching sites in the Middle Section should also be confirmed by reference to the Assistant Harbour Master beforehand, as certain of these may be occupied by commercial craft or otherwise obstructed.

Name of Site	*Location*	*Road Approach*
Johnson Draw Dock	Poplar ⎫	via Manchester
Newcastle Draw Dock	Poplar ⎬	Road or West Ferry
	⎭	Road.
Blackwall Causeway	Poplar	via Prestons Road or Blackwall Way.

* Can be used for beaching craft on the high water by permission of the Haven Master.

Barge House Draw Dock	West Ham ⎫	From Albert Road or Woolwich Manor Way.
East Ham Manor Way Draw Dock	East Ham ⎬	
Bugsby's Hole Causeway	East Greenwich	Blackwall Tunnel Avenue and Riverway.
Erith Causeway	Erith (Waterfront)	West Street and High Street.

Lower Section

Greenhithe Causeway	Greenhithe
Newbridge Causeway	Gravesend

It is strongly recommended that before a visitor uses these facilities he should previously study the warning notice regarding speed and also the general regulations regarding navigation, safety, etc. He should then apply to the Assistant Harbour Master, or to any Piermaster for the latest information regarding navigation on the river when he will be informed of the time and duration of any regattas or boat races that might be in progress during his visit.

Special events on the Thames (P.L.A. and T.W.A. Sections)

A diversity of aquatic pastimes belong to the Thames and they are as different as the great frost fairs of bygone days and dinghy sailing of today.

The Boat Race on the Thames between Oxford and Cambridge which is rowed each year from Putney to Mortlake is a national event, although it is not generally known that the first Boat Race between the universities was in 1829 and in those days Cambridge, who lost, had pink for their colours. No race could be arranged again until 1836 and this took place between Westminster and Putney, Oxford having dark blue stripes on their white jerseys, but Cambridge abandoned their pink when before the race started a supporter fixed a pale blue ribbon to the bow of the Cambridge boat, and as they won the race easily in 36 minutes, the light blue became their colour. Over the years the race went through several changes and the course had to be altered owing to the heavy river traffic below Putney.

The 1829 Oxford boat still exists and can be seen at the Science Museum in South Kensington. The boats have changed from stout clinker built eight-oared wherries, as in the year 1846 both crews used for the first time outrigged boats which were forerunners of the racing boat we know today. The 'Coach and Eight' in Upper Richmond Road, Putney, is the rowing man's museum, and amongst the many items of interest are Doggett's Coat and Badge. This is named after Thomas Doggett who founded in 1715 our oldest annual sporting event. The course rowed has remained unchanged and is from the 'Old Swan' at London Bridge to the 'White Swan' at Chelsea, a distance of $4\frac{5}{8}$ miles.

Henley is the Mecca of the rowing man as here takes place the grand meeting of international amateur oarsmen on the occasion of the annual regatta which had its beginnings in the first university boat races, and consisted of sculling and rowing races. Numerous other rowing events take place on the river including the various 'Head of the River' races sometimes on the tideway.

There is also yachting on many sections, the events being too numerous to list here, but they can be found in publications issued by the Royal Yachting Association. There was, also once the Thames and Medway barge races which had a devoted and enthusiastic following, but these are no more, as the Thames barge with its brown sails and topmast bowed a little forward is becoming a rare sight on the river. With their shallow draught, these barges could sail up many small creeks to deliver cargoes, but could not run to the time-table of a motor vessel and thus the long hours worked by the old-time skippers find few today who are willing to undertake them.

Numerous canoeing events are held on the river and the championship slaloms are held at Shepperton Weir and Marsh Lock Weir, Henley. The sport of canoeing would be greatly encouraged if the Canoeing National Championships for racing were held at Henley which was the venue in 1948 for the Olympic canoeing events, and clearly an ideal one.

A comparatively recent innovation is the annual Devizes to Westminster canoe race, which attracts an increasing number of entries from various youth organizations and the services each year. This race is the longest and toughest of its kind in the world, as the course is 125 miles long with 77 locks to portage, the first 54 miles of the course being along the Kennet and Avon Canal. From small beginnings in 1948, the idea of the race came from some Devizes business men who offered an award of £100 to local river scouts if they could canoe to London in 100 hours or less, they succeeded in doing so in 96 hours.

Not strictly a sport, but an event on the Thames which on occasions affords great interest to spectators, is what is known as swan-upping. This is a swan marking exercise which is carried out each year to mark the cygnets. When the boats taking part reach Romney Lock a short ceremony takes place as this lock is the nearest to the Queen's residence at the Royal Castle of Windsor. The Dyers' and Vintners' boats wait outside the lock so that they may salute the Queen's boats as they pass.

The swans on the Thames are not owned by the Conservators but belong to the Queen and to the Dyers' and Vintners' Companies. Anyone desirous of obtaining swans should consult the Comptroller of St. James's Palace, in London. There are three Swan Masters to whom all other enquiries should be directed.

Queen's Swan Keeper—Mr. F. J. Turk, Cookham, Berkshire.

Vintners' Company Swan Keeper—Mr. M. Turk, Thames Side Boathouse, Kingston-upon-Thames, Surrey.

Dyers' Company Swan Keeper—Mr. H. E. Cobb, 36 Rotherwood Road, Putney, London, S.W. 15

In the reign of Edward IV no one was permitted to keep swans who did not possess a freehold of at least five marks annual value, and by an Act of Henry VII robbers of eggs were fined 13 shillings and fourpence for each and the penalty for altering the markings of the birds was a year's imprisonment and a fine of £3. 6s. 8d. As a mark of favour the King sometimes granted to an individual or a corporation 'a game of swans' and along with it the right of a swan mark. Thus two City Companies, whose halls are on the banks of the river, have possessed, since the 15th. century the privilege of owning and marking the royal birds. These Companies are the Vintners' and the Dyers' Guilds, and the reason for the right being granted them was, probably, a desire on the part of the Crown to prevent trouble between the Royal Swanherd and the Conservancy of the Thames which was carried out with considerable firmness by the City Corporation.

Swans of a certain age, not marked, were claimed by the Crown, and were known as 'clear billed'. The marks were changed in the year 1878, after the Society for the Prevention of Cruelty to Animals had prosecuted, unsuccessfully, the swanherds employed by the Crown and the two City Companies.

The marking or 'upping' as it is technically called, is effected by cutting the upper mandible of the bird, and stopping the slight bleeding with pitch. The new system of marking, which omits at least half the old number of cuts, consists of two small nicks on either side of the mandible on birds belonging to the Vintners' Company, and one nick cut on the right side of birds belonging to the Dyers. The marking of Royal birds was discontinued about 1910. The two nicks on the Vintners' birds were corrupted and gave rise to the well known tavern sign 'The Swan with Two Necks'.

The process of swan-upping, conducted with much ceremony, takes place in July or August, when the markers of the three owners take count of all swans in the river, and mark the clear-billed birds which have reached maturity. Operations are conducted by officials in six boats, and upping is considered good sport from the vigorous resistance offered by the birds.

Many years ago a great cry was raised by anglers and others that the swans were enemies of the fish, haunting the spawning grounds and consuming the eggs. After analysis, however, it was proved that this was exaggerated, for the swans did not devour the spawn by preference, but only incidentally whilst feeding on the vegetable matter and river growths to which the spawn is frequently attached. The Crown nevertheless, has no desire to increase the number of birds on the river, which is maintained at about 500 grown birds and cygnets, thereby limiting the total to 610 allowing 65 to the Dyers and 45 to the Vintners.

Navigation offices Chief Navigation Inspector, Nugent House, Vastern Road, Reading, Berks. RG1 8DB. Tel. Reading (:0734) 593387.

No. 1 District (Cricklade to Wallingford Bridge). Osney Lock, Oxford. Tel. Oxford (0865) 721271

No. 2 District (Wallingford to Marlow Bridge). T.W.A., Nugent House, Vastern Road, Reading, Berks. Tel. Reading (0734) 593284.

No. 3 District (Marlow Bridge to Staines Bridge). Boulter's Lock, Maidenhead, Berkshire. Tel. Maidenhead (0628) 22491

No. 4 District (Staines Bridge to Teddington). Boundary Riverside Works, Footbridge Road, Sunbury on Thames, Middlesex. W16 4AP. Tel. Sunbury (093 27) 81946.

The Chief Engineer's Headquarters are at Nugent House, Vastern Road, Reading.

Branches Short Arm, known as Sheepwash Channel to Oxford Canal, is TWA water up to the tail of Isis (or Louse Lock). There is a railway swing bridge on this section, which is ⅛ mile long. (Now disused.)

Branch to Kennet and Avon Canal at Reading. Headway is only 9ft 8ins ins under Watlington Bridge but beware of lesser headways if you depart from the main channel. There is a maximum draught of 3ft 3ins only. TWA jurisdiction extends to a limit 70 yards eastwards of the High Bridge at Reading. There is one lock (Blakes) which is 122ft 8ins long by 18ft 11ins wide. Branch is ¼ mile along.

Branch to River Wey, at Shepperton, 200 feet long linking to the River Wey is TWA water. This section of TWA water is the remainder of a channel that used to go around an island but is now partly weeded up. St. Patrick's stream and part of the River Loddon form a by-pass route round Shiplake Lock. There is a public right of navigation but the route can be dangerous and the current is fast; headroom is limited to 4ft but there is about 10ft beam.

There are a number of side channels and tributaries that are possibly available for navigation but care is necessary and local enquiries are advised. The river Thame is navigable for small cruisers and light craft to Dorchester (Oxon).

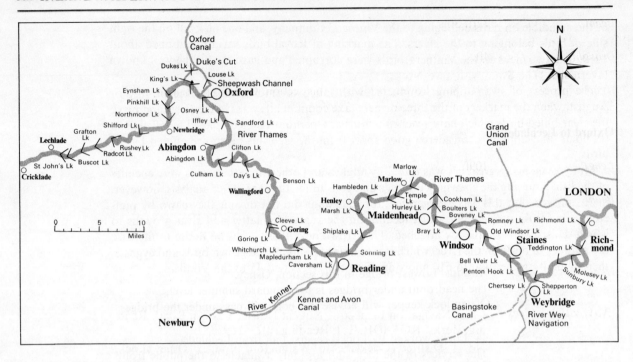

Teddington to Windsor

Length	174ft
Beam	19ft 10ins (Staines to Teddington 6ft 6ins)
*Draught**	5ft. 6ins.
Headroom	13ft. 2ins. Lowest bridge is in this section, Windsor. (Under certain water conditions headroom may be up to 1ft less)

Windsor to Reading

Length	130ft.
Beam	17ft. 6ins.
Draught	4ft. 6ins.
Headroom	12ft. 6ins. Lowest bridge in this section, Cookham Cut.

Reading to Oxford

Length	120ft.

* There is 6ft. 6ins. from Staines to Windsor.

Beam	17ft. 3ins.
Draught	4ft.
Headroom	11ft. 8ins. Lowest bridges in this section, Clifton and Culham.

Oxford to Lechlade

Length	109ft.
Beam	14ft.
Draught	3ft.
Headroom	7ft. 6ins Lowest bridge in this section, Osney.

The headroom under bridges is for standard summer level.
Osney lock keeper will advise if a boat will pass under the bridge.

Locks — 44. Locks worked by Lock-keepers. Fall from Lechlade.
The services of the lock staff are only available to the public from 9 a.m. to early evening, depending on time of year. Notices are placed at locks giving staff working hours. Outside these hours members of the public may work the locks themselves at their own risk and responsibility.
This does not apply to Teddington Lock where special conditions prevail, and where the services of the lock staff are always available. (24 hours a day throughout the year).

Lock chambers are cleaned during the summer months May to October every Wednesday morning between the hours of 0800 and 0930 hrs and at these times it will be necessary to close the locks to all traffic. When a lock-keeper is working on his own, having a meal break etc., members of the public may work the lock themselves at their own risk and responsibility. Instruction for the hand operation of the lock is posted on the operating pedestals. Always ensure gates are closed before operating sluices. It is important that the gates are closed as in many cases there is a public right of way over the gates.

Teddington Lock Signal Lights. A lighted signal, as shown below is placed at the lower end of Teddington barge lock to direct traffic proceeding upstream through Teddington Locks.

Bridges — 69, all fixed. For maximum headroom see Dimensions.

Approx. time taken to navigate — This, of course, depends upon the type of vessel, but a cruiser averages approximately 5 miles an hour which includes time taken up by lockage. This may be taken as a rough guide.

Bye-laws — A note of these bye-laws is made in the preamble to the Thames. The following notes based on the bye-laws should be noted.

The authority may refuse to register vessels capable of being driven at high speed, or otherwise considered unsuitable for use on the Thames. In addition to bye-laws referred to elsewhere *The Thames Launch Digest* should be consulted and this is obtainable from the authority free of charge.

Your launch must be registered with Thames Water (as must any pleasure boat including tenders and inflatables) *before it is used* in the river.

Thames Water is forbidden to register two or more launches in the same name.

For registration purposes the overall length of the hull and maximum beam are measured, excluding movable items such as a rudder or outboard motor.

Certificates of registration expire on a 31st December irrespective of the date of application and the full charge is payable without refund for periods of non-use in any year. Special facilities are available for vessels entering the Thames from other waterways for short periods and for those registered late in the year. Currently registered pleasure boats do not incur Thames Water lock tolls.

Licensing. Even if registered, no launch may navigate the freshwater Thames without a licence to do so. This is issued without charge but the registered owner must certify that the launch is constructed and equipped in accordance with the current specification made by Thames Water under the Thames Launch Bye-laws 1952. The licence is not transferable and the licence plate must be fixed to the launch to which it relates where it can easily be seen by Lock Staff and river patrols.

Applications. Application forms for registration and licensing are obtainable from and dealth with by A.D.M. (Finance), Thames Conservancy Division, Thames Water, Nugent House, Vastern Road, Reading RG1 8DB.

Change of ownership. If you transfer the ownership of your vessel before the expiry of a current certificate registration you are legally obliged to notify Thames Water, giving details of the new owner. Full instructions will be found on the reverse of the certificate.

The launch name as shown on the launch certificate must be marked clearly and conspicuously on each side of the bow and at the stern in a *contrasting colour* to the background and in plain letters of not less than the following sizes:

launch not exceeding 20ft in length 2in letters
launch 20ft to 30ft in length 3in letters
launch 30ft to 50ft in length 4in letters
launch exceeding 50ft in length 6in letters

The registered name should be sufficiently visible and clearly marked to avoid confusion with any trade name on the vessel.

Navigation notes

Fire extinguishers Owners of petrol motor launches are required to ensure that efficient fire extinguishing equipment is carried and maintained on board at all times. In case of fire, explosion or other similar accident on board a launch, notification should be given within 48 hours to The Divisional Manager, Thames Water Authority, Nugent House, Vastern Road, Reading, Berks. RG1 8DB or to the nearest navigation inspector, and the vessel must not be moved until an inspection has been made.

In case of vessels not registered and licensed with the Authority, which wish to proceed through their waters, application should be made in writing well in advance to the Thames Water Authority.

Charges A scale of charges will be issued on application.

Lights All launches navigating between sunset and sunrise must exhibit the following lights and no others:
(1) On the mast or staff at the bow, at a height of not less than 4 feet, a bright white light.
(2) On the starboard side a green light.
(3) On the port side a red light.
(4) On the stern a white light.
Tricolour or bicolour lights will not satisfy the requirements.

Navigation Navigate as near as possible in midstream and pass approaching launches 'port to port' when circumstances permit.

It is an offence to navigate a vessel on the river without care and caution, or to navigate it at such a speed or in such a manner as to endanger the safety of other persons or of other craft. A person convicted by a Magistrates Court of any of these offences may be fined up to £20 for each offence. If there are two convictions of offences of careless or improper navigation involving the same launch its registration ceases automatically to be in force: similarly, if a person is twice convicted of any such offence, any launch registration certificate held by him becomes void.

It is not the authority's wish to intervene unduly in the pleasure of users of the Thames. Where, however, the interests of the public in matters of safety and amenities are endangered, the authorities have a duty to perform and they will not hesitate to enforce regulations. As an instance of this, a case prosecuted by the authorities involving a launch travelling at high speed and towing a water skier resulted in a conviction and imposition of the maximum penalty.

Speed limit Launches are not allowed to navigate at high speed on the Thames. In narrow channels, such as lock cuts, speed must be carefully regulated so as not to cause a wash that will inconvenience other people, particularly those in racing, rowing and sculling boats, punts, skiffs and canoes. Slow down when passing moored craft, particularly punts and canoes, which may be swamped. You should realise that the wash of an average launch travelling at average speed will damage moored craft and it is good manners and good watermanship always to reduce speed when passing moored craft. Under no circumstances should your speed exceed 7 knots (8 m.p.h.) and you will often have to go much slower. It is your responsibility to ensure that other persons and property are not endangered. Watch your wash and its possible effect on moored craft.

It is obvious that many people in charge of launches are not heeding the advice given. Although their speed may not exceed the advised maximum, they nevertheless do travel faster than they should having regard to the prevailing conditions and circumstances. For instance, when you pass a sculler you should reduce speed to a minimum, to as low as 2 m.p.h. if necessary, so that he is not imperilled by your wash. The problem of speed and navigation is continually being considered by the Authority and launch owners and navigators should understand that the Authority will take appropriate action in cases where the lives of other river users are endangered by careless or dangerous navigation.

Sound Signals Every launch must be fitted with a whistle or horn on which navigation signals can be made: a bell is not suitable for this purpose. Only proper navigation signals, as follows, should be given:—
One short blast: 'I am directing my course to starboard' i.e. to the right.
Two short blasts: 'I am directing my course to port' i.e. to the left.
Three short blasts: 'My engines are going astern'.
Four short blasts: 'I am unable to manoeuvre'.
In addition to the above, you may hear the following local signals, particularly from commercial craft:—
Four short blasts followed by one short blast: 'I am turning round to starboard'.
Four short blasts followed by two short blasts: 'I am turning round to port'.

Sailing vessels When approaching or passing sailing vessels, especially those racing, slow down and manoeuvre as necessary to keep out of their way. Should it be found impossible to keep clear, give the proper navigation signal—four short blasts—in order to indicate your inability to manoeuvre. On their part, people in sailing boats should realize that a reach crowded with sailing boats engaged in racing can be a frightening hazard to launch drivers, particularly if they are inexperienced, and that, when tacking, they should not approach too near the launches.

Bridges and bends In the vicinity of bridges or sharp bends a launch going upstream should give way, as necessary, to any vessel coming downstream.

Dredgers Slow down when passing dredgers, and navigate to that side on which a white flag is displayed: keep clear of the dredger's mooring buoys and cables.

Bathers Always watch for and keep clear of bathers.

Underwater Divers Underwater divers may sometimes operate in the river. Their presence should be indicated by a safety boat and a white and blue burgess, International Code Flag A.

Locking When passing through a lock, act under and in accordance with the lock-keeper's instructions, and make your vessel fast head and stern. For safety reasons the lock-keeper may direct a passenger steamer or other large boat to enter the lock first. Do not moor above the white line painted down the lock side, which indicates the extent of the projection of the sill of the upper gates. See that you have the necessary mooring ropes on board. You should tend your boat and adjust the mooring ropes as the water in the lock rises or falls. It is necessary for you to take every care as regards the safety of your vessel and its passengers. If in a motor launch, stop your engine and do not open your fuel tank or strike matches. Petrol must not be transferred from one receptacle to another whilst the launch is in a lock or waiting outside a lock.

You are asked to switch off all radios in a lock. They can be an annoyance to other people, and in case of emergency they might prevent the lock-keeper's instructions from being heard.

When passing through a lockcut, launches must be navigated in single file and not overtake other launches until clear of the cut. Unless you are waiting to enter a lock you should not moor in a lock cut.

Lay-by facilities are provided for the convenience of craft waiting to enter locks. These may consist of piles and walling offshore, or bankside moorings. In most cases the offshore moorings are more suitable for larger craft and provide depth of water. Smaller boats should therefore use the bank side moorings if at all possible.

All craft should take up the nearest vacant position on the lay-bys to the locks so that craft arriving after them can moor astern.

Anchors It is desirable that an anchor be carried and rigged as necessary for immediate use in case of engine breakdown. Make sure that the anchor is stowed so as not to cause damage to other boats.

Weirs Always keep well away from weirs, particularly when tackle at the weir is drawn. When a strong stream is running large red notice boards are exhibited at the locks adjacent to the weirs concerned. At these time you are advised to moor up until the stream abates.

Overhead Cables Cables over the navigation channel are normally placed at a height of 40 feet above summer water level. A working clearance of at least 4 feet should be allowed when passing beneath electric cables. It is advisable for owners of craft with high masts or aerials to approach all cables with caution, and if in any doubt to lower their masts or aerials.

Over backwaters and smaller channels and the navigation channel in the higher reaches above Oxford, cables may be at a height well below 40 feet.

Regattas When approaching a Regatta course navigate very slowly and with caution and pay due regard to any instructions given by Thames Water Authority Inspectors, guard-boatmen and other authorized persons.

Mooring If you are stopping overnight or leaving the launch for any appreciable length of time, do not moor in shallow water, or with a tight rope or chain. For unavoidable reasons the water level may drop or rise by as much as two or three feet in a few hours. If it drops when you are moored aground or in shallow water the launch may be careened or damaged. If it rises when your mooring rope or chain is tight, the launch may

take on water, be pulled under or even broken free. Do not take the risk. Always ensure that there is at least two feet of water below your keel and at least two feet of vertical play on any mooring rope or chain.

Sanitary appliances No vessel is permitted to have on board any sanitary appliances connecting with the river by pipe or otherwise, and it is an offence to discharge from the vessel into the river any offensive or injurious matter.

Identification No two launches are registered in the same name, and each launch is required to have its name painted conspicuously upon each side of the bow and upon the stern, in light letters on a dark background or dark letters on a light background.

Moorings

Arrangements for mooring launches must be made with the owner of the land off which launches are to lie or with a boat-hirer who has vacant moorings.

If piles, buoys, mooring chains or any accommodations in the river are required, it is necessary to obtain the Authority's permission before the accommodations are placed and to submit plans showing the position of the accommodations. Facilities are available at many locks on the river for casual moorings during the summer months—application should be made to the lock-keeper for full particulars and charges. The Authority in co-operation with the Thames Hire Cruiser Association and the Association of Thames Motor Yacht Clubs have provided the following sites for the overnight mooring of launches free of charge. In each case the extent of the mooring site is indicated by notice boards:—

Towpath above Pinkhill Lock – Picnic site
Tow-path below Isis Bridge, near Iffley
Tow-path above Abingdon Lock
Tow-path below Goring Lock
Right bank below Gatehampton Railway Bridge
Tow-path above Sonning Lock
Tow-path at Lower Lashbrook Wargrave
Tow-path above Boveney Lock
Towpath at Laleham Wharf
Tow-path at Weybridge opposite Shepperton Lock
Stevens Eyot Kingston (Below Kingston Railway Bridge)

Fishing from the bank is not allowed from these sites between the 1st April and the 30th September.

Public slipways and launching sites

Although you may launch a boat at the following sites, there is not necessarily a right to park a car or a boat trailer, neither are these sites necessarily suitable for large and heavy boats and trailers. If in doubt, you are advised to make preliminary enquiries.

Teddington Drawdock
Kingston at Thameside
Thames Ditton by Swan Hotel
East Moseley Drawdock
West Moseley, Hurst Park
Walton Wharf by Anglers Hotel
Cowey Sale, Walton
Shepperton Village Wharf
Weybridge, Thames Street
Cookham Bridge by Ferry Hotel
Marlow, St. Peter's Street
Medmenham Ferry
Aston Ferry, from either bank
Henley, Wharf Lane
Wargrave, Ferry Lane
Caversham Bridge
Cholsey, Papist Way
Abingdon, St. Helen's Wharf

Further sites are listed in *Where to launch your boat* published by Link House.

Water points at locks	Water taps are provided for use by the public at locks. They are intended for replenishing water containers and not for bulk supplies which might delay traffic. A list of water points is given in *The Launch Digest* (T.W.A.)
Sewage and rubbish disposal facilities	As already mentioned, sewage and other polluting matter must not be allowed to pass into the river. In order to assist boat users, the authority have constructed sewage and rubbish disposal sites at various locks and certain boatyards and hotels have agreed to assist. A list of the sites and facilities is given in *The Launch Digest* (T.W.A.) When using the disposal sites, you are asked to take particular care to put rubbish etc. in the proper places. Please make sure that only sewage is emptied into the manhole, as anything else will clog the apparatus and put it out of action. Only dry combustible rubbish should be put into the incinerator. This should be placed in the dustbins and bottles in the special crates provided. Boatyards may, in some instances, make a small charge for the use of the disposal and mooring facilities.
Sewage Pump-out Stations	With the exception of Thames Water's 24 hour coin operated units at St. John's and Molesey Locks, all pump-out stations are under private management and all usually available only during the months of April to October. Operations can only be conducted during working hours and prior appointment is advised. At hire cruiser bases some delay will be experienced when craft are turned around from one hirer to another.

Markings of shoals, etc.

The Authority have adopted a uniform system of marking shoals and other obstructions in the river. This is particularly required in the early months of the year when the reeds, which add to the natural beauty of the river, have not grown through the surface of the water. Three shapes of topmarks used – can, triangle and sphere – are illustrated together with directions for passing them safely when you proceed upstream. Remember when you navigate downstream that the *can* and *triangle* shapes must be passed on your opposite side.

Wrecks or other temporary obstructions in midstream are marked by an isolated danger buoy which may be passed on any side. Where such obstructions must be passed on a particular side the appropriate *can* or *triangle* topmarks will be used.

In all cases craft should pass well clear of a marking buoy.

It is emphasised that Thames Water does not accept responsibility for the marking of obstructions that lie outside the fairway. You must therefore proceed with particular caution when approaching any bank or if you depart from the main navigation route.

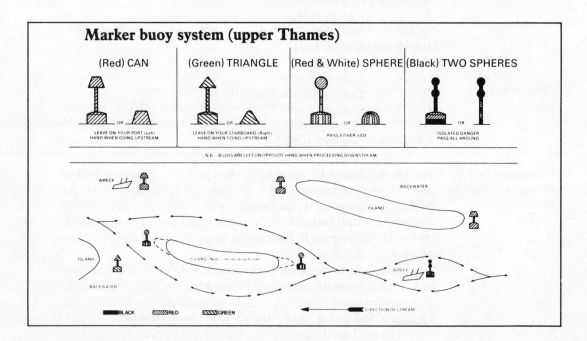

Thames Water Authority
Distance Table

Above Teddington				Between places		
M.	F.	Ch.		M.	F.	Ch.
142	0	0	Thames Head Bridge*	7	0	0
135	1	4	Cricklade Bridge and River Churn Left bank	0	7	5
134	1	9	Footbridge to Eisey	0	5	0

*Jurisdiction of the T.W.A. ends at Cricklade Bridge where the public right of navigation is used.

Distance Table

Above Teddington				Between places		
M.	F.	Ch.		M.	F.	Ch.
133	4	9	River Ray (right bank)	0	1	0
133	3	9	Bridge to Water Eaton House ...	2	4	3
130	7	6	Castle Eaton Bridge	1	3	9
129	3	7	St. Mary's Church, Kempsford ...	1	1	7
128	2	0	Hannington Bridge	3	1	1
125	0	9	St. John's Church, Inglesham ...	0	2	5
124	6	4	Inglesham Lock (closed)	0	0	2
124	6	2	River Coln (left bank)	0	5	4
124	0	8	Lechlade Bridge	0	3	9
123	4	9	River Cole (right)	0	1	3
123	3	6	St. John's Lock and Bridge ...	0	0	7
123	2	9	River Leach (left bank)	1	0	5
122	2	4	Buscot Lock	3	2	7
118	7	7	Grafton Lock	1	1	5
117	6	2	Radcot Bridge	0	5	3
116	7	1	Old Man's Footbridge	0	1	8
117	0	9	Radcot Lock	0	1	8
114	3	8	Rushey Lock	0	5	7
113	6	1	Tadpole Bridge	1	6	6
111	7	5	Tenfoot Footbridge	1	1	6
110	5	9	Shifford Weir	0	4	5
110	1	4	Shifford Lock	0	3	8
109	5	6	Old Shifford Farm	2	0	7
107	4	9	River Windrush, New Bridge (left bank)	1	1	3
106	3	6	Hart's Footbridge	1	0	1
105	3	5	Northmoor Lock	1	4	3
103	7	2	Bablock Hythe Ferry	2	2	6
101	4	6	Pinkhill Lock	1	3	0
100	1	6	Swinford Bridge, Eynsham	0	0	8
100	0	8	Eynsham Lock	1	1	7
98	7	1	River Evenlode (left bank)	0	7	8
97	7	3	Wytham Mill Stream, Hagley Pool (right bank)	0	4	2
97	4	6	*Junction with Duke's Cut entrance to Oxford Canal*	0	1	5
97	3	1	King's Lock	0	7	5
96	3	6	Godstow Bridge	0	1	5
96	2	1	Godstow Lock	1	7	8
94	2	3	Sheepwash Channel to Oxford Canal	0	1	7
94	0	6	Osney Bridge	0	1	7
93	6	9	Osney Lock	0	7	0
92	7	9	Folly Bridge	0	2	0
92	5	9	River Cherwell, old Mouth (left bank)	0	1	6
92	4	3	River Cherwell, new Mouth (left bank)	1	0	0
91	4	3	Iffley Lock	0	4	6
90	7	7	Kennington Railway Bridge ...	1	0	8
89	6	9	Sandford Lock	1	5	2
88	1	7	Radley Ferry	1	4	5

Above Teddington							Between places		
M.	F.	Ch.					M.	F.	Ch.
86	5	2	Nuneham Railway Bridge	...	...		0	7	3
85	5	9	Horseferry		...		0	3	7
85	2	2	Abingdon Lock		...		0	3	8
84	6	4	Abingdon Bridge ...		...	...	0	2	0
84	4	4	River Ock (right bank)		...	...	0	5	2
83	7	2	Culham Road Bridge ...		...	...	1	1	6
82	5	6	Culham Lock ...		...	...	0	0	6
82	5	0	Sutton Bridge ...		...	...	1	1	7
81	3	3	Appleford Railway Bridge		...		0	7	6
80	3	7	Clifton Weir		...		0	4	6
79	7	1	Clifton Lock		...		0	3	6
79	3	5	Clifton Hampden Bridge		...		2	4	2
76	7	3	Day's Lock		...		0	6	7
76	0	6	River Thame (left bank)		...		1	0	8
74	7	8	Keen Edge Ferry (closed)		...		0	6	2
74	1	6	Shillingford Bridge ...		...		1	2	0
72	7	6	Benson Lock		...		1	1	9
71	5	7	Wallingford Bridge ...		...		0	3	9
71	1	8	Chalmore Hole		...	...	2	1	5
69	0	3	Littlestoke Ferry (closed)		...		0	5	0
68	3	3	Moulsford Railway Bridge		...		0	5	5
67	5	8	South Stoke Ferry (Beetle and Wedge)				1	2	2
66	3	6	Cleeve Lock		...	...	0	5	0
65	6	6	Goring Lock		...	...	0	0	5
65	6	1	Goring Bridge ...		...	...	1	1	8
64	4	3	Gatehampton Railway Bridge			...	0	2	2
64	2	1	Gatehampton Ferry (closed) ...			...	2	4	0
61	6	1	Whitchurch Lock ...		...	...	0	1	0
61	5	1	Whitchurch Bridge ...		...	...	2	1	3
59	3	8	Mapledurham Lock ...		...	...	0	4	1
58	7	7	Upper Roebuck Ferry (closed)			...	0	2	7
58	5	0	Roebuck Ferry (closed)		...	...	0	3	1
58	1	9	Tilehurst Station ...		...	...	2	3	7
55	6	2	Caversham Bridge ...		...	...	0	4	2
55	2	0	Reading Bridge		...	...	0	1	4
55	0	6	Caversham Lock ...		...	...	0	6	0
54	2	6	River Kennet (right bank)		...	...	1	7	0
52	3	6	Sonning Lock		...	...	0	2	3
52	1	3	Sonning Bridge		...	...	2	5	0
49	4	3	Shiplake Lock		...	...	0	0	9
49	3	4	River Loddon (right bank)		...		0	0	8
49	2	6	Shiplake Railway Bridge		...		0	2	2
49	0	4	Wargrave Ferry ...		...		0	5	0
48	3	4	Lashbrook Ferry (closed)		...		0	7	2
47	4	2	Harpsden Ferry (closed)		...	...	0	4	6
46	7	6	Marsh Lock		...		0	7	6
46	0	0	Henley Bridge		...		1	3	2
44	4	8	Temple Island		...		0	7	1
43	5	7	Hambleden Lock ...		...	...	0	4	1

Above Teddington							Between places		
M.	F.	Ch.					M.	F.	Ch.
43	1	6	Aston Ferry (closed)	1	4	6
41	5	0	Medmenham Abbey and Ferry ...	1	4	6
40	0	4	Hurley Lock	0	5	1
39	3	3	Temple Lock	1	4	1
37	7	2	Marlow Suspension Bridge	0	1	3
37	5	9	Marlow Lock		0	7
35	5	2	Spade Oak Ferry closed	0	5	2
35	0	0	Bourne End Railway Bridge	0	2	8
34	5	2	River Wye (left bank)	0	5	6
33	7	6	Cookham Bridge	0	3	9
33	3	7	Cookham Lock	0	3	7
33	0	0	My Lady Ferry	1	5	0
31	3	0	Boulter's Lock	0	5	3
30	5	7	Maidenhead Bridge	0	1	6
30	4	1	Maidenhead Railway Bridge	1	2	1
29	2	0	Bray Lock	0	2	0
29	0	0	Maidenhaed M4 Bridge	0	1	9
28	6	1	Monkey Island (Hotel)	1	0	6
27	5	5	Oakley Court	0	7	9
26	5	6	Surly Hall Point	0	5	0
26	0	6	Boveney Lock	1	3	8
24	4	8	Windsor Railway Viaduct	0	3	4
24	1	4	Windsor Bridge	0	3	4
23	6	0	Romney Lock	0	2	9
23	3	1	Black Potts Railway Bridge	0	3	1
23	0	0	Victoria Bridge	1	3	9
21	4	1	Albert Bridge	0	6	1
20	6	0	Old Windsor Lock	0	6	8
19	7	2	'The Bells' of Ouseley	2	0	6
17	6	6	Bell Weir Lock	0	0	9
17	5	7	Colne Brook (left bank)	0	4	6
17	5	5	Runnymede Bridge	0	0	2
17	1	1	London Stone	0	2	5
16	6	6	Staines Bridge	0	0	6
16	6	0	River Colne (left bank)	0	1	9
16	4	1	Staines Railway Bridge	1	4	2
14	7	9	Penton Hook Lock	0	6	5
14	1	4	Laleham Ferry	1	1	1
14	0	3	M3 Bridge	1	1	1
13	0	3	Chertsey Lock	0	1	3
12	7	0	Chertsey Bridge	1	7	2
10	7	8	Shepperton Lock	1	3	0*
9	4	8	Walton Bridge via Desborough Channel	1	4	6
8	0	2	Sunbury Lock	2	1	3
5	6	9	Hampton Ferry	0	6	5
5	0	4	Molesey Lock	0	1	5
4	6	9	Hampton Court Bridge	0	2	5
4	4	4	River Ember right bank	0	5	1

Above Teddington				Between places		
M.	F.	Ch.		M.	F.	Ch.
3	7	3	Thames Ditton Ferry	0	1	7
3	5	6	Long Ditton Ferry	0	6	3
2	7	3	Raven's Ait (Middle)	0	7	1
2	0	2	Kingston Bridge	0	1	3
1	6	9	Kingston Railway Bridge	1	5	0
0	1	9	Teddington Lock	0	0	7
0	1	2	Teddington Barge Lock centre ...	0	1	2
0	0	0	Teddington Boundary Obelisk, approximately 293 yds. downstream of Teddington Lock			

Port of London Authority Section
Distances measured along the navigable Channel.

Sea Miles	Above London Bridge	Land Miles
16.08	P.L.A. Landward Limit	18.52
15.14	Eel Pie Island (Lower End)	17.43
15.04	Ham Landing Stage	17.32
14.55	Petersham Drawdock	16.75
13.97	Richmond Bridge	16.09
13.67	Richmond Railway Bridge	15.74
13.64	Twickenham Bridge	15.71
13.49	Richmond Lock & Footbridge (Recording Tide Gauge)	15.53
13.00	West Middlesex Sewage Outfalls	14.97
12.91	Church Ferry, Isleworth	14.87
11.88	River Brent and Grand Union Canal	13.68
11.33	Kew Bridge	13.05
11.30	Kew Pier (G.L.C.)	13.01
10.98	Kew Railway Bridge	12.64
10.22	Chiswick Bridge	11.77
10.16	University Stone, Mortlake	11.70
9.55	Barnes Railway Bridge	11.00
8.69	Chiswick Ferry Causeway	10.01
8.15	Hammersmith Pier (H.B.C.)	9.38
7.97	Hammersmith Bridge	9.18
7.73	Harrods Quay	8.90
6.92	Beverley Brook	7.97
6.54	Putney Pier (G.L.C.)	7.53
6.52	University Stone, Putney	7.51
6.45	Putney Bridge	7.43
6.31	Fulham Railway Bridge	7.27
5.74	Wandsworth Creek	6.61
5.46	Wandsworth Bridge	6.29
5.23	Fulham Generating Station	6.02
4.83	Battersea Railway Bridge	5.56
4.57	Chelsea Creek & Lots Rd. Generating Station	5.26
4.27	Battersea Road Bridge	4.92

Sea Miles	Above London Bridge	Land Miles
4.04	Albert Bridge	4.65
4.02	Cadogan Pier (P.L.A.)	4.63
3.40	Chelsea Bridge	3.92
3.31	Victoria Railway Bridge	3.81
3.18	Battersea Generating Station	3.66
2.46	Vauxhall Bridge	2.83
2.02	Lambeth Bridge	2.33
1.64	Westminster Bridge	1.89
1.60	Westminster Pier (G.L.C.)	1.84
1.32	Charing Cross Bridge	1.52
1.12	Waterloo Bridge	1.29
0.63	Blackfriars Road Bridge	0.73
0.24	Southwark Bridge	0.28
0.16	Cannon Street Railway Bridge	0.18
0.00	London Bridge	0.00
	Upper Pool	
0.00	London Bridge	0.00
0.33	Tower Pier (P.L.A. & G.L.C.) *(Recording Tide Gauge & Tower Bridge Headway Gauge)	0.38
0.49	Tower Bridge	0.56
0.73	St. Saviour's Dock	0.84
	Lower Pool	
1.05	Cherry Garden Pier *(Tower Bridge Signal Station & Headway Gauge)	1.21
1.26	Wapping Pier	1.46
1.34	Thames Tunnel	1.55
1.62	Rotherhithe Tunnel	1.87
	Limehouse Reach	
2.08	Regents Canal Dock Entrance	2.40
2.69	West India Dock Pier	3.10
3.18	Deadman Dock, Deptford	3.66
	Greenwich Reach	
3.71	Deptford Generating Station (U/end)	4.27
3.87	Deptford Creek	4.46
4.17	Greenwich Pier (G.L.C.) & foot tunnel	4.80
4.27	Greenwich Royal Naval College	4.92
	Blackwall Reach	
4.99	Victoria Wharf (U/end)	5.75
5.39	India & Millwall Dock Entrance	6.21
5.55	Blackwall Tunnel (Western)	6.39
5.73	Brunswick Wharf Generating Station (U/end)	6.60
	Bugsby's Reach	
6.08	Bow Creek (River Lee)	7.00
6.49	Blackwall Point Generating Station (U/end)	7.47
	Woolwich Reach	
7.40	Thames Flood Barrier	8.52
7.52	Thames Navigation Sub-Centre	8.66
7.76	Tate & Lyle's Jetty (U/end)	8.94
8.33	Woolwich Ferry & foot tunnel	9.59

*To ascertain tide level above Low Water datum from Tower Bridge Headway boards, subtract Headway reading from 14.8m (48.5ft)

Sea Miles	Below London Bridge	Land miles
	Gallions Reach	
8.89	Gallions or Bulls Point	10.24
9.10	King George V Dock Entrance	10.48
9.23	Thames House, Entrance Gallions (Recording Tide Gauge)	10.63
	Barking Reach	
9.87	Margaret Ness Lighthouse	11.37
10.12	Barking Creek (River Roding)	11.65
10.58	Barking Generating Station (U/end)	12.18
	Halfway Reach	
11.35	Crossness Point Lighthouse	13.07
11.68	Overhead Electric Transmission Cables	13.45
11.90	Dagenham Dock No. 4 Jetty (U/end)	13.70
12.15	Ford's Jetty (U/end) (Illuminated tide board, ferry)	13.99
12.57	Belvedere Generating Station (U/end)	14.47
	Erith Reach	
13.02	Jenningtree Point Lighthouse	14.99
13.88	Rainham Pumping Unit P.L.A.	15.98
14.41	Erith Causeway	16.59
	Erith Rands	
14.45	Coldharbour Point Lighthouse	16.64
14.85	Cunis Jetty	17.10
15.34	Rands Light	17.66
15.49	Crayfordness Lighthouse (Petroleum Limit for sea-going tankers)	17.84
	Long Reach	
15.89	Dartford Creek	18.30
16.29	Harrison's Jetty	18.76
17.22	Littlebrook Generating Station (U/end)	19.83
17.65	Dartford Tunnel	20.32
17.98	West Thurrock Oil Terminal (U/end)	20.70
	St Clements Reach	
18.75	Stoneness Lighthouse	21.59
19.14	Overhead Electric Transmission Cables	22.35
	Northfleet Hope	
20.11	Bradness Lighthouse	23.04
20.85	Tilbury Grain Terminal (U/end)	24.01
21.44	Northfleet Hope Container Terminal (L/end) Recording Tide Gauge	24.69
21.51	Tilbury Dock Entrance	24.77
21.78	Northfleet Lower Lighthouse	25.08
	Gravesend Reach	
22.00	Tilbury Cargo Jetty (U/end)	25.33
22.68	Tilbury Landing Stage (U/end)	26.12
23.13	Thames Navigation Centre, Gravesend	26.63
23.15	Royal Terrace Pier, Trinity House Pilot Station	26.66
23.52	Tilbury Generating Station (U/end)	27.08
25.12	Tilbury Buoy	28.93

Sea miles	Below London Bridge	Land miles
	Lower Hope	
25.55	Coalhouse Point Petroleum Limit (Night Navigation)	29.42
25.78	Ovens Buoy	29.67
26.49	Mucking No. 7 Buoy	30.50
27.23	Mucking No. 5 Buoy	31.36
	Sea Reach	
27.67	Lower Hope Point Beacon	31.86
27.88	Mucking No. 3 Buoy	32.10
28.50	Mucking No. 1 Buoy	32.82
28.95	West Blyth Buoy	33.34
29.20	Shell Haven Jetties (Tanker Warning Light)	33.62
30.50	Coryton Jetties (Recording Tide Gauge)	35.12
30.79	Mid Blyth Buoy	35.46
31.25	Holehaven Creek Entrance	35.99
31.85	North Thames Gas Board Jetty (Tanker Warning Light)	36.68
33.69	Chapman Buoy	38.79
33.82	Sea Reach No. 7 Buoy	38.94
34.29	East Blyth Buoy	39.49
35.58	Sea Reach No. 6 Buoy	40.97
36.08	Crowstone – London Stone Line	41.55
36.57	Sea Reach No. 5 Buoy	42.11
37.57	Southend Pier Head (Recording Tide Gauge)	43.26
38.32	Sea Reach No. 4 Buoy	44.13
39.83	Sea Reach No. 3 Buoy	45.87
41.85	Sea Reach No. 2 Buoy	48.19
43.62	Sea Reach No. 1 Buoy – P.L.A. former seaward limit Havengore Creek to Warden Point	50.23
51.44	Shivering Sand Tower (Recording Tide Guage)	59.23
	Seaward Limit	
64.82	When proceeding via Knock John Channel to a position near Black Deep No. 8 Buoy	74.64
66.32	When proceeding via North Edinburgh Channel to a position near the Tongue Light Vessel	76.37
65.82	When proceeding via Barrow Deep Channel to a position near the Barrow Deep Buoy	75.79

Note:– The above table gives the distances when the various marks are abeam of the normal Channel course.

For full coverage of the Lower Thames — Teddington to Southend see Imray Chart C2 River Thames.

Thames and Severn Canal (96)

There has been constant interest in the possible restoration of this waterway which was abandoned by orders on the 31st January 1927 (from Lechlade to Whitehall Bridge) and 9th June 1933 (from Whitehall Bridge to Walbridge). Running through the Upper Thames valley, through Sapperton Tunnel on the summit level, the canal travels through exceptionally fine countryside. The descent in Cotswold country through the Golden Valley is outstanding.

There are problems involved in the proposed restoration but none that cannot be solved. Particularly after 1840 and on the summit level leakage caused a shortage of water and techniques used recently on the Kennet and Avon Canal could be usefully employed. For many years navigation was impeded on the Upper Thames near Radcot by navigation weirs and shallows and although this problem has now been remedied it would not be possible to restore the canal entirely on its original route. As an alternative and as the Upper Thames is a navigation by statute to Cricklade Bridge the eastern end of the canal could easily be rerouted at that point.

The Stroudwater and Thames Severn Canal Trust have already restored the entrances to Sapperton Tunnel, part of the canal by Bow Bridge Lock and elsewhere.

Dimensions are given for the last years of the canal when in service.

Authority	None at present. David H. Boakes, Esq., C.Eng., M.I.Mech.E. Secretary of Stroudwater & Thames Severn Canal Trust Ltd., 1 Riveredge, Framilode, Gloucester can assist. Tel. Gloucester (0452) 740525
From and to	Junction with the Stroudwater Navigation at Wallbridge to Inglesham, junction with River Thames.
Remarks	Unnavigable at present. Canoeable in places. Rebuilt locks will have different dimensions.
Distance	28¾ miles.
Length	74ft.
Width	12ft 9ins.
Draught	3ft 6ins.
Headroom	8ft 6ins.

(The above dimensions were for craft using the waterway throughout. Wallbridge to Bourn Lock was 74ft x 16ft 1in x 5ft, Headroom 11ft 6ins. Bourn Lock was 90ft x 16ft 1in wide and was a trans-shipment lock. From Beale's Lock to Inglesham was 90ft x 12ft 9ins. This was because Brimscombe Basin was a trans-shipment point between Severn Trows and Thames Barges.

Summit Level 348ft 1in above Low Water, River Severn, 362ft 6ins above Ordnance datum.

Locks	44 (Locks 1 to 28 rise from Stroud. Locks 29 to 44 fall to Inglesham).
Branches	Cirencester 1½ miles.

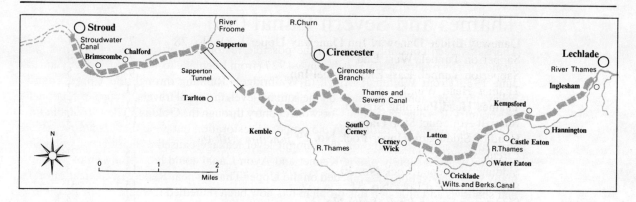

| | | Miles | Furlongs |

Tunnels   Sapperton 3808 yards.

Remarks   Restoration of the canal either side of Sapperton Tunnel and restoration work is also in progress in the area of Bowbridge Locks. Work has also taken place at South Cerney and elsewhere. Local council support has been encouraging and restoration work should go forward in a number of areas. Volunteers are urgently required.

Distance Table

Wallbridge Lower Lock No 1, junction with Stroudwater Navigation to:

	Miles	Furlongs
Wallbridge Upper Lock (Stroud) No. 2	–	2
Bowbridge Lock No. 3	–	7
Griffins Lock No. 4	1	3
Ham Mill Lock No. 5	1	5
Ridler's (Hope Mill) Lock No. 6	2	–
Gough's Orchard (Dallaway's or Lewis's) Lock No. 7	2	2
Brimscombe Basin (Trans-shipment Point)	2	4
Bourne (or Harris's) Lock No. 8	2	6
Beale's (or Wimberley) Lock No. 9	3	2
St. Mary's (or Clark's) Lock No. 10	3	5
Grist Mill (or Wallbank's) Lock No. 11	3	6
Ballinger's Lock No. 12	3	7
Chalford Wharf (Chalford Chapel) Lock No. 13	4	0½
Bell Lock No. 14	4	2½
Innell's (or Red Lion) Lock No. 15	4	4
Golden Valley Lock No. 16	4	6½
Baker's Mill, Lower Lock No. 17	5	4
Baker's Mill, Upper Lock No. 18	5	4½
Puck Mill Lower Lock No. 19	5	6½
Puck Mill Upper Lock No. 20	5	7
Whitehall Lower Lock No. 21	6	1
Whitehall Upper Lock No. 22	6	5
Bathurst Meadow Lock No. 23	6	6
Sickeridge Wood Lower Lock No. 24	6	6½
Sickeridge Wood Middle Lock No. 25	6	7
Sickeridge Wood Upper Lock No. 26	7	–
Daneway Basin, Daneway Lower Lock No. 27	7	0½

Daneway Bridge Daneway Inn Daneway Upper Lock No. 28	7	1
Sapperton Tunnel, West End	7	4
Sapperton Tunnel, East End, Tunnel Inn	9	5
Thames Head Wharf	11	3
Thames Head Pumping Station	11	5
Smerril Aqueduct Stop Gates	12	4
Head of Siddington Upper Lock No. 29 *junction with the Cirencester Branch*	15	2½
Siddington Second Lock No. 30	15	3
Siddington Third Lock No. 31	15	3½
Siddington Fourth Lock (Low) No. 32	15	4
South Cerney Upper Lock No. 33	16	5½
South Cerney Middle Lock No. 34	16	6
South Cerney Low Lock No. 35	16	6
Boxwell Spring (Little) Lock No. 36	17	4
Wilmoorway Lock (Upper) Lock No. 37	18	–
Wilmoorway Lock (Lower) Lock No. 38	18	3½
Cerney Wick Lock No. 39	19	3
Latton Junction, *junction with Wilts & Berks Canal North Wilts Branch*	20	1
Latton Lock No. 40	20	7
Latton Wharf, Cricklade	21	–
Eisey Lock No. 41	22	5
Dudgrove Double Locks (2) Nos. 42 & 43	28	1
Tail of Inglesham Lock No. 44 and *junction with River Thames*	28	6

Note on lock names
As is found on other navigations lock names tend to vary, and the names above have other designations. Mr. Boakes, Trust Secretary, suggests we list alternative names for certain locks:

Iles Mill Lock No. 11
Clothiers Lock (or Red Lion) No. 16
Twizzel's Mill Lower No. 17
Twizzel's Mill Upper No. 18
Bathurst's Meadow Upper No. 24
Daneway Basin Lock No. 27
Daneway Bridge Lock No. 28
Siddington Fourth Lock (lowest) No. 32
Boxwell Spring (Shallow) Lock No. 36
Humpback Lock No. 37
Wilmoorway Lock No. 38

Thames and Severn Canal
South Cerney Bottom Lock
in March 1951

River Trent (97)

The Trent is a very old navigation. The first Act to promote navigation was passed in 1699, but little was done to improve the river until an Act was passed in 1783. Further Acts were passed, the first in 1794 authorised the building of locks and weirs and the next in 1906 authorised the building of a further six locks, the seventh large lock at Newark was not built until 1952. These large locks are designed to a four boat standard, viz. 3 barges plus the tug can lock through together.

Powers were granted in 1955 to the British Transport Commission to fix Keadby opening railway bridge which now restricts craft to a little over 16 feet headroom at high water, and it must be noted that there is a tidal range here of 14 feet.

Originally the Trent was a navigation to Burton-on-Trent but is not now navigable above Wilden Ferry.

Nottingham is a good freight centre. The Castle houses the City Art Collection. The river is exceptionally popular in the very pleasant section from Hoveringham Ferry to Hazelford Lock. The village Cathedral, Southwell Minster, famous for its stone carvings, is only 3 miles from the river. Also nearby is Sherwood Forest.

Newark, with its Castle on the river bank has much historical interest due to its location at the junction of Fosse Way and the Great North Road. Below Newark there are only three road bridges, at Dunham (toll bridge), Gainsborough and Keadby (near Scunthorpe), although the distance is 60 miles.

The tidal reaches need great care and mooring is advised only at West Stockwith Basin or at the end of the Sheffield and South Yorkshire Navigation at Keadby. In both cases it is possible to obtain a non-tidal mooring but the right time must be selected to enter the locks. From its entrance at Trent Falls the river is tidal as far as Cromwell Lock about 52 miles above Trent Falls. Care is necessary during high spring tides in meeting the eagre or bore on the river below Gainsborough. This sometimes attains three or four feet in height, reaches Gainsborough at about the time of high water at Hull and can be felt above Torksey.

Through the towns of Newark and Nottingham the navigation leaves the river and follows parallel cuts. The river section from Beeston to Meadow Lane Lock, and from Averham Weir to Crankley Point is navigable to light craft only that can be portaged. Useful charts are issued by the Trent Boating Association for the river.

Authority	**Trent Falls to Gainsborough** Associated British Ports, Kingston House Tower, Bond Street, Hull HU1 3ER. Tel. Hull (0405) 2691/5. **Gainsborough to Wilden Ferry** British Waterways Board. (Newark Dyke is owned by the Newark Navigation Commissioners and is leased to BWB)
From and to	Trent Falls to Gainsborough. Gainsborough to Wilden Ferry (6 miles from Derby).
Connections	The River Trent has junction with the following waterways: The Grand Union Canal at Trent Junction. Trent and Mersey Canal at Derwent mouth. Beeston Cut and Nottingham Canal. Fossdyke Canal at Torksey. Chesterfield Canal and River Idle at West Stockwith. Sheffield and South Yorkshire Navigation at Keadby.

Distances
Trent Falls to Gainsborough, 26¼ miles.
Gainsborough to Wilden Ferry, 68½ miles.

Length
Below Cromwell Lock, unlimited
Cromwell Lock Top Gate to Intermediate, 187ft.
Cromwell Lock, 237ft. (Intermediate to Lower Gate, but, due to the apron at low water, the length is reduced to 195ft.) Cromwell Lock to Nottingham, 190ft.
Holme has a small lock as well as a barge lock length 94ft. 7½ins.
(Nottingham Canal 82ft)

Beam
Below Cromwell Lock, unlimited.
Locks are 30ft. wide but the limiting width is at Newark Nether Railway Bridge which is 19ft. 6ins.
(This dimension applies only to craft 120ft. long, and is reduced to 17ft. 9ins. for a vessel 142ft. long owing to the bend upstream of the lock).
(Nottingham Canal 14ft 6ins)

Draught
Below Cromwell Lock, 7ft. 3ins.
Tidal section, 7 to 10ft., depending on the tidal level.

Headroom
Newark Nether Railway Bridge, 11ft at ordinary level for craft with a width of 15ft or less, the headroom at ordinary water level is 12ft 3ins. (Nottingham Canal 8ft). Newark Nether Railway Bridge is upstream of **Newark Nether Lock**.

Locks
11. Lock gates worked by lock-keepers. Fall from Wilden Ferry.
There are two locks on the Nottingham Canal which forms a portion of the through route. This canal is listed separately.(82ft x 14ft 6ins x 8ft headroom)

Tow-path
Wilden Ferry to Gainsborough.

Bridges
Numerous bridges, including one fixed railway bridge at Keadby between Trent Falls and Gainsborough.

Speed limit and bye-laws

Excessive speed is contrary to the Bye-laws.
All users of the Trent should obtain a copy of the Bye-laws for the Trent and particular care should be taken to observe all signals. There are very few regulations affecting the use of pleasure craft on the river. Yachtsmen should apply to British Waterways Board or the Dock Office at Hull for information.

Approx. time taken to navigate	Up river, from Gainsborough, about 24 hours. Down river, to Gainsborough, about 15 hours.	

Pilotage — Pilotage is advisable below Cromwell Lock due to shoals, many of which are in the centre of the river and are often shifting. Enquiries should be made as pilotage may be compulsory by the time this book is issued.

Navigation — It is important to give way to vessels which cannot pass port to port due to tidal and draught considerations. Careful watch should be made for the weirs, which need to be avoided at times of high water; they total 11 in all. The river needs very careful navigation and pilotage in the tidal section is necessary. For strangers local enquiries are advised.

Canoeing note — Canoeing generally commences at Haywood Bridge, about 5 miles east of Stafford though there are a number of reports of canoeists coming down from as high up as Trentham. The Trent and Mersey Canal follows most of the route.

Special note — Below Nottingham there is some commercial traffic making a big wash and unable to give way to small craft. Great care is necessary. Pleasure craft using the river must carry adequate anchor and cable in case of breakdown. This river needs an experienced skipper and great care must be taken at the 9 weirs.

Tides — It is high water at Trent Falls between 45 minutes and one hour after Hull—Springs rise about 19ft., neaps about 12ft. It is high water at Gainsborough at about 2 hours 30 minutes after Hull.

Facilities — There are eleven boatyards and plenty of places for refreshment and shopping.

Distance Table
Wilden Ferry to:

	Miles	Furlongs
British Waterways, Shardlow Depot	—	1½
Derwent Mouth, *junction with Trent and Mersey Canal*	1	3
Sawley Flood Lock No. 1	2	0½
Sawley Lock No. 2 (two locks side by side)	2	4
Head of Cranfleet Cut, *junction with Grand Union Canal Erewash Section-left, and junction with Soar Mouth or Red Hill Branch-right*	3	3
Cranfleet, or Old Sal's, Lock No. 3	4	1
Thrumpton Ferry	4	5½
Barton Plaster Wharf	6	1½
Barton Ferry	6	3¼
Beeston Lock No. 4 and *commencement of Beeston Cut*	8	3½
Lenton Chain, *termination of Beeston Cut, and junction with Nottingham Canal*	11	—
Meadow Lane Lock, Nottingham, *termination of Nottingham Canal, and junction with Main River*	13	3½
Nottingham, junction with Grantham Canal (now abandoned except for 1st lock and short length)	13	5

Distance Table

					Miles	Furlongs
Holme Lock No. 5	...	...	...	...	15	6
Colwick Top Roving	...	...	...	...	16	6
Radcliffe Ferry	...	...	...	...	18	1
Stoke Bardolph Lock No. 6	...	...	...	...	18	6½
Stoke Bardolph Ferry	...	...	...	...	19	6
Burton Lane End	...	...	...	...	21	—
East Bridgford Wharf	...	...	...	...	23	4
Gunthorpe Lock No. 7	...	...	...	...	23	4½
Hoveringham Ferry	...	...	...	...	25	4
Hazelford Ferry	...	...	...	...	27	5½
Hazelford Lock No. 8	...	...	...	...	28	2½
Fiskerton Ferry	...	...	...	...	29	4½
Fiskerton Wharf	...	...	...	...	30	0½
East Stoke Wharf	...	...	...	...	31	3
Farndon Ferry	...	...	...	...	33	1½
Averham Weir, *commencement of Newark Dyke*					34	3½
Farndon Field Maltkiln	...	...	...	...	35	4
Newark, Plaster Wharf	...	...	...	...	36	1
Newark, Mill Bridge	...	...	...	...	36	3½
Newark, Town Lock No. 9	...	...	...	...	36	5
Newark, Town Wharf	...	...	...	...	36	6½
Newark, Cow Lane Wharf	...	...	...	37	0½
Newark, tail of Nether Lock No. 10	...	...			37	5
Crankley Point, and *termination of Newark Dyke*					38	2½
Muskham Ferry	...	...	...	...	40	4
Cromwell Lock No. 11	...	...	...	...	42	1½
Collingham Wharf	...	...	...	...	43	5
Carlton Ferry	...	...	...	...	45	1½
Carlton Wharf	...	...	...	...	45	2¼
Besthorpe Staithe	...	...	...	...	46	3½
Meering Ferry	...	...	...	...	46	7½
Sutton Wharf	...	...	...	...	47	1½
Girton Lane End	...	...	...	...	48	5
South Clifton Wharf	...	...	...	...	50	6
Marnham Ferry	...	...	...	...	51	2
North Clifton Lane End	...	...	...	...	52	3½
Dunham Bridge	...	...	...	...	54	1½
Laneham Ferry	...	...	...	...	56	—
Torksey, *junction with Fossdyke Canal*	...	...		58	2
Torksey Railway Bridge (E.R.)	...	...			58	7
Trent Port, Marton	...	...	...	...	60	4
Littleborough Ferry	...	...	...	...	61	6
Knaith	...	...	...	...	...	63	4
Gainsborough Road Bridge	...	...	...	68	4
Morton	...	...	...	...	...	70	3
Walkerith—Walkeringham Ferry	...	...		71	7
West Stockwith, *junction with Chesterfield Canal*				73	—
West Stockwith, *junction with River Idle*	...		73	1
Gunthorpe Lincolnshire	...	...	...	...	75	1
Wildsworth	...	...	...	...	...	75	6
Owston Ferry	...	...	...	...	...	76	3

Distance Table

									Miles	*Furlongs*
Kelfield	...	...	...	...	...	...	...	...	78	5
Susworth	...	...	...	...	...	...	...	...	79	4
Butterwick Ferry	...	...	...	...	...	...	...	81	6
Burringham Ferry	...	...	...	...	...	...	...	84	2
Althorpe Ferry	...	...	...	...	...	...	...	84	4
Keadby, Railway Bridge (E.R.)	...	...	...	...	...	...	85	1
Keadby, *junction with Sheffield and South Yorkshire Navigation-Stainforth and Keadby Canal*	...	...	...	...	...	85	6
Arncott's Ferry	...	...	...	...	...	...	...	88	5
Burton Stather Ferry	...	...	...	...	...	...	91	6
Trent Falls, *junction with River Humber and River Ouse*	...	...	94	6

Distances at and below the tail of Meadow Lane Lock, Nottingham, include the distance of 2 miles 3½ furlongs on the Nottingham Canal between Lenton Chain and Meadow Lane Lock as follows:

Nottingham Canal

Nottingham, Meadow Lane Lock, junction with River Trent to:

							Miles	*Furlongs*
Nottingham, Boot's Warehouses and *junction with Popular Cut* (¼ mile) to Manvers Street	...	...	...	...	...	—	6
Nottingham, British Waterways, Wilford Street, Warehouses	...	1	1
Castle Lock	...	...	...	...	...	...	...	1	1½
Lenton Chain, *junction with Beeston Cut*	...	...	...	...	2	3½

Trent Navigation: Stoke Bardolph Lock under repair Easter 1981

Trent and Mersey Canal (98)

This canal was formerly known as the Grand Trunk Canal, and was one of Brindley's but was not completed until after his death. His ancient and historic tunnel, the old Harecastle Tunnel, can still be seen though it has not been used for many years. Boatmen will notice on navigation far inside the tunnel, branch waterways leading into the Main Line which were constructed to lead right up to coal faces underground.

This canal was promoted by Acts in 1766, 1770, 1775, 1776, 1783, 1797 (two Acts), 1802, 1809 and 1827. A cross-country canal, it has many delightful sections, in spite of the Potteries which are encountered en route. Headroom is restricted at Harecastle Tunnel, where there is a height gauge to assist boatmen. Sections of the canal near the Anderton lift have been affected by salt mining. At Kidsgrove, a nearby village on the hill near Harecastle, is Brindley's tomb, now restored, which is often visited by students of his work. The area by Harecastle is in contrast to the section by Shugborough Park National Trust, where the canal skirts the outside of the park through a tunnel of trees. Sir Josiah Wedgwood had great faith in Brindley and backed the proposed canal from the Trent to the Mersey with a very vocal campaign. The section from Trent Lock to Great Haywood was completed in 1772 the year of Brindley's death, but the section on to the Mersey was held up by the work in Harecastle Tunnel which was not completed until 1777. The campaign of Sir Josiah Wedgwood bore fruit very quickly and the Potteries grew to become a very industrialised and prosperous area.

The works to build the canal were formidable for their time; there were 164 aqueducts, 109 road bridges and 5 tunnels. The summit at Harecastle is 395 feet above sea level. It is interesting to note that in Brindley's original survey he allowed for a draught of 5 feet 6 inches throughout, which is very different from its present state today.

The canal used to be famous for its electric tug at Harecastle. The second tunnel at Harecastle, built by Telford, suffered from subsidence which made the towing path unusable, and the tug used to tow strings of barges through at certain set hours but alas, commercial traffic on this section has now all but vanished. It will also be noticed that some of the tunnels had faulty alignments and vision through them is obstructed, special care and good headlights being necessary.

After passing the Anderton area, the canal goes through pleasant country although industrial development is not far away. Middlewich and Marston are salt towns and subsidence is noticeable. From Middlewich to Wheelock it is mainly industrial but nearby Sandbach is an interesting old town. The route follows through Harecastle and the Potteries, about which Arnold Bennett wrote; these include the towns of Burslem, Hanley, Tunstall, Stoke-on-Trent and Longton.

The Wedgwood Institute at Burslem is one of the show places of the area, which is very intensely industrialised. At Etruria is the Caldon Branch and in spite of surroundings at its commencement, it is a very lovely waterway, particularly the Churnet Valley. The Leek Branch Canal, though not open to Leek itself, is a novel engineering project with its 'up and over' section.

At Stoke the canal comes close to the Trent which follows it to Great Haywood and across to Trent Lock. There is attractive wooded country after the new Meaford Power Station, but the real scenic section of the waterway begins below Aston Lock when the Trent Valley opens out to parkland with country mansions such as Ingestre and Shugborough. Stone is a canal centre and a good place for excursions into the neighbourhood, this town has associations with the painter Peter de Wint and Admiral Jarvis.

After leaving Great Haywood Junction the canal passes Wolseley Park, near Colwich where the hills rise to 500ft. above sea level. At Great Haywood is the famous 14 arch private bridge built by the Earls of Essex as a short cut to Cannock Chase for hunting. At Cannock the canal runs into a coal mining area mixed with the wild natural scenery of the

Chase, and nearby is the lovely village of King's Bromley, the home of Lady Godiva. Places not to be hurried through are Armitage, where the tunnel has been opened out, and Handsacre. The Swan Inn at Fradley Junction, is a haunt of canal folk, and is not far from Lichfield which has a fine, if much restored cathedral.

The Trent enters the canal at Alrewas for a short distance, and great care should be taken after a spell of rainy weather. Burton-on-Trent is a famous brewing town and keen canal navigators claim that here beer tastes best. Burton's reputation dates back to the days when the monks discovered how good the water was for brewing.

The section on to Nottingham is mainly through pasture land. Swarkestone Bridge over the Trent is well known, this ancient structure is almost a mile long. Near Willington is the famous public school Repton, which dates from Tudor times. The aqueduct over the river Dove nearby is one of the longest in the Midlands and has nine arches.

One of the three main cross country routes, no inland waterway traveller should miss cruising on this canal with its extraordinary mixture of industrial landscape and scenic beauty.

At the time of going to press the British Waterways Board had removed the last of the old tow-path in Harecastle Tunnel which was an obstruction to some boats. This tunnel does seem to deter many navigators but their fears are groundless and the Trent and Mersey deserves to be better known. It is surprising that so little hire cruiser development has come to this waterway.

Authority	British Waterways Board.
From and to	Derwent Mouth, River Trent, to Preston Brook, Bridgewater Canal.
Connections	River Trent at Derwent Mouth.
	Coventry Canal at Fradley.
	Caldon Branch at Etruria.
	Staffordshire and Worcestershire at Great Haywood.
	Burslem Branch at Burslem.
	Macclesfield Canal at Hardingswood, via Hall Green Branch.
	Shropshire Union Canal at Middlewich, via Wardle Branch.
	River Weaver at Anderton, via Anderton Lift.
	Bridgewater Navigation at Preston Brook.
Distance	Main Line, 93½ miles.
	Caldon Branch, 17½ miles.
	Leek Branch, 2¾ miles. This was closed to navigation by Act of 1944. The first 2 miles act as a feeder to the Main Line.
	Leek Wharves to River Churnet aqueduct is now filled in.
	In navigating this branch it should be noted that a narrow boat can be winded only at the west end of Leek Tunnel.
Length	70ft.
Beam	7ft.
	Derwent Mouth to Horninglow Wharf, 10ft.
	Horninglow Wharf to Croxton Aqueduct, 7ft.
	Croxton Aqueduct to Preston Brook, 9ft.
	Croxton Aqueduct will only pass craft 7ft. beam.
Draught	3ft.

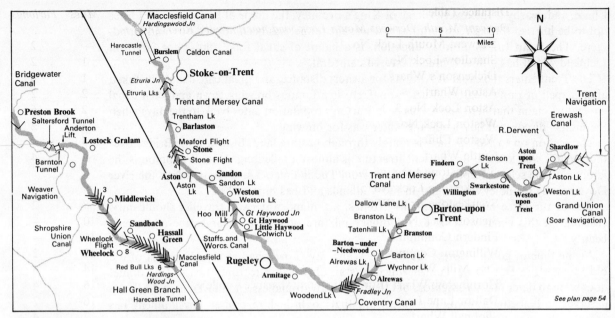

Headroom 5ft. 9ins.

Locks

76. Lock Nos. 1—40, rise from Derwent Mouth.
Lock Nos. 41—75, fall to Middlewich.
Nos. 76 is a stop lock—Level.
Hall Green Branch, 1 stop lock—Level.
Caldon Branch, 17 locks.
Nos. 1—9, rise from Etruria. Nos. 9—17, fall from Hazelhurst.
Wardle Lock Branch, 1 lock. Rise from junction with Main Line at
Middlewich to Middlewich Branch of S.U. Canal.
Main Line Locks Nos. 41—54, 57—66, are in duplicate side by side.
Flood warning lights on some locks.

Tunnels

Preston Brook—No Tow-path		1,239 yds.
Saltersford	,,	,,	424 yds.
Barnton	,,	,,	572 yds.
Harecastle*	,,	,,	2926 yds.
Froghall Caldon Branch—No tow-path		76 yds.
Leek (Leek Branch)†	,,	,,	130 yds.

Armitage Tunnel was opened out in 1971 due to mining subsidence.

Bridges

Numerous.

Tow-path

There is a tow-path throughout navigation except in certain tunnels.

Facilities

There are no less than nineteen boatyards and plenty of town and village shopping and inns.

* Navigation through this tunnel is under the control of the Tunnel Keeper.
† Leek Branch is closed above River Churnet Aqueduct.

Distance Table   Miles Furlongs

Derwent Mouth, Derwent Mouth Lock, and junction with River Trent to:

	Miles	Furlongs
Derwent Mouth Lock No. 1	—	2
Shardlow Lock No. 2	1	2
Dickenson's Wharf	1	6
Aston Wharf	2	2
Aston Lock No. 3	2	6
Weston Lock No. 4	4	2
Weston Cliffe	5	—
Cuttle Wharf	6	4

Swarkestone Junction, *junction with Derby Canal,** and head of

	Miles	Furlongs
Swarkestone Lock No. 5	7	—
Swarkestone Brick Wharf	7	2
Stenson Lock No. 6	10	—
Findern Common	11	—
Willington Common	12	2
Clay Mills Wharf	14	6
Horninglow Wharf (Burton-on-Trent distance ½ mile)	16	4
Dallow Lane Lock No. 7	16	7
Shobnall Wharf	17	4
Branstone Lock No. 8	18	4
Tatenhill Lock No. 9	21	—
Barton Turn Lock No. 10	21	3
Wichnor Lock No. 11 Wharf	23	—

Canal enters and leaves River Trent between Alrewas and Wichnor. When passing the weir, boats should navigate with care and close to protective fendering. In times of flood, a passage should not be attempted.

	Miles	Furlongs
Alrewas Lock No. 12	24	3
Bagnall Lock No. 13	25	—
Common Lock No. 14, Fradley Bottom	25	2

Then follows Hunt's Lock No. 15 and Keeper's Lock No. 16

Fradley Junction, *junction with Coventry Canal* and head of Fradley

	Miles	Furlongs
Junction Lock No. 17	26	2
Fradley Middle Lock No. 18	27	—
Shade House Lock No. 19	27	1
Wood End Lock No. 20	27	2
King's Bromley	28	4
Handsacre Wharf	30	4
Armitage	30	6
Armitage Tunnel	31	6
Brereton Wharf	32	6
Brereton Foundry	33	6
Rugeley Wharf	34	—
Rugeley Plaster Wharf	34	2
Brindley's Bank	35	—
Colwich Lock No. 21	37	5
Haywood Lock No. 22	38	7

Haywood Junction, *junction with Staffordshire and Worcestershire Canal*—Main Line

	Miles	Furlongs
Canal—Main Line	39	—
Hoo Mill Lock No. 23	39	6
Ingestre and Shirleywich	41	2
Shirleywich Salt Works	42	—

*Closed
throughout

Distance Table

	Miles	Furlongs
Weston Lock No. 24	42	4
Sandon Wharf	43	6
Sandon Lock No. 25	44	4
Aston Lock No. 26	46	5
Stone and Stone Lock Nos. 27, 28, 29 and 30	48	5
Meaford Lock Nos. 31, 32, 33 and 34	49	6
Meaford Power Station	50	4
Barlaston Boat Yard	52	—
Trentham Lock No. 35	53	2
Hem Heath	53	6
Sideway Flint Mills	55	6
Stoke Basin	56	2
Stoke Wharf	56	4
Stoke, junction with Newcastle Branch (derelict)	56	6
Stoke Lock No. 36	57	—
Cockshute Lock No. 37*	57	4
Etruria Bottom Lock No. 38*	57	6
Etruria Summit Lock No. 40 and Toll Office	57	7
Etruria, *junction with Caldon Branch*	58	—
Etruria, Wedgwood's Works	58	4
Etruria Ironworks	58	4
Burslem Junction, *junction with Burslem Branch*	59	2
Newport	59	4
Middleport Anderton Co.'s Boat Dock	59	6
Longport Wharf	60	—
Tunstall	61	—
Chatterley Basin	61	2
Chatterley, south end of Harecastle Tunnel	61	6
Kidsgrove, north end of Harecastle Tunnel	63	3
Harding's Wood Junction, *junction with Hall Green Branch leading to the Macclesfield Canal*	63	5
Red Bull Top Lock No. 41	63	6
Harding's Wood	63	7
Red Bull Wharf	64	1
Red Bull Bottom Lock No. 46	64	5
Lawton Lock No. 47 Top	65	3
Lawton Lock No. 52 Bottom	65	7
Snapes Aqueduct	66	1
Thurlwood Lock No. 53 and 54	66	6
Chellshill Aqueduct	67	3
Pierpoint Lock Nos. 55 and 56	68	3
Hassall Green Lock Nos. 57 and 58	69	—
Malkin's Bank Lock No. 59 Top	69	4
Malkin's Bank Lock No. 64 Bottom	70	—
Wheelock Lock No. 65	70	2
Wheelock Lock No. 66	70	2½
Wheelock Wharf	70	3
Rookery Bridge Wharf	71	7
Rookery Bridge, Bone and Manure Works	72	1

Portal of the Harecastle Tunnel in 1976

*Bradshaw lists different names for the following locks: No. 37 Fenton's, No. 38 Twyford's, No. 39 Johnson's.

Distance Table

	Miles	Furlongs
Moss Wharf	72	5
Crow Nest Lock No. 67	73	3
Booth Lane Lock Nos. 68 and 69	73	6
Rumps Lock No. 70	75	4
King's Lock No. 71	76	2
Middlewich, *junction with Wardle Lock Branch leading to Shropshire*		
Union Canal	76	3
Middlewich Top Lock No. 72	76	4
Middlewich Bottom Lock No. 74	76	5½
Middlewich Public Wharf	76	5
Middlewich Large Lock No. 75 ('Big Lock')	77	1
Croxton Aqueduct	77	5
Billinge Green	81	3
Broken Cross	82	3
Lostock Gralam	83	2
Wincham	84	3
Marbury Wharf	85	7
Anderton Public Wharf	86	3
Anderton, *junction with Anderton Lift Branch of River Weaver*		
Navigation	86	5
Soot Hill Wharf	86	7
Barnton Coal Wharf, and south end of Barnton Tunnel	87	3
North end of Barnton Tunnel	87	7
South end of Saltersford Tunnel	88	1
North end of Saltersford Tunnel	88	3
Saltersford Wharf	88	5
Little Leigh	89	5
Acton Bridge Wharf	90	1
Dutton Wharf	91	3
Dutton Stop Lock No. 76, south end of Preston Brook	92	4
North end of Preston Brook Tunnel, and *junction with Preston Brook*		
Branch of the Bridgewater Canal	93	3

Caldon Branch

Etruria, junction with Main Line, to:

	Miles	Furlongs
Etruria Wharf, Etruria Lock No. 1 and 2 staircases	—	2
Shelton	—	4
Caldon Place Lock No. 3 Planet Lock	—	6
Joiner's Square, Hanley Corporation Wharf	1	4
Joiner's Square	1	6
Hanley	2	—
Ivy House Wharf	2	2
Ivy House, Hanley and Bucknall Colliery	2	4
Prime's Pit	3	—
The Abbey, Gas Lime Wharf	3	6
Milton, junction with Foxley Branch Canal (now closed)	4	4
Engine Lock No. 4	5	4
Heakley Wharf	5	6
Stockton Brook Lock Nos. 5, 6, 7, and 8	6	6
Stockton Brook Lock No. 9	6	7
Stanley	7	4

Hazelhurst Lks (3)

Leek Branch

Leek Tunnel

Endon Basin

Aqueduct

Cheddleton Lks (2)

Trent and Mersey Canal

Engine Lk No.4

Stockton Brook Lks (5)

Milton

Woods Lk No.15

River Churnet

Caldon Canal

Hanley

Churnet Lk

Consall Quarry

Consall Mill Lk No.17

Froghall Tunnel

Froghall Basin

Planet Lk

Etruria Jn
Etruria Lks (2)

Stoke on Trent

Remains of Uttoxeter Canal

N

0 1 2 3 4 5 Miles

Caldon Canal: Etruria Lks

Photo: British Waterways Board

Distance Table

	Miles	Furlongs
Park Lane Wharf	8	4
Hazelhurst Junction, *junction with Leek Branch* and head of Hazelhurst		
Top Lock No. 10 Hazelhurst Lock Nos. 11 and 12 follow ...	9	4
Hollybush Inn, Denford	9	7
Wall Grange Public Wharf	10	2
Cheddleton Wharf and Cheddleton Lock Nos. 13 and 14	11	2
Woods Lock No. 15	12	—
Canal enters River Churnet, Churnet Lock No. 16*	13	4
Consall Quarry	14	2
Canal leaves River Churnet	14	6
Consall, Flint Mill and Consall Lock No. 17	15	—
Froghall	16	6
Froghall Tunnel	16	7
Froghall Basin	17	4

Leek Branch

Hazelhurst Junction, junction with Caldon Branch, to:

Leek Tunnel	2	—
Wall Grange Farm Bridge	2	4
River Churnet Aqueduct (canal filled in from this point)	2	6
Leek Wharves	3	2

Burslem Branch

Length from Burslem Junction, junction with Main Line, to:

Burslem	—	3

Hall Green Branch ... ...

Length from Harding's Wood Junction, junction with Main Line to:

Hall Green, *Junction with Macclesfield Canal,* halfway between the two stop locks	1	4

Wardle Lock Branch

Extends from a junction with the Main Line at the tail of Wardle Lock, Middlewich, to the head of Wardle Lock only, where it joins the Middlewich Branch of the Shropshire Union Canal Section (1 lock, Wardle).

River Tyne (99)

The River Tyne has always been a tidal navigation though no statutes were promoted to improve the navigation in early days. It is industrially developed on a considerable scale in the tidal reaches, but the stretches above the tidal limit are used by canoeists as they are very wild and beautiful and well wooded. Newcastle-on-Tyne, once a station on the Roman Wall has many interesting buildings particularly those dating from the Regency period.

Authority   Port of Tyne Authority, Berwick Street, Newcastle-upon-Tyne, NE 1 5HS
Tel. Newcastle (0632) 325541
Telegrams: Tyneport, Newcastle-upon-Tyne.

* Some times called Oakmeadow Lock.

From and to	Hedwin Streams to Harbour Mouth.
Distance	19 miles.
Length	Unlimited.
Beam	„
Draught	at Newburn L.W.S.T. 9ft. at Harbour Entrance 30ft.
Headroom	at Newburn H.W.S.T. 21ft.
Locks	None. Tidal throughout.
Tow-path	None on river or branches.
Connections	Lemington Gut ½ mile, is now filled in. River Derwent navigable ¾ mile River Team navigable ¾ mile River Ouseburn navigable ½ mile Navigable for small River Don navigable ½ mile craft only, at high tide.
General remarks	This navigation is used mainly by sea-going craft. Care should be taken in navigation and in passing the High Level Bridge, where the depth varies considerably.
Tides	High tide at Newcastle 12 minutes after Tynemouth. Spring Tides rise 15ft.
Canoeing note	The northern Tyne rises in the Cheviot Hills and is canoeable from Bellingham but the river is very shallow in dry weather to the confluence with the southern Tyne. This rises at Alston Common and is canoeable in high water from Haltwhistle. Below the confluence it is wider and needs to be navigated after rain to avoid portages.

Distance Table

Left Bank			Right Bank	
Miles	*Furlongs*		*Miles*	*Furlongs*
		Boundary Stone at Hedwin Streams to:		
		Ryton	—	5
1	4	Newburn Bridge		
		Stella...	2	5
		Blaydon	3	1
3	6	Junction with Lemington Gut		
4	3	Scotswood Suspension Bridge	4	3
		Junction with River Derwent	4	7
5	5	Opposite Elswick Station		
		Junction with River Team	6	5
7	3	Redheugh Bridge	7	3
7	4	King Edward Bridge	7	4
		Immediately above the High Level Bridge is a swing bridge.		

Distance Table

Left Bank				Right Bank	
Miles	Furlongs			Miles	Furlongs
7	7	Newcastle High Level Bridge, Newcastle-left;			
		Gateshead-right		7	7
8	6	*Junction with Ouseburn*			
		Pelaw Main Staithes		11	3
11	6	Walker, River Police Station			
		Hebburn Ferry Landing		12	5
12	7	Wallsend Shipyard			
13	5	Willington Gut ...			
		Jarrow, Palmer's Dock		14	2
14	3	Howdon Authorities Yard			
		West end of Jarrow Slake		15	—
15	4	East end of Jarrow Slake; *the River Don enters*			
		Jarrow Slake at the south-west corner		15	4
		Entrance to Tyne Dock		15	7
16	4	Entrance to Albert Edward Dock ...			
		South Shields Ferry Landing		16	8
17	1	North Shields Ferry Landing			
18	1	Tynemouth, opposite Black Middens.			
18	7	Mouth of Harbour		18	7

River Ure(100)

This extension to the Yorkshire Ouse Navigation was promoted by Acts in 1767 and 1820. This section is considerably more attractive than the Ouse below Linton Lock. Lonely country with only the small town of Boroughbridge en route, it forms ideal cruising country and from Boroughbridge upstream it is well wooded.

Authority	British Waterways Board, 1 Dock Street, Leeds 1. Tel. Leeds (0532) 36741/7. Telegrams: 'Britwater, Leeds'.
From and to	Junction with the River Ouse to junction with the Ripon Canal at Oxclose Lock.
Distance	7½ miles.
Length	57ft.
Beam	14ft. 6ins.
Draught	5ft.
Headroom	8ft. 6ins.
Locks	2. Lock gates worked by boat crews. Fall from junction with Ripon Canal.

Bridges	2.
Tow-path	Throughout navigation.
Connections	With the River Swale at Swale Nab. This is navigable to Myton, a distance of about 1 mile, but beware of dredger mooring wires.

Distance Table

Swale Nab, junction with River Ouse and junction with River Swale, to:

	Miles	Furlongs
Entrance to Boroughbridge Cut	2	3
Milby Lock No. 1	2	4
Boroughbridge Wharf	2	7
Warwick's Brewery	3	—
Langthorpe Landing	3	3
Green's Landing	4	—
Brampton Landing	5	1
Westwick Lock No. 2	5	1
Newby Hall Landing	6	4
Sugar Hill Landing	7	4
Junction with Ripon Canal	8	—

River Wansbeck (Northumberland) (101)

This is a new navigation formed by impounding the river which has created a riverside park, having general amenities for recreation including camp sites, car parks, picnic area etc.

Authority	Wansbeck District Council, Council Offices, Bedlington, Northumberland NE22 5TV. Tel. Bedlington (0670) 82212.

This is a new navigation and includes a new lock in the tidal estuary which will take craft up to 30ft long by 8ft beam with a draught of 5ft 3ins. Headroom is approximately 8ft 6ins. Lock gates are worked manually by the warden, who is normally at the riverside park upstream but will attend the lock by appointment. Lock gear can be mechanised if demand makes this necessary. Opening times of the lock are regulated by the tides. Craft drawing 5ft 3ins or less can enter the estuary one hour either side of HWOST. At HWON the draught is only 2ft 3ins. The lock is ⅔ of a mile from the sea and the amenity lake over 2½ miles long.

The Wash (102)

This section has been compiled with the assistance of Mr L. Critchley, whose help is gratefully acknowledged.

This is the sea area into which the rivers Welland, Witham, Nene and Great Ouse flow. It offers a sea link between these rivers, but the crossing is only suitable for craft capable of some off-shore sailing. Narrow beam craft with a lot of top hamper should not attempt to cross the Wash unless they are compelled and have sought local advice. The tides run fast in the channels which are well buoyed and lit, but the area abounds in sand banks which change frequently. The tides rise to 25 feet at springs and even on a fine day, when the tide turns against the wind a nasty short chop develops where an hour before it has been quite calm. To the experienced yachtsman a landfall in the Wash is not more difficult to make than any other, but those of lesser experience should seek advice from the authorities or members of local river clubs when planning to cross the Wash.

Members of local clubs are willing to escort or pilot boats if times are convenient. There are also a number of fishermen and retired pilots who are willing to do a trip for a fee, and the harbour masters are often willing to make the necessary introduction.

River Nene, Wisbech

Authority	Fenland District Council
Port Manager and Pilot Manager	Captain R. Kerr, Nene Parade, Wisbech. Tel. Wisbech (0954) 61369 and 2125, 2701 (night)

River Welland, Fosdyke

Authority	Anglian Water Authority, Welland and Nene River Division, North Street, Oundle. Tel. Oundle (083 22) 3366/7.
Pilotage	The pilotage authority is the Boston and Spalding Pilotage Authority, 5 South Square, Boston, Lincs and it is understood that the pilot is available to that authority on a casual basis. The AWA is the authority responsible for leisure and similar amenities. Yachtsmen would do well to seek the advice of local fishermen.

River Witham, Boston

Authority	Upstream of Boston Sluice the river is controlled by the British Waterways Board. Downstream of Boston Sluice, Boston Port Authority.
Port Manager	Captain A. T. Harris. Tel. Boston (0205) 65571
Harbour Master	Captain G. Hulland. Tel. Boston (0205) 62328
Pilotage	Boston and Spalding Pilotage Authority, 5 South Square, Boston, Lincs. Tel. Boston (0205) 62267.

River Great Ouse, Kings Lynn

Authority	The Kings Lynn Conservancy Board, Harbour Office, Common Staithe, Kings Lynn.
Harbour Master	Pilot Master and Tug Manager—Captain D.W. Garside, M.I.N., A.M. Inst.T.A.

Mr Lou Doubleday of 40 Church Drove, Outwell, Wisbech, Cambs. PE14 8RN, acts as Pilot for all rivers, particulary from the Middle Level, across the Wash. Tel. Wisbech (0945) 773285.

River Wear (103)

A number of Acts were promoted to establish this navigation in 1716, 1726, 1747, 1759 (two Acts), 1785, 1809, 1819 and 1830. This is a commercial waterway though the country above Sunderland is pleasant cruising country but it is only possible on a favourable tide. Spring tides flow to Chester-le-Street. Beyond this point is a very rocky stretch of river.

Authority	Port of Sunderland Authority, Barrack Street, Sunderland, Tyne and Wear SR1 2BU. Tel. Sunderland (0783) 40411
From and to	Sunderland, Wearmouth Bridge to Chester-le-Street. The Borough of Sunderland's jurisdiction ceases at Biddick Ford.
Distance	10⅜ miles.
Length	Unlimited.
Beam	,,
Draught	4ft. 4ins. M.H.W.S. at Biddick Ford. At the Port of Sunderland a minimum Depth of 18ft. 9ins. M.L.W.S.
Headroom	10ft.
Locks	None.
Tides	Spring Tidal range 14ft. 9ins. Neap Tidal range 7ft. 9ins.
Canoeing note	The river is very difficult above Chester-le-Street, and there is little useful water until Durham is reached. Here there is about 2½ miles of excellent water, but above and below is impracticable.

Distance Table					Miles	Furlongs
Chester-le-Street to:						
Biddick Ford	...	...	...	...	1	2
Lambton Castle	...	...	...	...	1	4
Fatfield	...	...	...	...	3	—
Cox Green ...	...	...	...	...	4	3
Hylton Boat House		...	...	...	6	7
Sunderland (Wearmouth Bridge)			...		10	3

River Weaver (104)

This river was originally made navigable under Acts passed in 1720, 1734, 1760, 1807, 1825 and 1829. The jurisidiction of the British Waterways Board commences at Winsford Bridge but under average conditions it is possible to go above the bridge into the top flash and bottom flash, a distance of just over 2 miles. There are shallows, and care is needed in the flashes which are lakes caused by subsidence of the ground, due to pumping the salt from underneath. The flashes should not be navigated without careful local enquiry.

This is 'salt country' where a number of towns have irregular streets and crooked buildings caused by the loss of the salt underground. Northwich is a pleasant town of black and white domestic architecture which shows dramatically the effect of brine pumping. The stately home Vale Royal is nearby. Winsford and Middlewich are also salt towns and are essentially industrial. The countryside, apart from the outskirts of the towns, is pleasant and the river is worth a visit, but care is needed as the river carries considerably more commercial traffic than is usual on our inland waterways.

Frodsham Lock, has been closed for many years as craft prefer to travel via Weston Marsh Lock. Downstream of Frodsham Lock is a BWB waterway but their jurisdiction ceases at Frodsham Bridge. From Frodsham Bridge to the junction of the River Weaver with the Manchester Ship Canal opposite the mouth of Weston Marsh Lock the river was not under the jurisdiction of the old Weaver Navigation Trustees and therefore was not transferred to the BWB. The Manchester Ship Canal Company have certain responsibilities with regard to the maintenance of navigable depths up to the mills at Frodsham Bridge but apart from this the river at this point is an unadopted water.

Frodsham can be visited to see a fine partly Norman church and the Bear's Paw Inn dating from 1632 but the main attraction to the canal voyages in this area is the Anderton Lift, the only lift in Britain, which takes boats from the Trent and Mersey Canal over 50 feet down to the river Weaver. Opened in 1875, it was worked hydraulically until it was electrified in 1907. The tanks are suspended from wire ropes which go round overhead pulleys to counter weights of 252 tons; little power, therefore, is needed to raise the boats in the tank or lower them as the case may be. The lift takes 15 minutes to move a boat up or down and a souvenir ticket is issued to users. Hours of operation are the same as for the Weaver Locks but journeys out of the usual hours can sometimes be arranged.

The opening bridges on the navigation are fine examples of early engineering and are opened for the coasting craft that use the navigation.

Authority	British Waterways Board. Winsford Bottom Flash is controlled by the Vale Royal District Council. Under the 1945 Weaver Navigation Act it would appear to be possible for B.W.B. to incorporate the flashes into the main navigation. The present situation appears to be unsatisfactory as the flashes are shallow and grounding of craft occurs. Refloating is difficult. Canoeable through the flashes to canal at Middlewich via Upper Weaver is usually possible.
From and to	Winsford Bridge to Weston Point Docks (junction with Manchester Ship Canal).
Distance	20 miles. Anderton Lift Branch ⅛ mile. Weston Marsh Branch, 2¼ miles, is closed as Frodsham Lock is now inoperative and legally closed.
Length	Northwich to Winsford, 130ft. Northwich to Weston, 150ft.
Beam	35ft.
Draught	10ft.
Headroom	To Hartford, 60ft. To Winsford, 30ft.

	Anderton Lift Branch
Length	72ft.
Beam	14ft. 6ins.

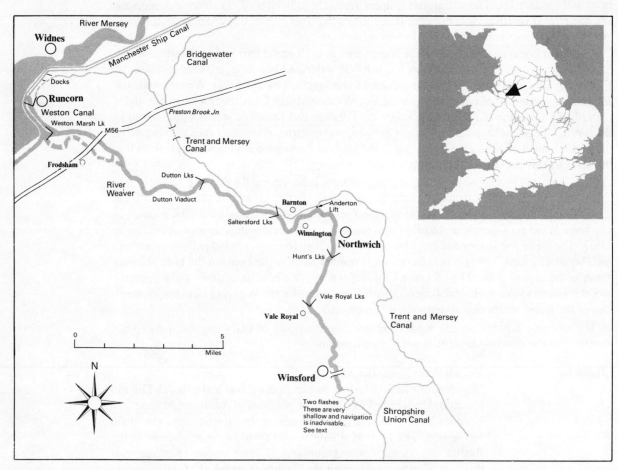

Connections	Manchester Ship Canal, at Marsh Lock and at Weston Point. Trent and Mersey Canal via Anderton Lift Branch. Runcorn and Weston Canal, at Weston Point.
Bridges	Numerous. There are 6 swing bridges.
Locks	5. Fall from Winsford. Weston Marsh Branch, 1 lock. Fall towards Weston Marsh at Low Tide. Locks have lock-keepers except Vale Royal Lock. Hours are Monday to Friday 0800–1700 hours, Saturday 0800–1100 hours For other times for opening apply to the authority beforehand.
Tow-path	Throughout navigation, except Anderton Lift Branch.
Tides	The tide flows up to the tail of Frodsham Lock, now closed, via the old line of navigation. High Spring tides flow past Frodsham Lock into the main line of the navigation up to Lock No. 4 (Dutton) and Weston Point Docks.

Distance Table

Winsford Bridge to:

	Miles	Furlongs
Salt Union Ltd. — Birkenhead, Salt Works	—	2
Wharton Grinding Mills	—	6
Cheshire Amalgamated Works	—	4
Little Meadow Works	1	—
National Works	1	2
Meadowbank Mine and Works	1	4
Falks Works	1	6
Newbridge Bridge opening	2	—
Vale Royal Locks No. 1	3	2
Hartford Bridge, 30ft. headway	3	7
Pimblott's Shipyard	4	6
Hunt's Locks, No. 2	5	1
Yarwood's Ship Yard	5	2
Northwich Repair Yard	5	3
Northwich, mouth of River Dane, Bridges (opening). ...	5	4
Northwich, Barons Quay	5	6
Witton Works and Witton Brook Works	6	—
Chemical Works	6	6
Junction with Anderton Lift Branch (Trent and Mersey Canal) ...	7	—
Winnington Chemical Works	7	—
Winnington Bridge openings	7	2
Wallascote Works	7	5
Saltersford Locks No. 3	9	2
Wilbraham's Quay, adjoining main road	10	2
Acton Bridge opening	11	1
Dutton Locks No. 4	12	3
Pickering's Wharf	13	2
Junction with Old Line of navigation—head of Frodsham Cut to Weston Marsh (now closed)	16	—
Sutton Weir and Sluices	16	4
Sutton Bridge opening	16	7
Parks Steel Works	17	1
Rock Savage Bridge opening	17	3
Weston Works Imperial Chemical Industries	18	3
Weston Marsh Side Lock, *giving access to Manchester Ship Canal and Old Line of Navigation*	19	—
I.C.I. Chemical Works	19	4
Junction with Runcorn and Weston Canal	19	6
Weston Point Docks, and *junction with Manchester Ship Canal* (Lock No. 5)	20	—

Old Line of Navigation—Head of Frodsham Cut to Weston Marsh

Junction with Main Line of Navigation and head of Frodsham Cut to:

	Miles	Furlongs
Frodsham Lock (now closed to navigation)	—	4
Frodsham Bridge (headway varies with tide)	1	—
Weston Marsh, *junction with Manchester Ship Canal, and Main Line of Navigation through Weston Marsh Side Lock.*	2	2

River Welland(105)

The river is tidal to Fulney, and continues above Spalding. Its navigation above Spalding is suitable for small cruisers but above the Folly River Outfall only light craft that can be portaged round old locks can be used. Navigation works to Stamford are derelict. Originally made navigable under Acts passed in 1571, 1772 and 1794.

Flat country, but famous for its bulb fields, Spalding is a very agreeable country town with very marked Dutch overtones. Much domestic architecture and the layout of the town show an influence of trading with the Netherlands, this is extensive in bulbs and horticultural produce. Fulney Lock has only come into operation in recent years and this has made it possible to go above Spalding to a point not far from the famous Crowland Abbey and triangular bridge. The Fosdyke Bridge Act 1870 is to be rescinded to allow opening bridge to be fixed. Port of Fosdyke Act 1987.

Authority	Anglian Water Authority, Oundle, Peterborough. Tel. Oundle 3366. Fulney Lock and Sluice Keeper. Tel. Spalding (0775) 3350
*From and to**	Fosdyke Bridge to Folly River Outfall.
Distances	Fosdyke Bridge to Spalding, 7½ miles. „ „ „ Market Deeping, 23¾ miles.
Length	To Spalding, 110ft. Above Spalding, Approx. 35ft.
Beam	30ft.
Draught	8ft. to Spalding at highest tides. 3ft. to Folly River Outfall.
Headroom	5ft. above Spalding Bridge. Below, Fosdyke unlimited. Fosdyke Bridge 7ft. 8 ins. H.W.S.T. 13ft. 7in. H.W.N.T.
Tow-path	Fosdyke Bridge to Spalding only.
Locks	One. Fall from Folly River Outfall.
Bridges	Fosdyke, opening bridge. Signal Flag at Masthead and three blasts.
Canoeing note	Canoeable to Market Deeping and up to Duddington Mill. Above this river is private.
Pilotage	Pleasure craft may use the outfall of the Welland without pilotage but cargo boats pay for pilotage up to Fosdyke Bridge to the Boston & Spalding Pilotage Authority.
Tides	High Water at Spalding about one hour after Fodsyke Bridge. Spring tides flow to Spalding, the rise being about 8ft. The river dries at Spalding at low tide except in freshets. There is only two hours flood tide at Fosdyke, after which the tide runs very strong. Vessels about to navigate the Welland should wait in Clayhole till after half-flood there.

* See The Wash.

Distance Table

Market Deeping Mill (*derelict lock*) *to:*

	Miles	Furlongs
Deeping St. James (derelict lock)	1	4
Folly River Outfall (Commencement of navigation)	3	4
Crowland (1 mile distant)	7	—
St. Guthlac's Cross	10	—
Sluice, entrance to Cowbit Drain (not navigable)	15	—
Spalding Bridge	16	—
Fulney Lock	17	—
Junction with River Glen (also called The Reservoir)*	20	6
Fosdyke Bridge	23	6
The Wash	25	7

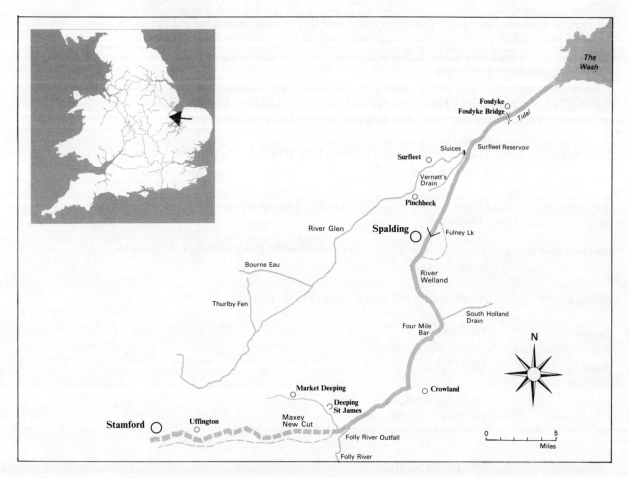

River Wey (106)

This was one of our earliest navigations. It was opened first to Guildford by an Act in 1651 and followed by two others in 1681 and 1683. It was continued to Godalming by an Act passed in 1760. Commercial traffic survived until 1970 although timber traffic to Guildford ceased in 1958. The Guildford navigation was for many years owned and managed by Mr. Harry W. Stevens who presented it to the National Trust in 1964. The Godalming Navigation which he also managed for a number of years was also presented to the Trust.

The entry from the Thames is below Shepperton Lock; leaving D'Oyly Carte Island astern vessels turn to port past Shepperton Lock and Weir, thence straight ahead to the entrance channel. The river, though close to London, has a remoteness of its own. Wisley, with a small Norman church has also yielded a 4,000 year old canoe and other prehistoric remains; the gardens run by the Royal Horticultural Society are famous. There are the remains of Newark Priory on a side stream, but Newark Mill a fine old timbered specimen has vanished after a disastrous fire. The Tudor mansion, Sutton Place, which now houses a fine art collection is on the route. Guildford Wharf is the home of the treadmill operated crane, over 200 years old and in excellent condition. Guildford city with its Guildhall, cobbled High Street, the Tudor Archbishop Abbott's Hospital and the castle remains should be visited. The new cathedral on Stag Hill dominates the west of the town.

All the way from the Thames the river avoids the suburban sprawl as it continues through the hills to Godalming past St. Catherine's Chapel at St. Catherine's Ferry where the Pilgrim's Way crosses the river. The Tillingbourne, a tiny stream once canalised for punts to carry gunpowder, enters the Wey near Shalford, a pretty village just off the river. Godalming at the head of the navigation is an interesting country town with some fine old buildings dating from Tudor times.

There are a number of side streams that can be explored, but in most cases they are very shallow. The area has extensive tree coverage and the river is ideal for winter cruising when one gets the feeling of passing through a series of Roland Hilder's paintings.

Authorities	The National Trust, Dapdune Lea, Wharf Road, Guildford, Surrey. Tel. Guildford 61389.
From and to	Junction with the River Thames just below Shepperton Lock to Godalming.
General remarks	The river is in good order for pleasure boats from the Thames to Godalming.
Distance	Junction with the River Thames to Godalming, 19½ miles.
Length	73ft. 6ins.
Beam	13ft. 10½ins.
Draught	To Coxes Lock, 4ft. To Guildford, 3ft. 3ins. To Godalming, 2ft. 6ins.
Headroom	To Guildford, 7ft. To Godalming, 6ft. Lowest bridge is Broadford Bridge, Shalford. It is sometimes possible, by special arrangement, to get another 2 or 3 inches headroom. All the above dimensions are at normal water levels.
Locks	16. Some of the locks have sloping turf sides, but chains are fitted and should be used in the locks. Fall from Godalming. There are lock-keepers at Thames Lock No. 16, New Haw No. 13, Walsham Gates No. 11, Paper Court No. 9, Triggs Lock No. 7 and Stoke Lock No. 5. All other locks are unattended. The entrance lock

from the Thames is preceded by a flood gate to provide extra draught. Visitors to the river with a draught of 1ft. 6ins. maximum, should moor just below the main lock chamber before locking through. If over 1ft. 6ins. draught it is advisable to moor just above the flood gate as this may have to be used to obtain extra depth. This flood gate has been referred to as a navigation weir, which is incorrect, it is always used in conjunction with Thames Lock.

Lock handles can be hired or bought at Thames Lock, Stoke Lock or the Guildford office.

In using the locks remember when operating the sluices to push the handle well on to the spindle and do not on any account let the sluices run down of their own accord. The navigation is a very old one and navigation works should be treated with extra care.

At Worsfold Gate Lock leave one paddle open, in the upper and lower gates. At Pyrford Lock leave upper gate sluices as indicated with both lower gates chained back.

Bridges	41.
Tow-path	Throughout navigation, except under Guildford High Street Bridge.
Speed limit	4 knots
Charges	On application to the National Trust.
Regulations	Licences for craft to navigate and/or remain on the River Wey Navigations are granted subject to the Bye-laws made under the National Trust Acts of 1907–53, and to the following additional conditions:

1 No unlicensed craft may use the River Wey and Godalming Navigations.
2 Licences are issued at the discretion of the River Wey and Godalming Navigations and may be withdrawn at any time following non-payment of dues or other infringement of the Bye-laws and/or conditions.
3 Persons bring craft on to the Navigations at their sole risk, and the River Wey and Godalming Navigations will accept no responsibility for damage or injury to their persons or property.
4 A speed limit of 4 knots to be observed by all power craft.
5 Speed to be reduced below 4 knots when passing moored craft or when propeller wash becomes excessive, and craft to be navigated with care and caution, and in such manner as not to cause damage, inconvenience or danger to persons or property.
6 No sanitary and other effluent or matter of any nature to be discharged into the Navigations; lock-keepers will advise owners regarding waste disposal.
7 The licence 'plate' must at all times be prominently displayed on the craft concerned. It is not transferable.
8 In the interests of safety and convenience, owners must moor or move their craft, and otherwise use the Navigations' installations according to such instructions as are given from time to time by persons authorised by the Navigations.

9 All craft navigating or mooring on the River Wey and Godalming Navigations shall be maintained in a good repair and proper order and afloat, or able to float in a safe and navigable state.

10 No craft may navigate, nor lock and sluice gear be operated after sunset, or at any time after 10 p.m.

11 In times of emergency or to avoid damage to property or danger and inconvenience to river users, the Navigations reserve the right to move any craft and its moorings. When taking such necessary action, the Navigation concerned to be considered as an appointed agent of the craft owner.

Canoeing note The river can be canoed from Frensham (Haslemere Branch) and Farnham (Alton Branch).

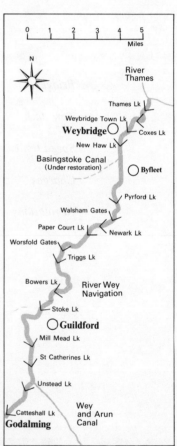

Distance Table

Junction with River Thames to:

	Miles	Furlongs
Thames Lock No. 16 and bridge	—	1
Old Weybridge Bridge and Lock No. 15	—	6½
Black Boy Bridge	1	0½
Coxes Railway Bridge	1	3½
Coxes Lock No. 14	1	5
New Haw Bridge and Lock No. 13 (the White Hart Inn)	2	2½
Junction with Basingstoke Canal, and Tow-path Bridge	2	7
Byfleet Railway Bridge	3	—
Parvis Bridge	3	4
Murray's Bridge	4	—
Dodd's Bridge	4	2½
Pyrford Bridge and Lock No. 12 (the Anchor Inn) ...	4	9
Pigeon House Bridge	5	3
Walsham Bridge and Gates (Walsham Gates Lock No. 11)	5	7½
Newark Lock No. 10	6	4
Newark Bridge (Seven Stars Inn)	6	5½
Paper Court Bridge	7	2
Paper Court Lock No. 9	7	2½
Tanyard Bridge	7	5½
High Bridge	8	1
Cart Bridge, Send (the New Inn)	8	5
Ashburton Bridge	8	5½
Worsfold Gates Lock No. 8	8	7
Triggs Lock No. 7 and bridge	9	5
Wareham's Bridge	9	6½
Send Church Bridge	10	2
Broad Oak Bridge	11	0½
Bowers Lock No. 6	11	6
Bowers Bridge	11	7
Stoke Lock No. 5	12	7½
Stoke Bridge (the Row Barge Inn)	13	3
Wood Bridge	14	1½

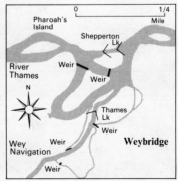

Distance Table

	Miles	Furlongs
Dapdune Railway Bridge and footbridge	14	$3\frac{1}{2}$
Dapdune Wharf	14	$4\frac{1}{2}$
Onslow Bridge	15	1
Guildford Wharf and footbridge	15	$1\frac{1}{2}$
Guildford Bridge	15	2
Mill Mead Lock No. 4 and bridge	15	3
Quarry Hill Footbridge	15	$4\frac{1}{2}$
St. Catherine's Ferry	16	$0\frac{1}{2}$
St. Catherine's Lock No. 3 and bridge	16	4
Railway Bridge (S.R.)	16	$6\frac{1}{2}$
Broadford Bridge (the Parrot Inn)	17	1
Mouth of Wey and Arun Junction Canal (now derelict but in use for $\frac{1}{2}$ mile for moorings)	17	$2\frac{1}{2}$
Railway Bridge (S.R.)	17	$3\frac{1}{2}$
Unstead Lock No. 2	17	6
Unstead Bridge	18	$0\frac{1}{2}$
Trowers Bridge	18	6
Catteshall Bridge	19	—
Catteshall Lock No. 1	19	$0\frac{1}{2}$
Godalming Wharf	19	4
Godalming Bridge	19	6

Wey-Arun Junction Canal(107)

For long the most talked about but derelict canal for over a century. Promoted by Act of Parliament in 1813 and closed in 1871, the Wey and Junction canal was the route through the Surrey border country rising from the Wey and dropping through the Arun valley to the sea. Enthusiasm and interest has been continuous and now a society has been formed, two locks restored and bridge repaired. A lifting bridge has been restored in a manner that would do credit to the BWB. This canal is part of London's Lost Route to the Sea.

Authority	None. (Wey Arun Canal Trust Ltd., 24 Griffiths Avenue, Lancing, West Sussex, BN15 0HW. Tel. Lancing (090 63) 3099)
From and to	Junction with Wey Navigation at Stonebridge (Guns Corner) to Newbridge (near Billingshurst) junction with the Arun Navigation.
Distance	18½ miles. *Beam* 12ft 2ins.
Length	68ft 6ins. *Headroom* 7ft.
Draught	3ft 1in. (These sizes applied when the canal was in operation).
Locks	23 (Rowner No. 1 and Malham (No. 2) Locks have been restored and work is proceeding on Lock 17 Rowley)
Bridges	Numerous. Three total rebuilds in brick. One lifting bridge at Northlands.

Towing Path	Through some of the waterways. Permission is needed to walk along the rest of the towpath.	
Restoration	This is a long job as separate lengths of canal have to be leased where possible from land owners to allow the work to proceed. Work sites should not be visited without first consulting the Society. Voluntary workers are needed.	

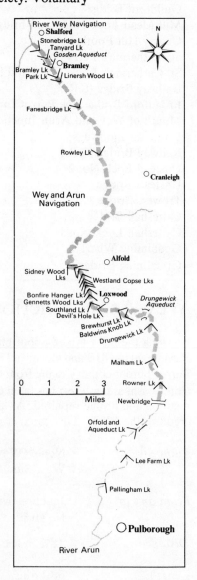

Distance Table

Junction with River Wey and Stonebridge to:

	Miles	Furlongs
Stonebridge Wharf	–	½
Stonebridge Lock No. 23	–	1
Tanyard Lock No. 22 and Gosden Aqueduct	–	2½
Bramley Lock No. 21	–	7
Linersh Wood or Wensby Lock No. 20 ...	1	2
Park Lock No. 19	1	4
Fanesbirdge Lock No. 18	1	7
Run Common Wharf	3	1
Rowley Lock No. 17	4	–
Elm Bridge Wharf (Cranleigh)	5	1
Bridge Wharf. Compass Inn	5	7
Tickners Heath and Cobdens Wharves ...	8	–
Sidney Wood Lock No. 16	8	6
Sidney Wood Lock No. 15	10	1½
Sidney Wood Lock No. 14	10	3½
Sidney Wood Lock No. 13	10	4½
Westland Copse Lock No. 12	10	5½
Westland Copse Lock No. 11	10	6½
Bonfire Hanger Lock No. 10	11	–
Gennets Wood Lock No. 9	11	1
Gennets Bridge Lock No. 8	11	2
Southland Lock No. 7	11	3½
Devils Hole Lock No. 6	11	6½
Loxwood. Onslow Arms Inn	12	1½
Brewhurst Lock No. 5	12	5
Baldwins Knob Lock No. 4	12	7
Drungewick Aqueduct	13	5
Drungewick Lock No. 3	14	3½
Malham Lock No. 2	15	–
Rowner Lock No. 1	16	5
Northlands Lifting Bridge	17	6
Newbridge – *Junction with Arun Navigation.*	18	4

River Wharfe (108)

Considerable difficulty may be experienced in reaching Tadcaster in the dry season. A weir at Tadcaster Church is the head of navigation.

Tadcaster is a pleasant Yorkshire country town with a 15th century church and some good domestic buildings. A fine railway viaduct which is never used, crosses the river above

Tadcaster Weir. In 1890 a company was formed to make the river a navigation but this was unsuccessful and was wound up in 1898.

Clay huts exist just above and below Ulleskelf Railway Bridge and there are a number of uncharted obstructions to be met elsewhere. Local enquiries are advised as the river is not recommended to strangers.

Authority	An open navigation.
From and to	Tadcaster to junction with the River Ouse.
Distance	9¼ miles.
Draught	Up to 5ft. 6ins. on Spring tides to Ulleskelf. Up to 3ft. 6ins. on Spring tides to Tadcaster, providing there is a good flow of land water.
Headroom	8ft. Unlimited to Ulleskelf.
Locks	None.
Tow-path	Throughout the navigation.
Canoeing note	Special care is needed to canoe above Tadcaster.
Tides	Spring tides flow to Ulleskelf and back up the water in the river to a height of about 10 inches at Tadcaster. A tide giving a depth of 28ft. on the Albert Dock Sill at Hull will raise the water at the mouth of the river 3ft.

Distance Table
Tadcaster Bridge to:

	Miles	Furlongs
Kirkby Wharf	2	4
Ulleskelf	3	7
Ryther	6	5
Nun Appleton Park	7	—
Junction with River Ouse (Yorkshire)	9	2

Wilts. and Berks. Canal (109)

Running through fine countryside this waterway was promoted by Acts of Parliament 1795, 1801, 1810, 1813, 1815 and 1821. It was closed in 1914 after having been unnavigable for several years. The waterway had a limited success for some years but closure of the Somerset coal mines seriously affected its future. Long considered unrestorable, there is a growing interest in repairing sections of it. Several long lengths are under inspection and work has already been carried out. Dimensions listed are as for the last years the canal was in service.

Authority	None. (Hon. Secretary: Wilts & Berks Amenity Group, Neil Rumbol, Esq., 14 Chestnut Avenue, Buckhurst Hill, Essex, 1G9 6EW

From and to   River Thames (Abingdon) to Semington. (Junction with Kennet & Avon Canal 52½ miles

Branches:
To Wantage		¼ mile
To Longcot Wharf		½ mile
To Calne		3⅛ miles
		(3 locks)
To Chippenham		2 miles
To Latton (North Wilts Canal. Junction with Thames & Severn Canal)		9 miles
		(12 locks)

Length	74ft.
Beam	7ft 6ins.
Draught	3ft 6ins.
Headroom	8ft
Towpath	Certain sections are usuable but care should be taken to obtain permission where there is no public right of way.
Remarks	Restoration work has commenced at Dauntsey Lock and work has started on the Calne Branch. A survey is being carried out on the section from Grove to Uffington. Work has been carried out at West Challow. Several other work sites are planned. The distance table for the canal is appended for interest but several parts have been lost for all time. Negotiations are taking place to link up from Dauntsey and the seven locks. Restoration of the seven locks and also Foxham locks is also envisaged.

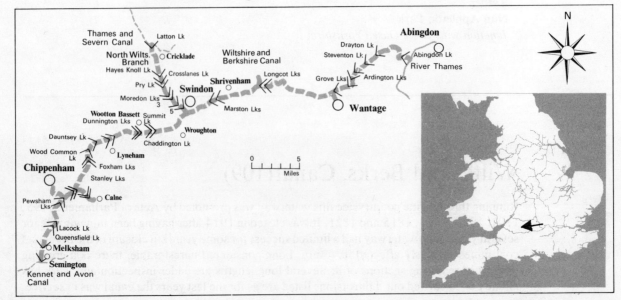

Distance Table

Abingdon Lock, junction with River Thames to:

	Miles	Furlongs
Tythe Barn Lock	–	6
Drayton Lock	2	4
Steventon Lock	4	
Ardington Marsh Lock	5	3
Ardington Top Lock	5	6
Grove Bottom Lock	7	1
Then follows Spirit Lock		
Smallmarch Lock		
Grove Common Lock		
Limekiln Lock		
Grove Top Lock		
	8	2
Challow Wharf	9	2
Uffington Wharf	14	6
Longcot Bottom Lock	16	4
Longcot Upper Lock		
Marston Bottom Lock	21	2
Marston Lock No. 3		
Marston Lock No. 2		
Marston Top Lock	21	7
Swindon Wharf	24	5
Junction with North Wilts Canal	25	1
Summit Lock	30	2
Chaddington Lock	30	5
Dunnington Top Lock	31	6
Dunnington Bottom Lock		
Seven Locks 1 to 7 (Lock No. 1)	34	1
(Lock No. 7)	34	5
Dauntsey Lock	36	3
Wood Common Lock	37	7
Foxham Upper Lock and Lower Lock (2)	39	1
Stanley Top Lock and Bottom Lock (2)	42	7
Pewsham Top, Middle and Bottom Lock (3)	45	1
Laycock Lock	47	5
Queensfield Lock	48	–
Melksham Forest Lock	49	1
Melksham Wharf	50	5
Semington Lock and *junction with Kennet & Avon Canal*	52	1

Witham Navigable Drains(110)

Witham Navigable Drains is the name given to the Drains which lie in the area north of the Witham and south of a line from Spilsby to Dogdyke. All are artificial cuts, or old streams improved, for drainage of the west and east fens. In the past these drains were used for transporting agricultural produce and coal but now are only used by pleasure and fishing craft, being mainly for drainage, and navigation rights have not been exercised in recent years to any great extent. Navigation is thus uncertain and the draught available largely depends on the wetness of the season. Local enquiries are advised. Entrance controlled by lock keeper, Cowbridge Lock key can be obtained from Keightly & Sons, 156 Willoughby Road, Boston. Tel. Boston (0205) 63616 (½ mile from lock).

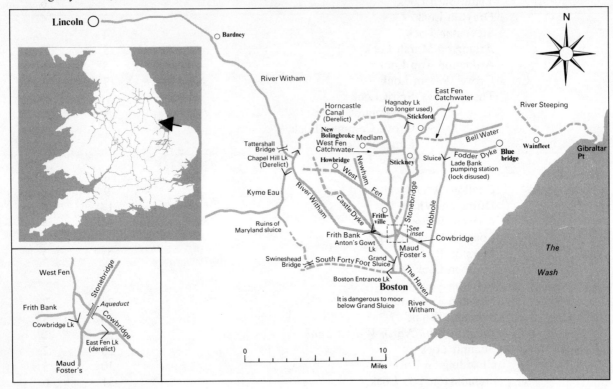

The names of the waterways are as follows:

Frith Bank Drain	West Fen Drain
Maud Foster Drain	Castle Dyke
Hobhole Drain	Medlam Drain
Cowbridge Drain	Lush's Drain
Newham Drain	West Fen Catchwater Drain
East Fen Catch water Drain	Stonebridge Drain
New Bolingbroke Drain	Bell Water Drain
Junction Drain	Howbridge Drain

In addition, there are several unnamed branches.

Craft over 60 feet in length but under 72 feet can pass through Anton's Gowt Lock into West Fen Drain and Medlam Drain, but there is no winding hole at Revesby Bridge for craft as long as a Narrow Boat. Special note should be made of the fact that there is no connection at Revesby Bridge between Medlam and West Fen Catchwater Drains. It is not possible to navigate from West Fen Drain via Lush's Drain to Stonebridge as the top end of this drain has silted up.

The area is flat and uninteresting, most of the drains being below ground level. The best section is in Boston where the drains allow a boat to enter the town, instead of having to be left above the Grand Sluice on the Witham. Boston Stump is this town's famous parish church.

It is possible to go from Boston to New York, passing Bunkers Hill on the way. The area merits the attention of enthusiasts to avoid loss of public rights.

Authority   Witham Fourth District Internal Drainage Board, 47 Norfolk Street Boston, Lincs. Tel. Boston (0205) 65226

From and to	Junction with River Witham at Anton's Gowt to Revesby Bridge. Thorpe Culvert and Stickford. There are numerous navigable branches.
Distances	Anton's Gowt to Revesby Bridge, 10½ miles. Anton's Gowt to Thorpe Culvert, 17¼ miles. Anton's Gowt to Revesby Bridge via Stickney, 12¾ miles.
Length	Through Anton's Gowt Lock, 72ft., otherwise 60ft.
Beam	Through Anton's Gowt Lock, 18ft., otherwise 10ft.
Draught	3ft. 6ins. Draught exceeds this in most places.
Headroom	8ft.
Locks	3. Entrance Lock at Anton's Gowt Lock is controlled by British Waterways Board. Fall from River Witham. The other two locks link waterways as follows: Cowbridge Lock, links Maud Foster Drain to West Fen Drain. Fall from Maud Foster Drain. East Fen Lock, links Maud Foster Drain to Cowbridge (or Kelsey) Drain. (Lock out of order). Rise to Cowbridge Drain. Locks have been dismantled at Lade Bank and Hagnaby.
Tow-path	Only in a few parts of the area.
Tolls	These are charged for Anton's Gowt Lock, for each passage through. Further details on application to the authority who own the entrance locks.
Facilities	No boatyards of any sort. A few scattered inns only.
Winter navigation	From approximately the end of September to the beginning of April the level in all Drains is lowered and craft may be trapped as this lowering of levels is carried out without warning to boatmen.

Distance Table
Frith Bank Drain

	Miles	Furlongs
Anton's Gowt Lock and junction with Newham Drain:		
Frith Bank Bridge	—	7
Junction with West Fen Drain	2	0½

West Fen Drain

	Miles	Furlongs
Cowbridge Lock Junction with Frith Bank Drain to:		
Junction with Short Drain to Aqueduct	—	2
Lush's Bridge and *junction with Lush's Drain*	—	7
Frithville, *junction with Medlam Drain*	2	—
Junction with Newham Drain and Howbridge Drain	5	7

Distance Table	Miles	Furlongs

Howbridge Drain
Junction with West Fen Drain and Newham Drain to:

	Miles	Furlongs
Inn, Bunker's Hill	1	1
Hough Bridge	2	3

Newham Drain
Junction with West Fen Drain and Howbridge Drain to:

	Miles	Furlongs
Junction with Castle Dyke	—	3
Canister Hall Bridge	1	5
Anton's Gowt, *junction with Frith Bank Drain*	3	4

Stonebridge Drain
Junction with West Fen Drain and Cowbridge Drain to:

	Miles	Furlongs
Canister Hall Bridge	1	5
Junction with Castle Dyke	2	1
Anton's Gowt, *junction with Frith Bank Drain*	3	4

Anton's Gowt
Entrance lock to
Witham Navigable
Drains in 1970

West Fen Catchwater Drain
Junction with Stone Bridge Drain and East Fen Catchwater Drain:

	Miles	Furlongs
Road Bridge, Stickney	2	2½
Hagnaby Old Lock (no gates, as there is now no change of level)	4	—
Revesby Bridge (no connection here with Medlam Drain)	6	3

East Fen Catchwater Drain
Junction with West Fen Catchwater Drain and Stonebridge Drain to:

	Miles	Furlongs
Road Bridge (Main Road, A.16)	—	4
Railway Bridge (E.R.)	2	7
Junction with Short Drain (not navigable)	3	3
Road Bridge, Stickford	4	4

Drain continues for another 3 miles but only a small portion of this is navigable.

Distance Table							*Miles*	*Furlongs*

Cowbridge Drain (or Kelsey Drain)

The Aqueduct (Stonebridge Drain passes over Cowbridge Drain) to:

Kelsey Main Road Bridge	...	...	...	...	...	...	—	7
Junction with Hobhole Drain	...	...	...	...	...	...	1	5

Junction Drain

Junction with Maud Foster and Stonebridge Drains and Cowbridge Lock to:

East Fen Lock and *Junction with Cowbridge Drain*	...	...	—	2

Maud Foster Drain

Junction with Stonebridge Drain, Junction Drain Cowbridge Lock to:

Rawson's Bridge	...	...	...	...	...	...	—	3½
Main Road Bridge	...	...	...	...	...	...	1	5
Sluice Doors (no junction with River Witham)...	...	...	...	2	5

Hobhole Drain

Hobhole New Pumping Station (no junction with River Witham) in 'The Haven' to:

Nunn's Road Bridge	...	...	...	...	...	...	1	—
Road Bridge	...	...	...	...	...	...	1	6
Road Bridge Freiston Bridge	...	...	...	...	...	2	4
Main Road Bridge	...	...	...	...	...	...	3	1
Junction with Cowbridge Drain	...	...	...	...	...	3	5
Bennington Road Bridge	...	...	...	...	...	6	4
Old Leake Station (British Railways E.R.)	...	...	...	8	2
Lade Bank Old Lock (now a sluice) and pumping Station	...	...	9	4
Junction, Drain to Blue Bridge (navigable for 2 miles approx)	...	11	—
Junction with Bell Water Drain, and Drain 2¼ miles long	...	...	11	6
Junction, Drain 1 mile long	...	...	...	...	...	12	4
Junction, Drain 1½ mile long	...	...	...	...	...	13	1
Head of Drain	...	...	...	...	...	...	13	6

Bell Water Drain

Junction with Hobhole Drain to:

Hemholme Road Bridge	...	...	...	...	...	1	2
Railway Bridge (E.R.)	...	...	...	...	...	2	3
Thorpe Culvert, junction with Steeping River (Craft cannot pass sluice into Steeping River)	...	...	...	...	...	5	2

Lush's Drain

This is only navigable for approximately 1½ miles from the Junction with West Fen Catchwater Drain at Lush's Bridge.

Castle Dyke

This is navigable to Thornton-le-Fen from the junction, with Newham Drain, near Anton's Gowt Lock, a distance of 2½ miles

New Bolingbroke Drain

Junction with Medlam Drain at Glebe Farm to:

New Bolingbroke Basin	...	...	...	...	...	...	—	4

Distance Table								*Miles*	*Furlongs*
Medlam Drain									
Junction with West Fen Drain to:									
Hakerley Bridge ...	...	...	...	...	...	...	...	1	4
Medlam Bridge ...	...	...	...	...	...	...	...	4	3
Glebe Farm and *Junction with New Bolingbroke Drain* (long craft should wind here) ...	...	...	...	...	...	...		5	2
Revesby Bridge (no connection with the West Fen Catchwater Drain)								6	6

River Witham Navigation (111)

This river navigation was promoted by Acts in 1671,1762,1808,1812,1826 and 1829. The city of Lincoln with its magnificent cathedral embodying every period of English architecture, was built between 1074 and 1380; the waterway commences at the Glory Hole (High Bridge), a famous bridge with buildings on it, of which one dates from 1540. The river has been straightened and the landscape below Lincoln is plain Fen country, though there are several interesting villages nearby and Carr Dyke commences at Washingborough. Much of the work done on drainage projects in this area was that of Sir John Rennie. Tattershall Castle and its large and very fine collegiate church are near the river. Boston at the end of the navigation is famous for its church of St. Botolph's (Boston Stump) 272 feet high.

The area, though flat, has a wealth of historical associations and an enthusiast could well explore the side drains providing suitable care is taken as many have seen no traffic since the demise of the Humber Keel. These side drainage channels are in fact old navigations, but do not appear to have been recorded in any canal history, article or technical paper. Several are large in scale and carried substantial traffic. Dogdyke Pumping Station has been reopened and the engine is steamed at intervals. See Appendix *Waterway Museums*.

The Fossdyke makes an open confluence on the west side of Brayford Mere. British Waterways are statutably forced to keep a channel 5 feet deep and 35 feet wide across the Brayford Mere, due west to east, entering the Witham at Brayford Mere open confluence. The short distance of the River Witham from Brayford Mere to High Bridge is disputed water, and all the tolls are listed from High Bridge to Boston Grand Sluice Lock. Brayford Mere belongs to the city of Lincoln, but is now controlled by the Anglian Water Authority, 50 Wide Bargate, Boston, Lincs. The Upper Witham Navigation from Brayford Mere is now closed and the railway bridge no longer opens but a right of navigation for light craft exists to Grantham.

Authority	British Waterways Board.
From and to	Junction with Fossdyke Canal at High Bridge, Lincoln, to outlet of Hobhole Drain.
Distance	36½ miles.
Length	78ft. Lock chamber, including tidal doors 59ft. (See Navigation notes).
Beam	15ft. 2ins.

Draught	5ft.
Headroom	7ft. 6ins. The headroom on the Lincoln to Boston Section is determined by the profile of the arch at High Bridge, Lincoln, the centre of which is 9ft. 9ins. above summer water level. Craft over 30ft. long will find difficulty in turning at the head of the old river on the branch from Bardney Lock to Barlings River.
Locks	3. Locks worked by lock-keepers. Fall from Lincoln. Grand Sluice is level at High Water.
Bridges	14 between Lincoln and Bardney; 5 between Bardney and Boston,
Speed limit	4½ miles an hour between Lincoln and Bardney 5 ,, ,, ,, ,, Bardney and Tattershall 5½ ,, ,, ,, ,, Tattershall and Boston
Tow-path	Towing path from Brayford Mere, Lincoln to Grand Sluice, Boston.
Navigation notes	The two swing bridges at Lincoln are situated west and east of the basin, the latter has a bridge-keeper. Below the lock is a large lifting bridge which gives only 5ft. headroom when closed and is dangerous to craft after dark. Boatmen can arrange for this bridge to be raised

River Witham
at Lincoln

for them, but some difficulty may be found in tracing the bridge-keeper after normal hours.

There is a lock and tide gate at Grand Sluice, Boston, boats can only pass through this on two occasions each tide, when the tidal water makes a level with the river, but as the lock will not take boats of more than 59ft. in length, craft exceeding this figure can only pass through once each tide, on the second level viz: about 2 to 2½ hours after high water.

Below Grand Sluice, the river through Boston dries to a trickle at low tides. Mooring is difficult, owing to the steepness of the mud bottom and the presence of many fishing boats. At high tide care should be taken as there are many large craft moving at high speed. No vessels are permitted to moor or anchor anywhere along the cut leading from the dock entrance to the sea, a distance of 5 miles.

A number of waterways that run into the Witham can be used for light craft that can be portaged around sluices. These are:–

Barlings Eau—Bardney to Langworth

River Bain—Dogdyke to Horncastle

Billinghay Skirth—Tattershall to Billinghay

Some boats may be found above sluices of such a size that it is obvious that they have not been portaged. It is dangerous to pass through the sluices as many are of a self-acting type and if any trip is contemplated therefore enquiries should first be made to the Divisional Manager, Lincolnshire River Division, 50 Wide Bargate, Boston, Lincs. Tel. Boston (0205) 5661.

Tides   High Water at Grand Sluice Boston, 30 minutes after Boston Deeps.

Distance Table

Lincoln, High Bridge, junction with Fossdyke Canal to:

	Miles	Furlongs
Lincoln, Stamp End Lock No. 1	—	4½
Washingborough	2	5
Five Mile House Station and Ferry	5	3
Horsley Deeps Lock, Bardney No. 2	8	4
Junction with Barlings Eau navigable for 1¾ miles to The Tyrwhitt Arms	8	4½
Bardney Station	9	4
Southrey Station and Ferry	12	2
Stixwould Station and Ferry	13	6
Kirkstead Station and Swing Bridge	15	7
Junction with Horncastle Canal (derelict)	19	3
Tattershall Bridge	20	—
Dogdyke Station and Ferry (Dogdyke Pumping Station)	20	7
Chapel Hill, *junction with Kyme Eau*	21	7
Langrick Station and Bridge	27	2
Anton's Gowt, *junction with Witham Navigable Drains*	29	3
Boston, Grand Sluice Lock No. 3	31	6
Boston Steel Bridge	32	1
Entrance to Boston Dock	33	2½
Outlet of Maud Foster Drain (no connection)		
Mouth of River and outlet of Hobhole Drain	36	1

Worcester and Birmingham Canal(112)

This canal was promoted by Acts in 1791, 1798, 1804, 1808 and 1815, and commences about half a mile from Birmingham city centre. The Bar Lock was built in 1815, as previous to that time the canal had no physical connection with the Birmingham Canal Navigation and everything had to be transhipped. After leaving the suburbs the canal passes through rolling country looking to the Lickey Hills with the Malvern Hills in the far distance. To maintain a level, cuttings and tunnels are more frequent than on some other canals, the 58 locks are within a distance of 16 miles. The top lock of the very fine Tardebigge flight of 30 locks is approximately 453 feet above sea level.

This is an ideal cruising waterway with black and white villages in profusion. Droitwich, an historic town is nearby, together with ancient Mere Hall, a Tudor manor house. The cathedral city of Worcester is at the end of navigation in delightful hilly country not far from the Cotswolds; here the Royal Porcelain works can be visited by arrangement, and among the many other buildings of interest are the Guildhall, Brittania House, King's School and St. Swithun's Church.

Nearby are Roman roads and other features of interest to the antiquarian, and as is generally the case, the canal reservoirs are haunts of wildfowl and wild life, the reservoir at Cofton Hacket being in a class of its own; the village of that name is in typical Worcestershire style.

The river crosses the Bourn, a stream which gives its name to Bourneville, famous for its cocoa products, and Stoke Prior which has important salt workings.

There is a Worcester and Birmingham Canal Society which is helpful to visitors. They erected a plinth and plaque at Tardebigge commemorating the Rolt-Aickman meeting in 1946 that started the waterways revival.

Authority	British Waterways Board.
From and to	Worcester to junction with the Birmingham Canal Navigations, Worcester Bar, Birmingham.
Connections	The canal has also junction with the Stratford-on-Avon Canal, 5½ miles below Birmingham.
Distance	30 miles. Bittell Arm, ½ mile long, (disused)
Length	70ft. Through Diglis Locks to Diglis Basin, 76ft.
Beam	7ft. Through Diglis Locks to Diglis Basin, 18ft. 6ins.
Draught	2ft. 6ins.
Headroom	6ft.
Locks	58. Lock gates worked by boat crews. Fall to Worcester. (The top lock has the highest rise of any narrow canal, 14ft)
Bridges	About 88, mostly fixed.

Tunnels   There are 5 tunnels as follows:

Dunhampstead	236 yards.	No tow-path
Tardebigge	580 ,,	,, ,, ,,
Shortwood	613 ,,	,, ,, ,,
West Hill King's Norton	2,726 ,,	,, ,, ,,
Edgbaston	105 ,,	Tow-path

Speed limit   4 miles per hour.

Tow-path   Throughout navigation except tunnels.

Facilities   Seven boatyards. A fair sprinkling of inns and villages apart from the 30 lock flight area.

Distance Table

Birmingham, Worcester Bar, junction with Birmingham Canal Navigations, Main Line, to:

	Miles	Furlongs
Birmingham, Granville Street Bridge	—	2
Birmingham, Sturge's and Bloxham's Wharves... ...	—	4
Edgbaston Tunnel	1	1
Stop Gates, Worcester end of Edgbaston Valley ...	1	6
Prichett's Wharf	2	2
Metchley Park Tip	2	4
Selly Oak Wharves		
Dudley Canal Line No. 2 (now closed at this end) ...	3	—
Stirchley Street Tip	4	—
Lifford Goods Station	4	3
Birmingham Corporation, Refuse Disposal Department	5	—
Kynoch's Works and Baldwin's Wharf	5	3
King's Norton *Junction with Stratford-on-Avon Canal*	5	4
King's Norton Wharves	5	6
King's Norton Tunnel	6	3
Hopwood Wharf	8	6
Junction with Bittel Arm ½ mile long	9	4
Bittell Wharf	9	6
Lane House Wharf...	10	—
Cooper's Hill Wharf	10	4
Withybed Green	10	6
Scarfield's Wharf	11	—
Grange Wharf	12	2
Shortwood Tunnel	12	2
Harris' Bridge	12	6
Tardebigge Old Wharf	13	2
Tardebigge Tunnel	13	4
Tardebigge New Wharf and Crane	14	—
London Lane, Engine House and Tardebigge Top Lock No. 58	14	1
(Then follows the longest flight of locks in the country Tardebigge, 30 locks Nos. 58 to 29.)		
Round Pond	15	—
Half-way House Bridge	15	2
Bate's Wharf (between Locks Nos. 29 and 28) ...	16	2

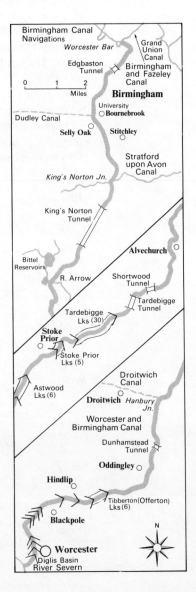

Distance Table

	Miles	Furlongs
(Then follows in a very short distance Stoke Prior Locks Nos. 28 to 23)		
Stoke Prior wharf (Lock No. 23)...	17	2
Stoke Prior Salt Works Central	18	—
Lock Nos. 22 to 17 Dodderhill or Astwood Locks	19	2
Grove's Brick Works	20	4
Hanbury Wharf and Junction with Droitwich Junction canal	20	6
Hadzor Wharf	21	2
Dunhampstead Tunnel	22	2
Dunhampstead Wharf	22	4
Oddingley Brick Works	23	2
Tibberton Wharf	24	2
Tibberton Lock No. 16 to 11 (sometimes called Offerton Locks) ...	24	6
Hindlip Wharf and Locks No. 9 and 10 (sometimes called Tolladine Locks)	25	2
Tolladine Private Wharf	26	—
Blackpole Wharf	26	6
Bilford Bridge, Locks Nos. 7 and 8	27	6
Worcester, Gregory's Mill and Lock Nos. 6 and 5	28	—
Worcester, Barker's Brick Works and Wharves	28	2
Worcester, Lansdown and Horn Lane Bridge	28	4
Worcester, Lowesmoor Wharves	29	—
Worcester, Tallow Hill, Blockhouse, Lock No. 4	29	2
Worcester, Sidbury Lock No. 3	29	1½
Worcester, Porcelain Works and Townshend's Mill	29	6
Worcester, Diglis Basin, Diglis Canal Locks and *junction with River Severn*, Locks Nos. 2 and 1	30	—

River Wye (113)

The river is navigable to Tintern, but above this it is tortuous and dangerous owing to weirs and rapids and should not be attempted except by those with good local knowledge, and then only in small craft.

From its entrance the river continues for more than 100 miles through Wales, and is perhaps one of the most beautiful in Great Britain, it is tidal to Bigsweir Bridge. A famous river for canoeists, a full itinerary can be obtained from the British Canoe Union.

Authority	An open navigation. There is a statutory and also common law right of navigation to Hay.
From and to	From junction with the River Severn at Beachley Point to Chepstow and Tintern (navigable limit for safety) thence to Bigsweir Bridge.
Distance	From River Severn to Bigsweir Bridge, 15 miles.
Length	Unlimited.
Beam	,,

Draught	To Chepstow, 12ft., to Bigsweir Bridge, 6ft., at low water spring tides.
Locks	None.
Tow-path	Although there was a path throughout the River Wye, it is now overgrown and useless.
Tides	High tides at Brockweir Ferry, 30 minutes after Bristol. High tide at Chepstow, 20 minutes after Bristol. Spring tides rise 38ft., neaps 28ft. 6ins. In summer there is sometimes a bore above Chepstow.

Distance Table

Bigsweir Bridge, to:

	Miles	Furlongs
Llandogo	1	2
Brockweir Ferry	3	1
Tintern Railway Bridge	3	7
Tintern Bridge	4	6
Lancaut Stone Quarries	9	6
Chepstow Bridge	12	—
Beachley Point, mouth of River and *junction with River Severn Estuary*	15	—

Inland Waterways of Scotland

INTRODUCTION

The canals and rivers of Scotland are not connected to the waterways of England and Wales, they were constructed for a different set of economic conditions and all have 'wide' locks. The two main canals are both 'sea-to-sea' waterways and are used by coastal craft. There is now a Scottish Inland Waterways Association.

Several of the Scottish rivers are navigable for a short distance in their estuaries and have not been listed, being used mainly by sea-going craft. The Dee (Kirkudbright) is navigable to Farland and small fishing vessels can, at high water, enter the River Spey through the gravel shoals which almost totally obstruct the entrance. The rivers Eden and Tweed are also used for short distances. None of the Scottish rivers have been canalised and made navigable but many of them provide exciting water for the canoeist. Fuller details can be obtained from the Scottish Tourist Board, 22 Ravelston Terrace, Edinburgh, EH4 3EU. Tel. 031-332 2433.

A considerable number of lochs in Scotland are used by pleasure craft, a list of the more important of these is given here for general interest.

A number of lochs are used for water supply and many are private. Enquiries are advised before attempting to use the lochs.

Name	Maximum length in miles (approx.)	Maximum width in miles (approx.)
Lomond	$20\frac{3}{4}$	5
Ness	$24\frac{1}{2}$	1
Awe	$22\frac{3}{4}$	$3\frac{1}{4}$
Maree	$12\frac{3}{4}$	$2\frac{1}{4}$
Tay	$14\frac{1}{2}$	$1\frac{1}{8}$
Shiel	$17\frac{1}{2}$	1
Leven	$3\frac{3}{8}$	2
Katrine	8	$\frac{3}{4}$
Arkaig	12	$\frac{3}{4}$
Earn	$6\frac{1}{2}$	$4\frac{5}{8}$
Loyal (Laoghal)	$4\frac{3}{8}$	$1\frac{3}{4}$
Naver	$6\frac{1}{4}$	$\frac{1}{2}$
Fannich	$6\frac{3}{8}$	$\frac{3}{4}$
Ken	4	$\frac{1}{2}$
Lochy	$9\frac{5}{8}$	$1\frac{1}{4}$
Lydock	$5\frac{1}{4}$	$\frac{1}{2}$
Morar	12	2
Rannoch	$9\frac{3}{8}$	$1\frac{1}{8}$
Shin	$3\frac{3}{4}$	$1\frac{1}{2}$
Menteith	$1\frac{1}{2}$	1
Vennacher	$3\frac{3}{4}$	$\frac{3}{4}$
Lubnaig	$3\frac{7}{8}$	$\frac{3}{8}$

Name	Maximum length in miles (approx.)	Maximum width in miles (approx.)
Assynt	6¾	⅜
Ericht	14¾	1⅛
St. Mary's	3	½
Doon	5⅝	¾
Garry (Perthshire)	2¾	⅜
Garry (Inverness-shire)	4½	½
Affric	3⅛	½
Glas	3¾	½
Luichart	4¾	¾
Treig	6	¾
Quoich	6⅛	¾
Cluanie	4⅜	½
Blackwater Reservoir	7	¼
Laggan (includes upper and lower portions)	12	½

Caledonian Canal (114)

This canal is one of the grandest and most beautiful in Europe. As long ago as 1726 Captain Burt had considered the linking of Loch Linnhe and the Moray Firth through Glen More, and later James Watt did a survey of the same route. Knox was moved to comment in 1785 that the canal would relieve distress in the Highlands and enable shipping to avoid the dangerous Pentland Firth.

In 1801 the Government asked Thomas Telford to survey the area for a canal route and the survey was carried out in 1801/2. An Act was passed in 1803 and the canal was opened in 1822 to through traffic. It has had a chequered history as Dr. Jean Lindsay records in her book 'The Canals of Scotland'. An Act of 1919 transferred the canal to the Ministry of Transport, and later it became part of the nationalised waterway organisation.

The British Waterways Board took over the canal in 1962 and now all locks have been mechanised and the basin at Corpach and the Sea Lock have been enlarged to take vessels of 1,000 tons. This development was made to accommodate trade from the new £20,000,000 pulp mill of Wiggins Teape & Co.

Less than half the canal is man-made, the rest consists of natural lochs (fresh water lakes) connected one to another and to sealocks at each end by relatively short lengths of canal. The entire system lies along a south-west to north-east axis in the Great Glen of Scotland, the straight-line characteristics of which is demonstrated by the fact that the distance by canal from end to end is only four miles longer than the distance as the crow flies.

The north-east end of the canal is close to Inverness and the south-west end is a few miles from Fort William. Fort Augustus is a considerable village alongside a flight of locks at the south-western end of Loch Ness. Pleasure cruises into Loch Ness are operated from above the locks at Muirtown (Inverness) and from below the locks at Fort Augustus. Small craft (with living accommodation) are available for charter. For details consult the Scottish Tourist Board.

The various natural lochs incorporated in the system are (starting from the north-east): Loch Dochfour (which is a mere offshoot of Loch Ness); Loch Ness, 22 miles long and mostly about 700 feet deep; Loch Oich, the summit level, smaller, shallower, with a buoyed channel; and Loch Lochy, 11 miles long and very deep. Apart from the scenery which is of unsurpassed grandeur (and which includes Ben Nevis, highest mountain (4,406 feet) in the

British Isles), chief points of interest are Castle Urquhart on the shores of Loch Ness and the Benedictine abbey at Fort Augustus.

Ben Nevis dominates the south-western entrance. It is always snow capped and overlooks Neptune's Starcase, the famous flight of locks at Banavie. Fort William is another tourist centre and also popular with the mountaineering fraternity.

This canal has enormous tourist potential and further details about the area can be obtained from the Scottish Tourist Board, 22 Ravelston Terrace, Edinburgh. Tel. 031-332 2433.

Authority	British Waterways Board, Caledonian Canal Office, Clachnaharry, Inverness, Scotland. Tel. Inverness (0463) 33140
From and to	The Caledonian Canal cuts across Scotland, linking the North Sea with the Atlantic Ocean, thus saving many miles of exposed navigation around the North Coast of Scotland. The Canal is entered at its north-eastern end from the Beauly Firth at Clachnaharry near Inverness, and runs to Corpach, Loch Linnhe, at its south-western end. The waterway consists of about 21½ miles of canal, the remaining 38½ miles being through fresh water Lochs Dochfour, Ness, Oich and Lochy.

Navigation through locks etc.	The navigation through Loch Ness and Loch Lochy presents no difficulties, but care must be exercised in navigating Loch Oich which, however, is well buoyed and beaconed. Buoys also mark the channel from the canal at the east end of Loch Ness. Along the canal and in the lochs all buoys, beacons and other markings are coloured as follows:

On the north-west side ... ... red
On the south-east side ... ... black

There are several recognised anchorages in the lochs, the most important of which are:

Loch Ness—at Invermoriston and in the inlet behind Urquhart Castle and at Temple Pier on the north-west side of the loch and Foyers on the south-east side.

Loch Oich—off Port MacDonnell pier.

Loch Lochy—in the inlet north-east of the glen of Loch Arkaig on the north-west side, and at Letterfinlay, half-way down the Loch on the south-east side.

At Clachnaharry Sea Lock.

Anchors may not be put out in the canal proper, but there are numerous places where craft can secure.

Tides	At Clachnaharry Sea Lock. Springs rise, 13ft. 6ins., Neaps rise, 6ft. 3ins. (average rise). At Corpach Sea Lock. Springs rise, 11ft., Neaps rise, 5ft. 9ins. Vessels cannot enter or pass out of the sea locks at either end of the canal for about two hours before or after low water springs.
Distance	From Clachnaharry to Corpach, 60 miles.
Length	150ft.

Beam	35ft.
Depth of water	Minimum 13ft. 6ins, maximum 770ft.
Headroom and maximum dimensions	120ft. Vessels over 150ft. long may be accepted up to a limit of 160ft. overall, providing draught does not exceed 9ft. Corpach basin and lock were enlarged in 1964/5 and they can now take vessels up to 1,000 tons. Corpach Sea Lock No. 29 can admit vessels 203ft. long and up to a beam of 35ft. Overhead power cables cross the canal at 125ft. above the water level. Masts must not exceed 120ft. above the water level.
Locks	29, 14 between Clachnaharry and the summit of the waterway at Laggan and Corpach. Lock gates worked by lock-keepers. All electro-hydraulically operated. Locks 1 to 14 rise from Clachnaharry to Loch Oich and 15 to 29 fall from Loch Oich to Corpach. Before each lock a heavy chain is suspended and it is dangerous for craft to approach any lock until this has been lowered. Vessels normally secure in each lock to the north-west side, i.e., the side on which the lock-keepers work, but when several vessels lock through together, both sides may be used.
Bridges	11 swing bridges, and one fixed bridge at Kessock (headroom 95 ft H.W.O.S.T)
Speed limit and bye-laws	Speed is restricted to 6 m.p.h. in the reaches. Notices giving instructions to vessels are posted along the canal bank and these should be carefully read and observed. A copy of the canal regulations may be obtained from the canal office if desired.
Fresh water	Fresh water supplies are available, for a small charge, with hosepipes at Muirtown, Inverness, Banavie and Corpach.
Approx. time taken to navigate	About one day and a half in summer, two days in winter.
Sunday navigation	The Canal is open for navigation between 0630 and 2030 hours each weekday in summer, and in daylight hours in winter, but vessels are not passed through locks on Sundays, except the sea locks on extra payment.
Charges	All charges for through passages in either direction are paid at Corpach.
Pilotage	Canal pilots are not usually necessary, but are available if required. Rates on application.
Towage	A canal tug is available for towing vessels through the canal on due notice being given to the office at Clachnaharry Works Lock at the seaward end of Muirtown Basin. The basis of charge per working day of tug can be obtained on application to the canal office.

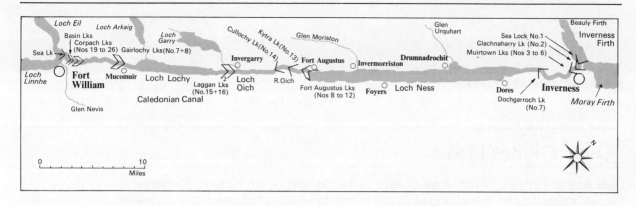

Facilities	There are seven hire bases with boating stores, equipment, etc. shopping at Fort Augustus, Inverness and Fort William.
Charts	Charts of the canal, as well as the canal bye-laws, may be obtained from the canal office. There is also an Admiralty chart of the canal, No. 1791 and numerous charts of the approaches.

Distance Table

	Miles	Furlongs
From Sea Lock No. 1 to:		
Clachnaharry Lock No. 2	1	—
Muirtown (Four Locks) Lock Nos. 3, 4, 5 and 6	2	—
Bught Bridge	3	—
Torvean	4	—
Dochgarroch Lock No. 7	6	—
Bona Ferry	7	—
Aldourie	9	—
Dores	10	—
Errichit Woods	12	—
Temple Pier	15	—
Inverfarigaig	18	—
Foyers	20	—
Aultsaye	23	—
Invermoriston	25	—
Portclair Point	27	—
Fort Augustus (5 locks) Lock Nos. 8, 9, 10, 11 and 12	31	—
Kytra Lock No. 13	34	—
Cullochy Lock No. 14	36	—
Port MacDonell	38	—
Bridge of Oich	40	—
Laggan (2 locks) Lock Nos. 15 and 16	42	—
Letterfinlay	46	—
Invergloy	49	—
Clunes	50	—
Achnacarry	51	—
Gairlochy (2 locks) Lock Nos. 17 and 18	53	—
Moy	54	—

Distance Table

	Miles	Furlongs
Muirshearlich	56	—
Banavie, Upper and Lower (8 locks) Nos. 19—26 (inclusive)... ...	59	—
Corpach Basin (2 locks) Lock Nos. 27 and 28	59	5
Corpach (Sea Lock) No. 29	60	—

River Clyde (115)

The firth of this river is very popular with yachtsmen and is the highway for seagoing vessels which come up to the docks at Glasgow. It is, however, of little interest to the inland navigator except that the Clyde makes a junction with the River Leven at Dumbarton and this river connects with Loch Lomond. There is no navigation authority as the Leven is not usually navigable under normal conditions.

The distance is 7¾ miles. There is a barrage across the Leven at Balloch about a mile south of the junction with Loch Lomond. In this barrage on the west side are ramps to facilitate the transport of boats around. The maximum dimensions are approximately 25 ft long by 7 ft 6 ins beam with unlimited height and a maximum deadweight of 3 tons. It takes approximately 1½ hours to go over the barrage.

Whilst no problems arise in navigating from the Loch to the north side of the barrage, the river downstream presents many obstacles to boat movement especially in the period May to September when the barrage is controlling river flow to the statutory amount of 133 mill/galls/day.

Because of the hazards of low water etc. in the lower section of the river only a few boats a year make the trip provided by the facilities at the barrage. The main access to Loch Lomond is via boat trailer to one of the many launching sites around the shore. The real problem with the Leven remains which is that navigators have to wait for a spate and then the current is too strong to make much headway against it. The barrage is controlled by the Central Scotland Water Development Board located at Balmore, Torrance, By Glasgow, G64 4AJ. (Tel. Balmore (036 02) 511.

Authority	Clyde Ports Authority, 16 Robertson Street, Glasgow Tel. 041-221 8733
From and to	Cambuslang to Greenock.
Distance	29½ miles.
Length	Unlimited.
Beam	,,
Draught	To Port of Glasgow, 21ft. at L.W. springs. To Cambuslang at H.W. springs, 3ft. only.
Headroom	Unlimited to George V Bridge.
Locks	None.
Tow-path	None.

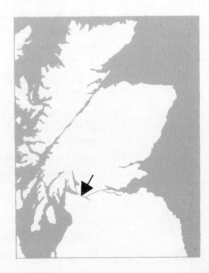

									Miles	Furlongs

Special note   The sailing of small boats east of Bowling Bay is prohibited by bye-law, except with special permission of the Clyde Ports Authority.

Tides   The range of the tide at Glasgow Docks is 12ft.

Distance Table

Cambuslang to:

	Miles	Furlongs
Rutherglen Bridge ...	5	4
Glasgow Bridge ...	7	2
Whiteinch ...	11	—
Bowling, *junction with Forth and Clyde Canal* ...	19	2
Junction with River Leven (not usually navigable) ...	21	4
Dumbarton ...	21	6
Greenock ...	24	9

River Leven

Junction with River Clyde to:

	Miles	Furlongs
Dumbarton Bridge ...	1	1
Renton Spring tides usually flow to within ½ mile of Renton. ...	3	6
Bonhill Bridge ...	5	6
Jamestown Bridge ...	6	6
Balloch Bridge ...	7	2
Balloch Pier ...	7	6

Crinan Canal(116)

This enchanting canal is only 9 miles long but its passage saves the journey around the Mull of Kintyre. The Act promoting the canal was passed in 1793 and opened finally in 1809. Many difficulties were encountered in its construction, including serious financial ones which continuously beset the promoters. Rennie surveyed the route and supervised James Hollingsworth the resident engineer and also the work of his father, but the work of both father and son suffered criticism. Telford produced a report in 1813 and later was responsible for directing repairs to the canal which eventually came under the control of Commissioners of the Caldedonian Canal.

One of the chief troubles in the canal's construction was the hardness of the whinstone which was found in places along the canal route between sections of peat moss, but in spite of early defective construction and a chequered history the canal is now in good order and a popular short cut. The basins at either end are invaluable as refuges in rough weather for yachtsmen but they are often crowded in the cruising season. However there are alternative moorings along the canal in Bellanoch Bay, 1½ miles east of Crinan.

The canal is beautiful and rural throughout. At its eastern end it is entered from Loch Gilp, a branch of Loch Fyne, one of the lochs of the Firth (Estuary) of Clyde at the village of Ardrishaig. After the sea-lock and the terminal basin there are three more locks within the confines of the village and thence a four mile pound to Cairnbaan, where four more locks lead to the summit pound which is only a little over one mile long at the end of which the descent begins through the five locks of Dunardry. After lock 13 there are no more locks until the western end of the canal at Crinan. After Bellanoch Bay (a kind of lagoon where there are moorings for yachts) the canal becomes narrow with sharp bends. Between Crinan Bridge (which is not at Crinan) and Lock 14 (which is at Crinan) one-way traffic is the rule, traffic being regulated by telephone between Crinan Bridge and Crinan. At the latter place Lock 14 leads down into the terminal basin from which the sea-lock leads into Loch Crinan. Only sea-going vessels should venture forth to sea from Crinan.

Authority	The Manager and Engineer, British Waterways Board, Canal Office, Ardrishaig, Argyll. Tel. Ardrishaig 210
From and to	Ardrishaig (Loch Gilp, Loch Fyne) to Crinan (Loch Crinan, Sound of Jura).
Distance	9 miles.
Length	88ft. Sea Locks 199ft.
Beam	20ft. Sea Locks 23 ft.
Draught	9ft. 6ins. Sea Locks 11ft. 10ft. draught is often passed through. but the canal authorities accept no responsibility.
Headroom	Approx. 90ft. Restricted by electricity cables near Lochgilphead.
Locks	15. Except for the sea-locks at each end where there are lock-keepers, all locks now have to be operated by boat crews which means that at least one hand must be landed at each group of locks and picked up again afterwards. The rule is that all gates and all sluices must be left shut. Bridges are operated by bridge-keepers. Locks 1-8, rise from Ardrishaig. Locks 9-15, fall to Crinan. Sea locks are at Ardrishaig and Crinan.
Bridges	6 opening bridges.
Speed limit	Speed must not be such as to cause wash on banks.
Charges	Dues for passage and Harbour Dues are payable to the canal office, at Ardrishaig.

Photo: Douglas Russell

No.4 Lock at Ardrishaig on the Crinan Canal

Fresh water	Supplies of fresh water can be obtained at terminal basins.
Hours of navigation	0830 hours until 1630 hours, lunch interval 1200 to 1230 hours. No through passage allowed on Sundays. Out of hours working bridges and sea-locks by special arrangement and extra payment.
Navigation	The distance from Ardrishaig to Crinan round the Mull of Kintyre is upwards of 132 miles. From the Clyde, a sheltered passage nearly 85 miles shorter than the exposed voyage around the Mull can be secured by boats passing through the canal. Entrance to the canal can be made at any state of the tide.

There is some confusion between Crinan Harbour and Crinan Basin. They are separate and distinct. The harbour is an anchorage just around the corner from the exit to the canal. It is not man-made and not a very good anchorage. The basin is a terminal basin of the canal and inside the sea-lock isolating it from salt water.

Care should be taken at sharp bends in the canal and a hooter should be sounded as there is considerable traffic on the canal particularly coastal 'puffers' and, at certain times of the year, fishing fleets.

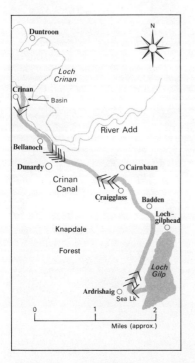

Distance Table				Miles	Furlongs
Ardrishaig Pier and Lock No. 1 to:					
Lochgilphead	...	...	...	2	2
Lock No. 5 ...	...	...	...	3	6
Lock No. 6 ...	...	...	...	3	7
Lock No. 7 ...	...	...	...	4	—
Lock No. 8 (summit)	...	...	...	4	1
Lock No. 13	...	...	...	5	—
Crinan, Lock No. 14	...	...	...	8	6
Lock, No. 15 Sea Lock	...	...	...	9	—

Forth and Clyde Canal (117)

Closed by Act of Parliament of the 1st January 1963, this canal has been left on the active list as the entrance lock and basin at Bowling are still in use, but the basin and lock at Grangemouth have been filled in and no trace of them remains. The canal ran from Bowling to Grangemouth through 39 locks, the dimensions of which were 69 feet 6 inches by 19 feet 8 inches length, draught 8 feet 6 inches and headroom 65 feet. The destruction of this large scale waterway linking the Forth to the Clyde should never have occurred, various societies are trying to preserve isolated sections for amenity.

About 20 miles can be used by light craft. The best sections at present are from Maryhill to Kirkintilloch and from Wynford Lock to Kirkintilloch. Restoration work is proceeding. Long term planning is going ahead, for the whole canal to be re-opened.

Authority	British Waterways Board.

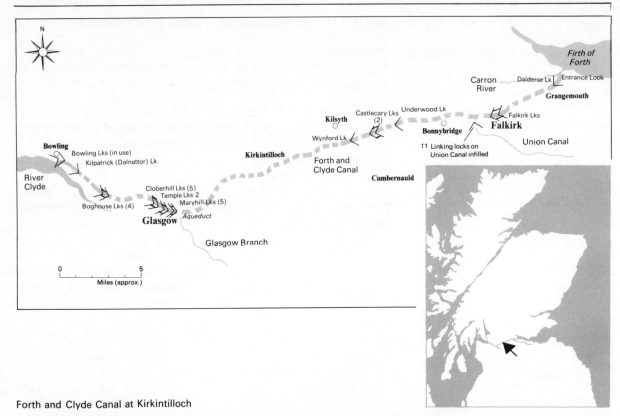

Forth and Clyde Canal at Kirkintilloch

Photo: Douglas Russell

River Forth(118)

This river is mainly a wide estuary but has many points of interest, including Inchcolm and other islands. There are considerable tidal variations to be taken into account.

Authority

Forth Ports Authority, Tower Place, Leith, Edinburgh. Tel. 031-554 2703.

From and to	Isle of May to Stirling.
Distance	62 miles.
Length	Unlimited.
Beam	,,
Draught	11ft. To Stirling at high water springs.
Headroom	Virtually unlimited.
Locks	None.
Tow-path	,,

Bridges

Forth Railway Bridge. Headroom at high water. 147ft.
Alloa Railway Bridge. Swing span, giving two clear openings.
Forth Road Bridge. Headroom at high water 148ft.
Kincardine Road Bridge. Swing span, two spans 150 feet wide.

Tides

High Water at Stirling 1¼ hours after Leith.

General remarks

This river is hardly in the category of an inland waterway and should only be navigated after careful local enquiry. From Alloa to Stirling it is tortuous and narrow and is obstructed by shallow ridges which can only be passed at high water.

Connections

Carron River which leads to the Forth and Clyde Canal at Grangemouth, but the canal is now closed.

Distance Table
Stirling to;

	Miles	Furlongs
Abbey Ford		4
Sow Ford	4	6
River Bannock Junction	6	6
Cambus	9	—
Alloa...	12	6
River Carron Junction	18	4
(Forth and Clyde runs from one mile up the Carron River)		
River Avon Junction	20	4
South Queensferry	30	4
Granton	37	4
Newhaven	38	5
Portobello	42	5
Isle of May	62	—

River Tay(119)

The Tay is a very fine river, one of the largest in Britain and it is claimed, discharges more water into the sea than any other. Its upper reaches are popular with canoeists though care should be taken during the fishing season.

The main navigable section is a wide estuary but there are numerous places of interest. Navigation near the Tay Railway Bridge needs caution as portions of the old bridge, which was destroyed in 1879, are still in being; local enquiries are advised for strangers, though in general it is better to keep to the south bank particularly after passing downstream through the Tay Bridge. The channel above the Tay Railway Bridge is buoyed.

Authority	**Buddon Ness to Balmerino** Dundee Harbour Trust, Harbour Chambers, Dock Street, Dundee. Tel. Dundee (0382) 4121 **Balmerino to Perth** The Perth and Kinross District Council, Perth. Tel. Perth (0738) 21161.
From and to	Buddon Ness to Perth.
Distance	31 miles.
Length	Unlimited.
Beam	,,
Draught	11ft. to Perth at high water springs.
Headroom	Tay Railway Bridge, 77ft.
Locks	None.
Tow-path	,,
Bridges	Tay Bridge is 2 miles long and consists of 86 spans. There is a road bridge downstream of the railway bridge.
General remarks	The entrance to the River Tay is marked by a lightship and a system of lighted buoys covering a navigation channel of ample width to deal with the largest vessels using the port. The minimum depth of water is 18 feet.
Connections	Two miles west of Newburgh is the River Earn. Navigable for 6 miles to Bridge of Earn for light craft.
Pilotage	Authority for pilots is the Dundee Harbour Trust, but pilotage is not compulsory for pleasure yachts.

Edinburgh and Glasgow Union Canal (120)

This canal was promoted by an Act in 1817 and was opened in 1822. It was made level for 31 miles and then descended 112 feet through 11 locks to the Forth and Clyde Canal. It traverses pleasant though not particularly exciting countryside. The canal has probably the most notable civil engineering works of any canal in Scotland. The ancient ruined palace of Linlithgow with excellent carvings is situated on a promontory in Linlithgow Loch and the nearby pre-reformation church of St. Michael still adjoins the palace. The canal crosses the battlefield where General Hawley was defeated by Prince Charles Edward in 1746, the site being near the entrance to the Falkirk Tunnel.

The locks connecting the canal to the Forth and Clyde Canal at Port Downie (Falkirk) were closed in 1936 and subsequently filled in. The canal then gradually deteriorated and became derelict, but in 1973 the British Waterways Board agreed to reopen it for pleasure craft including powered craft from Linlithgow to Broxburn (about ten miles) with the prospect of further reopening and to licence such craft for mooring and navigation. Details may be had from British Waterways Board, Glasgow.

Attempts are being made to save parts which have outstanding examples of engineering particularly the three aqueducts over the Water of Leith, River Almond and River Avon.

This wide waterway like the Forth and Clyde should never have been abandoned, particularly in view of the size of the navigation works, so unlike the English narrow canals. There are total of 6 places where portages are necessary. Useable sections are Linlithgow to Broxburn, outskirts of Edinburgh to M8 motorway via Ratho and a section to Kingsknowe. A boat serving meals operates from Ratho and a trip boat from Linlithgow. Slipways have been built and more are planned. BWB are now encouraging use of the canal and want to develop it.

Authority	British Waterways Board.
From and to	Edinburgh to Falkirk.
Distance	31 miles.
Length	66ft.
Beam	11ft. 3ins.
Draught	3ft. 6ins.
Headroom	5ft.
Locks	None.
Bridges	62. Lowest bridge, Redhall with 5ft. headroom.
Tunnels	Falkirk. Length 696 yards. Headroom 11ft. 9ins.
Speed limit	4 miles per hour for motor boats.
Main access points	Woodcockdale Stables – Off the A706 road to Armadale, 2 miles south of Linlithgow. Linlithgow – Main access point is at the Manse Basin, south of the railway station, off Manse Road. Park Farm – 2 miles east of Linlithgow via either the B9080 or A803 roads. Fawnspark – East of Philpstoun where the B8046 road crosses the canal.

Winchburgh – At the west end of Winchburgh next to the Old Brick Works.

Broxburn – Where Greendykes Road crosses the canal.

M8 – Off the A89 road at Powflats, 1 mile south of Broxburn.

Almond Aqueduct – Use road to Lins Mills off Clifton Mains Road from the M8 roundabout, and take right fork before aqueduct (Grid Reference 105/706)

Ratho – Next to Bridge Inn, Ratho.

Wester Hailes – Turn left off Calder Road into Calder Crescent, just before Calder Road crosses the Union Canal.

Slateford – East of Slateford Aqueduct adjacent to canal crossing. Slateford Road, by Craiglockhart Road junction.

Meggetland – Off Colinton Road, 200 yards west of Polwarth Terrace junction.

Harrison Park – Use Harrison Road off either Slateford Road or Polwarth Terrace.

Lochrin Basin – Behind the Scottish and Newcastle Breweries complex at Fountainbridge, use Gilmore Park Road.

(Reference should be made to an ordnance survey map before visiting the canal).

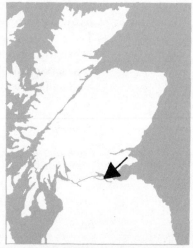

Distance Table					*Miles*	*Furlongs*
Port Hopetoun to:						
Slateford Aqueduct	...	...	...	...	2	2
Ratho	...	...	...	...	8	—
Lins Mill Aqueduct (over River Almond)				...	10	2
Broxburn	...	...	...	...	12	4
Winchburgh...	...	...	...	...	15	2
Phillipstoun	...	...	...	...	17	2
Linlithgow	...	...	...	...	21	—
Avon Aqueduct	...	...	...	...	23	4
Falkirk Tunnel entrance	...	...	...	29	4
Falkirk Tunnel exit	...	...	...	29	7
Falkirk	...	...	...	...	30	—

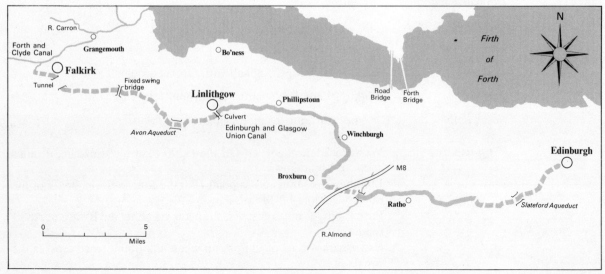

Appendix

HIRING CANAL AND RIVER CRAFT

The United Kingdom has the largest and best organised self-drive-live aboard boat fleets in the world. Certainly, the hire craft are the best available and most foreign operators in Europe use British boats. Firms advertise direct and others book through agencies.

The agencies are:

Blakes Holidays, Wroxham, Norwich, Norfolk NR12 8DH. Tel. Wroxham (060 53) 3221/2.

Boat Enquiries Ltd. 43 Botley Road, Oxford OX2 0PT. Tel. Oxford (0865) 511161.

Hoseasons Holidays Ltd. Sunway House, Oulton Broad, Lowestoft, Suffolk. Tel. Lowestoft (0502) 62211.

Whether you book a boat via an agency or direct is a matter of choice. Agencies do enforce standards but there are independent operators with equally exacting standards. Old pioneers of hiring used to visit the boatyards in the winter and select their boats and there is still some merit in doing this today possibly at the International Boat Show in January at Earl's Court which has hire boats on view. There are also those who visit popular sites in summer and see for themselves the boats with holiday-makers afloat.

Holidays afloat are longer established than is generally realised. Boats were being hired on the Broads at least as early as 1860 and the first agent to book craft was Mr. Brown of St. Olaves in 1890 in Broadland. The Blake Organisation was founded by Harry Blake in 1902 and the Hoseasons organisation came into being in 1945. Blakes and Hoseasons book the majority of boats available and also a large number of land based self catering holiday units.

The other agency has been in existence for many years and has some specialised craft on offer as well as conventional craft. It also has a number of hotel boats for booking. There are a lot of boats on offer for hire in Europe via the agencies. These overseas boatyards have in many cases been started by British firms.

Early, post war pleasure cruising was given an immense boost by the Inland Waterways Association which published a *Pink List* of Hire Craft. This grew over the years and became the Association of Pleasurecraft Operators, a separate body which has been mainly concerned with craft on the canal system. It is an association of a large number of operators and apart from hire craft, it includes day boats, tripper boats and other facilities. The yachting press also carries many useful advertisements.

As we go to press we are advised that British Waterways Board have launched a new overseas marketing consortium. BWB have run a hire fleet of their own for many years with bookings taken direct. The new concern, U.K. Waterway Holidays Ltd is a joint venture with BWB and hire cruiser operators through their trade association, the Association of Pleasure Craft Operators. The fleet consists of hire cruisers and hotel boats, from bases all over England, Scotland and Wales. The headquarters will be Melbury House, Melbury Terrace, London NW1 6JX. (Tel: 01-723 3700). The operation will at first deal only with enquiries and bookings from overseas but the scope of the operation may well make this new concern a new booking agency for home trade as well from U.K. residents.

CANOEABLE RIVERS

Particulars of several of the following rivers have already been given, the others are only of interest to the canoeist. The list has been prepared in conjunction with the British Canoe Union of England and Wales, Flexel House, 45/47 High Street, Addlestone, Weybridge, Surrey, KT15 1JV.

England and Wales.

Aire (Yorks.)
Arun (Sussex)
Avon (Devon)
Avon (Hants.)
Avon (Somerset)
Avon (Warwickshire) including the tributaries Arrow, Leam, Alne and Stour.
Dart (Devon)
Dee (Cheshire)
Derwent (Yorks.)
Eden (Cumberland)
Fal (Cornwall)
Lee (Herts.)
Lune (Lancs.)
Medway (Kent)
Nene (Northants.)
Norfolk and Suffolk Broads
Ouse (Great) including the tributaries Ouzel (Beds.), Brandon River, Lark and Cam, also the adjoining Middle Level Navigation.
Ribble (Lancs.) including the Calder and Hebble.
Severn, including the Vyrnwy, Tern and Teme.

Stour (Dorset)
Stour (Kent)
Tamar (Cornwall)
Torridge (Devon)
Tees (Durham/Yorks.)
Teifi (Cardiganshire)
Thames, including Thame, Cherwell, Churn, Colne, Coln, Kennet, Evenlode and Lodden. (Most of the lower tributaries are also canoeable.)
Tavy (Devon)
Towy (Carmarthenshire)
Trent (Derby/Staffs.) including Penk, Sow, Soar, Churnet, Dove, Derwent and Idle.
Tyne (Northumberland)
Ure (Yorks.) including Swale and Nidd.
Usk (Brecknock)
Wear (Durham)
Weaver (Cheshire)
Wey (Surrey)
Wharfe (Yorks.)
Wye (Hereford/Monmouth.) including Eithon, Lugg and Monnow.

Scotland

Clyde (Lanarkshire)
Dee (Aberdeenshire)
Dee (Kirkudbrightshire)
Don (Aberdeenshire)
Earn (Perthshire)
Forth (Perth/Stirlingshire)

Leven (Fife)
Ken (Kirkcudbrightshire)
Nith (Dumfrieshire)
Spey (Moray)
Tay (Perth)
Tweed (Finishes in Northumberland though mainly a Scottish river)

Canoeists can use many rivers and canals that are barred to other craft. Derelict canals holding water and rivers not controlled by navigation acts are usually private property and permission to traverse them should be obtained. If the canoeist's route is affected by the ebb and flow of ordinary tides then he has a right to navigation, but generally elsewhere he is in private water. But there are a large number of exceptions as some waterways enjoy a prescriptive right of navigation over their length. Canoeists are advised to join a club affiliated to the British Canoe Union or become a direct member of this body who issue a guide to the waterways and advise and help at national level.

On the canals controlled by the British Waterways Board, regulations vary as to whether tunnels can be used or not. The following is the present position but in case of doubt the nearest B.W.B. office should be consulted. The term canoe is also deemed to include small dinghies, small rowing boats and other small unpowered craft.

Small boats
The term 'unpowered' refers to canoes, dinghies, rowing boats, punts and other small unpowered boats.

Users of small boats should note the following points:

1. A valid Pleasure Boat Licence should be displayed whilst on any of the board's canals and as with other pleasure boats small boats are subject to the board's licensing conditions and bye-laws.

2. On the board's river navigations all boats should display either a valid Pleasure Boat Licence or a valid River Registration Certificate and are subject to the relevant bye-laws.

3. Unpowered boat users should take extra care near other craft particularly moving craft.

4. As the river navigations have a faster flow than canals and as some are tidal, unpowered boaters (especially novices) should be sure that they will not be swept away by current. Similarly users of small powered boats should ensure that their engine is capable of navigating against the current.

5. All boats should keep away from weirs and sluices, and the board strongly discourages boaters from 'shooting weirs' on safety grounds.

In addition to the normal licensing Conditions, special conditions apply to the use of certain tunnels and lengths of waterways. These are as follows:

1. No unpowered boat shall navigate through the following tunnels except if:

a. it is safely towed by a powered boat;
b. it is not manned;
c. it is fitted with satisfactory tunnel lights.

Canal	Name of tunnel	Yards	Canal	Name of tunnel	Yards
Ashby	Snarestone	250	Grand Union	Islington	960
BCN	Dudley	3154		Maida Hill	272
	Gosty Hill	557		Saddington	880
	Netherton	3027		Shrewley	433
Caldon	Froghall	76	Kennet and Avon	Savernake	502
	Leek	130			
Grand Union	Blisworth	3075⅝	Leeds and Liverpool	Foulridge	1640
	Braunston	2042		Gannow	559
	Crick	1528	Llangollen	Chirk	459
	Husbands Bosworth	1166		Ellesmere	87
				Whitehouses	191

426 INLAND WATERWAYS OF GREAT BRITAIN

Canal	Name of tunnel	Yards
Mon. and Brecon	Ashford	375
Peak Forest	Hyde Bank	308
	Woodley (Butterhouse Green)	176
Stratford-upon-Avon	Brandwood	352
Trent and Mersey	Barnton	572
	Harecastle	2926
	Preston Brook	1239
	Saltersford	424
Worc. and Birmingham	Dunhampstead	236
	Shortwood	613
	Tardebigge	580
	Wast Hill	2726

Boats are not permitted to run their engines in Dudley Tunnel (3172 yds) on the Birmingham Canal Navigation, and no boats are allowed into Standedge Tunnel (5698 yds) on the Huddersfield Narrow Canal.

2 The following tunnels may be used by unpowered boats provided that:
a All boaters are able to swim, wear life jackets, and have a suitable whistle attached to their bodies, by a substantial lanyard.
b All small boats have adequate buoyancy aids and a waterproof torch within them, and are fitted with an adequate white light fixed to the boat and showing ahead.

Canal	Name of tunnel	Yards
BCN	Coseley	360
	Galton	122
	Summit	103
Birmingham and Fazeley	Curdworth	57
Chesterfield	Drakeholes	147
Kennet and Avon	Bath No 1	59
	Bath No 2	55
Oxford	Newbold	250

Shopshire Union	Cowley	81
Staffs and Worcs.	Cookley	65
	Dunsley	23
Worc. and Birmingham	Edgbaston	105

3 On the following commercial waterways special conditions may be imposed on the use of small powered and unpowered boats:

Waterway	Length concerned
Aire and Calder Navigation	Leeds Lock to Goole: Fall Ings Lock, Wakefield to Castleford; Selby Canal from Knottingley to Haddesley Lock.
Calder and Hebble Navigation	Wakefield to Greenwood Lock.
Gloucester and Sharpness Canal	Sharpness Dock to Gloucester Lock.
New Junction Canal	Southfield to Bramwith
Sheffield and South Yorks. Nav.	Bramwith to bottom of Tinsley Flight at Sheffield

Details about the nature of the conditions may be obtained from the appropriate area engineer. In general the use of small boats on the Gloucester and Sharpness Canal is discouraged.

TYPES OF INLAND WATERWAY COMMERCIAL CRAFT

The commonest of these is the narrow boat, sometimes called long boat or monkey boat, which usually work in pairs, the leading boat towing the butty boat. They are the traditional craft and are mostly of a standard pattern, being approximately 70 feet long by 7 feet wide.
In the north of England a shortened and widened version of narrow boat used to go through the differently proportioned locks on certain canals, and in the Black Country will be found narrow boats without cabins, used for short journeys and called day boats. The 70-foot boat can carry about 30 tons, but due to the lack of dredging of British canals, 25 tons is the usual limit. In some cases the maximum is only 20 tons.

There is a short history of narrow boats published by Geoffrey Dibb Limited. There were a number of variations, and an expert could detect the difference between a Fellows, Morton and Clayton boat, a Yarwood's boat, a 'Town Class' Grand Union boat built by Harland and Woolf at Woolwich and others. Some boats were composite constructions (steel and wood) and some were all wood. The few narrow boats constructed at present are mainly all steel construction, although firms are still in existence that could build an all wooden narrow boat. There is a very thriving Narrow Boat Owners Club for enthusiasts.

In the Midlands will be found several batches of disused day-boats approximately 8ft. 6ins. beam. These would be used for certain sections of canal only and were called wharf boats.

Some narrow boats are painted in the traditional manner. This traditional painting is the only remaining folk art alive today in Britain. All canal boats used as dwellings are subject to George Smith's famous Acts of Parliament of 1877 and 1884. They must be registered under Regulations issued by the Ministry of Health for which a fee of 25p. is charged. This certifies the lettering, numbering and marking of the boat and the age, number and sex of the boat's occupants. The second Act places the responsibility on the local sanitary authorities for the enforcement of the Ministry of Health Regulations.

Wide boats were found in the Wey Navigation and Basingstoke Canal until recent years. They navigated the Thames Estuary to the Surrey Docks (now disused). Swim ended barges are towed by tugs on the Thames and can be seen on the lower section of the Grand Union, the Lee, Stort and elsewhere near the River Thames. They are known to the lightermen as 'punts'. Iron compartment boxes are seen on the Aire and Calder and are called 'Tom Puddings', they were towed in trains of up to nineteen boats, by tugs, but are no more. Use ceased in 1986.

Other specialised craft that were common to certain areas are the Severn Trows, Yorkshire Keels, Norfolk Wherries, Welsh Clippers and Mersey Flats. Thames sailing barges survive in a number of forms and a good deal of information is available about them, but the others, except for the wherry, virtually cease to exist apart from partly decayed hulks in estuaries.

Flats, trows, keels and clippers are poorly documented and the serious student could well make a study of these interesting craft. An attempt was made to preserve a keel some years ago but it was a failure, in spite of extensive restoration. The keel *Mayday* having laid at Goole for fourteen years is the subject of a further attempt to save her and rig her as a sailing keel. The Norfolk Wherry Trust has successfully restored *Albion*. Wherries were clinker built craft but *Albion* was the exception being carvel-built, but in other respects a typical wherry. Wherries were essentially river craft but some carried detachable keels to assist in the estuaries, one is known to have ventured as far as Prague. This sailing craft could almost sail into the wind's eye. The Norfolk Wherry Trust at Horning look after *Albion* and support for their work is well worth while as is also the work of the Sailing Barge Preservation Trust.

A few Thames Sailing Barges are still under sail, trading in the Thames and Medway

A PAIR OF NARROW BOATS

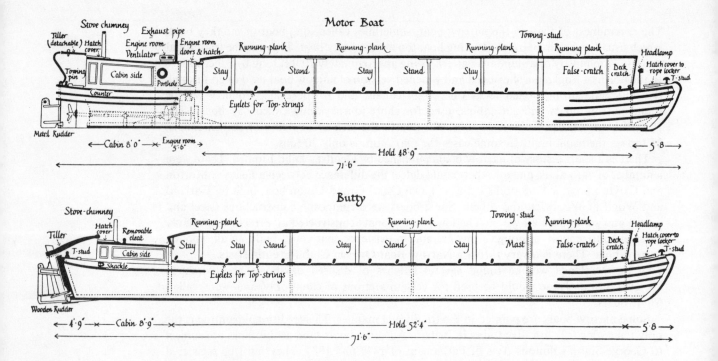

Estuaries to the south and east coast rivers, but many have become dumb lighters. Their story would form a book in itself and a number have been published. Norfolk wherries have been similarly well documented.

The Dolphin Sailing Barge Museum Trust plans to establish a museum with special emphasis on spritsail barges and it is hoped to acquire a sailing barge for preservation. There is an Exeter Maritime Museum interested in inland waterway craft and the National Maritime Museum is world famous. A number of provincial museums have models and plans of inland waterway craft.

In Scotland fishing boats are often seen on the canals, together with the famous 'puffers' which are common on the Crinan Canal.

New craft can be found operating on the broad English waterways. Ferrybridge power station is supplied with coal by a pusher-tug with three loaded compartment-barges, and new 500 ton barges have been built to take oil to Leeds. A new development is L.A.S.H. Which means 'lighter-aboard-ship'. These barge-carrying ships are now entering service, but their use is restricted in Britain owing to the size of the barges carried being too big for many of our waterways.

The large modern craft to be found on our waterways are the barges operating from Goole to York. Tonnage dead weight is 480 tons, length 134 feet 6 inches, draught 7 feet. These were the largest until recently. Now with craft carrying up to 700 tons using the Sheffield and South Yorkshire Navigation we shall see some new and exciting craft. B.A.C.T. or 'Barge Aboard Catarmaran' is another development that should soon be seen on our canals.

In recent years a number of craft are being salvaged and restored particularly sailing barges in the north. A Stour barge has been restored at Sudbury. The I.W.A. can put enthusiasts in touch with restoration schemes.

THE PUBLIC RIGHT OF NAVIGATION

This is a very emotive issue and there is little guidance for anyone who wishes to study the subject. Waterways were generally promoted by Act of Parliament, and in the very early days by Letters Patent and other means. In very few cases indeed did they restrict the right of navigation. In the author's researches only the Derby Canal Act was found to confer no statutory rights of navigation.

By kind persmission of the Inland Waterways Protection Society who sponsored the meeting at Manchester University, reproduced is the main text of the paper read by the author in 1977. An early document on the subject was published in the Law Society Journal dated 4th December 1953 but naturally parts of it are seriously out of date. A later study of the subject was carried out at the Trent Polytechnic at Nottingham on the 5th October 1979 when a Symposium on the *Public Rights of Navigation and Other Users of the Rivers* was held. The published report of the *Proceedings* makes interesting reading. Arthur Telling, barrister and principal lecturer in law at Trent Polytechnic, wrote a very useful and helpful article particularly to the layman in *Water Space* (Winter) 1980. This journal was the official organ of the Water Space Amenity Commission. The book, *The Law of Rivers and Watercourses* by A. S. Wisdom, published by Shaw & Sons Ltd., is a very useful work of reference.

The following is the text of a paper read by the author at Manchester University in 1977.

It should be simply stated that a public right of navigation is basically a right of way for the public in boats, and this right will entitle them to use the navigation works and to anchor or moor for reasonable periods so long as they do not cause obstruction or injure private rights. There is little difference between the right to use the road and exercising a right to use a highway by water. The right of navigation, like the right of way on land, should of course be used reasonably. You should not trespass on the sides of a highway or waterway.

The landowner's right of fishing is subject to the right of passage on a navigational waterway, and therefore it is unreasonable to moor for a long period or refuse to move on request from a popular salmon fishing pool. After all, no one may stable his horse on the Queen's highway.

Man has used river transport since the beginning of time and many of our early cathedrals had the stone for building them brought by water.

The first artificial cuts or canals appear to be made by the Romans, who constructed Caerdyke (or Carr dike), sections of which can be seen between Peterborough and the Trent. The Fossdyke Canal was a Roman waterway, and records show that as far back as 1121 King Henry I had improvements carried out on it, but no major canals for navigation were constructed until just before the middle of the eighteenth century.

The question of right of navigation has been challenged on a number of occasions, and as early as 1065 Edward the Confessor made a decree regarding four rivers, namely, the Thames, Trent, Severn and Yorkshire Ouse. He ordered that the mills and fisheries should be destroyed and the rivers made navigable. A very early feat of engineering was Alresford Pond. This was a reservoir to provide a head of water to enable craft to navigate through the early flash locks to Alresford and was constructed under the direction of Bishop Godfrey de Lucy.

If one is compiling a list of Acts dealing with rights of navigation of our waterways, the first should be Magna Carta (1225-9 Henry III). It is perhaps sometimes overlooked that, until recently, virtually the only section of Magna Carta that is unrepealed or unaltered relates to the uninterrupted navigation of our rivers. There are a number of early Acts relating to rivers, e.g. the Thames, 1425; Severn, 1430; and in 1462, among other Acts, a Charter of

Conservancy was granted to the Mayor and Burgesses of York, and this Charter related to the Aire, the Derwent and the Calder.

Perhaps the most interesting of the Acts to students of our subject was the Letters Patent granted to John Gilbert, who is claimed by some to be the inventor of the dredger. In 1563 John Trew constructed the Ship Canal to Exeter. There is a possibility that exceptions do exist, but in practice every canal and river which the public have used is generally regulated by private Act of Parliament which authorised the construction of a navigation. With very few exceptions, e.g. the Derby Canal, the Acts give a statutory right to navigate the waterway, generally on payment of a toll, and this right existed in most cases to pleasure craft and mechanically propelled boats. There was a famous case relating to the Midland Railway Company in 1859 where the railway company endeavoured to prohibit power driven craft, but the right of navigation for steamers was upheld.

The decline of the canal system from the middle of the last century onwards promoted the Royal Commission of 1906 to look at the problems relating to navigations, and it is interesting to note in 1905 a Canals Trust Bill was introduced into Parliament but never reached the Statute Book, but it is remarkably like the thinking behind the National Waterways Conservancy which was advocated by the Inland Waterways Association in post-war years.

The appalling state of navigations following the last war produced the Inland Waterways Association, the Inland Waterways Protection Society, the East Anglian Waterways Association – a regional body – and over the years societies have been formed for practically every navigation in the country. Many have been prompted because obstructions to navigations in various forms exist. In my early years in the waterway campaign I discovered before the war the unsatisfactory legal title in the case of the Basingstoke Canal. This canal has played a much greater part in waterway history than is generally realised.

In 1948 it became known that this canal was to be sold by auction, and a committee was formed to try and save it. The vigour with which the campaign was fought produced a press covereage which, for those days, was quite a feat. A Sheffield solicitor, the late Cyril Styring, whose memory is perpetuated in the IWA trophy of that name, came to the assistance of the committee with generous help, and it came to light that the company owning the canal were not linked with the rights and obligations of the Act of 1777. These rights and obligations in fact still exist but they are vested in the ghost of the original company which wound itself up in 1869 and disappeared. The canal was in fact acquired by a private company, although at the time I said that the best way to acquire these derelict waterways was to form a non-profit making company. It is interesting that these suggestions were taken up by those seeking to save the Lower Avon, and this has remained the pattern for the formation of a number of Trusts all over the country. Thus the failure on the Basingstoke led to success elsewhere. The company formed was never a success in putting the canal back into working order, although in the early days it made some attempt to do so. What also came to light after the war was the derelict state and curious legal position of the river Stour. The Commissioners running the river had disappeared and there was no competent body to administer it. It was discovered that Section 45 of the Railway & Canal Act of 1888 had empowered the Minister to order the repair of a derelict navigation, and if this was not done, transfer the navigation to a competent body to do so. Unfortunately, in the case of the Basingstoke this was never done for technical reasons, but when the Surrey & Hants Canal Society was formed in 1966 I did endeavour to get them to make an application under Section 45, but the very new society, faced with many problems, was not sure this was the right approach, and it is doubtful whether the society could have been converted into a Trust in time anyway, and therefore we had the tragedy presented to us by the notorious Transport Act of 1968 taking away the public right of navigation on canals and also the extinction of Acts such as the 1888 one with its valuable clauses.

Rights on Rivers, not on Canals

In attempting to assert one's right of navigation where they still exist, one is faced with the curious situation whereby the rights that still exist on the rivers have gone on the canals. I presume in the case of a canalised river the rights of navigation on the artificial lock cuts have been taken away, but on the river itself they still exist.

Investigations which I carried out dealing with the right of navigation in conjunction with extra material for my book 'Inland Waterways of Great Britain' from 1966 to 1971 showed a number of navigations, in addition to the Basingstoke, with defective titles. They are as follows:

The North Walsham & Dilham Canal, Norfolk (an exact parallel with the Basingstoke Canal)
The Royal Military Canal in Kent, which was constructed without an Act of Parliament
Brayford Mere on the Fossdyke Canal
River Stour, Essex and Suffolk
Witham Navigable Drains, Lincolnshire
Linton Lock Navigation, Yorkshire
River Derwent, Yorkshire
Market Weighton Canal, Yorkshire
The Sussex Ouse
Bow Back Rivers, East London
Driffield Navigation, Yorkshire
Chichester Canal, West Sussex

This list, unfortunately, is by no means the whole story. There are a number of cases where it is possible to navigate above the limit laid down in the Act controlling the navigation, and where this has been done from time immemorial there is a prescriptive right of navigation. Cases such as these are:

The river Thame to Dorchester
The river Medway above Tonbridge
The Western Rother, Sussex
The Great Ouse above Bedford
The river Wissey above Stoke Ferry in Norfolk

This list is not comprehensive, but in a number of cases persons exerting their right of navigation by prescription have been harassed and intimidated by claims that the river is private. Probably one of the most interesting cases is the river Avon in Hampshire which was constructed under an Act of Parliament in 1664 and was opened in 1684. This ran from Christchurch to Salisbury, a distance of 36 miles. Very little is known about this project, but no Act of Parliament or closure order ever seems to have been passed. It goes through one of the most heavily protected fishing areas in Britain where it is possible to pay up to £200 for a rod. There have been numerous skirmishes over the river and navigation rights, one of which occurred in 1907 with the residents of the village of Downton. There was a legal action in recent years which finished up in the High Court between Elkin's Boatyard at Christchurch and the Avon River Authority. Elkin lost, but what is interesting is that at no time in the proceedings was any mention made of the Act of 1664. The Avon case of 1907 highlights a problem with us today that whilst a public meeting set up a River Avon Public Rights Committee, insufficient money was raised to fight the battle and the judgment was lost.

There was for many years persistent obstruction on railway-owned canals to restrict navigation, such as forbidding the lighting of fires in the cabins during winter, refusal to allow ice to be broken, and as late as 1948 the nationalised successor, the Railway Executive, issued orders that navigation of the Kennet & Avon Canal after 4 p.m. on Wednesdays, after 11 a.m. on Saturdays and altogether on Sundays was forbidden, and this effectively killed pleasure traffic.

In view of the persistence of the argument that pleasure craft are something distinct from commercial vessels, it should be recorded that the upsurge of pleasure boating in recent years is not something new; it is merely a revival. Before the advent of the railways there was considerable passenger carrying and, indeed, passenger carrying occurred on the lesser known waterways as well. The most unlikely place for passenger boat traffic would be the deserted Fens in Lincolnshire, but nevertheless passenger traffic survived for shopping excursions down to the early 1920s, and the stone landing stages and steps still exist in Boston today. Similarly, if you look in obscure places these old landing stages are still to be found.

Some comment on towpaths ought to be made. After the passing of the 1968 Transport Act the British Waterways Board has not been responsible for the maintenance of the towpaths alongside canals. It appears the Board is only under an obligation to maintain the towpath for essential works or where it forms a public right of way. In other cases it has no obligations, but the local authorities had authority by the 1968 Act to contribute towards the upkeep of canal towpaths where they provided recreation for local inhabitants. There has been little interest from local authorities so far.

The BWB makes it clear that it is not prepared to permit towing paths to be used for horse towage except in special cases. You have, therefore, the absurd situation that whilst you can call it a towing path you cannot necessarily tow your boat from it, at least not with a horse. There are horse-drawn boats but BWB has not shown any particular keeness to have more of this type of business.

The towpath is part of the navigation as much as locks, bridges and aqueducts, and the Board must on many occasions need an effective towpath to carry out essential maintenance. The present situation is plainly absurd.

Over the last three years it has become increasingly common to see mooring rights being leased on the towpath side. This can cause problems both for boat owners and towpath walkers. Sometimes the moorings occupy the only reasonable access to a village and it may be almost impossible to moor a boat elsewhere – we have heard of someone being asked to pay to moor his boat overnight.

Inconvenience can also be caused to people using the towpath, when the person leasing the area may claim walkers have no right to pass. This has happened in Wheaton Aston on the Shropshire Union Canal where, possibly through a misunderstanding, some villagers believe they may be prevented from using part of the towpath, a favourite local walk.

Legal closure of navigations and also legalising structures which obstruct navigation are a problem still with us, and by far the worst cases are lowered bridges and other similar obstructions that are placed over navigations making headroom so small as to make navigation impossible. Until 1968, navigations were legally closed under Section 45 of the Railway & Canal Act of 1888 which gave the Minister of Transport power to issue a Warrant of Abandonment. Other navigations were extinguished by Section 41 of the Land Drainage Act of 1930, and also in recent years powers were given to river boards and their successors to close certain waterways. In all these cases official notification has to be put in a local newspaper as well as the *London Gazette,* and it is a matter of profound regret that even in recent years we have lost one of the navigations of the Bridgewater Canal network and the Black Sluice Drainage Navigation in Lincolnshire. Bridges have been lowered over the Driffield Navigation in Yorkshire and at Spalding in Lincolnshire over the Welland. No one apparently was able to effectively object. Therefore everybody concerned with the waterway movement should take particular care to look in his local paper every week at the official announcements column. All kinds of things will come to light this way, and there are some amusing attempts to divert towpaths which are established rights of way and close them. The Transport Act of 1968 has changed the picture considerably, and the vigilance watching the nationalised waterways network is such that no closure proposal by BWB will be unnoticed. But it is in the case of minor navigations and those privately owned that the danger lies. Canals that do not belong to the BWB come under Section 112 of the Transport Act 1968 whereby the Minister can by Order in effect close a navigation but, before making an Order, he must comply with Schedule 13 of the Act and consult with any organisations representing persons using the canal in question. Then he must publish the effect of his proposed Order in local newspapers, in a national newspaper and display this notice in places adjacent to the waterway. The local or river authority can require an inquiry to be held by the Minister, and any organisation can obtain an inquiry if the waterway was used to a significant extent for the purpose of navigation when notice of the proposed Order was published, provided the organisation had made an objection to the Order. An Order may include provisions similar to those in Section 109 and transfer the navigation to the local authority, a river authority or any body having public or charitable objects capable of discharging its responsibilities in consequence of the transfer of the navigation to it.

The case of the river Welland highlights the necessity of watching the public notices column as it appears unknown that an Order can be made by the Minister under Section 3 of the Highways Miscellaneous Provisions Act 1961. This Act refers back to the previous Act which is the Highways Act 1959. To find anyone to read the *London Gazette* is a far from easy task, but I would appeal to every waterway enthusiast in the country to watch this local paper.

In the past there have been a number of cases of a special Act of Parliament being passed to close a navigation, but this procedure does not seem to have been adopted in recent years. The last recorded successful closure was of the Stoudwater Navigation, but the climate of opinion has changed so much that this type of procedure is now not used, probably due to the fact that it attracts a lot of publicity!

Power lines have formed a dangerous obstruction to navigation in a number of cases. Various agreements have been made about power lines which on occasions present a hazard to navigation, but the legal position appears to be obscure. When an accident occurred at Peterborough in 1960 proceedings were threatened against the owner of a boat fouling overhead wires. After correspondence had been sent to the electricity authorities pointing out that in between the locks and bridges a prescriptive right of almost unlimited headroom had been obtained and enjoyed for over 20 years, the onus was clearly on the authorities not to put in an obstruction to navigation without proper consultation and making certain that headroom was sufficient. The interesting thing about this case was that proceedings were dropped against the boat owner and although many reminders were sent, the electricity authority over a good many years kept stalling and saying they would write in due course in further detail, but never did. In fact, the official who first dealt with correspondence eventually died as the correspondence carried on over such a long period.

As President of the Canadian Canoe Association of Great Britain I have been made familiar with the problems facing canoeists regarding rights of navigation. Where rivers are not regulated by statute and there is no prescriptive right of navigation, the waterway is private and the proper course is to obtain permission from the owner. The task of proving rights by prescription has always been difficult, but the Highway Act 1959 (sec 34-36) which provides that proof of 20 years uninterrupted use of a way as a right by the public shall be conclusive, has undoubtedly helped, providing of course there is not sufficient evidence on the other side that there was no intention to dedicate a right of way. The British Canoe Union has this matter under active concern, and the problem has been made worse in recent years by the match fishing competitions which take place on rivers where substantial monies are at stake and there are certainly a number of business interests involved.

In reading old navigation Acts care should be taken to note whether they *confirmed* old navigation rights, or *conferred* them. The distinction is important since in a number of cases although the navigation act has been rescinded by legal process, the rights of navigation by prescription remains.

MISCELLANEOUS WATERWAYS

The following is a list of inland waterways that are no longer navigable but of general interest and of benefit to canoeists and light craft users.

Some waterways under restoration at present but with long derelict sections have been included in the main section, so that more details can be given. Those listed below are in various states of dereliction and can in some cases be used for canoeing and towpath rambling and there are of course some canals that have virtually disappeared. Several of the waterways in the long term are restorable but in most cases only sections can be restored. Care should be taken in exploring old waterways as they are generally on private property and the old towpaths are not always public rights of way.

In case of the river navigations, the length now unnavigable is given, but whereas in some the locks are either derelict or have completely disappeared, the tidal portion of the river in most instances is still usable. Many of these rivers can be used by light craft such as canoes, but particular care should be taken in negotiating the old locks some of which can be shot by the expert canoeist, but the slow crumble and decay of old masonry may make this an extremely hazardous procedure. Portaging is recommended, although after preliminary reconnaissance from the bank it is possible in certain cases to shoot through the old lock-chambers. Do not trespass when portaging – seek permission.

Old maps marking waterways no longer in existence should be treated with reserve. Some projected canals appear on early maps as completed waterways, whereas in fact they were only started and then abandoned for one reason or another, and in other cases canals are marked as completed when, in actual fact, they did not pass the initial planning stage. Some of these navigations have been abandoned by Act of Parliament, others have been neglected and have not been maintained to statutory standards, with the result that traffic has been unable to use the waterway. Many canals have been lost in this manner to the detriment of our national economy.

Several of the waterways in the list have not been abandoned by Act of Parliament, they have merely been allowed to fall into a state of neglect which is apparently illegal and certainly contrary to every public interest. Canal and river navigations were usually promoted by Act of Parliament though there were numerous short private canals constructed from time to time, often to supply industrial premises.

Light craft users of navigations that have been abandoned should take great care as in most cases, they will be traversing private water and it is important to respect riparian interests so that the privilege of navigation is not lost.

Fuller details of most of these derelict waterways can be obtained from the works of Charles Hadfield, the canal historian. They are in the series 'Canals of the British Isles', published by David and Charles of Newton Abbot, Devon, and are recommended to those studying canal history. The help of Phillip Daniel of the British Waterways Board in preparing this section is gratefully acknowledged.

England and Wales.

Aberdare Canal. Now closed and converted to a road, after 1900. There were 2 locks and one stoplock. Length $6\frac{3}{4}$ miles.

Adelphi Canal. A private canal serving an iron foundry near Calow, close to the Chesterfield Canal. It was ½ mile long and ran to the nearest road, which linked to the canal. Closed in the middle of the 19th century.

Adur Navigation. Closed in 1875. Navigable for canoes from the upper lock near West Grinstead church. There were 2 locks on $3\frac{5}{8}$ miles closed section.

Aike Beck. A short river navigation, 1⅞ miles through 2 locks from the River Hull to Lockington landing.

Andover Canal. Closed in 1859. Over 14 miles of this was converted to a railway. Portions of the canal are still canoeable and they form part of the Test River but fishing rights are very keenly preserved and light craft are not permitted to the use of the river or old canal cuts.

Ashburnham Canal. Long derelict built prior to 1800, 1¼ miles long, and this ran near Pembrey, to the estuary of the Gwendraeth. There was a branch, a ¼ mile long to Coed built later.

Ashby Canal. Closed from Measham to Moira by Act of Parliament. The section from Moira to Donisthorpe has been closed for many years.

Avon Navigation (Wilts. and Hants.). Navigation works were constructed under an Act of Parliament in 1664, but were all destroyed by a flood soon afterwards. The river is canoeable from Salisbury to Christchurch on the old navigation route and, in good water conditions, from Pewsey. The river is strictly preserved for fishing and light craft are forbidden passage through the various properties though the Act of 1664 does not seem to have been rescinded.

Axe Navigation. Navigation above Bleadon ceased over 100 years ago. There was a tide lock at Bleadon, but the only navigable portion for many years has been the tideway up to the railway bridge.

Aylsham Navigation. (See Bure navigation).

Baybridge Canal. Alternative name for canalised section of the Adur.

Barnsley Canal. This canal ran from its junction with the Aire and Calder Navigation to Barnsley, a distance of 14½ miles, through 15 locks. Closed by Ministry of Transport Warrant in 1953. Derelict, though several pounds contain water since they are used by the National Coal Board as reservoirs. Restoration work has commenced.

Basingstoke Canal. Derelict and closed from Greywell to Basingstoke.

Bedale Beck. An unfinished canal from the junction with the River Swale to Bedale. There were to be 2 locks but the remains of only one at Leeming can be traced. About 2 miles long.

Bishop Monkton Canal. A water half a mile long that previously ran from south of Oxclose Lock on the River Ure to the canal head on the Westwick to Bishop Monkton Road. Closed mid-1800s.

Black Sluice Drainage and Navigation. Originally ran from Boston to Guthram Gowt, a distance of 21 miles. Closed 1967.

Blythe Navigation. In 1757 this river was made navigable from Halesworth to Blythburgh. Now closed, there were 4 locks on this section.

Bond End Canal. This connected the Trent and Mersey Canal at Shobnall to the River Trent. There was a stop lock and lock on the navigation, which has been disused since c.1875.

Bottisham Lode. This has never been closed but is very shallow. It ran from the Cam for 2½ miles to Lode village. The entrance staunch has long been demolished.

Bourne Eau. This led from the River Glen in Deeping Fen to Bourne, a distance of 3½ miles. There were 2 locks, now fixed sluices. The whole route can be used by light craft that can be portaged.

Bowser's Canal. A short length of waterway to link a small colliery near Ffrwd to the nearest road.

Bradford Canal. This canal was 3 miles long and had 10 locks. It connected Bradford to the Leeds and Liverpool Canal. It was closed in 1922 by Act of Parliament.

Braunton Canal. A short canal made after several grand schemes had come to nothing from Caen River and Knowle Water to Braunton.

Bridgewater Canal. West of Runcorn locks are closed and locks removed and there is no longer a connection with the Manchester Ship Canal.

Brue Navigation. Originally the lower portion of the Glastonbury Canal. Only a small part of the tideway is now navigable.

There were two short navigations Brown's and Galton's. These ran from the Brue northwards and were both approximately 1¼ miles long. They ran to North Drain but this does not seem to have been a navigation. There are some remains to be seen.

Bude Canal. This tub-boat canal was abandoned by Act of Parliament in 1891. There were routes running from Bude to Red Post, North Tamerton and Druxton. Also to Brendon and Blagdonmoor with a feeder from Alfordisworthy reservoir. Many miles are still open for water supply. The broad canal from Bude had 3 locks, but only the sea lock is now in use as the broad canal was closed in 1900 though the whole 2 miles can still be used for local boating. Canal was famous for its inclined planes.

Bungay Navigation. Canalised River Waveney. Three locks now derelict, closed 1934 by Order of the Ministry of Agriculture and Fisheries. This navigation ran from Geldeston to Bungay.

Bure Navigation. Canalisation of the Bure from Coltishall to Aylsham (Norfolk) through 5 locks, a distance of 9 miles. Closed by Warrant of the Ministry of Transport in 1927 though locks had been unusable since 1912.

Burry and Loughor Rivers. These rivers were improved under an Act of 1815 and were mainly used for coal traffic which lasted until the coming of railways.

Caistor Canal. This canal was never completed to Caistor in Lincolnshire but terminated at Moortown. It is now derelict. Originally 4 miles in length with 6 locks. Closed 1855.

Calder and Hebble Navigation (Halifax Branch). There were 14 locks on this branch which was 1¾ miles long. Closed by Warrant of the Minister of Transport dated 21st August 1942.

Caldon Branch Canal. The Branch to Leek was closed by L.M.S. Railway Act of 1944. The Branch was 3¼ miles long and left the main canal at Hazelhurst Junction. The canal can still be used to the River Churnet Aqueduct, a distance of 2 miles. Work on restoring the remainder is planned (1972.)

Cam, River (Gloucestershire). Used now only as a feeder to the Ship Canal nearby but previously navigable to Cam Village. Light craft can still use this route just over 1 mile long.

Cann Quarry Canal (Devon). A private canal 2 miles long built as a mill channel and a tub-boat canal. Disused about 1836.

Car Dyke. An ancient Roman waterway that ran from the Cam near Waterbeach to the River Witham near Lincoln. Modern research does not support previous theories that this was a transport canal except possibly at the Northern end.

Carlisle Canal. Length 11¼ miles. with 9 locks. Closed in 1853 and converted into a railway.

Cassington Cut. This was built by the Duke of Marlborough and ran from the Thames to the Cassington-Eynsham Road in Oxfordshire. It was ¾ mile long and there was one lock at the entrance.

Chard Canal. This canal was opened in 1842. Length 13½ miles, it ran from the Bridgwater and Taunton Canal at Creech St. Michael to Chard. None of the old route is usable but the huge embankments and sites of the inclined planes at Thornfalcon, Wrantage, Ilminster and Chard are worth visiting. Closed 1866.

Cinderford Canal. A private waterway connecting a Mill Pool to an ironworks at Cinderfoot in the Forest of Dean and was a mile long.

Charnwood Forest Canal. This canal was a failure largely due to troubles with the supply reservoir. It was 9¼ miles long and conveyed coal from Charnwood Forest to the Grand Union Canal. Disused 1801. Canal linked to G.U.C. by tramway.

Cod Beck. Junction of the River Swale to Thirsk. Though 5 locks were projected only 2 were Now being restored. Two locks when restored will link with the Severn. Listed in main section see page

Comstall Navigation. A short canal used in connection with the cotton mills at Etherow; used for coal supply.

Coombe Hill Canal. Short private canal constructed from the River Severn to the nearby road 3½ miles away. From here goods were taken to Cheltenham by road. Closed 1876. Now being restored. Authority: Severn Canal & Carrying Co. Ltd. Coombe Hill, Gloucestershire. Two locks when restored will link with the Severn.

Cromford Canal. This is 14⅝ miles long, with a branch to Pinxton Colliery 2 miles long. Connected to the Grand Union Canal and Nottingham Canal at Langley Mill. Butterley Tunnel closed due to colliery subsidence. Usable by light craft over part of its length. The portion above the closed tunnel is particularly beautiful. The railway remains that connected the canal to the Peak Forest Canal can still be inspected. There were 14 locks. Closed by L.M.S. Railway Act of 1944, except for ½ mile at the Langley Mill end of the canal. Buckland Hollow Tunnel was closed in 1969.

The Ambergate aqueduct has been demolished and Butterley tunnel has been long closed due to serious roof collapses. The 5½ miles from Cromford to Ambergate has been bought by the Derbyshire County Council in 1974, and the canal here has been restored. The section from Whatstandwell to Ambergate is now a nature reserve and the top section to Cromford, including the short Lea Wood Branch, now carries a horse drawn trip boat and this visits Lea Wood Pumping House and Engine; the original water supply is now restored. The bottom lock of the canal at Langley Mill has been restored, with a short length of canal, to connect with another short length of the top end of the Nottingham Canal, so craft from the Erewash Canal can use the Great Northern Basin.

Croydon Canal. Originally ran from Croydon to New Cross where it joined the Grand Surrey Canal. Closed in 1836 and converted into a railway.

Cuckmere, River. Navigable at high tide to Alfriston (site of Milton Lock). A bar at the entrance severely limits use of the river. Commercial traffic has used the river to Alfriston.

Cumberland Market Branch Canal. A short branch of the Grand Union in London that left the canal in Regent's Park. Filled in during the 1939-45 war, in part. A short length still open.

Cyfartha Canal. A South Wales tub-boat canal. Closed 1840.

Dearne and Dove Canal. Closed from Swinton to Barnsley (except Locks 1 to 4). There were a total of 19 locks and 2 branches.

Derby Canal. This canal was $14\frac{1}{2}$ miles long and ran from the Grand Union Canal at Sandiacre to the Trent and Mersey Canal at Swarkestone. There were branches to Little Eaton and the River Derwent.

Derwent River. This river was made a navigation by an Act of Parliament passed in 1720. From Derby to the Trent at Wilden Ferry, this navigation was later sold to the Derby Canal Company, who superseded this river navigation. The river is canoeable from as high up as Rowsley, though the old navigation section is unattractive.

Dick Brook. A very early canalisation from the River Severn to Yarranton Forge (three miles south of Stourport). It was ¾ mile long with 2 flash locks.

Doctor's Canal (listed in some books as Dr. Thomas's Canal). This ran from a junction with the Glamorganshire Canal at Denia to Treforest, a distance of 1 mile. Now derelict. Closed in 1914.

Dorset and Somerset Canal. This canal was only partially built. Eight miles of a branch were constructed, and the canal was then abandoned, though it is still remembered for its canal lift constructed at Mells to the design of Mr. Fussell.

Duke of Sutherland's Tub-boat Canal (Donnington Wood Canal). Commenced at Donnington with a junction with the Old Shropshire Canal and ran by Lilleshall Abbey to Pave Lane. There were 2 short branches. Total distance about 7 miles. Built by 1769 and closed completely by 1904.

Eardington Underground Canal. A canal ½ mile long linking lower and upper Eardington Forges. It was not linked directly to the Severn in the Bridgnorth area.

Eden, River. This river was made navigable for $10\frac{1}{4}$ miles, under an Act passed in 1721, but later was disused when the Carlisle Canal was opened. It was tidal throughout, but has silted up so that the tidal limit is 3 miles below Carlisle.

Emmet's Canal. Approximately 1 mile long, running to Birkenshaw Village. (Near Bradford). Disused by 1816.

Exeter and Credition Navigation. This canal was promoted by an Act in 1801 and was never completed and only just over ½ mile was excavated.

Fleet Canal. A canalisation of the river Fleet. This took traffic to Holborn Bridge from the Thames and became derelict in early 1700's. It has been covered over but is still a water channel.

Ffrwd Canal (Near Wrexham). A detached part of the Ellesmere Canal that was planned to run from the Dee to Trevor. The route was never built and this section was about 2 miles long and does not appear ever to be used.

Fletcher's Canal. A private canal once owned by the Clifton and Kersley Coal Co. Ltd. and was $1\frac{1}{2}$ miles long. It is now a water feeder to the Manchester, Bolton and Bury Canal. There was one lock only.

General Warde's Canal (Yspitty). This Carmarthenshire canal ran from a creek near Yspitty called Townsend's Pill and finally became two branches one leading to Bynea and the other to Pencrug.

General Warde's Canal (Dafen). A short extension of the Pill at Dafen to inland collieries.

Glamorganshire Canal. This canal commenced at Cyfartha and ran via Abercynon Treforest to Cardiff, a distance of $25\frac{1}{2}$ miles through 52 locks. The first half mile was closed in 1865 and the canal was disused above Abercynon after 1898. The Cardiff Corporation closed the canal by Act of Parliament in 1943, except for the bottom pound above the sea lock which was closed in 1950 under Section 27 of the Cardiff Corporation Act, 1943. The section between Tongwynlais and the Melingriffith Works at Whitchurch is maintained in order for fishing. The rest is virtually extinct.

Giant's Grave and Briton Ferry Canal. This canal formed a continuation of the Neath Canal at Giant's Grave. Length $\frac{1}{2}$ mile, no locks. It is now a water feeder to the local factories. One of group known as 'The Earl of Jersey's Canals'.

Glynne's, Sir John, Canal. This is sometimes called the Saltney Canal and was about a mile long. It was a local coal canal serving the Sandycroft colliery.

Glan-y-Wern Canal. This canal joined Red Jacket to Glan-y-Wern, a distance of $3\frac{1}{2}$ miles. Disused since 1910.

Glastonbury Canal. Joined Glastonbury to the river Brue at Highbridge. Closed in 1853, and sections of the bed were converted to a railway. Many sections are still usable by light craft. It was 14 miles long with 2 locks.

Grand Surrey Canal. An extension of the Surrey Docks now closed. Canal closed throughout. Ran originally from Surrey Docks to Camberwell, $2\frac{5}{8}$ miles with a branch to Peckham $\frac{1}{2}$ mile long. One entrance lock, from the Thames.

Grand Western Canal. Derelict from Taunton to Lowdwell. On this section were 8 canal lifts and 1 inclined plane. There was an entrance lock and exit lock to this section, length $13\frac{1}{2}$ miles. Closed 1867. There are no parts holding enough water for light craft. Portions of the lifts and aqueducts remain for the explorer.

Grantham Canal. Constructed under an Act of 1793, this canal ran from the Trent at Nottingham to Grantham, a distance of over 33 miles. There were 18 locks, 14 feet wide. There are long sections available for local boating. For permission apply to British Waterways Board, Dock Street, Leeds. Closed to barge traffic by Section 38 of the L.N.E.R. (General Powers Act) 1936. The entrance lock at Nottingham is still operable but not available for use.

Gravesend and Rochester Canal. Connected Gravesend to Strood. Derelict apart from the isolated section near Higham. Length $6\frac{1}{2}$ miles. Closed in 1845 when the canal tunnel was used for a railway though the Higham to Gravesend section remained open to 1937. Gravesend Basin is open for mooring. Dimensions: 80ft x 19ft x 4ft 3ins, details from Gravesend West Railway station. Owned by British Rail.

Greaseborough Canal (Park Gate). Made to serve coal mines near Greaseborough to link with the River Don. It was 1½ miles long with four locks and a ½ mile branch to Newbiggin. A private waterway that was totally disused by 1928.

Gresley's Canal. Built to connect the coal mines in Apedale to Newcastle-under-Lyne under an Act of 1775. 3 miles long. Derelict.

Hackney Canal. Constructed by Lord Clifford as a private canal for the export of china clay in 1843. The canal was half a mile long, and led from its junction with the River Teign estuary at Hackney to the main road nearby. The canal is derelict and the entrance lock has been bricked up. Closed 1955.

Hatfield Moors Peat Canals. These canals in the Thorne area were about 7 miles long and carried the peat from the bog land. Trade died out about 1835. There was a revival towards the end of the century and new canals were cut.

Hayle (or Copperhouse) Canal. This should not be confused with the Hayle-Camborne project that was never constructed. This was a tidal canal running from the Hayle River to the Tide Mill by Copperhouse Foundry.

Hereford and Gloucester Canal. Opened in 1798 to Ledbury, and in 1845 to Hereford, from its junction with the River Severn in the Maisemore Channel. Length 35½ miles. Closed 1889. Portions of the canal bed became a railway but very little of the rest has any water so it cannot be used by light craft. The Maisemore Lock, in the Maisemore Channel of the River Severn, has long been out of action. The canal at Monkhide is being restored as well as other sections.

Hopkin's Canal. A short canal half a mile long and long extinct, leading from Townsend's Poll, Yspitty.

Horncastle (or River Bain Navigation). Opened in 1802, this navigation ran from the River Witham, near Tattershall Bridge, to Horncastle. The canal was 11 miles long and there were 7 locks. Closed 1865. Most of the old route can be used by canoes.

Ipswich and Stowmarket Navigation. This joined the two towns mentioned and was the canalised River Gipping. Length nearly 16 miles. There were 15 locks. Closed 1934. The route apart from some lock cuts can be canoed throughout. Towpath is a right of way. Should be restored.

Distance Table

Stowmarket, Stowupland Bridge, to

	Miles	Furlongs
Stowupland Lock No. 1	–	6
Badley Lock No. 2	2	2
Needham Market and Needham Lock No. 3	3	7
Barking Lock No. 4	4	5
Bosmere Lock No. 5	5	3
Pips Lock No. 6	5	6
Baylham and Baylham Lock No. 7	6	4
Chamford Lock No. 8	7	3
Great Blakenham and Blakenham Lock No. 9	8	1
Claydon and Claydon Lock No. 10	8	7
Paper Mill Lock No. 11	10	3
Bramford and Bramford Lock No. 12	11	5
Sproughton and Sproughton Lock no. 13	12	6
Chantry Lock No. 14	13	6
Ipswich, Tide Lock No. 15	15	1
Ipswich, Stoke Bridge	15	7

Isle of Dogs Canal. This cut across the Isle of Dogs in the Thames to avoid the large bend in the river. It was little used and was merged into the West India Dock in 1829.

Itchen Navigation. Bishop Godfrey de Lucy made this river navigable to Alresford in 1200. It fell into disrepair and another navigation was made from Winchester to Southampton by an Act of 1662. An Act of 1710 authorised construction of a completely new navigation 10⅜ miles long. There were 15 locks. Most of the route is navigable by light craft but fishing rights are strictly preserved. Closed 1869. Clearance in the Allbrook area by local canal society. Navigation rights have not been abandoned. Four controlling Acts remain.

Ivel River (Bedfordshire). This river was made a navigation to Biggleswade in 1759 and to Shefford in 1810. The length was 11 miles of which over 3 miles were called the Shefford Canal. On the first section there were 6 locks and from Biggleswade to Shefford there were 5 locks. Closed 1876. Canoeable throughout.

Ivel River (Somerset) (sometimes called River Yeo). The river joins the Parrett one mile above Langport Bridge and under an Act of 1795, attempts were made to make this river a navigation from Langport to Ilchester, but the navigation was a failure. Light craft can still reach Load Bridge which carries the B 3165 road.

Ketley Canal. Short canal in Shropshire later incorporated into the Shrewsbury Canal. Long derelict, but remembered as it included the first canal inclined plane in England.

Kensington Canal. This originally ran from Warwick Road Basin in West London to the Thames. It was 1¾ miles long with one tide lock. Craft using the canal were 81ft x 18ft. Part was converted into a railway when it was acquired by the West London Extension Railway. The bottom section remained in use until 1970 but it has now been disposed of.

Kidwelly and Llanelly Canal. The first section was known as Kymer's Canal and was constructed under an Act dated 1766, this ran from the sea to Pwllyllgod. In 1812 another Act was passed and another 4½ miles added, part of which led to the direction of Llanelly and another part towards Pontyates. Other sections were completed but only a total of just over 9 miles were built and the canal was never completed. The canal was converted to a railway and part of the canal bed was used for the track.

Kilgetty Canal. A short canal in Pembrokeshire that does not ever appear to have been completed.

Kington, Leominster and Stourport Canal. Construction of this canal from Kington to the Severn via Tenbury and Leominster was commenced after the 1791 Act promoting the navigation. Only the section from Leominster to Mamble Wharf was completed. Totally derelict throughout the 18½ miles that were completed.

Kyme Eau. See Sleaford Canal.

Kymer's Canal. See Kidwelly and Llanelly Canal.

Lakenheath Lode. A drainage channel, once navigable for fen-lighters from Lakenheath Wharf to the Brandon River. There was one navigation weir three quarters of a mile downstream from Lakenheath. Length 3¼ miles. Usable for light craft only, except the short section three eights of a mile long downstream of the railway bridge which can be used by cruisers for mooring off the Brandon River.

Langford Cut. A short private canal from the Chelmer and Blackwater, near Beeleigh, to Langford Mill; about ½ mile long.

Leicester and Melton Mowbray Navigation. Opened in 1801 from near Leicester to Melton Mowbray. A river navigation using the Eye and Wreak rivers. The 11 mile route has long been derelict but some part is canoeable.

Leven Canal. A private canal constructed under Acts of 1801 and 1805. It ran from near Aike on the River Hull to Leven, a distance of $3\frac{1}{4}$ miles. The entrance lock has been replaced by a fixed sluice and the canal is used for fishing. Closed by Act of Parliament in 1935.

Liskeard and Looe Canal. Promoted under an Act of 1825. It ran from Tarras Pill to Moorswater (near Liskeard). Closed after the opening of the railway in 1860. There were 25 locks and the bottom end still retains water.

Little Punchard Gill. This was an underground canal to take away mined lead ore from Arkengarthdale in Swaledale.

Llansamlet Canal. This ran from Llansamlet, near Swansea, to the River Tawe at Foxhole. Long derelict. Three miles long.

Llechryd Canal. A cut made from the River Teifi to a tinplate works at Castle Malgwyn. The works closed early in the 1800s but stone material was carried on the River Teifi into the present century.

Lugg Navigation. A navigation was constructed in the mid-18th century from Leominster to the River Wye, a distance of 26 miles. Only flash locks appear to have been used. The route is usually canoeable throughout. Navigation was closed after the opening of the Hereford and Gloucester Canal which crossed the river by a low aqueduct at Wergins Bridge but this is now demolished.

MacMurray's Canal. This was a canal just over a ¼ mile long linking the Thames to The Lamb Brewery at Wandsworth. There was an entrance lock and two lifting bridges. There has been recently a scheme to link the nearby Bell Lane Creek to the Wandle to create a navigation to Wandsworth High Street. The canal became disused after the First World War.

Manchester, Bolton and Bury Canal. This linked the towns from which the canal takes its name. There were 17 locks rising from Salford to Littler Lever, and from here branches ran on the level to Bolton and Bury. A few isolated sections remain for amenity and recreation. Length 8 miles to Little Lever from Salford. Bury Branch $4\frac{1}{4}$ miles, Bolton Branch $2\frac{3}{4}$ miles.

Manchester & Salford Junction Canal. This linked the River Irwell at Water Street, Manchester with the Rochdale Canal.

Mardyke. Purfleet, junction with River Thames, to Bulphan Fen. This was about 5 miles long and some side drains to farms were also used. Used for farm produce and manure distribution. Disused since 1875.

Melton Mowbray Navigation. Linked the Grand Union Canal near Syston to Melton Mowbray via 12 Broad locks. It was mainly a canalisation of the River Wreak. Closed but sections are canoeable and there are many remains of the old navigation. This is a waterway which could be looked at for restoration, in part at least.

Mersey and Irwell Navigation. This was largely taken over by the Manchester Ship Canal works. In recent years the Runcorn and Latchford Canal has closed throughout including the section known as the Black Bear Canal and also Butchersfield Cut.

Morris's Canal. This canal in Glamorganshire, built before 1800, was a mile long and was incorporated into the Trewyddfa Canal which became part of the Swansea Canal.

Mundon Canal. A private waterway running from the River Blackwater to White House Farm, Mundon, Near Maldon. It was 1¼ miles long and had an entrance lock.

Nar Navigation. Promoted under an Act dated 1751 by which the river was canalised to Westacre. Locks are now fixed sluices. Original distance 15 miles. Closed 1884. Canoeable from Narborough to King's Lynn.

Nent Force Level. Nearly 5 miles long, this was a drainage and transport canal for and underground waterway underneath the valley of the River Nent, in Cumbria. A tourist attraction in later years, it is now lost and forgotten as mining has ceased at Alston. The navigable section was no less than 2 miles.

Newcastle-under-Lyme Canal. Promoted under Act of 1795. It was 4 miles long, now closed and derelict.

Newcastle-under-Lyme Junction Canal. Originally built with the intention of linking Gresley's Canal to the Newcastle-under-Lyme Canal to provide a link through to the Trent and Mersey. It however only ran a distance of 1⅛ miles from Stubb's Walk, Newcastle to link with the detached Gresley's Canal.

Newdigate Canals. A network of canals based on the Arbury Estate near Nuneaton. These were based on the area from the junction with the Coventry Canal to Seaswood Lake. There were 5½ miles of canals mainly for coal traffic but also for general goods and recreation. There were 14 locks including one stop lock, but the system was disused by 1820. The coal from the collieries at Griff were conveyed by a separate canal and this coal traffic remained until the early 1960s.

Newport Pagnell Canal. Promoted by Act of 1814 to link Newport Pagnell to the Grand Union Canal. Length 1¼ miles with 7 locks. Closed in 1864 and partly converted to a railway.

North and South Drove. Drains near Spalding Lincs, still in existence but disused.

North Wilts. Canal. See Wilts. and Berks. Canal.

Nottingham Canal. Promoted under Act of 1792 the canal ran from the Cromford Canal at Langley Mill to the Trent at Nottingham, a distance of 14⅞ miles with 29 locks. There was one short branch in Nottingham. Only the short section of 2½ miles is now used for traffic proceeding to or from the upper Trent. The canal is derelict in sections.

Nutbrook Canal. This canal, promoted under an Act of 1793, ran from a junction with the Erewash Canal at The White House to Shipley, a distance of 4½ miles, through 13 locks. All but the bottom ¼ mile was disused by 1895, and is now derelict.

Oakham Canal. Promoted by Acts in 1793 and 1800 and opened in 1802 from Melton Mowbray to Oakham, a distance of 15 miles, through 16 locks. Closed in 1853 and converted in part to a railway. Short sections are still canoeable.

Old Stratford and Buckingham Canals. A branch of the Grand Union to Buckingham, 10¾ miles long with 2 locks. Derelict except for a section at the lower end. The Old Stratford was a wide canal and the Buckingham Canal narrow. They were separate concerns.

Ouse, River (Sussex). Constructed under an Act of 1790 and four later Acts, from the sea at Newhaven to Cuckfield, a distance of nearly 30 miles, through 18 locks. Disused to Lindfield since 1861 and to Isfield in 1880. Usable in the tideway below Hamsey and is canoeable from the ruins of Isfield Lock to Hamsey. The original navigation Acts do not appear to have been rescinded.

Oxford Canal. There are a number of loops from the old route of the canal to be seen. These are not used now that the canal has been straightened. Some parts of these loops have been used for coal carrying, mooring etc. Main text notes use at present.

Par Canal. An early canal in Cornwall which ran from Par Harbour to Pontsmill, a distance of $1\frac{7}{8}$ miles through one lock. Now closed.

Parrott's Canal. This was a short canal that ran from bedworth to near Hawkesbury junction, a distance of ⅝ mile. Later, this coal canal was into the Coventry Canal.

Pembrey Canal. Opened in 1824 linking the Kidwelly and Llanelly Canal to Pembrey Harbour through one lock. Total distance 2 miles. Closed and partly converted to a railway.

Pen-clawdd Canal. Opened in 1814. This ran from Pen-clawdd to a point near the Llan River. Lockage is not known. Long derelict.

Penrhiwtyn Canal. A short canal running from Giant's Grave, $1\frac{3}{8}$ miles long. Derelict.

Pensnett Canal. This canal was built about 1810 by Lord Ward and was $1\frac{1}{4}$ miles long. It commences at its junction with the Dudley Canal at the top of Parkhead Locks and leads to Brierley Hill and Pensnett. Now derelict. It was never nationalised with the Birmingham Canal Navigations.

Petworth Canal. A branch of the Western Rother Navigation, it ran through 2 locks to Haslingbourne Bridge near Petworth from near Stopham Bridge.

Pidcock's Canal. This ran from Lydney for a distance of $1\frac{1}{2}$ miles. It has been long derelict.

Pillrow Cut. The artificial cut linking the Brue and Axe. It does not seem to have been used later than the Middle Ages and drainage works have ruined the Axe and Brue Navigations.

Plas Kynaston Canal. This Denbighshire canal was only about ⅝ mile long and was built in 1832 to connect the basins at Trevor on the Ellesmere Canal to works near Cefn-Mawr. Closed during the 1914-18 war.

Portsea Canal. Part of London's lost route to the sea. This route entered the sea by Chichester Harbour and craft went through the two entrance locks at Milton to Portsea Basins. This was a distance of nearly 2½ miles. To reach Milton Locks craft had a sea route from Chichester Channel around dredged channels via Thorney and Hayling Islands and across Langstone Harbour to Milton Common to enter the canal. Most of this route is now covered with roads and housing but the entrance lock has been restored.

Portsmouth and Arundel Canal. Part of the old London to Portsmouth route. Built under the Act of 1817. The canal left by a lock from the Arun near Ford and through another lock shortly after, it then ran level to the branch to Chichester. From here there were 2 locks to Chichester Harbour. Barges went round Thorney and Hayling Islands to Portsea Island and into a short canal to Portsmouth. A short section of the Chichester Canal remains open, but the bulk of the canal, apart from Chichester Branch, was closed about 1860. Total length nearly 31 miles.

Rhuddlan Canal. A very early canalisation of part of the River Clwyd up to Rhuddlan Castle carried out in the 13th century. This project was one of the earliest recorded canalisation projects bringing the castle within 2 miles of the sea. The cost was high, in modern terms it would be about £1 million. The engineer is now known but it is thought likely that James of St. George was responsible as he had overall direction of the King's works in North Wales.

Romford Canal. This canal was proposed from Collier Row Common, Romford, to the Thames via Dagenham. There were to be 5 locks but only one lock was partially constructed and the canal was never completed.

Rother, River (Western). Made navigable in 1793 and linked Midhurst to the River Arun at Stopham. Length 11⅛ miles with 8 locks. Canoeable from Midhurst. Disused since 1871.

Royal Arsenal Canal. (Sometimes called the **Woolwich Canal**). This left the Thames via an entrance lock to Woolwich Arsenal. The top part of the waterway has been filled in but the lower half may be re-opened for amenity purposes.

Runcorn and Weston Canal. This ran from the junction with the new line of locks of the Bridgewater Canal to Weston Point, junction with the River Weaver. Distance 1 mile 3 furlongs and two locks.

Runcorn and Latchford Canal. A section of canal holding water about 3 miles long is isolated and disused since construction of the Manchester Ship Canal.

St. Columb Canal. Promoted by an Act of 1773 from Mawgan Porth in Cornwall to Lower St. Columb Porth. Length about 6 miles, it has been derelict for over 150 years.

St. Helens Canal (Sankey Brook). This waterway from St. Helens to Fidlers Ferry and Widnes has been completely closed but final closure only took place in recent years. The main line was 13 miles 1 furlong long and there were 10 locks. There were double locks at Widnes, one of which is being restored to allow moorings for about 400 yards above it. The lock at Fidlers Ferry is also to be restored to allow moorings above it. A number of sections are to be restored in some way for recreation and amenity but they will be no more than isolated municipal duckponds. There were branches at Gerrards Bridge, Boardman's Bridge and Blackbrook, totalling approx. 3¾ miles. Originally, this canal was a canalised Sankey Brook; the canal still does take water from Sankey Brook and return it. It is still not certain whether or not this was the first true canal of the canal age.

Salisbury and Southampton Canal. This canal ran from Southampton to Redbridge and thence to Romsey via the Andover Canal and on to Michaelmarsh where it left the Andover Canal and ran through East Dean to Alderbury Common. It was opened in 1804 but never beyond Alderbury due to financial troubles. By 1808 the canal closed and was never reopened. There were 11 locks on the section to Alderbury and 2 sea locks at Southampton and Northam.

Shropshire Union Canal. This group was an amalgamation of canals of which two are closed throughout.

Ellesmere Canal. Promoted by Act 1793, the canal ran from Frankton Junction to Carreghofa where it joined the Ellesmere Canal. Distance 11½ miles with 7 locks. There was a branch to Weston 6 miles long. Most of the canal is open for light craft that can be portaged around locks and lowered bridges: part of the Weston Branch is now dry. Canal continued at Carreghofa into Montgomeryshire Canal. Under reconstruction (see below).

Montgomeryshire Canal. Promoted under an Act of 1794 and ran from Carreghofa where it joined the Ellesmere Canal to Newtown Basin, a distance of 23⅞ miles. There were 19 locks. A branch to Guildsfield was 2¼ miles long. Under reconstruction. See Shropshire Union Canal (Main Section).

Shrewsbury Canal. This ran from Shrewsbury to Donnington at first, later it was extended through Newport to Norbury Junction. Total length 25 miles. There were two branches to the Old Shropshire Canal Section at Wappenshall, and also to Lubstree Wharf. First section was opened in 1797 and the link to Norbury Junction in 1833. Portions were first constructed as a tub-boat canal and later to a narrow boat canal. The inclined plane has been disused since 1921 and raised for tub-boats so that they could continue to Donnington where a junction was made with the Duke of Sutherland's Tub-boat Canal. Closed throughout.

Shropshire Canal. A tub-boat canal running from Donnington (junction with Donnington Wood Canal and Old Shropshire Canal section) to Coalport on the River Severn. The canal did not lock into the Severn. There were 2 branches, one of which was the old Ketley Canal. There were inclined planes in use in several places. Parts were abandoned from 1818 onwards until by 1913 only 1¼ miles were in use at Blisser's Hill blast furnaces, but traffic ceased altogether that year.

Somersetshire Coal Canal. It was opened in 1802 when an inclined plane was brought into use. This proved unsuccessful and was replaced by 23 locks in 1805. It was 10½ miles long with a 7½ miles long branch from Midford to Radstock. The Radstock arm was never joined by water to the main arm, a tramroad connecting the terminus at Twinhoe with Midford (about one mile in length). This Radstock arm, which was little used, was converted into a tramway in 1815 and sold to the Somerset and Dorset Railway in 1871. The main line, ran from Dundas (junction with the Kennet and Avon) to Timsbury (Paulton Basin). A short length from the junction with the K. & A. is to be re-opened for moorings.

Speedwell Mine. This is an underground canal ½ mile long in Derbyshire. It was used in the past to transport lead ore but it is still open today as a tourist attraction.

Stover Canal. A short canal in Devonshire 1⅞ miles long through 4 locks, It ran from a backwater of the river Teign to Teigngrace. The bottom portion was in use until the Second World War and closed in 1944. Primitive and unique lock mechanism exists.

Surrey Canal. An extension of the Surrey Docks. This ran through a lock from the docks to Camberwell. A distance of 2 miles 5 furlongs. There was a branch to Peckham ½ mile long. The docks and canal are now closed. Owned by the PLA.

Swansea and Trewyddfa Canal. This was constructed under an Act of 1794 and runs from Swansea to Hen-Lloyd, a distance of 16¼ miles through 36 locks. Sections still hold water for water supply but the canal is derelict. The Trewyddfa canal is a section of the canal, 1⅜ miles long.

Tavistock Canal. Authorised by Act of 1803, was completed with branch to Mill Hill by 1819. The canal was 4 miles long and the branch 2 miles. There were no locks but 2 inclined planes. Canal closed, part canoeable and a part is used for a hydro-electric generating station.

Tennant Canal. This canal was constructed between 1817 and 1824. A private navigation, it joined the Neath Canal at Aberdulais to Swansea Docks. It was 8 miles long with one lock. A branch with one lock led to Red Jacket Pill. Now closed to navigation, though canoeable from Aberdulais to Jersey Marine and sections still hold water for water supply. Restoration now under way, see Main Section.

Tern, River. A tributary of the River Severn from the river to Upton Forge, 1½ miles, and other forges. There was an entrance lock from the Severn. Long derelict.

Thorne and Hatfield Moors Peat Canal. The Thorne Boating Dyke has been made redundant by the cutting of nearby Stainforth Canal but a new drain, about 2 miles long, was cut at the side of Thorne Waste. This was linked with about 4 miles of other drains for peat extraction. A new waterway system in the area was constructed late in the 19th century to extract the peat moss and this died out in the late 1920s.

Tremadoc Canal A short canal linking the town to the sea.

Thorney, River. This river was navigable from Dog-in-a-Doublet on the River Nene to Thorney Village, 3⅛ miles, through one lock. Lock now closed but whole of the route is canoeable. This lock was a double lock, staircase.

Tillingham, River. From Rye a portion of the river has in the past been used for navigation.

Tillingbourne, River. A short section of the river near Chilworth was canalised to serve the gunpowder mills. Still canoeable.

Tone, River. This was the old navigation route to Taunton from Burrow Bridge on the River Parrett. With the opening of the Bridgwater and Taunton Canal this route went out of use. Still navigable on a high tide to Knapp Bridge, a distance of 4⅞ miles.

Torrington Canal. A private canal about 6 miles long, which had an inclined plane. It linked the Torridge River to Torrington and a short distance above. Long closed.

Ulverston Canal. A short canal, 1¾ miles long, promoted under an Act of 1793 which linked the sea to Ulverston. Used by small sea-going coasters. Closed by Act of 1944.

Uttoxeter Canal. Constructed about 1805 by the Uttoxeter Canal Company, it left Froghall Basin by a sidelock to near Uttoxeter. It was 13 miles long and was closed when the Churnet Valley Railway was built.

Welland Navigation. Promoted under an Act of 1571 it made the Welland navigable from Stamford to Spalding. Locks are derelict from Stamford to Deeping St. James. River from Folly River Outfall to Spalding is still open. Navigation works were not completed until 1665.

Wendover Canal. Opened to traffic 1800 from the main line of the Grand Union near Tring to Wendover. Closed 1898. A feeder canal to the main line. This G.U.C. Branch should be restored.

Wern Canal (Llanelly). Short South Wales canal which ran from Copperhouse Dock to Wern Pits, a distance of one mile. (Also called Pen-y-fan Canal).

Westport Canal. A short canal leading to Westport (Somerset). This left the River Isle, a tributary of the Parrett, which was canalised with one lock at Mildeney. The canal was closed about 1880 but the Isle is canoeable.

Wisbech Canal. Constructed under an Act of 1794, it ran from the River Nene at Wisbech to Outwell where it made a junction with the Middle Level. The length was 5¼ miles and there were 2 locks, one at either end. Canal is now totally derelict, and was closed by Warrant of the Minister of Transport on 14th June 1926. The canal was filled with water each high tide, as there was no water supply.

Wombridge Canal. A private canal linking the coal and ironstone industry at Wombridge with the Shrewsbury Canal at Donnington Wood. Completed in 1789 and shortly after sold to the Shrewsbury Canal. Abandoned in 1931.

Woodeaves Canal. A detached canal just over 1¼ miles long built near Ashbourne Derbyshire to serve the cotton mills near Fenny Bentley.

Woolston Canal. A section of the Mersey and Irwell Navigation now closed. There were 2 locks, one at either end, Paddington and Woolston, and the total distance was 2¼ miles.

Worsley Underground Canals. This was a complex system of underground waterways in the coal mines at Worseley totalling 46 miles in length. There were locks, inclined planes and the waterways were on two levels. The system was last used in 1887 and was regularly maintained until 1969. It is now dangerous to enter and has been closed.

Wye, River. This river was navigable to Hay for barges but it was only by the use of primitive flash locks. It was never navigable in the usual accepted sense. The present head of navigation is usually Bigsweir Bridge over 80 miles downstream from Hay.

SCOTLAND

Aberdeenshire Canal. This canal was opened on 31st May 1805. The canal was 18¼ miles long with 17 locks and it ran from Aberdeen to Inverurie. Closed in 1853 and partly converted to a railway.

Bo'ness Canal. Built to link Bo'ness and Grangemouth but it was never finished due to financial problems.

Burnturk Canal. Two short canals (near Cupar) linking the lime kilns to Kingskettle. Two miles and a short length of half a mile.

Campbeltown Canal. This ran from Argyll colliery to Campbeltown, a distance of about 3 miles. Closed 1855 and its place taken by a light railway now also closed.

Carlingwark Canal. Two short lengths, 1¼ miles and ½ mile from Carlingwark Loch to the Dee.

Dingwall Canal. This waterway was tidal and took its water supply from the River Peffrey. It was 2000 yards long and is unique in having been constructed under the authority of an Act for building highland roads and bridges. It was completed in 1816. It suffered from silting and later railway competition, and the last meeting of the canal commissioners took place in 1884. The route is still traceable and holds water.

Forth and Cart Junction Canal. Constructed after an Act was passed in 1893, it ran from the Forth and Clyde Canal in Clydebank to the River Clyde to link up with Paisley. It was ¾ mile long and was closed in 1893. It linked Paisley via River Cart.

Glasgow, Paisley and Johnston Canal. This canal connected Glasgow to Johnston and it was 11 miles long. It came into use in 1810 but was closed by 1881.

Kilbagie Canal. This was a mile long to take grain from near Alloa to a distillery near Kilbagie. Closed 1862.

Loch Morlich. A canal system, mainly on existing river courses in the Cairngorms, closed about 1850. This system high up in the hills was used for floating timber and came into the news in recent years in a case dealing with rights of navigation on the River Spey.

Monkland Canal. This ran from the Glasgow Branch of the Forth and Clyde Canal to Woodhall, a distance of 12¼ miles through 6 locks. The canal still contains water in several places as it serves as a water feeder to the Forth and Clyde Canal. Canal was closed by Warrant of the Minister of Transport in 1950.

Muirkirk Canal. This Ayrshire Canal was built about 1790 for transporting coal and ore.

Perth Town Lode. After about 1824 coal was carried to the gas works from the River Tay. It was built to connect the River Almond and Tay.

Stevenston Canal. This was 2½ miles long running from Stevenston to Saltcoats. Closed about 1830.

WATERWAY MUSEUMS

The Waterway Museum (BWB), Stoke Bruerne, Towcester, Northants NN12 7SE. (Tel. Northampton (0604) 862229)

The North West Museum of Inland Navigation (Ellesmere Port) South Wirral, Cheshire L65 4EF (Tel. 051 355 1876)

The Black Country Museum, Tipton Road, Dudley, West Midlands DY1 4SQ. Tel. 021-557 9643.

Ironbridge Gorge Museum, Ironbridge, Telford, Salop. TF8 7AW

Wharf Museum and Gallery, Canal Wharf, Whaley Bridge, Stockport. Tel. Whaley Bridge (06633) 2226.

The Canal Exhibition Centre, The Wharf, Llangollen, Clwyd. Tel. Llangollen (0978) 860702.

Clock Warehouse Canal Exhibition, London Road, Shardlow, Derby. Tel. Derby (0332) 792844.

Exeter Maritime Museum, The Quay, Exeter. Tel. Exeter (0392) 58075.

Morwellham Museum, Near Tavistock, Devon. Tel. Gunnislake (0392) 766.

National Maritime Museum, Greenwich, London SE10. Tel. 01-858 4422.

The Science Museum, South Kensington, London SW7. Tel. 01-589 6371.

The Manchester Museum, Oxford Road, Manchester 13. Tel. 061-273 3333.

The Goole Museum, Carlisle Street, Goole. Tel. Goole (0405) 3784.

The Gloucester Folk Museum, Bishop Hooper's Lodgings, 99 Westgate Street, Gloucester. Tel. Gloucester (0452) 24131.

Hull Maritime Museum, Pickering Park, Hessle Road, Hull. Tel. Hull (0482) 27625.

East Anglia Maritime Museum, Marine Parade, Great Yarmouth. Tel. Great Yarmouth (0493) 2267.

Liverpool Museums, William Brown Street, Liverpool L3 8EN. Tel. 051-207 0001.

Manchester Ship Canal Company Museum, Ship Canal House, King Street, Manchester Tel. 061-832 2244. (A private Museum open only for students, research etc. by appointment.)

Nottingham Canal Museum, Canal Street, Nottingham. (Information: Tel. Nottingham (0602) 598 835).

Scottish Maritime Museum Trust, Laird Forge, Gotteries Road, Irvine, Ayrshire. Tel. Irvine (0294) 78283.

A number of the museums listed above have only a small part of their collection devoted to inland waterways. B.W.B. have opened another Museum in Gloucester Docks. The National Waterways Museum, The Dock Office, The Docks, Gloucester GL1 2EJ. Tel. Gloucester (0452) 25524.

There are a number of organisations devoted to preservation of old canal and river craft. These are:

> The Narrow Boat Trust
> The Norfolk Wherry Trust
> The Dolphin Sailing Barge Museum Trust
> The East Coast Sail Trust
> The Maritime Trust
> The River Stour Trust
> Oxford Colleges Barges Preservation Trust
> The Humber Keel and Sloop Preservation Society

Other craft may have preservation groups formed for their benefit, such as Mersey Flats, Severn Trows etc.

The following are some of the engines that are in use at intervals for the benefit of visitiors:

Crofton Pumping Engine. Kennet and Avon Canal, Crofton, Great Bedwyn, Wilts. Tel. Burbage (810) 575.

Claverton Pumping Station. A watermill, driving pumps. Ferry Lane, Claverton, Bath, Avon. Tel. (0225) 515954.

Dogdyke Pumping Station. River Witham. (Details from Dogdyke Pumping Station, Preservation Trust, Bridge Farm, Tattershall, Lincoln LN4 4JG). Tel. Coningsby (0526) 42583.

Lea Wood Pumping Station. Cromford Canal, near Cromford, Derbyshire. Tel. Wirksworth (062 982) 3737.

Stretham Pumping Engine. Old West River, Fenland. (Enquiries locally are needed to ascertain visiting times).

Broadland Wind Pumps, Stracey Arms, Horsey (National Trust), Thurne Dyke, How Hill Tower and How Hill Trestle Windpumps are open for inspection at intervals. Berney Arms is a windmill with associations of Broadland.

GLOSSARY

For most of the terms given below the author is indebted to *Bradshaw's Guide to the Canals and Navigable Rivers of England and Wales,* by the late Rodolph de Salis, and *Narrow Boat,* by L. T. C. Rolt.

Aegre.—See Bore.

Animals.—A boatman's name for donkeys, which until recently were much in use for towing purposes, particularly on the canals adjacent to the River Severn, a pair of them taking the place of one horse.

Balance Beam or Balance.—The beam projecting from a lock gate which balances its weight, and by pushing against which the gate is opened or closed.

Barge.—A term including a variety of vessels, both sailing and non-sailing, in use for canal or river traffic, whose beam is approximately twice that of a narrow boat. The name 'barge' is often applied erroneously to all vessels carrying goods on a canal or river, whether barge, wide boat, narrow boat, lighter or any other vessel.

Beck.—A dyke or drain.

Blow To.—To give warning when approaching a bridge-hole or other narrow place where the view ahead is restricted and there is therefore a danger of collision. Boatmen either crack their whips or blow a horn of polished brass which is kept in the cabin within reach of the steerer.

Bobbins.—Short wooden rollers, several of which are usually threaded on each of the traces of horses engaged in towing, to prevent the traces chafing. They are often painted in bright colours.

Bollard.—Wood or metal posts used for tying up boats at locks and moorings.

Bore.—A tidal wave.

Bow Hauling.—Hauling by men, in distinction from the more usual method of hauling by horses. When a motor-boat and butty are working through a flight of narrow locks the tow-line is usually detached and the butty bow hauled.

Breast or Mitre Post.—Of a lock gate, the vertical post of the gate farthest from its hanging; where the gates are in pairs, the two breasts are usually mitred to bed against each other when shut.

Bridge Hole.—The narrow channel beneath an over-bridge.

Butty Boat.—A boat working in company with another boat. The term is generally applied to a boat towed by a motor-boat.

Bye-Trader.—A term used to designate any trader on a canal other than the canal company itself when carriers. All canal companies are not carriers themselves, some merely providing the waterway and taking toll for its use.

Chalico.—A mixture of tar, cow-hair and horse-dung made hot, used for dressing the timbers of wooden boats.

Compartment Boats — Commonly called a 'Tom Pudding', a type of boat once used on the Aire and Calder Navigation, which was worked in trains with other similar boats.

Cratches.—The support of the gang-planks of a narrow boat at the fore end of the boat. The deck cratch is placed at the point where the fore deck terminates and the cargo space begins, the false cratch being situated a short distance abaft the deck cratch.

Cut.—A boatman's name for canal, so applied on account of its artificially cut channel, as distinguished from the natural channel of a river.

Day Boats.—Boats without cabins, used in working short-distance traffic and on which there is no sleeping accommodation. Also called open boats.

Doors.—A Fen term for gates; in the Fens all lock gates are called sluice doors.

Draw.—To draw a paddle, slacker, slat, weir or staunch is to open it in order to allow the water to escape. The reverse is to 'lower', 'drop' or 'shut in', or in the case of a staunch, to 'set'.

Dydle (Norfolk).—To dredge, to clean out.

Fender.—Wood plank or mat to protect boat sides in locks, wharves, etc.

Flash or Flush.—A body of accumulated water suddenly released, used for the purpose of assisting navigation on a river.

Flash.—An inland lake caused by subsidence of the ground due to salt-mining. This term is also used for the small inland lakes forming part of the Basingstoke Canal.

Flat.—A Mersey flat is a type of vessel which conducts the bulk of the traffic on that river and neighbouring canals. A black flat is a larger vessel trading between Liverpool and the River Weaver. The term 'flat' is also used to describe the shallow punts or rafts used by lock-keepers or lengthmen for canal maintenance.

Fleet (Norfolk).—Shallow.

Fly Boat.—Originally described a horse-boat which, using relays of horses, travelled day and night. The term now applies to any type of boat so travelling. A boatman so engaged is said to be 'working fly'.

Freshet.—An increase in the flow of a river due to rain.

Gang.—The number of Fen lighters or River Stour (Suffolk) lighters chained together for travelling. In the case of Fen lighters the number in a gang is five, on the River Stour always two.

Gang Planks.—Removable planks used to afford a means of passing from one end of a narrow boat to the other; when in place they run from the top of the cabin aft to the deck cratch forward, being supported in between by upright supports called stands. These stands, which are also removable, fit into mortices in the stretchers and boat's floor and have the gang planks tightly lashed down to them.

Gauging.—The means of ascertaining by the draught of a vessel the weight of cargo on board for the purpose of taking tolls. The first gauging of canal boats is carried out at a weigh-dock, where particulars of the boat's draught are taken when empty, and when fully loaded, and at intermediate points, such as at every ton of loading. The boat is loaded with weights kept for the purpose, which are lifted in and out by cranes; the result arrived at is then either transferred to graduated scales fixed to the boat's sides, which can be read at any time, or the particulars of each vessel are furnished to each toll office in a book, from which, on gauging the immersion of the boat, the number of tons on board can be at once ascertained. The usual method of gauging a boat for immersion is to take what is called the 'dry inches'—that is, the freeboard, at four points, at one point each side near the bow and at one point each side near the stern. This is done by an instrument consisting of a float in a tube having a bracket projecting from the side of the tube. The bracket is rested on the boat's gunwale and the float indicates the number of inches between that and the level of the water in the canal.

Give Way, To.—To concede the right of passage to another boat—e.g., empty boats usually give way to loaded, motors to horse-boats. The actual passing rule varies on different waterways, keeping to the right being now most general, but a motor-boat always gives a horse-boat the tow-path side for obvious reasons.

Gongoozler.—An idle and inquisitive person who stands staring for prolonged periods at anything out of the common. The word is believed to have its origin in the Lake District.

Handspike.—A bar of wood used as a lever; on some of the old-fashioned locks a handspike was required for working the lock paddles instead of rack and pinion gears. It is also used for working the anchor chain roller on river barges.

Hain (Norfolk).—Higher, 'The water is hain today'. That is: The water is higher today.

Haling Way.—A Fen term; a towing-path.

Heel Post.—The vertical post of a lock gate nearest to its hanging and the axis on which the gate turns, being rounded at the back to fit into the hollow quoin in which it partially revolves.

Hold In, Hold Out.—Boatmen's terms used as directions for steering, having reference to the position of the towing-path. 'Hold in' means hold the boat in to the towing-path side of the canal and vice versa.

Hollow Quoin.—The recess into which the heel post of a lock gate is fitted and in which it partially revolves when being opened and closed.

Horse Boat.—Strictly speaking, a small open boat for ferrying over towing horses from one side of a river to the other where no bridge is available. In common use in the Fen district where it is towed astern of a gang of lighters. One is also kept for use at Trent Junction to ferry horses from the mouth of the River Soar over the Trent to the junction of the Erewash Canal. Of recent years the term has come to be loosely used to describe any horse-drawn narrow boat as distinct from motor craft.

Horse Marines (Yorkshire).—Men who contract for the haulage of vessels by horses on the canals.

House Lighter.—A Fen term, used to denote a lighter provided with a cabin.

Inclined Plane.—A device on wheels which lifts boats from one level to another without using locks.

Invert.—An inverted arch of brickwork or masonry, used chiefly in canal work to form the bottom of locks and tunnels in cases where lateral or upward pressure has to be sustained.

Keb.—An iron rake used for fishing up coal or other articles from the bottom of a canal. Boatmen may often be seen fishing for coal in this way at coal wharves.

Keel.—A type of boat once in extensive use on the Yorkshire rivers and canals, they measure approximately 58 feet long by 14 feet beam.

Land Water.—A term used to denote the water in a river brought down from up country, in distinction from the water set up by the floodtide from seawards.

Legging.—A method used to propel horse-drawn boats through tunnels which have no towing-path, the boatman pushing with his feet against the tunnel walls. At one time leggers could be hired at most of the longer tunnels, notably Standedge on the Huddersfield Narrow Canal, 5,415 yards long, which is the longest in England, and Sapperton on the old Thames and Severn Canal, 3,808 yards long.

Lengthman.—A canal company's employee in charge of a particular section or length of waterway.

Let Off.—An appliance for getting rid of some of the water from a canal in rainy weather so that it may not overflow its banks. Originally a trapdoor sluice set in the bottom of the canal and worked by a chain, but now resembling the ordinary lock paddle.

Level.—When two reaches of water, one on each side of a lock or weir, from the flow of the tide or other cause become level, a level is said to be made.

Lighter.—A term including a variety of vessels in use on the Fens, the Thames, the River Stour (Suffolk) and the Bridgewater Canal. On an average they measure 42 feet in length by 10 feet beam, but Thames lighters equal barges in size, differing from them in the respect that they have 'swim ends', i.e., flat, sloping ends like a punt.

Lock, To.—To work a vessel through a lock.

Loodel.—A staff used to form a vertical extension of the tiller of a barge for the purpose of steering when loaded with high loads, such as hay or straw. The loodel, when required, is inserted in a mortice in the fore end of the tiller.

Narrow Boat.—A craft measuring approximately 70 feet long by 7 feet beam, extensively used throughout the Midland canal system. Sometimes also referred to as a monkey boat or long boat.

Nip (River Trent).—A narrow place.

Number Ones.—Boats owned by the boatmen who work them and who are consequently their own masters, in distinction from boats owned by a firm or company.

Paddle.—A sluice valve, by opening or closing which the water can either be allowed to pass or be retained. Sometimes also called a slacker or clough. Ground paddles or jack cloughs are those that admit water to the lock by culverts built in the ground, as distinct from the fly paddles, ranters or flashers, which are fitted to the gates themselves.

Pen (a Lock pen).—A Fen term; a lock chamber. Also 'to pen', to lock a vessel, e.g. 'A narrow boat is too long to pen at Stanground'.

Portage.—A term for lifting craft round locks and sluices. Light craft can use a derelict waterway even though the locks are out of order.

Pound.—The stretch of water on a canal between two locks.

Punt.—Thames lighter.

Quant (Norfolk).   A pole or shaft.

Ram's Head.—The boatman's name for the wooden rudder post of a narrow boat; usually it is bound with a pipe-clayed Turk's-head knot, and occasionally decorated with a horse's tail.

Rimers.—The posts in the removable portions of weirs on the Upper Thames against which the weir paddles are placed.

Roding.—A Fen term; cutting rushes or reed in a river, or cotting if they are uprooted.

Roving Bridge or Turnover Bridge.—A bridge carrying a towing-path from one side of a canal to the other.

Scour.—Bank of silt caused by a flow of water.

Screw.—A boatman's term for any boat driven by a screw propeller.

Set, To.—To set a staunch is to close it so that the water may accumulate.

Shaft, To.—To propel a boat through a tunnel with a long shaft as an alternative to legging.

Sill—Of a lock. The bar of masonry below water against which the bottom of the lock gates rest when closed.

Staircase Locks.—Also called risers. A flight or series of locks so arranged that the top gate or gates of each lock, except the highest, form the bottom gate or gates of the lock above. The best example of a staircase in England is the flight of five at Bingley on the Leeds and Liverpool Canal.

Staithe (Midlands and North).—A coal-loading wharf. In Norfolk the word refers to a general wharf.

Stands.—The intermediate supports for the gang-planks of a narrow boat.

Stank.—A temporary water-tight dam constructed of piling from which the water can be pumped to enable below-water repairs to be carried out. The word is also used as a verb, e.g., 'to stank off'.

Staunch or Navigation Weir.—An appliance for overcoming change of level in a navigable river. It consists of a weir provided with a gate through which vessels may pass, and which is equipped with paddles like a lock gate. When proceeding upstream, vessels close the gate behind them and wait until sufficient depth of water has accumulated in the reach above the gate to allow them to proceed. Travelling downstream the procedure is reversed. This is naturally a very slow business, examples are therefore no longer to be seen on the waterways.

Stemmed, Stemmed Up.—The boatman's term for running aground on a mud-bank.

Stop.—A stop or stop lock is generally a gate or lock erected at the junction of one canal with another, to prevent loss of water from one to the other if necessary, normally there being little or no change of level. There is generally a toll office at a stop lock where cargoes are declared and gauged and tolls paid.

Stop Gates.—They answer the same purpose as stop grooves and planks, but are made in the form of lock gates, and are always kept open except when required for use. In long canal pounds it is usual for stop gates to be fitted at intervals, so that in the event of a leak or burst the escape of water may be confined to that portion of the pound between two gates.

Stop Grooves.—Vertical grooves, usually provided at the head and tail of a lock and in other situations where under-water repairs may have to be carried out, into which stop planks can be inserted to form a temporary dam or stank.

Stoppage.—A temporary closing of a waterway for repairs.

Stud.—The tee-headed pin fitted on bow and stern of a narrow boat to which mooring lines are attached. The towing stud of a narrow boat is C-shaped, and is fitted to the top of a tall post called the mast.

Summit Level.—The highest pound of water in a canal, and therefore the pound into which the main supply of water for working the locks has to be delivered. Consequently, in dry weather it is the first to be affected as regards deficiency of navigable depth. The highest summit level in England is that of the Huddersfield Narrow Canal, which is 4½ miles long from Diggle to Marsden, and is 644 feet 9 inches above Ordnance Datum. For 3¼ miles of this summit level the course of the canal is through Standedge Tunnel.

Sweep.—A large oar.

Swim, To.—A boat light in draught and which answers readily to the helm is described by boatmen as 'a good swimmer', or may be said to "swim well'.

Tackle.—A boatman's name for the harness of a boat horse.

Tail—of a lock.—That portion immediately below the bottom gates. The equivalent portion above the top gates is called the head.

Toll.—The charge payable by a trader for the use of a canal.

Towing-path.—The path beside a canal for the use of towing horses, also called in different districts haling path or haling way.

Trow.—A type of vessel in use on the River Severn; they measure approximately 70 feet long by 17 feet beam.

Tub Boats.—Small box boats carrying from three to five tons, once used in Shropshire and on the Bude canal in Cornwall, and elsewhere.

Turns, Waiting Turns or Working Turns.—A system often adopted in dry weather in order to make the utmost use of the water. At any lock a boat must wait for the arrival of another coming in the opposite direction, thus making sure that the maximum of traffic is passed for the water consumed.

Tying Point.—The shallowest point in a navigation. For instance, the bottom sill of Cranfleet Lock, better known to boatmen as Old Sal's Lock, was at one time the tying point on the river Trent between Nottingham and the junction of the Erewash Canal; that is to say, any vessel that could float over this sill could find enough water everywhere else between these places.

Wash Lands or Washes.—Lands adjoining a river, so embanked that the river can overflow on to them when in flood.

Wherry.—The name given to the sailing vessels which trade over the rivers Bure, Yare and Waveney and their connecting dykes and broads; they varied considerably from a 12 ton boat about 35 feet long by 9 feet beam to the '*Wonder*' of Norwich, 65 feet long by 19 feet bean. Now almost extinct.

Wide Boat.—A type of boat in use on canals having wide locks. It is of a size between the the narrow boat and the barge, 70 feet long by 10 to 11 feet beam. Such craft navigate the Grand Union Canal from London as far north as Berkhamstead. They are not used for longer distances since they do not travel so well as a narrow motor boat and butty on account of their broader beam.

Wind, to.—To wind a boat is to turn a boat round.

Winding Place, Winding Hole, Winning Place or Winning Hole.—A wide place in a canal provided for the purpose of turning a boat round.

Windlass.—Also called in some districts a crank, is a handle or key for opening and closing lock paddles, shaped in the form of the Letter L and having a square socket at one end to fit on the square of the spindle operating the paddle gear.

Wings.—Flat pieces of board rigged for the purpose of legging in tunnels when the tunnel is too wide to permit of the leggers reaching the side walls with their feet from the boat's deck. A fully equipped narrow boat would carry two pairs of wings, a pair of 'narrow-cut wings' and a pair of 'broad-cut wings' that is, a pair of wings suitable for the full-size tunnels of narrow boat canals and also a pair suitable for the tunnels of barge canals.

BIBLIOGRAPHY

This list, prepared in mid 1984, is not exhaustive and does contain a number of books long out of print. Many can be obtained from public libraries and this source of information can be invaluable. Second hand bookshops can be very helpful in tracing old volumes. In preparing this list we are grateful for the assistance of the staff of the British Waterways Board.

BOATS AND BOATERS
Chaplin, T. *The Narrow Boat Book* Whittet Books 1978
Chaplin, T. *Short History of the Narrow Boat* Hugh McKnight 1974
Clark, R. *Black Sailed Traders* David & Charles 1972
Cook, G. F. (edit) *Decorative Arts of the Mariner* Cassell 1966
Cooper, F. S. *Handbook of Sailing Barges* Adlard Coles 1967
Faulkner, A. H. *A Short History of Fellows, Morton and Clayton* Robert Wilson 1975
Faulkner, A. H. *Claytons of Oldbury* Robert Wilson 1978
Faulkner, A. H. *Tankers Knottingley* Robert Wilson 1976
Faulkner, A. H. *The George & Mary (Grand Union Canal Carrying Company)* Robert Wilson 1973
Fletcher, Harry *A Life on the Humber* Faber & Faber 1975.
Hanson, Harry *The Canal Boatmen 1760-1914* Manchester Univ. Press 1976
Hanson, Harry *Canal People* David & Charles 1978
Landsell, A. *Clothes of the Cut* B.W.B. 1975
Lewery, A. J. *Narrow Boat Painting* David & Charles 1974
McDonald, Dan *The Clyde Puffer* David & Charles 1977
McKnight, H. *Canal and River Craft in Pictures* David & Charles 1969
Malster, R. *Wherries & Waterways* Terence Dalton 1972
O'Connor, J. *Canals, Barges & People* Art & Technics 1950
Pierce, A. J. *Canal People* A & C Black 1978
Smith, D. J. *Canals Boats and Boaters* Hugh Evelyn 1973
Smith, D. J. *Discovering the Craft of Inland Waterways* Shire Publications 1977
Smith, E. *Maiden's Trip* Macgibbon & Kee 1949
Inland Sailors Museum & Art Gallery Service for Yorkshire & Humberside 1974
Smith, G. *Our Canal Population (1878)* E.P. Publishing 1974
Smith, P. L. *Canal Barges & Narrowboats* Shire Publications 1977
Smith, P.L. *A Pictorial History of Canal Craft* Batsford 1979
Paget-Tomlinson, E. *Mersey and Weaver Flats* Robert Wilson 1973
Ware, M.E. *Narrow Boats at Work* Moorland 1980
Wheat, G. *Leeds & Liverpool Canal Craft* N. Counties Carriers Ltd. 1972
Wilson, J. K. & Faulkner, A. H. *Fenland Barge Traffic* Robert Wilson 1972
Wilson, R. *Knobsticks (Canal Carrying on the Trent & Mersey)* Robert Wilson 1974
Wilson, R. J. *Life Afloat* Robert Wilson 1976
Wilson, R. *Boatyards & Boatbuilding* Robert Wilson 1974
Wilson, R. J. *The Number Ones* Robert Wilson 1972
Wilson, R. J. *Roses & Castles* Robert Wilson 1976
Woolfit, S. *Idle Women* Benn 1947

BIOGRAPHY
Bode, H. *James Brindley* Shire Publications 1973
Bracegridle, B. and Miles, P. H. *Great Engineers & Their Works – Thomas Telford* David & Charles 1973
Boucher, C. T. G. *John Rennie* Manchester Univ. Press 1963
Boucher, C. T. G. *James Brindley, Engineer* Goose & Son 1968
Cruickshank, M. *Thomas Telford* Keele Teaching Unit 1971
Gibb, Sir A. *The Story of Telford* Maclehose London 1935
Hadfield, C. and Skempton, A.W. *William Jessop, Engineer* David & Charles 1979
Malet, H. *The Canal Duke* David & Charles 1961
Malet, H. *Bridgewater – The Canal Duke – 1736-1803* Manchester Univ. Press 1978
Rolt, L. T.C. *Thomas Telford* Longmans 1958
Rolt, L. T. C. *James Watt* Batsford 1962
Rolt, L. T. C. *Newcomen* David & Charles 1964
Smiles, S. *Lives of the Engineers (1861) Vol. 1 includes J. Brindley Vol. 2 includes J. Rennie & T. Telford* David & Charles 1968

CRUISING
Ball, E. & P. W. *Holiday Cruising on the Thames* David & Charles 1970
Colborne, C. L. *Practical Boat Handling on the Thames* David & Charles 1977
Cove-Smith, C. & Chase, R. E. *Pilotage on Inland Waterways* Yachting & Boating 1970
Cove-Smith, C. *London's Waterway Guide* Imray 1978
Link House *The Canals Books* Link House Annually
Edwards, L. A. *Holiday Cruising on the Broads & Fens* David & Charles 1972
Eyles, J. *Cruising along the Mon. & Brecon* Starling Press 1972
Hadfield, C. (ed) *Canal Enthusiasts' Handbook No. 2* David & Charles 1973
Hadfield, C. *Waterway Sights to See* David & Charles 1977
Hadfield, C. & Streat, M. *Holiday Cruising on Inland – Waterways* David & Charles 1971
Hankinson, J. *Canal Cruising* Ward Lock & Co. 1977
Liley, J. *Inland Cruising Companion* Stanford Martime 1978
Owen, D. E. *Water Rallies* J. M. Dent 1969
Ransom, P. J. G. *Holiday Cruising in Ireland* David & Charles 1971
St. Davids, Viscount *The Watney Book of Inland – Cruising* Queen Anne Press 1966
Westlake, R. J. *Britain's Holiday Waterways* Bradford Barton 1975
Wickham, H. & K. J. *Motor Boating – A Practical Handbook* Hollis & Carter 1977

DESCRIPTIVE CRUISES

B.B. *A Summer on the Nene* Kaye & Ward 1967
Bonthron, P. *My Holidays on Inland Waterways* Thomas Murby & Co 1916
De Mare, E. *Time on the Thames* Flare Books 1975
Doerflinger, F. *Slow Boat through England* Wingate 1970
Doerflinger, F. *Slow Boat through Pennine Waters* Wingate 1971
Farrant, A. *Rowing Holiday by the Canal in 1873* Oakwood Press 1977
Foster, A. J. *The Ouse* S.P.C.K. (pre 1914)
Gatt, J. *5000 Miles 3000 Locks* Arthur Barker 1973
Gardner, R. *Land of Time Enough* David & Charles 1977
Gayford, E. *The Amateur Boatwoman* David & Charles 1973
Hassal, J. *A Tour of the Grand Junction Canal in 1819* Cranfield & Bonfiel 1968
Hayward, Richard *Where the Shannon Flows* Dundalgan Press 1978
Liley, J. *Journeys of the Swan* Allen & Unwin 1971
Lloyd, M. & A. *Through England's Waterways* Imray 1948
Malet, H. *In the Wake of the Gods (Ireland)* Chatto & Windus 1970
Malet, H. *Voyage in a Bowler Hat (Eire & U.K.)* Hutchinson 1960
Owen, D. E. *Water Byways* David & Charles 1973
Pilkington, R. *Small Boat on the Thames* Macmillan 1966
Poole, J. *Narrow Boat Venture* Thornhill Press 1978
Rice, H. J. *Thanks for the Memory* Inland Waterways of Ireland (Athlone Branch)
Rogers, Mary *Prospect of Erne (N.I.)* Fermanagh Field Club 1967
Rolt, L. T. C. *Narrow Boat* Eyre & Spottiswood 1944
Rolt, L. T. C. *Green and Silver* Allen & Unwin 1949
Rolt, L. T. C. *Landscape with Canals* Allen Lane 1977
Seymour, J. *Sailing through England* Eyre & Spottiswood 1956
Seymour, J. *Voyage into England* David & Charles 1966
Smith, P. L. *Yorkshire Waterway* Dalesman Books 1977
Thurston, E. T. *The Flower of Gloster (1911)* David & Charles 1968
Wilkinson, T. *Hold on a Minute* Allen & Unwin 1971

GENERAL

Anderson, J. *Leicestershire Canals* A. B. Printers 1976
Balfe, Terry (ed) *The Shannon Book* Irish Shell & Bord Failte
Bowskill, D. *Northeast Waterways* Imray 1985
Braithwaite, L. *Canals in Towns* A & C Black 1976
Bursche, E. *A Handbook of Water Plants* Frek. Warne 1972
Burton, A. *The Canal Builders* Eyre Methuen 1972
Burton, A. *Back Door Britain* Andre Deutsch 1977
Burton, A. & Pratt, D. *Canals in Colour* Blandfords 1974
Burton, A. & Pratt, D. *Canal* David & Charles 1976
Cadbury & Dobb *Canals & Inland Waterways* Pitman 1929
Calvert, R. *Inland Waterways of Britain* Ian Allen 1963
Clew, K. R. *Wessex Waterway* Moonraker Press 1978
Darwin, A. *Canals and Rivers of Britain* J.M. Dent 1976
De Mare, E. *The Canals of England* Architect Press 1950 .0
Denny, M. *London & South East England's Waterways* Moorland Publishing Co. 1979
De Salis, H. R. *Bradshaw's Canals and Navigable Rivers of England and Wales (1904)* David & Charles 1968
Duckham, B. F. *Navigable Rivers of Yorkshire* Dalesman Pub. 1964
Edwards, L. A. *The Inland Waterways of Great Britain* Imray 1985
Ellis, E. A. *Wild Flowers of the Waterways & Marshes* Jarrold 1972
Eyre, F. & Hadfield, C. *English Rivers & Canals* Collins 1945
Forbes, V. A. & Ashford, W. H. R. *Our Waterways* John Murray 1906

Gagg, J. *Canals in Camera Vols 1 & 2* Ian Allen 1970/1
Gagg, J. *The Canaller's Bedside Book* David & Charles 1973
Gagg, J. *A Canal & Waterways Armchair Book* David & Charles 1975
Gladwin, D. D. *The Canals of Britain* Batsford 1973
Gladwin, D. D. *The Waterways of Britain* Batsford 1976
Hadfield, C. *The Canal Age* David & Charles 1968
Hadfield, C. *Canals and Waterways* David & Charles 1966
Hadfield, C. *A Brief Guide to Canals and Waterways* David & Charles 1966
Hadfield, C. *British Canals* David & Charles 1972
Hadfield, C. *Inland Waterways* David & Charles 1978
Harris, R. *Canals and their Architecture* Hugh Evelyn 1969
I.W.A. *Inland Shipping Group Fact Sheets* I.W.A.
Lyons, D. C. *The Leeds & Liverpool Canal* Hendon Pub. Co. 1977
Mabey, R. *The Unofficial Countryside* Collins 1975
May, R. *The Birmingham Canal Navigations* C. R. Smith Pub. 1973
McKnight, Hugh *Shell Book of Inland Waterways* David & Charles 1975
McKnight, Hugh *Canals, Locks & Canal Boats* Ward Lock 1974
McNeill, D. B. *Coastal Passenger Steamers and Inland Navigations in the North of Ireland* Belfast Museum & Art Gallery 1960
Metcalfe, L. & Vince J. *Discovering Canals* Shire Pub. 1968
Ogden, J. *Yorkshire's River of Industry – R. Calder* Dalton 1972
Ogden, J. *Yorkshire's River Aire* Dalton 1976
Owen, D. E. *Water Highways* Pheonix House 1967
Paget-Tomlinson, E. W. *The Complete Book of Canal and River Navigations* Waine Research Publications 1978
Paget-Tomlinson, E. *Britain's Canal & River Craft* Moorland 1979
Payne, R. *The Canal Builders* Macmillan 1959
Porteus, J. D. *Canal Ports: The Urban Achievement* Academic Press 1978
Pratt, D. *Discovering London's Canals* Shire 1977
Pratt, F. *Canal Architecture in Britain* B.W.B. 1976
Ransom, P. J. G. *Waterways Restored* Faber & Faber 1974
Ransom, P. J. G. *The Archaeology of Canals* Worlds Work 1979
Rolt, L. T. C. *The Inland Waterways of England* Allen & Unwin 1970
Rolt, L. T. C. *Navigable Waterways* Longmans 1969
Roulstone, A & M *Fenland Waterways* Balfour 1974
Rowbotham, F. R. *The Severn and its Bore* David & Charles 1970
Russel, R. *Waterside Pubs* David & Charles 1974
Russel, R. *Discovering Lost Canals* Shire Publications 1975
Seaman, K. *Canal Fishing* Barrie & Jenkins 1971
Sherwood, K. B. *Stoke Bruerne – impact of canal on village* Nene College, Northampton 1979
Smith, G. *Our Canal Population (1878)* E. P. Pub.1974
Smith, P. *Waterways Heritage* Luton Museum 1971
Smith, P.L. *Yorkshire Waterways* Dalesman 1978
Squires, R. W. *Canals Revived, The Waterways Restoration Movement* Moonraker Press 1979
Tibbs, R. *Fenland River* Lavenham Press 1971
Vince, J. *Canals & Canal Architecture* Shire Pub. 1973
Ward, J. R. *Finance of Canal Building in 18th Century England* O.U.P. 1974
Ware, M. E. *A Canalside Camera* David & Charles 1975
Ware, M. E. *Britain's Lost Waterways* Moorland Publishing Ltd 1979
Westall, G. *Inland Cruising* Lander Westall &c. 1908

RIVER THAMES

(There are more books written about the Thames than any other river. Several are listed elsewhere but reference to a public library in the Thames valley is essential).

Cove-Smith, C. *London's Waterway Guide* Imray 1987

Nicholson's Guide to the Thames Robert Nicholson 1969

The Thames Ward & Lock (Annually)

The Thames Book Link House

Salter's Guide to the Thames Salter Bros.

The Thames Guide Book L. Upcott 1890

Bunge, J. H. O. *Tideless Thames in future London* Frederick Muller 1944

Herbert, Sir A. *The Thames* Weidenfeld & Nicholson 1966

Pilington, R. *Thames Waters* Lutterworth Press 1956

Morley, F. V. *River Thames* Methuen 1926

Taunt, H. V. *A new map of the River Thames* (This is mainly a book with detailed maps) Taunt & Co. 1899

Thacker, F. S. *The Thames Highway (Locks and Weirs)* F.S. Thacker 1920. *The Thames Highway. A General History.* F. S. Thacker 1914. (This vol. 1 was reprinted by David & Charles in 1968).

FENLAND

Astbury, A. R. *The Black Fens* Golden Head Press 1958

Bloom, Alan *The Fens* Robert Hale 1953

Darby, H. C. *The Draining of the Fens* C.U.P 1968

Godwin, Sir H. *Fenland* C.U.P 1978

Harris, L. E. *Vermuyden and the Fens* Cleaver Hume Press 1953

Parker, A. K. & Pye, D. *The Fenland* David & Charles 1976

Storey, E. *Portrait of the Fen Country* Robert Hale 1971

Summers, D. *The Great Level* David & Charles 1976

Wedgwood, I. *Fenland Rivers* Rich & Cowan 1936

Wentworth-Day, J. *A History of the Fens* George Harrap 1954

(There is a good deal of data on Fenland in a variety of books. These are listed in *The Fen and Furrow,* compiled by W. E. Dring, F.L.A., and published by the Cambridgeshire County Library)

BROADLAND

Davies, G. C. *The Handbook to the Rivers and Broads of Norfolk & Suffolk* Jarrold (9th ed) 1887

Dutt, W. A. *The Norfolk Broads* Methuen (4th ed) 1930. *The Broads Book* Link House (Annually). *What to do on the Norfolk Broads* Jarrold (Annually)

Ellis, E.A. *The Broads* Collins 1965

Emerson, P. H. *On English Lagoons* D. Nutt 1892

Everitt, N. *Broadland Sport* R. A. Everitt 1902

May, John *Norfolk Broads Holiday Book* Hulton 1952

Manning, S. A. *Portrait of Broadland.* Robert Hale 1980. *The Making of the Broads* Royal Geographical Society 1960

Mottram, R. H. *The Broads* Robert Hale 1952

Payne-Jennings *Sun Pictures of the Norfolk Broads* Payne-Jennings 1892

Suffling, E. R. *The Land of the Broads* Benjamin Perry 1892

Wentworth-Day, J. *Norwich and the Broads* Batsford 1953. *Broadland Adventure* Batsford 1953. *Portrait of the Broads* Country Life 1951. *Marshland Adventure* Robert Hale 1967. George Harrap 1950

(The hire agencies are listed elsewhere. Blakes and Hoseasons have a wide range of booklets and guides to the Broads. From time to time The Norwich Central Library issue a bibliography of Broadland books.)

CANOEING

Bliss, W. *Canoeing* Methuen 1947

British Canoe Union *Guide to the Waterways of the British Isles* British Canoe Union (at intervals)

Prothero, F. E. and Clark, W. A. *A New Oarsman's Guide* George Philip 1896

CHILDRENS BOOKS

Banks, J. & Hume, P. *Fun on the Waterways* Penwork Ltd. 1972

Bibby, V. *Saranne (Fiction)* Longmans 1973

Carpenter, H. *The Joshers* Allen & Unwin 1977

De Mare, E. *Your Book of Waterways* Faber & Faber 1965.

Dorner, Jane *Canals* Wayland 1973

Farnworth, W. *Canals* Mills & Boon 1973

Gagg, J. *Boats and Boating* Blackwell 1973

Gagg, J. *Rivers in Britain* Blackwell 1971

Gagg, J. *Book of Locks, Canal Tunnels etc.* J. Gagg 1975

Grundy, B *The Flower of Gloster (Fiction)* Rupert Hart-Davis 1970

Harries, E. *The Narrow Boat* MacMillan 1973

Hutchings, C. *The Story of our Canals* Ladybird Books 1975

Lawrence, B. *Curlew on the Cut (Fiction)* Geoff. Dibb 1968

Pearce, R. *History at Source – Canals 1720-1910* Evans Bros. Ltd. 1972

Pick, C. *Canals and Waterways* Macdonald 1977

Purton, R. W. *Rivers and Canals* Routledge 1972

Ransom, P. J. G. *Your Book of Canals* Faber & Faber 1977

Rice, P. *Narrow Boats* Dinosaur 1976

Rolt, L. T. C. *Inland Waterways* E.S.A. Ltd. 1958

Ross, A. *Canals in Britain* Blackwell 1971

Samson, D. *Getting to Know Boats* Panda Public 1972

Smith, P. L. *Canals are Great* P. L. Smith 1977

Tate, S. *The Living River* J. M. Dent 1974

Vialls, Christine *Canals-Industrial Archaeology* A & C Black 1976

Vince, J. *River and Canal Transport* Blandford 1970

Wickson, R. *Britain's Inland Waterways* Methuen 1968

HISTORICAL

Bick, D. E. *The Hereford & Gloucester Canal* Pound House 1979

Biddle, G. *Pennine Waterway – Pictorial History* Dalesman Books 1977

Biddle, G. *Lancashire Waterways* Dalesman Books 1980

Body, A. H. *Canals & Waterways (It Happened Around Manchester)* Univ. London Press 1969

Extract Harpers Mag. *Through London by Canal 1885* B.W.B. 1977

Broadbridge, S. R. *The Birmingham Canal Navigations Vol 1* David & Charles 1974

Cameron, A. D. *The Caledonian Canal* Terence Dalton 1972

Cameron, A. D. *The Crinan Canal* A.D. Cameron 1978

Clamp, A. L. *Let's Explore Old Waterways in Devon* Westway Publications 1970

Clew, K. R. *The Kennet and Avon Canal* David & Charles 1973

Clew, K. R. *The Somersetshire Coal Canal Railways* David & Charles 1970

Clew, K. R. *The Dorset and Somerset Canal* David & Charles 1971

Compton, H. J. *The Oxford Canal* David & Charles 1976

Corbett, J. *The River Irwell (1907)* E. J. Morten 1974

Corbridge, J. *A Pictorial History of the Mersey and Irwell Navn.* E. J. Morten 1979

Cullimore, D. *Shadlow – 18th Century Port* D. Cullimore 1977

Dalby, L. J. *The Wilts & Berks Canal* Oakwood Press 1971

D'Arcy, G. *Portrait of the Grand Canal (Eire)* Trans. Research Assoc. 1973

Delany, V. T. H. & D. R. *Canals of the South of Ireland* David & Charles 1966

Delany, D. R. *The Grand Canal of Ireland* David & Charles 1973

Denney, Martin *London's Waterways* Batsford 1977

Duckham, B. F. *The Yorkshire Ouse* David & Charles 1967

Duckham, B. F. *The Inland Waterways of East Yorkshire (1700-1900)* E. Yorks Hist. Society 1973

Ewans, M. C. *The Haytor Granite Tramway & Stover Canal* David & Charles 1966

Faulkner, A. H. *The Grand Junction Canal* David & Charles 1972

Fife & Walls *River Foss* Sissons of York 1973

Flanagan, P. *The Balinamore & Ballyconnell Canal* David & Charles 1972

Gardner, P. & Foden, F. *Foxton, Locks and Barge Lift* Leicestershire C.C. 1978

Goodchild, J. & Morrell, W. J. *Waterways – Yorkshire Canals* E. P. Pub. 1972

Gladwin, D. D. *Victorian Canals* Batsford 1976

Gladwin, D. D. *A Pictorial History of Canals* Batsford 1977

Gladwin, D. D. & White, J. M. *English Canals (In 3 vols)* Gladwin & White 1969

Gladwin, D. D. & J. M. *Canals of Welsh Valleys & Their Tramroads* Oakwood Press 1974

Galdwin, D. D. *An Illustrated History of British Waterways* Spurbooks 1978

Hadfield, C. *Canals of the East Midlands (including part of London)* David & Charles 1966

Hadfield, C. *Canals of the West Midlands* David & Charles 1966

Hadfield, C. *Canals of South Wales & the Border* David & Charles 1960

Hadfield, C. *Canals of South West England* David & Charles 1967

Hadfield, C. *Canals of South & South East England* David & Charles 1969

Hadfield, C. *Canals of Yorkshire & North East England, Vols 1 and 2* David & Charles 1972

Hadfield, C. & G. Biddle *Canals of North West England Vols 1 and 2* David & Charles 1970

Hadfield C. & Norris, J. *Waterways to Stratford* David & Charles 1962

Hadley, D. *Waterway's Heraldry* Waterways Museum 1977

Handford, M. *The Stroudwater Canal 1729-1763* Moonraker Press 1976

Harris, H. & Ellis M. *The Bude Canal* David & Charles 1972

Harris, H. *The Grand Western Canal* David & Charles 1973

Household, H. *The Thames & Severn Canal* David & Charles 1973

Langford, Ian *Staffordshire & Worcestershire Canal* Goose & Son 1975

Lead, P. *The Caldon Canal and Tramroads* Oakwood Press 1979

Lead, P. *The Trent & Mersey Canal* Moorland Publishing Co. 1979

Leech, Sir B. T. *History of the Manchester Ship Canal 2 Vols* Sherratt & Hughes 1907

Lindsay, J. *Canals of Scotland* David & Charles 1968

Lindsay, J. *The Trent and Mersey Canal* David & Charles 1979

Lord, P. *Portrait of the River Trent* Robert Hale 1968

McCutcheon, W. A. *The Canals of the North of Ireland* David & Charles 1965

Ogden, J. *Yorkshire's River Derwent* Terence Dalton 1974

Owen, D. *Canals to Manchester* Manchester Univ. Press 1977

Phillips, J. *A General History of Inland Navigation (1805)* David & Charles 1970

Pratt, E. A. *A History of Inland Transport and Communications (1912)* David & Charles 1970

Pratt, E. A. *British Canals – Is their Resuscitation Practicable* John Murray 1906

Priestley, J. *A Historical Account of Navigable Rivers and Canals of Great Britain (1831).* David & Charles 1969

Russel, R. *Lost Canals of England and Wales* David & Charles 1971

Russel, R. & Boyes, J. *The Canals of Eastern England.* David & Charles 1977

Spencer, H. *London's Canal* Lund Humphries 1977

Stevens, P. A. *The Leicester Line* David & Charles 1972

Stevens, R. A. I. *Brecknock & Abergavenny and Monmouthshire Canals* Goose & Son 1974

Stevenson, P. *The Nutbrook Canal* David & Charles 1971

Summers, D. *The Great Ouse* David & Charles 1973

Tew, D. *The Oakham Canal* Brewhouse Press 1967

Thomas, J. *The Rise of the Staffordshire Potteries* Adams & Dent 1971

Tomlinson, V. I. *The Manchester, Bolton and Bury Navigation* Lancashire & Cheshire Antiq. Society 1969

Vine, P. A. L. *London's Lost Route to the Sea* David & Charles 1973

Vine, P. A. L. *Londons' Lost Route to Basingstoke* David & Charles 1968

Vine, P. A. L. *The Royal Military Canal* David & Charles 1972

Viner, D. J. *The Thames & Severn Canal* Hendon Publish. 1975

Viner, D. J. *Cirencester & the Thames and Severn Canal* Corinium Museum 1975

Waller, A. J. R. *The Suffolk Stour* Norman Adlard 1957

Ward, J. R. *The Finance of Canal Building in 18th Century* O.U.P. 1974

Welch, E. *The Bankrupt Canal* City of Southampton 1966

Wheat, G. *On The Duke's Cut* Northern Counties Carriers 1977

Willan, T. S. *River Navigation in England 1600-1750* O.U.P. 1936

Willan, T. S. *The Navigation of the River Weaver in the 18th Century* The Chetham Society 1951

Willan, T. S. *Early History of Don Navigation* Manchester Univ. Press 1962

Wilson, D. G. *The Making of the Middle Thames* Spurbooks 1977

Wilson, E. A. *The Ellesmere & Llangollen Canal* Phillimore 1975

Wright, I. L. *Canals in Wales* Bradford Barton 1977

OFFICIAL PUBLICATIONS

Report of Royal Commission on the Canals and Inland Navigations of the United Kingdom – 12 Volumes H.M.S.O. 1907-1909

Report of the Board of Survey – Canals and Inland Waterways Brit. Transport Commission 1955

Report of the Committee of Inquiry into Inland Waterways H.M.S.O. 1958

British Waterways Board *The Future of the Waterways* H.M.S.O. 1964

British Waterways Board *The Facts about the Waterways* B.W.B. 1965

British Waterways Board *Leisure and the Waterways* B.W.B. 1967

Ministry of Transport *British Waterways Recreation and Amenity (Cmnd 3401)* H.M.S.O. 1967

British Waterways Board *The Last Ten Years* B.W.B. 1973

London Canals Consultative Committee *London's Canals* G.L.C. 1976

British Transport *Annual Reports and Accounts 1948-1962* H.M.S.O.

British Waterways Board *Annual Reports and Accounts from 1963* H.M.S.O.

Ministry of Health and Local Government *Ulster Lakeland* H.M.S.O. Belfast 1963

Index